THE NEW

Wine, Lover's Companion

Third Edition

D0348436

THE NEW
Wine, Lover's Companion

Third Edition

Ron Herbst
and
Sharon Tyler Herbst

BARRON'S

All inquiries should be addressed to:
Barron's Educational Series, Inc.
250 Wireless Boulevard
Hauppauge, New York 11788
www.barronseduc.com

ISBN-13: 978-0-7641-4265-9
ISBN-10: 0-7641-4265-8

Library of Congress Catalog Card No. 2009025921

Library of Congress Cataloging-in-Publication Data

Herbst, Ron.
  The new wine lover's companion / Ron Herbst and Sharon Tyler Herbst. — 3rd ed.
      p. cm.
  Includes bibliographical references.
  ISBN-13: 978-0-7641-4265-9
  ISBN-10: 0-7641-4265-8
  1. Wine and wine making—Dictionaries. I. Herbst, Sharon Tyler. II. Title.

  TP546.H455 2010
  641.2'203—dc22   2009025921

PRINTED IN CHINA

9 8 7 6 5 4 3

Contents

Dedication

Dedicated with love to Sharon, who enriched and brightened so many lives when she entered them—especially mine. This book would never have existed had it not been for you. I miss you.

This book is also dedicated to the world's talented, hardworking winemakers and growers who, thankfully, so generously share their labors of love.

Acknowledgments

A bottle of wine begs to be shared;
I have never met a miserly wine lover.
—Clifton Fadiman, American author

My heartfelt thanks to:

Oscar Anderson and Holly Hartley, for sharing their exceptional, professional biweekly wine tastings (which always expand our knowledge) and, just as important, for being such good friends.

Lee and Susan Janvrin, dear friends with whom more bottles of excellent wine have been shared over the years than any of us care to admit —thanks for sharing the passion and making it so much fun.

Michael Boyd, for the wine knowledge he so generously shares, and for his wonderful shop, Michael's Wine Cellar, where we met many fellow wine lovers who've become great friends. And to Tammie Salas and Steve Hecht (former owners) and Bob and Sissy Blanchard (current owners) of my favorite wine shop on the Sonoma Coast, Gourmet au Bay.

Phil Hicks, friend and fellow wine enthusiast, for his thoughtful contribution toward the phonetics in the first edition of this book.

Pat Hunter, my wise and wonderful editor, for her talent, expertise and wisdom—and for her calm, cheerful understanding and good humor that is always able to soothe author angst.

And all the behind-the-scenes people at Barron's who were involved in the minutiae it takes to bring a book this size together.

For my friends and fellow wine lovers, who are all quite sure, as I am, that life's too short to drink bad wine: Jon Arnold, Gale Bach, Don Bailey, Leslie and David Bloom, Walt and Carol Boice, William Boyd, Jerry Bucher, Maria Cipriani, Marc Cuneo, Ron Cutler, Bruce Dukes, Howard Fields, Mike Folkes, Brian Halton, Bill Hassenzahl, Barry and Kathy Herbst, Ruth Hicks, Katy Karenbrock, Herb Kassler, Perry Marker and Marty Rudell, Gary and Suzann Mathers, Daniel Maye, Dan and Pat Metz, Larry Michalak, Christian Miller, Heino Nitsche, John and Gale Plane, Sid Sall and Debra Gray, Steven Schofield, Phil Shiota, Marc Shiota, David Shuh, Emma Swain and Wes Jones, Dennis Swanson, Joel Teller, Alan Tobey, Don and Marilyn Toms, Bob Tripp, Mark van Norman, and Stuart and Kirsten Williams.

And to the wonderful woman in my life, Bonnie Steele.

Introduction

*Good wine, well drunk, can lend majesty to the
human spirit. The rules are simple, and if followed
will add pleasure to the simplest palate, the simplest
meal, and make it grow.*
—M.F.K. Fisher, American author

The world has been having a love affair with wine since the moment
the first grape was stomped. And why not, for what other potable has
the ability to inspire, exhilarate, and nurture body, intellect, soul, and
spirit—all at the same time? Whether you say *vino, vin, Wein* or wine,
the word conveys contentment, satisfaction, gratification, inspiration,
comfort, joy, relaxation, poetry . . . in short, all things pleasurable.

The next best thing to consuming wine is talking about, learning
about, and (in my case) writing about it. So it should come as no surprise that, when my editor called asking if I wanted to update *Wine
Lover's Companion* for this third edition, I opened up a terrific bottle
of Zinfandel and started to think about how much the world of wine
has changed in the last few years and how many more people know
and talk about wine . . . and then I got to work.

My core objective was to keep the *New Wine Lover's Companion* true
to the original. It had to remain a straightforward, comprehensive reference, eminently user-friendly and packed with thousands of informative wine-related terms. Our work was cut out for us.

The past decade has seen a phenomenal number of changes in the
endlessly evolving world of wine, which correlates to a myriad of
changes in the second edition and now in this third edition. For example, even more new growing areas all over the world are being rec-

ognized for wines that are innovative and interesting; grape varieties, long out-of-favor or forgotten, have had a new awakening with today's improved winemaking techniques and are gaining worldwide recognition; continued exploration into winemaking processes is leading to new methods that solve age old problems resulting in higher quality wines all over the world; and on . . . and on.

Viticultural (winegrowing) terms have become much more a part of the winemaker-to-consumer lingo since we wrote the first edition. New definitions were added to the second edition and now additional ones have been added to this third edition—including new entries from ALLUVIAL SOIL to VERTICAL SHOOT POSITIONING. Likewise, more ENOL-OGY-related terms are part of the layman's language, so you'll find new entries from DEALCOHOLIZATION to WHOLE CLUSTER FERMENTATION in this edition.

In this book you'll find a myriad of details on grape varieties; wine styles; the world's wine-growing regions; official wine classifications; wine label terms; winemaking techniques; foreign wine terms; how to buy, store, and serve wine; what comprises a wine tasting; wine tasting terms; sizes and styles of glassware, wine bottles, and wine openers; ordering wine in a restaurant; opening and serving wine at home; temperatures for serving wine. Plus historical wine lore, etymological origins, phonetic pronunciations (*see* Pronunciation Guide, page xv), a completely revised Appendix section, and much, much more.

Great pains were taken *not* to editorialize in this book—a difficult task for two opinionated wine writers. But *The New Wine Lover's Companion* isn't about *our* opinions. As *Dragnet's* Sergeant Joe Friday always said, our aim was to present "just the facts, ma'am, just the facts." And hopefully in a clear, concise style. With this book as a guide, anyone can learn to speak the language of wine with ease, whether ordering it in a restaurant, buying it at a wine shop, or enjoying it at a friend's house.

And so we offer you this *New Wine Lover's Companion*, packed with over 4,000 terms, all wrapped up in a small, friendly little package. Whether you're a beginner, a collector, or just a compulsive reader, may it make the world of wine more enjoyable and less mysterious, informing the novice and offering the connoisseur new insights.

Lastly, fellow wine lovers, thank you for making *Wine Lover's Companion* so popular that it demanded a third edition. Writing this new tome has been a great gift. It took almost a year of hard work but, in the end, the most difficult part was . . . well, to stop writing. But I did.

Cheers!

Ron Herbst

No, Agnes, a Bordeaux is not a house of ill-repute.
—George Bain, Canadian author

How to Use This Book

ENTRIES ARE ARRANGED alphabetically and are cross-referenced. Alphabetization is by letter, rather than by word, so that multiple-word entries are treated as single words. For instance, the listing **closed** is positioned between **Clos du Roi** and **Clos Napoléon**. Common-usage acronyms and abbreviations appear in their natural alphabetical order. For example, **A.P.Nr.** follows **apéritif** and precedes **appellation**.

Entries are in lowercase, unless capitals are required for the proper form of the word (German nouns are always capitalized). All but the most basic words have pronunciations (*see* Pronunciation Guide, page xv). A term with several meanings will list all its definitions in numerical order within the main listing.

Words such as *aux, en, i, il, la,* and *les* are handled as the word *the.* For instance, the listings for **Aux Boudots** and **La Boudriotte** are in the *B* section, following the entry for **Bouchy**. However, the listing for **Mis au Domaine** comes before that of **Mis en Bouteille**.

CROSS-REFERENCES are indicated by SMALL CAPITALS and may appear in the body of a definition, at the end of a definition, or in lieu of a definition. Cross-references are used within the body of a definition when the term may not be familiar to the reader or to point out that there is additional information relevant to a term, as in the instance of **égrappage**, which states: "French term for DESTEMMING." Common entries such as **California**, **temperature**, or **wine** are not characterized with SMALL CAPITALS as cross-references. A cross-referenced word will be capitalized only once in each listing. Cross-references at the end of a definition refer to entries related to the word being defined.

When a word is fully defined elsewhere, a cross-reference rather than a definition is listed. For example, the listing for **malic acid** says: "*see* ACIDS; MALOLACTIC FERMENTATION." In the world of wine, many terms have more than one name, often depending on the region in which they're used. Cross-referencing is particularly extensive in *The New Wine Lover's Companion* because of the myriad synonyms for many terms (like grape varieties), as well as confusing, multifarious designations, such as those for German wine labels. For example, the terms **Blauburgunder**, **Pinot Nero**, and **Spätburgunder** are all cross-referenced to **Pinot Noir**, the more commonly known name of this grape. Different spellings of a term are also cross-referenced. **Silvaner**, for instance, refers the reader to the more common spelling of **Sylvaner**.

ITALICS are used in this book for several reasons. One is to point out that the term being defined also goes by another name. The Hungarian wine **Tokay**, for example, is also labeled as *Tokaji* or *Tokaji Aszu*. Additionally, italics are used to indicate foreign words and publication titles and to highlight cross-references at the end of a listing (the end of the entry for **maceration** states: "*see* CUVAISON; CARBONIC MACERATION").

BOLDFACE PRINT is used not only for main-entry headings but for subentries within a definition as well. For example, the definition for **Muscat** uses boldface to highlight the headings of the various types of this grape (such as **Muscat Blanc à Petits Grains** and **Muscat of Alexandria**), which are defined within the body of that entry. Boldface print is also used to highlight words like names of special brands or second labels.

BRACKETS surround an entry's pronunciation, which immediately follows the listing and precedes the definition. (*See* the Pronunciation Guide on the next page for complete information.)

Pronunciation Guide

All but the most basic words are accompanied by pronunciations, which are enclosed in brackets [—]. We've always thought that the standard phonetic alphabet and diacritical marks such as a tilde (~), diaeresis (¨), breve (˘) and circumflex (ˆ) slow readers down because they must often look up the symbol in a chart at the front of a book to see how it affects a word's pronunciation. As advocates of the most direct route, we use the "sounding-out" phonetic method, with the accented syllable indicated by capital letters. On a word like **Auslese**, for example, the common dictionary-style phonetic is *ous´ lā za*, which would force most readers to look up the sounds represented by the diacritics. In this book, however, the word is simply sounded out as *OWS-lay-zuh*.

A list of the basic sounds employed in this book's pronunciations follows:

a as in **can** or **add**
ah as in **father** or **balm**
ay as in **date** or **face**
ch as in **church** or **beach**
ee as in **steam** or **beer**
eh as in **set** or **check**
g as in **game** or **green**
i as in **ice** or **pie**
ih as in **if** or **strip**

j as in **gin** or **juicy**
k as in **cool** or **crisp**
o as in **odd** or **bottle**
oh as in **open** or **boat**
oo as in **food** or **boo**
ow as in **cow** or **flour**
uh as in **love** or **cup**
y as in **yellow** or **yes**
zh as in **beige** or **vision**

Note: A single *i* is used for the long *i* sound, as in *pie*. The exception to the single *i* rule is when an *i* is followed by a consonant, in which case, an *e* is appended. For example, both *i*'s are long in the word **weinkellerei**, which is phoneticized *vine-KEHL-ler-ri*.

Foreign Sounds

eu A sound made with the lips rounded as if to say *oo* (as in *food*) while trying to say *a* (as in *able*).

euh An *e* in French (not *é* or *è*) is often pronounced with an *oo*, as in *book* or *wood*.

n, m An italicized *n* or *m* is used to indicate that the *n* or *m* is not pronounced and that the preceding vowel has a nasal sound.

~~**ng**~~ Portuguese has a nasal vowel sound, indicated in this book by ~~**ng**~~, which serves simply to indicate the nasal quality of the preceding vowel. The "ng" is not pronounced.

r An italicized *r* indicates that the *r* sound should be diminished, with a sound more like *w*.

rr The appearance of *rr* indicates the sound of a rolling *r*.

A

abboccato [ah-boh-KAH-toh] Italian for "lightly sweet," indicating that a wine contains a small amount of residual sugar. Abboccato is used to describe a wide range of wines from semisweet to medium-dry.

Abfüller; Abfüllung [AB-few-ler; AB-few-lung] German for "bottler" and "bottling." For example, *erzeugerabfüllung* on a wine label means "bottled by the proprietor," which is equivalent to ESTATE BOTTLED in the United States.

Ablan *see* PALOMINO

abocado [ah-boh-KAH-doh] Spanish for "semisweet," indicating that the wine contains some RESIDUAL SUGAR.

Abona DO *see* CANARY ISLANDS

Abruzzi; It. Abruzzo [ah-BROOD-dzee] Abruzzi is a very mountainous region located east of Rome on the Adriatic Sea about midway down the coastline. There are approximately 82,000 vineyard acres. The main grape variety used for white wines is TREBBIANO, but there are a multitude of other white grapes allowed including BOMBINO BIANCO, MALVASIA, and Pinot Grigio (PINOT GRIS). MONTEPULCIANO is the main grape for ROSSO and ROSATO, followed by SANGIOVESE. There are three DOCs in this area: Controguerra, TREBBIANO D'ABRUZZO, and MONTEPULCIANO D'ABRUZZO.

Abtsberg *see* MAXIMIN GRÜNHAUS

AC Abbreviation for APPELLATION D'ORIGINE CONTRÔLÉE.

acescence; acescent *see* Glossary of Wine Tasting Terms, page 655

acetaldehyde [as-ih-TAL-duh-hide] A natural element found in grapes and wine, acetaldehyde is colorless, volatile, and water-soluble. It has a pungent fruitlike odor and is present in small amounts in good TABLE WINE and in high amounts in oxidized wines. OXIDATION is a detriment in a normal table wine but intentional in wines like SHERRY or MADEIRA. Most acetaldehyde eventually converts to ETHANOL, the ALCOHOL found in wine. If oxygen is introduced too fast or in excessive amounts, the production of acetaldehyde can temporarily cause a reaction like BOTTLE SICKNESS or, worse, give wine a permanent sherry-like trait.

acetic *see* Glossary of Wine Tasting Terms, page 655

acetic acid [uh-SEE-tihk] *see* ACIDS

acetification [uh-SEE-tuh-fih-KAY-shuhn] The process of wine turning into vinegar, the most common cause of which is spoilage, as acetic bacteria convert ALCOHOL to ACETIC ACID and ETHYL ACETATE.

acetobacter [uh-SEE-tuh-bak-tuhr] A microorganism that, when wines are exposed to oxygen, creates ACETIC ACID.

acetone *see* Glossary of Wine Tasting Terms, page 655

acid *see* ACIDS

acid adjustment *see* ACIDS

acidic *see* Glossary of Wine Tasting Terms, page 655

acidification *see* ACIDS

acidity A wine's acidity is exceedingly important. In proper balance with other components (TANNINS, ALCOHOL, FRUIT, etc.), it contributes a lively, refreshing quality. When acidity is too high, a wine can become tart and biting, sharp on the palate; too low and wine tastes dull and flat—FLABBY. The appropriate acid level of a wine varies, with sweeter wines generally requiring somewhat higher acidity levels in order to retain the proper BALANCE. Some wine labels list a wine's acidity. Acceptable acidity for TABLE WINE usually ranges between 0.6 and 0.75 percent; for sweet wine it's 0.7 to 0.85 percent. In a well-made wine, acidity will not be overt. *See also* ACIDIC; ACIDS.

acids Acids are present naturally in grapes; they're also produced during the FERMENTATION process. The acid content of grapes can be affected by several factors. Climate, for instance, plays a major role. Wines made from grapes grown in hot VITICULTURAL regions or during particularly hot seasons have lower levels of acid. Conversely, cooler regions or growing seasons produce wines with a higher acid concentration. Soil is another component affecting the acid concentration in grapes. For example, potassium-deficient soil may produce high-acid grapes. An additional determining factor is the grape variety itself—CHENIN BLANC is intrinsically high in acid, whereas MALBEC is a relatively low-acid grape. In the proper proportion, acids are desirable—they give wine CHARACTER, much as a dash of vinegar or lemon juice heightens the flavor of many foods. On the other hand, too much acid leaves a sharp, tart taste in the mouth, while too little makes wine seem flat and lifeless. The three primary acids in grapes are tartaric, malic, and citric, all of which are inherent to the fruit. **Tartaric acid**, the principal organic acid in grapes, contributes crisp flavor and graceful AGING to wine. **Malic acid**, the second principal acid in grapes, gives wine a fruity essence. **Citric acid** comprises only a fractional amount of a grape's acid. Wine also contains minute to trace amounts of other acids produced during fermentation including: **acetic**, **butyric**, **capric**, **caproic**, **caprylic**, **carbonic** (in SPARKLING WINES), **formic**, **lactic**, **lauric**, **propionic**, and **succinic**. The least desirable of these is **acetic acid**, which—when present in more than a nominal amount—gives wine a sour or vinegary aspect (*see* ACETIC; VOLATILE ACIDITY). **Volatile acids** (such as acetic and butyric) are those that can be altered—for instance, they can evaporate. **Fixed acids** are fruit acids (such as malic and tartaric) that are organic to the grape. **Total acidity**, also called *titratable acidity*, is the sum of the fixed and volatile acids, which is determined by a chemical process called **titration**. In the United States the total acidity is usually expressed in terms of tartaric acid, even though the other acids are measured. Total acidity is expressed either as a percentage or as grams per liter. In warm growing regions where grape acidity is lower (like California), natural grape acids can legally be added to wine to increase acid levels. This **acid adjustment** process is called **acidification** (sometimes *acidulation*). Less practiced by winemakers is **deacidification**, the acid adjustment process of lowerering acid in wines through any number of methods including COLD STABILIZATION and AMELIORATION. MALOLACTIC FERMENTATION also lowers acidity and helps soften the edges of an acidic wine. *See also* ACIDIC; ACIDITY; ASCORBIC ACID; PH; TARTRATES.

acidulation *see* ACIDS

Acolon *see* DORNFELDER

Aconcagua [ah-koan-KAH-gwah] A Chilean wine region located north and west of Santiago, CHILE's capital city. It has two major subregions—Aconcagua Valley and Casablanca Valley. The **Aconcagua Valley**, located in the northern interior of the country, is Chile's most northerly and hottest growing area. Within this subregion is the cooler Panquehue area, where Viña Errázuriz, the area's best-known producer, is headquartered. The **Casablanca Valley** is near the coastal city of Valparaiso, the location making it much cooler and therefore most promising for high-quality white wines. The ocean breezes combined with gently elevated slopes have made this subregion one of Chile's most popular areas. The most widely planted grape is CHARDONNAY, although SAUVIGNON BLANC can be quite distinctive here. Some producers are also successfully producing small quantities of CABERNET SAUVIGNON, MERLOT, and PINOT NOIR.

acrid *see* Glossary of Wine Tasting Terms, page 655

active wine cellar *see* WINE CELLAR

adamado [a-duh-MAH-doh] Portuguese for "sweet."

adega [ah-DAY-gah] A Portuguese term for a winery, cellar, or warehouse where wine is made, BLENDED, or AGED.

Adelaide This charming capital city of the state of SOUTH AUSTRALIA also lends its name to a wine zone. The name can be used on wine labels for wines that use grapes from the following wine regions in the Adelaide area: ADELAIDE HILLS, BAROSSA VALLEY, CLARE VALLEY, EDEN VALLEY, LANGHORNE CREEK, and MCLAREN VALE.

Adelaide Hills A wine-producing region about 10 miles east of the city of Adelaide in the Mount Lofty Ranges Zone of SOUTH AUSTRALIA. Its wine history dates back to the 1840s, and it was a popular growing area that thrived over many decades. It fell out of favor in the early 1900s, as the BAROSSA VALLEY became South Australia's dominant region. This change in popularity is credited to the bias for BIG, FULL-BODIED, high-ALCOHOL wines produced by the Barossa, but not possible in the cool-weather climate of the Adelaide Hills. These cooler hills (where most vineyards are planted above 1600 feet) are better suited to SPARKLING WINES made from CHARDONNAY and PINOT NOIR, and for elegant STILL WINES produced from Chardonnay, Pinot Noir, SAUVIGNON BLANC, SÉMILLON, and RIESLING grapes. Fortunately, these wines have caught on in the last couple of decades, and the Adelaide Hills is considered an area to watch. The climate varies throughout the Adelaide Hills, and red varieties like CABERNET FRANC, CABERNET SAUVIGNON, and MERLOT do better in the warmer northwestern sectors. Just over 6,000 acres are planted in the Adelaide Hills.

adulterated wine Wine that has been modified with either an inordinate amount of allowable ingredients or with unapproved substances.

aerate; aeration [AIR-ayt; air-AY-shun] The process by which air is deliberately introduced to wine. Aeration begins when the cork is removed from the bottle and the wine is exposed to outside air. The aeration process is accelerated when the wine is DECANTED into another vessel (a decanter) or poured into a wineglass and swirled. There's some debate about the benefits of letting wine breathe. Advocates believe that the practice allows wines to SOFTEN (especially younger red wines with high TANNINS) and the BOUQUET to evolve and develop COMPLEXITY. Detractors say breathing dulls a wine's flavor and diminishes its liveliness. There's no argument that many wines simply don't benefit from breathing—generally most white and ROSÉ wines, as well as many low- to medium-quality reds. Wines that do benefit are usually higher-quality VINTAGE red wines and some superior whites from BURGUNDY. Care should be taken with very old wines in that too much aeration may cause them to lose some of their fragile BOUQUET and flavor. In some wine circles, aerating wine is referred to as letting the wine "breathe."

aestivalis *see* VITIS AESTIVALIS

Affentaler [AH-fen-tah-ler] The shortened name of *Affentaler Spätburgunder Rotwein,* a German red wine made from Spätburgunder (PINOT NOIR) grapes in the BADEN region. The wine, which ranges from DRY to sweet, can be of QBA or QMP quality. Affentaler is produced in the area south of Baden-Baden around the villages of Bühl and Eisental. The word *Affental* translates to "monkey valley," which is why Affentaler wine bottles display an embossed image of a monkey.

Africa For the most part, Africa's excessive climate isn't very hospitable for wine grapes. They generally are grown only at the northern and southern ends of the continent, the farthest points from the Equator. *See also* ALGERIA; MOROCCO; TUNISIA; SOUTH AFRICA.

aftertaste *see* Glossary of Wine Tasting Terms, page 655

aggressive *see* Glossary of Wine Tasting Terms, page 655

Aghiorghitiko; Agiorgitiko [ah-yeor-YEE-tee-koh] A Greek red-grape variety, also known as *St. George.* It's thought to be one of Greece's oldest grape varieties and is the second most widely planted grape in the country. Its name comes from the town of Agios Georgios, now called Nemea. Only wines made from Aghiorghitiko can be labeled "Nemea," which is the large Greek APPELLATION located in the northeastern Peloponnese. Aghiorghitiko, considered by many to be Greece's noblest grape, is capable of producing a wide assortment of wine styles—from fruity ROSÉS to full-bodied, deeply colored reds. Higher-quality Aghiorghitiko wines are appearing from some of the cooler-climate areas in Greece, such as Koutsi and the Asprokambos valley in Nemea.

aging; age The process of maturing wines so that they can improve. Those wines that benefit from aging become less harsh, less TANNIC,

SMOOTHER, and more COMPLEX. Once wines complete FERMENTATION, they begin to change, mainly as a result of air contact but also because the natural components of the new wine begin interacting with one another. All ROSÉ wines and most white and LIGHT red wines should be bottled soon after fermentation and drunk while still young. But aging is necessary for some wines to reach their full potential. These include most fine red wines (such as those from France's BORDEAUX and RHÔNE regions, California's better CABERNET SAUVIGNONS and ZINFANDELS, and Italy's BAROLOS and BRUNELLO DI MONTALCINOS) and many white wines (SAUTERNES, BURGUNDIES, and some California CHARDONNAYS). Wines begin the aging process in the tanks or vats where they go through fermentation. After that, most high-quality wines receive some sort of wood aging and then bottle aging. **Wood aging**, sometimes referred to as **barrel aging**, **cask aging**, or **barrel maturation**, is a process of maturing wine in barrels or casks prior to bottling. This process allows young wines to SOFTEN and absorb some of the wood's flavors and TANNINS; the wine's flavors become concentrated because of slight evaporation. In modern winemaking, wood aging has become very complex, with considerations like size of container, origin and type of wood, and barrel-making techniques. Although the best sources for barrel oak are still being debated (*see* OAK), the small oak barrel has evolved as today's container of choice. **Bottle aging** further develops the nuances of wine. After a wine is bottled, the first few weeks of aging allow it to recover from BOTTLE SICKNESS. The length of further aging depends upon the type of wine. Many, including rosé, light white, and light red wines, are at their best soon after bottling and don't require further aging. White wines like California Chardonnay do well with a minimum of 6 to 12 months aging, whereas French white Burgundy and Sauternes develop better with extended bottle aging. Long-lived red wines—such as California Cabernet Sauvignon and Zinfandel, French Bordeaux, Italian Barolo, and vintage PORT— improve for many years, sometimes decades. Such wines evolve beautifully in the bottle as their tannins soften and the flavor and BOUQUET become more intriguing and complex. At some point, however, the wine hits its peak and begins declining in quality, making bottle aging no longer beneficial.

Agiorgitiko *see* AGHIORGHITIKO

Aglianico [ah-LYAH-nee-koh] One of the higher-quality red-wine grapes found in southern Italy, primarily in CAMPANIA and BASILICATA. Aglianico is thought to have been planted in this region as early as the seventh century B.C. The best 100 percent Aglianico wines come from

TAURAS DOCGI, followed by those from AGLIANICO DEL VULTURE DOC. The wines from these two areas are notably ROUGH when young due to high TANNINS, noticeable ACIDITY, and a dense concentration of flavors; they're definitely built for AGING. As these wines mature, they can exhibit great BALANCE, with subtle fruit flavors and EARTHY, TARRY, and CHOCOLATY characteristics. FALERNO DEL MASSICO also produces excellent wines that use a high proportion of Aglianico in their blend. Unfortunately, much of the wine produced from Aglianico grapes is low-quality and unexciting.

Aglianico del Vulture DOC [ah-LYAH-nee-koh del VOOL-too-reh] The only DOC zone in Italy's BASILICATA region. Although this DOC makes AMABILE and SPUMANTE wines, it's the STILL, DRY wines that are most highly regarded. These red wines are made from the AGLIANICO grape that's grown here and in the neighboring region of CAMPANIA (*see* TAURASI DOC). The better vineyards are on the east slope of Monte Vulture, an extinct volcano in the northern part of Basilicata. When young, the Aglianico del Vulture wines are noted for their ROUGHNESS, which is due to high TANNINS, noticeable ACIDITY, and a dense concentration of flavors. As they mature, these wines can show great BALANCE, with subtle fruit flavors and EARTHY, TARRY, and CHOCOLATY characteristics. They can AGE for 7 to 10 years or longer.

Agliano *see* ALEATICO

agrafe; agraffe [uh-GRAF] A metal clasp used to hold the temporary cork in place during BOTTLE FERMENTATION when making SPARKLING WINE via the METHODE CHAMPENOISE. The agrafe has, in most instances, been replaced by the CROWN CAP.

Agrelo *see* ARGENTINA

aguardente *see* LOURINHÃ DOC

Ahr [AHR] With only about 1,300 acres planted, Ahr is the fourth smallest of the thirteen German ANBAUGEBIETE (quality-wine regions). It's located on the river Ahr, a tributary of the Rhine, just south of the city of Bonn in western Germany. Winemaking in the Ahr region goes back to Roman times, and the region claims Germany's first cooperative cellar, which local growers established in 1868. Even though it is located the farthest north of all the Anbaugebiete, over 70 percent of its vineyards are planted with red varieties, which is unusual because of the cooler climate. The main varieties here are Spätburgunder (PINOT NOIR) and PORTUGIESER, and the red wines are usually pale and lightly flavored. The main white varieties are RIESLING and MÜLLER-

THURGAU. Even though Ahr's white wines are usually better than the reds, they're not as good as those made from the same varieties in some of the southern regions. Most of the wines are consumed locally, and few are exported. Ahr has one BEREICH, **Walporzheim/Ahrtal**; one GROSSLAGE, **Klosterberg**; and forty-three EINZELLAGEN. The principal wine-producing towns are Ahrweiler and Bad Neuenahr (the region's capital).

aigre [AYGR] French for "sour" or "vinegary." In wine parlance, *aigre* refers to an ACETIC trait.

aimable [ay-MAHBL] A French term used in the wine world to describe a pleasant, well-BALANCED wine.

Airén [i-REHN] A white grape that is Spain's most widely planted grape variety. Airén blankets central Spain's hot, arid regions of LA MANCHA and VALDEPEÑAS and is used for both red and white wines. The Airén grape's reputation for creating dull white wines is still widely dependable but—thanks to modern equipment and new winemaking techniques—these wines have been gaining a better image. There are now white Airén wines being produced that are light, crisp, fruity, and slightly aromatic. Spain's Valdepeñas region, which has a good reputation for red wines, actually grows much more Airén than it does the local red-grape favorite Cencibel (TEMPRANILLO). In fact, often a small amount of Airén is blended with the Cencibel to create the region's popular red wine. Much of the blander white wine made from Airén is processed further to create BRANDY. Airén is also known as *Lairén, Manchega,* and *Valdepeñera Blanca.*

air lock; airlock A device made of glass or plastic and designed to prevent wine contamination and to release carbon dioxide gas during FERMENTATION. The air lock fits into the top of the vessel containing the fermenting wine and is filled about halfway with water. As the carbon dioxide gas builds up during fermentation, it forces its way through the water barrier and out of the container. Outside air doesn't have enough pressure to force its way into the air lock so the wine is protected from outside contaminates.

aisle In VITICULTURE, the vineyard floor between the grapevine rows.

Aix *see* COTEAUX D' AIX-EN-PROVENCE

Ajaccio AC [ah-YAHT-choh] An APPELLATION that encompasses the wines made in the hills around the city of Ajaccio on the west coast of the French island of CORSICA. The appellation designation covers red and

ROSÉ wines made primarily from the local Sciacarello grape and white wines made primarily from VERMENTINO and Ugni Blanc (TREBBIANO).

Alba [AHL-bah] An important wine town of about 30,000 people situated in the wine-producing area south of Turin in Italy's PIEDMONT region. Several Italian DOCs use Alba in their name—BARBERA D'ALBA, DOLCETTO D'ALBA, NEBBIOLO D'ALBA, and Dolcetto di Diano d'Alba. The well-known DOCGs of BAROLO and BARBARESCO are also near Alba. In addition to red wines, the area around Alba is also known for its white truffles.

Albana [ahl-BAH-nah] Grown principally in northern Italy's EMILIA-ROMAGNA region and environs, this white wine grape has been cultivated in this area since the thirteenth century. The wines it produces are of extremely variable quality and rarely considered great. ALBANA DI ROMAGNA wines are designated DOCG (Italy's highest official classification); however, many experts question this high ranking. At their best, Albana wines are SMOOTH yet CRISP, with hints of nuttiness. The Albana grape is processed into many styles of wine including AMABILE, DRY, PASSITO, SPARKLING, and sweet. Albana is also known as *Biancame, Greco di Ancona,* and *Greco* (although it's totally unrelated to the true GRECO variety used in GRECO DI TUFO).

Albana di Romagna DOCG [ahl-BAH-nah dee roh-MAH-nyah] When the wines from this area were upgraded from DOC to DOCG status in 1987, the event sparked much controversy. Many wine reviewers had hoped the DOCG designation would be reserved for outstanding high-quality wines, and the Albana di Romagna wines weren't viewed as such. At their best, these wines, which are made from the ALBANA grape, are SMOOTH yet CRISP, with hints of nuttiness. Their quality, however, is quite variable, and the wines are generally not considered world class. The area for producing these wines is extremely large and is located in the EMILIA-ROMAGNA region in northern Italy. Albana di Romagna covers the vineyards surrounding over twenty villages between Bologna and Rimini. The DOCG designation allows many styles of wine including AMABILE, SECCO, PASSITO, and DOLCE. The SPUMANTE wines may still only be classified as DOC. The best versions are the sweet ones, passito and dolce.

Albani *see* COLLI ALBANI DOC

Albany *see* GREAT SOUTHERN

Albariño *see* ALVARINHO

albariza *see* JEREZ-XÉRÈS-SHERRY Y MANZANILLA DE SANLÚCAR DE BARRAMEDA DO

Alcamo DOC [AHL-cah-moh] A DOC that is located in the western part of SICILY and includes the vineyards surrounding the village of Alcamo and eleven other small villages. The wines, also called *Bianco Alcamo* or *Bianco d'Alcamo,* are made mainly from CATARRATTO grapes but use small amounts of others like Damaschino, Grecanico, and TREBBIANO. Many are of mediocre quality, but several producers make CRISP, LIVELY wines with class and CHARACTER.

Alcanol *see* MACABEO

Alcobaça *see* ESTREMADURA

alcohol [AL-kuh-hawl] Alcohol is the intoxicating element produced by the yeast FERMENTATION of certain carbohydrates—the sugar in fruit, in the instance of wine. If a wine is fully fermented, from 40 to 45 percent of the grapes' sugar content is converted into carbon dioxide and from 55 to 60 percent is converted into **ethyl alcohol** (the only alcohol suitable for drinking). Therefore, a wine whose grapes were picked at 23° BRIX will end up with 12.6 to 13.8 percent alcohol if VINIFIED completely DRY. Ethyl alcohol, also known as *ethanol,* lends little if any flavor to wine but must be present in the right proportion to give wine a desirable BALANCE. Wine with a low alcohol level might be too sweet because not enough of the grape's sugar was converted. This results in RESIDUAL SUGAR, an undesirable trait in some wines. Wines with excessive alcohol are characterized by a burning sensation in the mouth and are, in fact, referred to as HOT. Wines with full, CONCENTRATED fruit flavors can withstand higher alcohol levels without becoming hot; more delicate wines don't fare as well. *See also* ALCOHOL BY VOLUME.

Alcohol and Tobacco Tax and Trade Bureau (TTB) The U.S. Treasury Department agency that oversees enforcement of alcohol-related legislation. Some wine-related areas that the TTB controls in this capacity are winery licensing, regulation of wine label content, and the petitioning and approval process for AVAS. The TTB assumed these functions from the BATF (Bureau of Alcohol, Tobacco and Firearms) toward the end of 2002, when the Homeland Security Act of 2002 was passed. Under this Act, the BATF (now abbreviated ATF) was transferred to the Department of Homeland Security and continues with its other responsibilities for firearms, explosives, arson, and criminal enforcement. *See also* BUREAU OF ALCOHOL, TOBACCO, FIREARMS AND EXPLOSIVES.

alcohol by volume The percentage of ALCOHOL content, which must be included on American wine labels. For TABLE WINE, the United States requires a minimum alcohol level of 7 percent and a maximum of 14 percent. Because alcohol can be difficult to measure precisely, the label variance can be up to 1.5 percent. For example, a wine stating "Alcohol 12.5% By Volume" can legally range anywhere from 11 to 14 percent. However, wines cannot exceed the upper or lower limit. The alcohol-by-volume range for SHERRIES is 17 to 20 percent; for PORTS it's 18 to 20 percent. The label variance for both of these FORTIFIED WINES is 1 percent.

alcohol-free wine *see* DEALCOHOLIZED WINE

alcoholic *see* Glossary of Wine Tasting Terms, page 655

alcool [al-KOOL] The Italian and French word for "alcohol."

Aleatico [ah-leh-AH-tee-koh] An Italian red grape that some theorize is a variation of the MUSCAT family because of its flowery Muscat characteristics. Its noncharacteristic deep color, however, seems to discount this theory. The wines created from this grape are RICH, sweet, ALCOHOLIC, and well-ROUNDED. Two DOCS are focused on this variety— Aleatico di Puglia in southern Italy and Aleatico di Gradoli in LAZIO, northwest of Rome. Aleatico wines that are FORTIFIED as LIQUOROSOS can serve as less expensive PORT substitutes. This grape is also called *Agliano, Allianico, Leatico, Moscatello,* and *Muscateller.*

Alejandro Fernández *see* RIBERA DEL DUERO DO

Alella DO [ah-LEH-lyah] A small DO zone located on the outskirts of Barcelona in the CATALONIA region in northeast Spain. As the urban sprawl of Barcelona grows toward the small village of Alella, the vineyards around it are disappearing, being replaced with houses. In 1989 this designated area, which has been shrinking since the 1970s, added the vineyards of four other towns to increase its size. This move has been criticized because the added vineyards aren't as good as those in the original zone. Alella primarily produces semisweet and DRY white wines. The main white grapes used in them are Pansá Blanca (XAREL-LO) and Garnacha Blanca (GRENACHE). CHARDONNAY and CHENIN BLANC have also been approved and are used. A small amount of red and ROSÉ wines are produced from Ulle de Llebre (TEMPRANILLO) and

Garnacha Tinta (GRENACHE). The area's white wines, which should be consumed young, are considered its best.

Alenquer DOC [EHR-lay~~ng~~-kehr] Designated region in and around the town of Alenquer in the western Portuguese region of ESTREMADURA. Principal white grape varieties are ARINTO and FERNÃO PIRES. Red wines are made primarily from João de Santarém (PERIQUITA).

Alentejano (ALENTEJO).

Alentejo; Alentejo DOC [ah-LEN-tehzh] A Portuguese DOC located in the vast area of southeast Portugal. It's also a VINHO REGIONAL designation, which appears on labels as "Alentejano." Known as the "bread basket" of Portugal, the Alentejo region covers about one third of Portugal's available agricultural (and wine-producing) area. In addition to the improving quality of its wines, Alentejo is also known for the large number of CORKS produced from the *Quercus suber* oak trees, which are so abundant in this region. Alentejo comprises eight subregions that now have their own DOC status, most of which are named after nearby towns. They are **Alentejo/Borba, Alentejo/Evora, Alentejo/Granja-Amareleja, Alentejo/Moura, Alentejo/Portalegre, Alentejo/Redondo, Alentejo/Reguengos,** and **Alentejo/Vidigueira.** Although the white wine quality here is starting to improve, the Alentejo region is best known for its red wines which can be full-bodied and complex. Principal red-grape varieties are Aragonêz (TEMPRANILLO), Trincadeira (TINTA AMARELA), PERIQUITA, and Alfrocheiro Preto. The principal white grape is Rouperio, sometimes called *Perrum* or *Síria*.

Alexander Valley AVA A VITICULTURAL AREA just north of San Francisco in northern Sonoma County. It borders the Russian River from just south of Healdsburg, north to the Sonoma-Mendocino County line. Alexander Valley temperatures are somewhat on the warm side because fog is not as prevalent as in other growing areas. It generally falls into the Region III category (*see* CLIMATE REGIONS OF CALIFORNIA). The region, however, is versatile enough to do well with a wide variety of grapes including CABERNET SAUVIGNON, CHARDONNAY, GEWÜRZTRAMINER, MERLOT, RIESLING, SAUVIGNON BLANC, and ZINFANDEL. Approved in 1988, the Alexander Valley AVA comprises 76,000 acres, of which approximately 15,000 acres are planted with vines at this writing. Producers such as Silver Oak Cellars (based in the Napa Valley, with a winemaking facility in the Alexander Valley) make

Cabernet Sauvignon with an "Alexander Valley" designation, indicating that the grapes came from this growing region.

Alexandria Lakes AVA Established in August 2005, this is Minnesota's first VITICULTURAL AREA. It's located near the city of Alexandria in Douglas County, northwest of Minneapolis. The AVA, which contains 10,880 acres, was petitioned by Carlos Creek Winery, which grows a variety of CROSSES and HYBRIDS that are able to survive the Minnesota environment; they include Edelweiss, FRONTENAC, King of the North, La Crescent, MARÉCHAL FOCH, Swenson Red, and Valiant. There are also some European varieties that have been grafted to winter resistant rootstock including CABERNET SAUVIGNON, CHARDONNAY, GEWÜRZTRAMINER, MERLOT, MUSCAT, and RIESLING.

Algeria [al-JEER-ee-uh] Algeria, along with its neighbors TUNISIA and MOROCCO, was once a significant wine producer. During the time it was a colony of France, Algeria produced good-quality wines. Because Algeria's Muslim-dominated population drank little alcohol, most of its wine was exported to France, either in bottles or in BULK to be blended with French wine. Since Algeria's independence in 1962, when most of the French left, wine quality has dropped, exports have dwindled, and production has diminished. The 900,000 acres of vineyard land has been reduced to less than 40,000 acres, and wine production has been reduced to less than 1 percent of the pre-1962 levels. The French established a VDQS system with twelve regions, which exists to some extent today. The current demarcated areas are Aïn Bessem-Bouria, Coteaux du Zaccar, Médéa, Monts du Tessalah, Coteaux de Tlemcen, Coteaux du Mascara, Oued-Imbert, Mostaganem, Mostaganem-Kenenda, and Haut-Dahra. Although these areas have a climate like that of southern Italy, this Moslem-dominated country has not shown the desire to move forward with modernizing its wine industry. The grape varieties grown in Algeria include ALICANTE BOUSCHET, CARIGNAN, CINSAUT, CLAIRETTE, GRENACHE, MOURVÈDRE, SYRAH, Ugni Blanc (TREBBIANO), and, occasionally, CABERNET SAUVIGNON.

Alianca *see* CAVES ALIANCA

Alicante *see* ALICANTE BOUSCHET; ALMANSA DO; GRENACHE

Alicante Bouschet [al-eh-KAN-tay (Fr. ah-lee-KAHNT) boo-SHAY] Frenchman Louis Bouschet de Bernard and his son Henri created this prolific HYBRID vine that produces intensely colored, red-fleshed grapes. They developed Alicante Bouschet in 1866 by crossing GRENACHE and Petit Bouschet (the latter variety a cross of

A

Teinturier du Cher and ARAMON). By itself, the Alicante Bouschet grape produces wines that are decidedly unexciting. It's cultivated mainly to add color to wines made from less vivid varieties. This grape is widely planted in the MIDI region of southern France, Spain, and North Africa. It was quite popular in California during PROHIBITION (for use by home winemakers), where there are still a number of acres planted, mainly in the CENTRAL VALLEY. This grape is sometimes simply called *Alicante,* but shouldn't be confused with the ALICANTE DO wines of southeastern Spain. Nor should it be confused with the wine called *Bouchet,* which is the name sometimes used for CABERNET FRANC in BORDEAUX'S SAINT-ÉMILION. In parts of Spain it's called *Garnacha Tintorera.*

Alicante DO [al-eh-KAN-tay (Fr. ah-lee-KAHNT)] DO located in the Alicante province in the Levante region of southeastern Spain, south of the VALENCIA DO. Alicante consists of two areas—a large one spreading out to the west of the city of Alicante and a smaller one, referred to as La Marina, northeast of the city. The larger area produces mostly BIG, full-bodied (*see* BODY) red wines, as well as some ROSÉS from Monastrell (MOURVÈDRE) and Garnacha Tinta (GRENACHE). The DRY, white wines, made from Verdil and Merseguera grapes, aren't particularly well regarded. The smaller zone, La Marina, produces good, sweet white wines made from Moscatel (MUSCAT). A unique wine called **Fondillon** is also produced in the Alicante area. It's a RANCIO-style wine made from the Monastrell grape and AGED for 6 to 10 years in barrels. The ALCOHOL content is a potent 16 to 18 percent.

Alicante Ganzin *see* RUBIRED

Aligoté [ah-lee-gaw-TAY] White wine grape that is widely cultivated in and around BURGUNDY. It's considered less important and distinguished than the CHARDONNAY grape, and, in most cases, wines developed from the Aligoté are not as rich or long-lived as those from Chardonnay. Older Aligoté vines have been known to produce some very nice wines, which often exhibit citrusy and, occasionally, nutty characteristics. Burgundian wines made from this grape are labeled BOURGOGNE ALIGOTÉ AC or, when they come from the village of Bouzeron in the COTE CHALONNAISE, BOURGOGNE ALIGOTÉ DE BOUZERON AC. The Aligoté grape is losing out to Chardonnay, and vineyard plantings have been reduced in the last 15 years. However, it remains popular in some eastern European countries including Bulgaria and Romania. The Aligoté grape is also called *Blanc de Troyes, Chaudenet Gris,* and *Plant Gris.*

Allianico *see* ALEATICO

A

Alluvial soil [ah-LOO-vee-uhl] A type of soil that contains clay, mud, sand, silt, and/or gravel deposited by running water such as rivers or streams. Soil such as this can be prized in the viticultural world since it often produces grapes with a higher concentration of flavors.

Almansa DO [ahl-MAHN-suh] DO situated in Spain's CASTILLA-LA MANCHA region east of the LA MANCHA DO and next to the Levante. Although there's a small amount of white wine made from Merseguera grapes, about 75 percent of the wine produced is red, made with Monastrell (MOURVÈDRE), Cencibel (TEMPRANILLO), and Garnacha Tintorera (ALICANTE BOUSCHET). This last variety, which is also called *Alicante* here, has red flesh and imparts plenty of color, flavor, and TANNINS to the blends. It is unrelated to the Garnacha Tinta (GRENACHE). Although the Garnacha Tintorera grape gives these Almansa wines a special character, the better red wines use only a small amount of it. Experimental plots of CABERNET SAUVIGNON have also been planted.

Almerim *see* RIBATEJO DOC

Aloxe-Corton; Aloxe-Corton AC [ah-loss kor-TAWN] An important wine-producing village at the northern end of the CÔTE DE BEAUNE district in France's BURGUNDY region. The most celebrated wines come from the vineyards on Montagne de Corton, a vast hill rising above the village. This area's red wines are made from PINOT NOIR grapes; the whites, from CHARDONNAY. Within Aloxe-Corton (and extending into the villages of LADOIX-SERRIGNY and PERNAND-VERGELESSES) are the two GRANDS CRUS of CORTON (red wines) and CORTON-CHARLEMAGNE (white wines). The wines from these grand crus are ranked among the world's finest, with the reds from Corton considered some of the best and longest aging in Burgundy, and the white wines from Corton-Charlemagne compared favorably to other top white wines from the region. Within the grand cru of Corton, there are twenty-seven other individual grand cru vineyards in addition to le Corton vineyard. These vineyards may simply use Corton on the label or add their name to Corton, as in Corton Bressandes or Corton Clos du Roi. Nine of these same vineyards are also permitted to produce grand cru white wines under the Corton-Charlemagne AC. Aloxe-Corton also has a number of fine PREMIER CRU vineyards. The wines produced under the general village appellation of Aloxe-Corton AC are also generally of good quality.

Alpine Valleys An Australian wine region located in the North East Victoria Zone of VICTORIA. It's situated in the foothills of the Great

A

Dividing Range about 165 miles northeast of Melbourne around the town of Myrtleford. Vineyards in this area were planted in the 1850s and 1860s, and the local wine industry prospered until the 1890s. That's when the area was hit with a double whammy—a nationwide depression and the appearance of PHYLLOXERA. The Alpine Valleys region began its revival in the 1980s, and it now has eight wineries and over 1,250 acres of vineyards. The two main winegrowing areas are **Ovens Valley** and the **Kiewa River Valley**. The high growing areas have warm days and cool nights, though spring and autumn frosts are a concern. The main varieties planted here are CHARDONNAY, CABERNET SAUVIGNON, MERLOT, PINOT NOIR, and Shiraz (SYRAH). Chardonnay and Pinot Noir are used for both SPARKLING WINES and STILL WINES.

Alsace [al-SASS (Fr. al-ZASS)] Located on the German border in northeast France, east of CHAMPAGNE and north of BURGUNDY, Alsace is one of France's most beautiful wine regions. Its vineyards (about 33,000 acres) extend along the foothills of the Vosges Mountains, and numerous picturesque villages like Eguisheim, Kayserberg, and Riquewihr dot the landscape. Alsace, which consists of the modern French DÉPARTEMENTS of Haut-Rhin and Bas-Rhin, is not your usual French winemaking region because of the extensive use of VARIETAL WINE labeling on bottles. The Alsace APPELLATION was the first in France to implement varietal labeling, which is a system similar to that in the United States and therefore easier for Americans to understand. Alsace also differs from other French winemaking regions because of its widespread German influence. Germany ruled this region from 1870 until 1919, and its influence persists not only in the Germanic names but also in the tall, slender, green MOSEL-like bottles and in the bias of the approved grape varieties—GEWÜRZTRAMINER, RIESLING, SYLVANER, PINOT GRIS, PINOT BLANC, PINOT NOIR, and MUSCAT. Unlike the Germans, however, Alsace VINTNERS make DRY wines with higher ALCOHOL content and usually with riper, more scented fruit. Almost all Alsatian wines are varietal wines and must be 100 percent of the chosen grape variety. The exception is **Edelzwicker**, which means "noble wine" and consists of a blend of the approved white Alsace grape varieties. Pinot Noir is the only approved grape for red wine. Because this grape variety has difficulty in fully ripening in this climate (except during warmer years), Pinot Noir often appears as a ROSÉ wine. Since the 1985 VINTAGE, the very best Alsatian vineyards have been designated Alsace GRAND CRU, a distinct appellation for which fifty vineyards have qualified so far. These vineyards are allowed to put "Grand Cru" on their labels. SPARKLING WINES have their own appellation—CRÉMANT D'ALSACE AC. LATE

HARVEST wines, made from late-picked grapes with higher sugar levels and more pronounced flavors, are bottled under the appellation **Alsace Vendange Tardive**. A specialty of the Alsace region, the rich, extremely flavorful VENDANGE TARDIVE wines are usually vinified totally DRY. **Sélection de Grains Nobles** are wines made with late harvest grapes that are affected by BOTRYTIS CINEREA, which results in very sweet and CONCENTRATED wines. Alsace Grand Cru, Vendange Tardive, and Sélection de Grains Nobles appellation wines can be made only from Gewürztraminer, Riesling, Pinot Gris, and Muscat.

Alta Mesa AVA This VITICULTURAL AREA was established in August 2006. Its 55,400 acres are located within the larger LODI AVA, which is between Sacramento and Stockton in northern California. Alta Mesa means "high table" in Spanish and refers to its higher elevation (35 to 140 feet) versus the surrounding area. It's one of the warmer areas within the Lodi area. Red varieties such as CABERNET FRANC, CABERNET SAUVIGNON, MERLOT, SYRAH, and ZINFANDEL are most common.

Altenberg *see* KANZEM

alte reben [AHL-teh RAY-behn] *see* OLD VINE

Altesse [ahl-TESS] Good-quality white-wine grape cultivated mainly in and around France's SAVOIE region, where it's also called *Roussette*. Vines from this variety are thought to have been brought to the Savoie from CYPRUS in the Middle Ages. Altesse wines are described as full-bodied (*see* BODY) and AROMATIC with SPICY, PEPPERY characteristics. This grape is often blended with other varieties to produce desirable white wines. A substantial portion of the Altesse crop finds its way into SPARKLING WINES. The Savoie village of Seyssel is well known for its SEYSSEL MOUSSEUX sparkling wines, which are described as CREAMY, with a sharp peppery bite. Altesse is sometimes referred to as *Maconnais* or *Altesse Vert*.

Alto Adige DOC [AHL-toh AH-dee-zhay] DOC zone that covers most of the northern portion of Italy's TRENTINO-ALTO ADIGE region, Alto Adige. It's located in northeastern Italy, bordered by LOMBARDY on the west, VENETO on the east, and Austria on the north. Many of the vineyards are planted on steep hillsides as the Alps drop down toward the Adige River and its tributary, the Isarco. There are seven subzones (which may be used on the label)—Colli di Bolzano, LAGO DI CALDARO, Meranese, SANTA MADDALENA, Terlano, Valle Isarco, and Valle Venosta. Alto Adige, which is also known as **South Tyrol** or **Südtirol**, is officially bilingual, with a German-speaking majority that still has strong

A

ties to Austria (which ceded this area to Italy in 1918). The Alto Adige wines reflect this bilingual approach in their labels—a wine made from the PINOT BLANC grape might be referred to as both Weissburgunder and Pinot Bianco (both of which mean Pinot Blanc). There are seventeen VARIETAL WINES—Cabernet (from CABERNET SAUVIGNON and CABERNET FRANC), CHARDONNAY, LAGREIN (labeled as *Lagrein Rosato* or *Lagrein Kretzer* for ROSÉ wines and *Lagrein Scuro* or *Lagren Dunkel* for red wines), MALVASIA (also labeled *Malvaier*), MERLOT, MUSCAT (labeled *Moscato Giallo* or *Goldenmuskateller* for white wines and *Moscato Rosa* or *Rosenmuskateller* for rosé wines), MÜLLER THURGAU (also labeled *Riesling-Sylvaner*), Pinot Blanc (labeled *Pinot Bianco* or *Weissburgunder*), PINOT GRIS (labeled *Pinot Grigio* or *Rulander*), PINOT NOIR (labeled *Pinot Nero* or *Blauburgunder*), WELSCHRIESLING (also labeled *Riesling Italico*), RIESLING (labeled *Riesling Renano* or *Rheinriesling*), SAUVIGNON BLANC, SCHIAVA (also labeled *Vernatsch*), SYLVANER, and GEWÜRZTRAMINER (also labeled *Traminer Aromatico*). SPUMANTE is also made from some of these approved grapes.

Altus AVA A 12,800-acre VITICULTURAL area within the huge OZARK MOUNTAIN AVA in northwestern Arkansas. It's situated around the town of Altus and has a climate moderated by the Ozark Mountains to the north and the Arkansas River Valley to the south.

Alvarinho [ahl-vah-REE-nyoh] Low-yielding, high-quality white wine grape grown in Portugal's VINHO VERDE, as well as in Spain's Galicia region, where it's called *Albariño*. Although reasonably productive, these grapes are so thick-skinned that only a small amount of juice can be extracted from them. Alvarinho grapes can produce CREAMY, rich wines with complex flavors of apricots, peaches, and citrus. Although Alvarinho wines are some of the most expensive and highly prized white wines in both Portugal and Spain, this variety is rarely cultivated elsewhere.

amabile [ah-MAH-bee-lay] An Italian word describing wines that are medium-sweet. Amabile wines are usually less sweet than those labeled DOLCE but sweeter than ABBOCCATO.

Amador County [AM-uh-dor] Important California wine-producing area located in the Sierra Foothills, north of Calaveras County and west and slightly south of Sacramento. There are two smaller VITICULTURAL AREAS in the county, FIDDLETOWN and SHENANDOAH VALLEY, and the large SIERRA FOOTHILLS AVA, which also includes parts of several other counties. Amador County is very warm in most parts, generally rating a Region III classification and sometimes a Region IV (*see* CLIMATE

REGIONS OF CALIFORNIA). By a very considerable margin, ZINFANDEL is the
most widely planted grape variety here. Rhône varieties including
SYRAH, GRENACHE, MARSANNE, ROUSSANNE, and VIOGNIER are becoming
increasingly popular, as is the Italian SANGIOVESE. Interesting SAUVIGNON
BLANC is still being made. Tiny amounts of CABERNET SAUVIGNON,
CHARDONNAY, and a variety of other grapes are also grown.

amaro; pl. amari [ah-MAH-roh] 1. An Italian word used to
describe wines that are bitter or very DRY. The words *amarognolo* or
ammandorlato, which denote a bitter, toasted-almond flavor, are considered more flattering. 2. A bitter and sweet herbal liqueur from Italy.
Amari are made using a variety of ingredients such as herbs, roots,
flowers, citrus rinds, and bark macerated in alcohol with caramel
added for sweetness. Alcohol content can be as high as 35 percent.
Amari are generally drunk as an after-dinner beverage.

amarognolo *see* AMARO

amarone *see* RECIOTO

Amboise [ahm-BWAHZ] A quaint little town in France's TOURAINE AC
that produces higher-quality wine and is allowed to append its name
to the label Touraine-Amboise. The white wines are made from CHENIN
BLANC and resemble those from VOUVRAY. The red and ROSÉ wines are
made from CABERNET FRANC, GAMAY, and MALBEC. The Touraine province
is known as the "château country," and Amboise has a well-known
château that's quite popular.

Ambonnay [ahm-baw-NAY] An important wine-producing village
located in the Montagne de Reims area of France's CHAMPAGNE region.
Ambonnay, whose vineyards are planted with PINOT NOIR, is one of
only seventeen villages to have obtained a GRAND CRU rating of 100
percent (*see* CHAMPAGNE for explanation of percent system).

ambra *see* MARSALA DOC

amelioration [uh-MEEL-yuh-RAY-shuhn] A catchall term for various methods of improving a wine, some of which are illegal in commercial winemaking. These methods include adding sugar, water,
and/or ACID to the grape juice or wine to correct deficiencies. Most
countries have regulations pertaining to these practices with regard to
commercial winemaking.

American grapes *see* NATIVE AMERICAN GRAPES

Americano *see* ISABELLA; TICINO

A

American Viticultural Area (AVA) An American system implemented in 1978 to identify U.S. wines in a fashion similar to the French APPELLATION D'ORIGINE CONTRÔLÉE (AOC or AC) system. Unlike the French regulations, however, the rules governing American VITICULTURAL AREAS (under the jurisdiction of TAX AND TRADE BUREAU, previously BATF) are very lax. An AVA is defined strictly by a geographic area, whereas in France the parameters are much more precise. A French AOC identifies the grape varieties that may be grown in a geographic area, the maximum production per acre, the minimum level of alcohol required for wines produced in the area, and so forth. The only requirement for wine with an AVA designation on the label is that 85 percent of the grapes must be grown in that viticultural area. Growers must petition the Tax and Trade Bureau to obtain an AVA designation for a region. The Bureau's decision is based on such characteristics as an area's topography, soil type, climate, elevation, and, to some extent, historical precedent. AVAs range in size from several hundred acres to several million; some reside within other larger AVAs. For example, California's NAPA VALLEY is an AVA that encompasses other AVA's including HOWELL MOUNTAIN, STAGS LEAP DISTRICT, and RUTHERFORD BENCH. It also includes part of the CARNEROS AVA, whose area spills over into SONOMA COUNTY. The first AVA in the United States was the AUGUSTA AVA in MISSOURI, established in 1980.

ammandorlato *see* AMARO

amontillado *see* SHERRY

Amorgiano *see* MANDELARIA

amoroso *see* SHERRY

Les Amoureuses *see* CHAMBOLLE-MUSIGNY

ampelography [am-peh-LAW-gra-fee] The study and classification of grape varieties.

amphora; pl. amphorae [AM-fuhr-uh] An ancient earthenware vessel used by the Greeks and Romans to store wine. It usually had two handles and an oval body and was tapered to a point at the base. In order for it to stand upright, the amphora was seated on a round foot or base. Josko Gravner, a winemaker in the FRIULI-VENEZIA GIULIA region in northeastern Italy, has resurrected the use of amphorae for aging his white wine. He uses giant terra-cotta amphorae (about 660 gallons) from the Republic of Georgia, coats them with beeswax and then buries them up to their opening.

Ampurdán-Costa Brava DO [ahm-poor-DAHN KOH-stah BRAH-vah] *see* EMPORDÀ-COSTA BRAVA DO

Amtliche Prüfungsnummer [AM-tlish-eh PROOF-unz-snoo-mer] A German phrase meaning "official test number," usually abbreviated on a wine label as A.P.Nr. The Amtliche Prüfungsnummer indicates that the wine has met the minimum standards required by the law. It's granted by an official testing control center where the wine is tasted and the results of a chemical analysis (performed by an officially recognized laboratory) reviewed. The number, which must appear on the label, identifies the control center that tested the wine, bottling location, bottler's registration number, bottler's application number (indicating the wine lot), and year the wine was tested (not the VINTAGE year).

Anbaugebiet; pl. Anbaugebiete [AHN-bow-geh-beet] A German term referring to a growing region for quality wine, either QbA (QUALITÄTSWEIN BESTIMMTER ANBAUGEBIET) or QmP (QUALITÄTSWEIN MIT PRÄDIKAT). There are now thirteen of these regions, and their regional name is required on labels of quality wines. Eleven were initially established in 1971 by German law in an effort to meet European Common Market rules. They are AHR, BADEN, FRANKEN, HESSISCHE BERGSTRASSE, MITTELRHEIN, MOSEL-SAAR-RUWER, NAHE, RHEINGAU, RHEINHESSEN, PFALZ, and WÜRTTEMBERG. Two more Anbaugebiete have been added from the former East Germany—SAALE-UNSTRUT and SACHSEN. Each Anbaugebiet may be further divided into BEREICHE (districts), GROSSLAGEN (general sites), and EINZELLAGEN (individual sites or vineyards).

Andalucía; Andalusia [ahn-dah-LOO-syah; ahn-dah-LOO-zhuh] A well-known region covering the southernmost part of Spain. Andalusia encompasses eight provinces and spans from the Atlantic Ocean to the Mediterranean. There are four DO areas—MONTILLA-MORILES, MÁLAGA, CONDADO DE HUELVA, and JEREZ-XÉRÈS-SHERRY Y MANZANILLA DE SANLÚCAR DE BARRAMEDA. The best-known potables from the region are FORTIFIED WINES, the most famous of which is SHERRY.

Anderson Valley AVA An AVA located in California's Mendocino County, north of Sonoma County and San Francisco. The area starts just south of Boonville and extends northwest for about 25 miles ending close to the Pacific Ocean at its northwest tip. Most of the Anderson Valley Viticultural Area is a cool growing area—a Region I to Region II rating (*see* CLIMATE REGIONS OF CALIFORNIA). It does well with PINOT NOIR, CHARDONNAY, GEWURTRAMINER, and RIESLING; CABERNET SAUVIGNON, MERLOT, and ZINFANDEL are also grown. In addition to STILL WINES,

A

this region successfully grows the style of grape required for good SPARKLING WINES, such as those from Pacific Echo (formerly Scharfenberger Cellars) and Roederer Estate.

anejo; anejado por [ah-NYAY-yoh; ah-nyay-YAH-doh por] Spanish terms for "old" or "aged," and for "aged by."

angelica wine [an-JEHL-ih-kuh] An inexpensive FORTIFIED WINE, typically made from MISSION or MUSCAT grapes and enhanced with BRANDY. Angelica wine usually contains 10 to 15 percent RESIDUAL SUGAR. It's associated with California, its name being a reference to the city of Los Angeles.

angular *see* Glossary of Wine Tasting Terms, page 655

Aniane *see* TERRASSES DU LARZAC AC

Anjou [ahn-ZHOO] Area that is located in the western LOIRE near the city of Angers and is part of a larger growing region known as Anjou-Saumur. Anjou is best known for its rosés—ROSÉ D'ANJOU AC (a sweetish, pale pink wine produced from Cot (MALBEC), GAMAY, GROSLOT, and Pineau d'Aunis grapes) and CABERNET D'ANJOU AC (generally regarded as a higher-quality rosé made from CABERNET FRANC and CABERNET SAUVIGNON). White wines from Anjou have traditionally been on the sweet side, made mostly from CHENIN BLANC (locally called *Pineau d'Anjou* or *Pineau de la Loire*). However, there are also some drier styles made with up to the legal maximum of 20 percent CHARDONNAY and/or SAUVIGNON BLANC, which produce attractive, fruity wines. Beside the basic Anjou APPELLATION, white wines are produced in a number of smaller appellations in the area including BONNEZEAUX AC, COTEAUX DE L'AUBANCE AC, COTEAUX DU LAYON, QUARTS DE CHAUME, and SAVENNIÈRES AC. Red wines are made from Cabernet Franc, Cabernet Sauvignon, and Gamay, and those from the basic Anjou appellation are gaining in reputation. The **Anjou-Villages AC** is made up of forty-six villages scattered throughout Anjou that produce higher-quality red wines made from Cabernet Franc and Cabernet Sauvignon. There are also a number of white and rosé SPARKLING WINES made by the MÉTHODE CHAMPENOISE and produced under the **Anjou Mousseux AC** and the higher-quality CRÉMANT DE LOIRE AC.

Annaberg *see* KALLSTADT

annata [an-NAH-tah] Italian for "year of the vintage."

año [AHN-yoh] Spanish for "year."

anthesis *see* FLOWERING

anthocyanins [an-tho-SIGH-uh-nins] The pigments that contribute the red colors in wine and grapes.

antioxidant In winemaking, reference to additives such as ASCORBIC ACID and SULFUR DIOXIDE. When added in the right quantities, these substances limit the effect of oxygen contact with wine during various winemaking processes such as RACKING, FILTERING, and bottling. *See also* PHENOLIC COMPOUNDS

AOC Abbreviation for APPELLATION D'ORIGINE CÔNTROLÉE.

Aosta *see* VALLE D'AOSTA

apéritif [ah-pehr-uh-TEEF; ay-pehr-ee-TEEF] A French term referring to a light alcoholic drink taken before a meal to stimulate the appetite. Popular apéritifs include CHAMPAGNE, VERMOUTH, SHERRY, and FORTIFIED and flavored wines such as Lillet and Dubonnet.

A.P.Nr. Abbreviation for AMTLICHE PRUFÜNGSNUMMER.

appellation [ap-puh-LAY-shuhn; Fr. ah-pel-lah-SYAWN] In the wine world, a designated growing area governed by the rules and regulations established by its central government and local governing body. Such rules vary from country to country but are somewhat similar in their attempt to stimulate the production of quality wines. These regulations are established by the APPELLATION D'ORIGINE CONTRÔLÉE (AOC) in France, the DENOMINAZIONE DI ORIGINE CONTROLLATA (DOC) in Italy, the DENOMINAÇÃO DE ORIGEM CONTROLADA (DOC) in Portugal, and the DENOMINACIÓN DE ORIGEN (DO) in Spain. Canada has introduced the Vintners Quality Alliance (VQA) to define quality wines produced in that country. In the United States, the TAX AND TRADE BUREAU (previously BATF) is responsible for approving designated growing areas called AMERICAN VITICULTURAL AREAS (AVA). AVAs in the United States are not focused on quality, as is the French model, but rather on defining an area's unique growing environment. Besides AVAs, the United States also has **appellations of origin**, which can be any of the following: the United States, a single state, up to three contiguous states, a single county, or up to three counties in the same state (in which case the word "County" must appear on the label). In order to use an appellation name on a wine label, a wine must adhere to various rules on the percentage of grapes used from that area. For example, for "California" to be used on a label, 100 percent of the grapes must be grown in the state. For a county designation (such as "Monterey

A

County" or "Sonoma County"), 75 percent of the grapes must come from the named county. However, if "Monterey AVA" is used, then 85 percent of the grapes must be grown in that viticultural area. If two contiguous counties are used such as "Napa County" and "Sonoma County" then all the grapes must come from the two counties and the percentage of the wine that comes from each county must be identified on the label. Australia has implemented a system, called geographic indications, that is closer to the United States AVA structure than to the European appellation systems.

Appellation Contrôlée *see* APPELLATION D'ORIGINE CÔNTROLÉE

Appellation d'Origine Contrôlée (AOC or AC) [ah-pehl-lah-SYAW*N* daw-ree-JEEN kaw*n*-traw-LAY] The top category in the French system for ensuring quality wines. Appellation d'Origine Contrôlée, which means "Controlled Appellation of Origin," is sometimes shortened to Appellation Contrôlée and abbreviated as either AOC or AC. The French initiated the Appellation d'Origine Contrôlée system in 1935 as a means of safeguarding the more quality-conscious winemakers, vineyards, and areas from unethical producers who were taking advantage of the better-known names. Although the French AC system can't guarantee the quality of a producer's wine, it can control most of the elements that go into making it. This control is accomplished by the demanding criteria necessary for qualifying as an AC. These criteria fall into the following seven categories: (1) the land—acceptable vineyard acreage is precisely defined based on centuries of recorded usage and issues such as the land's soil, configuration, and altitude; (2) the grape varieties—the grape varieties are defined for each geographic area and based on historical data, clarifying which varieties perform well in particular soils and climates; (3) viticultural practices—this category considers such things as the number of vines per HECTARE, pruning techniques, and fertilization methods; (4) permissible YIELD—because large yields decrease the grapes' quality, and one way to improve caliber is to restrict the crop, maximum yields are established for each AC; (5) alcohol content—all ACs must guarantee a minimum alcohol level, which means that the grapes must reach a certain ripeness (sugar content), which in turn ensures flavor, although in some areas it's legal to add sugar (CHAPTALIZE) to reach the required alcohol level; (6) winemaking practices—each AC has regulations regarding winemaking procedures, usually based on historical practices that produced favorable results; (7) official tasting—since 1979 tasting panels sample all wines that apply for AC status. Wines that meet all seven of these criteria are entitled to use the phrase

Appellation Contrôlée on their labels; not following these regulations disqualifies a wine from AC status. Multiple ACs can exist within the geographic area of a larger AC. Such is the case with the PAUILLAC AC, which is within the HAUT-MÉDOC AC, which is within the BORDEAUX AC. Generally, the smaller ACs produce the highest-quality wines. The categories below Appellation d'Origine Contrôlée are, from top to bottom: VIN DÉLIMITÉ DE QUALITÉ SUPÉRIEURE, VIN DE PAYS, and VIN DE TABLE. Although the French system is being paralleled by other countries, so far none seem to be as successful. These include the AMERICAN VITICULTURAL AREA (AVA) in the United States, the DENOMINAZIONE DI ORIGINE CONTROLLATA (DOC) in Italy, the DENOMINAÇÃO DE ORIGEM CONTROLADA (DOC) in Portugal, and the DENOMINACIÓN DE ORIGEN (DO) in Spain.

Applegate Valley AVA Established in 2001, this AVA is located in southern OREGON south of Grants Pass and west of Medford and Ashland. It's a subregion of the ROGUE VALLEY AVA and is comprised of approximately 235 planted acres in thirty different vineyards. With its warm climate, the Applegate Valley tends to produce intense, full-bodied red wines.

appley; apples *see* Glossary of Wine Tasting Terms, page 655

Aprilia DOC [ah-PREE-lyah] DOC zone that is south and slightly east of Rome in the CASTELLI ROMANI district of Italy's LATIUM region. Three wines are made here: A DRY red from MERLOT; a DRY ROSATO from SANGIOVESE; and a dry white from TREBBIANO. The named grape must make up at least 95 percent of the grapes used.

Apulia [ah-POOL-yuh] Located in Italy's southeast section, Apulia (*Puglia* in Italian) is the wine region lying in the "heel" of Italy's boot-shaped land mass. There are over 260,000 vineyard acres planted with numerous grape varieties in the Apulia region. The primary red grapes are Negroamaro, Primitivo (*see* ZINFANDEL), MALVASIA Nera, and UVA DI TROIA. The white grape varieties, led by Verdeca, include Bianco d'Alessano, BOMBINO BIANCO, Malvasia Bianca, and TREBBIANO. The wine output from this area is tremendous and usually competes with SICILY for the largest production of Italy's twenty wine regions. The quality of the wines, however, is generally not very high. This is somewhat evidenced by the tiny amount of DOC-quality wine produced (less than 2 percent of the region's total production), although many of the region's good wines are not qualified to be DOCs. Apulia's twenty-five DOCs are Aleatico di Puglia, Alezio, Brindisi, Cacc'e mmitte di Lucera, CASTEL DEL MONTE, Copertino, Galatina, Gioia del Colle, Gravina, Leverano, Lizzano, Locorotondo, Martina or Martina Franca, Matino,

A

Moscato di Trani, Nardò, Orta Nova, Ostuni, Primitivo di Manduria, Rosso Barletta, Rosso Canosa or Canasium, Rosso di Cerignola, SALICE SALENTO, San Severo, and Squinzano. Much of this region's wine production is further processed into VERMOUTH or other APÉRITIF-type wine.

Aquileia DOC [ah-kwee-LAY-ah] A DOC area located in the southern part of the FRIULI-VENEZIA GIULIA region in northeastern Italy. The DOC covers a ROSATO plus thirteen different VARIETAL WINES, which must contain at least 90 percent of the main grape variety. The varietal wines are Cabernet (from CABERNET SAUVIGNON and CABERNET FRANC), Cabernet Sauvignon, Cabernet Franc, CHARDONNAY, MERLOT, Pinot Bianco (PINOT BLANC), Pinot Grigio (PINOT GRIS), Refosco dal Peduncolo Rosso (REFOSCO), Riesling Renano (RIESLING), Sauvignon (SAUVIGNON BLANC), FRIULANO, Traminer Aromatico (GEWÜRZTRAMINER), and VERDUZZO FRIULANO. The Rosato is mainly Merlot but can include up to 30 percent of some of the other approved red grapes. Most Aquileia wines have a light to medium BODY and should be drunk fairly young.

Aragon; Sp. Aragón [AH-rah-goan] Aragon, one of Spain's seventeen autonomous regions, is located in the northeast section of the country. Much of this area is subject to intense heat, which tends to push the grapes to an overripe stage, resulting in high-alcohol wines. Garnacha (GRENACHE) is the dominant red grape here; MACABEO, the primary white variety. Although mediocre, high-alcohol (many reaching 18 percent) wines prevail in Aragon, there are signs that a movement to better wines is underway. Four DOS—CAMPO DE BORJA, CARIÑENA, CALATAYUD, and SOMONTANO—are using more modern winemaking methods to produce higher-quality wines. Of these, Somontano, located in the cooler foothills of the Pyrenees, shows the most promise.

Aragonêz *see* TEMPRANILLO

Aramon [ah-rah-MAWN] This high-yielding, red-wine grape is extensively planted in France's LANGUEDOC-ROUSSILLON region. It's responsible for immense amounts of inferior wine, most of which has low alcohol and little flavor—France's contribution to the notorious European WINE LAKE. Because Aramon produces such pale red wine, a more darkly colored variety such as ALICANTE BOUSCHET is usually added for color. France is encouraging the replanting of many areas like the Languedoc-Roussillon with more respectable varieties. As a result, Aramon acreage has been decreasing over the last 25 years. Aramon is also known as *Pisse-vin, Plante Riche,* and *Ugni Noir.*

Arbois AC [ahr-BWAH] A large APPELLATION located in the Jura region of eastern France surrounding the town of Arbois. White wines are made from SAVAGNIN and CHARDONNAY. Light red and ROSÉ wines are made from Trousseau, PINOT NOIR, and Poulsard grapes. A good SPARKLING WINE, **Arbois** MOUSSEUX, is made by MÉTHODE CHAMPENOISE from Chardonnay grapes.

Aretini *see* CHIANTI DOCG

Argentina Even though Argentina is the world's fifth largest wine-producing country, a great majority of the wine is inexpensive and ordinary. However, progress has been made since the late 1990s in elevating the quality of wines, especially those exported to the international market. Total vineyard acreage has been reduced and new vineyards are being planted with higher quality grapes using improved planting methods. Still, there is a tendency for many growers to produce high yields out of their vineyards, resulting in lower quality wines. If this inclination is overcome, Argentina is positioned to become a major provider of high-quality wines. It's achieved notice for its MALBEC wines and gained an international audience for them. Malbec is the recognized star of the red-grape varieties. It's the most widely planted *quality* grape here and produces rich, deep-colored wines. Most of Argentina's wine is consumed within the country, which also happens to have one of the higher per capita consumption rates. The largest growing region is in the **Mendoza** province, which produces 70 to 75 percent of Argentina's wine and 85 percent of its quality wine. Mendoza has evolved the furthest in the development of recognized subregions, which include Luján de Cuyo, Maipú, San Rafael, and Uco Valley (around the village of Tupungato). Other growing regions include **Agrelo, Catamaraca, Jujuy, La Rioja, Neuguén, Rio Negro**, San Juan, and **Salta. San Juan**, the second most productive region, has three major subregions—the valley areas of Tulum, Ullum, and Zonda. A majority of the growing areas are not far from the Andes Mountains and benefit from irrigation water from melting snow. Most of Argentina's better wines come from the high, cool mountainous areas, with red wine comprising the majority. The most widely planted red-grape variety is Criolla (MISSION), followed by Malbec. There are a variety of other red grapes planted in Argentina including BARBERA, BONARDA, CABERNET SAUVIGNON, MERLOT, NEBBIOLO, PINOT NOIR, SANGIOVESE, SYRAH, and TEMPRANILLO. The most popular white varieties (used mostly for FORTIFIED WINES), are PALOMINO, Torrontes, and PEDRO XIMÉNEZ. There is also acreage planted with CHARDONNAY,

A

CHENIN BLANC, SÉMILLON, and SAUVIGNON BLANC, most of which go into higher-quality white wines, particularly from the Rio Negro area.

argol(s) [AHR-guhl] A natural tartar produced during FERMENTATION that appears as little crystals in wine vats and sometimes in bottles. Argols can sometimes be found clinging to a cork when it's extracted.

Arinto [ah-RIHN-toh] Cultivated in Portugal, this good-quality white-wine grape is known for its high ACID content, even when grown in the hottest areas. A well-made Arinto wine can be very aromatic with a fresh citrus feature. Arinto is a recommended variety throughout much of Portugal. Many growers, however, prefer to plant higher-yielding but lower-quality varieties. Arinto is also known as *Pedernão*.

Arizona Southwestern state that is one of the oldest winegrowing regions in the United States. Franciscan missionaries planted MISSION grapes over 400 years ago, many years before they moved into California. There are a few wineries in the northern part of the state; however, the major growing area is in the southeast corner in the mountainous regions south and east of Tucson. The **Sonoita AVA** (currently the only one recognized in the state) is southeast of Tucson around Elgin in Santa Cruz County. Other VITICULTURAL areas include the Sulphur Springs Valley (between Bisbee and Willcox) and Dos Cabezas (east of Willcox). The best-known winery, Callaghan Vineyard, has been making wines since 1990. Others include Arizona Vineyards, Charron Vineyard, Dark Mountain Winery, Domaines Ellam, Dos Cabezas Wineworks, Echo Canyon, Florence Vineyards, Fort Bowie Vineyards, Kokopelli Winery, Palo Verde, Paradise Valley Vineyards, San Dominique, Santa Cruz Winery, Sonoita Vineyard, Village of Elgin Winery, and Whispering Peak Vineyards. Arizona has less than 1,000 acres planted, primarily to popular grape varieties like CABERNET SAUVIGNON, MERLOT, SYRAH, CHARDONNAY, SAUVIGNON BLANC, and SANGIOVESE.

Arkansas In the early 1900s, Arkansas enjoyed abundant vineyards, mostly of CONCORD grapes, an indigenous American variety of the VITIS LABRUSCA species. Unfortunately, wines from these grapes don't have the popular appeal of VITIS VINIFERA species (the basic European varieties like CABERNET SAUVIGNON and CHARDONNAY). Today, Arkansas wine-making is mostly from HYBRIDS and *Vitis vinifera* grapes. The state has three AMERICAN VITICULTURAL AREAS, all located in the northwestern portion of the state—the large OZARK MOUNTAIN AVA (which Arkansas shares with MISSOURI and OKLAHOMA) and the smaller AVAs of ALTUS and Arkansas Mountain, both subzones of the Ozark Mountain AVA. Area wineries produce a variety of STILL WINES from Cynthiana (NORTON) grapes or hybrids (like NIAGRA and SEYVAL BLANC), as well as from Cabernet Sauvignon, MERLOT, and Chardonnay grapes. Arkansas also produces SPARKLING WINES. The Wiederkehr Winery, which was started in the late 1800s, is in operation today by the founder's descendants. It has shifted from American varieties and hybrids to grapes like Cabernet Sauvignon, RIESLING, and MUSCAT.

Arkansas Mountain AVA *see* OZARK MOUNTAIN AVA

Armagnac [ahr-muhn-YAK] A fine French BRANDY from the Armagnac region, which is situated southeast of BORDEAUX. The region consists of three subregions—Bas-Armagnac, Tenareze, and Haut-Armagnac. Although almost as highly regarded as COGNAC, Armagnac is of a different style. It's distilled (*see* DISTILLATION) only once and, therefore, has a lower alcoholic strength (generally about 53 percent alcohol) than Cognac (about 70 percent), which undergoes a double distillation process. This single distillation also leaves more flavoring elements in the distilled spirit. Armagnac employs the local black oak for AGING instead of the Limousin oak used for Cognac. Black oak imparts more flavor to the Armagnac and allows for faster aging. The result is that Armagnac is silky smooth but fuller-flavored than Cognac, although it generally doesn't have the finesse of the finest Cognacs.

arms *see* HEAD PRUNED VINE

Arneis [ahr-NAYZ] White-wine grape that originated (and is still primarily grown) in the Roero hills of Italy's southern PIEDMONT, just north of ALBA. Once nearly extinct, Arneis has made a comeback in recent years. It can produce very good wines with PERFUMY characteristics of apples, pears, and a hint of licorice. The wines, usually sold as ROERO ARNEIS DOC, are in limited supply.

Arnsburger [AHRNS-behrk-er] A German white-wine grape derived in 1939 from a CROSS of two RIESLING CLONES (88 and 64). Arnsburger found its way to MADEIRA where its disease resistance is useful and it's blended with VERDELHO to diminish that grape's high acidity in creating a better balanced dry TABLE WINE.

aroma *see* Glossary of Wine Tasting Terms, page 655

aromatic *see* Glossary of Wine Tasting Terms, page 655

Arrábida *see* PALMELA DOC

A

arresting fermentation A technique of preserving RESIDUAL SUGAR in wines by stopping FERMENTATION. There are several methods to arrest fermentation including chilling the wine to the point where YEASTS become inactive and using a CENTRIFUGE to remove the yeast cells prior to completing fermentation.

Arribes DO [ah-*RR*EE-bhehs] An up-and-coming DO located in the CASTILE AND LEÓN region next to the Portuguese border. Over 1,800 acres of vineyards are planted in the provinces of Salamanca and Zamora. Red and ROSÉ wines are made with a minimum of 60 percent of the JUAN GARCIA variety blended with TEMPRANILLO and RUFETE. Whites are made with a minimum of 60 percent MALVASIA combined with AIRÉN and VERDEJO. Arribes DO is sometimes referred to as *Arribes del Duero.*

arroba [ah-ROH-bah] A Spanish measure used for grapes and the resulting wines. It's equivalent to just over 25 pounds of grapes (about one basketful), which yields about 4¼ gallons.

arrope *see* MALAGA DO

Arroyo Grande Valley AVA [uh-ROY-oh GRAN-day] 42,880-acre AVA located in central California about halfway between San Francisco and Los Angeles. It's southwest of San Luis Obispo, encompasses the town of Arroyo Grande, and extends to the northeast. The western part of the area has a long cool growing season, a Region I rating (*see* CLIMATE REGIONS OF CALIFORNIA), but the eastern part of the area is warmer and falls into Region III. CHARDONNAY is the most popular variety by a considerable amount, followed by PINOT NOIR and other grapes like CABERNET SAUVIGNON, SAUVIGNON BLANC, SÉMILLON, and ZINFANDEL.

Arroyo Seco AVA [uh-ROY-oh SEH-koh] Small, 18,240-acre VITICULTURAL AREA located in Monterey County, California, southeast of Monterey. Arroyo Seco, which is a subzone in the larger MONTEREY AVA, begins just south of Soledad and extends to south of Greenfield. The major white grapes grown here are CHARDONNAY and RIESLING, along with some GEWÜRZTRAMINER. PINOT NOIR does well in this cooler area, and some CABERNET SAUVIGNON is grown. Jekel Vineyard is the main winery in this region, although a number of other wineries obtain grapes from this area's vineyards and use the "Arroyo Seco AVA" designation on their labels.

Arruda *see* ESTREMADURA

Les Arvelets *see* FIXIN

asciutto [ah-SHOO-toh] An Italian word that, when used to describe STILL WINES, means "very DRY." *See also* SECCO.

ascorbic acid Known commonly as vitamin C, ascorbic acid is used in winemaking primarily as an ANTIOXIDANT.

Asian lady beetle Insect introduced to the United States in the 1960s to help control aphids inhabiting various crops. When other crops are picked, the Asian lady beetle will spread into vineyards and enjoy the grape juice available to them, particularly of VITUS VINIFERA grapes. When frightened, the beetles will emit a yellowish secretion, which often happens during grape harvesting. This is becoming a concern to the wine industry because, if concentrated, the secretion can taint a wine causing an objectionable, musty, peanut character. The Asian lady beetle is also known as *Harlequin ladybird, Halloween lady beetle, Asian ladybug.*

Asprinio [ah-SPREE-nee-oh] A white-grape variety used in SPARKLING WINES and DRY, LIGHT, STILL WINES produced in Italy's BASILICATA and CAMPANIA regions. The Aversa DOC wines are made primarily from the Asprinio grape.

Asprino [ah-SPREE-noh] A DRY, LIGHT, lower-ALCOHOL wine produced in the BASILICATA and CAMPANIA regions of Italy. This VINO DA TAVOLA (table wine) is made from the ASPRINIO grape.

assemblage [ah-sahm-BLAHJ] French for "assembling," referring to the art of BLENDING. In BORDEAUX assemblage describes the activity of judging the wines made from different lots (which can come from different varieties, the same variety from different parts of the vineyard, or grapes picked at different times and therefore showing different levels of sugar) and determining which lots are suitable for a CHÂTEAU'S final wines. In some cases, the wine will go into the premium brand; in other cases, it'll go into a SECOND LABEL or even be sold off in BULK. In a poor year, a château may decide not to produce any of its premium brand wines at all. In CHAMPAGNE, a similar process is employed (particularly with NON-VINTAGE champagnes) in order to achieve a "house style" that's consistent from year to year. This requires reviewing batches of wines from different vineyards, grapes, and years to blend the appropriate CUVÉE.

Assmannshausen [AHS-mahns-how-zuhn] A German village located in the RHEINGAU region, north of RÜDESHEIM, where the Rhine shifts north toward the town of Koblenz. Assmannshausen produces a

A

famous and expensive red wine made from Spätburgunder (PINOT NOIR). Internationally, these wines are not as well received as they are in Germany because they're generally lighter and can be sweet.

Assyrtico; Assyrtiko [ah-SYR-tih-koh] A high-quality white grape that's not only the main variety grown on the Greek island Santorini but also increasingly grown throughout Greece. Assyrtico has citrus and honeysuckle traits and a trademark ACIDITY that perseveres even as it fully ripens in the hot Greek climate. It's often used as a BLENDING WINE with wines from grapes with low acidity.

Asti [AH-stee] Name of an important wine-producing town and province situated south of Turin in Italy's PIEDMONT region. In addition to the ASTI DOCG (which produces the area's famous SPARKLING WINE), several other DOCS and DOCGS use Asti in their names—BARBERA D'ASTI, Dolcetto d'Asti, Freisa d'Asti, Grignolino d'Asti, and MOSCATO D'ASTI.

Asti DOCG; Asti [AH-stee] Located in the southeastern portion of the PIEDMONT region near the town of Asti, this DOCG area produces Italy's most famous SPARKLING WINE, formerly called *Asti Spumante*. It shares this DOCG with a related wine, **Moscato d'Asti**, which is made similarly, but in a FRIZZANTE (instead of fully sparkling) style. In 1994, when Asti Spumante was upgraded to DOCG status, its name was simplified to *Asti*. These wines, which are generally semisweet to sweet, are so popular that the amount produced by this DOCG is now second only to the CHIANTI DOCG. The wines are made in a modified version of the CHARMAT (or *autoclave*) process. In this procedure the grape MUST is filtered and then stored in tanks at near freezing temperatures so that FERMENTATION can't begin. The producers make batches according to demand so that the resulting wines can be as fresh as possible. To produce the wine, the must is allowed to warm and then is innoculated with yeast so that fermentation can begin. This process all occurs inside large sealed tanks so that the carbon dioxide produced during fermentation isn't lost. After the desired ALCOHOL and RESIDUAL SUGAR levels are reached, the wine is rapidly chilled to stop fermentation. The wine is then filtered, bottled, and corked—ready for shipment. The main difference between the Asti DOCG wines and the Moscato d'Asti DOCG wines is that fermentation of Moscato d'Asti wines is stopped sooner so that the residual sugar content is higher, the alcohol level is lower, and the wine is less effervescent because less carbon dioxide is produced. Additionally, Asti is normally packaged like CHAMPAGNE with a wired-down cork, and Moscato d'Asti generally has the standard cork used by most STILL

WINES. The wines are made from the MUSCAT grape (called *Moscato Bianco* or *Moscato di Canelli* in this region), and the resulting wine has a fresh grapey taste. Asti Spumante and Moscato d'Asti wines should be drunk young and fresh.

astringent; astringency *see* Glossary of Wine Tasting Terms, page 655

asztalibor; asztali bor [AHS-tah-lih-bahr] Hungarian term for "common TABLE WINE" (*bor* means wine).

Aszú [ah-SOO] The Hungarian term for grapes infected with BOTRYTIS CINEREA and therefore shriveled and full of CONCENTRATED flavors and sugar. TOKAJI ASZÚ, the famous DESSERT WINE, is made from botrytis-infected FURMINT grapes.

ATF *see* BUREAU OF ALCOHOL, TOBACCO, FIREARMS AND EXPLOSIVES

Atlas Peak AVA A subregion located within the NAPA VALLEY AVA but east of Napa Valley proper. Approved in 1992, this AVA takes its name from Atlas Peak, the highest point in the Vaca Mountain range at 2,700 feet. It encompasses most of the Foss Valley and consists of approximately 11,400 acres, although only a small percentage is planted. Atlas Peak Vineyards, owned by Marchese Piero Antinori, is the primary winery in the area. High-end producer, Pahlmeyer, also has several hundred acres planted in this region.

atmosphere; atm Atm is the abbreviation for *atmosphere,* which in the wine world is the measurement for pressure used to produce SPARKLING WINES. Technically, it's the normal air pressure at sea level, approximately 14.7 pounds per square inch. In the production of a standard sparkling wine such as CHAMPAGNE or SPUMANTE, the pressure should be 6 atm. A CRÉMANT-style sparkling wine has about half that pressure, and some FRIZZANTE-style Italian wines may have only 2 atm of pressure.

attack *see* Glossary of Wine Tasting Terms, page 655

attenuated *see* Glossary of Wine Tasting Terms, page 655

Attica An important wine-producing region situated near Athens in southeastern Greece. The grapes used are the local varieties—Savatiano, Mandilaria, and Rhoditis. Most of the production is made into RETSINA.

Aubance *see* COTEAUX DE L'AUBANCE AC

A

Aube *see* CHAMPAGNE

Auckland New Zealand winegrowing region located on the North Island around Auckland, New Zealand's largest city. Although a few wineries are located east and south of the city, most are northwest of the city in the growing areas around **Henderson, Kumeu,** and **Huapai.** Winegrowing started in the early 1900s in the Henderson area and continued to expand with significant activity during the late 1920s and early 1930s. In the 1960s, the need for more vineyards increased interest in the Kumeu/Huapai area. During the middle of that decade, the Auckland region comprised about half the vineyard land in all of New Zealand. Today, with the growth of other prominent areas like MARLBOROUGH, HAWKES BAY, GISBORNE, and CANTERBURY, the Auckland region has less than 4 percent of the country's vineyards—about 1,100 acres. However, the majority of the large and significant wine producers are located in the Auckland region and source their grapes from other areas. Auckland is known for its high-quality red wines made from CABERNET FRANC, CABERNET SAUVIGNON, and MERLOT (in particular when these are blended). CHARDONNAY is the most popular white variety followed by SÉMILLON and SAUVIGNON BLANC. Whereas Auckland has one of the wettest climates, **Waiheke Island**, which is just in the Hauraki Gulf, receives less than 10 percent of Auckland's annual rainfall. With its dry climate and ideal temperatures, this small growing area has gained a sterling reputation for consistent production of high-quality Cabernet and Merlot wines. Also technically in the Auckland region is **Matakana**, located about 50 miles north of the city of Auckland. It also has been developing a reputation for high-quality wines—reds from Cabernet and Merlot and whites from Chardonnay and PINOT GRIS.

Aude [OHD] A large DÉPARTEMENT in France's LANGUEDOC-ROUSSILLON, or *Midi,* as it's sometimes called. Aude, located in southern France along the Mediterranean not too far from the Spanish border, produces millions of bottles of very ordinary wine, most of it red wine made from CARIGNAN, CINSAUT, and GRENACHE. Along with départements of L'HÉRAULT and GARD, Aude contributes to what is called the European WINE LAKE—huge amounts of nondescript wine. There are signs that the quality is improving, in part as a result of increased planting of popular varieties like CABERNET SAUVIGNON, CHARDONNAY, and SAUVIGNON BLANC. Under existing APPELLATION rules, these varieties cannot qualify for higher classification so the wines made from them must be sold as VIN DE PAYS. The best-known appellations in Aude are BLANQUETTE DE LIMOUX (which produces decent SPARKLING WINE via MÉTHODE CHAMPENOISE), CORBIÈRES, MINERVOIS, and FITOU.

Auflange *see* NIERSTEIN

Augusta AVA The first viticultural area to be approved in the United States was Augusta in 1980—and it's not in California but in MISSOURI. This area encompasses approximately 15 square miles around the historic town of Augusta, west of St. Louis. In the mid-1800s, German immigrants settling in valleys along the Missouri River discovered that the area provided a safe haven where grapes could be cultivated. Today, HYBRIDS like CHAMBOURCIN, SEYVAL BLANC, VIDAL BLANC, and Vignoles (RAVAT) are the favorites along with NORTON (also known as *Cynthiana*). Mount Pleasant, probably the best-known winery in the region, has planted red BORDEAUX varieties (CABERNET SAUVIGNON, CABERNET FRANC, and MERLOT) in addition to the hybrids.

Aurora;Aurore [aw-ROAR-ah; aw-ROAR] White-wine grape that is one of the most widely planted varieties in the northeastern United States, where the cool climate suits its early ripening properties. Aurora is a French-American HYBRID, officially known as **Seibel Hybrid 5279**. It's used to make SPARKLING WINES, as well as OFF-DRY, STILL WINES.

Ausbruch A quality category for Austrian wines. Wines allowed into this category are made from grapes that have been infected with BOTRYTIS CINEREA and then dried naturally. This shrivels the grapes, thereby concentrating the sugar. The superior wine made from these grapes is very sweet but has enough ACIDITY for proper BALANCE. The required sugar levels (a minimum 139° OECHSLE) place Ausbruch wines between BEERENAUSLESE and the highest-quality level, TROCKENBEERE-NAUSLESE.

Auslese [OWS-lay-zuh] German for "selection," used in the wine trade to describe specially selected, perfectly ripened bunches of grapes that are hand-picked and then pressed separately from other grapes. Auslese is one of the six subcategories of QmP (QUALITÄTSWEIN MIT PRÄDIKAT) and ranks above KABINETT and SPÄTLESE but below BEERE-NAUSLESE, EISWEIN, and TROCKENBEERENAUSLESE. To attain the Auslese category, the natural sugar content of the grapes must reach a certain minimum (83 to 105° OECHSLE, approximately 20 to 25 percent sugar by weight), depending on the region and the variety. The grapes are often subject to BOTRYTIS CINEREA (called *Edelfäule* in German), which can give them that extra push toward the high sugar levels. The superior wine made from these grapes is sweet and expensive and is often categorized as a DESSERT WINE, although many are fermented to contain less residual sugar (resulting in high alcohol levels) and labeled as

TROCKEN. AUSTRIA has an Auslese category that's similar and requires a minimum 105° OECHSLE.

austere; austerity *see* Glossary of Wine Tasting Terms, page 655

Australia Although Australia has had vineyards since the late 1700s, it wasn't until the late 1950s that Australian winemakers really started to focus on TABLE WINES. By the 1980s Australian wines were commanding the attention of the rest of the world. Australia, not content with its place as a major wine producer, developed **Strategy 2025** in 1996. Introduced by the Winemakers Federation of Australia (with considerable government backing), this mission statement and plan was designed to make Australia the world's most influential and profitable supplier of branded wines. In 1999 Australia was the world's seventh largest producer with major exports to the United Kingdom, United States, New Zealand, Canada, Germany, and a number of other countries. To achieve its Strategy 2025 goals, Australia must more than double its production. As in California, the European (particularly French) grape varieties are the most popular in Australia. Shiraz (SYRAH) is the most popular grape variety, followed by CABERNET SAUVIGNON, CHARDONNAY, SÉMILLON, MERLOT, COLOMBARD, RUBY CABERNET, PINOT NOIR, RIESLING, SAUVIGNON BLANC, CHENIN BLANC, and VERDELHO. A fair amount of PALOMINO and PEDRO XIMÉNEZ is still grown for the production of Australian SHERRY. SULTANA is also widely grown, and although most of the production is used for table grapes or raisins, some finds its way into BULK WINES. Australia is about four-fifths the size of the United States. The vineyard land, like the population, is clustered primarily in the southeast and the southwest. The vast quantity of wine comes from areas collectively known as the Riverlands, which are located along the Murry, Darling, and Murrumbidgee Rivers in the states of NEW SOUTH WALES, SOUTH AUSTRALIA, and VICTORIA. These areas are RIVERINA in New South Wales, RIVERLAND in South Australia, and MURRAY DARLING and SWAN HILL, which lie in both New South Wales and Victoria. The better-quality wines come from a variety of distinct regions: In New South Wales—HUNTER VALLEY, MUDGEE, and new regions like COWRA, ORANGE, and HILLTOPS; in Victoria—GEELONG, GOULBURN VALLEY, GRAMPIANS, RUTHERGLEN, and YARRA VALLEY; in Southern Australia—ADELAIDE HILLS, BAROSSA VALLEY, CLARE VALLEY, COONAWARRA, PADTHAWAY, and MCLAREN VALE; and in Western Australia—GREAT SOUTHERN, MARGARET RIVER, and SWAN DISTRICT. In Queensland the only area of note is the Granite Belt. On the Australian island of TASMANIA, with its somewhat cooler climate, there are high viticultural hopes for areas like Piper River and Tamar Valley in the north and Coal River, Derwent Valley,

Huon Valley, and the East Coast in the southern portion. If an Australian wine label indicates a single grape variety, the wine must be made of at least 80 percent of that grape. If the label indicates multiple varieties—such as Cabernet-Shiraz or Semillon-Chardonnay—the varieties must be listed in descending order of quantity. If the label indicates a particular region, 80 percent of it must be from that region. A wine blended from wines of different regions (which many Australian winemakers prefer) must label the regions in descending order of volume. The gigantic zone called SOUTH EASTERN AUSTRALIA covers three states and parts of two others and accounts for 95 percent of the Australian growing regions. VINTAGE Australian wine must be at least 95 percent from that vintage. Australia's APPELLATION system (necessary in order to satisfy trade agreements with key trading partners) is known as GEOGRAPHIC INDICATIONS.

Austria The world of wine in Austria is similiar to that of Germany in many ways, but it is also quite different. Austria is generally warmer than Germany; therefore, the grapes ripen more fully, which produces stronger wines. Austrians also generally like their wines drier (*see* DRY) than Germans. Since the wine scandal of 1985, where traces of poisonous diethylene glycol were found in wines that were supposed to contain only natural sugars, Austria enacted tougher wine-quality laws very similar to those in Germany. The lowest wine-quality category is TAFELWEIN, with a subcategory of LANDWEIN. The middle category is QUALITÄTSWEIN, with a subcategory of KABINETT (which in Germany is in the highest category). Austria's highest category is PRÄDIKATSWEIN, with the subcategories (lowest to highest) of: SPÄTLESE, AUSLESE, STROHWEIN (not a German subcategory), EISWEIN, BEERENAUSLESE, AUSBRUCH (not a German subcategory), and TROCKENBEERENAUSLESE. In most cases, the Austrian requirements are somewhat stricter—for example, higher required sugar levels. If the name of a RIED ("vineyard") is used on the label, 100 percent of the wine used must be from that vineyard location. This is also true for any local or regional name. If a VARIETY or VINTAGE appears on the label, 85 percent of the wine must come from the named grape or vintage. In 2001, Austria implemented new laws regarding an appellation system called DISTRICTUS AUSTRIA CONTROLLATUS (DAC). Over time, this appellation approach may replace the more traditional approach based on sugar levels. **Weinviertel** was the first area in Austria to receive a DAC designation. Per capita, Austrians consume over three times the wine of Americans. In fact, they consume more than they produce so imported wines fill the gap. More than 80 percent of the Austrian wine production is white. The most popular white grape is GRÜNER VELTLINER, which produces pale, CRISP, light- to medium-bodied (*see* BODY), slightly SPICY wines of good quality. Other popular white varieties are GEWÜRZTRAMINER, Muscat-Ottonel (MUSCAT), Rhine Riesling (RIESLING), MÜLLER-THURGAU, Weissburgunder (PINOT BLANC), WELSCHRIESLING, Rotgipfler, Zierflander, and Neuburger (a cross of Pinot Blanc and SYLVANER). The red wines, which are typically very light, are made from Blauburgunder (PINOT NOIR), PORTUGIESER, BLAUFRÄNKISCH, and Zweigelt. Austria produces most of its wines in the eastern part of the country—over half in the region of Lower Austria (Niederösterreich), followed by Burgenland, then Styria (Steiermark) and Vienna. Most of Austria's wines are dry, the exceptions being the sweet, BOTRYTISED wines from Burgenland, which are sometimes compared to those from SAUTERNES.

autoclave [AW-toh-klayv] Italian name for the sealed tanks used in the CHARMAT PROCESS (bulk process) of producing SPARKLING WINES. Occasionally the process itself is referred to as autoclave. ASTI sparkling wines rely heavily on the use of the autoclave.

autolysis [aw-TAHL-uh-sihss] A decomposition of dead yeast cells that occurs in wines that are aged SUR LIE ("on the LEES"). Winemakers believe that certain wines—like those made with CHARDONNAY or SAUVIGNON BLANC grapes—benefit from autolysis because they gain complexity during the process. Autolysis affects SPARKLING WINES made via MÉTHODE CHAMPENOISE because yeast cells and a mixture of sugar and wine (DOSAGE) are added to create a second fermentation in the bottle. The sparkling wine is then aged with the yeast cells in the bottle (sometimes for up to 10 years), which adds complexity to both BOUQUET and flavor.

autovinification [AW-toh-vihn-ih-fih-KAY-shun] The use of large, pressure-locked stainless steel or concrete tanks (called autovinificators) during the FERMENTATION of PORT. The naturally produced gases create enough pressure to force open the locks, pumping the juice up and over the CAP (seed, skins, stems, etc.) and thereby extracting TANNINS, color, and full fruit flavors. This technique replaces the traditional method of using long poles to push the cap down into the juice.

Auvergne *see* CÔTES D'AUVERGNE VDQS

Auxerre *see* CÔTES D'AUXERRE

Auxerrois *see* MALBEC

Auxerrois Blanc [awk-sehr-WAH (oh-zher-WAH) BLAHN (BLAHNGK)] A white wine grape grown primarily in France's ALSACE region. The good-yielding Auxerrois Blanc produces a rather bland wine with high ACIDITY and high ALCOHOL. It's most often used as a blend for EDELSWICKERS. There's some confusion about its name because, in various locales, MALBEC is called *Auxerrois,* CHARDONNAY is called *Auxerrois Blanc,* and PINOT GRIS is called *Auxerrois Gris.*

Auxerrois Gris *see* PINOT GRIS

Auxey-Duresses AC [awk-SAY dew-RESS] A minor wine-producing APPELLATION centered around the village of Auxey-Duresses in the CÔTE DE BEAUNE area of France's BURGUNDY region. This area produces good wines—reds from PINOT NOIR and white wines from CHARDON-NAY—but they're overshadowed by the superb wines of neighboring MEURSALT. Auxey-Duresses contains several PREMIER CRU vineyards, but much of the wine produced in this appellation is sold under the name Côte de Beaune-Villages AC.

AVA *See* AMERICAN VITICULTURAL AREA

Avellino *See* FIANO DI AVELLINO DOC

awkward *see* Glossary of Wine Tasting Terms, page 655

AxR1 *see* PHYLLOXERA

Aÿ [AH-ee; Ah-yee] Very famous GRAND CRU village in the Montagne de Reims district in the CHAMPAGNE region near Epernay. Its full name is Aÿ-Champagne. The hillside vineyards, located on the north bank of the Marne, are planted almost entirely with PINOT NOIR along with a small amount of MEUNIER (Pinot Meunier). The high quality of the grapes and the wines produced here has been recognized as far back as the sixteenth century.

Ayala *See* CHAMPAGNE

azienda agricola [ah-DZYEHN-dah ah-GREE-koh-lah] Italian for "agrarian concern," *azienda agricola* is an Italian term for "wine estate." It's used in conjunction with the estate's name on some Italian wine labels. **Azienda vinicola** on a label refers to the winery, the place where the wine was actually made; **azienda vitivinicola** to the concern that grew the grapes.

azienda vinicola *see* AZIENDA AGRICOLA

azienda vitivinicola *see* AZIENDA AGRICOLA

BA Abbreviation for BEERENAUSLESE.

Bacchus [BAK-uhs] 1. A white-wine grape that is a very successful cross of MÜLLER-THURGAU and a SYLVANER-RIESLING HYBRID. Bacchus generally produces wines with good BODY, CHARACTER, and AROMA but low ACIDITY. The best ones show MUSCATlike attributes. Most Bacchus wines are blended with Müller-Thurgau and go into lower-quality LIEBFRAUMILCH. 2. The Roman god of wine in classical mythology, Bacchus is often confused with DIONYSUS, the Greek god of wine before the age of Rome.

Bacharach, Bereich *see* MITTELRHEIN

back blending The New Zealand term for adding SÜSSRESERVE (sweet unfermented grape juice) to sweeten a wine.

backbone *see* Glossary of Wine Tasting Terms, page 655

backward *see* Glossary of Wine Tasting Terms, page 655

Baco Blanc [BAH-koh BLAHN (BLAHNGK)] White French-American HYBRID that is grown mainly in France's ARMAGNAC district, where it replaced FOLLE BLANCHE, which had GRAFTING and BLACK ROT problems. Baco Blanc was developed by French hybridizer Maurice Baco who CROSSED the American hybrid Noah with Folle Blanche. Baco Blanc is very prolific and produces the high-ACIDITY, low-ALCOHOL wines much sought after by Armagnac's BRANDY makers. It's also known as *Baco 22A* and *Piquepoul de Pays.*

Baco, Maurice [BAH-koh] A late eighteenth-century French hybridist who developed a number of HYBRIDS that are still in use today including BACO BLANC and BACO NOIR.

Baco Noir [BAH-koh NWAHR] A French-American HYBRID developed by French hybridizer Maurice Baco by crossing FOLLE BLANCHE with a native American vine. Baco Noir is grown in the eastern United States, primarily in New York State. It produces red wines that range from light, fruity styles that are reminiscent of BEAUJOLAIS' GAMAY to slightly heavier versions that are more suggestive of light BORDEAUX-style wines. Much of the modest Baco Noir acreage finds its way into BLENDS.

Badacsonyi [BAH-dah-CHAW-nyih] Hungary adds an *i* to the end of the names of its high-quality wine-producing regions, thereby identifying the wine's source. Badacsonyi refers to wines coming from the Mount Badacsony area in western Hungary on Lake Balaton's north shore. The best known of these wines is Badacsonyi Kéknyelü, made from the KÉKNYELÜ grape. Others are Badacsonyi Szürkebarát (PINOT GRIS) and Badacsonyi FURMINT.

Bad Dürkheim [baht DUHRK-hime] An important German wine center as well as a spa town. The name *bad* translates to "bath" or "spa" and usually indicates an area with mineral springs. Bad Dürkheim is located west of the city of Mannheim in the PFALZ region. The vineyards around Bad Dürkheim, which is also famous for its annual Sausage Fair, are known for producing excellent RIESLING wines. There are three GROSSLAGEN—Feuerberg, Hochmess, and Schenken-böhl. The EINZELLAGE Spielberg is one of the best sites.

Baden [BAHD-uhn] A large German ANBAUGEBIET (quality-wine region) with about 41,000 vineyard acres that is the southernmost of the thirteen Anbaugebiete, with its southern edge touching up against the Swiss border. The major portion of Baden starts along the river Main, just north of Heidelberg, and extends south about 300 kilometers (180 miles) to the city of Basel. Most of the vineyards are situated in the southern portion, from the spa-resort town of Baden-Baden to Basel. One small part of Baden sits next to the FRANKEN Anbaugebiete, which is farther north, and another section is around Bodensee (also called *Lake Constance*). Baden's climate is the warmest of the thirteen Anbaugebiete and, as a result, over 70 percent of Germany's Spätburgunder (PINOT NOIR) vines are planted here. MÜLLER-THURGAU is the most widely planted variety, with Rülander (PINOT GRIS) quite popular as well. The area's warm climate contributes to wines that are generally higher in ALCOHOL and lower in ACIDITY than those from other parts of Germany. The unusual ROSÉ wine, BADISH ROTGOLD, which is a local specialty, is made from a combination of Spätburgunder and Rülander grapes. The pale pink WEISSHERBST wines, generally made from Spätburgunder, are also a local favorite. Baden contains 7 BEREICHE (including KAISERSTUHL-TUNIBERG and MARKGRÄFLERLAND), 16 GROSSLAGEN, and over 300 EINZELLAGEN. Production in Baden is carried out primarily by cooperative cellars including the huge **Badischer Winzerkeller**, Europe's largest wine-producing cellar.

Badischer Winzerkeller, Bereich *see* BADEN

Badisch Rotgold [BAHD-ish ROHT-golt] A quality ROSÉ wine that used to be quite popular in Germany's BADEN region. It's made by combining Rülander (PINOT GRIS) and Spätburgunder (PINOT NOIR) grapes and then PRESSING and FERMENTING them together.

Bad Kreuznach [baht KROYTS-nahkh] The center of Germany's NAHE wine region, Bad Kreuznach is a spa-resort town (*bad* translates to "bath" or "spa"). In addition, it gives its name to the BEREICH **Kreuznach**, which covers the southern portion of the Nahe ANBAUGE-BIETE. **Kronenberg** is the well-known GROSSLAGE, whose vineyards surround Bad Kreuznach. Some of the best EINZELLAGEN include **Brückes**, **Kahlenberg**, **Krötenpfuhl**, and **Steinweg**.

Badstube, Grosslage Bernkasteler *see* BERNKASTEL

Baga [BAH-guh] Portugal's most widely cultivated red wine grape variety. It's particularly heavily planted in BAIRRADA, where it accounts for 80 to 90 percent of the region's red wine production. Baga is also widely grown in the regions of DÃO, DOURO (where its known as *Tinta Bairrada*), and Minho. Although extremely productive, Baga generally produces only medium-quality wines. These deeply colored wines are very TANNIC and ASTRINGENT, especially when VINIFIED in the traditional way by leaving the skins *and* stalks in the fermenting juice for a week or longer. Newer processing methods, which use only the skins (and for shorter periods) during fermentation, produce rich, colorful wines that are fragrant and fruity and certainly not as ROUGH.

bag-in-a-box wine An Australian invention conceived in the mid 1960s specifically to provide lighter, non-breakable packaging for large amounts of less-expensive wines. Inside each box (which typically holds the equivalent of four to five bottles of wine) is a polyethylene bag filled with wine. The bag operates on the principle of the traditional leather European wine bladder—as the wine is drawn off (by a spigot built into the box) the bag collapses, thereby keeping out much of the air that begins a wine's deterioration. Bag-in-a-box wines are best consumed within six months of being filled, and most are dated for the consumer's awareness. In Australia and New Zealand, this packaging is also called *cask* or *bladder pack*.

Baiken *see* RAUENTHAL

Bairrada DOC [bi-RAH-dah] A DENOMINAÇÃO DE ORIGEM CONTROLADA (DOC) area located in northern Portugal near the Atlantic coast, west of the DÃO DOC and south of Oporto. The region is known for its TANNIC, high-ACIDITY red wines made primarily from the BAGA grape along with PERIQUITA, Bastardo, and Tinta Pinheira. The best of these wines will, with AGING, become SOFTER and richer. Newer techniques have been introduced to remove grape stalks prior to FERMENTATION and to shorten the period that the skins are in contact. This method produces rich,

B

colorful wines that are fragrant and fruity and much less tannic. About 90 percent of the wines produced are red. Small amounts of SPARKLING WINE and white STILL WINE are also produced. Grapes used for the white wines are mainly local varieties, primarily Maria Gomes (FERNÃO PIRES), but also BICAL and Rabo de Ovelha.

baked *see* Glossary of Wine Tasting Terms, page 655

baking A term that relates to MADEIRA wine production. Baking refers to a process called *estufagem*. During this procedure, the wines are placed in hot rooms or heated tanks (*estufas*) where they're allowed to bake slowly for a minimum of 90 days. The temperatures during this process range from 85°F to 130°F. Finer Madeiras are stored in wooden casks and left in attics or other extremely warm areas for years to develop slowly the tangy, burnt-caramel, slightly bitter flavor that's unique to this wine.

balance; balanced *see* Glossary of Wine Tasting Terms, page 655

Balaton [bah-lah-TAWN] Term that refers to Europe's largest lake, Lake Balaton, located in western Hungary. It also refers to the general wine-producing region surrounding the lake. Specific growing districts around Lake Balaton include Badacsony (BADACSONYI) and Balatonfüred-Csopak.

Balbi *see* ARGENTINA

Balbi *see* PROSECCO

balling scale *see* BRIX

Balthazar *see* Wine Bottles, page 609

Bandol AC [bahn-DAWL] An APPELLATION for red, white, and ROSÉ wines that covers the area around the resort town of Bandol, located between Marseille and Toulon on the Mediterranean coast in France's Provence region. The MOURVÈDRE variety is the principal component (comprising at least 50 percent) in the BANDOL red and rosé wines, with GRENACHE, CINSAUT, and SYRAH generally used in the blend. The red wines, which are considered some of the best in Provence, must be AGED in wood for at least 18 months and can handle extensive BOTTLE AGING (10 years or so). The white wines, made from CLAIRETTE, UGNI BLANC, BOURBOULENC, and SAUVIGNON BLANC, are rather neutral in character and account for only about 5 percent of the total wine production.

Banyuls AC [bah-NYUHLS] An APPELLATION in the LANGUEDOC-ROUSSILLON in southern France known for its rather unusual FORTIFIED WINES,

B

which are classified as VIN DOUX NATUREL. Many of the vineyards are located in the sheer rocky terraces of the Pyrenees as they sweep down into the ocean close to the Spanish border. Even though Banyuls wines are sometimes vinified moderately DRY, they're best when sweet. They must contain at least 15 percent alcohol and be made from a minimum of 50 percent GRENACHE grapes. Banyuls GRAND CRU must be made from a minimum of 75 percent GRENACHE and aged in wood for 30 months. RANCIO is a variation that's purposefully OXIDIZED by placing small barrels of wine in the sun during summertime. This procedure gives the wine a tawny color and a rich but unique flavor. Banyuls wines are consumed as both APÉRITIFS and DESSERT WINES.

Barbaresco DOCG [bar-bah-RESS-koh] One of the small number of DOCG areas in Italy, Barbaresco shares this status in northwestern Italy's PIEDMONT region with BAROLO, ASTI, GATTINARA, GAVI, and GHEMME. The DOCG zone encompasses the villages of Barbaresco, Tresio, and Neive, just east of Alba. The wines, which are made from the NEBBIOLO grape, must be AGED for 2 years, one of which is in wooden barrels. A RISERVA must be aged for 4 years, one of those in wood. Considered some of Italy's best, these wines have rich, spicy flavors, and, although DRY, they have a perfumed sweetness. Barbaresco wines are often compared to Barolo wines because they're both made from Nebbiolo grapes. In the comparison, Barbaresco wines are usually regarded as more elegant and refined; the Barolos are thought to be more robust and longer-lived.

Barbera [bar-BEH-rah] Italian red-wine grape that can produce marvelous wines but that has become so plentiful in some of the hotter growing regions around the world that its image is beginning to tarnish. Barbera wines from these hotter areas—such as southern Italy and California's SAN JOAQUIN VALLEY—have higher ALCOHOL and ACIDITY. Because they're low in flavor, they're primarily used as BLENDING WINES. Superior Barbera wines can exhibit a ripe currant flavor with a nuance of SMOKINESS. Five DOCS in Italy's PIEDMONT region produce the most noteworthy Barbera wines. BARBERA D'ALBA makes wines that are 100 percent Barbera, while BARBERA D'ASTI, Barbera del MONFERRATO, Colli Toronesi, and Rubino di Cantavenna may produce BLENDS. Good Barbera wines are also made by the DOCs of OLTREPÒ PAVESE in Lombardy and COLLI BOLOGNESI and COLLI PIACENTINI in Emilia (look for "Gutturnio" on the label). The PIEDMONT region uses Barbera grapes to produce **Verbesco**, a light, DRY, slightly effervescent (FRIZZANTE) white wine made as a BLANC DE NOIR.

B

Barbera d'Alba DOC [bar-BEH-rah DAHL-bah] DOC located in the PIEDMONT region in northwestern Italy near the town of Alba. The wines from this area are regarded as some of the best made from the BARBERA grape. Although they're some of the more robust of the Barberas, they should be drunk within 3 to 4 years of the VINTAGE date.

Barbera d'Asti DOC [bar-BEH-rah DAH-stee] Wines produced in Italy's PIEDMONT from the vineyards around the towns of Asti, Alexandria, and Casale Monferrato. These wines are generally regarded as slightly less full-bodied (*see* BODY) than those from BARBERA D'ALBA, even though both are made from the BARBERA grape. They should be drunk young.

Barco Reale *see* CARMIGNANO DOCG

Bardolino DOC; Bardolino Superiore DOCG [bar-doh-LEE-noh] DOC area that lies in the western part of the VENETO region in northeast Italy. It encompasses vineyards on the southeastern shore of Lake Garda, in and around the town of Bardolino. The grapes used for these ROSSO and ROSATO wines are mainly CORVINA, Rondinella, Molinara, and Negrara. Although the blend of grapes used is similar to that for the better-known VALPOLICELLA DOC wines, Bardolino wines are usually not as full-bodied (*see* BODY). Wines labeled **Bardolino Classico** are made with grapes from a smaller site (the original Bardolino area) that's thought to have better vineyard land. **Bardolino Chiaretto** is the name for the ROSÉ wine, which is made in both STILL and SPUMANTE (sparkling) versions. **Bardolino Novello** is a young, fresh wine that must be bottled prior to the end of the VINTAGE year (like a French BEAUJOLAIS NOUVEAU). **Bardolino Superiore**, which received DOCG status in 2001, is only for DRY, still wines that have at least one year of aging.

barnyard *see* Glossary of Wine Tasting Terms, page 655

Barolo DOCG [bah-ROH-loh] Many view the red wines from Barolo as Italy's best—so much so that they're sometimes called the "King" of Italian wines. The Barolo DOCG area lies just southwest of Alba and includes the vineyards on the steep hills around the towns of Barolo, Castiglione Falletto, Serralunga d'Alba, Monforte d'Alba, and La Morra. It's one of the small number of DOCG areas in Italy, sharing this status in northwestern Italy's PIEDMONT region with ASTI, BARBARESCO, BRACHETTO D'ACQUI, GATTINARA, GAVI, and GHEMME. Like the Barbaresco DOCG, the grape used here is the NEBBIOLO. DOCG rules require Barolo wines to AGE for a minimum of 3 years, two of which

B

must be in wooden barrels. RISERVA wines must have 5 years of aging. In general young Barolos, which are tough, TANNIC, and need 5-plus years to SOFTEN, are somewhat of an acquired taste for most. Once they SOFTEN and open up, however, they're RICH, full-bodied (*see* BODY), and COMPLEX and can have earthy, truffly, and CHOCOLATY characteristics with an aroma reminiscent of violets. The five communes, which produce about 87 to 88 percent of the wines from the Barolo DOCG, have differing styles based on the soils of the region. They sit in two primary valleys that run through the appellation, each with different soil types. The vineyards around the town of **Barolo**, located near the center of this DOCG in the western valley, contain clay soils that are denser and more productive. The resulting wines are powerful, yet fruity and elegant, and they tend to age more quickly than some of the other areas. The vineyards here produce 12 to 13 percent of the DOCG wines. The famous Cannubi vineyard lies near the town. The area around **La Morra** is located in the western valley to the north of the town of Barolo and shares the same soil type. Its clay soils are also denser and more productive and its wines are similar to those of the village of Barolo—aromatic, fruity and elegant and likely to mature quicker. There are a large number of vineyards around La Morra which produce 32 to 34 percent of the appellation wines. The Brunate, Cerequio, and Rocche di La Morra vineyards are highly regarded. **Castiglione di Falletto** lies northeast of the town of Barolo but in the eastern valley. The less productive sandstone soils in the area produce more concentrated, well-structured wines that age more slowly than the wines from the villages of Barolo and La Morra. They are, however, not as intense as the wines from the other two eastern valley communes, Monforte d'Alba, and Serralunga d'Alba. Castiglione di Falletto produces about 10 percent of the appellation's wines. Montprivato, Rocche di Castiglione, and Villero are some of the top rated vineyards. The vineyards of **Monforte d'Alba** area sit at the southern end of the appellation in the eastern valley where the sandstone soils are the norm. Vineyards to the north and east of the town are considered the best. They include Brussia, Santo Stefano di Perno, Castelletto, Ginestra, and Mosconi. The wines from here are considered some of the most intense, concentrated, and long-lived. Around 16 to 17 percent of the Barolo DOCG wines are produced from these vineyards. **Serralunga d'Alba** sits on the eastern edge of the Barolo DOCG in the eastern valley with its sandstone soils. Like the wines from Monforte d'Alba, wines from Serralunga are considered some of the most powerful, well-structured, and long-lived. The grapes from here have long been in demand especially from the vineyards of

Baudana, Ceratta, Fontanafredda, Gabutti, Parafada, Lazzarito, and Vigna Rionda. The Serralunga d'Alba area produces around 16 to 17 percent of the Barolo DOCG wines.

B

Barossa Valley [bah-RAH-suh; bah-ROH-suh] One of the most important wine-producing regions in Australia. It's located in the state of SOUTHERN AUSTRALIA in the Barossa Zone, which also includes the EDEN VALLEY to the southeast. The Barossa Valley is about 40 miles northeast of the city of Adelaide. In the late 1830s and early 1840s, dissident German Lutherans and English settlers began populating the Barossa Valley. Vines were first planted in 1847, and wine soon became a part of the local culture, with the industry continuing to grow slowly over the next few decades. Growth accelerated during the 1880s and continued into the twentieth century, thereby establishing the Barossa as one of Australia's best-known wine regions. The climate here is generally warm and dry, but the eastern hills offer a cool growing area. There are about 23,000 acres of vineyards (Barossa and Eden Valley combined) and tons of grapes are shipped into this region's wineries for processing. The most popular grape grown for white TABLE WINES is RIESLING, followed by CHARDONNAY and SÉMILLON. PALOMINO and PEDRO XIMÉNEX are still grown for use in FORTIFIED WINES, which have historically been a part of this area's winemaking tradition. The most popular red grape is Shiraz (SYRAH), and the Barossa Valley is world-famous for these wines, some made from vines dating back to the mid-1800s. Other very successful red VARIETIES are CABERNET SAUVIGNON, GRENACHE, and Mataro (MOURVÈDRE).

Barossa Zone *see* SOUTH AUSTRALIA

barrel A wooden container of varying size used to AGE, store, and sometimes FERMENT and ship wine. OAK is the wood of choice, although redwood and chestnut are sometimes used. BARRIQUES, BUTTS, FEUILLETES, HOGSHEADS, PIÈCES, and PUNCHEONS are some of the names for different barrels used in the wine-producing process. *See also* COOPERAGE.

barrel aging *see* AGING

barrel fermentation; barrel fermented The process of fermenting wines in small barrels instead of large vats or stainless steel tanks. The barrels are usually made of **oak** and are about 60 gallons in size, although larger ones are used occasionally. Even though barrel fermentation is more expensive and less controllable than fermentation in larger tanks, it's thought to imbue certain wines with complexity, rich creamy flavors, delicate oak characteristics, and better aging capabili-

B

ties. On the downside, this technique contributes to some loss of fruit flavor. Barrel fermentation is usually associated with white wine grapes like CHARDONNAY and SAUVIGNON BLANC, although occasionally CHENIN BLANC and SÉMILLON are processed this way. *See also* FERMENTATION.

barrel-making *see* COOPERAGE; TOAST

barrel maturation *see* AGING

barrica [bahr-REE-kah] The Spanish name for the wooden barrels similar to the French BARRIQUES.

barrique [ba-REEK] The term used in BORDEAUX to specify the 225-liter (almost 60-gallon) oak barrels that are used for storing and aging wine. It's similar in size to the PIÈCE used in BURGUNDY.

barro [BAH-roh] *see* JEREZ-XÉRÈS-SHERRY Y MANZANILLA DE SANLÚCAR DE BARRAMEDA DO

Barsac AC [BAHR-sak; ba*r*-SAK] The largest of the five townships within the SAUTERNES district, Barsac is the most recognizable APPELLATION after Sauternes itself. It's part of France's BORDEAUX region and is located approximately 25 miles from the city of Bordeaux. Because Barsac is part of the Sauternes appellation, producers may also use "Sauternes" on their label, although most top producers simply use "Barsac." Like their Sauternes neighbors, Barsac wines are sweet and luscious, although generally lighter and more refined. The wines are made from SÉMILLON, SAUVIGNON BLANC, and a little MUSCADELLE. The best producer is Château Climens followed by Châteaux Coutet and Doisy-Védrines and then by Châteaux Broustet, Doisy-Daëne, and Nairac. The very rare Cuvée Madame from Château Coutet is specially produced in exceptional years and thought by some to be second only to the renowned Château d'Yquem.

Basilicata [bah-see-lee-KAH-tah] An obscure region located in southern Italy next to APULIA, CALABRIA, and CAMPANIA. Of Italy's twenty regions, Basilicata is the third smallest wine producer and has only one DOC, AGLIANICO DEL VULTURE, which produces a well-regarded red wine from the AGLIANICO grape. It has less than 30,000 vineyard acres. This region's principal grapes for red and ROSÉ wines are Aglianico, Aglianicone, and MALVASIA Nera; for white wines they're Asprinio and Malvasia Bianca.

basket *see* DECANTING

Bas-Médoc *see* MÉDOC

Basses Mourottes *see* CORTON; CORTON-CHARLEMAGNE

bastard A sweet wine of uncertain origin that was popular in England during the sixteenth century. It's thought to have come from either Spain, Portugal, or the Portuguese island of MADEIRA. The wine is said to have been made from the Bastardo grape (hence the name), which is still grown in parts of Portugal.

B

Les Baux de Provence AC [lay bow duh praw-VAHNSS] A wine-producing APPELLATION located in the western part of the PROVENCE region. Its name comes from the medieval village of the same name. RED and ROSÉ wines are made of various blends of CABERNET SAUVIGNON, CINSAUT, GRENACHE, and MOURVÈDRE. The RHÔNE-like red wines are the most notable. Small amounts of white wine are made from CLAIRETTE, Grenache Blanc (GRENACHE), SAUVIGNON BLANC, and Ugni Blanc (TREBBIANO).

Bâtard-Montrachet AC [bah-TAHR mohn-rah-SHAY] A 29-acre GRAND CRU vineyard located in the CÔTE DE BEAUNE just east of the famous LE MONTRACHET vineyard in France's BURGUNDY region. Although mostly associated with the village of PULIGNY-MONTRACHET, part of the vineyards are in the village of CHASSAGNE-MONTRACHET as well. These wines, made from CHARDONNAY grapes, are among the world's best and most-expensive white wines. The best examples have honeyed aromas, have rich and CONCENTRATED flavors with lots of fruit, and deserve 8 to 10 years of AGING.

BATF *see* BUREAU OF ALCOHOL, TOBACCO, FIREARMS AND EXPLOSIVES; ALCOHOL AND TOBACCO TAX AND TRADE BUREAU

bâtonnage *see* LEES

Baumé [boh-MAY] A system used by the French and other Europeans to measure SPECIFIC GRAVITY, which indicates the sugar content of unfermented grape juice. One degree Baumé is equivalent to 1.8° BRIX (the measurement system used in the United States). The Baumé measurement system helps winemakers forecast the finished wine's **potential alcohol** content, with 1° roughly equal to 1 percent alcohol when the wine is fully fermented. Germany has a similar system measured on the OECHSLE scale.

Bay of Plenty *see* WAIKATO

Béarn AC [bay-ARN] This APPELLATION, which lies in Basque country in the Pyrenees in SOUTHWEST FRANCE, covers red, white, and ROSÉ wines. Red and rosé wines are made from various grapes including

CABERNET SAUVIGNON, CABERNET FRANC, Tannat, and Manseng Noir. White wines are produced from Gros Manseng, Petit Manseng, and Courbu. Within the Béarn area are the appellations of IROULEGUY, JURANÇON, and MADIRAN. Generally these are pretty basic wines; the best are the rosés and the sweet white wines from Jurançon.

Beaujolais [boh-zhuh-LAY] The Beaujolais area, located in the southern part of France's BURGUNDY region, starts just north of Lyons and extends for about 35 miles north to the city of Mâcon. Beaujolais is different from most of Burgundy because of its focus on the GAMAY grape for its red wines, instead of PINOT NOIR. As with many of France's regions, years of experience have proven which grape is best for an area, and for the granite-laden hills of Beaujolais, it's Gamay. To date, no other location in the world has been able to produce Gamay-based wines as well as Beaujolais. Most of the wines from Beaujolais are red, with tiny amounts of ROSÉ and white. Beaujolais winemakers employ a different red winemaking process called *macération carbonique* (*see* CARBONIC MACERATION), a technique used during primary FERMENTATION to make light red wines with intense color, a fresh fruity flavor, and low TANNINS—in short, a wine that can be drunk early. Most wines for the basic APPELLATION **Beaujolais AC** are produced in the southern part of the region. These wines must contain minimum alcohol levels of 9 percent for red and rosé wines and 9½ percent for white. **Beaujolais Supérieur AC** wines, which are produced in the same areas as the Beaujolais AC, must have lower yields per acre (usually an indicator of higher-quality wines) and minimum alcohol levels that are 1 percent higher. The next highest-quality appellation is **Beaujolais-Villages AC**, a collection of thirty-nine villages with superior vineyard sites in the northern part of Beaujolais. The highest-quality level is comprised of ten individual, CRU-status villages, each with its own individual appellation. They are BROUILLY, CHÉNAS, CHIROUBLES, CÔTE DE BROUILLY, FLEURIE, JULIÉNAS, MORGON, MOULIN-À-VENT, RÉGNIÉ, and SAINT-AMOUR. These villages produce the best and most-expensive wines, with Moulin-à-Vent, Morgon, and Chénas considered the most full-bodied (*see* BODY) and longest AGING. **Beaujolais Nouveau** is a special category of 7- to 9-week-old wine that's released annually on the third Thursday of November. This "new" wine, sometimes called **Beaujolais Primeur**, is meant to be drunk very young. It's made from the better grapes of the basic Beaujolais appellation and is usually quite good.

Beaulieu-sur-Layon *see* COTEAUX DU LAYON

Beaumes-de-Venise [bohm duh vuh-NEEZ] A small attractive village in the southern RHÔNE best known for its sweet MUSCAT DE BEAUMES-DE-VENISE, a VIN DOUX NATUREL style of white wine. The red wines, made from CINSAUT, GRENACHE, SYRAH, and MOURVÈDRE, and bottled as Côtes Du Rhône-Villages AC wines, are generally good and hearty.

Beaune [BOHN] An important French town that many consider the wine capital of the CÔTE D'OR, if not of all BURGUNDY. It not only is in an area of important vineyards but also houses many influential wine merchants. Beaune gives its name to the southern portion of the Côte d'Or, CÔTE DE BEAUNE. The **Beaune AC** itself produces mainly red wines from the PINOT NOIR grape. Most of these wines, although they'll AGE 5 to 10 years, are made in a SOFTER, low-TANNIN style that allows them to be appreciated young. Even though there are no GRAND CRU vineyards in the Beaune AC, there are number of PREMIER CRU vineyards—many of which are excellent. Usually included in the top tier are **Les Boucherottes**, **Les Bressandes**, **Les Cents Vignes**, **Clos du Roi**, **Le Clos des Mouches**, **Les Fèves**, **Les Grèves**, **Les Marconnets**, and **Les Teurons**. *See also* CÔTE DE BEAUNE.

Beaunois *see* CHARDONNAY

Beauroy *see* CHABLIS

Beerenauslese (BA) [BAY-*r*uhn-OWS-lay-zuh; BEH-*r*uhn-OWS-lay-zuh] The German term for "selected bèrries," which is used in the wine trade to describe specially selected, overripe grapes that are hand-picked and then pressed separately from other grapes. Beerenauslese is one of the six subcategories of QmP (QUALITÄTSWEIN MIT PRÄDIKAT) and ranks above KABINETT, SPÄTLESE, and AUSLESE but below TROCKENBEERENAUSLESE. To attain the Beerenauslese category, the natural sugar content of the grapes must reach a certain minimum (110 to 128° OECHSLE, approximately 26 to 30 percent sugar by weight), depending on the region and the variety. The grapes are usually infected with BOTRYTIS CINEREA (called *Edelfäule* in German), which shrivels them, thereby concentrating the sugar. The superior wine made from these grapes is very sweet but has enough ACIDITY for proper BALANCE. Beerenauslese wines are quite rare, extremely expensive, and considered one of the world's top DESSERT WINES. These wines will AGE for many years, during which they develop even more complexity. AUSTRIA has a Beerenauslese category that's similar and requires a minimum 107° OECHSLE.

beeswing [BEEZ-wing] Named for its translucent appearance, beeswing is a flaky deposit sometimes found in older, BOTTLE-AGED wines, particularly PORT. Such wines are usually DECANTED, thereby eliminating the residue.

B

Beira Interior DOC [BAY-reh] Portuguese DOC located in the eastern part of the country within the larger BEIRAS VINHO REGIONAL near the Spanish border. It sits east of the DÃO DOC and south of the PORT DOC. It's made up of three former IPRS that are now subregions of the Beira Interior DOC: **Castelo Rodrigo**, located around the town of Figueira de Castelo Rodrigo, **Pinhel**, positioned around the town of Pinhel, and **Cova da Beira**, encompassing the municipalities of Belmonte, Covilhã, and Fundão. The wines vary depending on the subregion; Castelo Rodrigo produces full-bodied red wines, Pinhel produces full-bodied white wines used mostly for SPARKLING WINES, and Cova da Beira is mainly known for lighter red wines. The primary red grapes grown in the Biera Interior DOC are Bastardo, Marufo, RUFETE, Tinta Roriz (TEMPRANILLO), and TOURIGA NACIONAL. The dominant white-grape varieties are ARINTO, MALVASIA, Rabo de Ovelha, and Síria.

Beiras [BAY-resh] Portuguese VINHO REGIONAL located in the north central part of the country. It encompasses the DOCS of BAIRRADA, BEIRA INTERIOR, and DÃO. However, in general, wines labeled "Beiras" do not meet the standards established for these classified areas. Some Beiras wines now include popular grapes neither native to this area nor allowed in the DOCs, such as CABERNET SAUVIGNON and CHARDONNAY. The inland areas of Beiras contain a number of IPRS that are showing promise for their red wines.

Beli Pinot *see* PINOT BLANC

Bell Mountain AVA *see* TEXAS HILL COUNTRY AVA

Belle Epoque *see* CHAMPAGNE

Bellet AC [behl-LAY] A tiny APPELLATION in France's PROVENCE region, located in the hills behind Nice near the French Riviera. It produces red, white, and ROSÉ wines from the 100-plus acres that qualify for AC status. Red grapes are CINSAUT, GRENACHE, and the local varieties BRACHET and Folle (or Fuelle) Noire. White grapes are the local Rolle (VERMENTINO) and small amounts of CHARDONNAY.

Bellina *see* ISABELLA

bench grafting *see* GRAFTING

Bendigo An Australian wine region located in VICTORIA's Central Victoria Zone. It's situated about 90 miles north and slightly west of

Melbourne, around the town of Bendigo. This area's wine history dates to about the time gold was discovered in 1851. In the late 1800s, however, PHYLLOXERA ended the wine industry's efforts, and it wasn't until the late 1960s that Bendigo began to revive. The recovery here is riding the reputation of the rich, minty Shiraz (SYRAH) and CABERNET SAUVIGNON wines. CHARDONNAY, PINOT NOIR, CABERNET FRANC, MERLOT, and SÉMILLON are also grown. There are over 1,000 planted acres and over twenty wineries in the Bendigo region.

Ben Lomond Mountain AVA The 38,000-acre subzone located in the SANTA CRUZ MOUTAINS AVA that was formed in 1988. Few wineries use this APPELLATION on their labels.

Benmore Valley AVA *see* LAKE COUNTY

bentonite [BEN-tn-ite] A powdery clay found in Wyoming, South Dakota, and Germany that is used as a FINING agent to CLARIFY wines (especially white). When added to wine, bentonite settles to the bottom carrying with it any suspended particles.

Bereich; pl. Bereiche [beh-RIHK] German for "region." Under the German wine laws established in 1971, a Bereich is a district or subregion within an ANBAUGEBIET (quality-wine growing region). There are forty-three Bereiche throughout the thirteen Anbaugebiete. Within a Bereich, there are GROSSLAGEN (general sites) and EINZELLAGEN (individual sites or vineyards). If a wine label carries a Bereich name (instead of a Grosslage or Einzellage), it's considered to be of satisfactory quality (much like a French regional wine from ANJOU, BORDEAUX, BURGUNDY, or CÔTES-DU-RHÔNE). However, the higher-quality wines will generally carry the name of an individual vineyard (Einzellage) from one of the better Bereiche.

Berg *see* ERSHERNDORF; RÜDESHEIM

Bergerac [behr-jeh-RAK] The town that gives its name to the surrounding region and sits on the Dordogne River just over 60 miles from the city of Bordeaux. The Bergerac APPELLATIONS abut the BORDEAUX region and use many of the same grapes. **Bergerac AC** produces red wines that are made from CABERNET SAUVIGNON, CABERNET FRANC, and MERLOT and that are similiar to lighter Bordeaux reds. MUSCADELLE, SAUVIGNON BLANC, and SÉMILLON are the main white varieties and are used in the basic **Bergerac Sec AC** wines. **Côtes de Bergerac AC** wines are required to have a higher minimum alcohol content and are generally of better quality. The **Côtes de Bergerac Moelleux AC** is for sweet wines produced in the Bergerac area. Other appellations in the Bergerac area include MONBAZILLAC, MONTRAVEL, PÉCHARMANT, ROSETTE, and Saussiggion.

Bergeron *see* ROUSSANNE

Bermejuela *see* MARMAJUELO

Bergwein [BEHRK-vine] Austrian wine category for wines made from grapes grown on slopes with an angle of over 26 degrees. Bergwein is a special form of TAFELWEIN that's able to bypass normal QUALITÄTSWEIN criteria and be sold in standard size bottles (750 ml) and labeled with the name of the viticulture region.

Berici *see* COLLI BERICI DOC

Bernkastel [BEHRN-kah-stl] The name Bernkastel applies to a town, a BEREICH, and as part of two GROSSLAGEN. The town is situated on the Mosel River in Germany's MOSEL-SAAR-RUWER region and is noted for its narrow, picturesque streets. The town, which is also known as Bernkastel-Kues (Kues is the larger town across the river), is located near many important vineyard sites, including the world-famous DOC-TOR vineyard. **Bereich Bernkastel** is one of the five Bereiche in the Mosel-Saar-Ruwer region and covers the vineyards around the middle portion of the Mosel River area, what's often referred to as the Mittelmosel. The Bereich begins northeast of Trier and encompasses the area to the northeast, including Bernkastel-Kues, and ends just short of ZELL. Ten Grosslagen are included in the Bereich, including two that encompass vineyards around the town of Bernkastel. These two, which are entitled to add Bernkasteler in front of their name, are Bernkasteler **Badstube** and Bernkasteler **Kurfürstlay**.

berry A VITICULTURAL term for an individual grape.

berrylike *see* Glossary of Wine Tasting Terms, page 655

Biancame *see* ALBANA

bianco; Bianco [BYAHN-koh] 1. Italian for "white," *vino bianco* meaning "white wine." 2. In Italy, the term *Bianco* (with a capital *B*) is also used to indicate a white wine that's made from specific, approved grape varieties, which can differ depending on the DOC and region.

Bianco Alcamo; Bianco d'Alcamo *see* ALCAMO DOC

Bianco di Custoza DOC [be-YAHN-koh dee koos-TOH-tzah] DOC that makes a DRY white wine from a blend of TREBBIANO, GAR-

GANEGA, FRIULANO, CORTESE, MALVASIA, and Riesling Italico (WELSCHRIES-
LING). These wines, once thought to be a cheaper, lesser-quality alternative to those from the SOAVE DOC, have established themselves as
high-quality contenders (except against the better SOAVE SUPERIORE
DOCG wines). Bianco di Custoza is located on the southeastern shore
of Lake Garda in the eastern portion of Italy's VENETO region (in the
same area as the BARDOLINO DOC).

Bical [BEE-kahl] White Portuguese grape variety known in the DÃO
DOC as *Borrado das Moscas* ("fly droppings"), assumably because of
the small specks on the skin. Bical is also a popular grape in the BAIR-
RADA DOC. It has good ACIDITY and AROMA and is often used as a BLEND-
ING WINE.

Bienvenues-Bâtard-Montrachet AC [byan-veh-NOO bah-
TAH*R* mohn-rah-SHAY] A 9-acre GRAND CRU that is located in France's
BURGUNDY region and situated in the village of PULIGNY-MONTRACHET in
the CÔTE DE BEAUNE. The vineyard is bordered on two sides by the
larger and better-known BÂTARD-MONTRACHET vineyard. The wines from
these two vineyards are often compared, although the Bâtard-
Montrachet is usually considered superior. Still, the rich, flavorful
Bienvenues-Bâtard-Montrachet wines, made from CHARDONNAY grapes,
are among the world's best white wines and are priced accordingly.

Bierzo DO [be-YEHR-soh] Spanish DO located in the northwestern
part of the country around the city of Ponferrada. It's part of the
Castile and León region and sits next to the VALDEORRAS DO, which borders it on the southwest. The region is known as El Bierzo, but the DO
is designated as *Bierzo*. The growing areas are concentrated around
the towns of Cacabelos and Villafranca del Bierzo along the River Sil
at the 1,600- to 2,000-foot level. The climate ranges from mild to hot,
depending on the location of the vineyard. There are about 9,500
acres of vineyards in the DO. The primary grape is MENCÍA, a red VARI-
ETY once thought to be related to CABERNET FRANC, which produces the
most interesting wines. Garnacha Tintorera (ALICANTE BOUSCHET) is
planted in small amounts, and CABERNET SAUVIGNON is being introduced
in some vineyards. White varieties, which make up a minority, include
Doña Blanca, Godello (VERDELHO), MALVASÍA, and PALOMINO.

Biferno DOC *see* MOLISE

big *see* Glossary of Wine Tasting Terms, page 655

Bigney *see* MERLOT

Big Rivers Zone *see* NEW SOUTH WALES

Bikaver *see* EGRI BIKAVÉR

Bildstock *see* NIERSTEIN

Billecart-Salmon *see* CHAMPAGNE

Bingen [BING-uhn] An important wine town directly across from RÜDESHEIM, where the Nahe River joins the Rhine River. Its name is also used for the BEREICH that covers this area. Both are part of the RHEIN-HESSEN region, with **Bereich Bingen** covering the northwestern portion of the Rheinhessen. The Bereich contains six GROSSLAGEN, including Grosslage Sankt Rochuskapelle, of which the vineyards around the town of Bingen are a part. The town's best-known vineyard is the 87-acre **Scharlachberg** (which means "scarlet hill," referring to its red soil). RIESLING grapes produce the area's top wines, which can be among the best from the Rheinhessen region.

Binissalem DO [be-NEE-sah-lem] Spanish wine region located on the northwest part the island of Mallorca that's gaining some recognition. It shares the island with the PLA I LLEVANT DO. This island has a very mild climate, cooler than the mainland, which translates to a longer growing season. The Binissalem DO produces red, ROSÉ, white and sparkling wines. The red and rosé wines are made of at least 50 percent of the local Manto Negro, which is often blended with Callet. But other red grapes are planted, including CABERNET SAUVIGNON, Fogoneu, MERLOT, Monastrell (MOURVÈDRE), PINOT NOIR, and Ull de Llebre (TEMPRANILLO). The main white variety is Moll, also called Prensal Blanc. Other white varieties include CHARDONNAY, MACABEO, MOSCATEL, PARELLADA, and RIESLING.

Bischofsberg *see* RÜDESHEIM

bishop A type of MULLED WINE, usually made with PORT, sugar, oranges, and cloves, which are combined and heated.

bite *see* Glossary of Wine Tasting Terms, page 655

bitter; bitterness *see* Glossary of Wine Tasting Terms, page 655

bitter rot Recognized as a grape disease since 1887, bitter rot is caused by the fungus *Melanconium fuligineaum*. The name comes from the bitter taste of infected berries. Although bitter rot is often confused with BLACK ROT, the latter infects only green berries; bitter rot can affect young shoots, fruit cluster stems, and the fruit itself. The most obvious symptom of this fungus is a brownish, wet lesion on the grapes. Spraying with fungicides is the most commonly used form of control. *See also* DISEASES, VINEYARD.

B

blackcurrant *see* Glossary of Wine Tasting Terms, page 655

black dead arm *see* DEAD ARM

Black Hamburg *see* MUSCAT

Black Muscat *see* MUSCAT

black rot A fungal disease caused by the fungus *Guignardia bidwellii* that attacks both grapes and vines. Usually brought on by hot, extremely humid weather, black rot discolors leaves and stems and causes the grapes to shrivel and turn brownish-black, at which point they're called "mummies." Copper sulfate is the common treatment. *See also* DISEASES, VINEYARD.

Blackwood Valley An Australian wine region located in the South West Australia Zone of WESTERN AUSTRALIA. It's situated about 160 miles south and slightly east of Perth around the towns of Bridgetown, Nannup, and Balingup. Blackwood Valley is east and inland of the famous MARGARET RIVER region, which gives it hotter summers and cooler winters. There was very little VITICULTURAL activity in this area until the 1990s. It's still relatively undeveloped, with only about 1,000 acres planted. CHARDONNAY, RIESLING, CABERNET SAUVIGNON, and Shiraz (SYRAH) are the most widely planted varieties, along with smaller amounts of PINOT NOIR, MERLOT, SAUVIGNON BLANC, and SÉMILLON.

bladder pack *see* BAG-IN-A-BOX WINE

Blagny [blah-NYEE] A tiny village that straddles the borderline of the MEURSAULT and PULIGNY-MONTRACHET appellations in the CÔTE DE BEAUNE district of France's BURGUNDY region. Both areas have PREMIER CRU vineyards for white wines, which are made from CHARDONNAY and labeled either Puligny-Montrachet, Meursault, or Meursault-Blagny. The Blagny APPELLATION is only for red wines made from PINOT NOIR grapes.

blanc [BLAHN; BLAHNGK] French for "white." *Blanc* is commonly used as a suffix for white-grape varieties.

Blanca-Roja *see* MALVASIA

blanc de blanc(s) [BLAHN duh BLAHN; BLAHNGK duh BLAHNGK] French phrase meaning "white wine from white grapes." The term originated in France's CHAMPAGNE region (where most cham-

B

pagnes are made from a combination of the white CHARDONNAY grape and the red PINOT NOIR grape) to describe champagne made entirely from Chardonnay. Blanc de blancs are usually light and delicate. The term also refers to STILL WINES. *See also* BLANC DE NOIR.

Blanc de Cabernet Sauvignon *See* CABERNET BLANC

Blanc de Morgex *see* VALLE D'AOSTA

blanc de noir(s) [blah*n* (blah*ngk*) duh NWAHR] The French term used for "white wine from red grapes." In particular, the phrase *blanc de noir* is used with those CHAMPAGNES (and other SPARKLING WINES) that are made entirely from the PINOT NOIR grape. In the United States, *blanc de noir* sparkling wines sometimes contain small amounts of CHARDONNAY. Occasionally this phrase refers to STILL WINES made from CABERNET SAUVIGNON, Pinot Noir, or ZINFANDEL. In the United States, however, these BLUSH WINES usually go by other names such as BLANC DE PINOT NOIR, CABERNET BLANC, or WHITE ZINFANDEL. Blanc de noirs are produced by quickly removing the skins from the juice after the grapes have been pressed. This technique prevents the pigment in the grape's dark skin from transferring too much color to the wine. These wines may vary in hue from pale pink to apricot to salmon; seldom are they clear or "white." *See also* BLANC DE BLANC; SAIGNÉE.

Blanc de Pinot Noir [blah*n* (blah*ngk*) duh PEE-noh NWAHR] One of the names used for BLUSH WINE, describing that made from PINOT NOIR grapes. *See also* SAIGNÉE.

Blanc de Troyes *see* ALIGOTÉ

Blanc Fumé [blah*n* (blah*ngk*) foo-MAY] Around the village of Pouilly-sur-Loire, in the central part of France's LOIRE region, Blanc Fumé is the name used for the SAUVIGNON BLANC grape. Wine from this grape is usually labeled POUILLY-FUMÉ AC, but, occasionally, **Blanc Fumé de Pouilly AC**. *Blanc* is French for "white," *fumé* means "smoke," and it's said the name comes from the SMOKY (also known as FLINTY) quality of these wines.

Blanchots [blah*n*-SHOH] One of the seven GRAND CRU vineyards in CHABLIS. Blanchots consists of just over 30 acres and sits southeast of the other six grand cru vineyards.

blanco [BLAHNG-koh] Spanish for "white."

Blanquette *see* CLAIRETTE

Blanquette de Limoux AC [blah*n*-KEHT duh lee-MOO] APPELLA-
TION for sparkling wines made in the hills surrounding the town of
Limoux in Southern France's LANGUEDOC-ROUSSILLON region. Mauzac,
also called *Blanquette*, is the main grape, of which the wines must
contain at least 90 percent. CHENIN BLANC and CHARDONNAY make up the
balance. The wines, sometimes referred to as *vins mousseux*, are primarily made by MÉTHODE CHAMPENOISE, although the *méthode rurale*
(RURAL METHOD) is still occasionally used. Blanquette de Limoux wines,
which are generally quite good, are described as having a "green
apple" or "cidery" flavor. *See also* CRÉMANT DE LIMOUX AC.

blau [BLOUW] German for "blue." The word *blau* is often used in
wine-producing circles to refer to grapes used to produce red wines,
such as Blauer Portugieser (PORTUGIESER) or Blauer Spätburgunder
(PINOT NOIR).

Blauburgunder *see* PINOT NOIR

Blauer Klevner *see* PINOT NOIR

Blauer Limberger *see* BLAUFRANKISCH

Blauer Portugieser *see* PORTUGIESER

Blauer Spätburgunder *see* PINOT NOIR

Blaufränkisch [blouw-FRAHN-keesh] A red-wine grape widely
planted in Austria and in smaller amounts in Germany's WÜRTTEMBERG
region, where it's called *Blauer Limberger* (also *Limberger* and
Lemberger). In the United States, it's planted in Washington, where it's
known as Lemberger and where there are over 200 acres, in the FIN-
GER LAKES AVA in New York and in Oregon. Blaufränkisch, which buds
early and ripens late, doesn't do well in the colder climates. The wines
it produces are lighter-styled reds, usually with plenty of ACIDITY.
Blaufränkisch is known as *Kékfrankos* in Hungary, *Franconia* in the
FRIULI-VENEZIA GIULIA of Italy, *Frankovka* in Slovakia, and *Gamé* in
Bulgaria. It's not, as is sometimes thought, the same variety as GAMAY.

Blaye [BLA-yuh; BLI] A historic town on the Gironde estuary across
from the HAUT-MÉDOC in France's BORDEAUX region. It's the center of a
large winegrowing region of the same name that has three appellations. **Blaye AC** (or *Blayais*) and **Côtes de Blaye AC** produce white
wines using SÉMILLON, SAUVIGNON BLANC, and COLOMBARD as the main
grape varieties. For the most part, these wines are fairly undistinguished. **Premières Côtes de Blaye AC** produces mostly red wines
from MERLOT, CABERNET SAUVIGNON, CABERNET FRANC, and MALBEC and a

B

small amount of white wine. Although this is the inferred superior appellation for this region, many of the better white wines use only the Côtes de Blaye designation. The quality of the red wines is increasing, but, except in isolated cases, they still have a reputation for being below-average wines.

blend(s); blending Blend is a general term used for a wine made from more than one grape VARIETY. **Blending** is the process of combining different wines with the goal of creating a composite that's better than any of the wines separately. The wines used for blending might be from different varieties (for instance, CABERNET SAUVIGNON, MERLOT, and CABERNET FRANC), different regions (such as NAPA VALLEY and PASO ROBLES), varying types of COOPERAGE (some new barrels, some older barrels, barrels from different forests or coopers, etc.), and even different VINTAGES (as in non-vintage CHAMPAGNE created by combining wines from different years).

blending wine Also called *cutting wine*, a blending wine is added, in small quantities, to other wines to enhance them or to correct deficiencies in them. For example, wines with high alcoholic content are often added to wines with low alcoholic content, and wines with dark color, to those lacking color. In France a blending wine is called a *coupage*.

blind tasting *see* Tasting Wine, page 648

blunt *see* Glossary of Wine Tasting Terms, page 655

blush wine Called BLANC DE NOIR or ROSÉ in France, blush wine is an American generic name given to wines that vary in color from pale pink to apricot to salmon. Such wines are generally produced from red grapes by quickly removing the skins from the juice after the grapes are pressed. This technique stops the transfer of color from the dark pigments in the grape's skin, and the wine continues its processing as for white wine. Introduced in the United States in the late 1970s, blush wines found popularity in the early 1980s as the white-wine boom took off and producers searched for a channel for the red-grape surplus. Today, some producers create blush wine by mixing red and white wines. Blush wines usually go by other names, such as BLANC DE PINOT NOIR, CABERNET BLANC, WHITE ZINFANDEL, or PINOT VIN GRIS. Most of these wines are slightly sweet, although some are quite DRY with just a whisper of RESIDUAL SUGAR. Wines labeled VIN GRIS are usually fairly dry and often have some wood aging.

Boal; Bual [boh-AHL; boo-AHL] 1. A white-wine grape historically associated with the island of MADEIRA. Boal is now found there only in limited quantities. After PHYLLOXERA attacked the Madeira vineyards in the 1870s, the vineyards were eventually replanted, but the classic Madeira varieties like Boal were replaced with the hardier TINTA NEGRA MOLE. However, because of Common Market labeling regulations (see following discussion), Boal is expected to make a comeback. 2. After MALMSEY, Boal is the darkest and richest of the Madeira wine styles. Originally made primarily with the Boal grape, cheaper versions of this style of Madeira began using more Tinta Negra Mole. However, in 1986, when Portugal entered the Common Market, regulations required that by 1993 any Madeira wine naming a variety on its label would have to contain at least 85 percent of that grape. This labeling requirement has caused an upsurge in replanting of the classic vines such as Boal. Wines labeled "Boal-style" can contain less than the required 85 percent and most likely contain more Tinta Negra Mole.

Bobal [boh-BAHL] Spanish red-grape variety native to the UTIEL-REQUENA DO in eastern Spain. It's also grown in the ALICANTE, BULLAS, JUMILLA, RIBERA DE GUADIANA, VALENCIA and YECLA DOS. However, it is not currently approved for use in all these DO wines. It's very dark colored, has good acidity and the wines are usually lower in alcohol than those of many other red VARIETIES. It's Spain's third most heavily planted variety with hundreds of thousands of acres of vineyards. Although mostly sold as bulk wine, Bobal is being rediscovered and appearing in some higher quality wines. It's also known as *Requena* or *Tinto de Requena.*

Boberg Region *see* SOUTH AFRICA

Boca DOC [BOH-kah] A DOC in the Novara hills near the village of Boca, just north of GATTINARA in Italy's PIEDMONT region. It makes DRY red wines from NEBBIOLO, Vespolina, and BONARDA grapes. These wines must have 3 years of AGING, two of which must be in wooden barrels.

Bocksbeutel [BAWKS-boy-tuhl] A squat, flagon-shaped, green or amber bottle used for quality wine (QbA or QmP) from Germany's FRANKEN region. Badisches Frankenland, a wine produced in the northern part of German's BADEN region, also uses a bocksbeutel. *Bock* is German for "goat," and it's said that the bottle is patterned after the scrotum of that animal. Others feel that the name is taken from a bag used to carry religious books called a **Bockesbeutel** in Low German.

Bockstein *see* OCKFEN

B

bodega [boh-DAY-gah] A versatile Spanish term used for "wine cellar," as well as "winery," "wine storage area," and "wine-producing firm."

Bodega Norton *see* ARGENTINA

Bodegas Trapiche *see* ARGENTINA

boden [BOH-duhn] German for "soil" or "ground." Like the French GOÛT DE TERROIR, *bodengeschmack,* which means "taste of the soil," refers to wines with a flavor that reflects the vineyard in which the grapes were grown. RIESLING grapes grown in slate-based terrain, such as that found in the MOSEL-SAAR-RUWER region, are said to absorb a slate flavor and transmit it to the wines.

body *see* Glossary of Wine Tasting Terms, page 655

Böhlig *see* WACHENHEIM

Bolgheri DOC; Bolgheri Sassicaia DOC [bohl-GEH-ree] Located south of Livorno in Italy's TUSCANY region, the Bolgheri DOC includes the sloping coastal vineyards south of the village of Bolgheri in an area whose wines are much in demand. The DRY rosé (ROSATO) wines—made primarily from SANGIOVESE, blended with some CANAIOLO and other red grapes—are highly regarded. The area's dry white wines (BIANCO) are made chiefly from TREBBIANO, blended with VERMENTINO and other white grapes. But the superior wines made from BORDEAUX varieties—CABERNET SAUVIGNON, CABERNET FRANC, and MERLOT—have created so much of a sensation in this area that, in 1994, the Italian government granted two changes to this DOC. It added Cabernet Sauvignon and Merlot to its list of acceptable grapes and granted Sassicaia (the PROPRIETARY name for a CABERNET SAUVIGNON/CABERNET FRANC blend) its own DOC status as subzone of Bolgheri. Indeed, **Bolgheri Sassicaia** wines were at the vanguard of the Tuscany region's trend toward non-DOC wines called SUPER TUSCANS. The first Sassicaia was released in 1968, although the wine had been made for numerous vintages before that. Produced by the Marchesi Incisa della Rocchetta estate, Sassicaia is made in a Bordeaux style from vines originally planted with CUTTINGS from the Château Lafite-Rothschild estate (previously owned by Lodovico Antinori). It's AGED in BARRIQUES for 18 to 24 months prior to release. Other Bolgheri-area super Tuscans include Antinori's *Guado al Tasso* and Podere Grattamacco's *Rosso* (both of which are a blend of Cabernet Sauvignon, Merlot, and Sangiovese) and the recently purchased Mondavi/Frescobaldi estate's *Ornellaia* (a Cabernet Sauvignon, Cabernet Franc, and Merlot blend).

Bolognesi *see* COLLI BOLOGNESI DOC

Bombino Bianco [bom-BEE-noh BYAHN-koh] White-wine grape that is grown in southeast Italy, primarily in APULIA and ABRUZZI but also in MARCHE and LATIUM. Bombino Bianco generally produces bland, low-ALCOHOL wines used primarily with other grape varieties for BLENDS, and sometimes for VERMOUTH. In Abruzzi, a DOC called TREBBIANO D'ABRUZZO uses this grape, which is also called *Trebbiano d'Abruzzo* (although it's unrelated to TREBBIANO). Some producers in this DOC carefully prune the Bombino Bianco vines, thereby reducing the YIELD and generating more flavorful grapes, which result in wines that can be quite good. The better examples exhibit CREAMY and CITRUSY characteristics. Bombino Bianco is also known as *Pagadebit* or *Pagadebito* and *Zapponara Bianca.*

Bonarda [baw-NAHRR-dah] 1. The shortened name given to *Bonarda Piemontese,* a red-wine grape grown in Italy's PIEDMONT region. Though once widely planted in Piedmont, this grape fell out of favor over the years. Only recently has it been making a slight comeback. Bonarda Piemontese wines are generally LIGHT, FRUITY, and immediately drinkable. This variety is also known as *Bonarda di Chieri* and *Bonarda di Gattinara.* 2. A synonym for a grape variety officially known as CROATINA.

Bonarda dell'Oltrepo Pavese *see* CROATINA

Bonarda di Chieri *see* BONARDA

Bonarda di Gattinara *see* BONARDA

Bonarda Piemontese *see* BONARDA

bond; bonded A *bond* is a federal permit to produce and store wine commercially. A *bonded winery* is an enterprise that produces and stores wine under a bond that guarantees payment of the federal excise tax.

Bonnes Mares AC [bawn MAHR] A famous GRAND CRU vineyard located in the CÔTE DE NUITS area of France's BURGUNDY region. Of its 37 acres of PINOT NOIR grapes, 33.5 acres are in the village of CHAMBOLLE-MUSIGNY, and 3.7 acres are in MOREY-SAINT-DENIS. Bonnes Mares AC red wines are full-bodied (*see* BODY) and TANNIC and can AGE for 10 to 20 years. They're quite different from the wines from the village's other grand cru vineyard, MUSIGNY, which are lighter, more elegant, and earlier maturing. Most critics agree that Bonnes Mares AC red wines can be some of the best in the world.

B

Bonnezeaux AC [bawn-ZOH] Small APPELLATION that nestles in the ANJOU region of France's LOIRE Valley. Located within the larger CÔTEAUX DU LAYON appellation, Bonnezeaux is one of the two premier DESSERT WINES from the Loire—QUARTS DE CHAUME is the other. Both have GRAND CRU status. The grapes used are CHENIN BLANC, which, in better years, are attacked by BOTRYTIS CINEREA (noble rot). This mold produces shriveled, raisiny, intensely sweet grapes that in turn create rich, luscious wines. The Chenin Blanc grape's naturally high ACID content helps these wines AGE well—some for 20 years or more.

bor [bahr] Hungarian for "wine."

Borba DOC *see* ALENTEJO

Bordeaux [bohr-DOH] An area in southwestern France considered by most wine enthusiasts as the world's greatest wine-producing region because of the large quantity (ranging from 700 million to 900 million bottles annually) and the high quality of the wines. This large region has about 280,000 vineyard acres and essentially covers the same territory as the DÉPARTEMENT of GIRONDE. At its center lies the seaport city of Bordeaux, which sits on the Garonne River upstream from the Gironde estuary, which empties into the Atlantic Ocean. The Bordeaux region's fame dates back some 2,000 years when Romans first sang the praises of its wines. The wide popularity of Bordeaux wines in the United Kingdom (where they're called CLARETS) can be traced back to the period from 1152 to 1453, when the English owned this region, which was acquired through a royal marriage and then lost in the 100 Years' War. Bordeaux gains most of its fame from its red wines, which generally make up over 75 percent of the production. Nevertheless, the region's rich, sweet white wines from SAUTERNES are world renowned, and its DRY white wines from GRAVES have a serious following. Bordeaux's primary APPELLATIONS (*see also* APPELLATION D'ORIGINE CONTRÔLÉE), which cover the entire region, are **Bordeaux AC**—for red, white, and ROSÉ wines—and **Bordeaux Supérieur AC**—a designation for red and rosé wines that requires lower grape yields and slightly higher alcohol levels than basic Bordeaux. However, Bordeaux is broken up into many districts and contains numerous individual appellations. The five main districts that have individual appellations are POMEROL, SAINT-ÉMILION, Graves, Sauternes, and, most important of them all, MÉDOC. Within Médoc, there are many individual COMMUNES with specific appellations as well. Some of them, like MARGAUX, PAUILLAC, SAINT-ESTÈPHE, and SAINT-JULIEN, are quite well known. Minor Bordeaux districts with appellations include BLAYE,

BOURG, ENTRE-DEUX-MERS, and PREMIÈRES CÔTES DE BORDEAUX. There are over fifty individual appellations in Bordeaux, and, generally, the smallest ACs produce the highest-quality wines. There are also thousands of individual châteaux—some are quite impressive, while others are simply tiny farmhouses. This number has resulted in attempts at classifying the better châteaux in addition to using appellations as a quality guide. At the top of the list sit the CRU CLASSÉ (classed growths) whose classifications are, for the most part, quite old and frequently raise questions regarding the accuracy of the rankings in today's environment. For example, the 1855 Official Classification of Bordeaux (*see* Official Wine Classifications of Bordeaux, page 678) divided the crus classés for the Médoc red wines into five subcategories—PREMIER CRU (FIRST GROWTH) through CINQUIÈME CRU (fifth growth)—and the white wines of Sauternes into two subcategories—*premier cru* (first growth) and DEUXIÈMES CRU (second growth). The quality of the wines from châteaux ranked in the second through fifth growths has changed over the years, but there hasn't been any official classification change. However, the first growth châteaux—Haut-Brion, Lafite-Rothschild, Latour, Margaux, and Mouton-Rothschild (added in 1973)—have continued to maintain their standards for high quality (and high prices). Over the years, additional cru classé classifications were declared for other areas like Graves and Saint-Émilion. Today there are fewer than 200 châteaux classified as crus classés, and the Pomerol district châteaux have never been classified. This has not deterred wine lovers from seeking out the higher-quality wines— Pomerol's Château Pétrus is consistently one of the most desired and expensive of all Bordeaux wines. Below the cru classé ranking is another grouping of classifications called CRU BOURGEOIS, which ranks several hundred better Bordeaux châteaux not included in the cru classé. Below this are thousands of châteaux of lesser stature grouped together as PETITS CHÂTEAU (the categories of CRU ARTISAN and Cru Paysan are no longer commonly used). The primary red-grape varieties used in Bordeaux are CABERNET SAUVIGNON, CABERNET FRANC, MERLOT, and occasionally MALBEC and PETIT VERDOT. In fact, it may surprise many American ENOPHILES to learn that Merlot has almost twice as much acreage as Cabernet Sauvignon. SAUVIGNON BLANC, SÉMILLON, and MUSCADELLE are the primary white grapes. Bordeaux winemakers tend to blend grape varieties when making their wines, as opposed to the most common practice in the United States of making VARIETAL WINES. It should be noted that winemakers in the United States are now making more blended wines, coining the term MERITAGE for those comprised of the approved Bordeaux grape varieties. In general, the vineyards of Saint-Émilion and Pomerol are planted more heavily in Merlot and thus produce SOFTER, more SUPPLE wines, whereas the vineyards of Médoc and Graves favor the Cabernet varieties and produce more intense, TANNIC, and long-lived wines.

Bordeaux Blend [bohr-DOH] A term used for blended wines made with two or more of the traditional BORDEAUX grape varieties. The Bordeaux red grapes are CABERNET FRANC, CABERNET SAUVIGNON, Carmenere, Gros Verdot, MALBEC, MERLOT, PETIT VERDOT, and St. Macaire; white grapes are SAUVIGNON BLANC (Sauvignon Musque), MUSCADELLE (Sauvignon Vert), and SÉMILLON. In the United States, such blends are referred to as MERITAGE wines, providing they meet certain requirements.

Bordeaux Classifications of 1855 *see* Official Wine Classifications of Bordeaux, page 678

Bordeaux mixture [bohr-DOH] Known as *bouillie bordelaise* in France, a Bordeaux mixture is a compound of copper sulfate, slaked lime, salt, and water. It's used throughout Europe and other parts of the world as a spray to combat MILDEW, especially powdery mildew.

Borden Ranch AVA This VITICULTURAL AREA was established in August 2006. Its 70,000 acres are located in the east central section of the larger LODI AVA, which is between Sacramento and Stockton in northern California. It has a higher elevation (73 to 520 feet) versus much of the surrounding Lodi area. It's home to vineyards owned by Woodbridge by Robert Mondavi, Sutter Home and Delicato. Red varieties such as CABERNET FRANC, CABERNET SAUVIGNON, MERLOT, SYRAH, and ZINFANDEL are most common.

Bordertown SOUTH AUSTRALIA wine-producing region located about 165 miles southeast of the city of Adelaide in the Limestone Coast Zone. It's situated around the town of Bordertown in the far southeast corner near the VICTORIA state border. The Bordertown area is north of the more famous COONAWARRA and PADTHAWAY regions. It has about 2,500 acres of vineyards dominated by red VARIETIES—CABERNET SAUVIGON is the most widely planted, followed by Shiraz (SYRAH), MERLOT, PETIT VERDOT, and Mataro (MOURVÈDRE). CHARDONNAY is the most widely planted white variety.

Bordo *see* CABERNET FRANC

Borrado das Moscas *see* BICAL

bota [BOH-tah] 1. A Spanish term referring to a goatskin bag that holds about a liter of wine. The bota has a nozzle on one end—when the bag is squeezed, the wine is forced out and into one's mouth. 2. A Spanish wine barrel equivalent to a sherry BUTT, holding about 132 U.S. gallons.

botrytis bunch rot *see* BOTRYTIS CINEREA

Botrytis cinerea; botrytis [boh-TRI-tihs sihn-EHR-ee-uh] The fungus that causes *botrytis bunch rot*. Depending on the conditions, *Botrytis cinerea* can be either exceedingly beneficial or devastating to grapes. In its benevolent form, botrytis is called **noble rot**—and when wine writers use the term "botrytis," they are typically referring to this form. The ideal conditions under which this beneficial mold develops include cool, misty mornings (during which the fungus grows) and warm, sunny afternoons that dry the grapes, controlling the growth of the fungus. However, if the weather's unremittingly damp, or rains come shortly before harvest, botrytis bunch rot turns malevolent, in which case it's known as **gray rot**. In such circumstances, the botrytis spores run rampant, spreading quickly throughout the grape clusters and spoiling the fruit. When carefully cultivated in its noble-rot form, *Botrytis cinerea* causes the grape to shrivel, concentrating and intensifying both sugar and flavor. The grape's ACID level remains high, which prevents the resulting wines from being cloyingly sweet. Most winemakers are exhilarated when noble rot descends on their grapes because it gives them fruit from which to make very elegant, intensely flavored DESSERT WINES. In California, BOTRYTISED wines are usually referred to as LATE HARVEST or SELECT LATE HARVEST. In France, where noble rot is called *pourriture noble,* the best-known beneficiaries are the famous wines of SAUTERNES. Noble rot is called *Edelfäule* in Germany, where winemakers are experts at producing a large variety of elegant wines such as TROCKENBEERENAUSLESE and BEERENAUSLESE. The renowned Hungarian TOKAJI ASZÚ is also a popular botrytis-infected wine. In Italy, *Botrytis cinerea* is called *muffa nobile*. A wide range of grape varieties are subject to the positive effects of noble rot including CHENIN BLANC, FURMINT, GEWÜRZTRAMINER, HÁRSLEVELÜ, OPTIMA, ORTEGA, RIESLING, SAUVIGNON BLANC, SCHEUREBE, and SÉMILLON.

botrytised *see* Glossary of Wine Tasting Terms, page 655

botte [BOAT-tay] Italian for "cask" or "barrel."

bottiglia [boat-TEE-lyah] Italian for "bottle."

bottle *see* Wine Bottles, page 609

bottle aging *see* AGING

B

bottled by By itself, the phrase *bottled by* indicates that the winery played a very small part in the wine's production. The most likely role was simply to purchase and bottle wine made somewhere else. *See also* ESTATE BOTTLED; GROWN, PRODUCED AND BOTTLED BY; MADE AND BOTTLED BY; PRODUCED AND BOTTLED BY.

bottle fermentation; bottle-fermented Reference to the second fermentation that occurs in the bottle during the production of SPARKLING WINE via MÉTHODE CHAMPENOISE. *See also* FERMENTATION.

bottle shock *see* BOTTLE SICKNESS

bottle sickness A reaction that occurs in wine immediately after corking, resulting from the large amount of oxygen it absorbed during bottling. Bottle sickness can also result if SULFUR DIOXIDE was added during the bottling process. The effect on the wine is a flat flavor and aroma, sometimes accompanied by an off-putting odor. Bottle sickness, sometimes referred to as *bottle shock,* dissipates within a few weeks. *See also* ACETALDEHYDE.

bottle stink *see* Glossary of Wine Tasting Terms, page 655

bottling dosage *see* DOSAGE

Bouche *see* CABERNET FRANC; CABERNET SAUVIGNON

Les Boucherottes *see* BEAUNE

Bouchet *see* CABERNET FRANC; CABERNET SAUVIGNON

Bouchy *see* CABERNET FRANC

Aux Boudots *see* NUITS-SAINT-GEORGES

La Boudriotte *see* CHASSAGNE-MONTRACHET AC

Bougros [boo-GROH] One of the seven GRAND CRU vineyards in CHABLIS. Bougros consists of just over 35 acres and is adjacent to and northwest of LES PREUSES.

bouquet *see* Glossary of Wine Tasting Terms, page 655

Bourboulenc [boor-boo-LAHNK] Also known as *Malvoisie du Languedoc,* Bourboulenc is one of the principal white-grape varieties of the CÔTES-DU-RHÔNE. It requires considerable heat to ripen properly. Bourboulenc's high ACID content makes it popular for use in BLENDS to which it brings BODY and spicy flavors. On its own, this grape produces fresh, floral, low-alcohol wines that are best drunk young.

Bourg [BOOR] A small town in France's BORDEAUX region located north of the city of Bordeaux and across the Gironde River from MARGAUX. It's in the BLAYE region but has its own appellation, **Côtes de Bourg AC**, whose wines have a better reputation than the rest of Blaye. Red wines, which represent the largest percentage of production, are made from MERLOT, CABERNET FRANC, CABERNET SAUVIGNON, and MALBEC grape varieties. Although these wines don't have the reputation of those produced across the river in MÉDOC, they're full-flavored, pleasant, and moderately priced.

Bourgeois *see* CRU BOURGEOIS

Bourgogne AC [boor-GON-yuh] A general regional APPELLATION for red, ROSÉ, and white wines. It covers all the wines produced in France's BURGUNDY region that, although they don't qualify for a higher-rated appellation, meet the qualifications of this basic appellation. Red Burgundy (*Bourgogne Rouge*) must be made from PINOT NOIR, although the GAMAY grape variety is allowed in BEAUJOLAIS; in the Yonne DÉPARTEMENT, the local varieties Tressot or Cesar are also approved. CHARDONNAY is the main variety used for white Burgundy (*Bourgogne Blanc*), although PINOT BLANC and PINOT GRIS are also approved varieties. Bourgogne AC wines are usually not as interesting as those with village or vineyard appellations, but they're generally good and moderately priced. The best are usually from single growers who couldn't put their wine into premium labels because it didn't quite meet specifications. *See also* BOURGOGNE ALIGOTÉ AC; BOURGOGNE GRAND ORDINAIRE AC; BOURGOGNE PASSE-TOUT-GRAIN AC; BURGUNDY.

Bourgogne Aligoté AC; Bourgogne Aligoté de Bouzeron AC [boor-GON-yuh ah-lee-goh-TAY] These APPELLATIONS are specifically for the ALIGOTÉ variety, a white-wine grape cultivated in some parts of BURGUNDY. Compared to CHARDONNAY, Aligoté is not as important or distinguished, and, in most cases, the wines it produces aren't as rich or long-lived. Some Aligoté wines can be sharp and sour, but older Aligoté vines have been known to produce some very pleasant wines that exhibit citrusy and, occasionally, nutty characteristics. Burgundian wines made from this grape are labeled **Bougogne Aligoté AC** or, when they come from the village of Bouzeron in the northern CÔTE CHALONNAISE, **Bourgogne Aligoté de Bouzeron AC**.

Bourgogne Grand Ordinaire AC [boor-GON-yuh grah*n* ohr-dee-NEHR] The general regional APPELLATION, known as BGO, that is rarely used today. Its requirements are even lower than those for the BOURGOGNE AC, so most winemakers opt for the latter. The grape varieties are the same as allowed for Bourgogne AC wines, with the addition of MELON DE BOURGOGNE for white wines. In the Yonne DÉPARTEMENT, the local Sacy grape variety is also allowed in white wines. As the name implies, the wines are fairly ordinary.

Bourgogne-Hautes Côtes de Beaune *see* HAUTES-CÔTES DE BEAUNE

Bourgogne-Hautes Côtes de Nuits *see* HAUTES-CÔTES DE NUITS

Bourgogne Mousseux AC *see* CRÉMANT DE BOURGOGNE

Bourgogne Passe-Tout-Grain AC [boor-GON-yuh pahss too GRA/N] An APPELLATION that covers the entire BURGUNDY region for wines that are comprised of at least one-third PINOT NOIR and up to two-thirds GAMAY grapes and that are fermented together. This is primarily a red wine AC, although a small amount of ROSÉ is also produced. The wine from this AC is fairly basic and ordinary; however, ongoing vineyard replanting is gradually increasing the available Pinot Noir grapes, which in turn is improving wine quality. Most of Bourgogne Passe-Tout-Grain AC wines come from the CÔTE CHALONNAISE, with small amounts from CÔTE D'OR.

Bourgogne Vézelay AC *see* VÉZELAY AC

Bourgueil AC [boor-GEUH-yuh] One of the few APPELLATIONS in the LOIRE Valley focused on red wines. Located in the TOURAINE region, the area around the village of Bourgueil—like that of its neighbors CHINON and SAINT-NICOLAS-DE-BOURGUEIL—is dry enough to grow CABERNET FRANC and limited quantities of CABERNET SAUVIGNON. The wines from this AC are normally light and fruity. They're certainly no match for better BORDEAUX reds, but hot years can produce good, full-bodied (*see* BODY) wines with AGING capabilities of 10 to 15 years.

Bourguignon Noir *see* GAMAY

Bousse d'Or *see* VOLNAY

Boutenac *see* CORBIÈRES AC

Bouzeron *see* BOURGOGNE ALIGOTÉ DE BOUZERON AC

Bouzy [boo-ZEE] An outstanding wine-producing village on the Montagne de Reims in France's CHAMPAGNE region. Its vineyards have GRAND CRU status with a top rating of 100 percent under the region's percentage system (*see* CHAMPAGNE for more information). The grapes are PINOT NOIR, most of which are used to produce SPARKLING WINE, although a small amount of still red wine is bottled under the CÔTEAUX CHAMPENOIS AC.

boxed wine *see* BAG-IN-A-BOX WINE

Brachet [brah-SHAY] French VARIETY also known as *braquet*. It's grown primarily in the BELLET AC in PROVENCE where it's used to make VARIETAL WINES and also blended with CINSAUT and GRENACHE. Both ROSÉ and light-bodied red wines are produced. It's unrelated to the Italian variety, BRACHETTO.

Brachetto; Brachetto d'Acqui DOCG [brah-KAY-toh dah-KWEE] **Brachetto** is a red-grape variety grown mainly in Italy's PIEDMONT region. It's light red in color with an aroma like MUSCAT and a strawberry trait. Brachetto is used to produce a variety of styles from STILL, DRY wines to the more common SWEET, SPARKLING ones. **Brachetto d'Acqui** is a DOCG located in the southeastern portion of the Piedmont region in the provinces of Asti and Alessandria near the town of Aqui Terme southeast of Asti. This zone's version of Brachetto is primarily FRIZZANTE, although there are also STILL versions, which, in most cases, are slightly sweet.

Bramaterra DOC [brah-mah-TEHR-uh] DOC located in Italy's PIEDMONT region just to the west of GATTINARA near the villages of Roasio and Villadel Bosco. The DRY, red wines—made from NEBBIOLO, CROATINA, BONARDA, and Vespolina—are much lighter and more elegant than those from BAROLO or GATTINARA. They require 2 years AGING, with 18 months in wood barrels. A RISERVA requires 3 years, with 2 years in wood barrels.

brambly *see* BRIARY in the Glossary of Wine Tasting Terms, page 655

branco [BRAHN-koh] Portuguese for "white."

brandy A liquor distilled (*see* DISTILLATION) from wine and aged in wood, which contributes flavor and color. The finest of all brandies is COGNAC, closely followed by ARMAGNAC. The name *brandy* comes from the Dutch *brandewijin,* meaning "burned (distilled) wine." Brandy can also be made from fermented fruits other than grapes (such as the apple-based Calvados), but they are generally qualified by adding the name of the fruit, as in apple brandy. The term brandy by itself generally refers to those made from grapes.

Braquet *see* BRACHET

Brauneberg [BROUW-nuh-beh*r*k] A well-known village located just southwest of its more famous neighbor, BERNKASTEL, on the Mosel River in Germany's MOSEL-SAAR-RUWER region. Vineyards belonging to the village are in BEREICH Bernkastel and GROSSLAGE Kurfürstlay. **Juffer** is the most famous EINZELLAGE, and the wines from this vineyard are very expensive. Wines from this village have had an esteemed reputation for centuries.

Braune Kupp *see* WILTINGEN

Braunfels *see* WILTINGEN

brawny *see* Glossary of Wine Tasting Terms, page 655

Brazil In South America, Brazil now ranks third in wine production, after Argentina and Chile. Although grape growing and winemaking were first introduced to Brazil by the Portuguese in the 1530s, it wasn't until the 1870s with the arrival of Italian and German immigrants that VITICULTURE took hold in a permanent fashion. Most of their efforts occurred in the mountainous Serra Gaúcha area in the northeast part of Rio Grande do Sul. The early plantings were NATIVE AMERICAN GRAPES, HYBRIDS, or CROSSES. Varieties such as CONCORD, DUTCHESS, ISABELLA, NIAGARA and SEYVAL BLANC still proliferate. Eventually European varieties (VITIS VINIFERA) such as BARBERA, BONARDA, MUSCAT and TREBBIANO were planted. Now other varieties have been added and CABERNET FRANC, CABERNET SAUVIGNON, CHARDONNAY, GEWÜRZTRAMINER, MERLOT, PETITE SIRAH, SÉMILLON, and SYRAH can be found. In general these varieties do best in areas far from the Equator, where the climate is cooler. **Rio Grande do Sul**, Brazil's southernmost state, still grows the majority of the grape crop. Within Rio Grande do Sul is **Serra Gaúcha**, the primary wine producing zone, which is divided into five growing areas. The best known of these is **Vale dos Vinhedos**, which was the first area to receive Brazil's Geographical Indication of Origin certificate (established in 2001). Also within Rio Grande do Sul is **Campos de Cima da Serra**—at about 3,300 feet it's one of the coolest growing areas in Brazil. In the south of Rio Grande do Sul is **Campanha** (previously known as **Fronteira**), which sits near the Uruguay border. Wines from Campanha are starting to attract attention in the international market. In northeast Brazil is **Vale do São Francisco**, which is the closest to the equator of any winegrowing region in the world. Surprisingly, it's semi-arid and requires some irrigation during the growing seasons. Being so close to the equator means there is no winter and vines can produce two crops a year. Some wines from here are also receiving good reviews.

breathe *see* AERATION

breed *see* Glossary of Wine Tasting Terms, page 655

Breede River Valley Region *see* SOUTH AFRICA

B

Breganze DOC [breh-GAHN-zeh] Located in the VENETO region in northeast Italy, this DOC zone is north of Vicenza and encompasses the vineyards around the village of Breganze. This DOC produces five VARIETAL WINES—Cabernet (made with CABERNET FRANC and CABERNET SAUVIGNON), Pinot Bianco (PINOT BLANC), Pinot Grigio (PINOT GRIS), Pinot Nero (PINOT NOIR), and Vespaiolo. Breganze DOC also produces blended red and white wines. The BIANCO combines Pinot Bianco, Pinot Grigio, Riesling Italico (WELSCHRIESLING), Sauvignon (SAUVIGNON BLANC), FRIULANO, and Vespaiolo. The ROSSO is made with Cabernet Franc, Cabernet Sauvignon, Gropello, MERLOT, Marzemino, and Pinot Nero.

Brenton *see* CABERNET FRANC

Les Bressandes *see* BEAUNE; CORTON

brett *see* BRETTANOMYCES

brettanomyces; brett [breht-tan-uh-MI-sees; BREHT] A spoilage yeast that grows on grapes and in wineries. Because brettanomyces (*brett*, for short) is almost impossible to eradicate, most winemakers take great pains to avoid it. When it does occur, vintners generally use special filters to reduce the prospect of continued growth in the bottle. Low levels of this pesky yeast can add complexity to a wine's aroma, while overt amounts can ruin it. An organism called *dekkera* is virtually identical to brettanomyces and produces the same odoriferous results. *See also* DIMETHYL DICARBONATE; Glossary of Wine Tasting Terms, page 655.

briary *see* Glossary of Wine Tasting Terms, page 655

bricco [BREE-koh] Label term found on wines from Italy's PIEDMONT region, referring to a vineyard's summit or highest point and relating to the belief that hillside vineyards are superior for grape growing. *See also* SORI.

brick red *see* Glossary of Wine Tasting Terms, page 655

bright; brightness *see* Glossary of Wine Tasting Terms, page 655

brilliant *see* Glossary of Wine Tasting Terms, page 655

British Columbia Although British Columbia can point to a wine history dating back to the 1860s, it wasn't until the late 1980s that this western Canadian province really got serious about making quality wines. The trigger was the North American Free Trade Agreement (NAFTA), which, once enacted, would mean that Canadian wineries would no longer enjoy the protection of not having to compete with imported wines. Faced with losing what wine industry there was, the British Columbia Wine Institute was created in 1990, mandating standards for British Columbia wine. These criteria followed ONTARIO's lead in embracing the VQA program, establishing designated viticultural areas (VA), and setting standards and certification criteria for wine. British Columbia now has four VAs—Fraser Valley, Okanagan Valley, Similkameen Valley, and Vancouver Island. The **Okanagan Valley VA**, with over 40 wineries and 4,000 acres of vineyards, is the largest and most important—it produces about 95 percent of the province's wines. The 120-mile-long valley is situated around the deep Okanagan Lake, which is in south central British Columbia about 200 miles east of the city of Vancouver and about 10 miles from the Canada-United States border. Unlike the far west of British Columbia, this area is arid. The valley's southern section, which is Canada's only classified desert area, is warmer and drier than the northern end. This range of climates allows a wide variety of grapes to be grown in the valley including Cabernet Franc, Cabernet Sauvignon, and Merlot in the south, and Chardonnay, Pinot Blanc, Pinot Gris, and Pinot Noir in the north. The **Similkameen Valley VA** is a small area just west of the southern part of the Okanagan Valley. It has only a couple of wineries and less than 200 acres of vineyard. The **Fraser Valley VA** is another small growing area (three wineries) just outside of Vancouver—east and slightly south of the city. The **Vancouver Island VA** covers not only all of Vancouver Island but also the neighboring islands west of British Columbia's mainland and south of the fiftieth parallel. Vineyards here are primarily around the city of Duncan on the eastern side of the island about 30 to 35 miles north of the city of Victoria. The climate is cool, and the focus is on early-ripening grape varieties. There are about 135 acres of vineyards and ten small wineries in the area. The most popular white variety grown in British Columbia is CHARDONNAY, followed by GEWÜRZTRAMINER, PINOT GRIS, PINOT BLANC, RIESLING, and SAUVIGNON BLANC. The reds in order of popularity are MERLOT, PINOT NOIR, CABERNET SAUVIGNON, and CABERNET FRANC. British Columbia now has over seventy wineries.

British Sherry *see* BRITISH WINE

British Wine In England, the term "British Wine" (or "British Sherry") indicates that imported MUST or grape concentrate was used to make the wines, as opposed to ENGLISH WINE, which uses grapes grown in country. British wine is also known as *Made Wine*.

B

Brix [BRIHKS] Named for A. F. W. Brix, a nineteenth-century German inventor, the Brix scale is a system used in the United States to measure the sugar content of grapes and wine. The Brix (sugar content) is determined by a HYDROMETER, which indicates a liquid's SPECIFIC GRAVITY (the density of a liquid in relation to that of pure water). Each degree Brix is equivalent to 1 gram of sugar per 100 grams of grape juice. The grapes for most TABLE WINES have a Brix reading of between 20° to 25° at harvest. About 55 to 60 percent of the sugar is converted into ALCOHOL. The estimated alcohol that a wine will produce (called **potential alcohol**) is estimated by multiplying the Brix reading by 0.55. Therefore, a 20° Brix will make a wine with about 11 percent alcohol. The **Balling** scale was a comparable measurement procedure that has since been replaced by the Brix system. *See also* BAUMÉ.

Brochon *see* CÔTE DE NUITS

Brouilly AC [broo-YEE] This is the largest and southernmost of the ten CRUS in France's BEAUJOLAIS region. It includes five villages surrounding Mont de Brouilly and has almost 3,000 acres of vineyards. Made from GAMAY grapes, these wines are delicate and fruity with nuances of strawberries, bananas, and peaches. Though perhaps lighter than some of the other crus, they're still considered to be fairly typical of Beaujolais wines. CÔTE DE BROUILLY is a different cru located next to Brouilly.

browning *see* Glossary of Wine Tasting Terms, page 655

Brown Muscat *see* MUSCAT

brown sherry *see* SHERRY

Brückes *see* BAD KREUZNACH

Bruderberg *see* MAXIMIN GRÜNHAUS

Brunello *see* SANGIOVESE

Brunello di Montalcino DOCG [broo-NELL-oh dee mawn-tahl-CHEE-noh] The wines from Brunello di Montalcino are regarded as some of Italy's best. They're made totally from a SANGIOVESE clone, a strain of Sangiovese Grosso called *Brunello* ("little dark one"), so named for the brown hue of its skin. The wines are BIG, deep-colored, and powerful, with enough TANNINS and STRUCTURE to be quite LONG-LIVED. Brunello di Montalcino wines have one of the longest AGING requirements in Italy—4 years, 2 of which must be in wooden barrels. The RISERVA must age for 5 years. Brunello di Montalcino is one of the small number of DOCG areas in Italy and one of the six (along with CHIANTI, CHIANTI CLASSICO, CARMIGNANO, VERNACCIA DI SAN GIMIGNANO, and VINO NOBILE DI MONTEPULCIANO) located in the TUSCANY region. This DOCG zone encompasses the vineyards around the hillside town of Montalcino, which is south and slightly east of Siena in the southern portion of Tuscany. The wine owes its beginning to Ferruccio Biondi-Santi, who, in the 1860s, planted Brunello on the hills with the belief that he could produce great wines. His family continues the tradition today under the Biondi-Santi label. *See also* ROSSO DI MONTALCINO DOC.

brut [BROOT] A label term applied to the driest (*see* DRY) CHAMPAGNE and other SPARKLING WINES. Brut wines are drier (contain less RESIDUAL SUGAR) than those labeled "extra dry." **Extra Brut** denotes a wine that's extremely dry, sometimes totally dry. Totally dry sparkling wines (those that aren't sweetened with a little DOSAGE) are also sometimes called *Brut Nature* or *Brut Integral.*

Bual *see* BOAL

Bucelas *see* ESTREMADURA

bud break; budbreak In the warmth of early spring (typically March in the northern hemisphere, September in the southern hemisphere), the growing season begins as buds open after a winter of dormancy, revealing SHOOTS and tender green leaves. Buds growing on the previous season's CANES will produce shoots that will be fruitful. *See also* VITICULTURE.

budwood A shoot or stem of a plant bearing buds suitable for bud GRAFTING. *See also* VITICULTURE.

Bugey VDQS [boo-JAY] This small area (less than 1200 acres) with VDQS status is located in the DÉPARTEMENT of Ain next to SAVOIE in eastern France. It produces red and ROSÉ wines, mainly from GAMAY, PINOT NOIR, MONDEUSE, and Poulsard. The main grape varieties for white wines are JACQUÈRE, CHARDONNAY, and ALTESSE. Generally, the wines from the Bugey area are light but good, and the white wines in particular are improving as Chardonnay begins to play a more important role. Most wines are labeled **Vin du Bugey VDQS**, although wine made from Chardonnay and Altesse, called *Roussette* locally, can be labeled **Roussette de Bugey VDQS**. The name of certain CRU villages

(Cerdon, Machuraz, Manicle, Montagnieu, and Virieu-le-Grand) can be added to the label of wines. These cru villages have established vineyard YIELDS that are lower and minimum ALCOHOL levels that are higher. Sparkling (MOUSSEUX) and semisparkling (PÉTILLANT) wines are labeled "Vin du Bugey Mousseux" or "Vin du Bugey Pétillant."

Buisserate *see* JACQUÈRE

Bulgaria [buhl-GEHR-ee-uh] An important wine-producing country in eastern Europe. Of the eastern European countries, Bulgaria has done the best job of getting wines into the markets of western Europe and the United States. This success is related to establishing approved growing regions (similiar to APPELLATIONS) and modernizing the wine-producing industry; however, it is primarily the result of Bulgaria's quicker adaptation to popular Western grapes like CABERNET SAUVIGNON and MERLOT (which are now the top two red varieties here), along with ALIGOTÉ, CHARDONNAY, GEWÜRZTRAMINER, PINOT GRIS, RIESLING, and WELSCHRIESLING. Wines are also still made from eastern European varieties like the white Dimiat, Mistket, and Rkatzitelli and the red Gamza, Mavrud, Melnik, Pamid, and Tamianka. Bulgarian wines of a **Declared Geographical Origin** (DGO) must be labeled with one of twenty-six specifically approved wine-producing district designations. Of these DGOs, the best areas for white wines are Khan Krum, Novi Pazar, Preslav, Shumen, Targovishte, and Varna. The best DGOs for red wines include Assenovgrad, Lorzitza, Oriachovitza, Pavlikeni, Pleven, Plovdiv, Sakar Mountain, Stambolova, Suhindol, and Svischtov. **Controliran** wines, the highest-quality level, must be from an approved vineyard site in one of the twenty-six DGOs and be from a specified grape variety. Currently there are twenty-one approved Controliran wines—Assenovgrad Mavrud, Harsovo Melnik, Kahn Krum Traminer, Liaskovetz Aligote, Lorzitza Cabernet, Novi Pazar Chardonnay, Novo Selo Gamza, Oriachovitza Cabernet-Merlot, Pavlikeni Gamza, Preslav Chardonnay, Rozovata Dolina Misket, Russe Riverside White, Sakar Merlot, South Coast Rosé, Stambolovo Merlot, Suhindol Gamza, Sungulare Misket, Svischtov Cabernet Sauvignon, Treasure of Kralevo, Varna Chardonnay, and Yantra Valley Cabernet Sauvignon. Use of the word *"Reserve"* on the label requires 2 to 3 years of AGING for white varieties and 3 to 4 years for red varieties.

bulk; bulk wine Although sometimes erroneously used to describe wine sold in jugs or boxes, the term *bulk wine* actually refers to wine that's not yet packaged for retail sale.

bulk process *see* CHARMAT PROCESS

Bullas [BOOL-lyahss] A Spanish DO of just over 6,000 acres, located in the Levante region in eastern Spain around the town of Bullas. It's in the province of Murcia, running south from the JUMILLA DO to the Mediterranean Sea. As with Jumilla, the main grape variety in this area is Monastrell (MOUVEDRE), which has been used primarily for producing ROSÉ wines or as a red BLENDING WINE. Today, however, some producers are using it to make more elegant red wines closer in style to the French Mouvedre wines. There are small amounts of Garnacha (GRENACHE) and Cencibel (TEMPRANILLO) grown in this DO. The primary white varieties are MACABEO and AIRÉN.

Bull's Blood *see* EGRI BIKAVÉR

bunch The portion of the vine to which individual grapes are joined. Also called a *cluster*.

Bundesweinprämierung [BOONT-ehs-vine-prai-myeh-roog] An official federal wine award (gold, silver, and bronze) given in Germany. Wines must have won a regional wine award to participate.

bung A plug that's used for sealing a wine barrel. It's inserted into the **bung hole,** through which wine can be added or withdrawn.

Bureau of Alcohol, Tobacco, Firearms and Explosives (ATF) The Bureau of Alcohol, Tobacco, Firearms and Explosives (now abbreviated ATF) is an agency within the Department of Homeland Security with responsibilities for firearms, explosives, arson, and illegal activities involving alcohol and tobacco products. Until the latter part of 2002, when the Homeland Security Act of 2002 was passed, BATF (as it was previously called) was part of the U.S. Treasury Department. The Homeland Security Act that transferred the ATF also transferred alcohol-related revenue generation and public protection regulatory responsibilities relating to alcohol to a new entity, the ALCOHOL AND TOBACCO TAX AND TRADE BUREAU.

Burger *see* ELBLING

Burgundac Crni *see* PINOT NOIR

Burgunder Term used in Germany to refer to members of the Pinot family of grapes like PINOT NOIR, which are referred to as Spätburgunder and Frühburgunder, or PINOT BLANC, which is called Weissburgunder.

Burgundy [BER-gun-dee] One of the world's most famous wine-growing areas, located in eastern France, southeast of Paris.

B

Bourgogne, as it's called in France, has about 110,000 vineyard acres, which is about 40 percent of what exists in BORDEAUX. Burgundy consists of five basic regions—CHABLIS in the north, the CÔTE D'OR, the CÔTE CHALONNAISE, the MACÔNNAIS, and BEAUJOLAIS, which is farthest south. The Côte d'Or is futher divided into two well-known sections—CÔTE DE BEAUNE in the south and CÔTE DE NUITS in the north. Burgundy and its wines have a long history going back at least to the time when the Romans ruled this region. In the fourteenth and fifteenth centuries, the Grand Duchy of Burgundy flourished, controlling an area that included what are now parts of Belgium, the Netherlands, Luxembourg, and a large portion of northern France. It was a rich and powerful empire, and the great Dukes of Burgundy savored the region's marvelous wines as part of their opulent lifestyle. The Burgundy region has established a reputation over the centuries not only for its fine wines but also for its marvelous food. The wines vary considerably from region to region throughout Burgundy, but the focus is on three grape varieties—PINOT NOIR and GAMAY for red wines and CHARDONNAY for whites. Though other varieties are grown—such as the white ALIGOTÉ, PINOT BLANC, SAUVIGNON BLANC, and Sacy and the red Cesar—they're being replaced in many areas by the three most prominent grapes. Gamay is the dominant red grape in Beaujolais, while Pinot Noir prevails in the other regions. The very best red wines come from the GRANDS CRUS in the Côte d'Or. Chardonnay is grown throughout the region and reaches its zenith in the Côte de Beaune. Although the wines made of Pinot Noir and Chardonnay get most of the attention, more wines are produced in Beaujolais (where they make Gamay-based wines) than in the rest of Burgundy. In some ways, the Burgundian system for identifying quality wines is much more straightforward than that of BORDEAUX. In addition to the APPELLATION D'ORIGINE CONTRÔLÉE (AC), Bordeaux uses a complex and inconsistent château classification system. Burgundy uses only the AC system to classify regions, villages, and individual vineyards into appellations, the theory being that the smaller and more precise the appellation, the higher the general quality of the wine. At the lowest quality level (usually), the AC system starts with general regional appellations that cover all of Burgundy, such as BOURGOGNE AC, BOURGOGNE ALIGOTÉ AC, BOURGOGNE GRAND ORDINAIRE AC, and BOURGOGNE PASSE-TOUT-GRAIN AC. Less general are the specific regional appellations like Chablis AC, Beaujolais AC, HAUTE-CÔTES DE BEAUNE AC, and HAUTE-CÔTES DE NUITS AC. Next up on the quality scale are the village appellations, which allow single villages to use their name on the label (for example, GEVREY-CHAMBERTIN, GIVRY, MEURSAULT, POMMARD, and VOLNAY). In the Beaujolais

B

region, there are ten villages (called CRUS) with the right to specific village appellations: BROUILLY, FLEURIE, MORGON, and MOULIN-À-VENT, to
name a few. Some vineyards are now adding the vineyard name after
the village name to further differentiate themselves. Ranking next to
the top of this appellation progression are the PREMIER CRU (first-
growth) vineyards, which are individual vineyard sites that have historically produced superior wine. (Note that premier cru is the very
top rating for châteaux in Bordeaux.) Burgundy premier cru wines use
the village name, the vineyard name, and the term *"Premier Cru"* on
the label. The only exception is when the wine is a blend of several
premier cru vineyards, in which case the village name and the term
"Premier Cru" appear. At the very top of the quality hierarchy are the
GRANDS CRUS (great growths), which are the few very select sites that
traditionally produce exceptional wines. Grand cru wines need only
the vineyard name and the term *"Grand Cru"* on the label. Burgundy's
seemingly straightforward ranking of appellations deteriorates, however, because the ownership structure in Burgundy, triggered by
events that began with the French Revolution in the late eighteenth
century, results in myriad small owners. The oft-used example is Clos
de Vougeot, a 125-acre grand cru vineyard that now has around eighty
different owners, each with a small parcel. The quality of wines made
from this vineyard by the multitude of producers varies widely, yet all
have the right to call their wine Clos de Vougeot, Grand Cru. It's
thought that many of the best producers do a better job with their premier cru vineyards than some of the poorer producers with their
grand cru vineyards. The same holds true with the best producers and
their village-appellation vineyards versus the lesser producers with
premier cru vineyards. So, although the appellation system is fairly
straightforward, true Burgundy lovers study the individual producers
to determine which wines they like best.

Burgundy basket *see* DECANTING

Burgweg *see* NAHE

burning *see* HOT in the Glossary of Wine Tasting Terms, page 655

burnt matches *see* SULFUR in the Glossary of Wine Tasting Terms,
page 655

La Bussière *see* MOREY-SAINT-DENIS

butt A very large CASK used for wine or other SPIRITS. A butt normally
holds 132 gallons and is commonly used to ship SHERRY.

Buttafuoco *see* OLTREPÒ PAVESE DOC

buttery *see* Glossary of Wine Tasting Terms, page 655

butyric acid [byoo-TIHR-ihk] *see* ACIDS; Glossary of Wine Tasting Terms, page 655

buying wine *see* Tips on Buying Wine, page 607

Buzet AC [boo-ZAY] APPELLATION in SOUTHWEST FRANCE that is right next to ARMAGNAC, not far from BORDEAUX. Formerly called **Côtes de Buzet**, it achieved AC status in 1973. Its main grapes are those of Bordeaux—CABERNET SAUVIGNON, CABERNET FRANC, MERLOT, and MALBEC for red and ROSÉ wines; SÉMILLON, SAUVIGNON BLANC, and MUSCADELLE for whites. The red wines, which dominate the area's production, are similar to good Bordeaux wines but are more moderately priced. The series of good vintages in the 1980s have helped this little-known appellation gain attention. Most of the wines come from a large cooperative, **Les Vignerons de Buzet**, at Buzet-sur-Baise. It produces good wines under the Cuvee Napoleon label.

C **Cabardès AC** [kah-bahr-DAY] French AC upgraded from VDQS status in 1998 and is beginning to gain attention. It's located in France's LANGUEDOC-ROUSSILLON region north of the city of Carcassonne and just west of the MINERVOIS AC. RED and ROSÈ wines are made from a combination of BORDEAUX and RHÔNE grape varieties including CABERNET SAUVIGNON, CABERNET FRANC, CINSAUT, Cot (MALBEC), FER, GRENACHE, and SYRAH.

Cabernet Blanc [KA-behr-nay BLAH*N* (BLAH*N*GK)] One of the names used for a BLUSH WINE (white wine made from red grapes) produced from CABERNET SAUVIGNON grapes. Such wines are also known as *Blanc de Cabernet Sauvignon* and *Cabernet Blush*. *See also* SAIGNÉE.

Cabernet Blush *see* CABERNET BLANC

Cabernet d'Anjou AC [KA-behr-nay dah*n*-ZHOO] An APPELLATION for ROSÉ wine located in the ANJOU region in the central part of France's LOIRE Valley. These almost DRY, raspberry-flavored wines are based on CABERNET FRANC grapes (with some CABERNET SAUVIGNON) and regarded with more respect than the sweet ROSÉ D'ANJOU AC wines that are also produced in this region.

Cabernet di Pramaggiore *see* LISON-PRAMAGGIORE

Cabernet Dorio *see* DORNFELDER

Cabernet Dorsa *see* DORNFELDER

Cabernet Franc [KA-behr-nay FRAH*N* (FRAH*N*GK)] A red wine grape that's similar in structure and flavor to CABERNET SAUVIGNON, but not quite as full-bodied (*see* BODY), and lower in TANNINS and ACIDS. It is, however, more AROMATIC and HERBACEOUS. Unlike Cabernet Sauvignon, Cabernet Franc grows in cooler climates and ripens early. Therefore, this grape can be particularly important when weather conditions produce a less-than-perfect Cabernet Sauvignon crop. Under such circumstances, the French have found that the addition of Cabernet Franc might salvage the VINTAGE. In BORDEAUX, Cabernet Franc is most often blended with MERLOT and Cabernet Sauvignon, though it's usually not the dominant grape in these blends. The most noteworthy examples of French wines made primarily from Cabernet Franc grapes are those from Château Cheval Blanc, whose vineyards are planted with about 66 percent Cabernet Franc and 33 percent Merlot. In California, Cabernet Franc has not been widely planted, primarily because the climate produces consistently higher-quality Cabernet Sauvignon grapes than in France. Only fairly recently has

Cabernet Franc's popularity grown as an enhancement for Cabernet Sauvignon-based wines. In 1997, researchers at UNIVERSITY OF CALIFORNIA, DAVIS determined that Cabernet Franc and SAUVIGNON BLANC were the likely parents of the renowned Cabernet Sauvignon grape. Cabernet Franc is also called *Bordo, Bouchet, Bouchy, Brenton, Carmenet,* and *Trouchet Noir.*

Cabernet Sauvignon [ka-behr-NAY soh-vihn-YOHN (soh-vee-NYAW*N*)] If not the king of the top-quality red-wine grapes, as many argue, Cabernet Sauvignon is certainly the most successful and popular. It's the primary grape of most of the top vineyards in France's MÉDOC and GRAVES districts. It's also the source for most of California's superb red wines and, with about 70,000 acres as of the year 2000, the state's most widely planted red variety. Cabernet Sauvignon's reputation for excellence has made it popular around the world. There's been heavy planting (which continues) in CHILE, AUSTRALIA, and eastern Europe, especially Bulgaria. Cabernet Sauvignon has also begun making inroads into SPAIN and ITALY in areas where local grapes have dominated for centuries. In 1997 researchers at UNIVERSITY OF CALIFORNIA, DAVIS determined that Cabernet Sauvignon is an offspring of SAUVIGNON BLANC and CABERNET FRANC. Since Cabernet Sauvignon appeared in the late seventeenth century prior to plant hybridization practices, UC Davis scientists believe that its origin was a natural occurrence rather than a planned CROSS of the two parents. This serendipitous union turned out to be viticulturally historical. The flavor, STRUCTURE, COMPLEXITY, and longevity of wines made from Cabernet Sauvignon are what make this grape so popular. Its fruity flavors have been described as CHERRY, black cherry, BLACKCURRANT (or *cassis*), and raspberry. In addition, other flavor descriptions include MINTY, CEDAR, CHOCOLATE, and bell pepper; the word TOBACCO is often used to describe older vintages. The ACIDITY and TANNINS found in Cabernet Sauvignon wines help form the basis for its structure and longevity. In Bordeaux, Cabernet Sauvignon is most often blended with one or more of the following: MERLOT, CABERNET FRANC, PETIT VERDOT, or MALBEC. In California, wines are more often made with 100 percent Cabernet Sauvignon grapes, although the trend is now toward some blending, as in Bordeaux. In Australia, there is a predilection to blend Cabernet Sauvignon with SHIRAZ, which is widely grown there. Although the Cabernet Sauvignon grape has been grown in Italy for over 150 years, it has only recently become more popular there. Italian winemakers are now blending small amounts of Cabernet Sauvignon with SANGIOVESE, the country's top red wine grape. They also make a few top-quality wines with a majority of Cabernet Sauvignon. In Spain, there are blends of Cabernet Sauvignon and the local favorite, TEMPRANILLO. Throughout the world you'll find a multitude of well-made Cabernet Sauvignon-based wines. Among the most notable are those from France's Château Lafite-Rothschild, Château Latour, Château Mouton-Rothschild, and Château Margaux and California's Beaulieu Vineyards, Caymus Vineyards, Heitz Wine Cellars, and Robert Mondavi Winery. Although known as Cabernet Sauvignon throughout most of the world, in parts of France this grape is also called *Bouche, Bouchet, Petit-Cabernet, Sauvignon Rouge,* and *Vidure. See also* RUBY CABERNET.

Cabinet *see* KABINETT

Caccione Nero *see* CANAIOLO

Cadarca *see* KADARKA

Cadillac AC [kah-dee-YAHK] A small APPELLATION located in the area around the picturesque little town of Cadillac in the southern end of the PREMIERES CÔTES DE BORDEAUX in France's BORDEAUX region. It sits on the Garonne River across from CÉRONS and BARSAC. The appellation is only for white wines made from SÉMILLON, SAUVIGNON BLANC, and MUSCADELLE, which must be semisweet or sweet (minimum of 1.8 percent RESIDUAL SUGAR). Although some of the grapes in the Cadillac AC are infected by BOTRYTIS CINEREA, the resulting wines aren't generally as intense or luscious (nor are the prices as high) as those from SAUTERNES, which is just across the river.

cage, champagne *see* MUSELET

Cahors AC [kah-OR] Located in SOUTHWEST FRANCE, this APPELLATION produces red wines, mainly from MALBEC (locally called Auxerrois) BLENDED with small amounts of MERLOT and Tannat. Cahors has a reputation for its "black wines," which are made with grapes from the high limestone plateau vineyards and are so named because they're very dark, TANNIC, and LONG-LIVED. Newer vineyards on the lower slopes produce much lighter-style red wines.

Les Caillerets *see* CHASSAGNE-MONTRACHET AC; VOLNAY

Les Cailles *see* NUITS-SAINT-GEORGES

Cairanne [keh-RAHN] A small village in the southern portion of France's RHÔNE region. It's entitled to use the CÔTES DU RHÔNE-VILLAGES AC, and wine labels usually also include the village name. These wines generally exhibit dark color, spicy fruit, and enough TANNINS to age well. The main grapes used are GRENACHE, SYRAH, CINSAUT, and MOURVÈDRE.

Calabrese *see* NERO D'AVOLA

Calabria [kah-LAH-bree-uh] A wine region positioned in the "toe" of Italy's boot-shaped land mass. This beautiful, mountainous region is still quite antiquated in terms of winemaking technology and generally produces mediocre wine. Calabria has twelve DOCs, the best known being CIRÒ, Greco di Bianco, and Melissa. Others are Bivongi, Donnici, Lamezia, Pollino, San Vito di Luzzi, Sant'Anna di Isola Capo Rizzuto, Savuto, Scavigna, and Verbicaro. There are about 60,000 vineyard acres. The primary grapes here are GAGLIOPPO and Marsigliana for red and ROSÉ wines and GRECO for white wines.

Calatayud DO [kah-lah-tay-YOOD] The largest DO in Spain's Aragón region with about 19,000 acres of vineyards. It's located in the north central part of the country northeast of Madrid around the city of Calatayud. The area is hot with low annual rainfall. Garnacha (GRENACHE), the principal red grape VARIETY, comprises nearly two thirds of the vineyards. Other reds include TEMPRANILLO, Monastrell (MOURVÈDRE), and Mazuelo (CARIGNAN). MALVASIA is the main white variety along with Garnacha Blanca (GRENACHE) and Moscatel (MUSCAT). Calatayud is best known for its ROSADO (ROSÉ) WINES but some smaller producers are starting to make decent full-bodied reds. Although CABERNET SAUVIGNON, SYRAH, and MERLOT grapes are planted, they're not currently allowed in DO-labeled wines. Most wines are produced by the area COOPERATIVES.

calcium alginate beads *see* RIDDLING

Caldaro *see* LAGO DI CALDARO

California The California wine industry is said to have started during the period from 1769 to 1823 when the Franciscan monks began planting vineyards as they worked their way from southern to northern California establishing their missions. Unfortunately, the grape they planted was the MISSION, which produces wines of poor to medium quality. It wasn't until about 1830 that Jean-Louis Vignes began to import higher-quality VITIS VINIFERA grapevines. In the 1850s and 1860s, AGOSTON HARASZTHY expanded the effort by trying to determine which grape varieties would work best in various locations in the state. To this end, he imported thousands of CUTTINGS of about 300 different grape varieties. In addition to planting these vines in SONOMA COUNTY, he sold cuttings in various parts of the state, primarily in the

San Francisco Bay and Los Angeles areas. The California wine-producing industry went through numerous ups and downs over the next
80 years, but the PHYLLOXERA infestation in the 1890s and PROHIBITION
from 1920 to 1933 severely curtailed wine business growth. The industry continued to grow sporadically from 1933 on, but most of the production was fairly ordinary wine from the giant CENTRAL VALLEY. At the
time, most wines were made from grapes like THOMPSON SEEDLESS,
Emperor, and Flame Tokay, which could also be used for table grapes
or raisins. This trend began to change in the 1960s when Joe Heitz
started Heitz Wine Cellars in 1964, Dick Graff established Chalone
Vineyard in 1965, and Robert Mondavi left the family (Charles Krug)
winery and established his own in 1966. At that time, the boom for
quality wine took off, with dramatic increases in acreage allotted to
grapes like CABERNET SAUVIGNON and CHARDONNAY. In the year 2000, the
California Department of Food and Agriculture estimated that there
were about 568,000 acres of wine grapes planted. Chardonnay is the
most widely planted white wine grape, with over 103,000 acres, followed by French COLOMBARD, with less than half that amount. (This
compares with a 1959 total of about 80,000 acres for all of California's
wine grapes.) After Chardonnay and French Colombard, the white
grapes in order of total acreage are CHENIN BLANC, SAUVIGNON BLANC, RIES-
LING, GEWÜRZTRAMINER, PINOT BLANC, and MUSCAT. The most widely
planted red grape (with about 70,000 acres) is Cabernet Sauvignon;
ZINFANDEL has about 50,000 acres. These two varieties are followed in
order of total acreage by MERLOT, PINOT NOIR, RUBIRED, BARBERA,
GRENACHE, SYRAH, RUBY CABERNET, CARIGNANE, PETITE SIRAH, and CABERNET
FRANC. At this writing, California produces about 90 percent of the
wine made in the United States. Although it now competes favorably
in producing some of the world's finest wines, it also still produces
plenty of ordinary wine with over 70 percent of California wine production coming from the hot Central Valley. Much of this wine is still
undistinguished, although the quality is higher than in the past
because of modernized equipment and better crop selection. For fine
California wines, the climate of the cooler growing areas along the
coast is best. Because of this, the NAPA VALLEY has become one of the
premier wine-producing areas in the world. But it is not alone in the
production of fine wine, as evidenced by other areas of the NORTH
COAST in the counties of LAKE, SONOMA, MENDOCINO, SOLANO, and SONOMA.
As the California wine industry continues to grow, other quality VITI-
CULTURAL AREAS are being discovered, including numerous locations in
the CENTRAL COAST region and selected areas in the SIERRA FOOTHILLS. In
an effort to define growing areas around the state, California uses a

system known variously as degree days, heat summation method, Winkler Scale, and Regions I–V (*see* CLIMATE REGIONS OF CALIFORNIA). California has almost ninety AMERICAN VITICULTURAL AREAS (AVA); however, this system is still in its infancy, and there are myriad issues yet to be resolved. As California growers and winemakers understand more about the elements of what the French call TERROIR, petitions are being submitted for subsections of larger AVAs to further define the areas where wines are produced.

California Shenandoah Valley AVA [shen-uhn-DOH-uh] A 10,000-acre VITICULTURAL AREA located east of Sacramento, California, in portions of AMADOR and El Dorado Counties. It's part of the large SIERRA FOOTHILLS AVA in an area northwest of Fiddletown and northeast of Plymouth. ZINFANDEL and SAUVIGNON BLANC are the two most popular varieties here.

Caluso Passito DOC [kah-LOO-soh pah-SEE-toh] DOC area located in the northern part of Italy's PIEDMONT region north of Turin. The vineyards are located in thirty-five different villages in and around the town of Caluso. The rich, sweet DESSERT WINES are made from the ERBALUCE grape by the PASSITO process—grapes are dried on mats so that their sugars and flavors are concentrated before they're made into wine. The wines are then AGED for a minimum of 5 years (different VINTAGES may be combined). This area also produces **Caluso Passito Liquoroso**, a wine FORTIFIED with grape ALCOHOL to a minimum alcohol level of 17.5 percent. *See also* ERBALUCE DI CALUSO DOC.

Caluso Spumante *see* ERBALUCE DI CALUSO DOC

Camobraque *see* FOLLE BLANCHE

Campanha *see* BRAZIL

Campania [kahm-PAH-nyah] A wine-producing region that runs along the eastern coast of southern Italy and encompasses Naples and the surrounding area. Naples is the major city of Campania, Italy's second most populous region. There are just over 100,000 vineyard acres. Most Campania wines are mediocre at best, as somewhat evidenced by the less than 4 percent of the total wine production that qualifies for DOC status—amazingly this percentage has increased significantly in the last decade. There is one DOCG, TAURASI, and nineteen DOCs in the area—Aglianico del Taburno, Aversa, Campi Flegrei, CAPRI, Castel San Lorenzo, Cilento, Costa d'Amalfi, FALERNO DEL MASSICO, FIANO DI AVELLINO, Galluccio, GRECO DI TUFO, Guardia Sanframondi or Guardiolo, ISCHIA, Penisola Sorrentina, Sannio, Sant'Agata dei Goti, Solopaca,

Taburno, and VESUVIO. The standout among premium wine producers in this region is the family-run firm of Mastroberardino, which produces over half the DOC wine. The primary varieties here are AGLIANICO and Piedirosso for red and ROSÉ wines and Asprinio, Fiano, GRECO, and Falanghina for white wines.

Campden tablets *see* POTASSIUM METABISULFITE

Campo de Borja DO [KAHM-poh day BOR-hah] A small DO located in northern Spain's ARAGON region, west of the city of Zaragoza in the Ebro Valley. Like much of this region, Campo de Borja is known for its heavy, high-ALCOHOL (from 13 to 18 percent) red wine, much of which is sold off in BULK as a BLENDING WINE. In addition to the large volumes of red wine, about 20 percent of the production is ROSÉ; there's also a small amount of white wine. The main grape for red wine is Garnacha (GRENACHE) although smaller amounts of TEMPRANILLO and CABERNET SAUVIGNON are sometimes added. The white wines are made from MACABEO (which is also used in small amounts in the red wines) and Moscatel (MUSCAT). Producers in Campo de Borja are experimenting with different grapes, lower-alcohol wines, and shorter AGING periods in an attempt to produce the lighter, fruitier wines that are more popular today.

El Campo de Tarragona *see* TARRAGONA DO

Campos de Cima da Serra *see* BRAZIL

Canada Canada is not a large wine producer and, in fact, consumes almost seven times what it produces. The cold climate severely limits the areas in which grapes can be grown successfully. However, Canada is making a serious effort to produce excellent wines. The province of ONTARIO is the leader in this effort, followed by BRITISH COLUMBIA and, to a much smaller degree, Nova Scotia and Quebec. Bodies of water play a critical role in successful Canadian wine production, especially in the emerging quality-wine areas of southern Ontario and the Okanagan Valley in British Columbia. The climate of both areas is tempered by the surrounding lakes (*see* LAKE EFFECT). Southern Ontario produces about 80 percent of Canada's wines and has three quality growing areas—Pelee Island, Lake Erie North Shore, and the Niagara Peninsula (*see* ONTARIO, for more detail). **Quebec**, with over thirty wineries, produces hardy HYBRIDS that can withstand the cold weather and the short growing season. **Nova Scotia** also has a small evolving wine industry. Ontario was the first to implement the VINTNERS QUALITY ALLIANCE (VQA), an APPELLATION-regulating system.

British Columbia has since adopted the VQA, Quebec and Nova Scotia are about to accept it, and there is a move to implement it on a national scale. VQA is important because it distinguishes quality wines made with Canadian grapes from wines labeled simply "Product of Canada," which can comprise up to 75 percent imported grapes or wine. For many decades grapes grown in Canada were mainly HYBRIDS (like BACO NOIR, DE CHAUNAC, MARÉCHAL FOCH, SEYVAL BLANC, and VIDAL BLANC) or North American varieties (like CATAWBA, CONCORD, Elvira, and NIAGARA). Until the late 1980s, Canada grew limited amounts of VITIS VINIFERA grapes—since then, increased plantings have produced a significant amount of these varieties. The quality growing areas now cultivate increasing amounts of CABERNET FRANC, CABERNET SAUVIGNON, CHARDONNAY, GAMAY NOIR, GEWÜRZTRAMINER, MERLOT, PINOT GRIS, PINOT NOIR, RIESLING, and SAUVIGNON BLANC. Needless to say, cool weather varieties do best in Canada's climate. One advantage that Canada's cold weather provides is the ability to produce consistently superior icewine (*see* EISWEIN).

Canaiolo [kah-nah-YAW-loh; kah-nay-YOH-loh] A red wine grape grown in the Italian regions of TUSCANY, UMBRIA, LATIUM, MARCHE, and EMILIA-ROMAGNA. *Canaiolo Nero*, as it's officially known, produces slightly bitter, rather bland wine that becomes part of the traditional BLEND for CHIANTI wine. Chianti's DOCG rules for allowable grapes were changed in 1984, and Canaiolo's role was reduced from the 10–30 percent range to less than 10 percent. Naturally, this stimulated an acreage reduction in some areas. This variety, sometimes called *Cagnina*, is occasionally made into a red DESSERT WINE by that same name. Canaiolo has many synonyms including *Caccione Nero, Tindilloro, Uva Canina,* and *Uva Merla.*

Canard-Duchêne *see* CHAMPAGNE

Canary Islands Spanish islands located in the Atlantic about 65 miles off the southwestern coast of Morocco and approximately 685 miles southwest of Spain. The winemaking history of the Canary Islands dates back hundreds of years and the dessert wines were particularly famous in the seventeenth and eighteenth centuries. In recent years, the Canary Islands have become a flourishing wine region. Five of the islands in this subtropical archipelago now have DOS: El Hierro **(Hierro DO)**, Gran Canaria **(Elmonte DO)**, La Palma **(La Palma DO)**, Lanzarote **(Lanzarote DO)**, and Tenerife, which has five DOs **(Abona, Tacoronte-Acentejo, Valle de Güímar, Valle de La Orotava,** and **Ycoden-Daute-Isora)**. The first DO in these islands was

Tacoronte-Acentejo, which is also the largest with over 4,000 vineyard acres. It's also the most progressive in adopting modern winemaking methods. This DO is primarily red-wine country, with Listán Negro and Negramoll (NEGRA MOLE) the dominant red VARIETIES. Wines from these two varieties, along with traditional La Palma dessert wines made from MALVASÍA, are attracting the most attention.

Canberra District Australian wine region located in the Southern New South Wales Zone of NEW SOUTH WALES and situated around Canberra, the nation's capital. However, most wineries are located outside the Australian Capital Territory (an area around Canberra set aside in the early 1900s for the new national capital), mainly to the north near Murrumbateman. The exception is Kamberra, a large BRL Hardy winery located near the Canberra racecourse. For the most part, this region is hot and dry, but the autumns are cool and sometimes rain-laden. The Canberra District comprises approximately 1,200 acres planted primarily with CHARDONNAY, RIESLING, SAUVIGNON BLANC, SHIRAZ, CABERNET SAUVIGNON, PINOT NOIR, and MERLOT.

cane Viticulture term referring to a one-year-old woody shoot with numerous NODES growing out of the vine trunk. Canes are thin, smooth and light tan and contrast to the darker color and rough texture of the permanent wood. Canes are never over one year old because each year the primary canes are pruned back and only the strongest shoots are left unpruned to become next year's primary canes. Cane-trained vines contrast to another vine training approach using SPURS. *See also* VITICULTURE.

Cannonao; Cannonau *see* GRENACHE

Canon-Fronsac AC [kah-NAWN fwawn-SAK] Small APPELLATION for red wines that is found at the southern end of the FRONSAC district in France's BORDEAUX region, not far from SAINT-ÉMILION. In the eighteenth and nineteenth centuries, the wines from this area were better known than the now-more-famous POMEROL. MERLOT is the dominant grape, followed by CABERNET FRANC, CABERNET SAUVIGNON, and small amounts of MALBEC. The Canon-Fronsac hillside vineyards generally produce better wines than the neighboring Fronsac appellation, as indicated by the required ½ percent higher minimum ALCOHOL content. Wines from both appellations are reputed to be BIG and full-flavored, though somewhat HARD and TANNIC; they require extensive AGING. A new SOFTER style and the improved quality of recent vintages have created renewed interest in this area.

canopy A grapevine's "curtain" of leaves and shoots that surround the grape clusters.

canopy management A complex series of techniques including vine spacing, trellising (*see* TRELLIS SYSTEM), SHOOT positioning, and leaf removal to improve both light and air circulation in an effort to create the optimal grape-growing environment for maximum flavor, color, and ripeness of the grapes. Such techniques are specific to the vineyard site, contingent on such things as soil, grape VARIETY, and MICROCLIMATE. Proper CANOPY management can affect the color, flavor, and/or structure of grapes. It can also help prevent disease. For instance, removing leaves and shoots improves aeration, thereby reducing susceptibility to rot and mildew on grape clusters. There's an art to removing excess foliage, however. Enough leaves must be left on the vine to provide the required energy for grape maturation; excessive leaf removal can bleach the fruit's color, cause sunburn, or impede ripening. On the other hand, vineyards in warmer areas require less leaf removal than those in cooler climes. In the end, the perfect balance between vegetative growth and grape production will mean the difference between an ordinary wine and one of distinction. *See also* VITICULTURE.

Canterbury New Zealand winegrowing region located on the east coast of the South Island near Christchurch, the island's largest city. There are vineyards southwest of Christchurch on the Canterbury Plain and southeast on Banks Peninsula; north of the city is **Waipara**. Although considered part of the Canterbury region, Waipara has different soils and climate, which make it a candidate for its own region in the future. History records that French colonists were making wine here as early as the 1840s. There were other sporadic efforts at winemaking over time, but it wasn't until the 1970s that interest was revived. Growth began in earnest in the mid-1980s. Today, with about 1,200 acres, Canterbury is New Zealand's fourth largest growing area—barely ahead of AUCKLAND, but significantly behind GISBORNE. This is New Zealand's coolest commercial growing area (although parts of CENTRAL OTAGO would also contend for this distinction), and good wines require early-ripening grape varieties. The Waipara area is slightly warmer and drier than most of the Canterbury region because it's sheltered from the coast by the Teviotdale Hills. The most popular varieties are CHARDONNAY, PINOT NOIR, RIESLING, and SAUVIGNON BLANC (Waipara's most popular). Other varieties include CABERNET SAUVIGNON (which requires a great year to ripen properly), GEWÜRZTRAMINER, MÜLLER-THURGAU, PINOT GRIS, and SÉMILLON.

Cantenac *see* MARGAUX AC

cantina [kan-TEE-nuh] Italian for "cellar" or "winery."

cantina cooperativa *see* CANTINA SOCIALE

cantina sociale [kan-TEE-nuh soh-CHAH-lay] Italian for a "cooperative cellar" or "cooperative winery." Sometimes abbreviated as CS, cantina sociale is also called *cantina cooperativa*.

cap In winemaking, the mass of grape solids (skins, stems, seeds, pulp, etc.) that floats on the surface of the juice during the FERMENTATION of red wine. The cap needs to be broken up and pushed down into the wine frequently to help extract color, flavor, and TANNINS, as well as to ensure that the cap doesn't dry out and develop unwanted bacteria. In some wineries, workers employ the old method of using a long paddle to punch down the cap into the wine several times a day during active fermentation. Newer techniques include pumping the juice over the cap, thereby breaking it up and forcing it down into the juice. There are also specially designed tanks with screens fixed part way up in the tank. These screens stop the cap from rising to the top, thereby keeping it suspended in the juice. Other specially designed tanks rotate periodically, blending the cap and juice together.

Cape Agulhas WO [ah-GUHL-uhs] Demarcated SOUTH AFRICA wine district located south and east of Cape Town along the African continent's southernmost tip. The cape, whose name means "cape of needles," is the southernmost point of Africa and separates the Atlantic and Indian Oceans. This wine area is very cool due to the maritime climate and is developing a solid reputation for the SAUVIGNON BLANC wines, especially those from the ward of Elim.

Cape blend Term used in South Africa for wines made with PINOTAGE blended with other grapes, usually BORDEAUX varieties such as CABERNET SAUVIGNON and MERLOT. Although there's no consensus, most producers feel that a minimum of 30 percent Pinotage is necessary.

Cape Riesling *see* CROUCHEN

Capri DOC [KAH-pree] DOC situated on the island of Capri south of Naples in the Gulf of Naples. It produces red wines mainly from Piedirosso grapes and white wines from Falanghina, GRECO, and Biancolella; these wines are considered fairly ordinary.

capsule [KAP-suhl; KAP-sool] The wrapping that covers the cork and neck of a wine bottle. Historically, the favored material for capsules has been lead, but concerns over lead's safety are the basis for its replacement. Current capsule alternatives are plastic, tin, aluminum, and laminates. Frequently a capsule is referred to as a *foil* because of its association with a metal covering. Robert Mondavi Winery has eliminated the traditional capsule and now uses a natural-paper and beeswax cap that's attached directly to the cork—a few other wineries are using this as well.

En Caradeux *see* PERNAND-VERGELESSES

carafe [kuh-RAF] A simple clear glass (occasionally metal) container with a wide mouth used for serving wine or other beverages. Restaurants often use carafes to serve inexpensive wines. Carafes can also be used to DECANT older wines that have thrown SEDIMENT; however, finer wines are customarily transferred to a more elaborate container, such as a DECANTER.

carafe wine [kuh-RAF] Another name for HOUSE WINE. Generally a young, inexpensive wine served in restaurants, usually in a CARAFE. In France, this is referred to as a *vin de carafe*.

Caramany *see* CÔTES DU ROUSSILLON AC

caramel *see* Glossary of Wine Tasting Terms, page 655

carbonation [kar-buh-NAY-shuhn] A method of making SPARKLING WINE (and other beverages) by injecting it with carbon dioxide. This technique is the least-effective way to create effervescence and is used only for inexpensive wines. Such wines must be labeled "carbonated" in the United States, *gazéifié* in France. They're characterized by large, crude bubbles that quickly lose their effervescence, whereas MÉTHODE CHAMPENOISE sparklers have smaller, more refined and longer-lived bubbles.

carbon dioxide A colorless, odorless, incombustible gas. Carbon dioxide (CO_2) is one of the two by-products of FERMENTATION, the other being ALCOHOL. Yeast acts on the natural grape sugar and converts 40 to 45 percent of it to carbon dioxide, which in most cases escapes into the air. In the production of SPARKLING WINES, however, carbon dioxide is purposely trapped in the wine to create effervescence.

carbonic maceration [kar-BAHN-ihk mas-uh-RAY-shuhn] Also called *macération carbonique*, this technique is used during primary FERMENTATION to produce light red wines with low tannins, intense color, and fresh, fruity flavors and aromas. Such wines—like French BEAUJOLAIS—should be consumed early. The carbonic maceration process begins by dumping whole bunches of freshly picked, uncrushed grapes into large vats filled with carbon dioxide and, if native yeasts are undesirable, a good wine yeast. In this process, the bottom grapes are crushed by the weight of the grapes above them, and fermentation begins with the exuded juice. This beginning fermentation develops more carbon dioxide gas, which envelops the upper layers of uncrushed grapes and blocks air exposure that normally would occur. Soon, fermentation begins within the whole grapes, and they begin to ooze more juice. Finally, the whole batch is pressed, and fermentation is finished in a standard way.

carboy [KAHR-boy] A large narrow-necked bottle of glass, plastic, or earthenware often used with a FERMENTATION LOCK as a SECONDARY FERMENTATION vessel.

Carcavelos DOC [kar-kuh-VEH-lyoosh] A small Portuguese DENOMINAÇÃO DE ORIGEM CONTROLADA (DOC) located just west of Lisbon near the seaside resort of Estoril. Carcavelos is known for its sweet, white FORTIFIED WINES made from local grape varieties of Boais, Cerceal do Douro (SERCIAL), Galego Dourado, and Rabo de Ovelha. They also make an almost-DRY style that's more appropriate as an APÉRITIF.

cardboard see Glossary of Wine Tasting Terms, page 655

Carema DOC [kah-REE-mah] DOC zone located in the far northern portion of Italy's PIEDMONT region in a mountainous area next to the VALLE D'AOSTA DOC. This is a red-wine area, and the primary variety used is NEBBIOLO, which must make up a minimum of 85 percent of the wine's varietal blend. The cool mountain climate doesn't ripen the grapes as effectively as some of the warmer Nebbiolo regions so the wines are not as powerful as those from BAROLO DOCG or BARBARESCO DOCG, but rather more DELICATE and AROMATIC.

Carignan; Carignane [kah-ree-NYAHN] Although this red grape (also called *Carignano, Cariñena, Mazuelo, Monestel, Roussillonen,* and *Samsó)* originated in northern SPAIN'S CARIÑENA district, it's become the most widely grown red grape in FRANCE, especially throughout the LANGUEDOC-ROUSSILLON region. It's also extensively grown in other countries ringing the Mediterranean including Italy, Spain, Algeria, and Israel. It was also once the most widely planted red grape in California (where it's spelled *Carignane)*, mostly in the San Joaquin Valley. With its high yields, Carignan produces more red wine than any other grape variety—most of it very ordinary. The wines are noted for their deep purple color, high TANNINS, and high ALCOHOL. It generally produces wines that are FRUITY and SPICY although wines from OLD WINE Carignan with lower yields, such as some from PRIORAT or SARDINIA, can also be rich and of very high quality. Carignan is most often blended with wines from softer grapes, primarily GRENACHE and CINSAUT. In France most of these wines end up as VIN DE TABLE or VIN ORDINAIRE—"ordinary TABLE WINES." In many areas, Carignan vineyards are being torn out and replanted with higher-quality vines, but it's still extensively grown in a number of regions.

Carignan Rosos *see* GRENACHE

Cariñena; Cariñena DO [kah-ree-NYEH-nah] 1. A popular red grape (*see* CARIGNAN). 2. A DO encompassing the town of Cariñena in northern Spain's Aragón region. It's the region's largest DO with about 45,000 vineyard acres. It is also the oldest, having been established as a demarcated zone in 1932. The Cariñena DO produces large quantities of red and ROSÉ wine made primarily from Garnacha Tinta (GRENACHE), TEMPRANILLO, and Cariñena (CARIGNAN). The Cariñena grape, which is also called *Mazuelo,* is thought to have originated in this region but is now more widely planted in Spain's NAVARRA and RIOJA DOs and in southern France. As part of a campaign to increase the quality of their wines, Cariñena growers are being encouraged to plant more Tempranillo, Monastrell (MOURVÈDRE), and even CABERNET SAUVIGNON, an approved variety. White wines here are made from Viura (MACABEO), Garnacha Blanc (GRENACHE), PARELLADA, and Moscatel Romano (MUSCAT). Because of this region's dry, hot weather, the grapes ripen quickly, which results in high-ALCOHOL wines. Although the minimum alcohol content for this DO was lowered from 14 to 12 percent, the maximum is still 18 percent. Area COOPERATIVES, which dominate the production, include Covinca Cooperativa, San José Cooperativa, and San Valero Cooperativa.

Carmelin *see* PETIT VERDOT

Carmel Valley AVA VITICULTURAL AREA approved in 1983 that's located in Monterey County, California. It's southeast of the city of Monterey and the resort town of Carmel and west of the Salinas Valley. Though Carmel Valley encompasses over 19,000 acres, it has only a few wineries. Carmel Valley generally falls into a Region I classification (*see* CLIMATE REGIONS OF CALIFORNIA), although it's a bit warmer (and does better with red wines) than the north end of Salinas Valley.

Carmenère; Carmenere [car-men-EHR] Sometimes called BORDEAUX's sixth red-grape variety (along with CABERNET SAUVIGNON, CABER-

NET FRANC, MALBEC, MERLOT, and PETIT VERDOT). Although it had a significant presence in Bordeaux in the past, it was phased out in the twentieth century. However, it turns out that many "Merlot" vines growing in Chile are really Carmenère, and the Chileans are bottling varietal wines from this grape. Such wines are occasionally called **Grand Vidure**, although that's changing since Carmenère is gaining name recognition. When yields are reduced and grapes fully ripened, Carmenère can produce full-bodied, full-flavored, deeply colored wines that combine some of the best qualities of Cabernet Sauvignon and Merlot. Although Chile is currently the most noted for Carmenère wines, there's evidence that there may be significant vineyards of Carmenère in northern Italy that have previously been identified as Cabernet Franc.

Carmenet *see* CABERNET FRANC

Carmignano DOCG [kahr-mee-NYAH-noh] Small area that was recently upgraded to DOCG status. It's one of only a small number of DOCG areas in Italy and one of six (along with CHIANTI, CHIANTI CLASSICO, BRUNELLO DI MONTALCINO, VERNACCIA DI SAN GIMIGNANO, and VINO NOBILE DI MONTEPULCIANO) in the TUSCANY region. It's located just west of Florence inside the northeast section of the CHIANTI Montalbano sub-zone. These red wines, which are similar to those from Chianti, use a variety of grapes—SANGIOVESE being predominate. Carmignano wines differ from Chiantis in that they must include between 10 and 20 percent CABERNET SAUVIGNON/CABERNET FRANC grapes, which have been justified for DOCG qualification because they've been grown here since the 1700s. ROSATO and VIN SANTO wines from Carmignano have DOC status. **Barco Reale di Carmignano**, a lighter version of the Carmignano DOCG red wines, received its DOC status in 1994.

Carnelian [kahr-NEEL-yuhn] A red-wine grape that is the result of a cross of GRENACHE with an earlier cross of CABERNET SAUVIGNON and CARIGNAN. This variety was developed in California during the early 1970s in an attempt to produce a grape that would do well in hot climates and still have Cabernet Sauvignon characteristics. The result was not widely successful, and there are only modest plantings of this grape. To the disappointment of all, the generally LIGHT, rather bland Carnelian wines did not acquire the desired Cabernet Sauvignon traits.

Carneros AVA; Los Carneros AVA [kahr-NEH-rohs] Also known as *Los Carneros,* this AVA lies at the northern end of San Pablo Bay (the northern section of San Francisco Bay) and includes vineyards in both SONOMA and NAPA COUNTIES. Because of the Bay's cooling effects, and the fog that the hotter inland areas draw over the land, Carneros has become an increasingly popular growing area. Its climate is ranked a Region I (*see* CLIMATE REGIONS OF CALIFORNIA), although some areas protected from the cooling breezes can be warmer than Region II. There are approximately 8,000 acres planted. The dominant grapes in Carneros are PINOT NOIR and CHARDONNAY, 20 percent of which are made into SPARKLING WINE. Small amounts of CABERNET SAUVIGNON and MERLOT are grown here as well. Carneros has attracted foreign investment in the form of three sparkling wine facilities: Artesa (formerly Codorníu Napa) from the Spanish giant Codorníu; Domaine Carneros from the French CHAMPAGNE house Taittinger; and Gloria Ferrer from Freixenet, another Spanish firm. All three wine facilities also make STILL WINES. The Carneros area supplies grapes to many wineries not located in the AVA itself. Carneros is Spanish for "sheep," referring here to the numerous sheep ranches that once populated the area.

Les Carrières *see* CORTON

Cartaxo *see* RIBATEJO DOC

Casablanca Valley *see* ACONCAGUA

casa vinicola [KAH-suh vee-nee-KOH-luh] The Italian term for a wine house or a firm that makes wine primarily from purchased grapes.

cascina [kah-SHEE-nuh] The northern Italian term for a farm or estate that makes wine.

casein [KAY-seen; KAY-see-ihn] A form of milk protein used for FINING wines. Casein is often obtained in the form of powdered skim milk.

cask [KASK] 1. A large, strong, barrel-shaped, leak-proof container generally used for storing wines and other SPIRITS. Most wine casks are made of oak. 2. The quantity such a container holds.

cask aging *see* AGING

cask number; cask # A cask number is often used to denote a very special wine, such as Stag's Leap Wine Cellars "Cask 23," which is a RESERVE-style CABERNET SAUVIGNON. In the true sense, a cask number is supposed to indicate that a wine spent its entire aging period in one cask and that the wine was produced in limited quantities. However, there's no legal requirement as to how this term is used, and it's too often employed simply as a marketing ploy.

cask wine *see* BAG-IN-A-BOX WINE

cassis *see* Glossary of Wine Tasting Terms, page 655

Cassis AC [kah-SEES] APPELLATION that surrounds the resort town of Cassis located on the Mediterranean just southeast of Marseille in France's PROVENCE region. Although this appellation also covers red and ROSÉ wines made from GRENACHE, CINSAUT, and MOURVÈDRE, white wines predominate and make up a majority of the production. The best examples of these white wines, which are made from Ugni Blanc (TREBBIANO), CLAIRETTE, MARSANNE, and a small amount of SAUVIGNON BLANC, are FRESH, LIGHT, DRY, and FRAGRANT. Wines from the Cassis AC should not be confused with crème de cassis liqueur, which is made from a European blackcurrant called *cassis*.

Castelão, Castelão Frances *see* PERIQUITA

Castel del Monte DOC [kas-TEHL del MON-tay] A well-known DOC located in Italy's APULIA region. It's located in the hilly region west of Bari not far from the Adriatic. It covers ROSSO, BIANCO, and ROSATO wines; the reds and rosés are highly regarded. UVA DI TROIA is the main grape for the red wines, which also include AGLIANICO, MONTEPULCIANO, Pinot Nero (PINOT NOIR), and SANGIOVESE. Bombino Nero is the dominant grape for the rosé wine, which can also include most of the aforementioned red grapes. The white wine, which is made mainly from Pampanuto, is considered rather bland.

Casteller DOC [kass-TEH-ler] DOC located in the Trentino province, which is part of the TRENTINO-ALTO ADIGE region in northeastern Italy. It covers a wide area and includes vineyards around twenty-seven different villages in the province. The rather ordinary, DRY, light red wine produced here is made from SCHIAVA, LAMBRUSCO, and MERLOT. It should be drunk young.

Castelli di Jesi *see* VERDICCHIO DEI CASTELLIDI DI JESI DOC

Castelli Romani; Castelli Romani DOC [kah-STEHL-ee roh-MAH-nee] A group of hills southeast of Rome in the LATIUM region. The Castelli Romani area contains a number of DOCs including COLLI ALBANI, COLLI LANUVINI, Cori, FRASCATI, MARINO, MONTECOMPATRI, Velletri, Zagarolo and the **Castelli Romani DOC**, which encompasses the entire area. These DOCs produce some 80 percent of Latium's DOC wines and help supply wine to the large populace of Rome. This area primarily produces white wines using mainly MALVASIA and TREBBIANO grapes.

castello [kahs-TEHL-loh] Italian for "castle." The word "*castello*" can be used only on labels of DOC/DOCG wines.

Castiglione di Falletto [kah-STEH-lyo-neh dee fah-LEH-toh] *see* BAROLO

Castile and León; Sp. Castilla y León [kah-STEEL and lay-YON] Spain's largest autonomous region, which comprises just under 20 percent of the country's land mass. It's located in the north central part of the country north of Madrid. Castile and León encompasses eight provinces—Burgos, León, Palencia, Salamanca, Sergovia, Soria, Valladolid, and Zamora. It contains five DO areas—BIERZO, CIGALES, RIBERA DEL DUERO, RUEDA, and TORO. This region's best known for the red wines from Ribera del Duero and the white wines from Rueda. Toro is a rising star here because of its shift from the traditional, dull, heavy red wines to powerful, fresh, fruity ones.

Castilla-La Mancha [kahs-TEE-yuh lah MAHN-chuh] A huge winegrowing region in the center of Spain. It includes the provinces of Albacete, Cuenca, Ciudad Real, Guadalajara, and Toledo plus the cities of Madrid and Toledo. The summer climate is so hot and forbidding that the YIELD is very low. Yet there are so many acres of vineyard planted that this region generates almost half of all the wine produced in Spain—most of it white. The main white grape is the AIRÉN, and this vast region helps Airén claim the title of the world's most widely planted grape variety. Cencibel (TEMPRANILLO) is the region's most widely planted red variety. Much of the wine produced is sold in BULK as a BLENDING WINE to other Spanish regions and even other European countries. Large quantities find their way to distilleries for further processing into ALCOHOL. DOS in Castilla-La Mancha include—ALMANSA, LA MANCHA (Europe's largest designated quality-wine-producing area), MÉNTRIDA, RIBERA DEL JÚCAR, VALDEPEÑAS, and VINOS DE MADRID.

Castillon *see* CÔTES DE CASTILLON AC

Catalonia; Sp. Cataluña [katl-OH-nee-uh; katl-OHN-yuh (Sp. kah-tah-LOO-nyuh)] An extensive and well-known region in the northeastern part of Spain. Its northern border is adjacent to France, and the Mediterranean is to the east. Catalonia is an autonomous bilingual region whose people speak both Spanish and the local Catalan. The region covers the four provinces of Barcelona, Gerona, Lérida, and Tarragona; its capital is the city of Barcelona. Catalonia has one DOCA, PRIORAT, and eight DO areas making STILL WINE—ALELLA, CONCA DE

BARBERÀ, COSTERS DEL SERGRE, EMPORDÀ-COSTA BRAVA, PENEDÈS, PLA DEL BAGES, TARRAGONA, and TERRA ALTA. The CAVA DO, which has multiple locations spread throughout northern Spain producing SPARKLING WINE via MÉTHODE CHAMPENOISE, is centered in Catalonia.

Catamaraca *see* ARGENTINA

Catarratto [kah-tahr-RAHT-toh] Although only grown in SICILY, this important white grape is Italy's most cultivated white VARIETY, second only to SANGIOVESE. There are several related varieties including **Catarratto Bianco Comune** and **Catarratto Bianco Lucido**. Although much of the grape production is distilled (*see* DISTILLATION), it's also approved for use in the BIANCO (white) wines of the Sicilian DOCS of ALCAMO, Contea di Sclafani, Contessa Entellina, ETNA, Menfi, Sambuca di Sicilia, Santa Margherita di Belice, and Sciacca.

Catawba [kuh-TAW-bah] This light red grape is native to North America and thought to be a natural HYBRID of other indigenous varieties. It's believed to have first been found along North Carolina's Catawba River, hence its name. It's popular on the East Coast of the United States, particularly in the FINGER LAKES region of New York State. Catawba grapes produce light-colored juice in various shades of pink, with flavor characteristics of the native VITIS LABRUSCA. They're used in ROSÉ and white STILL WINES, as well as in inexpensive SPARKLING WINES.

Catena *see* ARGENTINA

Catoctin AVA [kah-TAHK-tin] Established in 1987, this 170,000-acre VITICULTURAL AREA in western MARYLAND encompasses parts of Frederick and Washington Counties.

cat pee *see* Glossary of Wine Tasting Terms, page 655

Cava DO [KAH-vah] Cava is the official name for SPARKLING WINE produced in designated areas in various parts of northern Spain. The use of the word *cava* came about as a result of legal conflicts with France over the use of *champán*, Spain's word for *champagne*. The word *cava* (Catalan for "cellar") was chosen for Spain's sparkling wines because almost all such wines are made in the Catalan region. The Cava DO was established in 1986 and, unlike other Spanish DOS, it has multiple geographic areas. In fact, eight specified regions have been authorized for sparkling wine production. Three of the provinces—Barcelona, Girona, and Tarragona (in the CATALONIA region around Barcelona)—make over 95 percent of the country's cava. The other regions are Álava, Aragón, Extremadura, Navarra, and Rioja. To qual-

ify for Cava DO status, wines must be made by the MÉTHODE CHAMP-
ENOISE. Sparkling wines that aren't geographically qualified for Cava
DO status but that are made by méthode champenoise are called *vino
espumoso natural método tradicional.* The grapes used for most Cava
DO wines are MACABEO, PARELLADA, and XARELLO. However, CHARDONNAY
is allowed in the CUVÉE (some producers use it extensively), and the
companies using it as a major component include Codorníu, Raimat
(owned by Codorníu), and Segura Viudas (owned by Freixenet).
Additionally, some *rosado* (ROSÉ) cava is produced using Garnacha
(GRENACHE), Monastrell (MOURVÈDRE), and PINOT NOIR. Cava DO rules
require a minimum aging of 9 months. Top producers here are now
producing CRISP, FRUITY sparkling wines, which was not always the
case. Still, they differ from the French models because they're more
EARTHY and have less ACIDITY.

cave [CAHV] The French term meaning "cellar." Although often referring to an underground storage place, the word *cave* is also used to
identify a collection of wines wherever they are stored.

cave cooperative *see* COOPERATIVE

Cayuga Lake AVA *see* FINGER LAKES AVA

Cayuga White [kay-YOO-guh; ki-YOO-guh] A white-wine HYBRID
created by the New York State Agricultural Office at its Geneva experimental station by crossing SEYVAL BLANC (a European hybrid) with a
native American vine. It's grown mostly in New York's FINGER LAKES
region and is named after that region's Cayuga Lake.

cedar *see* Glossary of Wine Tasting Terms, page 655

cellar *see* WINE CELLAR

cellared by An imprecise term that appears on some wine labels,
usually meaning that the winery purchased the wine from somewhere
else and then bottled and AGED it prior to release. Because there's no
requirement for the length of aging, this term doesn't necessarily
mean the wine received special attention. *See also* BOTTLED BY; ESTATE
BOTTLED; GROWN, PRODUCED AND BOTTLED BY; MADE AND BOTTLED BY; PRO-
DUCED AND BOTTLED BY.

cellar rat Term used affectionately to describe someone who does
odd jobs (grunt work) around a winery. Cellar rats usually work on a
seasonal basis during the harvest.

Cencibel *see* TEMPRANILLO

centiliter *see* METRIC

Central Coast AVA Established in 1985, this huge VITICULTURAL AREA encompasses vineyards from Los Angeles to San Francisco. It originally covered areas in Alameda, Monterey, San Benito, San Luis Obispo, Santa Barbara, Santa Clara, and Santa Cruz Counties. In 1999 the Central Coast AVA was expanded to include the SAN FRANCISCO BAY AVA, adding areas in San Francisco, San Mateo, and Contra Costa Counties. There are numerous smaller AVAS within the large Central Coast area. Some winemakers use the smaller AVA names on their labels, although those who use grapes from more than one of these must use the Central Coast AVA.

Central Delaware Valley AVA A 96,000 acre VITICULTURAL AREA located along both sides of the Delaware River in southeast Pennsylvania and New Jersey. The southern end of the area starts around Titusville, New Jersey, just north of Trenton, and runs north to Musconetcong Mountain. Area wineries use HYBRIDS like CHAMBOURCIN, CHANCELLOR, LEON MILLOT, SEYVAL BLANC, and VIDAL BLANC; AND VITIS VINIFERA grapes like CHARDONNAY, RIESLING, CABERNET SAUVIGNON, and PINOT NOIR.

Central Otago New Zealand wine growing region located far south on the South Island and inland toward the central part of the island around the small towns of Alexandria, Cromwell, Gibbston, Queenstown, and Wanaka. This region evolved in the 1860s when gold was discovered, and it was about this time that Frenchman Jean Désire Feraud planted vines and began making prize-winning wines. In 1895, Bordeaux-trained wine expert Romeo Bragato identified this area's potential as a premium grape-growing region. Central Otago is New Zealand's and the world's most southerly wine region. The southernmost location and high altitude also make it one of New Zealand's coolest areas. But, being inland, Central Otago does not have a maritime climate and therefore is subject to higher fluctuations in daily and seasonal temperatures. Surprisingly, because the region is protected, days can be very warm with temperatures ranging from mid 80°F to low 90°F, but dropping dramatically overnight, all of which helps maintain the grapes' ACIDITY levels. PINOT NOIR has overtaken CHARDONNAY as the most popular VARIETY and continues to increase its hold as the most dominant. Other varieties planted here include GEWÜRZTRAMINER, PINOT GRIS, RIESLING, and SAUVIGNON BLANC. With approximately 1,100 acres, Central Otago is New Zealand's sixth largest growing area, right behind CANTERBURY and AUCKLAND and just ahead of WELLINGTON.

Central Ranges Zone *see* NEW SOUTH WALES

Central Valley 1. Huge California growing area that runs inland from north of Chico (which is north of Sacramento) to south of Bakersfield. The Central Valley can actually be broken into two parts—the **Sacramento Valley** at the north and the **San Joaquin Valley** at the south. The area is so large (it encompasses 55 percent of California's vineyard acreage) and the yields are so bountiful that over 75 percent of California's total wine production comes out of this region. There are three VITICULTURAL AREAS in the valley—MADERA, MERRITT ISLAND, and CLARKSBURG. Most of the wine from the Central Valley is pretty ordinary, but implementation of modern winery facilities has gradually improved the quality. Because of the Central Valley's high temperatures and short growing season, ACID in the grapes isn't fully developed. For this reason, high-acid grapes like BARBERA, CHENIN BLANC, and French Colombard (COLOMBARD) have been planted in increasing numbers. The leading red varieties are ZINFANDEL and GRENACHE, followed by Barbera, CARIGNANE, RUBIRED, RUBY CABERNET, CABERNET SAUVIGNON, and MERLOT. Other white varieties include CHARDONNAY, SAUVIGNON BLANC, and MALVASIA. 2. CHILE's Central Valley, situated between the giant Andes and the shorter coastal mountains, is the country's most important wine-producing region. The vineyard areas start around Santiago, Chile's capital city, running south for over 200 miles and varying in width from about 25 to 50 miles. The Central Valley, known as *el Valle Central*, consists of four main subregions—the MAIPO VALLEY, RAPEL VALLEY, Curico Valley, and MAULE VALLEY. Each valley has an eponymously named river that runs east to west from the Andes to the ocean. Wines made from grapes grown thoughout the region use the Central Valley appellation on their labels. Wines made from grapes grown in only one of the subregions may use the subregion name.

Central Victorian High Country Formerly called Strathbogie Ranges, this Australian wine region is located in the Central Victoria Zone of VICTORIA. It's situated about 60 miles north and slightly east of Melbourne around the towns of Seymour and Mansfield. This is cool, high country, and most vineyards are planted at about the 1,000- to 1,600-foot level, meaning that the focus is on cool-weather VARIETIES. CHARDONNAY is used for both STILL WINES and SPARKLING WINES (the latter also utilize much of the PINOT NOIR crop). Domaine Chandon and giant Southcorp use grapes from this area for their sparkling wines. Varieties like RIESLING, GEWÜRZTRAMINER, and SAUVIGNON BLANC produce CRISP, fruity wines.

Central Victoria Zone *see* VICTORIA

centrifuge; centrifuging [SIHN-truh-fyooj] A high-speed, rotating apparatus that separates substances of varying densities through centrifugal force. **Centrifuging** is used in winemaking to remove yeast cells from a wine before it completes the FERMENTATION process. It's also used instead of other processes (such as FILTERING) to remove particles from wine.

Les Cents Vignes *see* BEAUNE

Centurian; Centurion [sihn-TOOR-ee-uhn; sihn-TYOOR-ee-uhn] This red-wine grape is a cross (similar to CARNELIAN) of CARIGNAN, CABERNET SAUVIGNON, and GRENACHE. It was developed in California for hotter growing areas and has been planted on a limited basis in California's CENTRAL VALLEY. Like Carnelian, Centurion didn't acquire enough Cabernet traits to make it valued, and it's received only limited acceptance.

cepa [THEH-pah] A Spanish term literally meaning "vine" or "root"; also often used to mean "grape variety."

cépage [say-PAHZH] French for "grape variety." In France, **Vin de cépage** is a wine labeled by its principal grape VARIETY, rather than by an APPELLATION CÔNTROLÉE. Historically, Vin de cépage has had a disparaging connotation. **Cépages nobles** refers to the NOBLE GRAPE varieties.

cerasuolo [cheh-rah-SWAW-loh] Italian for "cherry red" or "cherry-colored." Cerasuolo is used to describe some darker ROSÉ wines.

Cerceal *see* SERCIAL

Cérons AC [say-RAWN] Small APPELLATION that is located southeast of the city of Bordeaux along the Garonne River, abuts BARSAC, and is surrounded by the much larger appellation GRAVES. Cérons AC produces only sweet white wines, similiar to those from SAUTERNES though not as intense, sweet, or expensive. The grapes used are SÉMILLON, SAUVIGNON BLANC, and MUSCADELLE. Decreasing interest in sweet wines has led many producers in this area to shift to DRY white wines, which must be labeled with the Graves appellation.

Cerveteri DOC [chayr-veh-TEH-ree] Located northwest of Rome in Italy's LATIUM region, this DOC zone produces both ROSSO and BIANCO wines. The reds are made from SANGIOVESE, MONTEPULCIANO, Cesanese, Carignano (CARIGNAN), CANAIOLO Nero, and BARBERA. The white wines are a blend of numerous white varieties but predominately TREBBIANO and MALVASIA.

Chablais [shah-BLAY] One of the three main growing areas in the Swiss canton of VAUD. Chablais is located just north of the canton of VALAIS and just south of the eastern end of Lake Geneva in the valley of the Rhône. It's a white-wine area where the dominant grape is CHASSELAS (locally known as *Dorin*). This area's best wines come from the villages of Aigle and Yvorne.

Chablis [sha-BLEE; shah-BLEE] Small growing district located 110 miles southeast of Paris that encircles the town of Chablis in France's BURGUNDY region and produces some of the world's best-known white wines. Chablis' vineyards, which are fairly far north, are closer to the CHAMPAGNE region than they are to most of the rest of Burgundy. There are just over 7,000 acres with AC status. This acreage has increased in recent years because of improved methods of protecting the vineyards when the temperature drops below freezing, which isn't uncommon in this northerly region. CHARDONNAY is the approved grape for Chablis' appellations, which are, in increasing order of quality, **Petit Chablis AC**, **Chablis AC**, **Chablis Premier Cru AC**, and **Chablis Grand Cru AC**. The majority of the production comes from the Chablis AC vineyards followed by those of the Chablis Premier Cru AC vineyards. There are forty vineyards with PREMIER CRU status, but some smaller premier cru vineyards have the right to use the names of certain larger, better-known premier cru vineyards so that the practical number of names in use is around twenty. The best known of these are **Beauroy**, **Fourchaume**, **Les Fourneaux**, **Côte de Léchet**, **Mont de Milieu**, **Montée de Tonnerre**, **Montmains**, **Mélinots**, **Vaillons**, **Vaucoupin**, **Vau de Vey**, and **Vosgros**. The best wines come from the grand cru vineyards—BLANCHOTS, BOUGROS, LES CLOS, GRENOUILLES, LES PREUSES, VALMUR, and VAUDÉSIR—which cover a total of about 250 acres. The term *"grand cru"* appears on the labels of these special wines, followed by the name of the originating vineyard. There is one vineyard, **La Moutonne**, that's an "unofficial" grand cru; although it's not recognized by the INAO, it's allowed to use *"grand cru"* on its label. It's located between Les Preuses and Vaudésir. The Chablis Grand Cru can rank among the best white wines in Burgundy, and therefore in the world, but Chablis wines are at the mercy of the weather more than any place else in Burgundy. Cool growing seasons inhibit the Chardonnay grapes from fully ripening, whereas warm seasons can produce luscious ripe grapes that produce magnificent wines. Chablis wines are somewhat different from other Burgundy white wines in that they're generally known for being drier (*see* DRY) and slightly more AUSTERE and for having a FLINTY or MINERALLY quality. Oak-barrel AGING lends added complexity and a hint of vanilla. However, most producers in Chablis VINIFY only in stainless steel tanks or employ minimal use of oak barrels, thereby achieving their desired goal of wines that are CRISP and more precise. As with other parts of Burgundy, wine quality varies even from the same PREMIER CRU or GRAND CRU vineyard so it's best to get to know the various producers.

chai [SHEH; SHAY] A French term usually referring to an aboveground building for storing wine. Although CAVE and chai are often used interchangeably, cave more typically denotes underground cellars.

Chalk Hill AVA APPELLATION that is just east of the town of Windsor in SONOMA COUNTY, California, and is a subzone of and encompasses the northeast corner of the larger RUSSIAN RIVER AVA. Chalk Hill differs from the rest of the Russian River area in that it's warmer (the hills block the fog and cooling ocean breezes) and the soil is white, derived from volcanic ash. While most of the Russian River area is rated as a Region I growing area, Chalk Hill is considered a Region II (*see* CLIMATE REGIONS OF CALIFORNIA). The more widely planted varieties are the white grapes, CHARDONNAY and SAUVIGNON BLANC, but CABERNET SAUVIGNON and MERLOT are grown as well. Chalk Hill Winery is this area's best-known winery. Rodney Strong Vineyards also has land in this area and produces a Chalk Hill-designated Chardonnay.

Chalone AVA [shuh-LOHN] Small 8,600-acre AVA located in Monterey County, California. It has only one winery—CHALONE VINEYARD, which is in the hills southeast of Salinas and northeast of Soledad. In the 1990s Michael Michaud, general manager and winemaker at Chalone, bought land from Chalone and began to develop Michaud Vineyard, to which he devoted full attention starting in 1998. So far he has not built a winery on the property. Because the Chalone area sits above the Salinas Valley fog, it has higher temperatures than the valley floor. The Chalone VITICULTURAL AREA falls into the Region II or Region III category (*see* CLIMATE REGIONS OF CALIFORNIA), depending on a particular year's weather. CHARDONNAY and PINOT NOIR are the area's major grapes, followed by CHENIN BLANC, PINOT BLANC, and SYRAH.

Chalonnaise *see* CÔTE CHALONNAISE

Chambertin [shah*m*-behr-TAN] A world-famous, GRAND CRU vineyard located in the village of GEVREY-CHAMBERTIN in the CÔTE DE NUITS district of France's BURGUNDY region. This 32-acre PINOT NOIR vineyard adjoins a 38-acre parcel called **Clos de Bèze**, which is also a GRAND CRU vineyard and whose wine may use **Chambertin AC** or **Chambertin-Clos de Bèze AC** on their labels. Chambertin may not be called Chambertin-Clos de Bèze, however. The Clos de Bèze vineyard was initially cleared and planted back in the seventh century by monks from the Abbey of Bèze, which owned the land. Legend has it that it wasn't until the twelfth century that Chambertin was planted by a Monsieur Bertin, who felt that he could also make good wines if he grew the same grape varieties as his famous next-door neighbor. His vineyard was called Champ de Bertin ("Bertin's field") and later shortened to Chambertin. The Chambertin wines were one of Napoleon's favorites, and it's said that he insisted that they be available to him even during his various military campaigns. As with most of Burgundy's vineyards, both Chambertin and Clos de Bèze have had numerous owners, twenty-three and eighteen, respectively. Unfortunately, quality varies from producer to producer, and, although Chambertin has been called "King of Wines," less accomplished vintners don't make wines that live up to that reputation. The quality of wines from Clos de Bèze is considered higher and more consistent than those from Chambertin. The best wines from these two vineyards are quite powerful. They have CONCENTRATED fruit flavors, intense, rich, perfumed aromas, and long AGING capabilities. There are seven other GRANDS CRUS that may use "Chambertin" on their labels followed by their vineyard name. They are CHAPELLE-CHAMBERTIN, CHARMES-CHAMBERTIN, GRIOTTE-CHAMBERTIN, LATRICIÈRES-CHAMBERTIN, MAZIS-CHAMBERTIN, MAZOYÈRES-CHAMBERTIN, and RUCHOTTES-CHAMBERTIN.

Chambertin-Clos de Bèze AC *see* CHAMBERTIN

Chambolle-Musigny [shah*m*-BAWL mew-see-NYEE] Well-known village located in the the CÔTE DE NUITS district of France's BURGUNDY region. It's one of the smaller villages in this famous area and contains approximately 550 vineyard acres, all planted in PINOT NOIR except for a ¾-acre plot that grows CHARDONNAY. The highest-quality wines are from two well-known GRAND CRUS—BONNES MARES AC and MUSIGNY AC—and they produce wines of quite different styles. The Musigny wines are flavorful but better known for their elegance and finesse; they can be drunk relatively young. Wines from Bonnes Mares, however, are full-bodied (*see* BODY), TANNIC, and require AGING a number of years before they mature. The small plot of Chardonnay is planted in

Musigny. It produces very good wines, but they're limited, very expensive, and generally not the quality of other top GRAND CRU white wines. Chambolle-Musigny also has twenty-four PREMIER CRU vineyards with **Les Amoureuses** and **Les Charmes** generally regarded as the two finest. Chambolle-Musigny AC wines, though generally light and elegant, normally have good STRUCTURE.

Chambourcin [shahm-boor-SAN] Red wine HYBRID that was introduced in 1963 by Joannes Seyve and that has gained favorable acceptance, particularly in France's LOIRE region. In the United States' mid-Atlantic region, states like Maryland, New Jersey, New York, and Pennsylvania have planted Chambourcin to the extent that more is grown in the area than any other part of the world. Chambourcin produces good-quality, ruby-colored wines that have a reasonably full, slightly herbaceous flavor and aroma. This grape is VINIFIED both as a ROSÉ and a red wine. Chambourcin is also known as *Joannes Seyve 26205*.

chambrer [shahn-BRAY] A derivative of the French word *chambre* ("room"), the term *chambrer* means "bring to room temperature." It's associated with the older traditional environment where cellars were very cool (55°F or less) and dining rooms were frequently about 60°F. Bringing to room temperature meant simply taking the bottle of wine out of the wine cellar several hours before serving so that it could warm to this room temperature. Today, dining rooms are usually much warmer, and most wines are better when served at 65°F or less, so bringing them to room temperature could make them too warm. *See also* WINE CELLAR; Temperatures for Serving Wine, page 641; Optimum Serving Temperatures by Wine Type, page 642.

Champagne; champagne [sham-PAYN (Fr. shahm-PAH-nyuh)] 1. Even though effervescent wines abound throughout the world, *true* Champagne comes only from France's northernmost winegrowing region of Champagne, just 90 miles northeast of Paris. This renowned region has about 75,000 vineyard acres and consists of four main growing areas—**Montagne de Reims**, **Côte des Blancs**, **Vallée de la Marne**, and the **Aube**—and a fifth area that's evolving, **Côte de Sézanne**. Because it's so far north, Champagne's cool weather creates a difficult growing environment for grapes to ripen fully. The main grape varieties grown in the Champagne region are PINOT NOIR, MEUNIER (Pinot Meunier), and CHARDONNAY, all of which require warmer weather for optimum development. Grapes that don't completely ripen tend to have high ACIDS and less-developed flavors, which just happens to be the perfect formula for SPARKLING WINES. This region's chalky soil adds its magic to create just the right flavor composition in these grape varieties. Champagne region villages and their associated vineyards are classified (from 80 to 100 percent) according to the quality of the grapes produced. Of the approximately 270 villages, only 17 have obtained GRAND CRU ratings of 100 percent. The next level, called PREMIER CRU, consists of villages with ratings from 90 to 99 percent. The remaining villages have ratings of between 80 and 89 percent. Most of the better-known Champagne houses buy grapes to supplement their own vineyards, and this percentage rating system helps set the prices growers receive. The art of blending wines to create Champagnes with superior flavor is credited to DOM PÉRIGNON, seventeenth-century cellarmaster of the Abbey of Hautvillers. Today, some Champagne makers mix as many as thirty to forty or more different base wines to create the blend, or CUVÉE. Most major Champagne houses strive for a cuvée that's consistent from year to year. Good Champagne is expensive not only because it's made with premium grapes but also because it's made by the MÉTHODE CHAMPENOISE. This traditional technique requires a second fermentation in the bottle, as well as some 100 hand operations (some of which are mechanized today). **Vintage Champagnes** are made from the best grapes of the harvest in years when the *chef de cave* of an individual Champagne house believes that the grapes are better than average. Wines from the declared year must comprise at least 80 percent of the cuvée for vintage Champagnes, with the balance coming from reserve wines from prior years. Vintage Champagnes must be aged for 3 years prior to their release. **Non-vintage Champagnes**, which make up 75 to 80 percent of those produced, are blends of 2 or more years. They're usually made in a definitive house style, which is maintained by meticulous cuvée blending. **Rosé Champagnes** are generally made by adding a small amount of red still wine to the cuvée, although some producers extract color through MACERATION of the juice with red grape skins. These sparkling wines are usually full-flavored and full-bodied (*see* BODY) and have an intriguing salmon-pink color. The pale pink, full-flavored **Blanc de Noirs Champagnes** are made entirely from red Pinot Noir and/or Meunier grapes. **Blanc de Blancs Champanges**, which are usually more delicate and the lightest in color, are made entirely from Chardonnay grapes. **Crémant Champagnes** are made with only slightly more than half the pressure of standard sparkling wines and therefore have a creamier MOUTHFEEL. Champagne can be LIGHT and FRESH, TOASTY to YEASTY, and DRY to sweet. A Champagne's BOUQUET and flavor gain complexity through a process called AUTOLYsis, whereby the wine ages with the yeast cells in the bottle (sometimes for up to 10 years) before DISGORGEMENT. A sugar-wine mixture, called a DOSAGE, added just before final corking, determines how sweet a Champagne will be. The label indicates the level of sweetness: **EXTRA BRUT** (totally dry to very dry—less than 0.6 percent sugar); **BRUT** (very dry to almost dry—less than 1.5 percent sugar); **EXTRA SEC** or **EXTRA DRY** (slightly sweeter—1.2 to 2 percent sugar); sec (medium sweet—1.7 to 3.5 percent sugar); **DEMI-SEC** (sweet—3.3 to 5 percent sugar); and **DOUX** (very sweet—over 5 percent sugar). The last two are considered DESSERT WINES. **Grande Marque** is a French term for "great brand" and is used unofficially to refer to the best Champagne houses. An organization called the *Syndicat des Grandes Marques* has about thirty members, and most of the better-known firms belong, including **Ayala**, **Billecart-Salmon**, **Bollinger**, **Canard-Duchêne**, **Deutz**, **Charles Heidsieck**, **Heidsieck Monopole**, **Henriot**, **Krug**, **Lanson**, **Laurent Perrier**, **Mercier**, **Moët & Chandon**, **Mumm**, **Perrier-Jouët**, **Joseph Perrier**, **Piper Heidsieck**, **Pol Roger**, **Pommery and Greno**, **Louis Roederer**, **Ruinart**, **Salon**, **Taittinger**, and **Veuve Clicquot-Ponsardin**. Some of these Grandes Marques produce a premium brand (an expensive, high-end sparkling wine) variously known as **cuvée de prestige** or **cuvée spéciale**. Moet & Chandon was the first to produce such a wine with their **Dom Perignon** bottling. Today there are numerous offerings including **Diamant Bleu** from Heidsieck & Co., **Comtes de Champagne** from Taittinger, **Grand Siècle** from Laurent-Perrier, **Cristal** from Louis Roederer, **Grand Cuvée** from Krug, and **Belle Epoque** from Perrier-Jouët. In recent years, a number of high-quality Champagnes have come from small producers like Baptiste-Pertois, Paul Bara, Bonnaire, Cattier, Delamotte, Egly-Ouriet, Guy Larmandier, and Tarlant. Some of these producers are growers that provide grapes to the large Champagne houses. STILL WINES are also made in the Champagne region. The **Coteaux Champenois AC** covers red, white, and rosé still wines made from the three primary Champagne grapes—Pinot Noir, Meunier, and Chardonnay. These wines don't have a great reputation primarily because the grapes used aren't generally fully ripe. The **Rosé des Riceys AC** covers Pinot Noir-based rosé still wines made around Les Riceys in the Aube. Though hard to find and relatively expensive, these wines are more full-flavored because the Aube, which is warmer than other parts of the Champagne region, produces riper grapes. 2. The term "champagne" is also used generically for sparkling wines made outside of the Champagne region. Most countries bow to French tradition by not using the word "champagne" on their labels. Their sparkling wines are called by other names such as SPUMANTE in Italy, SEKT in Germany, *vin mousseux* (*see* MOUSSEUX) in other regions of France, or simply *sparkling wine*. In the United States and some South American countries, it's legal to use the word "champagne" for sparkling wine, but the label must conspicuously identify the appellation of origin. However, most top-quality, U.S. sparkling-wine producers don't use the term but rather indicate that the wines were made by the French *méthode champenoise*. *See also* Opening and Serving Wine at Home, page 636

champagne method *see* MÉTHODE CHAMPENOISE

champán *see* CAVA

Les Champans *see* VOLNAY

Champenois, Coteaux AC *see* CHAMPAGNE

champenoise *see* MÉTHODE CHAMPENOISE

Les Champs Fulliot *See* MONTHÉLIE

Chamusca *see* RIBATEJO DOC

Chancellor [CHAN-suh-luhr; CHAN-sluhr] Red-wine grape that is a French-American HYBRID widely grown in the eastern United States. Chancellor, also known as Seibel 7053, produces fruity but somewhat bland red wines.

chapeau [sha-POH] French for "CAP," referring in the wine world to the mass of grape solids that floats on the juice's surface during the FERMENTATION process.

Chapelle-Chambertin AC [shah-PEHL shah*m*-behr-TA*N*] A small GRAND CRU vineyard located in the village of GEVREY-CHAMBERTIN in the CÔTE DE NUITS district of France's BURGUNDY region. It takes its name from a chapel built by the monks from the Abbey of Bèze. Its 13.6 acres of PINOT NOIR grapes generally produce the lightest red wines of this village's grands crus. *See also* CHAMBERTIN.

chaptalization [shap-tuh-luh-ZAY-shuhn] The procedure of adding sugar to grape juice or MUST prior to or during FERMENTATION; also called *sugaring*. When natural grape sugars aren't high enough to produce reasonable ALCOHOL levels (sugar is converted to alcohol during fermentation), chaptalization is used to attain the necessary sugar levels. Chaptalization is usually practiced when grapes don't fully ripen, which can happen in cool-weather regions or during poor-growing seasons. When used properly, chaptalization allows the production of full, rich wines with sufficient alcohol levels to give them BALANCE. This procedure is legal (with certain restrictions) in France and Germany, but it is illegal in California and Italy, although addition of GRAPE CONCENTRATE is allowed. Chaptalization is legal in other parts of the United States such as Oregon and New York.

character *see* Glossary of Wine Tasting Terms, page 655

Charbono [shar-BOH-noh] An uncommon red-wine grape grown in California's NAPA VALLEY and MENDOCINO COUNTY. Charbono wines are very dark in color, lackluster in flavor, and tend to be high in both TANNINS and ACIDITY. Charbono is thought to have links to *Corbeau* (or *Charbonneau*), a rare French variety.

Chardonel [SHAHR-duh-nehl] A HYBRID created by New York State Agricultural Experiment Station from CHARDONNAY and SEYVAL BLANC (which itself comes from a long line of hybrids). Released in 1991, Chardonel has become popular in colder U.S. climates because of its hardiness, plus it can produce high-quality wines because of its Chardonnay parentage.

Chardonnay [shar-dn-AY; shar-doh-NAY] Just as CABERNET SAUVIGNON has become the most popular high-quality red-wine grape, Chardonnay has taken the lead for first-class white-wine grapes—and with even greater ardor. Although some argue that the RIESLING grape produces the finest white wines, Chardonnay is being extensively planted throughout the world. In addition to being highly prized, Chardonnay is easy to grow and quite versatile. It's high in EXTRACT and, unless picked late, has good ACID levels. The wide range of growing soils, as well as the winemaker's influence, produces a diverse spectrum of Chardonnay wines with varying characteristics. Their flavors can be described as BUTTERY, CREAMY, NUTTY, SMOKY, and STEELY; popular fruit descriptors include APPLEY, lemon, melon, and pineapple. Chardonnay's origins are believed to be from the Pinot family (PINOT NOIR, PINOT GRIS, PINOT BLANC) on one side and a mediocre variety called Gouais Blanc on the other. Gouais Blanc, which is no longer grown in France, appears to be identical to Heunischweiss, a variety once widely grown in eastern Europe. Chardonnay's reputation was established in France, particularly in the BURGUNDY region. The highly prized Chardonnay wines from CHABLIS, CORTON CHARLEMAGNE, MÂCON, MEURSAULT, MONTRACHET, and POUILLY-FUSSÉ are imitated by winemakers around the world. Chardonnay is also an important grape in the CHAM-

PAGNE district where it's picked before fully ripe while it still has high ACID and understated fruit flavors—the perfect combination for champagne. California has adopted this grape with a fervor and has come into prominence with its delightful Chardonnay wines from a number of wineries across the state. In addition to the hundreds of wineries in California, over 200 wineries in other parts of the United States are producing Chardonnay wines. Chardonnay has also seen a tremendous planting surge in Australia, with excellent wines from several wineries including Petaluma and Leeuwin. As this grape's popularity grows, new vineyards of Chardonnay are being planted throughout the world in Italy, Lebanon, New Zealand, Spain, South Africa, and other parts of France. Chardonnay is also called *Beaunois, Gamay Blanc, Melon d'Arbois,* and *Pinot Chardonnay.* It's sometimes mistakenly referred to as PINOT BLANC, which is a different variety.

En Charlemagne; Le Charlemagne *see* CORTON; CORTON-CHARLEMAGNE

Charmat; Charmat process [shar-MAH; shar-MAHT] A BULK method for making SPARKLING WINES developed around 1910 by Frenchman Eugène Charmat. The Charmat process involves faster and less expensive production techniques using large pressurized tanks throughout production. These interconnecting tanks retain the pressure (created by the production of CARBON DIOXIDE during FERMENTATION) throughout the entire process. For many winemakers, the Charmat process replaces the expensive MÉTHODE CHAMPENOISE technique of secondary fermentation in bottles, thereby enabling them to produce inexpensive sparkling wines. Charmat wines can be good (although, once poured, they often lose their bubbles quickly) but are usually not as esteemed as méthode champenoise sparkling wines. The Charmat process is superior, however, to the technique used by some producers of simply pumping carbon dioxide gas into STILL WINE (as carbonated soft drinks are made). The Charmat process is also called *bulk process,* and in the United States, wines may be labeled "Bulk Process" or "Charmat Process" (the latter being preferred). In France, this process is also called *cuve close*; in Italy, it's known as *metodo charmat* or sometimes *autoclave* (the Italian name for the sealed tanks). In Spain, it's called *granvas,* and in Portugal, *método continuo.*

Les Charmes *see* CHAMBOLLE-MUSIGNY; MEURSAULT

Charmes-Chambertin AC [SHARM shahm-behr-TA(N)] A well-known GRAND CRU vineyard located in the village of GEVREY-CHAMBERTIN in the CÔTE DE NUITS district of France's BURGUNDY region. The grand cru adjoining it, **Mazoyères-Chambertin**, may legally use the name Charmes-Chambertin on its wine labels, and most producers do. Few producers actually use Mazoyères-Chambertin AC on their labels so it isn't well known, and the two parcels are often viewed as one large (76-acre) vineyard (referred to as Charmes-Chambertin). Because of the size of the production from the two parcels, Charmes-Chambertin is one of the better known grands crus of Gevery-Chambertin. These wines are highly prized although considered to be more variable than most of the other grand crus of Gevrey-Chambertin.

Charta [KAR-tah] A German association founded in 1983 by leading producers in the RHEINGAU region to encourage production of TROCKEN (DRY) and HALBTROCKEN (off-dry) RIESLING wines. This was in sharp contrast to the German wine laws of the early 1970s that sent German winemakers in the direction of making sweet wines. As part of this new effort, Charta classified Rheingau-region vineyards in a fashion similar to what had been done in the mid-1800s, focusing on those vineyards with the best capability to fully ripen Riesling grapes. Charta also established (and enforced) strict regulations as to how these dry wines were to be made, including low YIELDS, a minimum ALCOHOL level of 12 percent, and the use of 100 percent Riesling grapes. The grapes cannot have been affected by Edelfäule (BOTRYTIS CINEREA), which the Charta members believed only occurred in lesser vineyards. Wine labels identify the classified vineyard that produced the grapes. These dry, high-quality Charta-approved wines are bottled in tall brown bottles embossed with a double Romanesque arch.

Chassagne-Montrachet AC [shah-SAH*N*-yuh moh*n*-rah-SHAY] A significant village in the southern part of the CÔTE DE BEUNE in France's BURGUNDY region. Although best known for its CHARDONNAY-based white wines, until the late 1980s the 800-plus acres in Chassagne-Montrachet actually produced more red wines, which are made from PINOT NOIR. The popularity of these white wines reversed this situation. Chassagne-Montrachet has one GRAND CRU vineyard (CRIOTS-BÂTARD-MONTRACHET) and nearly half of each of two others (LE MONTRACHET and BÂTARD-MONTRACHET). Many consider Le Montrachet's top white wines the best in the world, and those from the other two grand cru aren't far behind. Wines from the Chassagne-Montrachet AC and the village's thirteen PREMIER CRU vineyards are of generally high quality, and, because the Chassagne-Montrachet doesn't have the notoriety of the neighboring village of PULIGNY-MONTRACHET, prices are somewhat less. The best premier cru vineyards for white wines include **En Caillerets**, **Les Embrazées**, **Morgeot**, **Les Grandes**

Ruchottes, and **Les Vergers**. Because of the attention focused on the white wines, the red wines are sometimes overlooked. There are no grand cru red wines, but the red wines from the Chassagne-Montrachet AC and the premier cru vineyards can be quite good and reasonably priced relative to other red Burgundies. The best premier cru vineyards for red wines include **Clos Saint-Jean**, **La Boudriotte**, **La Maltroie**, and **Morgeot**.

C

Chasselas [shas-suh-LAH] A very ancient white-wine grape that is grown in Switzerland and in small sections of France, Germany, Italy, and New Zealand. Chasselas—one of the oldest cultivated varieties— is thought to have originated in the Middle East. Even though this grape's still one of Switzerland's leading varieties, Chasselas' acreage in general has dwindled over the years. Chasselas wines are low in ACIDITY and ALCOHOL and generally lacking in CHARACTER. There are numerous subvarieties of this grape, one being the *Chasselas Dore*, which is cultivated on a very limited basis in California. As with many older grape varieties, Chasselas is known by a variety of names including *Dorin, Fendant, Gutedel, Marzemina Bianca, Perlan,* and *Weisser Gutedel.*

château; pl. châteaux; châteaus [sha-TOH] Although this is the French word for "castle," in wine parlance château refers to "wine estate" or "vineyard." The name is most often used in France's BORDEAUX region. The buildings occupying the wine estate or vineyard range from simple farmhouses to true castlelike structures. The French only allow the word "château" to appear on a label name when an authentic vineyard with the traditional use of the name has produced the wine. Note that American chateaus do not generally use the diacritical mark ∧ above the first *a*.

château bottled *see* ESTATE BOTTLED

Château-Chalon AC [sha-TOH shah-LAWN] This tiny APPELLATION, located in the Jura region in eastern France, specializes in VIN JAUNE (yellow wine), which is made from a rather rare, high-quality white grape called SAVAGNIN. AGED for 6 years, vin jaune undergoes a process simliar to SHERRY, whereby a film of YEAST covers the wine's surface, which prevents OXIDATION but allows evaporation and the subsequent concentration of the wine. The result is a sherrylike wine with a delicate, nutty richness that can age for decades. Unlike sherry, Château-Chalon wines are not FORTIFIED. Most wine critics think that they're not quite as good as the better Spanish sherries but Château-Chalon wines are capable of AGING for decades.

Château-Grillet AC [sha-TOH gree-YEH] A celebrated vineyard located in France's northern RHÔNE region. The 6½-acre plot, which has its own APPELLATION, is planted entirely with VIOGNIER grapes. The MESOCLIMATE appears to be just right for this variety because some of the best Viognier wines are produced here. These DRY white wines have a floral BOUQUET, a hint of apricot in the flavor, and a spicy FIN-ISH. Only a small amount is produced so these wines are generally expensive.

Châteaumeillant VDQS [shat-toh-may-AHN] An area with VDQS status for producing red and ROSÉ wines made mainly from GAMAY even though PINOT GRIS and PINOT NOIR are also permitted. It's located around the village of Châteaumeillant, south of the city of Bourges in central France's Cher DÉPARTEMENT. The wines, which are a lighter style, are seldom seen outside of the local area.

Châteauneuf-du-Pape AC [shah-toh-nuhf-doo-PAHP] Important APPELLATION that surrounds the village of Châteaneuf-du-Pape, which is located between Orange and Avignon in the southern portion of France's RHÔNE region. Its name means "new castle of the pope," refer-ring to the summer palace built in the area during the 1300s and used by the popes from Avignon. In 1923 Châteauneuf-du-Pape was the first area to adopt strict rules for grape growing and winemaking. These rules were the basis for France's national system, APPELLATION D'ORIGINE CONTRÔLÉE, which was implemented in 1936. Châteauneuf-du-Pape AC permits thirteen red and white grapes; it's quite unusual for a French AC to have so many varieties. GRENACHE, the dominant variety in the area, exists in both a red (Grenache Noir) and white (Grenache Blanc) form. Other red varieties include CINSAULT, Counoise, MOURVÈDRE, Muscardine, SYRAH, Terret Noir, and Vaccarèse. Permitted white vari-eties are BOURBOULENC, CLAIRETTE, Picardan, ROUSSANNE, and Piquepoul (or Picpoule)—this last variety had a red version, but it's not widely grown. Red wines make up approximately 97 percent of this appella-tion's production; however, the white varieties may be used in red wines, mainly to SOFTEN some of the bigger, bolder wines. The mini-mum ALCOHOL level of 12½ percent is the highest minimum of any AC. Generally, it's not difficult to reach this alcohol level because of the warm climate. The area's stony soil retains the day's heat into the evening hours, which allows the grapes to ripen to their fullest. Fully ripened grapes have a high sugar content that can convert into higher alcohol levels. Châteauneuf-du-Pape's red wines are traditionally BIG, RICH, and full-bodied (*see* BODY) with SPICY, raspberry flavors. They're capable of AGING for 5 to 20 years. A lighter BEAUJOLAIS-style red, made with CARBONIC MACERATION, is also produced. The white wines are usually CRISP with flavors that hint of peaches, pears, melons, and, sometimes, licorice. Wines with the papal coat of arms embossed on the bottle above the label indicate that they are ESTATE BOTTLED.

châteaux [sha-TOH] Plural of CHÂTEAU.

C

Chatillon-en-Diois AC [shah-tee-YAW*N* ahn dee-WAH] An obscure APPELLATION located near the village of Die on the eastern (middle) edge of France's RHÔNE region. Red and ROSÉ wines are produced from GAMAY, PINOT NOIR, and SYRAH; white wines are made from ALIGOTÉ and CHARDONNAY.

Chauche Gris *see* TROUSSEAU GRIS

Chaudenet Gris *see* ALIGOTÉ

Chaume *see* COTEAUX DU LAYON

Les Chaumes *see* CORTON

Les Chaumes de la Voirosse *see* CORTON

De Chaunac [duh SHAW-nak] A red HYBRID grape that is widely grown in the eastern United States and further north in Canada's Ontario province. De Chaunac, also known as *Seibel 9549*, is the most extensively planted variety in New York's FINGER LAKES region. This grape produces fairly fruity wines of ordinary quality; much of it is further processed into SHERRY.

Chautauqua *see* NEW YORK STATE

Chaves IPR *see* TRÁS-OS-MONTES

Chehalem Mountains AVA [sha-HAY-lum] APPELLATION created in December 2006 within the larger WILLAMETTE VALLEY AVA. Its 68,235 acres are located in Clackamas, Yamhill, and Washington counties of northwestern Oregon starting about 19 miles southwest of Portland. Chehalem Mountains AVA has approximately 31 wineries and 1,600 acres planted with wine grapes. PINOT NOIR is the primary variety but CHARDONNAY, PINOT BLANC, PINOT GRIS and RIESLING are also grown. Oregon's smallest VITICULTURAL AREA, RIBBON RIDGE AVA, is located with the Chehalem Mountains AVA. Top vineyards include Chehalem's Ridgecrest, Ponzi's Abetina and Gypsy Dancer.

Cheilly-lès-Maranges *see* MARANGES AC

Chelois [shehl-WAH] A French-American HYBRID also known as *Seibel 10878*. Chelois is popular in the mid-western and eastern

United States, particularly in the FINGER LAKES region of New York. It's made into LIGHT red or ROSÉ wines.

Chénas AC [shay-NAH] The smallest of the ten CRUS in France's BEAU-JOLAIS region. These GAMAY-based wines are full-bodied (*see* BODY) and CONCENTRATED, with more intense color but less fruitiness than some of the lighter-style wines from other Beaujolais crus. They usually benefit from 2 years or more of AGING and peak at about 5 years. Wines from Chénas are very similar in style to those from its larger and better-known neighbor to the south, MOULIN-À-VENT. Because portions of Chénas are in Moulin-à-Vent, growers can sell their wines under either label. It's even been suggested that Chénas be absorbed by Moulin-à-Vent. Because many producers opt for Moulin-à-Vent on the label, wines labeled Chénas aren't well known and are difficult to find.

Chenin Blanc [SHEN-ihn BLAHN (BLAHNGK)] French white-wine grape that is the basis for many superior wines coming out of France's LOIRE region. These include lively, DRY wines from SAVENNIÈRES; medium-sweet wines from VOUVRAY; rich, LATE HARVEST wines from COTEAUX DU LAYON; and fragrant SPARKLING WINES from SAUMUR. French Chenin Blanc has an intense, fascinating aroma; its high ACIDITY enables some of these wines to balance the sweetness and age for years. Two notable areas from the Coteaux du Layon are QUARTS DE CHAUME and BON-NEZEAUX, where BOTRYTISED grapes produce intensely sweet, rich, fla-vorful wines. Although sometimes called *Pineau de la Loire* or *Pineau d'Anjou*, Chenin Blanc is not related to PINOT NOIR. Chenin Blanc is widely grown outside of France in South Africa and California and is planted to a lesser extent in Chile, Australia, and New Zealand. In the mid-1960s, it was discovered that South Africa had been growing this grape for centuries but referred to it as *Steen* or *Stein*. Unfortunately, most of the Chenin Blancs produced around the world—particularly those from hotter growing areas—don't compare to the quality of the top French efforts. Most Chenin Blanc grapes are more neutral and much less exciting. Wines from cooler regions can be well balanced with delicate, FLORAL characteristics and hints of melon. Because of the grape's high ACID content, Chenin Blanc wines outside of France are often combined with other wines to cut Chenin Blanc's sharpness and enliven the final blend. Chenin Blanc is also called *Gros Pineau de Vouvray, Pineau de Savennières,* and *Pinot Blanco.*

cherry *see* Glossary of Wine Tasting Terms, page 655

Chevalier-Montrachet AC [shuh-vahl-YAY mohn-rah-SHAY] Esteemed 18-acre GRAND CRU vineyard that is located in France's BUR-

GUNDY region and sits just above the famous LE MONTRACHET grand cru vineyard in the village of PULIGNY-MONTRACHET in the CÔTE DE BEAUNE. This sloping vineyard with its stony, chalky soil produces some of the best white wines in the world from the CHARDONNAY grapes. The wines are intense and SPICY with a unique GOÛT DE TERROIR. Many wine lovers not only believe that the best white wines from Chevalier-Montrachet rank second only to the best from Le Montrachet but that the former also produces more top-quality wines. Although quite expensive, Chevalier-Montrachet wines aren't nearly as costly as those from Le Montrachet.

Cheverny AC [sheh-vehr-NEE] An AC area located in France's LOIRE Valley southwest of the village of Blois. It produces red and ROSÉ wines from GAMAY, CABERNET FRANC, and CABERNET SAUVIGNON and white wines from CHARDONNAY, CHENIN BLANC, and SAUVIGNON BLANC. **Cour-Cheverny AC** was established for white wines based on the local variety, Romorantin. These Romorantin-based wines are light, dry, and floral-scented.

Chevrier *see* SÉMILLON

chewy *see* Glossary of Wine Tasting Terms, page 655

Chianti DOCG; Chianti Classico DOCG   [kee-AHN-tee; KYAHN-tee] Large well-known Italian wine-producing area that runs from the Florence area south to the Siena region in central Italy's TUS-CANY region. The **Chianti Classico** region is the central zone of this area and its most famous. Historically, the Chianti Classico zone was Chianti until the Chianti area began to enlarge over time. In 1996 Chianti Classico was awarded DOCG status separate from the rest of Chianti. The wines from Chianti Classico, which are usually identifiable by a black rooster (*gallo nero*) on the label, are generally more well known and of better quality than those from Chianti's other areas. The rest of Chianti is included in the Chianti DOCG. It's a single APPELLATION divided into seven subzones—**Chianti Colli Aretini**, **Chianti Colli Fiorentini**, **Chianti Colli Senesi**, **Chianti Colline Pisane**, **Chianti Montalbano**, **Chianti Montespertoli**, and **Chianti Rufina**. A wine made in one of the subzones may be labeled either with the name of the subzone or simply with that of Chianti. Chianti Rufina wines are generally considered the best of the various subzones. **Superiore** is a category that requires an additional 3 months of aging over the regular Chianti DOCG wines. The word "RISERVA" on the label indicates that the wine has been aged for at least 2 years and 3 months before being released. A federation called **Chianti Putto** is made up of growers in the Chianti DOCG—their labels often sport a pink cherub called a *putto*. Chianti's STURDY, DRY red wines were once instantly recognizable by their squat, straw-covered bottles called FIASCHI. However, Chianti wines—particularly those from better producers—are now more often found in the traditional Bordeaux-type bottle. Only a few VINTNERS use the straw-based bottle, which today usually designates a cheaper, and often inferior, product. Chianti wines are made from four grape varieties—SANGIOVESE (minimum 75 percent), CANAIOLO, TREBBIANO, and MALVASIA. Today, however, CABERNET SAUVIGNON and/or MERLOT are being added to some Chianti blends. During the 1970s and 1980s, Chianti's reputation was tarnished by the expansion of production and lack of quality control, but in the 1990s it has regained some of its stature as quality leaders improved both vineyard practices and winemaking approaches.

chiaretto [kyah-REH-toh] Italian for "light red," referring in the wine world to the lively but delicate ROSÉ wines made from GROPPELLO in the LOMBARDY region's DOC of Riviera del Garda Bresciano.

Chiavennasca *see* NEBBIOLO

Chicama Vineyards *see* MARTHA'S VINEYARD AVA; MASSACHUSETTS

Chile; Chilean [CHILL-ee; CHEE-leh; CHIL-lee-uhn] Chilean vineyards were first established in the mid-sixteenth century by Spanish missionaries. These viticultural pioneers planted the grape known as *Pais*, which is similiar to both the MISSION grape widely grown in California and to Argentina's Criolla variety. For the next 300 years, Pais was Chile's primary grape and still comprises about half the total vineyard acreage. In 1851 a Spaniard, Silvestre Ochagavía, brought in French wine experts and, subsequently, CUTTINGS of CABERNET FRANC, CABERNET SAUVIGNON, MALBEC, MERLOT, PINOT NOIR, SAUVIGNON BLANC, and SÉMILLON. Later, other varieties were planted, including CHARDONNAY, GEWÜRZTRAMINER, and RIESLING. The next four decades saw the establishment of numerous wineries that are still prominent estates today including Cousiño Macul (1861), San Pedro (1865), Errázuriz (1870), Santa Rita (1880), Concha y Toro (1883), and Viña Undurraga (1885). These six wine estates, plus those of Caliterra, Los Vascos, Santa Carolina, Saint Morillon, and Walnut Crest, account for almost 90 percent of the Chilean wines exported to the United States. Chile has an ideal environment for growing grapes—the vineyards are protected by the Andes Mountains, the oceans, and the desserts, and they've never been infected with PHYLLOXERA. To the envy of viticulturists in other areas like France and California, this means that Chilean vineyards can be planted with original rootstock, rather than having to be grafted onto those that are phylloxera-resistant. Most Chilean vineyards are in the country's central section from about 50 miles north of the city of Santiago to about 150 miles south. Chile's regional APPELLATION system is quickly evolving. Currently there are five major growing regions, within which are smaller subregions. The subregions also have smaller divisions called zones, within which are even smaller categories called areas. Some subregions don't have zones but jump directly to areas. From north to south the five main growing regions are Atacama, Coquimbo, ACONCAGUA, CENTRAL VALLEY, and Southern. **Atacama** and **Coquimbo** are both very hot and dry, and very limited TABLE WINE is made. The crops consist mainly of table grapes or grapes destined for distilled (*see* DISTILLATION) spirits. **Aconcagua** has a rising subregion called CASABLANCA VALLEY. The **Central Valley** has four main subregions—the MAIPO VALLEY, RAPEL VALLEY, Curicó Valley, and MAULE VALLEY. The **Southern Region**, where País and MUSCAT are the dominate varieties, has the subregions of Itata Valley and Bío Bío Valley. Most of the areas are dry and aren't beleaguered by rains spoiling the harvest, but they do get plenty of water from the melting snows of the Andes. The tremendous potential of the Chilean wine industry is attracting the investments of several foreign wine-producing companies including Spain's Miguel Torres, France's Lafite-Rothschild, and California's Franciscan Vineyards, Kendall-Jackson Vineyards, and Robert Mondavi Winery.

Chiles Valley AVA A small 6,000-acre California AVA that's a sub-zone of the NAPA VALLEY AVA. Approved in 1999, it's located east of the towns of St. Helena and Calistoga and southeast of the HOWELL MOUNTAIN AVA. The surrounding hills block the fog that the Napa Valley receives, which means Chiles Valley is hotter and has a shorter growing season. ZINFANDEL is the grape that grows best in this area, although CABERNET SAUVIGNON and SAUVIGNON BLANC can also do well.

chilling wine *see* Temperatures for Serving Wine, page 641; Optimum Serving Temperatures by Wine Type, page 642

Chinon AC [shee-NOHN] Located in the TOURAINE area, Chinon is one of the few villages in the LOIRE valley focused on red wines, which some wine lovers believe are the Loire's best. Like its neighbors BOUR-GUEIL and SAINT-NICOLAS-DE-BOURGUEIL, this picturesque village with its medieval hilltop fortress grows CABERNET FRANC (known locally as Brenton) and minor amounts of CABERNET SAUVIGNON. Although normally LIGHT and fruity with a heady raspberry aroma, these red wines have enough BODY to age a few years. Hot years can produce good, full-bodied wines with AGING capabilities of 10 to 15 years. The Chinon APPELLATIONS also make ROSÉ wines and white wines made from CHENIN BLANC grapes. Chinon is known as the birthplace of François Rabelais, sixteenth century satirist and humorist, who was an ardent admirer of Chinon wines and coined the phrase "taffeta wines," meaning that they are soft and smooth.

Chiroubles AC [she-ROO-bl] Of the ten CRUS in France's BEAUJOLAIS region, Chiroubles produces the softest and lightest wines. Located between the crus of MORGON and FLEURIE, Chiroubles is one of the smallest crus at less than 700 acres. The best Chiroubles wines, which are meant to be drunk very young, are highly sought after; they can be fairly expensive for Beaujolais wine.

chocolaty; chocolate *see* Glossary of Wine Tasting Terms, page 655

Chorey-lès-Beaune AC [shaw-REH lay BOHN] APPELLATION located in France's BURGUNDY region in the CÔTE DE BEAUNE district just north of the city of Beaune. Although the village of Chorey-lès-Beaune has no GRAND CRU or PREMIER CRU vineyards, area producers make highly rated red wines from the principal variety PINOT NOIR.

Chusclan *see* CÔTES DU RHÔNE

Cienega Valley AVA A VITICULTURAL AREA established in 1982 in San Benito County, California. It lies about 25 to 30 miles inland from the Monterey Bay along the foothills of the Gabilan Range, which separates San Benito County from Monterey County. Almaden Vineyards once had a big presence here. Pietra Santa Vineyard & Winery grows ZINFANDEL, SANGIOVESE, DOLCETTO, CABERNET SAUVIGNON, MERLOT, and small amounts of CHARDONNAY and Pinot Grigio (PINOT GRIS). DeRose Vineyards grows Zinfandel, NÉGRETTE, VIOGNIER, and CABERNET FRANC.

Cienna Australian red-wine grape created by crossing CABERNET SAUVIGNON with Sumool, a Spanish variety. Cienna was developed to produce high-quality wine and be productive in Australia's drier, warmer growing environments. It compares favorably with Cabernet Sauvignon and in some of the evaluations scored as well or better. Cienna takes its name from its color, which has a reddish hue like Sienna. *See also* TYRIAN and RUBIENNE.

Cigales DO [thee-GAH-lehs] A small DO in Spain's Castile and León region, located northwest of Madrid near three other DOs—RIBERA DEL

DUERO, RUEDA, and TORO. Whereas Rueda is known for high-quality white wines and Ribera Del Duero and Toro for their red wines, Cigales is known for ROSADO (ROSÉ) wines. In the best rosados, the red Tinta del País (TEMPRANILLO) is the primary grape variety. This area also allows Garnacha Tinta (GRENACHE) and the white varieties of Albillo, PALOMINO, VERDEJO, and Viura (MACABEO). Cigales DO also produces red wines, which are improving in quality but generally are not yet as good as those of the neighboring DOs.

cigar box *see* CEDAR in the Glossary of Wine Tasting Terms, page 655

Cinque Terre DOC [CHEENG-kweh TEHR-*r*uh] Italian word that means "five lands" and refers to the five fishing villages that dot the coast of the LIGURIA region in northwestern Italy. This DOC area includes the steeply terraced vineyards around the town of La Spezia and the five villages of Monterosso, Vernazza, Corniglia, Manarolo, and Riomaggiore. The rather mediocre, DRY white wine made here is at least 60 percent Bosco and up to 40 percent Arbarola and VERMENTINO. Producers also make limited amounts of the highly regarded **Sciacchetrà** wine, a PASSITO version made from the same grapes. Sciacchetrà can range from AMABILE (medium-sweet) to DOLCE (sweet) and also comes in a LIQUOROSO version.

cinquième cru [san-kyem KROO] French phrase that means "fifth growth," signifying the lowest category of the MÉDOC area's CRUS CLASSÉS (classed growths), which were established in the Classification of 1855 (*see* Official Wine Classifications of Bordeaux, page 678). At that time, eighteen châteaux were given the *cinquième cru* classification, and that number remains unchanged today.

Cinsaut; Cinsault [SAN-soh] Red-wine grape that is widely planted in France. It's extensively grown throughout LANGUEDOC-ROUSSILLON, with particular emphasis in AUDE, L'HÉRAULT, and Gard. Because Cinsaut can withstand very hot weather and is highly productive, it contributes greatly to the huge volumes of wine from this area. Cinsaut grapes create wines that are light in BODY and neutral in flavor. Because of their high ACIDITY and low TANNINS, Cinsaut wines are usually BALANCED with a blend of GRENACHE and/or CARIGNIN (in Languedoc-Roussillon and surrounding areas). In the southern RHÔNE where its YIELD is strictly controlled (a limited volume per acre), Cinsaut produces wines that are more deeply colored, CONCENTRATED, and flavorful. Here, Cinsaut is blended with a variety of other grape varieties including CLAIRETTE, Grenache, MOURVÈDRE, and SYRAH. This grape was once heavily grown in North Africa (particularly Algeria) and is still widely cultivated in South Africa. The South Africans also crossed Cinsaut with PINOT NOIR to create PINOTAGE. Cinsaut is also called *Espagne, Hermitage, Malaga, Ottavianello, Œillade, Picardan Noir,* and *Prunella.*

Cirò DOC [CHEER-oh] The best-known DOC in southern Italy's CALABRIA region. It's said that the ancient Greeks served these wines (then called *Cremissa*) to Olympic winners. Many consider the past reputation to be better than the current one. The Cirò DOC produces ROSSO, BIANCO, and ROSATO wines. The main varieties used for the red and rosé wines are the red GAGLIOPPO and the white TREBBIANO and GRECO grapes. The white wines are made from Greco and Trebbiano. Cirò DOC red RISERVA wines have been AGED for 2 years.

citric acid *see* ACIDS

citrusy; citrus *see* Glossary of Wine Tasting Terms, page 655

clairet *see* CLARET

Clairette [kleh-RHEHT] White-wine grape that is widely cultivated in southern France. It is also known by its full name *Clairette Blanc.* Clairette is one of the white grape varieties allowed by the French government for use in the red CHÂTEAUNEUF-DU-PAPE and the white CÔTES-DU-RHÔNE wines. Its name is tied to the AOCS of **Clairette du Languedoc** and **Clairette de Bellegarde** in the Languedoc-Roussillon region and to the CLAIRETTE DE DIE in the central RHÔNE. By themselves, Clairette wines are generally high in ALCOHOL, low in ACID, and rather bland. The Clairette de Die SPARKLING WINES have a good reputation, but that's primarily because the BLEND includes Muscat Blanc à Petits Grains (MUSCAT), which provides the distinctive aroma and flavor. Clairette is also grown in Australia, where it's known as *Blanquette,* as well as in South Africa, where it's known as *Clairette Blanche.*

Clairette de Die AC; Clairette de Die Tradition AC [kleh-RHEHT duh DEE] APPELLATIONS, centered around the village of Die on the eastern edge of France's RHÔNE region that produce SPARKLING WINES. **Clairette de Die AC** wines are made from the CLAIRETTE grape using the MÉTHODE CHAMPENOISE; **Clairette de Die Tradition AC** wines are made with at least 50 percent MUSCAT grapes (usually much higher) and the rest Clairette via the **méthode dioise** (also called **méthode tradition**). Méthode dioise is a variation of the RURAL METHOD and unique to this appellation. To create effervescence using this method, the MUST is chilled (which slows FERMENTATION) before the wine is bottled. When the chilled, bottled wine begins to warm, the fermentation process is renewed. As with *méthode champenoise*, the by-product of this fermentation is carbon dioxide, which creates bubbles in the bottled wine. The *méthode dioise* technique for removing sediment is to decant and FILTER the wines under pressure, which eliminates the sediment while retaining as much effervescence as possible. The wines are then rebottled. The Muscat-based wines usually receive higher praise than the Clairette-based ones.

Clairette Ronde *see* TREBBIANO

Clairette Rosé *see* TREBBIANO

La Clape [lah KLAHP] The vineyards surrounding this village are part of the COTEAUX DU LANGUEDOC AC but have CRU status, which indicates that the wines are of better quality and allows the name "La Clape" to be added to the label. This area is located along France's Mediterranean coast near Narbonne. The white wines, made from BOURBOULENC, CLAIRETTE, GRENACHE Blanc, and Terret Noir, are considered quite good because of the chalky soil, which contributes a unique flavor composition. The soil, which is unique for this area, is a result of the unusual mountain that rises up dramatically in this fairly flat region. The red and ROSÉ wines, which are made from CARIGNAN, CINSAULT, and GRENACHE, are LIGHT and should be drunk young.

Clare Riesling *see* CROUCHEN

claret [KLAR-eht] 1. A term used by the English when referring to the red wines from BORDEAUX. It's derived from the French *clairet*, which refers to a BORDEAUX wine with a style somewhere between a RED and ROSÉ—in short, a light refreshing red wine. It's made by drawing fermenting wine off after very short skin contact. 2. Elsewhere, the word *claret* is sometimes used as a general reference to light red wines. Even though "claret" sometimes appears on labels, it has no legal definition.

clarete [klah-REH-teh] A Spanish term for light red wines. Clarete has no official definition or application.

Clare Valley A beautiful Australian wine region located in SOUTH AUSTRALIA'S Mount Lofty Ranges Zone. It's situated about 65 miles north of Adelaide around the town of Clare. Vines were first planted in this region in 1840, but the wine industry was slow to get established. Starting in 1890, there was rapid expansion for a decade; then it slowed again until the 1980s. Today there are thirty-six wineries and almost 11,000 acres of vineyards in Clare Valley. RIESLING is clearly the star of the white VARIETIES and is the most widely planted. CHARDONNAY, SÉMILLON, and SAUVIGNON BLANC are the next most popular whites. As for red grapes, CABERNET SAUVIGNON and Shiraz (SYRAH) both produce highly regarded, FULL-BODIED wines. CABERNET FRANC, GRENACHE, MERLOT, and PINOT NOIR are also grown.

C

clarify; clarification   The process of making wine clear by removing particles of yeast and grape matter (pulp, skins, stems, and seeds). One way to clarify wine is to simply let the particulates fall to the bottom of the storage container, after which the wine is racked (*see* RACKING). Sometimes the wine is fined (*see* FINING) to assist in getting the particles to separate from the wine. FILTERING and STABILIZATION may be used as well. The objective is to make a wine that will be clear and bright after bottling.

clarity   *see* Glossary of Wine Tasting Terms, page 655

Clarksburg AVA   California AVA that is southwest of the city of Sacramento, stretching southward for about 16 miles around the small town of Clarksburg. It includes the MERRIT ISLAND AVA subregion. Although it's part of the generally hot CENTRAL VALLEY, Clarksburg's climate is moderated by the Sacramento River delta and breezes from San Francisco Bay. It's generally considered a Region II growing area (*see* CLIMATE REGIONS OF CALIFORNIA). In the past, wines made here from CHENIN BLANC and PETITE SIRAH grapes had a good reception. Today, many other varieties are grown including CABERNET SAUVIGNON, CHARDONNAY, MERLOT, PINOT GRIS, SAUVIGNON BLANC, SYRAH, VIOGNIER, and ZINFANDEL. Bogle Vineyards and River Grove Winery are both located in the Clarksburg area.

classed growth; classified growth   The English translation of the French "CRU CLASSÉ," signifying a top-ranked vineyard in the Bordeaux Classification of 1855 (*see* Official Wine Classifications of Bordeaux, page 678). This famous classification system ranked the red wines of the MÉDOC and the white wines of SAUTERNES.

classic   *see* GERMANY; Glossary of Wine Tasting Terms, page 655

classical method   *see* MÉTHODE CLASSIQUE

classico   [KLA-sih-koh; KLAH-see-koh] 1. Italian for "classic." 2. An area within a larger geographic region defined by the Italian classification system (DOC); also the wines from that area. Such a terrritory is usually the oldest in terms of grape cultivation and wine production and often has the best wines within the larger region. The famous CHIANTI CLASSICO DOCG, located within the larger CHIANTI DOCG, is such an area.

Classic wines *see* GERMANY

Classification of 1855 *see* Official Wine Classifications of Bordeaux, page 678

classified châteaux A term used for top BORDEAUX châteaux that have been classified under the Official Wine Classifications of Bordeaux (page 678) and are known to produce superior wine.

clavelin [klav-LAN] A short fat bottle traditionally used in France's Jura region for VIN JAUNE from the CHÂTEAU-CHALON AC and in some of the region's other ACs. The clavelin holds 62 centiliters (equivalent of about 21 ounces) and is also used for more robust potables like EAU DE VIE.

clean *see* Glossary of Wine Tasting Terms, page 655

Clear Lake AVA Located in southwestern Lake County, north of SONOMA and NAPA COUNTIES and east of MENDOCINO COUNTY. This extremely large AVA area encompasses the territory around California's largest fresh-water lake, Clear Lake. This viticultural area's climate, which consists of hot days and cold nights, categorizes it as a Region II or III (*see* CLIMATE REGIONS OF CALIFORNIA), depending on the area location. SAUVIGNON BLANC grapes seem to do best, although CABERNET SAUVIGNON, CHARDONNAY, and ZINFANDEL are also planted. Kendall-Jackson Vineyards started out here and still has about 80 acres of vineyard land. Despite the large size of the Clear Lake AVA there are only a few wineries here. In 2004 the RED HILLS LAKE COUNTY AVA was established as a sub-appellation.

Clements Hills AVA This VITICULTURAL AREA was established in August 2006. With 85,400 acres, it's the second largest sub-appellation within the larger LODI AVA and is located in San Joaquin County in northern California. Its terrain moves from the flatlands to foothills of the Sierra Nevada Mountains and elevations range from 90 to about 400 feet. Although some CHARDONNAY is grown, mostly red varieties such as BARBERA, CABERNET SAUVIGNON, DOLCETTO, GRENACHE, MALBEC, MERLOT, MOURVEDRE, PETITIE SIRAH, SYRAH, and ZINFANDEL are planted on about 22,000 acres of vineyards.

Clevner *see* PINOT BLANC; PINOT NOIR

climat [klee-MAH] French for "climate," this Burgundian term refers to a specifically defined vineyard area, usually an individual field. Such a vineyard area is distinguished by various factors including soil, drainage, angle of the slope, bearing of the sun, and altitude. *See also* TERROIR.

Climate Regions of California A method for classifying wine climate regions that was developed in the 1930s at the UNIVERSITY OF CALIFORNIA, DAVIS by Professors A. J. Winkler and Maynard Amerine. This system is referred to variously as *degree days, heat summation method, Winkler Scale,* and *Regions I–V.* The method is based on the theory that no vine shoot growth occurs below 50°F and that each degree a day averages above 50°F is considered a *degree day.* For example, if during a 24-hour period the temperature ranges from 57 to 81°F, the average is 69°F, which is equivalent to 19 degree days (69 minus 50). The *heat summation* (sum of all the degree days between April 1 and October 31) of a growing region determines its classification, which is described in total degree days. There are five climate region classifications, which suggests that California has growing environments that are comparable to the various traditional winemaking regions throughout the world. **Climate Region I** (up to 2,500 degree days) is the coolest and is similiar to regions like CHAMPAGNE and CÔTE D'OR in France and the RHINE in Germany. It includes portions of the following areas: ANDERSON VALLEY, CARNEROS, EDNA VALLEY, Marin, MENDOCINO, MONTEREY, NAPA, RUSSIAN RIVER VALLEY, SANTA CLARA, SANTA CRUZ MOUNTAINS, and SONOMA. Suggested varieties for Region I include CABERNET SAUVIGNON, CHARDONNAY, PINOT NOIR, RIESLING, and SAUVIGNON BLANC. **Climate Region II** (from 2,500 to 3,000 degree days) is similiar to France's BORDEAUX region and includes portions of the following areas: ALEXANDER VALLEY, Anderson Valley, CHALK HILL, Edna Valley, Mendocino, Monterey, Napa, POTTER VALLEY, Russian River Valley, Santa Clara, and Sonoma. Suggested varieties include those for Region I plus MERLOT. **Climate Region III** (from 3,000 to 3,500 degree days) is equivalent to France's RHÔNE region and includes portions of the following areas: ALAMEDA, Alexander Valley, CONTRA COSTA, EL DORADO, KNIGHT'S VALLEY, LAKE, MCDOWELL VALLEY, Mendocino, Monterey, Napa, PASO ROBLES, PLACER, REDWOOD VALLEY, RIVERSIDE, SAN BENITO, Santa Clara, and Sonoma. Suggested varieties include CARIGNAN, RUBY CABERNET, Sauvignon Blanc, SÉMILLON, and ZINFANDEL. **Climate Region IV** (3,500 to 4,000 degree days) is similar to southern Spain and includes portions of the following areas: AMADOR, CALVERAS, El Dorado, Fresno, MERCED, Riverside, SACRAMENTO, San Diego, SAN JOAQUIN, and YOLO.

Suggested varieties include BARBERA, EMERALD RIESLING, Ruby Cabernet, and those used for PORT-style wines. **Climate Region V** (more than 4,000 degree days) is the hottest region and is similar to North Africa. It includes portions of the following areas: Amador, Calveras, Fresno, Kern, MADERA, Merced, Sacramento, San Bernardino, San Diego, San Joaquin, Stanislaus, and Tulare. Suggested varieties include SOUZÃO, TINTA MADERA, and VERDELHO. The authors of this approach have acknowledged that within these broader regions there are MESOCLI-MATES capable of growing other varieties. Other states, such as OREGON and WASHINGTON, also use this method to classify their regions.

clonal selection The practice of identifying and taking CUTTINGS from vines that embody the best of specific desired traits—such as aroma, flavor, ripening ability, YIELD, and/or vine health. The cuttings are then propagated through GRAFTING to other ROOTSTOCK. Clonal selection allows growers and winemakers to balance the objectives of their vineyard and winemaking practices. If flavor is the key objective, then selecting a PARENT VINE with superior flavor characteristics is cru-cial. If the growing area has a short season, then early ripening ability may be the key factor. Determining plant characteristics can take decades. In the United States, The Foundation Plant Material Service (FPMS) at UNIVERSITY OF CALIFORNIA, DAVIS assists with this process. In France, the principal organization involved with clonal selection is ENTAV-INRA. They've established a trademark that guarantees French CLONE authenticity and license a small number of nurseries around the world the right to propagate and sell grafted vines and BUDWOOD of trademarked materials. Although clonal selection is the approach taken by many winegrowers, it doesn't mean they use a single clone—many use a mix of clones to achieve their desired objectives. A process that bypasses clonal selection is called **mass selection**, where many vines are used as a source. This practice produces a vari-ety of characteristics, which means WINEGROWERS usually cannot achieve specific objectives as well as they can with clonal selection. However, some winemakers feel using mass selection produces more complex wines.

clone; cloning [KLOHN] In vineyard parlance, a clone is a plant that has been propagated asexually, usually by CUTTINGS or by GRAFT-ING. Cloning is done to reproduce plants with the distinctive traits of its PARENT VINE, such as high productivity, disease resistance, and/or better adaptability to environmental conditions. Within a given variety, PINOT NOIR for example, there are a large number of clones (subvari-eties) that differ from each other in aroma, flavor, ripening ability,

YIELD, and/or vine health. For instance, in Germany they use *Frühburgunder* for an early ripening version of Pinot Noir and *Spätburgunder* for a late ripening form. *See also* CLONAL SELECTION; CROSS; HYBRID.

clos [KLOH] French for "closed" or "enclosed," usually expanded to mean "enclosed field" or "enclosed vineyard." This term, generally associated with BURGUNDY, may not appear on a French wine label unless a vineyard by that name produces and bottles the wine—for example, CLOS DE LA ROCHE or CLOS DE VOUGEOT.

Les Clos [lay KLOH] Probably the most famous of the seven GRAND CRU vineyards in CHABLIS. Les Clos consists of just over 61 acres and sits between BLANCHOT and VALMUR. Some of the best wines of Chablis come from this vineyard.

Clos Blanc de Vougeot *see* VOUGEOT

Clos de Bèze *see* CHAMBERTIN

Clos de la Maréchale *see* PRÉMEAUX

Clos de la Perrière *see* FIXIN; VOUGEOT

Clos de la Roche AC [kloh duh lah RAWSH] The largest and the best GRAND CRU vineyard in the village of MOREY-SAINT-DENIS in the CÔTE DE NUITS district of France's BURGUNDY region. From its 41.8 acres of PINOT NOIR come some of the longest-lived red wines in Burgundy. Clos de la Roche boasts a cadre of good producers, and their wines are RICH, full-bodied (*see* BODY), and intense. They're best after about 10 years and can AGE for as long as 30 years.

Clos des Chênes *see* VOLNAY

Clos des Ducs *see* VOLNAY

Clos des Lambrays AC [kloh day lah*m*-BRAY] Elevated from PRE-MIER CRU status in 1981, this GRAND CRU vineyard is located in the village of MOREY-SAINT-DENIS in the CÔTE DE NUITS district of France's BURGUNDY region. Planted with PINOT NOIR, this 21.8-acre vineyard is one of the few Burgundian grands crus almost totally owned by one set of own-ers, the Saier brothers. The vineyards have been extensively replanted over the last few years, and the younger vines are currently producing LIGHT red wines. Older wines from vintages prior to the replanting indicate that this vineyard can produce RICH, full-bodied (*see* BODY) wines with good AGING capabilities.

Clos des Maréchaudes *see* CORTON

Clos des Meix *see* CORTON

Clos des Mouches, Le Clos des Mouches *see* BEAUNE

Clos des Ormes *see* MOREY-SAINT-DENIS

Clos des Réas *see* VOSNE-ROMANÉE AC

Clos de Tart AC [kloh duh TAHR] An 18.6-acre GRAND CRU vineyard located in the village of MOREY-SAINT-DENIS in the CÔTE DE NUITS district of France's BURGUNDY region. This vineyard is very unusual in that it is totally owned by the Mommessin family who purchased it in 1932 (most Burgundian grand cru vineyards have multiple owners). The vineyard is planted with PINOT NOIR and is capable of producing exceptional red wines.

Clos de Vougeot AC [kloh duh voo-ZHOH] A very famous GRAND CRU vineyard located in the COMMUNE of VOUGEOT in the CÔTE DE NUITS district of France's BURGUNDY region. The Cistercian monks first planted portions of the vineyard in the twelfth century, adding to it during the thirteenth and fourteenth centuries. Its 125 walled acres make it the largest single vineyard in the CÔTE D'OR. Only red wines from PINOT NOIR grapes are produced. Although Clos de Vougeot's reputation has been stellar in the past, today the wines can vary considerably—choosing a wine from this vineyard isn't easy. Clos de Vougeot is often used as the example of Burgundy's fragmented ownership patterns. There are approximately eighty owners of individual parcels within Clos de Vougeot, and the location of the parcels within the vineyard has an impact on the quality of the wine. The upper portion of the vineyard is capable of producing the best wines, followed by the middle section. While the lower portion has poor drainage and is the least effective land, better producers can coax excellent wines out of it. Conversely, there are examples of less-than-impressive wines from the upper section. The bottom line is that choosing a good Clos de Vougeot wine requires knowledge of both the producer and the vineyard parcel.

Clos du Chapitre *see* FIXIN

Clos du Roi; Le Clos du Roi *see* BEAUNE; CORTON

closed; closed-in *see* Glossary of Wine Tasting Terms, page 655

Clos Napoléon *see* FIXIN

Clos Saint-Denis AC [kloh sa*n* duh-NEE] A 16-acre GRAND CRU vineyard located in the village of MOREY-SAINT-DENIS in the CÔTE DE NUITS district of France's BURGUNDY region. In 1927 the village of Morey appended the name of this vineyard to its own (a widespread practice among Burgundian villages). The red wines, produced from PINOT NOIR, are not as full-bodied (*see* BODY) as those from the neighboring CLOS DE LA ROCHE grand cru, but they're fruitier and have more delicacy and finesse.

Clos Saint-Jacques *see* GEVREY-CHAMBERTIN AC

Clos Saint-Jean *see* CHASSAGNE-MONTRACHET AC

closures For eons, natural corks have been the closure of choice for most high-end wines. However, because of the problem with CORKED WINES (though the severity level of this predicament is controversial), several other closure alternatives are now being explored. Some wine producers are pioneering the move for change by using synthetic corks or manufactured hybrids (*see* CORKS) or SCREW CAPS. Few are willing to use the CROWN CAP that many sparkling wine producers use during TRIAGE or SECONDARY FERMENTATION. Another alternative is the glass closure, like Aloca Closure Systems' Vino-Seal (or Vino-Lok), which consists of a glass stopper (much like a decanter glass stopper) with flexible O-rings that provide a sterile seal. The glass stoppers are then covered with a tin or aluminum cover cap to give the look of a traditionally packaged wine bottle. Initially synthetic corks had the best reception but screw caps have become the most popular in the last few years. However, many wine producers are waiting before they decide to make changes because they're worried about consumer acceptance of these other alternatives for higher-quality wines. While these forays into alternative closures are proceeding, the Portuguese cork industry is attempting to reduce the rate of problematic corks by spending a great deal of money on new equipment, modernized production areas, and quality control improvements. Closures are sometimes referred to as **stoppers**.

cloudy; cloudiness *see* Glossary of Wine Tasting Terms, page 655

cloying *see* Glossary of Wine Tasting Terms, page 655

cluster The portion of the vine to which individual grapes are joined. Also called a *bunch*.

coarse *see* Glossary of Wine Tasting Terms, page 655

Coastal Region *see* SOUTH AFRICA

cocktail sherry *see* SHERRY

co-fermentation Term used to describe when two or more grape varieties are FERMENTED together in the same FERMENTATION CONTAINER. This is necessarily done with FIELD BLENDS where a single vineyard has several grape varieties that are intermixed. It's also done purposefully in areas like the CÔTE RÔTIE AC in the northern Rhone where SYRAH and a small amount of VIOGNIER have long been co-fermented. Winemakers in this area believe the resulting wines are improved through this technique.

Cognac [KOHN-yak; KON-yak; Fr. kaw-NYAK] Hailing from the town of Cognac and the surrounding areas in western France, this potent potable is the finest of all brandies (*see* BRANDY). The Cognac region is divided into six APPELLATIONS, which radiate outward from the town of Cognac from the most to least desirable. They are Grande Champagne, Petite Champagne, Borderies, Fins Bois, Bons Bois, and Bois Ordinaires. The higher desirability of the first two districts comes from their high-ACID grapes, made possible by chalky soil. Cognac is made primarily from TREBBIANO grapes (known in France as *Ugni Blanc* and *Saint-Émilion*) and double-distilled (*see* DISTILLATION) immediately after FERMENTATION. Freshly distilled Cognac is strong, sharp, and harsh and needs wood aging (usually in LIMOUSIN oak) to mellow it and enhance the aroma and flavor. Stars on a Cognac bottle's label vary in meaning from producer to producer, although three stars usually indicate longer aging and therefore higher quality than two stars or one star. Older Cognacs are labeled **V.S.** (very superior), **V.S.O.P.** (very superior old pale), and **V.V.S.O.P.** (very, very superior old pale). A Cognac label can no longer legally claim more than 7 years aging. It has been difficult for authorities to accurately keep track of Cognacs aged longer than this, so they've limited what producers may claim. The label terms **X.O.**, **Extra**, and **Reserve** usually indicate that a Cognac is the oldest put out by a producer. The term **Fine Champagne** on a Cognac label indicates that 60 percent of the grapes came from a superior grape-growing section of Cognac called *Grande Champagne*. A label designating *Grande Fine Champagne* proclaims that all the grapes for that Cognac came from that eminent area.

Colares DOC [kuh-LAH-rush] A small DENOMINACÃO DE ORIGEM CONTROLADA (DOC) area located northwest of Lisbon on the Atlantic coast. The vineyards are situated on a sandy plateau where the vines must be planted deep into the clay subsoil below. Because of the sandy soil, the vines are free of PHYLLOXERA and, therefore, have never been grafted to a different rootstock. Colares is best known for its red wines, which are made primarily from the Ramisco grape blended with Molar, Parreira Matias, and PERIQUITA. The wines are generally TANNIC and full-bodied (*see* BODY) and require considerable AGING. A small amount of white wine is made from ARINTO, Galego Dourado, and MALVASIA.

cold duck Originating in Germany, this pink sparkling wine is supposedly a mixture of CHAMPAGNE, SPARKLING BURGUNDY, and sugar. In practice, however, cold duck is simply pink and sparkling, and the wines used are often of inferior quality. The resulting potation is quite sweet with few other distinguishable characteristics. Its origin is traced back to the Bavarian practice of mixing bottles of previously opened champagne with cold sparkling Burgundy so that the champagne wouldn't be wasted. This mixture was called *kalte ende* ("cold end"); over the years, *ende* transliterated to *ente* ("duck").

cold maceration *see* MACERATION

cold soak *see* MACERATION

cold stabilization *see* STABILIZATION

Cole Ranch AVA A small California AVA located in MENDOCINO COUNTY southwest of the town of Ukiah and northeast of Boonville. There's a single, 61-acre vineyard in this 150-acre viticultural area. CABERNET SAUVIGNON is the dominant variety grown, along with small amounts of RIESLING and CHARDONNAY. Fetzer Vineyards puchases most of the grapes from this area. It has the distinction of being the smallest AVA in the United States.

colheita [cuhl-YAY-tah] Portuguese for "vintage." On the label of a bottle of PORT, "*colheita*" indicates that the bottle is not VINTAGE PORT but rather a TAWNY PORT harvested in the indicated year and aged in wood for a minimum of 7 years. Colheita port is sometimes called *dated port.*

collage [koh-LAHZH] French for "FINING."

Colli Albani DOC [KAWL-lee ahl-BAH-nee] A DOC area located in Italy's LATIUM region just south of Rome near Lake Albano. The area produces inexpensive white wines that vary in sweetness from DRY to DOLCE (sweet), and they can be STILL or SPUMANTE. The primary grapes used are MALVASIA and TREBBIANO.

Colli Berici DOC [KAWL-lee beh-REE-tchee] DOC located in the central section of the VENETO in northeast Italy. It extends south from the edge of the city of Vicenza to include the vineyards of twenty-eight small villages. A number of VARIETAL WINES are produced here—Cabernet from CABERNET SAUVIGNON and CABERNET FRANC, CHARDONNAY, GARGANEGA, MERLOT, Pinot Bianco (PINOT BLANC), Sauvignon (SAUVIGNON BLANC), FRIULANO, and Tocai Rosso. Many of these wines allow for up to 15 percent of other approved varieties to be used.

Colli Bolognesi DOC   [KAWL-lee baw-law-NYAY-zee] DOC located in the Appennine foothills southwest of Bologna in Italy's EMILIA-ROMAGNA region. It produces VARIETAL WINES made from BARBERA, CABERNET SAUVIGNON, MERLOT, Pignoletto, Pinot Bianco (PINOT BLANC), Riesling Italico (WELSCHRIESLING), and SAUVIGNON BLANC. Each of these varietals can have up to 15 percent of other approved grapes blended with them. There is also a BIANCO wine that's a blend of ALBANA and TREBBIANO grapes. The Bianco and Pignoletto wines are made in both AMABILE and DRY versions. The red Barbera and the white Sauvignon Blanc wines are more highly regarded than others. The Colli Bolognesi DOC has seven subzones, the names of which may be added to certain of the varietal wines: **Colline di Riosto**, **Colline Marconiane**, **Zola Predosa**, **Monte San Pietro**, **Colline di Oliverto**, **Terre di Monebudello**, and **Serravalle**.

Colli Euganei DOC [KAWL-lee eh-yoo-GAH-neh] A DOC area located southwest of Padova (Padua) in the south central part of Italy's VENETO region. The area produces VARIETAL WINES plus a ROSSO and a BIANCO. The varietal wines are Cabernet (from CABERNET SAUVIGNON and CABERNET FRANC), CHARDONNAY, MERLOT, Moscato (MUSCAT), Pinot Bianco (PINOT BLANC), and FRIULANO. The Rosso is made mainly from the widely planted Merlot but can include up to 40 percent of other approved varieties. The Bianco is made from GARGANEGA, Serprina (PROSECCO), FRIULANO, and other grapes.

Colli Fiorentini *see* CHIANTI DOCG

Colli Lanuvini DOC [KAWL-lee lah-noo-VEE-nee] Colli Lanuvini is located in Italy's LATIUM region just south of Lake Albano, which is south of Rome. The DOC zone makes white wines, both DRY and AMABILE, from MALVASIA and TREBBIANO.

Colline Pisane *see* CHIANTI DOCG

Collio DOC; Collio Goriziano DOC [KOH-lee-oh goh-ree-zee-AH-noh] Also known as *Collio Goriziano*, Collio is an important

DOC located in the FRIULI-VENEZIA GIULIA region in northeast Italy. It spreads out north and west of the city of Goriziano and borders Slovenia on the eastern edge. The area, which has a reputation for high-quality white wines, produces Collio Bianco, which is made from Ribolla Gialla (RIBOLLA), MALVASIA, and FRIULANO grapes, as well as VARIETAL WINES from CABERNET FRANC, CABERNET SAUVIGNON, CHARDONNAY, MALVASIA, MÜLLER-THURGAU, MERLOT, PICOLIT, Pinot Bianco (PINOT BLANC), Pinot Grigio (PINOT GRIS), Pinot Nero (PINOT NOIR), RIBOLLA, Riesling Italico (WELSCHRIESLING), Sauvignon (SAUVIGNON BLANC), Friulano, and Traminer (GEWÜRZTRAMINER). The wines from Collio are generally considered the best of the Friuli area.

Colli Orientali del Friuli DOC [KAWL-lee oh-ryayn-TAH-lee free-OO-lee] Colli Orientali del Friuli means "eastern hills of Friuli," which describes this area's location in the FRIULI-VENEZIA GIULIA region in northeastern Italy. It's east of Udine and northwest of the COLLIO DOC; part of the zone borders Slovenia. The wines are generally well regarded and considered right behind those of the Collio DOC in quality. The DOC covers 20 types of wines, 17 of which are VARIETALS. RAMANDOLO, a subzone known for sweet DESSERT WINES made from the VERDUZZO grape, was given DOCG status in 2001. There are two other subzones—**Cialla** and **Rosazzo**. Another of this area's unusual (as well as prized and expensive) dessert wines is made from the PICOLIT varietal. The other varietal wines are Cabernet (from Cabernet Sauvignon and Cabernet Franc), CABERNET SAUVIGNON, CABERNET FRANC, CHARDONNAY, MALVASIA, MERLOT, Pinot Bianco (PINOT BLANC), Pignolo, Pinot Grigio (PINOT GRIS), Pinot Nero (PINOT NOIR), Refosco dal Peducolo Rosso (REFOSCO), RIBOLLA, Riesling Renano (RIESLING), Sauvignon (SAUVIGNON BLANC), SCHIOPPETTINO, FRIULANO, Traminer Aromatico (GEWÜRZTRAMINER), and Verduzzo Friulano. All the varietal wines are required to use a minimum of 90 percent of the named varietal. This DOC also produces a ROSATO, which must be made with 90 percent Merlot.

Colli Piacentini DOC [KAWL-lee pyah-tchen-TEE-nee] In 1984 this DOC combined three previous DOC areas (Gutturnio dei Colli Piacentini, Monterosso Val d'Arda, and Trebbianino Val Trebbia) plus several other areas under this one designation. It's located south of Piacenza in the western part of Italy's EMILIA-ROMAGNA region. This DOC allows VARIETAL WINES made from BARBERA, BONARDA, MALVASIA, Orturgo, Pinot Nero (PINOT NOIR), and SAUVIGNON BLANC. Each of these varietal wines can have up to 15 percent of other approved grapes blended with them. They all have DRY and STILL or FRIZZANTE versions; some can be semisweet or sweet, some SPUMANTE. **Gutturnio** is a blend of Barbera and Bonarda that can be made DRY or sweet and also FRIZZANTE. Other approved blended wines are **Monterosso Val d'Arda**, **Trebbianino Val Trebbia**, and **Val Nure**—all are made from approved white varieties and can be dry or AMABILE (medium-sweet) and still, frizzante, or spumante.

Colli Senesi *see* CHIANTI DOCG

Collioure AC [kol-YOOR] Small APPELLATION that comprises the vineyards surrounding the villages of Collioure and Port-Vendres in France's LANGUEDOC-ROUSSILLON region along the Mediterranean near the Spanish border. Collioure AC produces full-bodied (*see* BODY) red wines based primarily on GRENACHE and blended with CARIGNAN, CINSAUT, MOURVÈDRE, and SYRAH.

Colomba Platino *see* CORVO

Colombar *see* COLOMBARD

Colombard; Columbard [KAHL-uhm-bahrd (Fr. kaw-law*n*-BAH*R*)] Highly productive white-wine grape that is one of the most widely planted vines in California, where it's called *French Colombard*. The California acreage expanded dramatically (mostly in the SAN JOAQUIN VALLEY) during the 1970s and early 1980s because of this grape's ability to grow in hot climates and still create decent wine. Colombard produces a crisp, moderately DRY, SPICY wine with FLORAL attributes and good ACIDITY. It's used extensively in blending—usually with CHENIN BLANC—to make JUG WINES and less-expensive SPARKLING WINES. The Colombard VARIETAL WINES, which are usually produced in cooler growing regions like MENDOCINO COUNTY and LAKE COUNTY, are not as popular as other California whites. In France's Charente district where it originated and was used mainly in the production of COGNAC, Colombard has largely been replaced by the Saint-Émilion (TREBBIANO) variety. It's still grown in parts of BORDEAUX, although the Colombard wines are generally uninteresting. Colombard is, however, making a comeback in France, mainly because French winemakers in some of the hotter growing areas have observed that they can produce quality wines from this grape by adopting some of California's more modern VINIFICATION techniques. Colombard is popular in South Africa, where it's called *Colombar*, and is now being grown in the hotter growing regions in Texas.

color *see* Glossary of Wine Tasting Terms, page 655

Colorado It might surprise some people that this high-altitude Rocky Mountain state is home to over thirty wineries and two AMERICAN VITICULTURAL AREAS. Most Colorado vineyards are located in the temperate river valleys and plateaus of Mesa and Delta counties in western Colorado. Here the vineyards are at the 4000- to 7000-foot level, which makes them some of the world's highest vineyards. Terror Creek Winery in Paonia stands at 6,417 feet above sea level, making it the highest *commercial* vineyard currently on record. True, there are a couple of vineyards at higher altitudes (the kingdom of Bhutan in the Himalayas at 7,200 feet and Colorado's Locke Mountain Vineyards, which is just over 6,500 feet), but they only make wine for private consumption. Colorado's **Grand Valley AVA** encompasses some 32,000 acres and is located on the western slope, east of Grand Junction in Mesa County. The **West Elks AVA** is located in eastern Delta County covering approximately 48,000 acres of the North Fork of the Gunnison Valley, extending from Bowie to Hotchkiss. Much like California coastal areas, the long hot days allow Colorado grapes to mature and ripen to proper sugar levels; cool nights help set the grape's ACID content. There are an estimated 450 acres of vineyards and, in order of popularity, the most widely planted grape varieties are CHARDONNAY, MERLOT, RIESLING, CABERNET SAUVIGNON, CABERNET FRANC, PINOT NOIR, and GEWÜRZTRAMINER.

Colorino [koh-loh-REE-noh] Red-grape VARIETY grown mainly in TUSCANY. Its dark red color and high TANNINS make it a good BLENDING partner for SANGIOVESE, particularly when added STRUCTURE is desired. Colorino is allowed in red wines from zones like CHIANTI DOCG, Colline Lucchesi DOC, MONTECARLO DOC, and VINO NOBILE DI MONTEPULCIANO DOCG.

Columbard *see* COLOMBARD

Columbia Gorge AVA APPELLATION established in July 2004 that encompasses 179,200 acres that lie on both sides of the Columbia River in Oregon and Washington. On the Oregon side, the area extends east to west from the town of Biggs Junction to Hood River and on the Washington side, it stretches from Goldendale to White Salmon. The Columbia Gorge AVA sits on the western border of the larger COLUMBIA VALLEY AVA. The climate is somewhat unique in this area as its location is blocked from the rains by Mount Adams and Mount Hood and the gorge itself is narrow and creates a bit of wind tunnel effect. So far CHARDONNAY and GEWÜRTRAMINER have received the most attention but BARBERA, CABERNET SAUVIGNON, CHENIN BLANC, MERLOT, PINOT

BLANC, PINOT GRIS, PINOT NOIR, SANGIOVESE, SAUVIGNON BLANC, SYRAH, VIOG-NIER and ZINFANDEL are also grown.

Columbia Valley AVA A very large AVA in south-central Washington and northern Oregon. The Columbia Valley AVA encompasses 1,152,000 acres, taking up almost a third of Washington State plus a small part of Oregon. Of this, approximately 29,000 acres are planted, including the smaller VITICULTURAL AREAS of HORSE HEAVEN HILLS, YAKIMA VALLEY, RED MOUNTAIN, and WALLA WALLA. Columbia Valley AVA represents 99 percent of Washington's vineyards. Because it's protected by the Cascade Mountains from the cool weather coming in from the Pacific Ocean, the Columbia Valley is the warmest growing area in the Pacific Northwest. Its growing areas range from Region I to Region III (*see* CLIMATE REGIONS OF CALIFORNIA). Because of the contrasting temperatures throughout the region, different grape varieties do well in various locations. This means that MERLOT, a warm-weather grape, and RIESLING, a cool-weather grape, both can ripen properly here. CABERNET SAUVIGNON, CHENIN BLANC, SAUVIGNON BLANC, and SÉMILLON are also grown, as are CONCORD and other VITIS LABRUSCA varieties. While there are a few wineries in the northern part of the Columbia Valley, almost all of them are in southern Washington nearer the Oregon border in the Yakima Valley and the Red Mountain and Walla Walla areas.

La Comarca de Falset *see* MONTSANT DO

Combe aux Moines *see* GEVREY-CHAMBERTIN

Les Combes *see* CORTON

Comblanchien *see* CÔTE DE NUITS

Commandaria *see* CYPRUS

commerciante [koh-mayr-CHAHN-tay] An Italian term for a producer (merchant) who works primarily with grapes or wines that are purchased before being bottled and sold.

commune [KAHM-myoon] A word used to describe a small administrative district, generally comprised of a village and the land (including vineyards) surrounding it.

complex; complexity *see* Glossary of Wine Tasting Terms, page 655

Complexa Red-wine grape grown primarily on Madeira island and used in making MADEIRA wines. It was created in the 1960s by crossing

CASTELÃO, Muscat Hamburg (*see* MUSCAT), and Tintinha. Complexa and TINTA NEGRA MOLE have become the prominent varieties for use in making Madeira, with Complexa providing deep color and lower tannins to the blend.

Comtes de Champagne *see* CHAMPAGNE

Conca de Barberà DO [KAWN-kuh deh bahr-BEH-rah] Located north of the PENEDÈS DO in Spain's CATALONIA area, this small DO was approved in 1989. It's in the middle of the neighboring DOs of COSTERS DEL SEGRE, PENEDÈS, and TARRAGONA, and has about 15,000 acres of vineyards. White grapes, mainly Viura (MACABEO) and PARELLADA, account for about two-thirds of the crop (down from a decade ago). Traditionally, much of what is grown here is sold off to CAVA DO producers in the Penedès area. The traditional wines in this area are reds and ROSÉS made from Garnacha Tinta (GRENACHE) and Ull de Lebre (TEMPRANILLO). However, things are changing as producers are recognizing the potential for this area. This is particularly true with TORRES, which is producing high-quality wine with CHARDONNAY and CABERNET SAUVIGNON grapes, as well as a blend made with Garnacha (GRENACHE), Garró, Samsó (CARIGNAN), and Monastrell (MOURVÈDRE). Other producers are joining in with blends of Chardonnay and Viura and of Cabernet Sauvignon, Merlot, and Ull de Lebre (TEMPRANILLO).

concentrate, grape *see* GRAPE CONCENTRATE

concentrated *see* Glossary of Wine Tasting Terms, page 655

Concord [KAHN-kord] Native American variety that is widely grown in the eastern states, particularly in New York, and in Michigan and Washington. Ephraim Bull first planted these native grape seeds in 1843 in his garden in Concord, Massachusetts—hence the name. The vine's beautiful blue-black grapes often appear to have been powdered with silver. They're most often used for jams, jellies, and unfermented juice and as table grapes. Concord wines aren't well regarded by most wine lovers because of their FOXY characteristics, which are often associated with members of this VITIS LABRUSCA species.

Condado de Huelva DO [kohn-DAH-doh day-WAYL-bah] DO located northwest of the JEREZ Y MANZANILLA DO in southern Spain. In the past, this area grew grapes that were shipped to the Jerez y Manzanilla area and eventually made into SHERRY; it also produced its own sherrylike wines. Because this style of wine isn't as popular as it once was, the number of vineyard acres has been reduced, and producers have shifted much of their production to DRY white wines.

Zalema is the primary grape used, but it's losing ground to higher-quality grapes like Palomino Fino (PALOMINO), Garrido Fino, and Moscatel (MUSCAT). Some sherry-style wines are still produced such as *Condado Palido* (a FINO style) and *Condado Viejo* (an OLOROSO style).

Condrieu AC [kawn-D*R*EE-yuh] An APPELLATION located near the village of Condrieu, south of CÔTE-RÔTIE in France's northern RHÔNE region. Condrieu AC produces only white wines made from VIOGNIER. These DRY, RICH wines have a perceptible spiciness and aromas and flavors reminiscent of apricots, peaches, and pears. They're very expensive because they're quite good and difficult to find.

Conegliano [koh-nehl-YAH-noh] A small city in the VENETO region and home of Italy's foremost ENOLOGY school and experimental VITICULTURE station (*Istituto Sperimentale per la Viticoltura*). An area around Conegliano, which is located about 35 miles north of Venice, is entitled the **Prosecco di Conegliano-Valdobbiadene DOC**. This DOC produces FRIZZANTE and SPUMANTE wines (chiefly from PROSECCO grapes) in styles that can range from DRY to AMABILE to DOLCE.

Conero *see* ROSSO CONERO

Connecticut Commercial wineries didn't get started in this state until 1978, when the Connecticut Winery Act was passed with the encouragement of Haight Winery. The state now has over ten wineries, most of which are located in the SOUTHEASTERN NEW ENGLAND AVA, which it shares with Massachusetts and Rhode Island. The few other wineries in the state are in the **West Connecticut Highlands AVA**, which encompasses a little over 1 million acres in the state's southwestern section. Although this region is the cooler of the two areas, it gains a warming influence from Long Island Sound, which runs along the state's southern edge. The most popular grapes here are HYBRIDS like VIDAL BLANC, SEYVAL BLANC, CHANCELLOR, CAYUGA, MARÉCHAL FOCH, and AURORA. VITIS VINIFERA varieties like CHARDONNAY, CABERNET SAUVIGNON, PINOT NOIR, MERLOT, CABERNET FRANC, and RIESLING are also grown.

confectionary *see* Glossary of Wine Tasting Terms, page 655

consejo regulador *see* DENOMINACIÓN DE ORIGEN

consorzio [kawn-SOHRD-zyoh] Local growers' associations found throughout Italy that supervise and control wine production, as well as promote and market the wine. Although these consortiums are voluntary, most producers join. The best-known *consorzio* is the Gallo Nero ("black rooster") of the CHIANTI CLASSICO region.

Constantia WO A demarcated South African wine ward (*see* SOUTH AFRICA) located on the fringes of Cape Town. This historic area is considered the birthplace of the South African wine industry. In the eighteenth and nineteenth centuries, this area was the source of sweet MUSCAT-based wines, the reputation of which rivaled those of the sweet wines from SAUTERNES and TOKAJI. Today area producers are making "Vin de Constance," a modern-day version of this famous wine. Constantia sits on a peninsula south of Cape Town that is cooled by the Atlantic Ocean on the south and east and by False Bay on the west. This cool climate lends itself to white wines more than to reds—CHARDONNAY, GEWÜRZTRAMINER, SAUVIGNON BLANC, SÉMILLON, and RIESLING get the most attention. However, red wines including CABERNET SAUVIGNON, MERLOT, and Shiraz (SYRAH) occasionally also get high praise. Groot Constantia Estate, founded in 1685, is South Africa's oldest winery.

consumption *see* Main Wine Producing Countries—Production and Consumption, page 688

cooked *see* Glossary of Wine Tasting Terms, page 655

cooking wine A wine labeled "cooking wine" is generally an inferior wine that would not be drunk on its own. It lacks distinction and flavor, and some have been known to be adulterated with salt. The rule of thumb when cooking with wine is only to use one you'd drink and to be sure the wine's flavor complements the food with which it's paired.

cooler *see* WINE COOLER

cooling wine *see* Temperatures for Serving Wine, page 641; Optimum Serving Temperatures by Wine Type, page 642

Coonawarra An important Australian wine-producing region with over 12,000 vineyard acres located in the Limestone Coast Zone of SOUTH AUSTRALIA. It's located around the town of Penola, a rather remote location about 240 miles southeast of the city of Adelaide, near the border of VICTORIA. Coonawarra was first planted with vineyards in 1890, but it wasn't until the 1950s that the quality of this region's grapes began to be recognized. The highly regarded red wines from Coonawarra (which means "honeysuckle" in Aborigine) are the result of the cool climate and the terra rossa over limestone soil. The two most popular red grapes (and the ones that make this area's reputation) are CABERNET SAUVIGNON, which produces some of Australia's best VARIETAL WINES, and Shiraz (SYRAH). Small amounts of PINOT NOIR, MERLOT, and CABERNET FRANC are also grown. RIESLING is the most appreciated white variety, followed by CHARDONNAY, Traminer (GEWÜRTZTRAMINER), and SAUVIGNON BLANC. However, the most widely planted grape is Chardonnay, much of which goes into SPARKLING WINES.

cooperage; cooper [KOO-per-ihj] 1. The work, as well as the place of business of a **cooper**, a craftsman who makes or repairs BARRELS or CASKS. 2. Cooperage also describes the articles (barrels, etc.) made by a cooper. 3. In wineries, cooperage refers to the wine storage capacity in such containers.

cooperativa *see* CANTINA SOCIALE

cooperative A winery or cellar that's jointly owned and operated by a group of small producers. A cooperative is usually started in an effort to spread the cost of facilities, equipment, and marketing among the participants. Europe in particular has hundreds of cooperatives, some of which have grown into huge organizations. For many small producers, these cooperatives continue to be extremely important because it would be prohibitively expensive for each one to upgrade to the latest technology and produce wine that's competitive with the rest of the world. In Italy, a cooperative is called a CANTINA SOCIALE or *cantina cooperativa;* in Germany, it's called a WEINGÄRTNERGENOSSEN-SCHAFT, WINZERGENOSSENSCHAFT, or ZENTRALKELLEREI. The French term is *cave cooperative.*

copita [koh-PEE-tah] A traditional glass for tasting sherry that originated in Jerez, Spain. *See also* Glassware, page 647

Corbières AC [kawr-BYAYR] District located in Frances' LANGUEDOC-ROUSSILLON region that was finally upgraded from VDQS to APPELLATION D'ORIGINE CONTRÔLÉE status in 1986. This is a large area with diverse growing conditions—because of this it has been divided into eleven unofficial zones in a move toward defining it more distinctly. It's possible that in the future these will be established as officially recognized subzones or APPELLATIONS in their own right. The best of these subzones are Alaric, Boutenac, Lézignan, Sigean, and Termenes. In 2005 one of these subzones, **Boutenac**, was granted APPELLATION status as **Corbières-Boutenac AC**. This sub-appellation was established for red wines consisting of from 30 to 50 percent CARIGNAN blended with a maximum 30 percent SYRAH and a maximum of 70 percent of GRENACHE and SYRAH combined. Alcohol levels for these wines must be at least 12 percent. A huge majority of the wines produced in Corbières are red, produced largely from Carignan blended with small amounts of CINSAUT, Grenache, MOURVÈDRE, and Syrah. Small quantities of ROSÉ are made from these same red varieties; a miniscule amount of white wine is produced mainly from BOURBOULENC, CLAIRETTE, GRENACHE BLANC, and MACABEO. The red wines are considered best and, since the introduction of CARBONIC MACERATION, they're BIG and full-bodied (*see* BODY) yet have a fruitiness that doesn't exist in the older traditionally made wines.

cordon Somewhat permanent extension of a grapevine's trunk. Occasionally cordons are removed during pruning if they interfere with the proper growth of the vine but most are left intact. Cordons are two years or older and are generally seen positioned horizontally along a trellis wire.

Cordisco *see* MONTEPULCIANO

Corgoloin *see* CÔTE DE NUITS

cork *see* CORKS

corkage [CORK-ihj] A fee charged by restaurants to open and serve a bottle of wine brought to the establishment by the patron. A quick call to the restaurant will confirm the amount of the corkage fee. Some restaurants charge a lower fee if the patron's wine is not on the restaurant's wine list, such as might be the case with an older or particularly distinctive wine.

corked wine Wine professionals estimate that 2 to 5 percent of wines are ruined because of faulty corks, which generate the chemical compound 2,4,6-Trichloroanisole (also called *TCA* or *246-TCA*) that humans can perceive at levels as low as 30 ppt (parts per trillion). High levels of this compound produce an unmistakably putrefying odor and flavor that many compare to that of moldy, wet cardboard or newspapers. At moderate levels, a corked wine takes on a musty quality; at low levels, it seems AUSTERE and lacking in FRUIT. *See also* CORKS; **METHOXY-DIMETHYLPYRAZINE**, Glossary of Wine Tasting Terms (CORKED), page 655

corks Corks are made from the bark of a type of oak tree (*Quercus suber*) found in Spain and Portugal. Once a tree has matured, which takes from 16 to 25 years, the bark can be stripped every 9 years without harming the tree. The stripped bark is then processed and graded. Cork lengths generally range from 1¼ to 2¼ inches, although longer corks can be specially ordered. Fine wines with good aging potential are typically sealed with longer, higher-quality corks; wines made for early consumption are often sealed with shorter, lower-quality corks. Although corks have long been associated with fine wine (versus screw-top lids for JUG WINE), much controversy surrounds their use. True, corks have many desirable attributes—they're very light, they compress enough to be forced into the neck of a wine bottle (and then swell back to fill the neck tightly), and their honeycomb texture grips the bottle snugly, forming a tight seal. When wine is properly stored on its side the cork stays moist and fully expanded, thereby providing an airtight seal. However, if a wine isn't suitably stored, a cork can dry out and leak, spoiling the wine. Additionally, faulty corks generate the chemical compound 2,4,6-Trichloroanisole (TCA) which produces a musty, moldy character that ruins a wine, in which case it's referred to as CORKED WINE. Some professional tasters estimate that 2 to 5 percent of wines are ruined because of defective corks, and many feel the problem is escalating. Many leading authorities are suggesting that it's time to reconsider the screw-cap, arguing that it preserves the wine just as well and would eliminate many of the cork-attendant problems, not to mention the need for corkscrews (*see* Wine Openers, page 639). Another answer to natural cork issues is the synthetic "cork," which has made great progress in the last decade. **SupremeCorq**, made from food-grade thermoplastic elastomeric material, has become the leader in this market. It comes in natural, beige, and tan colors, as well as vivid shades of blue, green, purple, tangerine, and yellow, which make it obvious that it isn't the real thing. **Neocork Technologies**, a Napa company funded by Beringer, Clos du Bois, Kendall-Jackson, Robert Mondavi, and Sebastiani, is a recent newcomer to the synthetic cork market. Because synthetic cork doesn't need to be kept moist to retain its seal, proponents claim that wine can be stored upright. On the other hand, critics point out that these "plastic corks" haven't yet demonstrated their viability over the long term. **Altec**, made by the French company Sabaté SA, is a closure made from both synthetic and natural materials. It uses natural cork suberin particles (a waxy waterproof substance, which is less suscep-tible to TCA) combined with Sabaté's proprietary polymer particles (called "microspheres") and an FDA-approved binder that's free of plasticizing additives. Proponents like these manufactured hybrid corks because they're closer to natural cork closures with little of the TCA risk. Meanwhile, the Portuguese cork industry is spending lots of money on new equipment, modernized production areas, and quality-control improvements in an attempt to lower the ratio of cork-related problems. *See also* CLOSURES.

corkscrew *see* Wine Openers, page 639

Cornas AC [kor-NAH] APPELLATION that sits south of the better-known HERMITAGE AC in France's northern RHÔNE region. Fast developing a following of its own, Cornas AC produces only red wines made from the SYRAH variety. These wines are some of the biggest, most full-bodied (*see* BODY) wines made in the region. Other growing districts in the Rhône cut the boldness of their wines by blending in other red or white varieties, but Cornas does not. From better vintages, the wines can be dark red, almost black, with an intense fruitiness and plenty of TANNINS. Some producers are making wines in a style that is accessible earlier, but the more traditionally made wines can require 5 to 10 years of AGING before they SOFTEN and become fully enjoyable.

Corse *see* CORSICA

Corsica [KOHR-sih-kuh] Large Mediterranean island located southwest of the Italian mainland and just north of Sardinia. Corsica is a French DÉPARTEMENT and has four main APPELLATIONS—**Vin de Corse AC**, which covers most of the island's wines; the smaller AJACCIO AC (at the island's west side); PATRIMONIO AC, which is on the northwestern side; and **Muscat Du Cap Corse AC**, an appellation covering the sweet VIN DOUX NATUREL wines made from Muscat Blanc à Petits Grains (MUSCAT). The Vin de Corse AC has five small subzones or CRUS, which can append their name to the label. They are Calvi, Coteaux du Cap Corse, Figari, Porto Vecchio, and Sartène. Most of the wine is red and ROSÉ; the red grapes used include CARIGNAN, CINSAUT, GRENACHE, Nielluccio (SANGIOVESE), and Sciacarello. The main white grape is VERMENTINO, which is usually blended with Ugni Blanc (TREBBIANO). Some producers are trying the popular French varieties like CABERNET FRANC, CABERNET SAUVIGNON, CHARDONNAY, CHENIN BLANC, and MERLOT.

Cortese [kohr-TEH-zeh; kohr-TAY-zee] A white-wine grape grown in northwest Italy, primarily in PIEDMONT and in parts of LOMBARDY. Cortese generally produces good-quality wines with high ACIDITY and an aroma and flavor that's DELICATE, fruity, and sometimes citrusy. Much of this wine is sold as *Cortese del Piemonte*. Higher-quality wines come from the DOCG of GAVI, with those known as *Gavi di Gavi* being among the most expensive Italian whites. Other Cortese wines come from the DOCS of Colli Tortonesi and Cortese dell'Alto Monferrato.

Cortese di Gavi *see* GAVI DOCG

Corton AC [kor-TAW*N*] A famous GRAND CRU whose vineyards are located on the Montagne de Corton, a vast hill rising above ALOXE-CORTON, an important wine-producing village at the northern end of the CÔTE DE BEAUNE district in France's BURGUNDY region. Although usually associated with Aloxe-Corton, the Corton appellation is also part of the villages of LADOIX-SERRIGNY and PERNAND-VERGELESSES. The Corton grand cru ranking is only for red wines made from PINOT NOIR. Certain vineyards are also permitted to produce white wines made from CHARDONNAY, PINOT BLANC, and PINOT GRIS and to use the name of the other grand cru in this area, CORTON-CHARLEMAGNE. Vineyards not authorized to produce white wines under the Corton-Charlemagne name can produce it under Corton, but the wines are not entitled to grand cru status. There are twenty-eight individually named vineyards that may label their wines with Corton by itself or use Corton followed by the individual vineyard name such as *Corton Bressandes* or *Corton Clos du Roi*. Blended wines using grapes from two or more of these vineyards may only use the designation "*Corton.*" The twenty-eight vineyards are **Clos des Cortons**, **Les Bressandes**, **Le Meix Lallemand**, **Les Chaumes de la Voirosse**, **Les Chaumes** (the previous two are usually grouped as one vineyard referred to as Les Chaumes), **Les Combes**, **Le Corton**, **Les Fiètres**, **Les Grèves**, **Les Languettes**, **Les Maréchaudes**, **Clos des Maréchaudes** (usually included with Les Maréchaudes), **Clos des Meix**, **Les Paulands**, **Les Perrières**, **Le Village** (usually included with Les Perrières), **Les Pougets**, **Les Renardes**, **Le Clos du Roi**, **La Vigne au Saint**, **Les Carrières**, **Les Grandes Lolières**, **Basses Mourottes**, **Hautes Mourottes** (the previous two are often referred to as **Les Mourottes**), **Les Moutottes**, **Le Rognet et Corton**, **La Toppe au Vert**, and **Les Vergennes**. The Corton AC red wines are usually regarded as the best and the longest-lived of the Côte de Beaune.

Cortona DOC [kohr-TOH-nah] A DOC zone located in the TUSCANY region just north of the VINO NOBILE DI MONTEPULCIANO DOCG and close to the Tuscany-UMBRIA border. Cortona allows VARIETAL wines containing a minimum of 85 percent of the variety and is establishing a name for CHARDONNAY, MERLOT, and SYRAH. This area also produces VIN SANTO from TREBBIANO, GRECHETTO, and/or MALVASIA.

Corton-Charlemagne AC [kor-TAW*N* shah*r*-luh-MAH*N*-yuh] A celebrated GRAND CRU that produces CHARDONNAY-based white wines, which are considered by many as second only to those from the most famous white-wine grand cru LE MONTRACHET. The Corton-Charlemagne vineyards are located high on the Montagne de Corton, a vast hill-rising above the village of ALOXE-CORTON. Although the individual vineyards of **Les Pouget**, **Les Languettes**, **Le Corton**, **Les Renardes**, **Basses Mourottes**, **Hautes Mourottes** (the previous two are often referred to as **Les Mourottes**), and **Le Rognet et Corton** are permitted to produce white wines and use the Corton-Charlemagne AC name, they currently are planted only with PINOT NOIR and produce red wines as part of the grand cru CORTON AC. In actuality, the white wines come from only two vineyards, **En Charlemagne** and **Le Charlemagne**, which make up what is commonly referred to as Corton-Charlemagne. The story goes that these vineyards were planted with red-wine grapes until the eighth century when the Emperor Charlemagne's wife, tired of seeing red stains in his white beard, nagged him until he ripped out the vines and replanted them with white-wine grapes. Although the Corton-Charlemagne AC resides mainly in the village of Aloxe-Corton, it also extends into the villages of LADOIX-SERRIGNY and PERNAND-VERGELESSES. These full-bodied (*see* BODY) white wines are long-lived and thought to be at their best after 7 to 8 years of AGING.

Coruche *see* RIBATEJO DOC

Corvina [kohr-VEE-nuh] This Italian red-wine grape is the principal ingredient in the VALPOLICELLA and BARDOLINO wines of the VENETO region. In both of these wines, Corvina is blended with Rondinella and Molinara to produce light-colored, light-BODIED (*see* BODY) wines that are characterized by a tart, cherry flavor and a slightly bitter almond character. This grape is also called *Corvina Veronese* and *Cruina*.

Corvinone [kohr-VEE-noh-neh] Red-wine grape grown in Italy's VENETO region. Long thought to be a clone of CORVINA, it's now regarded as a separate variety. As such, Corvinone can now be used as a substitute for Corvina in the VALPOLICELLA DOC wines, where traditionally Corvina was required to make up from 40 to 80 percent of the grape varieties used. However, Corvinone may never make up more than 50 percent of the blend. In the BARDOLINO DOC, it may make up no more than 10 percent of varieties used in the DOC wines.

cosecha [koh-SAY-chah] Spanish for "harvest" or "crop."

Costers del Segre DO This DO, which was established in 1988, is located in and around the city of Lerida, west of Barcelona in the CATALONIA region in northeastern Spain. The only wines of consistently high quality come from Ramait, a wine estate owned by Codorníu, the giant SPARKLING WINE firm located in PENEDÈS.

Costières de Nîmes AC [kaws-TYEH*R* duh NEEM] Formerly called **Costières du Gard AC**, this large APPELLATION is located in France's LANGUEDOC-ROUSSILLON region between Nîmes and Montpellier. It produces red, white, and ROSÉ wines. White wines, made mainly from BOURBOULENC, CLAIRETTE, GRENACHE BLANC, and Ugni Blanc (TREBBIANO), make up only about 5 percent of the production. A small amount of rosé wine is made, but the majority is red—both are produced from CARIGNAN, CINSAUT, GRENACHE, MOURVÈDRE and SYRAH.

Costières du Gard AC *see* COSTIÈRES DE NÎMES AC

Cosumnes River AVA This VITICULTURAL AREA was established in August 2006. Its 54,700 acres are located in the northwestern section of the larger LODI AVA, that's located between Sacramento and Stockton in northern California. Of these, about 3,500 acres are planted with vines. Because of a maritime environment, it's cooler than other sections of the Lodi AVA. Therefore, varieties like CHARDONNAY, PINOT GRIS, SAUVIGNON BLANC, and VIOGNIER are popular (compared to a predominance of red grape in most of Lodi.) Some CABERNET SAUVIGNON, MERLOT, and SYRAH are also grown.

Cot *see* MALBEC

côte; côtes; coteau; coteaux [KOHT; koh-TOH] French terms meaning "slope" or "slopes" that are often used as prefixes to French growing areas. *Côtes* is the plural of *côte; coteaux,* the plural of *coteau.* The use of these terms relates to the belief that hillside vineyards are superior for grape growing. The famous area in BURGUNDY, CÔTE D'OR, means "slope of gold."

La Côte [lah KOHT] This is one of the three main growing areas in the Swiss canton of VAUD. It's located between Geneva and Lausanne on the sloping northern shore of Lake Geneva. La Côte is chiefly a white-wine area, and CHASSELAS (locally known as Dorin) is the dominant grape. The best wines come from the areas around Féchy, Luins, Perroy, Montsur-Rolle, and Vinzel.

coteau; coteaux *see* CÔTE

Coteaux Champenois AC *see* CHAMPAGNE

Coteaux d'Aix-en-Provence AC [koh-toh dehks ahn proh-VAH*N*S] APPELLATION, elevated from VDQS in 1985, that is located around the French city of Aix-en-Provence, northeast of Marseille. Red and

ROSÉ wines are made from CABERNET SAUVIGNON, CINSAUT, GRENACHE, MOURVÈDRE, and SYRAH; white wines are made from CLAIRETTE, GRENACHE BLANC, SAUVIGNON BLANC, SÉMILLON, and Ugni Blanc (TREBBIANO). Rosé wines make up over half the production followed by red wines and a very few white wines.

Coteaux de l'Aubance AC [koh-toh duh loh-BAH*N*S] APPELLATION that is located south of Angers on the river Aubance in the center of France's LOIRE region. It produces limited amounts of white wine, in varying degrees of sweetness, from CHENIN BLANC.

Coteaux du Languedoc AC [koh-toh deu LAH*N*G-dahk] Large APPELLATION in southern France that encompasses the vineyards of over 160 different COMMUNES and stretches from near Montpellier to Narbonne in the LANGUEDOC-ROUSSILLON region. This huge area has a number of named CRUS, TERROIRS, and subzones that have been identified as providing better quality wines than standard Coteaux du Languedoc AC wines and so they're allowed to add their name to the label. Of these, LA CLAPE, **Montpeyroux**, and **Pic Saint-Loup** produce some of the best wines. The reds and rosés are made from CARIGNAN, CINSAUT, GRENACHE, MOURVÈDRE, and SYRAH. White wines are made from BOURBOULENC, CLAIRETTE, Grenache Blanc, MARSANNE, Picpoul, ROLLE, and ROUSSANNE. Within Coteaux du Languedoc AC are two smaller appellations—FAUGÈRES AC and SAINT-CHINIAN AC—whose names also appear on the label.

Coteaux du Layon AC; Coteaux du Layon-Villages AC [koh-toh deu leh-YAW*N*] APPELLATIONS located south of Angers along the river Layon in the ANJOU district of France's LOIRE region. They produce only white wines (usually semisweet or sweet) from CHENIN BLANC grapes. The *villages* appellation applies to seven villages—**Beaulieu-sur-Layon**, **Chaume**, **Faye-d'Anjou**, **Rablay-sur-Layon**, **Rouchefort-sur-Loire**, **Saint-Aubin-de-Luigné**, and **Saint-Lambert-du-Lattay**. All may append their own name to the label if their wines have at least 1 percent more alcohol than the standard appellation (a minimum of 12 percent versus 11 percent). The grapes in this area are subject to BOTRYTIS CINEREA on occasion. When it strikes, the resulting wines can be RICH, intensely sweet, and luscious. BONNEZEAUX AC and QUARTS DE CHAUME AC are two small appellations located within the Coteaux du Layon area that are noted for their superb DESSERT WINES.

Coteaux du Lyonnais AC [koh-toh deu lee-oh-NAY] APPELLATION that is located around the city of Lyon at the southern end of France's BURGUNDY region just south of the vineyards of BEAUJOLAIS. Upgraded from VDQS status in 1984, it produces mostly light red wines and small amounts of ROSÉ and white wines. The red wines are made from GAMAY and are similiar in style to those from neighboring Beaujolais. The white wines are made from CHARDONNAY, ALIGOTÉ, and MUSCADET.

Coteaux du Tricastin AC [koh-toh deu tree-kahss-TAN] Area that is noteworthy because it was established only in the 1960s in an effort to accommodate French winemakers fleeing from North Africa after several nations there gained independence. This fairly large APPELLATION is located in the southern portion of France's RHÔNE region, north of Bollene. It produces mainly red and some ROSÉ wines from CARIGNAN, CINSAUT, GRENACHE, MOUVÈDRE, and SYRAH. The red wines, which have historically been rather light, are gaining BODY as more Syrah is being planted and used in the BLEND. Small amounts of white wine are produced mainly from BOURBOULENC and MARSANNE.

Coteaux Varois AC [koh-toh vah-RWAH] Coteaux Varois is a large APPELLATION located west of the CÔTES DE PROVENCE AC in France's Provence region. Standard grapes for making red and ROSÉ wines are CARIGNAN, CINSAUT, GRENACHE, and MOURVÈDRE, but plantings of CABERNET SAUVIGNON and SYRAH have been improving the quality of the red wines, giving them more BODY and flavor. Minimal amounts of white wine are made from CLAIRETTE, GRENACHE BLANC, and Ugni Blanc (TREBBIANO).

Côte Blonde *see* CÔTE-RÔTIE

Côte Brune *see* CÔTE-RÔTIE

Côte Chalonnaise [koht shah-law-NEHZ] A winegrowing area located just south of the CÔTE D'OR in France's BURGUNDY region. This area has no APPELLATION of its own, and unless the wines are part of one of the five villages entitled to an individual appellation, the wines go into one of the basic Burgundy appellations such as BOURGOGNE AC or BOURGOGNE PASSE-TOUT-GRAIN AC. The five villages with AC status start in the north with Bouzeron and its BOURGOGNE ALIGOTÉ DE BOUZERON AC, which produces white wines from the ALIGOTÉ variety. The rest of the villages—RULLY, MERCUREY, GIVRY, and MONTAGNY—produce red wines from PINOT NOIR and white wines from CHARDONNAY. Mercurey is the largest appellation of the area and has a high enough profile that there is some pressure to rename formally the Côte Chalonnaise to what occasionally is used now, Région de Mercurey. The VINS MOUSSEUX of the Côte Chalonnaise, which fall under the CRÉMANT DE BOURGOGNE AC designation, are a specialty of the area and considered quite good by many sparkling wine enthusiasts.

Côte de Beaune; Côte de Beaune AC; Côte de Beaune-Villages AC [koht duh BOHN] The southern half of BURGUNDY's famous CÔTE D'OR, which contains the GRAND CRU, PREMIER CRU, and village vineyards responsible for many of the renowned Burgundy wines. The Côte de Beaune includes twenty different villages, seventeen with their own APPELLATIONS—ALOXE-CORTON, AUXEY-DURESSES, BEAUNE, BLAGNY, CHASSAGNE-MONTRACHET, CHOREY-LÈS-BEAUNE, LADOIX-SER-RIGNY, MEURSAULT, MONTHÉLIE, PERNAND-VERGELESSES, POMMARD, PULIGNY-MONTRACHET, SAINT-AUBIN, SAINT-ROMAIN, SANTENEAY, SAVIGNY-LÈS-BEAUNE, and VOLNAY. Three other villages—Cheilly-lès-Maranges, Dezize-lès-Maranges, and Sampigny-lès-Maragnes—are grouped in a separate appellation, MARANGES AC. The Côte de Beaune area is well known for both its red wines, made from PINOT NOIR grapes, and white wines, made from CHARDONNAY. Even though the Côte de Beaune produces superb red wines, led by the grand cru CORTON, they are somewhat overshadowed by the red wines from the CÔTE DE NUITS in the northern half of the Côte d'Or. However, the white wines from the Côte de Beaune area are considered to be the best in the world. The superstars are the wines from the grands crus of MONTRACHET, BÂTARD-MONTRACHET, BIENVENUE-BÂTARD-MONTRACHET, CHEVALIER-MONTRACHET, CORTON-CHARLE-MAGNE, and CRIOTS-BÂTARD-MONTRACHET, and from the numerous outstanding premiers crus vineyards. Wines from individual villages like Meursault also have stellar reputations. In addition to the appellations for grands crus, premiers crus, and the individual villages, there are two others—Côte de Beaune AC and Côte de Beaune-Villages AC. **Côte de Beaune AC** is an appellation for four vineyard sites, located on a hill above the town of Beaune, that don't qualify for higher-quality appellations. **Côte de Beaune-Villages AC** is an appellation for wines from sixteen of the area's villages (Aloxe-Corton, Beaune, Pommard, and Volnay are exempted). This appellation applies to wines BLENDED from the various villages, and it's used by villages that are not well known and benefit from using the better-known Côte de Beaune-Villages AC on their labels. The area has a famous vineyard owner HOSPICES DE BEAUNE, a charitable organization that was founded in 1443. *See also* HAUTES-CÔTES DE BEAUNE; BEAUNE.

Côte de Brouilly AC [koht duh broo-YEE] One of the ten premier growing areas with its own APPELLATION (called CRU) in France's BEAU-JOLAIS region. It's located upslope from the BROUILLY AC on Mont de Brouilly, where an annual pilgrimage is made each September to the

Notre-Dame du Raisin (Our Lady of the Grape) chapel at the summit to ask protection for the coming harvest. These fruity wines, made from GAMAY grapes that tend to get more sunlight and therefore become riper, are more full-bodied (*see* BODY) and CONCENTRATED than those of Brouilly and some of the other Beaujolais cru. They have the highest minimum alcohol level (10.5 percent) in Beaujolais, which isn't hard to achieve because of the high sugar content of the fully ripened grapes. Côte de Brouilly AC wines can AGE well for 2 to 3 years. The acreage of this AC is smaller, making the wines more difficult to find than those from Brouilly.

Côte de Léchet *see* CHABLIS

Côte de Nuits; Côte de Nuits AC [koht duh NWEE] The Côte de Nuits makes up the northern half of Burgundy's famous CÔTE D'OR and contains the GRAND CRU, PREMIER CRU, and village vineyards responsible for many of the renowned red BURGUNDY wines. PINOT NOIR is the grape of choice in this region, although minute amounts of white wine are produced from CHARDONNAY, PINOT BLANC, and PINOT GRIS. The Côte de Nuits, which takes its name from the village of NUITS SAINT-GEORGES, is made up of numerous villages, including eight that have their own APPELLATIONS—CHAMBOLLE-MUSIGNY, FIXIN, GEVREY-CHAMBERTIN, MARSANNAY, MOREY-SAINT-DENIS, Nuits Saint-Georges, VOSNE-ROMANÉE, and VOUGEOT. The villages of **Brochon**, **Comblanchien**, **Corgoloin**, **Prémeaux**, and **Fixin** can bottle their wines under the designation **Côte de Nuits-Villages AC**. The quality of the red wines from the seven village appellations and from the Côte de Nuits-Villages AC is generally quite high. However, the grand cru and premier cru vineyards have created this area's esteemed reputation. The grands crus include famous names like BONNES MARES, CHAMBERTIN, CHABERTIN-CLOS DE BÈZE, CLOS DE ROCHE, CLOS DE VOUGEOT, GRANDS ÉCHEZEAUX, MUSIGNY, RICHEBOURG, ROMANÉE-CONTI, and LÂ TACHE. Most wine lovers agree that these vineyards produce some of the very best red wines in the world. *See also* HAUTES-CÔTES DE NUITS.

Côte des Blancs *see* CHAMPAGNE

Côte de Sézanne *see* CHAMPAGNE

Côte d'Or [koht DOR] The name of this very famous area in France's BURGUNDY region means "slope of gold." It's said that the name comes from the golden color of the vineyard-covered hills during autumn, not from the fact that the wines are so expensive. The Côte d'Or *is* Burgundy to many people. For all its notoriety, the Côte d'Or is rather small—just over 30 miles in length and measuring about 1½ miles at its widest point and only a few hundred yards wide at its narrowest. The Côte d'Or runs from the outskirts of Dijon in the north to just past SANTENAY in the south. It divides neatly into two parts—the CÔTE DE BEAUNE in the south and CÔTE DE NUITS in the north. The Côte de Nuits is famous for its red wines, while the Côte de Beaune, although it also produces superb red wines, is more celebrated for its white wines. The area's red wines are based on PINOT NOIR; the white wines are based on CHARDONNAY. The Côte d'Or contains numerous GRAND CRU and PREMIER CRU vineyards that turn out some of the greatest wines in the world, which, because of the limited vineyard area, are extremely high priced. This list of famous wines includes BONNES MARES, CHAMBERTIN, CLOS DE VOUGEOT, CORTON-CHARLEMAGNE, MONTRACHET, ROMANÉE-CONTI, and LA TÂCHE. These grand cru vineyards are part of the many villages that produce wine in their own right under their village or communal APPELLATIONS such as CHAMBOLLE-MUSIGNY, GEVREY-CHAMBERTIN, MEURSAULT, MOREY-SAINT-DENIS, and PULIGNY-MONTRACHET. Wines that don't qualify for grand cru, premier cru, or the individual village appellations may fit into either the CÔTE DE BEAUNE-VILLAGES AC or the CÔTE DE NUITS-VILLAGES AC. If not, then they may simply fall into one of the general regional appellations such as BOURGOGNE AC or BOURGOGNE PASSE-TOUT-GRAIN AC.

Côte Roannaises AC [koht roh-ah-NEHZ] A French APPELLATION located in the upper LOIRE, northwest of the city of Lyon and around the town of Roanne. Côte Roannaises produces LIGHT red and ROSÉ wines made from GAMAY with some PINOT NOIR. The wines are similiar in style to those from Beaujolais.

Côte-Rôtie AC [koht roh-TEE] The most northerly and one of the oldest APPELLATIONS in France's RHÔNE region. Its name means "roasted slope," and it consists of 300 acres of *sunbaked* vineyards, most of which are located on the steep hillside above the village of Ampuis near the town of Vienne, south of Lyon. The vineyards are built on terraces so narrow and steep that tending and harvesting the vineyards must be done manually. There are two sections that produce the best wines—one with lighter-colored soil called **Côte Blonde** and one with darker soil called **Côte Brune**. Legend has it that Maugiron, a nobleman in this area, gave one of the two sections to his blond daughter and the other section to his brunette daughter and that over time the two sections took on the traits of their respective owners. Côte-Rôtie produces only red wines made from SYRAH, with up to 20 percent of the white grape VIOGNIER in the blend. The wines are noted for their exotic fragrance, deep color, RICH, spicy flavor, and full BODY. Most of the better Côte-Rôtie wines will age easily for 10 or more years.

côtes *see* CÔTE

Côtes d'Auvergne VDQS [koht doh-VERN-yuh] This VDQS area, which produces red and ROSÉ wines, is located in central France around the village of Clermont-Ferrand in the upper LOIRE (east of the northern RHÔNE region). The wines, which are very BEAUJOLAIS-like, are based on the GAMAY grape blended with a small amount of PINOT NOIR. There are over fifty small villages making these wines, but only the better ones can add their name to the label. They include Boudes, Châteaugay, Chanturgue, Corent, and Médargues.

Côtes de Bergerac *see* BERGERAC

Côtes de Blaye AC *see* BLAYE

Côtes de Bourg AC *see* BOURG

Côtes de Buzet *see* BUZET

Côtes de Castillon AC [koht duh kass-tee-YAWN] APPELLATION that takes its name from the village of Castillon-la-Bataille, which is famous for being the site where the English lost a decisive battle, thus ending the Hundred Years' War and England's 300-year control of the Bordeaux region. The area is located east of SAINT-ÉMILION in France's BORDEAUX region. Côtes de Castillon produces red wines from standard Bordeaux grapes but primarily uses MERLOT and CABERNET FRANC.

Côtes de Duras AC [koht duh doo-RAH] APPELLATION that is located east and just outside of the BORDEAUX region in SOUTHWEST FRANCE. It's centered around the town of Duras in the French DÉPARTEMENT of Lot-en-Garonne. White wines dominate the production and are made from the favorite white Bordeaux varieties of SAUVIGNON BLANC, SÉMILLON, and MUSCADELLE. The red wines are made from CABERNET SAUVIGNON, CABERNET FRANC, MERLOT, and MALBEC. Both red and white wines should be consumed while they're young.

Côtes de Francs AC; Côtes de Francs Liquoreux AC [koht duh frahn] A small, obscure APPELLATION located northeast of SAINT-ÉMILION in France's BORDEAUX region. Many think that the Côtes de Francs area (also referred to as *Bordeaux Côtes de Francs*) has plenty of potential because of its ideal soil and warm weather. This region primarily produces red wines from CABERNET SAUVIGNON, CABERNET FRANC, MERLOT, and MALBEC. A small amount of white wine is made from SAUVI-

C

GNON BLANC, SÉMILLON, and MUSCADELLE. The **Côtes de Francs Liquoreux AC** is for sweet white wines.

Côtes de la Malepère AC [koht duh lah mahl-PEHR] A small APPELLATION located in France's LANGUEDOC-ROUSSILLON region southwest of the city of Carcassonne. RED and ROSÉ wines are made from a mix of BORDEAUX and RHÔNE grape VARIETIES. For red wines, MERLOT is the primary VARIETY, along with CABERNET SAUVIGNON and CABERNET FRANC. Cot (MALBEC), GRENACHE, CINSAUT, and SYRAH can also be used. Rosé wines are made from Cinsaut, Grenache, Cabernet Franc, and Cot.

Côtes de Provence AC [koht duh praw-VAHNSS] The largest APPELLATION in France's PROVENCE region, which covers some 45,000 acres. One section stretches from Toulon on the Mediterranean, eastward along the coast to above Saint Tropez. Another reaches from Toulon inland in a northeastern direction, while a third section heads west from Toulon toward Marseille. ROSÉ is the dominant wine produced in this AC, followed by red wines and a tiny amount of white. The red and rosé wines are made from Barbaroux, CABERNET SAUVIGNON, CARIGNAN, CINSAUT, GRENACHE, MOURVÈDRE, SYRAH, and others, while the whites are made from CLAIRETTE, Rolle, SÉMILLON, Ugni Blanc (TREBBIANO) and VERMENTINO. Even though the quality of Côtes de Provence AC wines varies considerably, they appear to be generally improving, primarily because of increased planting of high-quality grape varieties like Cabernet Sauvignon, Mourvèdre, and Syrah. Sainte-Victoire is a subappellation located east of Aix-en-Provence along the base of Mount Sainte-Victoire. Wines from here may be labeled **Côtes de Provence Sainte-Victoire AC**. The wine production is almost 80 percent rosé and 20 percent red wines that are made up of a minimum of 50 percent Grenache and Syrah, a maximum of 50 percent Cinsaut blended with a maximum of 30 percent Barbaroux, Cabernet Sauvignon, Carignan and Mourvèdre. The wines from another subappellation, Fréjus, may be labeled **Côtes de Provence Fréjus AC**. This area lays southwest of Cannes near the Mediterranean in the Côte D'Azur.

Côtes de Saint-Mont VDQS [koht duh sahn-MOHN] A VDQS area located in SOUTHWEST FRANCE just south of Armagnac and next to MADIRAN. Côtes de Saint-Mont produces red and ROSÉ wines from Tannat, a local variety, blended with FER, CABERNET SAUVIGNON, CABERNET FRANC, and MERLOT. Small amounts of DRY white wine are produced mainly from Arrufiac, Courbu, and Manseng.

Côtes du Frontonnais AC [koht deu frawn-tawn-NAY] Small APPELLATION whose vineyards surround the towns of Fronton and Villaudric just north of the city of Toulouse in SOUTHWEST FRANCE. Côtes du Frontonnais produces red and ROSÉ wines that must include a minimum of 50 percent of a local grape variety called NÉGRETTE. It's blended with CABERNET SAUVIGNON, CABERNET FRANC, SYRAH, and GRENACHE, among others. The wines can be very smooth and supple, have flavor aspects of strawberry and raspberry, and be capable of medium-term AGING.

Côtes du Jura AC [koht deu zhoo-RAH] Large APPELLATION that covers most of eastern France's Jura region near the Swiss border. The Côtes du Jura AC encompasses red, white, and ROSÉ wine, as well as VIN JAUNE, VIN DE PAILLE, and SPARKLING WINE. The grapes used for the red and rosé wines are PINOT NOIR, Poulsard, and Trousseau; for white wines they're CHARDONNAY, PINOT BLANC, and SAVAGNIN, the Jura specialty. Among the region's vineyards that have their own appellation are ARBOIS AC, CHÂTEAU-CHALON AC, and L'ÉTOILE AC.

Côtes du Lubéron AC [koht deu leu-bay-RAWN] Located in the southern part of France's RHÔNE region, southeast of Avignon and just south of CÔTES DU VENTOUX AC, this APPELLATION was accorded AC status in 1988. A majority of the wine is red and ROSÉ produced from CINSAUT, GRENACHE, MOURVÈDRE, and SYRAH. The white wines are made from CLAIRETTE, CHARDONNAY, SAUVIGNON BLANC, and Ugni Blanc (TREBBIANO). Similar to the lighter-style wines of CÔTES DU RHÔNE AC, those from Côtes du Luberon are generally LIGHT and fruity and made for early consumption.

Côtes du Marmandais AC [koht deu mah*r*-mah*n*-DEH] APPELLATION in SOUTHWEST FRANCE around the town of Marmande, which is on the Garonne River just east of BORDEAUX. Nearby are the ACS of CÔTES DE DURAS, BUZET, and ENTRE-DEUX-MERS. The red wines are made from the Bordeaux favorites (CABERNET SAUVIGNON, CABERNET FRANC, MERLOT) as well as from the local varieties of Abouriou and FER, and occasionally SYRAH. The DRY white wines primarily employ the Bordeaux varieties of MUSCADELLE, SAUVIGNON BLANC, and SÉMILLON. Generally, the wines from Côtes du Marmandais are meant for early consumption.

Côtes du Rhône AC; Côtes du Rhône-Villages AC [koht deu ROHN; koht deu ROHN vee-LAHZH] The **Côtes du Rhône AC** is a regional APPELLATION covering various areas throughout France's RHÔNE region. It accounts for about 80 percent of the region's wines, most of which come from a large area north of Avignon in the southern Rhône. Although white wines are made, about 90 percent of Côtes du Rhône wines are red and ROSÉ. The principal red grape is GRENACHE, but CARIGNAN, Counoise, MOURVÈDRE, Terret Noir, and SYRAH are also grown. The white grapes used are BOURBOULENC, CLAIRETTE, MARSANNE, Muscardine, Picardan, ROUSSANNE, and Piquepoul (or Picpoule). Though Côtes du Rhône red wines have in the past been rather heavy, the implementation of modern winemaking techniques (including CARBONIC MACERATION) has resulted in lighter, fruitier wines. The quality of these wines varies immensely. **Côtes du Rhône-Villages AC** is a higher-quality appellation that requires lower crop YIELDS and a higher minimum level of ALCOHOL (12½ percent versus 11 percent for Côtes du Rhône AC wines). Sixteen villages are allowed to produce wines under this appellation: BEAUMES DE VENISE, CAIRANNE, **Chusclan**, LAUDUN, RASTEAU, **Roaix**, **Rochegude**, **Rousset-les-Vignes**, **Sablet**, **Saint Gervais**, **Saint Maurice-sur-Eygues**, **Saint-Pantaléon-les-Vignes**, **Séguret**, **Valréas**, **Vinsobres**, and **Visan**. These wines are generally more full-bodied (*see* BODY) than the regular Côtes du Rhône AC wines, and single estate wines are generally the best. If the wine is from a single village, the label may have the village name appended, as in *Côtes du Rhône-Chusclan*. If the wine is a blend from two or more villages, the designation Côtes du Rhône-Villages must be used.

Côtes du Roussillon AC; Côtes du Roussillon-Villages AC [koht deu roo-see-YAW*N*; koht deu roo-see-YAWN vee-LAHZH] An area located in southern France's LANGUEDOC-ROUSSILLON region, not far from the Spanish border. The **Côtes du Roussillon AC** is the basic APPELLATION for the area and produces red, white, and ROSÉ wines. The reds and rosés, which constitute about 95 percent of the production, are based on CARIGNAN with some CINSAUT, GRENACHE, and MOURVÈDRE. Most red grapes are processed using CARBONIC MACERATION, which results in LIGHT, fruity wines that are best drunk young. The white wines, which are generally DRY and CRISP, are made mostly with MACABEO and MALVOISIE grapes. **Côtes du Roussillon-Villages AC** is an appellation for higher-quality red wines requiring lower YIELDS and a higher minimum ALCOHOL content (12 percent versus 11½ percent for regular Côtes du Roussillon AC). This appellation, which includes the better vineyard areas from 28 villages around the Argly River, is north of Perpignan. The villages of **Caramany**, **Latour-de-France**, **Lesquerde**, and **Tautavel**, which generally produce the best wines, are the only ones allowed to add their names to the label.

Côtes du Ventoux AC [koht deu vaw*n*-TOO] Large APPELLATION located in the southern RHÔNE, east of CHÂTEAUNEUF-DU-PAPE. It produces red, white, and ROSÉ wines from the vineyards planted on the slopes of Mount Ventoux. The red and rosé wines are made from CARIGNAN, CINSAUT, GAMAY, GRENACHE, MOURVÈDRE, and SYRAH. White wines are produced from BOURBOULENC, CLAIRETTE, GRENACHE BLANC, and Ugni Blanc (TREBBIANO) grapes. Côtes du Ventoux wines are similar to those from the CÔTES DU RHÔNE AC.

Côtes du Vivarais VDQS [koht deu vee-vah-RAY] A VDQS area that produces LIGHT, easy-to-drink, mostly red wines. Côtes du Vivarais is located in the southern RHÔNE, northeast of CHÂTEAUNEUF-DU-PAPE. The grape varieties used for red and ROSÉ wines are those popular throughout the Rhône—CARIGNAN, CINSAUT, GAMAY, GRENACHE, and SYRAH—as well as CABERNET SAUVIGNON, which is now also being planted. Increasing use of Syrah and Cabernet Sauvignon is resulting in a more full-bodied (*see* BODY), full-flavored style. The area's small amount of white wine is made from BOURBOULENC, CLAIRETTE, GRENACHE BLANC, and Ugni Blanc (TREBBIANO).

Cotnari Winegrowing area in the Moldavia region that produces what was once ROMANIA's most famous wine. Now rarely seen outside of Romania, Cotnari wines were extremely popular in France in the 1920s, and their reputation goes back many centuries. When the local grapes (Feteasc Alb, Frîncus, Gras, and Tamiîoas Romaneasc) are infected with BOTRYTIS CINEREA, the resulting wines can be RICH, intensely sweet, and luscious with excellent ACIDITY.

cotto *see* MARSALA DOC

coulure [coo-LYUR] The failure of grapes to develop after flowering. Coulure may occur because of extended rains or very frigid weather during the flowering season. If blossoms are not pollinated, the grape fails to develop and falls off. Other grapes on the same vine may develop, and their quality will not suffer, but the YIELD from a vine with coulure may drop considerably.

coupage; coupe [koo-PAHZH; KOOP] *Coupe* is French for the noun form of "cut." *Coupage* refers to a cutting wine or BLENDING WINE. Such wines are added in small quantities to other wines either to correct deficiencies in them or to enhance them.

Cour-Cheverny AC *see* CHEVERNY AC

courtier [koor-TYAY] In the wine world, this French term means "wine broker." Such a person is the middleman between a small producer and a NÉGOCIANT, who bottles and ships the wines. The courtier helps establish the price that a small producer will get from the négociant for the wine.

Covelo AVA APPELLATION created in April 2006 in northern Mendocino County about 45 miles north of Ukiah. Although there are 38,000 acres in Round Valley, Williams Valley and the foothills that surround them, there are currently only 2 acres with vines planted. The Covelo AVA is part of the larger NORTHCOAST AVA.

Covisa *see* SOMONTANO DO

Cowra An emerging Australian wine region located in the Central Ranges Zone of NEW SOUTH WALES. It's situated about 190 miles west of Sydney on the western side of the Great Dividing Range. It is as warm as the HUNTER VALLEY but is less humid and not as cool at night. There are approximately 4,000 vineyard acres. The most widely planted white varieties are CHARDONNAY, SÉMILLON, VERDELHO, and SAUVIGNON BLANC; the main reds are Shiraz (SYRAH), CABERNET SAUVIGNON, CABERNET FRANC, PINOT NOIR, and MERLOT. Initially, white varieties were the mainstay, but red varieties have been planted in higher quantities over the last few years, including BARBERA, SANGIOVESE, and TEMPRANILLO. Much of the Cowra grape harvest is trucked to wineries to the south or west to MUDGEE or Hunter Valley.

Crabutet *see* MERLOT

crackling Term used in the United States to describe wine that's only slightly SPARKLING, much less so than CHAMPAGNE. Standard champagne is measured at 6 ATMOSPHERES of pressure, whereas crackling wines have only 1 to 2 atm, similar to Italian FRIZZANTE and French PETILLANT wines. Even though a crackling wine's effervescence sometimes occurs naturally, it's often created by pumping in CARBON DIOXIDE. The crackling style is popular with moderately priced red, white, and particularly ROSÉ wines such as Portugal's Lancers and Mateus. Occasionally, the word *crackling* appears in the wine's name, as with Paul Masson Vineyards' Crackling Rosé and Crackling Chablis.

cradle; wine cradle *see* DECANTING

Cramant [kra-MAHN] An important wine-producing village located in the Côtes des Blancs area of France's CHAMPAGNE region. Cramant, whose vineyards are planted with CHARDONNAY, is one of only seventeen villages to have obtained a GRAND CRU rating of 100 percent for its vineyards (*see* CHAMPAGNE for an explanation of the percent system). The grapes from these vineyards are highly regarded, and the resulting champagne, which is often sold unblended, uses the village name on the label.

cream of tartar *see* TARTRATES

cream sherry *see* SHERRY

creamy *see* Glossary of Wine Tasting Terms, page 655

crémant [kray-MAHN] French for "creaming," which in CHAMPAGNE describes wines that are moderately SPARKLING. This means that they've been made with slightly more than half the pressure of champagne or MOUSSEUX-style sparkling wines but more pressure than wines described as PÉTILLANT, FRIZZANTE, or CRACKLING. Even though *crémant* is included in the name of three APPELLATION D'ORIGINE CONTRÔLÉES (CRÉMANT D'ALSACE, CRÉMANT DE BOURGOGNE, and CRÉMANT DE LOIRE), their wines are not moderately but rather fully sparkling. The sparkling wines from these three areas are made by the MÉTHODE CHAMPENOISE and have strict regulations regarding their production.

Crémant d'Alsace AC [kray-MAHN dahl-SASS (dahl-SAYSS)] An APPELLATION in France's ALSACE region that produces DRY SPARKLING WINES that must be aged for a minimum of 9 months. The grapes allowed in these wines include AUXERROIS BLANC, CHARDONNAY, PINOT BLANC, PINOT GRIS, PINOT NOIR, and RIESLING. The quality of the Crémant d'Alsace wines, which are made using the MÉTHODE CHAMPENOISE, is generally quite good, although they're a bit more expensive than some of the other non-CHAMPAGNE alternatives.

Crémant de Bourgogne AC [kray-MAHN deh boor-GON-yuh] APPELLATION that covers France's BURGUNDY region and features DRY SPARKLING WINES. These wines are made via MÉTHODE CHAMPENOISE from the principal grapes of ALIGOTÉ, CHARDONNAY, PINOT BLANC, and PINOT NOIR. Most of the wines produced are white, with a small amount of ROSÉ. Crémant de Bourgogne wines must be aged for a minimum of 9 months. Their quality is much higher than the wines from the region's older appellation **Bourgogne Mousseux AC**, which is being phased out. Today's Burgundian sparkling wines are viewed very positively and are regarded as good, lower-priced alternatives to the wines of CHAMPAGNE.

Crémant de Jura AC [kray-MAHN deh zhoo-RAH] An APPELLATION covering the same area as the CÔTES DU JURA AC—eastern France's Jura region near the Swiss border. It produces DRY SPARKLING WINES (white and ROSÉ) via MÉTHODE CHAMPENOISE. The grapes used are CHARDONNAY,

PINOT GRIS, PINOT NOIR, Poulsard, SAVAGNIN, and/or TROUSSEAU. Because the Crémant de Jura AC's quality standards are so high, the sparking wines from this area are taking precedence over other Jura-region ACs such as ARBOIS, Côtes du Jura, and L'ÉTOILE.

Crémant de Limoux AC [kray-MAH*N* deh lee-MOO] APPELLATION established in 1990 for SPARKLING WINES made via MÉTHODE CHAMPENOISE. This area is located in the hills surrounding the town of Limoux in Southern France's LANGUEDOC-ROUSSILLON region. These wines differ from the area's better-known BLANQUETTE DE LIMOUX AC sparkling wines in that they cannot be made with *méthode rurale* (RURAL METHOD) and they may use a maximum 70 percent of Mauzac (known locally as *Blanquette*), with the remaining grapes being CHARDONNAY and CHENIN BLANC. Blanquette de Limoux wines must use a minimum 90 percent of Mauzac. In addition, Crémant de Limoux wines are aged for a minimum of 12 months—3 months longer than those of Blanquette de Limoux.

Crémant de Loire AC [kray-MAHN deh LWAH*R*] An APPELLATION covering the ANJOU, SAUMUR, and TOURAINE districts in the LOIRE Valley. It produces DRY SPARKLING WINES using the MÉTHODE CHAMPENOISE. CHENIN BLANC is the primary grape, but CABERNET FRANC, CHARDONNAY, GAMAY, and Pineau d'Aunis are also used. Although there's a plentitude of sparkling wine produced in these districts, the quality standards for Crémant de Loire AC are higher. For example, this appellation requires lower yields, a higher proportion of FREE-RUN JUICE, and longer AGING periods (1 year versus 9 months for most others in the area). These higher standards are translating into better sparkling wines, which are generally SOFTER and fruitier than those from the ACs of Anjou Mousseux or Saumur Mousseux.

crème de tête [krehm deh TEHT] Term used by some French producers, notably those in SAUTERNES, to identify their best wines. Similar to *tête de cuvee* (*see* CUVEE).

Cremevo *see* MARSALA DOC

Crepy AC [kray-PEE] Crepy is located in eastern France's SAVOIE region very close to the Swiss border, near the south shore of Lake Geneva. This small APPELLATION produces white wines that seem more Swiss than French—they're LIGHT and low-ALCOHOL and made from one of Switzerland's leading grape varieties, CHASSELAS.

criadera [kree-ah-DEHR-ah] A Spanish term that translates as "nursery." In the sherry-making region around JEREZ DE LA FRONTERA, however, criadera is part of the SOLERA SYSTEM for aging and ensuring the consistency of SHERRY wines. It is the nursery where young wines are managed, cared for, and evaluated. To be very precise, all levels of wine in the solera system are referred to as criaderas, with the exception of the oldest level, the solera. The next level up (next oldest) from the solera is referred to as the first criadera, the level after that, the second criadera, and so forth. Some producers have up to fourteen levels in their solera systems.

crianza [kree-AHN-zah] The Spanish term meaning "breeding" or "upbringing." "Con crianza" or "vino de crianza" on a wine label refers to the AGING a wine receives. The exact rules are defined by the governing body of each DENOMINACION DE ORIGEN (DO). If a DO has no specific rules, a crianza wine must receive a minimum of 2 years aging either in a tank, an oak barrel, or a bottle. Many of the DOs require that 1 year of the 2 years be in oak barrels. By contrast, red RESERVA wines require a minimum of 3 years of aging with at least 1 year in oak barrels; ROSÉ and white RESERVAS require a minimum aging of 2 years with no less than 6 months in oak barrels. The words **"Sin crianza"** on a label indicate that the wine did not receive minimum aging and was bottled young.

Crljenak Kastelanski *see* ZINFANDEL

Criolla *see* MISSION

Criots-Bâtard-Montrachet AC [kree-oh bah-TAHR mohn-rah-SHAY] A 3.9-acre vineyard that is the smallest of the GRANDS CRUS in the CÔTE DE BEAUNE district of France's BURGUNDY region. The vineyard is next to the grand cru BÂTARD-MONTRACHET and is the only grand cru located entirely in the village of CHASSAGNE-MONTRACHET. Considered among the world's best, Criots-Bâtard-Montrachet AC wines are made from CHARDONNAY grapes. They're similar to, although perhaps slightly LIGHTER than, those from the neighboring Bâtard-Montrachet AC.

crisp *see* Glossary of Wine Tasting Terms, page 655

Cristal *see* CHAMPAGNE

Croatina; Croattina [kraw-ah-TEE-nah] Red-wine grape that is grown in the southwest area of Italy's LOMBARDY region. The best-known Croatina wines are from the OLTREPÒ PAVESE area, where this grape is called *Bonarda* (not to be confused with a different variety, *Bonarda Piemontese*, also called BONARDA). To add to the confusion, Croatina has achieved DOC status in this area under the name *Bonarda dell'Oltrepò Pavese*. These DOC wines are SOFT and ROUND, yet LIVELY and fruity with characteristics of plums and cherries; they generally have a bitter FINISH. Croatina is often BLENDED with terrific results, as in EMILIA-ROMAGNA'S GUTTURNIO, where it's used to soften the BARBERA in this blend. Croatina's also known as *Neretto* and *Uva Vermiglia*.

cross; crossing *n.* A vine or grape created by breeding two varieties of the same genus (VITIS VINIFERA, for example). Crosses are created in an effort to produce a plant with the best traits of its parents, such as high productivity, disease resistance, and/or better adaptability to environmental conditions. Some of the better-known crosses are Germany's MÜLLER-THURGAU (a RIESLING and SYLVANER cross), California's RUBY CABERNET (a CABERNET SAUVIGNON and CARIGNAN cross), and South Africa's PINOTAGE (a PINOT NOIR and CINSAUT cross). *See also* CLONE; HYBRID. **Cross** *v.* The act of creating or breeding a cross from members of the same species. *See also* HYBRIDIZE.

Crouchen [kroo-SHEN] In South Africa, where this white-wine grape is known variously as *South African Riesling, Cape Riesling,* and *Paarl Riesling*, Crouchen has long been thought to be RIESLING. The Australians believed it was SÉMILLON but, strangely, called it *Clare Riesling*. It wasn't until the mid-1970s that this grape was identified as Crouchen, a variety from the Landes region of SOUTHWEST FRANCE (where it's now almost extinct). Crouchen continues to be grown in both South Africa and Australia, where it produces pleasant, lightly AROMATIC wines that are sometimes vinified DRY and other times with a bit of RESIDUAL SUGAR. Other names for Crouchen include *Cruchen Blanc* and *Navarre Blanc*.

crown cap A cap, resembling that on a beer bottle, that is used during BOTTLE FERMENTATION when making SPARKLING WINE via MÉTHODE CHAMPENOISE. The crown cap has a small plastic receptacle attached to it that fits inside the bottle, into which the yeast sediment settles during the RIDDLING process.

Crozes-Hermitage AC [krawz ehr-mee-TAHZH] The largest APPELLATION in France's northern RHÔNE region. The vineyards of the eleven villages that make up Crozes-Hermitage AC surround the more famous HERMITAGE vineyards. Crozes-Hermitage produces red wines from SYRAH and white wines from MARSANNE and ROUSSANNE. The wines from the area vary considerably in quality because some of the vineyards are located in the superior hilly areas, while others are situated on the less-desirable flatlands. The better Crozes-Hermitage wines bear a resemblance to those of the Hermitage AC, but usually without the concentrated flavors and richness. Generally the red wines are better than the whites.

cru [KROO] French term for "growth." When related to wine, *cru* is usually combined with another descriptor (as in PREMIER CRU, CRU BOURGEOIS, or CRU CLASSÉ) to indicate a vineyard's ranking. In BEAUJOLAIS, the term refers to the top ten villages that have their own APPELLATIONS. In other areas in France, such as the COTEAUX DU LANGUEDOC AC, *cru* identifies villages with exceptional-quality wines that deserve special reference.

cru artisan [kroo AHR-tih-san] Although the term is rarely used, *cru artisan* describes a category for châteaux in BORDEAUX that ranks below CRU BOURGEOIS.

cru bourgeois [kroo boor-ZWAH] A category for châteaux of the MÉDOC that ranks just below that of CRU CLASSÉ. When the Classification of 1855 (*see* Official Wine Classifications of Bordeaux, page 678) was completed, thousands of châteaux had been excluded. The cru bourgeois category was created as a means of including the best of these. In 1932 the first list of cru bourgeois châteaux was created by the Bordeaux Chamber of Commerce. It included 444 châteaux classified in three categories. The highest ranking—*cru bourgeois supérieurs exceptionnel* (sometimes called *cru exceptionnel* or *cru bourgeois exceptionnel*)—originally included only six châteaux and was limited to those from the area in the HAUT-MÉDOC where the cru classé châteaux were located. The next category was *cru bourgeois supérieurs* with 99 châteaux; the third category was *cru bourgeois* with 339 châteaux. However, châteaux in any of these three categories may only use the term "cru bourgeois" on their wine labels. An organization known as *Syndicat des Crus Bourgeois* updated this list in 1966 and again in 1978. However, their list includes only member châteaux, which eliminates many good châteaux who choose not to join. The Syndicat's 1978 list included 127 châteaux, of which only 18 are included in the top category. Ranked below crus bourgeois is a category that's rarely used—CRU ARTISAN.

cru bourgeois exceptionnel *see* CRU BOURGEOIS

cru bourgeois supérieurs *see* CRU BOURGEOIS

cru bourgeois supérieurs exceptionnel *see* CRU BOURGEOIS

cru classé; pl. crus classés [kroo klah-SAY] 1. French for "classed growth," indicating that a CHÂTEAU (most often in BORDEAUX) is ranked in the top category. 2. The famous Classification of 1855 (*see* Official Wine Classifications of Bordeaux, page 678) divided the crus classés for Bordeaux's MÉDOC region red wines into five subcategories—PREMIER CRU (first growth) through CINQUIÈME CRU (fifth growth). The white wines of SAUTERNES were divided into only two subcategories—premier cru and DEUXIÈMES CRU (second growth). 3. The term *cru classé* is also used in a similar fashion when referring to other classifications such as the one established in 1953 for the red wines of GRAVES, which didn't create any subcategories but simply listed thirteen crus classés châteaux. In 1959, eight white-wine châteaux in Graves were given cru classé status and—as with the red-wine châteaux—the right to use "GRAND CRU CLASSÉ" (Great Classed Growth) on their labels. In the SAINT-ÉMILION region, there was a 1954 classification (which was revised in 1969 and 1985) that ranked the châteaux in three major categories—PREMIER GRAND CRU CLASSÉ (First Great Growth Class), Grand Cru Classé, and Grand Cru. Saint-Émilion's Premier Grand Cru Classé is similiar to the Médoc's Cru Classé.

cru exceptionnel *see* CRU BOURGEOIS

Cruian *see* CORVINA

crush A term used in California and other parts of the United States referring to the time when grapes are harvested and crushed to make wine.

crusher; crusher-stemmer A **crusher** is a mechanical device consisting of paddles and rollers that break the grape berries and extract the juice. Crushing must be delicate enough so that the grape seeds are not broken, which would release their bitterness into the wine. With a crusher, a screen is necessary to separate the juice, skins, and seeds from the stems and leaves. With a **crusher-stemmer**, however, the stems and leaves are automatically expelled. Large commercial wineries have continuous-feed crusher-stemmers that can process up to 150 tons of grapes an hour.

crushing The most common way of extracting the juice from grapes. (PRESSING is the second most frequent method.) At commercial wineries, grape clusters are dumped into a receiving hopper that feeds the recently picked grapes into a CRUSHER (or crusher-stemmer). There the grapes are broken, and the juice, skins, and seeds are separated from any stems and leaves that are attached. White-wine juice is normally separated from the skins and seeds, which are pressed for further juice extraction. For red wines, the juice, skins, and seeds (MUST) are then placed in tanks or vats for FERMENTATION.

crust Another name for the SEDIMENT thrown off by red wines as they age in bottles. The use of the term *crust* is generally associated with vintage port (*see* PORT).

crusted port *see* PORT

cryoextraction [kri-oh-ex-STRAK-shuhn] French term for the practice of subjecting grapes to very low temperatures (around 20°F) so that only the most concentrated grape juice will be extracted during PRESSING. The cryoextraction process begins by putting freshly culled grapes into cold storage until they reach a desired temperature (the temperature can be adjusted upward or downward in accordance with the quality level of the grapes). Because riper, better-quality grapes have a higher concentration of sugars, their freezing point is lower than that of less ripe grapes. When the grapes reach the proper temperature, they're immediately pressed. As a result of the cryoextraction process, only the premium juice is expressed because the lower-quality (not perfectly ripe) grapes are still frozen. The results are similar to those that occur naturally when frozen grapes are picked to make EISWEIN. Cryoextraction is now being used by some SAUTERNES estates in poorer VINTAGES (particularly wet years) when the quality of individual grapes is inconsistent. With the help of this process, vintners can produce the renowned DESSERT WINES for which Sauternes is famous.

crystals Small, innocuous fragments of tartaric acid (*see* ACIDS) found in some wines.

Cucamonga Valley AVA A 109,000-acre southern California VITI-CULTURAL AREA located about 45 miles east of Los Angeles. Established in 1985, its history goes back to the nineteenth century when MISSION grapes were first planted. Although there were as many as 35,000 acres planted here in the 1950s, today there are only about 1,000 acres. Urban sprawl continues to spread eastward toward San Bernardino, and grapevines have succumbed to the GLASSY-WINGED SHARPSHOOTER and PIERCE'S DISEASE.

Cugnette *see* JACQUÈRE

cultivar *see* VARIETY

cult wines An American term used to describe high-quality, extremely expensive wines that are produced in very small quantities and highly sought after by collectors. It refers primarily but not exclusively to CABERNET SAUVIGNON wines produced by a group of NAPA VAL-LEY wineries such as Araujo, Bryant Family, Colgin, Grace Family, Harlan Estate, and Screaming Eagle. Other wines that fall into this category include CHARDONNAYS from Kistler, Koonsgaard, and Marcassin and ZINFANDEL from Turley. *See also* GARAGE WINES.

Cumberland Valley AVA AVA that encompasses 765,000 acres in MARYLAND and PENNSYLVANIA. It stretches from the Potomac River in Washington County in west central Maryland across the Pennsylvania state line through Franklin and Cumberland counties and ends at the Susquehanna River at Harrisburg. Approved in 1985, the Cumberland Valley AVA is home to three wineries and about 100 acres of vineyards.

Currency Creek An Australian wine region located in the Fleurieu Zone of SOUTH AUSTRALIA. It's situated about 45 miles southeast of Adelaide around the town of Currency Creek and adjacent to the better known LANGHORNE CREEK region. Like Langhorne Creek, Currency Creek has a cool, even growing season influenced by Lake Alexandrina and the Southern Ocean. CABERNET SAUVIGNON, Shiraz (SYRAH), MERLOT, and CHARDONNAY are the most widely planted VARIETIES. At this writing, there are only two wineries in the region.

custom crushing; custom crush facility A term used in the United States for the process whereby winemakers without the capital-intensive equipment required for a full-fledged winery can have their grapes VINIFIED at a facility with the necessary equipment in place. Such a location might be a winery producing its own wines that has extra capacity, or a winery operation (known as a **custom crush facility**) set up specifically to service a number of different winemakers. In either case, each winemaker's wine is processed and marketed separately.

Custoza *see* BIANCO DI CUSTOZA DOC

cutting(s) In the world of VITICULTURE, a cutting refers to a short, woody shoot removed from a grapevine to propagate a new plant through GRAFTING. The plant from which a cutting is taken is called a "parent vine."

cutting wine *see* BLENDING WINE

cuvaison [koo-veh-ZOHN] The French term for the period when grape juice is kept in contact with the skins and seeds during both FERMENTATION and MACERATION. Critical in the making of red wines, cuvaison allows color, TANNINS, and AROMA to be transferred from the skins and seeds to the juice. For ROSÉ or BLUSH WINES the cuvaison would be very short (measured in terms of hours) so that not much color or tannin would be extracted from skins and seeds.

cuve [KOOV] The French term for "vat" or "tank," generally associated with a large vat or tank used for fermenting or blending.

cuve-close *see* CHARMAT PROCESS

cuvée [koo-VAY] Term derived from the French CUVE (which means vat) that denotes the "contents of a vat." In France's CHAMPAGNE region, it refers to a blended batch of wines. In Champagne, the large houses create their traditional (and very secret) house-style cuvées by blending various wines before creating the final product via MÉTHODE CHAMPENOISE. A deluxe version is often referred to as *cuvée speciale*; VIN DE CUVÉE refers to wine from the first pressing. Outside Champagne the term *cuvée* is also used for still wines. It may refer to wines blended from different vineyards, or even different varieties. Occasionally, the word *cuvée* followed by a number is used to identify a specific batch of wines blended separately and distinctly from others. Some French producers identify their best wines with the term, **tête de cuvée**.

cuvée de prestige *see* CHAMPAGNE

cuvée speciale *see* CHAMPAGNE

cuverie [KOO-vay-ree] French word for the building in which FERMENTATION takes place.

Cynthiana *see* NORTON

Cyprus [SI-pruhs] Independent island republic located south of Turkey in the Mediterranean. Most of the better vineyards are situated in the foothills on the south side of the Troodos Mountains. Because it's a former British colony, Cyprus is, to a degree, still tied to the British idea of wines and winemaking. The best Cypriot wines are their Spanish-style SHERRIES and a DESSERT WINE called **Commandaria**. The latter, which is light red- or amber-colored and can be rich, intense, and luscious, is made from various varieties of dried, raisined grapes. The island's primary grape is the red Mavron, which is used in their full-bodied red wines and ROSÉS and for the Commandaria. Small amounts of two red grapes—Opthalmo and Marathefticon—are also grown. The primary white grapes are Xynisteri and Muscat of Alexandria (MUSCAT). Other European varieties are being introduced to Cyprus, but with caution, because the island has never been afflicted with PHYLLOXERA.

DAC *see* DISTRICTUS AUSTRIA CONTROLLATUS

Dame Jeanne *see* DEMIJOHN

Les Damodes *see* NUITS-SAINT-GEORGES

Dão DOC [DOWNG] Located in north central Portugal, this well-known wine-producing region's vineyards are situated in the mountainous area surrounding the city of Viseu. Dão, a DENOMINAÇÃO DE ORIGEM CONTROLADA, is best known for BIG, full-bodied (*see* BODY) red wines that require considerable AGING to SOFTEN. Some feel the lengthy aging is a detriment because the wines lose much of their fruitiness. Since Portugal joined the European Economic Community, control has been taken from the local cooperatives that had a monopoly on winemaking. Such changes are allowing independent producers to become more involved, and those who use more modern winemaking techniques are producing fruitier, more youthful wines. The huge SOGRAPE company is leading this new trend with its Quinta dos Carvalhais estate. The red wines here are made from a large variety of approved grapes, but mostly from Alfrocheiro Preto, Alvarelhao, Bastardo, Tinta Amarela, and TOURIGA NACIONAL. A small amount of DRY white wine is made from ARINTO, Assario, Barcelo, Borrado das Moscas (BICAL), Branco, Cerceal (SERCIAL), ENCRUZADO, and VERDHELO.

Daphnes *see* GREECE

dated port *see* COLHEITA

Davis, University of California *see* UNIVERSITY OF CALIFORNIA, DAVIS

deacidification [dee-uh-SIHD-ih-fih-KAY-shuhn] The process of reducing the titratable acidity (*see* ACIDS) in wine, grape juice, or MUST. There are numerous methods for doing this including COLD STABILIZATION and AMELIORATION.

dead arm This is the generic name, also known as *side arm* or *dying arm,* for a number of fungal diseases that affect vineyards all over the world. Sometimes the whole vine dies, but it often manifests with only the death of some of the arms (or branches) of the vine. Almost all varieties of grape species are susceptible to dead arm— both VITIS VINEFERA and NATIVE AMERICAN GRAPES. The fungi are most active in winter or early spring when the environment is cool and moist. Early pruning is recommended along with sprays such as benomyl or captan and sometimes sodium arsenite. **Eutypa dieback**, called **eutypiose** in France, is one of these diseases and is caused by the fungus *Eutypa armeniacae*. Some believe that pruning wounds may likely be the entry point for this fungus. They recommend applying a Benlate paste to the wound to inhibit infection. **Black dead arm** is another type caused by several different members of the *Botryosphaeria* family of fungi. **Phomopsis** is another example that's caused by *Phomopsis viticola*. The symptoms of each of these are somewhat different and the solutions for inhibiting the fungi vary as well. Some vintners, like D'Arnberg in SOUTH AUSTRALIA, indicate that the grapes from the unaffected arms are very intensely flavored and in fact they label a highly regarded SHIRAZ wine made from some of these grapes as *The Dead Arm*.

dealcing *see* DEALCOHOLIZATION

dealcoholization The process of lowering the alcohol level of wine. This may be done to reduce a winery's tax obligation since wines with 14 percent alcohol and under have a lower tax rate than those with over 14 percent. Dealcoholization, sometimes shortened to **dealcing**, may also be done to improve the BALANCE in HOT wines or to create DEALCOHOLIZED WINE. Processes for lowering alcohol levels include REVERSE OSMOSIS, SPINNING CONE, and WATERING BACK.

dealcoholized wine A category of wine produced by one of several special processes that remove the ALCOHOL (*see* DEALCOHOLIZATION). Although the wine industry prefers the term "dealcoholized wine," such wine is also called *alcohol-free wine* and *nonalcoholic wine*. It's legally a nonalcoholic product, which means it contains less than 0.5 percent alcohol (about the same amount in most freshly squeezed orange juice). That in itself makes this product appealing to many, but weight watchers love the fact that dealcoholized wine has less than half the calories of regular wine. Add to that the fact that *The American Journal of Clinical Nutrition* tells us nonalcoholic red wine is also good for the heart. That being said, dealcoholized wine simply doesn't have the subtlety, BODY, and MOUTHFEEL of real wine, primarily because alcohol contributes to all of those characteristics. Still, there are some fairly decent dealcoholized wines on the market in a variety of styles including reds, whites, ROSÉS, and SPARKLING WINES. You can even find some varietals like CHARDONNAY, CABERNET SAUVIGNON, MERLOT, and RIESLING. However, most tasting panels agree that the simpler styles, such as Ariel Blanc and Sutter Home Fré Premium White, have the best flavor. Such wines can be found at liquor stores and some supermarkets and are typically grouped together.

débourbage [day-boor-BAZH] French term for the winemaking phase when suspended solids fall from the MUST to the bottom of the storage vessel.

decant; decanting [dee-KANT-ing] Decanting is done either to separate the wine from any sediment deposited during the AGING process or to allow a wine to BREATHE in order to enhance its flavor. When decanting an older wine, care should be taken not to disturb the sediment. A wine basket (also called *cradle* or *Burgundy basket*) can be used to move the bottle in a horizontal position from where it was stored to where it will be decanted. This position keeps the sediment from disseminating throughout the wine. If such a basket isn't available, stand the bottle upright for an hour so that the sediment can settle to the bottom of the bottle. Once the foil and cork are removed, gently wipe the mouth of the bottle. Then begin slowly pouring the wine into a DECANTER, placing a strong light (a candle is charming, but a flashlight is more practical) behind or below the neck of the bottle. The light lets you see the first signs of sediment, at which point you stop pouring. *See also* Opening and Serving Wine at Home, page 636.

decanter A glass container into which wine is decanted (*see* DECANT; DECANTING). A decanter can be a simple CARAFE but is generally more elegant and often made of hand-cut crystal.

De Chaunac [duh SHAHW-nak] This French-American HYBRID, originally known as *Siebel 9549*, was brought to North America by Ademar De Chaunac. It performs well in the cool vineyard environs of the Midwest and Northeast United States and in southern Canada. De Chaunac ripens early and produces fruity wines with moderate acid, alcohol and tannin levels.

Declared Geographical Origin *see* BULGARIA

declassify Primarily associated with Europe, this term describes wine that is placed in a lower classification. In BORDEAUX, a CHATEAU might declassify a portion of the wine produced from their vineyards and bottle it under their SECOND LABEL instead of as their primary offering. In BURGUNDY, a producer might declassify a portion of wine from a PREMIER CRU vineyard and bottle it as a village or regional wine. Wines are often declassified for quality-related reasons, but sometime producers are forced to declassify because APPELLATION restrictions were not met. Outside of Europe some quality-wine producers use the term "declassify" similarly by indicating that they won't produce their high-end wine, such as a RESERVE.

deep *see* Glossary of Wine Tasting Terms, page 655

dégorgement *see* DISGORGEMENT

degree days *see* CLIMATE REGIONS OF CALIFORNIA

Deidesheim [DI-duhss-hime] One of several adjoining towns, including FORST, RUPPETSBERG, and WACHENHEM, that produces some of the best wines of Germany's PFALZ region. This picturesque town has a number of fine estates including BASSERMAN-JORDAN, von Buhl, and Deinhard. Deidesheim is located in the BEREICH Mittelhaardt/Deutsche Weinstrasse and has vineyards located in three of the area's GROSSLAGEN—Hofstück, Mariengarten, and Schnepfenflug. There are a number of excellent EIZELLAGEN including **Grainhübel**, **Herrgottsacker**, **Hohenmorgan**, **Kieselberg**, **Langenmorgen**, **Leinhöhle**, and **Paradiesgarten**. Over 50 percent of the vineyards attached to Deidesheim are planted with RIESLING, the variety used to produce Deidesheim's most distinguished wines. The town's reputation for fine wines extends back several centuries.

dekerra *see* BRETTANOMYCES

delicate; delicacy *see* Glossary of Wine Tasting Terms, page 655

demi [DEHM-ee] A French term meaning "half" or "lesser," used in combination with other words as a modifier, such as with DEMI-SEC.

demijohn [DEHM-ee-jon] A large squat bottle with a short narrow neck and usually covered in wicker. Demijohns can hold from 1 to 10 gallons. The word is thought to be derived from the French *Dame Jeanne* (Lady Jane), a term which is also still used to describe this bottle.

demi-sec [DEHM-ee sehk] A French term meaning "half DRY," used to describe a sweet SPARKLING WINE. *See also* SEC.

Denmark *see* GREAT SOUTHERN

Denominação de Origem Controlada (DOC) The highest quality wine category in Portugal. The old term *Região Demarcada* ("Demarcated Region") was replaced by *Denominação de Origem Controlada (DOC)*, which means "Controlled Denomination of Origin." This category is roughly equivalent to the French APPELLATION D'ORIGINE CONTRÔLÉE in that there are rules relating to yields, density of planting, and the like. Although Portugal was actually the first country to implement a national APPELLATION system (in 1756), there has been much confusion as the country tries to adjust to its entry into the European Economic Community (1987). Officials are also reorganizing a category called *Indicação de Proveniencia Regulamentada (IPR)* for lower-quality wines.

D

Denominación de Origen (DO) [deh-naw-mee-nah-THYON deh aw-REE-hen] The Spanish system for wine classification that fits the requirements of the European Economic Community's top-quality wine category. This "designation of origin" is similar to France's APPELLATION D'ORIGINE CONTRÔLÉE. Most experts, however, don't think the Spanish standards are as high because approximately 50 percent of the Spanish wines qualify, compared to only about 25 percent of those in France. To qualify for *Denominación de Origen (DO)* status, wines must meet specific requirements including geographic areas where the grapes must be grown and the wines made, grape varieties permitted in that area, vineyard practices, maximum YIELD, minimum ALCOHOL content, and winemaking practices. The first DO—RIOJA—was established in 1926; there are now close to forty areas with DO status. Each DO has its own governing body (*consejo regulador*) that may implement stricter rules for the CRIANZA, RESERVA, and GRAN RESERVA wines than those imposed by federal standards. A **Denominación de Origen de Pago** is given to Spanish estates that have consistently produced high-quality wines and have an international following. *See also* DENOMINACIÓN DE ORIGEN CALIFICADA.

Denominación de Origen Calificada (DOCa) [deh-naw-mee-nah-THYON deh aw-REE-hen kah-lee-fee-KAH-dah] A term meaning "qualified designation of origin," referring to the top category for Spanish wines. It was presumably introduced as a response to the criticism that many of the holders of DENOMINACIÓN DE ORIGEN (DO) status did not produce wines of acceptably high quality. This DOCa classification adds the word *calificada* ("qualified"), indicating that it has more exacting standards than those established for DOs. Spain's RIOJA region was the first to meet the definitive standards of the new DOCa category, PRIORAT the second.

Denominazione di Origine Controllata (DOC) [deh-NAW-mee-nah-TSYAW-neh dee oh-REE-jee-neh con-traw-LAH-tah] Established in 1963 and implemented in 1966, the *Denominazione di Origine Controllata (DOC)* ("Controlled Denomination of Origin") is Italy's system for ensuring quality wines, equivalent to France's APPEL-

LATION D'ORIGINE CONTRÔLÉE. DOCs are defined by the geographic area of production for each wine, the varieties that can be used, the minimum ALCOHOL content, the maximum YIELD, and the specifications for AGING. In 1990, tasting commissions introduced standards for appearance, color, bouquet, and flavor. In addition, chemical analysis is performed to determine levels of ALCOHOL, ACIDITY, and RESIDUAL SUGAR. As with the systems implemented in France, Spain, and other countries, the DOC system doesn't guarantee quality, but it does nudge a majority of the wines in that direction. There are now over 320 DOC zones, including a small group belonging to a more elite level called DENOMINAZIONE DI ORIGINE CONTROLLATA E GARANTITA. An issue that many wine experts have with the DOC rules is their strict disposition toward traditional winemaking techniques and grape varieties. They haven't adapted to the many new techniques or the successful production of wines from nontraditional varieties (for each particular growing region). As a result, many excellent wines that are being produced by these modern methods or using nontraditional grapes can't qualify for DOC status. Instead, they must use the lower-ranking VINO DA TAVOLA classification on their labels.

Denominazione di Origine Controllata e Garantita (DOCG) [deh-NAW-mee-nah-TSYAW-neh dee oh-REE-jee-neh con-traw-LAH-tah eh gah-rahn-TEE-tah] A premium wine category that embodies a premier group of Italian growing areas whose regulations encompass all laws of the DENOMINAZIONE DI ORIGINE CONTROLLATA but are even more demanding. Meaning "Controlled and Guaranteed Denomination of Origin," the *Denominazione di Origine Controllata e Garantita* focuses on the key word *garantita*—the Italian government's quality "guarantee." Government testers examine and taste the wines prior to awarding DOCG status. The producers then bottle the qualifying wines, securing them with a government seal (a colored strip placed over the capsule or cork). The words "Denominazione di Origine Controllata e Garantita" are incorporated into the label. The first five DOCGs were BAROLO and BARBARESCO in the PIEDMONT region and BRUNELLO DI MONTALCINO, VINO NOBILE DI MONTEPULCIANO, and CHIANTI in the TUSCANY region. These five areas all received general approval, but the addition of the sixth area, ALBANA DI ROMAGNA, has been quite controversial. Many experts believe that the quality of this area's wines aren't comparable to the other five DOCGs. Other DOCG zones include Acqui or BRACHETTO D'ACQUI, ASTI, BARDOLINO SUPERIORE, CARMIGNANO, FRANCIACORTA, GATTINARA, GAVI or CORTESE DI GAVI, GHEMME, MONTEFALCO SAGRANTINO, RAMANDOLO, RECIOTO DI SOAVE, SOAVE SUPERIORE,

TAURASI, TORGIANO RISERVA, VALTELLINA SUPERIORE, VERMENTINO DI GALLURA, and VERNACCIA DI SAN GIMIGNANO.

département [day-pahr-tehr-MAHN] A French term referring to an administrative area that's similiar to a county within a state in the United States. The French mainland has ninety-five départements grouped into twenty-two regions.

deposit The SEDIMENT that settles in the bottle as a wine ages. Such deposits occur in many red wines and occasionally in some whites. It's a natural process and doesn't signify that there's anything wrong with the wine.

depth see Glossary of Wine Tasting Terms, page 655

dessert wine Generally speaking, any of a wide variety of sweet wines (sometimes FORTIFIED with brandy), all of which are compatible with desserts. More specifically in the United States, *dessert wine* is a legal term referring to all FORTIFIED WINES (whether or not sweet), which typically range from 16 to 21 percent in ALCOHOL BY VOLUME. Some of the more popular dessert wines are LATE HARVEST RIESLING, PORT, SAUTERNES, SHERRY, and BEERENAUSLESE.

destalking see DESTEMMING

destemming [dee-STEHM-ming] The process of removing grape stems from the MUST (juice, pulp, skin, and seeds) prior to FERMENTA-TION so that, during fermentation, bitter TANNINS in the stems won't transfer to the wine and make it HARSH. During the fermentation of red wines, the juice is in contact with the skins and seeds, which also con-tain tannins. Destemming (also called *destalking*) is important so that such wines, which obtain enough tannins from the skin and seeds to give them BALANCE, don't become overtly tannic. The French call this process *égrappage*.

Deutscher Sekt see SEKT

Deutscher Tafelwein (DTW) [DOYT-shur TAH-fuhl-vyn] A phrase indicating that a wine is 100 percent "German TABLE WINE," used to distinguish it from other European countries using German-style labeling. *Deutscher Tafelwein* is Germany's lowest category of wine and must contain a minimum of 8½ percent of ALCOHOL BY VOLUME. The labels for such wine must indicate the name of one of Germany's broad growing regions—Bayern, Neckar, Oberhein, or Rhein-Mosel. The term *Deutscher Tafelwein* is officially recognized by the European Economic Community, meaning other members must abide by the labeling conventions. When used by itself, the word *Tafelwein* on a label indicates that the wine is not German; the label should specify the country of origin. *See also* GERMANY; LANDWEIN; QUALITÄTSWEIN BESTIMMTER ANBAUGEBIETE; QUALITÄTSWEIN MIT PRÄDIKAT.

Deutschherrenberg *see* ZELTINGEN

deuxième cru [deu-zyem KROO] French phrase that means "second growth," the second-highest subcategory of the MÉDOC and SAUTERNES area's CRUS CLASSÉS (classed growths). Fifteen of the Médoc's châteaux were included in this category when it was established in the Classification of 1855 (*see* Official Wine Classifications of Bordeaux, page 678); that number remains unchanged today.

deuxième taille *see* TAILLE

developed *see* Glossary of Wine Tasting Terms, page 655

Dézaley [day-zah-LEH] One of the top wine-producing COMMUNES in Switzerland's VAUD canton. It's located in the LAVAUX growing zone, where steep vineyards slope down toward Lake Geneva. The primary grape is CHASSELAS, which is generally viewed as producing white wines of neutral character. Here, however, it performs extremely well and produces LIVELY, AROMATIC wines.

Dezize-lès-Maranges *see* MARANGES AC

DGO *see* BULGARIA

Diablo Grande AVA A 30,000-acre California AVA established in 1998 in the western foothills of the San Joaquin Valley in Stanislaus County. The area is located 25 to 30 miles east of San Jose and west of Modesto near Patterson. Isom Ranch Winery make's wines from its own vineyards and for Diablo Grande Vineyards. The grapes grown here are BARBERA, CABERNET SAUVIGNON, CABERNET FRANC, CHARDONNAY, MERLOT, PINOT NOIR, RIESLING, SANGIOVESE, SAUVIGNON BLANC, and SYRAH.

diacetyl *see* MALOLACTIC FERMENTATION

Diamant Bleu *see* CHAMPAGNE

Diamond Mountain AVA A 5,000-acre California viticulture area located on Diamond Mountain in the Mayacamas Range. Established in 2001, this small subzone is in the northwestern part of the NAPA VALLEY AVA. It runs west and is south of the town of Calistoga. Approximately 500 acres are planted to mostly CABERNET SAUVIGNON,

MERLOT, and ZINFANDEL. Sterling Vineyards has made wines from its Diamond Mountain vineyards for a number of years.

Die *see* CLAIRETTE DE DIE

Dienheim [DEEN-hime] An important wine-producing town located just south of OPPENHEIM in the RHEINHESSEN region. Although overshadowed by the reputation of Oppenheim, Dienheim is nonetheless recognized for producing high-quality wines from RIESLING and SYLVANER. Vineyards attached to Dienheim are found in GROSSLAGEN Oppenheimer **Krötenbrunnen** and Güldenmorgen. The better EINZELLAGEN associated with Dienheim include **Falkenberg**, **Herrengarten**, and **Tafelstein**.

dimethyl dicarbonate (DMDC) A yeast inhibitor used along with cold STABLIZATION techniques to add stability to wines as they are being bottled. During cold stablization, wines are filtered and if sterile filtration techniques (*see* FILTERING) are used then many microorganisms are eliminated. However, this doesn't ensure that problems, such as overt amounts of BRETTANOMYCES, don't resurface once the wine is bottled. Dimethyl dicarbonate, when added, helps promote stability of the bottled wines. It's thought to be superior to other chemicals such as potassium sorbate or sodium benzoate in conjunction with sulfur dioxide because DMDC doesn't affect the quality of the bottled wine, whereas these other chemicals might.

Dimiat *see* BULGARIA

Dionysus; Dionysos [di-uh-NI-suhs] The mythical Greek god of wine, fertility, and drama, Dionysus (also called *Bacchos* and known as *Bacchus* by the Romans) was the son of Zeus and Semele. Although known for his following of those who enjoyed licentious binges, it's said that Dionysus also dispersed information about the art of vine cultivation. The *bacchanals* (annual festivals held in his honor) became so outrageously lewd that the Roman Senate finally banned them in 186 A.D.

dirty *see* Glossary of Wine Tasting Terms, page 655

dirty sox *see* Glossary of Wine Tasting Terms, page 655

diseases, vineyard *see* BITTER ROT; BLACK ROT; BORDEAUX MIXTURE; GRAY ROT; LEAF-ROLL VIRUS; MILDEW; PIERCE'S DISEASE; PHYLLOXERA

disgorge; disgorgement The step in winemaking where sediment is removed during the MÉTHODE CHAMPENOISE process of making fine SPARKLING WINES. In a prior step called REMUAGE, sediment slowly collects around the CORK or CROWN CAP (the bottle is positioned upside-down). The neck of the bottle is then placed in an icy brine or glycol solution, which causes the neck's contents (mainly sediment) to freeze into a solid plug. During disgorging the cork or crown cap is removed, and the pressure in the bottle causes the frozen plug of sediment to pop out. The procedure is followed by the remaining méthode champenoise steps including adding the DOSAGE, topping off the bottle with additional wine, and recorking it. The French term for this process is *dégorgement*. The unofficial term **late disgorged** is used on some wine labels to indicate that a SPARKLING WINE has been AGED longer than normal bottlings and, through this longer aging, absorbed more flavor from the LEES.

distillation *v.* The process of purifying and concentrating a liquid through separating its components by heating it to the point of vaporization and collecting the cooled condensate (vapor that reverts to liquid through condensation). The apparatus used for distillation is a still, of which there are two types—pot still and continuous still. **distillation** *n.* The end product of the distillation process. Distilled spirits (such as BRANDY) are typically based on fermented (*see* FERMENTATION) fruit or cereal grains. After distillation, many are flavored in some way, either with added ingredients or by barrel AGING, or both.

distinguished *see* Glossary of Wine Tasting Terms, page 655

district *see* SOUTH AFRICA

Districtus Austria Controllatus (DAC) A new APPELLATION system being initiated in Austria. It's similar to the French AOC and Italian DOC(G) systems but allows a little more flexibility. To implement this, interprofessional committees consisting of cooperatives, grape growers, wine makers, and wine vendors were established in the eighteen Austrian wine districts. Their role is to determine whether their district should continue traditional methods of basing wines on sugar levels or implement the appellation approach with wines labeled with DAC. This approach is still in its infancy and so far the following have been given DAC status: **Kamptal DAC** (for both GRÜNER VELTLINER and RIESLING), **Kremstal DAC** (for both Grüner Veltliner and Riesling), **Mittelburgenland DAC** (for BLAUFRÄNKISCH), **Traisental DAC** (for both Grüner Veltliner and Riesling), and **Weinviertel DAC** (for Grüner Veltliner).

disulfides [di-SUHL-fides] *see* HYDROGEN SULFIDE

Dizy [dee-ZEE] An important wine-producing village in the Montagne de Reims area of France's Champagne region. It's planted chiefly with PINOT NOIR grapes. Dizy is classified as a PREMIER CRU village; its vineyards have a rating of 95 percent (*see* CHAMPAGNE for explanation of percent system).

DMDC *see* DIMETHYL DICARBONATE

DNA fingerprinting; DNA profiling; DNA typing DNA stands for *deoxyribonucleic acid*. Strands of DNA are long polymers composed of millions of nucleotides linked together. The sequence of nucleotides determines individual hereditary characteristics (the fingerprint) for all living matter, including grape vines. DNA fingerprinting (also called *DNA profiling* or *DNA typing*) allows small tissue samples of various grape VARIETIES to be compared and analyzed to determine if they are similar or identical. In the United States, UNIVERSITY OF CALIFORNIA, DAVIS researchers have been at the forefront of DNA profiling. In the early 1990s, Davis researchers used DNA fingerprinting to establish a relationship between California's ZINFANDEL and Italy's Primitivo. They established that some (but not all) examples of Primitivo were identical to Zinfandel, which caused speculation that Zinfandel might have originated in Italy. However, in late 2001, through collaborative efforts of researchers at UC Davis and the University of Zagreb in Croatia, DNA analysis determined that Crljenak (a little-known grape from Croatia) and Zinfandel had identical DNA profiles. Further analysis proved that a more popular Croatian grape, Plavac Mali, was a descendant of Crljenak (and therefore of Zinfandel). In 1997 researchers at UC Davis determined that CABERNET SAUVIGNON is an offspring of SAUVIGNON BLANC and CABERNET FRANC. Since Cabernet Sauvignon appeared in the late seventeenth century prior to plant hybridization practices, UC Davis scientists believe that its origin was a natural occurrence rather than a planned CROSS of the two parents. This serendipitous union turned out to be viticulturally historical. Based on DNA profiling, Chardonnay's origins are believed to be from the Pinot family (PINOT NOIR, PINOT GRIS, PINOT BLANC) on one side and from Gouais Blanc (a mediocre variety) on the other. Gouais Blanc, which is no longer grown in France, appears to be identical to Heunischweiss, a variety once widely grown in eastern Europe. Information on these varieties has been added to the DNA profiles of about 700 grape varieties, a database developed in collaboration with UC Davis researchers' colleagues in Montpellier, France. These profiles will contribute to the efforts of the International Grape Genome Project—groups of research teams in ten countries that map the genetic material of grapes to better understand various characteristics of grapes.

DO Abbreviation for DENOMINACIÓN DE ORIGEN utilized in the Spanish appellation system.

doble pasta [DOH-blay PAHSS-tah] Spanish for "double paste," referring to red wine that is made by fermenting a second batch of MUST over the LEES of a prior batch. This essentially doubles the dead YEAST cells, grape skin, and pulp particles that are in contact with the new must, which results in a much heavier wine. Doble pasta wines are often used as BLENDING WINES to boost lighter-weight reds.

DOC The abbreviation for the APPELLATION system of two countries—Italy (DENOMINAZIONE DI ORIGINE CONTROLLATA) and Portugal (DENOMINAÇÃO DE ORIGEM CONTRALADA).

DOCa Abbreviation for DENOMINACIÓN DE ORIGEN CALIFICADA utilized in the Spanish appellation system.

doce [DOAH-sehr] Portuguese for "sweet," typically referring to wines with a high degree of RESIDUAL SUGAR.

DOCG Abbreviation for DENOMINAZIONE DI ORIGINE CONTROLLATA E GARANTITA utilized in the Italian APPELLATION system.

Doctor [DAHK-tohr] A world-famous EINZELLAGE located on the steep hills above the town of BERNKASTEL in Germany's MOSEL-SAAR-RUWER region. According to the German laws established in 1971, the minimum size of an Einzellage is 5 HECTARES (12.35 acres) and Bernkasteler Doctor, at about 8 acres, is only one of two vineyards that are given special dispensation. The grapes from this steep vineyard are normally riper than others in this renowned area and possess a slate flavor that's exhibited in the superb wines.

dolce [DOHL-chay (It. DAWL-cheh)] Italian for "sweet," usually referring to wines with a high degree of RESIDUAL SUGAR.

Dolceacqua *see* ROSSESE DI DOLCEACQUA DOC

Dolcetto [dohl-CHEHT-oh; dohl-CHEHT-uh] Red-wine grape, whose name translates to "little sweet one," that is grown mainly in the southwest section of Italy's PIEDMONT region. There are several theories for Dolcetto's name. One suggests that it's because of the sweetness of the grapes and the juice they produce. Another says it's because there's a perception of sweetness in Dolcetto wines, even though they're usually VINIFIED as DRY wines without RESIDUAL SUGAR.

Dolcetto wines have high ACIDITY and are usually deep purple in color. They have perfumy BOUQUETS and rich, fruity, ripe-berry flavors, sometimes with a slightly bitter aftertaste. They should be drunk young before the fruit starts to fade. There are seven DOCs for Dolcetto, all in the Piedmont region. They are Dolcetto d'Aqui, Dolcetto d'Asti, Dolcetto di Diano d'Alba, Dolcetto delle Langhe Monregalesi, Dolcetto di Dogliani, Dolcetto di Ovada, and, probably the best known, DOLCETTO D'ALBA. This variety's also grown in the Piedmont's neighboring region LIGURIA, where it's known as *Ormeasco*. Other names for Dolcetto include *Dolsin* and *Dolsin Nero*.

Dolcetto d'Alba DOC [dawl-CHEHT-toh DAHL-bah] DOC zone that is considered the best of the seven DOCs in Italy's PIEDMONT region because of the number of high-quality producers making wine. It specializes in wines made with the DOLCETTO grape and the better wines are SMOOTH, with just enough TANNINS to be well BALANCED. This DOC zone encompasses an area around the town of Alba in the southeastern part of Piedmont. Part of the vineyards covered are in the same area as BAROLO and BARBARESCO.

Dôle *see* VALAIS

Dolsin; Dolsin Nero *see* DOLCETTO

domaine [doh-MAYN; Fr. daw-MEHN] French for "estate" or "property." The term is most often used in BURGUNDY where it pertains to a single property, although the property might be made up of several vineyards in different locations. If a wine is ESTATE BOTTLED (made and bottled by the grower), it's labeled "MIS AU DOMAINE," "MISE DU DOMAINE," "MIS EN BOUTEILLE AU DOMAINE," or "MIS EN BOUTEILLE A LA PROPRIETE."

domaine bottled *see* ESTATE BOTTLED

Domäne [daw-MEH-nuh] German for "domain" or "estate" (*see also* WEINGUT). The word domäne generally is used only for state-owned estates or for private estates owned by nobility or other officially recognized family. As is the German habit, "Domäne" is often combined with others names, such as in *Staatliche Weinbaudomäne* or *Domänenweingut Schloss Schönborn*. The word Domäne may be used on the label only if the wine is made exclusively from grapes grown on the estate's property.

Domdechaney *see* HOCKHEIM

Dom Pérignon [dom pay-ree-NYON] The seventeenth-century cellarmaster of France's Abbey of Hautvillers. Contrary to what some believe, Dom Pérignon did not invent sparkling wines. His important contribution was the creation of a method to prevent Champagne bottles and corks from exploding by using thicker bottles and tying the corks down with string. Even then, it's said that the venerable monk lost half his Champagne through bursting bottles. Dom Perignon is also celebrated for developing the art of blending wines to create Champagnes with superior flavor. *See also* CHAMPAGNE.

Domprobst *see* GRAACH

Donnaz *see* VALLE D'AOSTA

Doosberg *see* OESTRICH

Dorado *see* RUEDA DO

Dorin *see* CHASSELAS

Dornfelder [DORN-fehl-tehr] An effective German red-wine grape derived in 1955 from a CROSS of Helfensteiner and Heroldrebe, both of which are also crosses. Helfensteiner is a cross between Frühburgunder (PINOT NOIR) and Trollinger (SCHIAVA); Heroldrebe is a cross of PORTUGIESER and Limberger (BLAUFRÄNKISCH). Dornfelder, grown primarily in Germany's PFALZ, RHEINHESSEN, and WÜRTTEMBERG regions, produces wines considered very good, but not great. It's considered a good alternative to the German PINOT NOIR varieties *Frühburgunder* and *Spätburgunder,* which often don't meet expectations in these regions. Dornfelder is also grown in England, where it's often used as a BLENDING WINE. Because of its success, Dornfelder itself has been crossed to created additional varieties—with Limberger (BLAUFRÄNKISCH) to create **Acolon** and with CABERNET SAUVIGNON to create both **Cabernet Dorsa** and **Cabernet Dorio**.

dosage [doh-SAHJ] A syrupy mixture of sugar and wine (and sometimes BRANDY and/or citric acid) that's added to CHAMPAGNE and other SPARKLING WINE. A dosage is used in a couple of ways. A **bottling dosage** (*dosage de tirage* or *liqueur de tirage*) plus yeast is added to a CUVÉE (a blend of still wines) in order to cause a SECONDARY FERMENTATION in the bottle. A **shipping dosage** (*dosage d'expédition* or *liqueur d'expédition*)—usually sugar plus some of the same wine that's been reserved for this purpose—is added to a wine immediately prior to final bottling to increase its level of sweetness. The percentage of sugar in the shipping dosage determines the degree of sweetness in the final wine. Depending on this level of sweetness, sparkling wines are described as BRUT, EXTRA DRY or EXTRA-SEC, SEC, DEMI-SEC, or DOUX. *See also* MÉTHODE CHAMPENOISE.

dosage de tirage *see* DOSAGE

dosage d'expédition *see* DOSAGE

Dos Rios AVA Another small APPELLATION, which lies in the larger MENDOCINO AVA and the even larger NORTH COAST AVA. It was created in November 2005 and contains 15,500 acres. Only about 6 acres are planted to grape vines and these belong to the lone winery of the AVA, Vin de Tevis. The grapes grown are CABERNET FRANC, CABERNET SAUVIGNON, MERLOT and ZINFANDEL.

double blind tasting *see* Tasting Wine, page 648

double magnum *see* Wine Bottles, page 609

Douro; Douro DOC [DOO-roh] Douro is a wild mountainous region located around the Douro River starting at the Spanish border and extending west into northern Portugal. The Douro region contains two DENOMINAÇÃO DE ORIGEM CONTROLADA (DOC) areas—Douro DOC for TABLE WINES and PORT DOC (see listing) for port wines. Although they share much of the same area, the Douro DOC is larger because it includes vineyards that aren't acceptable for the Port DOC because many of the Douro DOC vineyards sit at higher altitudes than are optimum for port vineyards. At the higher altitudes in this hot region, grapes don't ripen quite as fully, which makes them better suited for table wines than for port. The Douro DOC allows a multitude of grapes to be used in the wines. The main varieties for red wines are TOURIGA NACIONAL, TOURIGA FRANCESA, and Tinta Roriz (TEMPRANILLO). The primary white grapes used are Esgana Cão (SERCIAL), Folgosão, and VERDELHO. Some of Portugal's best and most sought after wines (like the *Barca Velha* from FERREIRA) come from this region.

Douro bake *see* PORT

doux [DOO] French for "sweet." On a CHAMPAGNE label, "doux" means the wine is very sweet—over 5 percent sugar. *See also* LIQUOREUX; MOELLEUX.

downy mildew *see* MILDEW

Drachenstein *see* RÜDESHEIM

dried-grape wines Wines made from partially dried grapes—most are sweet, some are DRY. This centuries-old technique of drying grapes for wine was developed in the Mediterranean region and used by the Phoenicians, Greeks, and Romans. Whether the grapes are dried in the sun or indoors on mats, the end result is similar to wine made with BOTRYTIS CINEREA-infected grapes or frozen grapes (for EISWEIN)—all have concentrated flavors, ACIDITY, and sugar levels, as well as added complexity. When drying grapes, producers must be careful that they don't get infected with undesirable molds, which would ruin the grapes. Even Botrytis cinerea is avoided by many producers. This requires the grapes to be dehydrated in dry areas with good air circulation. Today Italy is the strongest supporter of this traditional winemaking method, which Italians call PASSITO. The VIN SANTO produced in the TUSCANY, UMBRIA, TRENTINO-ALTO ADIGE, and VENETO regions is made using this technique. Other Italian APPELLATIONS making dried-grape wines include CALUSO PASSITO DOC, CINQUE TERRE DOC, MONTEFALCO SAGRANTINO DOCG, MOSCATO PASSITO DI PANTELLERIA DOC, RECIOTO DI SOAVE DOCG, RECIOTO DELLA VALPOLICELLA DOC, and RECIOTO DELLA VALPOLICELLA AMARONE DOC (the latter being one of this wine style's few dry forms). Other wines made in this fashion include Austria's STROHWEIN, France's VIN DE PAILLE, and Commandaria, a dessert wine specialty of CYPRUS.

dried out *see* Glossary of Wine Tasting Terms, page 655

dry *see* Glossary of Wine Tasting Terms, page 655

Dry Creek Valley AVA Located in the northern part of SONOMA COUNTY, this APPELLATION runs from north of the town of Geyserville to just south of Healdsburg and spreads west from these towns. Most of the vineyards and wineries are scattered around Dry Creek, a tributary of the Russian River. The warmer northern and middle sections of this VITICULTURAL AREA favor ZINFANDEL grapes, which have been planted in this area since the 1880s. Other varieties that do well here include SAUVIGNON BLANC, CHARDONNAY, and CABERNET SAUVIGNON. RHÔNE varieties are increasingly being planted in some of the warmer areas as well. In the cooler southern portion (near the RUSSIAN RIVER AVA), even RIESLING can do well.

dry sherry *see* SHERRY

DTW *see* DEUTSCHER TAFELWEIN

dulce [DOOL-thay; DOOL-say] Spanish for "sweet."

dull *see* Glossary of Wine Tasting Terms, page 655

dumb; dumb phase *see* Glossary of Wine Tasting Terms, page 655

Dundee Hills AVA This is a sub-AVA of the larger WILLAMETTE VALLEY AVA. It was established in January 2005 and comprises 6,490 acres. It's located just north of the town of Dundee and about 28 miles southwest of Portland. There are over 25 wineries and autonomous vineyards with about 1,500 acres planted mostly with PINOT NOIR, but also with CHARDONNAY, MULLER-THURGAU, PINOT BLANC, PINOT GRIS and RIESLING. Archery Summit, Domaine Drouhin and Domaine Serene control some of the top vineyards.

Dunnigan Hills AVA Located in Yolo County northwest of Sacramento and northeast of San Francisco, this area encompasses 89,000 acres in the foothills of the Coast Range Mountains about 30 miles east of the Napa County line. R.H. Phillips Wine Company has approximately 1600 acres planted with CABERNET SAUVIGNON, CHARDONNAY, SAUVIGNON BLANC, SYRAH, TEMPRANILLO, and VIOGNIER.

Duras *see* CÔTES DE DURAS AC

Durbanville WO A small demarcated South African wine ward (*see* SOUTH AFRICA) located on the northeast edges of Cape Town. It is one of the country's coolest growing regions due to breezes blowing off False Bay to the south and Table Bay to the east. Durbanville is best known for premium red wines, particularly Shiraz (SYRAH), although SAUVIGNON BLANC has also attracted attention recently.

Durif [dyoor-IF; DUR-if] A red-wine grape grown in France's RHÔNE region in the late nineteenth century and up to the middle of the twentieth century. Long-viewed as a rather common and minor variety, Durif is seldom found in French vineyards today. In the late 1990s, DNA analysis indicated that Durif was in fact a CROSS between SYRAH and a variety called Peloursin. A vast majority of the variety called PETITE SIRAH in California is actually Durif. Durif is also known as *Pinot de Romans* and *Pinot de l'Ermitage*, although it's not a member of the PINOT NOIR family.

Dürkheim *see* BAD DÜRKHEIM

dusty *see* Glossary of Wine Tasting Terms, page 655

Dutchess [DUH-chess] A VITUS LABRUSCA and VITIS VINIFERA HYBRID developed in the United States and grown mostly in the eastern states. Even though the white wines it produces have FOXY characteristics, they're generally of good quality. Dutchess is not widely planted, so these wines are difficult to find.

earthy; earthiness *see* Glossary of Wine Tasting Terms, page 655

East India *see* SHERRY

eau de vie; pl. eaux de vie [oh duh VEE] French for "water of life." This term describes any colorless, potent BRANDY or other spirit distilled (*see* DISTILLATION) from fermented fruit juice. Among the grape-based eaux de vie are *eau de vie de marc* (from MARC), *eau de vie de lie* (from LEES), and *eau de vie de vin* (from wine). Probably the two most popular eaux de vie in the world are Kirsch (from cherries) and Framboise (from raspberries).

Échezeaux AC [ay-shuh-ZOH] A lesser-known GRAND CRU vineyard that is located in the CÔTE DE NUITS area of France's BURGUNDY region. Even though it's located in the village of Flagey-Échezeaux, it is often grouped with the famous grands crus of the neighboring village of VOSNE-ROMANÉE. Échezeaux has 93 acres, all planted with PINOT NOIR grapes, making it the second largest Burgundian grand cru after CLOS DE VOUGEOT. These red wines are generally LIGHTER, more refined, and earlier maturing than those from neighboring grands crus—the acclaimed GRANDS-ÉCHEZEAUX in particular, which is recognized as producing superior wines with more depth of aroma and flavor. As a large Burgundian vineyard, Échezeaux has many (80 plus) owners, all of whom produce wines of varying quality and use the Échezeaux name.

Edelfäule [ay-duhl-FOY-luh] A German term meaning "noble rot," referring to BOTRYTIS CINEREA, the beneficial mold responsible for the TROCKENBEERNAUSLESE wines.

Edeltraube *see* GEWÜRZTRAMINER

Edelzwicker *see* ALSACE

Eden Valley An Australian wine region located in the Barossa Zone of SOUTH AUSTRALIA. It's situated about 40 miles northeast of Adelaide around the towns of Angaston and Eden Valley. It shares much of its history with the BAROSSA VALLEY, which borders it on the west. Vines were first planted in 1847—the same year vines first arrived in the Barossa Valley. Eden Valley has not developed like the Barossa and today has only sixteen wineries. It's cooler and windier so site selection is very important. RIESLING is Eden Valley's most famous and widely planted grape. Shiraz (SYRAH) is the next most heavily planted, followed by CABERNET SAUVIGNON, PINOT NOIR, SÉMILLON, SAUVIGNON BLANC, and MERLOT. Shiraz has the same sterling reputation as Riesling here.

Especially esteemed are those wines from Henshke, whose Hill of Grace Shiraz comes from vines planted in the 1860s and is thought by many to be second only to the great GRANGE from Penfold.

edes [A-dehsh] Hungarian for "sweet."

eggs *see* SULFUR in the Glossary of Wine Tasting Terms, page 655

Egiodola Egiodola, which means "pure blood" in Basque, is a CROSS between FER SERVADOU and Arbouriu created in the 1950s. It's grown in SOUTHWEST FRANCE and also found in BRAZIL. This red wine grape produces fruity, spicy wines with deep color, high alcohol and a good dose of tannins.

E

égrappage [ay-grah-PAHZH] French term for DESTEMMING. *Éraflage* is sometimes used as well. An *égrappoir* is a machine that removes stems.

Egri Bikavér [EH-grih BIH-kah-vahr] The town of Eger is located northeast of Budapest in notably mountainous country. Egri Bikavér, which means "bull's blood from Eger," is Hungary's best-known red wine. According to legend, the wine got its name in the sixteenth century after the Eger was attacked by Turkish troops. Fortified with the local wine, the valiant Hungarian soldiers bravely defeated the attacking hoard. Thankfully, there's no bull's blood in the wine, which is made from at least three of the following varieties: KADARKA, Kékfrankos (BLAUFRÄNKISCH), MENOIR, Kékoportó (PORTUGIESER), CABERNET SAUVIGNON, CABERNET FRANC, MERLOT, PINOT NOIR, SYRAH, Blaugurger and Zweigelt. At one time, Egri Bikavér was a very highly regarded, full-flavored, full-bodied (*see* BODY) wine. It's now considered quite average, which some believe is the result of using less of the high-quality Kadarka grapes and more of the rather ordinary Kékfrankos variety. **Egri Bikavér Superior** must contain four of the recommended grape varieties and is generally of higher quality.

Ehrenfelser [EHR-en-fehl-zuhr] A good-quality, white-wine, HYBRID grape developed at GEISENHEIM, Germany in the 1920s. Ehrenfelser is a CROSS of RIESLING and SYLVANER that—except for its lower ACID levels—closely resembles Riesling. It has some advantages over Riesling in that Ehrenfelser grows in less desirable locations and ripens earlier, which makes it increasingly popular in some of Germany's northern growing regions.

1855 Official Classification of Bordeaux *see* Official Wine Classifications of Bordeaux, page 678

Einzellage; pl. Einzellagen [I'n-tsuh-lah-guh; I'n-tsuh-lah-gehn] As defined by the German wine laws of 1971, an Einzellage is an individual vineyard site with a minimum size of 5 HECTARES (about 12½ acres). This law caused the absorption of many tiny vineyards into larger ones, reducing the total number of vineyards from approximately 25,000 to about 2,600. The result is a situation similar to France's BURGUNDY region where a vineyard may be divided among many different growers. Nearly all the vineyard sites in Germany are officially registered as Einzellagen, each with their own officially assigned number. Einzellagen are the smallest defined areas under the German system, which includes GROSSLAGEN (general sites), BEREICHE (districts), and ANBAUGEBIETE (growing regions). On labels, the name of the Einzellage is most often preceded by the name of the village where the vineyard is located. When this is done, the village name has an *er* attached to it. For example, the Einzellage Daubhaus from the village of Oppenheim would appear on the label as "Oppenheimer Daubhaus," and the Einzellage Sonnenberg in the village of Eltville appears as "Eltviller Sonnenberg."

Eiswein [ICE-vyn] A German term meaning "ice wine," referring to a rich, flavorful DESSERT WINE. Eiswein is made by picking grapes that are frozen on the vine and then pressing them before they thaw. Because much of the water in the grapes is frozen, the resulting juice is concentrated—rich in flavor and high in sugar and ACIDITY. The resulting wines, although different than Germany's famous BEERENAUSLESEN and TROCKENBEERENAUSLESEN, are similarly extraordinarily sweet, yet balanced by high acidity. Eiswein is an excellent candidate for long AGING. In 1982, Eiswein became one of the six subcategories of QUALITÄTSWEIN MIT PRÄDIKAT. In order to thus qualify, a wine's MUST needs to reach the minimum natural sugar levels of BEERENAUSLESE category wines—110 to 128° OECHSLE (approximately 26 to 30 percent sugar by weight), depending on the region and the variety. AUSTRIA has an Eiswein category that's similar and requires a minimum 127° OECHSLE. Eiswein is a specialty of Canada (where it's spelled "icewine"), whose cold weather produces excellent examples of this specialty. In fact, Canadians now produce more Eiswein than Germany, and has VQA regulations that define the sugar content required for this designation to be used on labels. Other cold weather areas, such as the more northern of the United States, are now also producing Eisweins.

Eitelsbach [I-tls-bahkh] A small village that's part of the city of TRIER in Germany's MOSEL-SAAR-RUWER region. Eitelsbach, which sits on the Ruwer River and is part of the BEREICH SAAR-RUWER, is well known because of one famous wine estate—**Karthäuserhofberg**. This estate's vineyards, which are situated on the steep hills just above Eitelsbach, are considered one of the two best along the Ruwer (the other being MAXIMIN GRÜNHAUS). Karthäuserhofberg, which means "Carthusians' Hill," gets its name from the Carthusian monastery that owned the vineyard for nearly 500 years. Although the estate has five named vineyards—Burgberg, Kronenberg, Orthsberg, Sang, and Stirn—the vineyard names have not been used on labels since 1985, and all wines are labeled "Eitelsbacher Karthäuserhofberger."

elaborado por [ay-lah-boh-RAH-doh poor] Spanish term for "made by."

Elba DOC [EHLL-bah] DOC zone on the island of Elba, which is located off the coast of (and is considered part of) Italy's TUSCANY region. The island is famous as the place where Napoleon was exiled. Elba's BIANCO wines are produced mainly from TREBBIANO and Procanico grapes—a SPUMANTE version may also be made. Their ROSSO wine is made from a blend of at least 75 percent SANGIOVESE, plus CANAIOLO, Trebbiano, and Biancone.

Elbling [EHL-bling] A very productive white-wine grape with origins prior to the Middle Ages—possibly to Roman times. Elbling's grown mainly in Germany's MOSEL region, particularly in environments where RIESLING has trouble ripening. This grape produces rather ordinary wines with neutral flavors and high ACIDITY. Although much of it is made into SPARKLING WINE (called SEKT in Germany), Elbling is occasionally found as either a DRY or medium-dry STILL WINE. This grape is also called *Burger, Grossriesling, Kleinberger,* and *Rheinelbe.*

El Dorado AVA [ehl doh-RAH-doh] APPELLATION that covers the foothills (which range from 1,200 to 3,500 feet in altitude) in El Dorado County, east and slightly north of Sacramento, California. The boundaries of the larger SIERRA FOOTHILLS AVA include the El Dorado AVA. This growing area ranges from a Region II to a Region III (*see* CLIMATE REGIONS OF CALIFORNIA), depending on the location and the year. **Fair Play AVA,** sometimes called South County, is a subzone created in 2001 within the El Dorado and Sierra Foothills AVAs. The Fair Play region is mostly in the 2,500- to 3,500-foot level, which is extremely high for California growing areas. El Dorado wines are known for their high ACIDITY. ZINFANDEL, CABERNET SAUVIGNON, CHARDONNAY, SAUVIGNON BLANC, SYRAH, and three dozen other varieties are all grown here.

elegant; elegance *see* Glossary of Wine Tasting Terms, page 655

éleveur [eh-leh-VUHR] A word taken from the French *élevage,* which means "bringing up" or "raising." In the French wine trade, an éleveur is someone who buys recently fermented wine and then "raises" it by performing such functions as BLENDING, FINING, FILTERING, AGING, and bottling. These activities are sometimes performed by a NEGOCIANT, who then labels the wines with the phrase *négociant-éleveur.*

Elgin WO *see* OVERBERG WO

Elmonte DO *see* CANARY ISLANDS

Elysium *see* MUSCAT

E

embotellado de/en origen [aym-boa-tay-LYAH-doh deh/ehn oh-REE-gehn] A Spanish phrase meaning ESTATE BOTTLED.

embotellado por [aym-boa-tay-LYAH-doh poor] Spanish for "bottled by."

Les Embrazées *see* CHASSAGNE-MONTRACHET AC

Emerald Riesling [EHM-uhr-uhld REEZ-ling; REES-ling] White HYBRID grape that was developed by the UNIVERSITY OF CALIFORNIA, DAVIS in 1948 in an attempt to create high-quality, highly productive grapes for California's hotter growing areas. Emerald Riesling's parents are the highly regarded RIESLING and the rather ordinary MUSCADELLE. The resulting grape produces wines that are fairly AROMATIC, high in ACIDITY, and medium-bodied, but lacking in flavor. These wines are generally used for blending, although there are some medium-DRY VARIETAL WINES made, the most famous being Paul Masson's Emerald Dry. Emerald Riesling has never been extremely popular—most of its acreage is in California's CENTRAL VALLEY, with limited amounts in South Africa and Australia.

Emilia-Romagna [eh-MEE-lyah raw-MAH-nyah] Diverse wine-producing region located in northern Italy, north of TUSCANY and south of LOMBARDY and VENETO. Its capital city is Bologna. Emilia-Romagna is renowned for its food and food products and is the home of Parmesan cheese and Parma hams. There are about 145,000 vineyard acres in a diverse number of winegrowing areas spread among the plains and the hills of both the Emilia and Romagna sectors. The great flat plain of the Emilia area around Modena produces huge volumes of red wine from the LAMBRUSCO grape and its many subvarieties. In the hilly regions around Colli Bolognesi and Colli Piacentini the principal grapes for red wine are BARBERA and BONARDA. In Romagna, ALBANA and

TREBBIANO are the primary white grapes, and SANGIOVESE is the primary red grape. Emilia-Romagna has one DOCG, ALBANA DI ROMAGNA, about which there is a great deal of controversy. The general sentiment is that this growing area received DOCG status more through political posturing than through the quality of its wines. Emilia-Romagna also has the following DOC areas: **Bosco Eliceo**, **Cagnina di Romagna**, COLLI BOLOGNESI, **Colli della Romagna Centrale**, **Colli di Faenza**, **Colli di Parma**, **Colli di Rimini**, **Colli di Scandiano e Canossa**, **Colli d'Imola**, COLLI PIACENTINI, **Lambrusco di Sorbara**, **Lambrusco Grasparossa di Castelvetro**, **Lambrusco Salamino di Santa Croce**, **Pagadebit di Romagna**, **Reggiano**, **Reno**, **Romagna Albana Spumante**, **Sangiovese di Romagna**, and **Trebbiano di Romagna**.

Empordà-Costa Brava DO [ahm-poor-DAHN KOH-stah BRAH-vah] A small DO located at the very northeastern tip of Spain in the CATALONIA region. (Empordà-Costa Brava is the Catalan spelling; Ampurdán-Costa Brava is the Spanish.) This region's northern border is France; the Mediterranean lies to the east. It consists of many small landowners, and most of the wines are made by thirteen large cooperatives. Empordà-Costa Brava DO produces mostly ROSÉS, but also red and white wines. The red wines are made with Garnacha Tinta (GRENACHE) and Cariñena (CARIGNAN); rosé wines use those grapes plus the two white VARIETIES—MACABEO and XAREL-LO. White wines are made from these last two grapes. There are a variety of wine styles made here, including RANCIOS and FORTIFIED WINES, of which **Garnatxa**—the local VINO DE LICOR made from Garnacha (GRENACHE)—is a specialty. Producers are experimenting with nonlocal varieties like CABERNET SAUVIGNON, CHARDONNAY, CHENIN BLANC, GEWÜRZTRAMINER, MERLOT, MUSCAT, RIESLING, and TEMPRANILLO, all of which are allowed in DO wines.

empty *see* Glossary of Wine Tasting Terms, page 655

encapsulated yeasts *see* RIDDLING

encépagement [ahn-say-PAHZH-mah*n*] The French term used for the assortment of grape VARIETIES planted on a particular property.

Encostas d'Aire *see* ESTREMADURA

Encruzado [ayng-kroo-ZAH-doo] A Portuguese white-grape variety heavily planted in the DÃO DOC. Better examples of Encruzado based wines have good ACIDITY and a medium to full BODY and can exhibit hints of melon.

engarrafado; engarrafado na origem [ayn-gar-rah-FAH-doh nah oh-REE-zhem] Portuguese for "bottled" and "ESTATE BOTTLED," respectively.

Engelsberg *see* NACKENHEIM

Engelsmannberg *see* HATTENHEIM

England The Romans are thought to have been the VITICULTURAL pioneers in England. There were also numerous vineyards producing wine during the Middle Ages, although English rule (through a royal marriage) of France's Bordeaux region from 1152 through 1453 seemed to shift allegiance to the wines of Bordeaux permanently. Most vineyards were associated with monasteries, but when Henry VIII renounced the monasteries, the vineyards were ripped up, and the land was planted with other crops. It wasn't until the 1950s that English winemaking began its revival. Britain's northerly climate isn't particularly hospitable for grape growing, but the southern portions of England and Wales contain about 2,000 acres of grapevines. There are over 400 wineries (most are small) producing wine in areas like Essex, Hampshire, Hereford, Kent, Somerset, Suffolk, Sussex, and the Thames Valley. Because of its severe climate, England is white-wine country, with the most popular grapes being MÜLLER-THURGAU, SEYVAL BLANC and the German CROSSES of HUXELREBE, KERNER, ORTEGA, Reichensteiner, Schönburger, and Siegerrebe. Tiny amounts of PINOT NOIR and CHARDONNAY are also planted. English wines are generally DRY, LIGHT, CRISP, and FLOWERY with good ACIDITY. *See also* ENGLISH WINE and BRITISH WINE.

English Wine This term on a label indicates that the wine was produced using grapes grown in England. *See also* BRITISH WINE.

Eola-Amity Hills AVA This is a sub-APPELLATION of the larger WILLAMETTE VALLEY AVA. It was established in August 2006 and covers 37,900 acres. It starts just northwest of Salem and runs about 15 miles north until it reaches the town of Amity. The climate is temperate and the area receives cool air flowing from the Pacific Ocean which helps set the grape's ACID levels. CHARDONNAY, DOLCETTO, PINOT BLANC, PINOT GRIS, PINOT NOIR, SYRAH, and VIOGNIER are the most widely planted varieties in the 1,500 acres of vineyards. Top producers include Bethel Heights Vineyard and Cristom Vineyards.

enologist *see* ENOLOGY

enology [ee-NAHL-uh-jee] The science or study of winemaking. One trained in the science is called an **enologist** or **enologue**. Also spelled *oenology*. The word VINICULTURE is synonymous, although not as commonly used. *See also* ACETALDEHYDE; ACETIFICATION; ACETOBACTER; ACIDITY; ACIDS; ACIDULATION; AGING; ALCOHOL; AMELIORATION; ANTHOCYANINS; ANTIOXIDANT; ASSEMBLAGE; AUTOCLAVE; AUTOLYSIS; BAKING; BARREL; BARREL FERMENTATION; BENTONITE; BLENDING; BORDEAUX BLEND; BOTTLE FERMENTA-TION; BOTTLE SICKNESS; BRIX; BUNG; CAMPDEN TABLETS; CAP; CAPSULE; CARBON DIOXIDE; CARBONIC MACERATION; CARBOY; CHAPTALIZATION; CHARMAT PROCESS; COOPERAGE; CORKS; CRUST; CRYOEXTRACTION; CUSTOM CRUSHING; DEACIDIFICA-TION; DESTEMMING; DISGORGEMENT; DOSAGE; ESTERS; ESTUFAGEM; FERMENTA-TION; FERMENTATION CONTAINERS; FERMENTATION LOCK; FIELD BLEND; FILTERING; FINING; FLAVONOIDS; FLOR; FORTIFICATION; FRUCTOSE; GLUCOSE; GLYCEROL; GRAPE CONCENTRATE; GRAPES; HYDROGEN SULFIDE; HYDROMETER; INOCULATE; ISINGLASS; LEAF REMOVAL; LEES; MACERATION; MALOLACTIC FERMENTATION; MÉTH-ODE CHAMPENOISE; MUST; MUST WEIGHT; MUTAGE; MUTÉ; MYCODERMA; OAKING; OXIDATION; PASSITO; PASTEURIZATION; PH; PHENOLIC COMPOUNDS; PLASTERING; POMACE; POTASSIUM METABISULFITE; POTENTIAL ALCOHOL; PRESS; PULP; PUMPING OVER; PUNCHING DOWN; RACKING; RESIDUAL SUGAR; RIDDLING; RIPASSO PROCESS; SECONDARY FERMENTATION; SEDIMENT; SKIN CONTACT; SOLERA SYSTEM; SPECIFIC GRAVITY; STABILIZATION; STAINLESS STEEL TANKS; STARTER; SULFUR DIOXIDE; SUR LIE; TANNINS; TOPPING; TARTRATES; ULLAGE; VARIETY; VINTAGE; VITICULTURE; VOLATILE ACIDITY; WHOLE BERRY FERMENTATION; WINEGROWER; YEAST.

enophile [EE-nuh-file] Someone who enjoys wine, usually referring to a connoisseur. Also spelled *oenophile*.

enoteca [ay-noh-TEH-kah] Italian for "wine cellar," but referring to a wine shop that has an extensive, high-quality offering of wines. Wine regions sometimes establish an enoteca to showcase the wines of the area.

en primeur *see* FUTURES

en tirage *see* TIRAGE

Entre-Deux-Mers [ah*n*-truh duh MER*R*] Meaning "between two seas," the area of Entre-Deux-Mers sits between two rivers, the Dordogne and the Garonne, in the eastern portion of France's BOR-DEAUX region. With approximately 7,400 acres, it's the largest subdis-trict within Bordeaux. Its undulating hills make it one of the most beautiful as well. The Entre-Deux-Mers AC applies only to white wines made from MUSCADELLE, SAUVIGNON BLANC, and SÉMILLON. These wines are now made in a CRISP, DRY fashion, a change from the rather bland, semisweet versions made in the past. Within the southern por-tion of Entre-Deux-Mers is the small **Haut-Benauge AC**, which produces white wines of somewhat higher quality. Red wines produced from the Entre-Deux-Mers region are sold as BORDEAUX AC or Bordeaux Supérieur AC.

Les Epenots *see* POMMARD

Epitrapezios Inos *see* GREECE

Épernay [ay-pehr-NAY] Very famous commune located in the heart of the CHAMPAGNE region in northern France. Épernay lays claim to the unofficial title of the "Capital of Champagne" not because the vineyards around Épernay are so highly regarded (they rate 88 percent— *see* CHAMPAGNE for description) but because it is the main distribution center for the Champagne region. Many of the famous Champagne producers have grand buildings along the Avenue de Champagne. Beneath Épernay there are hundreds of millions of bottles of Champagne aging in the huge cellars that are built into the underground chalk formations.

éraflage *see* ÉGRAPPAGE

Erbach [EHR-bahkh] Located in Germany's RHEINGAU region, this town is known for its esteemed wines, particularly those from **Marcobrunn**, a celebrated EINZELLAGE. Marcobrunn is actually located only partly in the village of Hattenheim, but in 1971 a dispute was settled to the effect that all wines produced in the area are attached to the village of Erbach, and therefore labeled "Erbacher Marcobrunn." Wines from the Marcobrunn site are generally full-bodied (*see* BODY) and long-lived. Erbach has also made its mark with wines from other sites including **Hohnenrain**, **Honigberg**, **Michelmark**, **Rheinhell**, **Schlossberg**, **Siegelsberg**, and **Steinmorgen**.

Erbaluce [ehr-bah-LOO-chay] A white-wine grape grown mainly in the northwest area of Italy's PIEDMONT region. Erbaluce yields highly ACIDIC wines of rather ordinary quality. LEAN, DRY wines and SPARKLING WINES are produced under the DOC banner of ERBALUCE DI CALUSO. In the DOC of CALUSO PASSITO, the Erbaluce grapes are laid out in the sun to dry and then FERMENTED into a rich DESSERT WINE that ranges in color from pale yellow to golden. A LIQUOROSO—or FORTIFIED version—of the Caluso Passito is also produced. Erbaluce is most renowned for these PASSITO wines.

Erbaluce di Caluso DOC [ehr-bah-LOO-tchay dee kah-LOO-soh] DOC area located in the northern part of Italy's PIEDMONT region north of Turin. The vineyards are located in thirty-five different villages in and around the town of Caluso. These are ordinary DRY white wines made from the ERBALUCE grape, although a rich, sweet DESSERT WINE called CALUSO PASSITO is also made. A sparkling version called **Caluso Spumante** is produced as well.

Erben [EHR-buhn] German for "heirs" or "successors." Erben is sometimes used on labels much like "& Sons" might be used in England or the United States. Examples include Weingut Bürger-meister Anton Balbach Erben and Weingut Bürgermeister Carl Koch Erben.

Erden [EHR-duhn] A small village located in Germany's MOSEL-SAAR-RUWER region, along the Mosel River downstream from the town of BERNKASTEL in the BEREICH Bernkastel. Erden is surrounded by gently sloping vineyards, but its best vineyards are across the river on the steep hills next to the village of Urzig. The top EINZELLAGEN are **Herrenberg**, **Prälat** (the best known), and **Treppchen**.

Ermitage *see* HERMITAGE; MARSANNE

Erste Lage [AYR-sters lah-guh] *see* GERMANY

Erstes Gewächs [AYR-sters GER-vehks] German for "first growth," Erstes Gewächs is a vineyard classification established in September 2000, for Germany's RHEINGAU region. The area involved is relatively large—just over 35 percent of the entire region. However, to use "Erstes Gewächs" on the label (the equivalent of the French PREMIER CRU), vineyards must comply with a complex set of criteria, including a maximum yield of 50 hectolitres per hecatre and the tasting test of the finished wine.

Erzeugerabfüllung [AYR-tsoy-guhr-AB-few-lung] A German term meaning "producer bottled" and having a meaning somewhat similar to ESTATE BOTTLED. The major difference is that German COOPERATIVES, which blend wines from various members, can use the term. The term GUTSABFÜLLUNG is much more restrictive and is much closer to the use of the term "estate bottled" in the United States.

erzeugergemeinschaft [AYR-tsoy-guhr-geh-MYN-shawft] German phrase referring to a VITICULTURE producers' association, which is not the same as a winemaking COOPERATIVE.

Escherndorf [ESH-uhrn-dorf] This well-known village produces some of the best wines coming from Germany's FRANKEN region. Escherndorf, which is located on the Main River northeast of Wurzburg, lies at the base of steep hillside vineyards. The best EINZEL-LAGEN are **Berg**, **Fürstenberg**, and **Lump**.

Escondido Valley AVA A VITICULTURAL AREA approved in 1992 in the Trans-Pecos region of west TEXAS just east of Fort Stockton. It covers approximately 32,000 acres in Pecos County. Cordier Estates/Ste. Genevieve, a subsidiary of French wine giant Domaines Cordier, is the largest wine producer in Texas. It farms just over 1,000 acres in this region and imports BULK wine from France's vast LANGUEDOC-ROUSSILLON region and South Eastern AUSTRALIA, which enables it to produce more than 700,000 cases per year under the labels of Ste. Genevieve, Escondido Valley, and L'Orval.

Esgana Cão *see* SERCIAL

Espagne *see* CINSAUT

espumante [ish-poo-MERN-teh] Portuguese for "sparkling."

espumoso [ehs-poo-MOH-soh] Spanish for "sparkling." *See also* CAVA DO.

Essencia *see* MUSCAT; TOKAJI

esters [EHS-tuhrs] Compounds produced by the reaction between ACIDS and ALCOHOL, which happens in wine during FERMENTATION as well as AGING. The contribution of esters (the most prominent of which is ETHYL ACETATE) to wine is an ACETONE smell that's sweet and slightly fruity. Esters also contribute COMPLEXITY to wine.

Est! Est!! Est!!! di Montefiascone DOC [EHST EHST EHST dee mawn-teh-fyahs-KAW-neh] The name of a DOC area located in Italy's LATIUM region, northwest of Rome near Lake Bolsena. According to legend, a twelfth-century German bishop on his way to Rome sent his servant ahead to identify places where wines were particularly good. When the servant found one, he was to identify it by writing the word *Est* (Latin for "it is") on its wall. The servant apparently found the wine at a tavern in Montefiascone to be so fantastic that he enscribed the enthusiastic *Est! Est!! Est!!!* on the wall. According to the story, the bishop (who apparently agreed with his servant's opinion) never left Montefiascone. It produces a light, DRY white wine from TREBBIANO, Procanico, and MALVASIA grapes. The wine is generally viewed as quite ordinary—certainly not worth all the exclamation points.

Estremadura [ish-trer-mah-DOO-rah] A VINHO REGIONAL located in western Portugal near Lisbon. Included in its boundaries are eight DOC areas—ALENQUER, **Arruda**, **Bucelas**, CARCAVELOS, COLARES, LOURINHÃ, **Obidos**, and **Torres Vedras**. It also has two IPRS—**Alcobaça** and **Encostas d'Aire**. The Estremadura region is Portugal's largest volume producer and is generally thought of as a source of cheap, mediocre, easy-drinking wine. Quality is starting to improve in the region, especially for the wines coming out of the DOC designated areas.

estufa *see* MADEIRA

estufagem *see* MADEIRA

ethanol *see* ALCOHOL

ethyl acetate [ETH-uhl ASS-ih-tayt] An ESTER that is a by-product of FERMENTATION. When ethyl acetate exists in sufficient quantity, it produces a slightly sweet, fruity, vinegary smell. Even though ethyl acetate exists in all wines and can be complementary (especially in rich, sweet wines), noticeable amounts are considered a flaw.

ethyl alcohol *see* ALCOHOL

Etna DOC [EHT-nuh] A DOC area located in eastern SICILY on the eastern slopes of Mount Etna, a famous volcano. It covers ROSSO and ROSATO wines made from NERELLO and other grapes (including up to 10 percent white grapes), and white wines made from Carricante, CATARRATTO, TREBBIANO, and Minnella Bianca. The best Etna wines are the *Bianco Superiore*, which are made predominantly from Carricante grapes.

L'Étoile AC [lay-TWAHL] French for "the star," L'Étoile is the name of this tiny APPELLATION and the village it encompasses. It's located in eastern France's Jura region, near the Swiss border. This appellation produces white wines made from SAVAGNIN, CHARDONNAY, and the red grape Poulsard. L'Étoile AC also covers VIN JAUNE, VIN DE PAILLE, and MOUSSEUX wines.

eucalyptus *see* Glossary of Wine Tasting Terms, page 655

EU Abbreviation for EUROPEAN UNION.

European Union (EU) A federation of European nations set up after World War II. The original European Union members were Belgium, Germany, France, Italy, Luxembourg, and the Netherlands. These countries were later joined by Austria, Denmark, Finland, Greece, Ireland, Portugal, Spain, Sweden, and the United Kingdom. Other countries preparing to join the current group of fifteen are Bulgaria, Czech Republic, Estonia, Cyprus, Latvia, Lithuania, Hungary, Malta, Poland, Romania, Slovenia, Slovakia, and Turkey. As it relates to the world of wine, the EU has established a standard set of regulations for wines entering EU countries from the United States; some member countries might also have additional individual requirements. Essentially, U.S.

exporters must follow the TAX AND TRADE BUREAU (previously BATF) production regulations described in Circular 86-2—Certification and Analysis of U.S. Wine for Export to the European Economic Community (EEC). In addition to a host of required information that must appear on the labels, it's interesting to note what is not allowed. Items that cannot appear on labels include European APPELLATION names, such as "Champagne" and "Beaujolais." In fact, the label can't show the use of generic or semigeneric wine class or type designations having European significance. For instance, "*méthode champenoise*" cannot be used and must be replaced by any of the following: "bottle-fermented by the traditional method," "traditional method," "classical method," or "classical traditional method." Labels are not allowed to have quality terms that have no TAX AND TRADE BUREAU (previously BATF) standard, such as "reserve" and "select." Furthermore, a geographic indication of "American" is too broad—the label must indicate a smaller area, such as "California" or "New York," or one of the AMERICAN VITICULTURAL AREAS. Interestingly, items required on U.S. labels, like the government warning statement and the sulfites declaration, are not allowed either.

Eutypa dieback *see* DEAD ARM

eutypiose *see* DEAD ARM

Evora DOC *see* ALENTEJO

extended maceration *see* MACERATION

extra brut *see* BRUT

extract The total of all nonvolatile substances (such as minerals, sugars, and pigments) that give a wine substance. Some winemakers determine extract by simply evaporating the liquid and weighing the residue. Extract contributes to the BODY, flavor, CHARACTER, and color of a wine. Wines made from grapes that provide heavy extract are usually described as full-bodied, and have dense, CONCENTRATED flavors and dark (for the type), opaque colors. *See also* Glossary of Wine Tasting Terms, page 655

extra dry The term "extra dry" (or *extra sec*) appears on SPARKLING WINE labels to indicate that a wine is fairly DRY, but with some RESIDUAL SUGAR. Extra dry sparkling wines usually contain 1.2 to 2 percent sugar, making them sweeter than BRUT but drier than SEC, DEMI SEC, or DOUX.

extra sec A French term meaning "EXTRA DRY."

exuberant *see* Glossary of Wine Tasting Terms, page 655

Faber [FAH-bur] German HYBRID that was developed in the 1920s but that wasn't commercially popular until the 1960s. Faber's parents are Weissburgunder (PINOT BLANC) and MÜLLER-THURGAU. It's viewed as a good-quality grape with RIESLING-like characteristics—fruity, SPICY, and, in particular, high in ACIDS. Although often used for BLENDING, Faber also produces some high-quality, Riesling-style VARIETAL WINES. In addition to its good quality, one of Faber's big advantages is its ability to grow under conditions where Riesling would not properly ripen. The fact that it's not as productive as some of the other varieties is one of its drawbacks. A majority of Faber's acreage is in Germany's RHEIN-HESSEN region, with some plantings in the NAHE region, as well. This grape is also known as *Faberrebe*.

Factory House A grand mansion in northern Portugal that houses the Association of British Port Shippers. Built during the late eighteenth and early nineteenth centuries, this superb granite structure is the site of some of the world's best PORT tastings. Its dual dining rooms allow attendees to retire after formal dinners to the second dining room in order to enjoy their port properly. The term *factory* refers to an establishment for factors (trading agents) and merchants conducting business in a foreign country.

faded *see* Glossary of Wine Tasting Terms, page 655

Fair Play AVA *see* EL DORADO AVA

Falanghina; Falangina [fah-lahn-GEE-nah] A white-wine grape that may have historical connections to Falernian (or Falernum), the most acclaimed wine of ancient Rome. Falanghina's grown along the coast in the FALERNO DEL MASSICO DOC, northwest of Naples, and in the hills of the Sannio DOC northeast of Naples; both DOCs are in the CAMPANIA region. The wines produced range from CRISP and FRESH (similar to PINOT GRIGIO) to full-bodied (*see* BODY), well-structured (*see* STRUCTURE) and COMPLEX.

Falerian *see* FALERNO DEL MASSICO DOC

Falerno del Massico DOC [fah-LEHR-noh del MAHSS-see-koh] Falernian (or Falernum), the most acclaimed wine of ancient Rome, was produced along the northern coast of the CAMPANIA region near Mondragone. Today in that same area (which is northwest of Naples), the modern DOC of Falerno del Massico produces BIANCO made from the Falanghina grape and ROSSO, which is made primarily from AGLIAN-ICO and Piedirosso, although small amounts of Primitivo (*see* ZINFAN-

DEL) and BARBERA can be added. In addition, there is a Primitivo VARI-
ETAL WINE that must contain at least 85 percent Primitivo. Today's wines
are promising, but they have little connection to the highly regarded
Falernian of Roman times.

Falernum *see* FALERNO DEL MASSICO DOC

Falkenberg *see* DIENHEIM; PIESPORT

false wine *see* SUGAR WINE

Far South West Victoria *see* HENTY

fat *see* Glossary of Wine Tasting Terms, page 655

fattoria [fah-toh-REE-ah] An Italian term used in and around TUS-
CANY to refer to a large farm or estate. Use of the term on a label, however, does not always guarantee that the wine is ESTATE BOTTLED. *See
also* MASSERIA.

F

Faugères AC [foh-ZHEHR] APPELLATION located in the hilly region
around the village of Faugères, which is north of Béziers in southern
France's LANGUEDOC-ROUSSILLON region. The area encompasses about
5,000 acres around the villages of Autignac, Cabrerolles, Caussiniojouls,
Faugères, Fos, Laurens, and Roquessels. Faugères is best known for
making good, sturdy red wines, which are made up of CARIGNAN (no
more than 40 percent), CINSAUT (no more than 20 percent), GRENACHE (no
more than 20 percent), MOURVÈDRE, and SYRAH (these last three must
make up at least 50 percent). GRENACHE BLANC, MARSANNE, ROUSSANNE (must
be at least 30 percent), and VERMENTINO make up the white offering.

Favorita *see* VERMENTINO

Faye-d'Anjou *see* COTEAUX DU LAYON

Federspiel [FEE-der-schpeel] A specialty wine category of Lower
Austria's Wachau area. Federspiel wines are medium-bodied and must
have an alcohol content of no more than 12 percent.

Federweisser [FEE-der-VICE-ehr] Semi-fermented grape juice
made at the beginning of the grape harvest in a number of Germanic
countries. It's usually made from white wine grapes and is cloudy with
a yellowish tint. It has a low alcohol level, is faintly effervescent and
semi-sweet. In Austria and some parts of Germany, it's also called
Sturm. Elsewhere, it also goes by *Suser* and *Sauser*. The French make
a version called *vernache*. Federweisser does not age and should be
purchased young and consumed as soon as possible; thus, it's usually

only available in the fall. A rare version made from red wine grapes is called *Roter Raushcer.*

feeble *see* Glossary of Wine Tasting Terms, page 655

fehér [FEH-hayr] Hungarian for "white."

Feinherb [FIN-hehrb] *see* HALBTROCKEN

Felsenberg *see* SCHLOSSBÖCKELHEIM

Fendant *see* CHASSELAS

Fennville AVA *see* MICHIGAN

Fer; Fer Servadou [FAIR; FAIR sehr-vah-DOO] A red-grape variety that's grown primarily in SOUTHWEST FRANCE. It's a minor ingredient in a number of growing areas like the CÔTES DU MARMANDAIS AC, CÔTES DE SAINT-MONT VDQS, GAILLAC AC, and MADIRAN AC. However, Fer plays a more prominent role in the wines of Vins d'Entraygues et du Fel VDQS, Vins d'Estaing VDQS, and MARCILLAC AC. A small amount is also used in the CABARDÈS AC in the LANGUEDOC-ROUSSILLON. Fer provides good color, concentrated spicy flavors and aromas, and a softness that helps balance some of its BLENDING partners in the rustic southwest wines. Argentina's Fer variety is believed to be MALBEC.

fermentation; fermenting [fer-men-TAY-shuhn] The natural process that turns grape juice into wine, fermentation is actually a chain reaction of chemical responses. During this process, technically called the **primary fermentation**, the sugars in the grape juice are converted by the enzymes in yeasts into ALCOHOL (55 to 60 percent) and CARBON DIOXIDE (40 to 45 percent). In addition, fermentation generates minor amounts of numerous incidental by-products that affect the aroma and taste of wine including ACETALDEHYDE, acetic acid (*see* ACIDS), ETHYL ACETATE, GLYCEROL, and alcohols other than ETHANOL. One of the potential problems winemakers must avoid is a **stuck fermentation**. This occurs when the yeast stops converting the sugar into alcohol and carbon dioxide, thereby prematurely leaving undesirable RESIDUAL SUGAR in the wine. As more is learned about fermentation, techniques are evolving to manage the process in order to produce optimum wines. For example, managing the temperature during the fermentation—cooler temperatures (45 to 60°F) for white wines, warmer temperatures (70 to 85°F) for heavier red wines—leads to superior wines. Red wines are usually fermented with their skins, seeds, and pulp to extract color and tannins—something not desirable in white wines. YEAST strains are also being experimented with to determine which ones work best for different wines under various conditions. Many winemakers believe BARREL FERMENTATION adds flavor and complexity to some white wines. CARBONIC MACERATION is a specialized fermentation process for producing light fruity red wines. *See also* BOTTLE FERMENTATION; CO-FERMENTATION; FERMENTATION CONTAINERS; MALOLACTIC FERMENTATION; SECONDARY FERMENTATION; WHOLE BERRY FERMENTATION.

fermentation containers A variety of containers have been used over the years for fermenting wine. These include barrels and vats of oak or redwood, concrete vats lined with glass or coated with epoxy, and the huge LAGERS of Spain and Portugal, in which the grapes are stomped and then fermented. Today, most modern wineries use stainless steel tanks with temperature-controlled jackets because they're easy to clean (important in keeping unwanted bacteria out of the wine) and the temperature can be managed throughout the fermentation process. *See also* FERMENTATION.

fermentation in bottle *see* BOTTLE FERMENTATION

fermentation lock Also called a *fermentation trap*, this low-pressure valve atop a fermenting vessel allows carbon dioxide gas to escape but inhibits air or bacteria from entering. *See also* FERMENTATION.

fermentation trap *see* FERMENTATION LOCK

fermentation yeasts *see* YEAST

fermentazione [fayr-mayn-tah-TSYOH-nay] Italian for "fermentation." On labels of sparkling wines (like SPUMANTE), the term *fermentazione naturale* indicates that carbon dioxide gas has been instilled in the wine through a natural method (usually the CHARMAT PROCESS).

fermentor [fer-MEN-tor] A vessel used to FERMENT grape juice. *See also* FERMENTATION CONTAINERS.

Fernão Pires [FER-nerng PEE-rish] Portugal's most widely planted white-grape variety. The versatile Fernão Pires can produce a variety of wine styles, from CRISP and DRY, to sweet BOTRYTISED wines, to SPARKLING WINES. It is reasonably aromatic with a distinctive PEPPERY quality. Fernão Pires is also called *Maria Gomes, Fernam Pires,* and *Fernão Pirão.*

Fernam Pires *see* FERNÃO PIRES

Fernão Pirão *see* FERNÃO PIRES

Feteasca; Feteaska; Fetiska *see* LEÁNYKA

feuillette [fuh-YET] A small oak barrel traditionally used in France's CHABLIS region. The feuillette, which holds approximately 136 liters (36 U.S. gallons), was eventually replaced by the 228-liter (60 U.S. gallons) PIÈCE, which is used primarily in the rest of BURGUNDY. Today, however, most producers in Chablis have eliminated oak barrel aging and instead use stainless steel tanks for storage until bottling.

Les Fêves *see* BEAUNE

Fiano di Avellino DOC [fee-AH-noh dee ah-veh-LEE-noh] Highly regarded, DRY white wines that are made with at least 85 percent of the indigenous Fiano grape. This DOC zone is located in the hills surrounding Avellino and 25 other villages, east of Naples in Italy's CAMPANIA region. "Fiano di Lapio" on the label indicates that the wine was made from grapes grown in the classical area just northeast of Avellino near the village of Lapio.

fiasco; pl. fiaschi [fee-YAHS-koh; fee-YAHS-kee] Italian for "flask," the word *fiasco* is most often connected with the squat, round-bottomed, straw-covered bottle containing cheaper wine from the CHIANTI region. The straw covering not only helps the bottle sit upright, but protects the thin, fragile glass. Fiaschi are seldom seen today because the cost of hand-wrapping each flask for cheaper wines has become prohibitive, and the more expensive wines with aging potential need bottles that can be laid on their sides.

Les Fichots *see* PERNAND-VERGELESSES

Fiddletown AVA A small APPELLATION located east of Sacramento in northern California's AMADOR COUNTY. This area's altitude ranges from 1,500 to about 2,500 feet, which makes it cooler than the lower neighboring SHENANDOAH VALLEY AVA. ZINFANDEL is the most popular grape variety here. Eschen Vineyard is a respected Fiddletown grower that sells to a number of wineries.

field blend The practice of planting a single vineyard with several grape varieties that will make up a single wine. Rather than picking and processing each variety separately and then blending them together, the grapes are all picked and crushed together. This method was practiced in Europe and was quite popular in California at one time, although it's not much in evidence today. *See also* CO-FERMENTATION.

field grafting *see* GRAFTING

Les Fiètres *see* CORTON

fifth growth *see* CINQUIÈME CRU

fill level The level of a wine's surface in its bottle. In a bottle with a high fill level, the surface will be just below the bottom of the cork. A fill level that comes only midway up a bottle's shoulders means that more oxygen can reach the wine, causing deterioration through OXI-DATION. Fill levels reduce over time owing to several factors. A faulty cork may allow for leakage, or extreme temperatures can cause the wine's expansion, which can loosen the cork and cause leakage. It's a good idea to check the fill level of older wines. *See also* ULLAGE.

filtering A step used by some winemakers to CLARIFY wine just prior to bottling. The purpose of filtering is to remove yeast cells and other microorganisms that could spoil the wine, as well as any remaining sediment that would keep it from being crystal clear (which is what most of the public expects). The wine is pumped through one or more various filters including those made of cellulose, pads coated with diatomaceous earth, or especially fine membranes. Today's modern winery has filters so fine that they can remove infinitesimal particles. When such fine filters are used, the process is called **sterile filtering**. Some winemakers argue that this precise filtering extracts flavor and character that the sediment lends the wine. *See also* FINING; RACKING; UNFILTERED.

finca [FEENG-kah] Spanish for "estate."

finesse *see* Glossary of Wine Tasting Terms, page 655

Finger Lakes AVA APPELLATION located in northern New York State just south of Lake Ontario. Its name comes from its four largest glacial lakes (Canandaigua, Keuka, Seneca, and Cayuga), which look like the fingers of a giant hand. Grape growing survives in this region because the environment around the lakes moderates the temperatures and extends the growing seasons (*see* LAKE EFFECT). MESOCLIMATES in this area are extremely important. Although there are a dozen lakes in the area, the areas around the larger lakes of **Cayuga** (which has it own AVA) and Seneca are considered best because the water is deeper and thereby stores more warmth, and because the lower altitude is warmer. Finger Lakes AVA was approved in 1987; the Cayuga Lake AVA, one year later. Finger Lakes AVA encompasses approximately 2,600,000 acres with over 10,000 acres planted. Growers in this area still plant a lot of NATIVE AMERICAN GRAPES (CATAWBA, CONCORD, DELAWARE, and NIAGARA) and HYBRIDS (AURORA, BACO NOIR, CHELOIS, DE CHAUNAC, and SEYVAL BLANC). However, VITIS VINIFERA grapes continue to increase in popularity, gaining acreage at the rate of 20 percent per year since the mid-1990s. The most popular of these are CABERNET FRANC, CHARDONNAY, GEWÜRZTRAMINER, PINOT NOIR, and RIESLING. There are over 70 wineries in the Finger Lake AVA.

fining [FI-ning] A winemaking process that removes microscopic elements such as protein particles that would cloud the wine and PHENOLIC compounds like TANNINS that could cause bitterness and astringency. The most frequently used **fining agents** are activated carbon, activated charcoal, BENTONITE, CASEIN, egg whites, gelatin, ISINGLASS, nylon, and polyvinyl poly-pyrrolidone (PVPP). When added to wine, fining agents capture suspended particles by absorption or coagulation, causing them to settle to the bottom of the container. Once the particles sink, the wine can be RACKED, FILTERED, or CENTRIFUGED to separate it from this sediment. In addition to clarifying wines, various fining agents can also be used to remove color from white wines, deodorize wines with an off odor, and reduce ACIDS.

fining agents *see* FINING

finish *see* Glossary of Wine Tasting Terms, page 655

fino *see* SHERRY

firm *see* Glossary of Wine Tasting Terms, page 655

first growth The English translation of the French "PREMIER CRU." The precise meaning of the term *first growth* refers to the original four red-wine châteaux ranked in the Classification of 1855 (*see* Official Wine Classifications of Bordeaux, page 678)—**Lafite-Rothschild**, **Latour**, **Margaux**, and **Haut-Brion**—plus **Château Mouton-Rothschild**, which was added in 1973. Sometimes the meaning of first growth is expanded slightly to include Châteaux **Ausone** and **Cheval Blanc** (ranked in a separate classification for SAINT-ÉMILION in 1954) and Château **Pétrus** from POMEROL (which has never been classified but has the status, wine quality, and premium pricing to rank it with the others). Although Château D'YQUEM of SAUTERNES is also a premier cru, it produces white wines, and the narrower use of first growth typically applies only to red wines. Even though BURGUNDY and CHAMPAGNE also have a premier cru class, the first growth designation doesn't usually refer to these areas.

Fitou AC [fee-TOO] APPELLATION located in the LANGUEDOC-ROUSSILLON region in southern France. It is surrounded by the CÔTES DU ROUSSILLON-VILLAGES AC on one side and on the other side by the large CORBIÈRES AC of which Fitou AC is actually a part. Fitou is split into two sections—one area on the Mediterranean coast between Narbonne and Perpignan and the other inland around the village of Tuchan. Fitou AC makes red wines that are considered some of the best in the Languedoc-Roussillon region. They're made from CARIGNAN, GRENACHE, MOURVÈDRE, and SYRAH and require a minimum of 9 months AGING in wooden barrels.

fixed acids *see* ACIDS

Fixin AC [fee-SAN] Fixin is one of the most northerly villages in the CÔTE DE NUITS district of France's BURGUNDY region. It's not as well known as some of the neighboring villages in this famous area because it contains no GRAND CRU vineyards. However, Fixin produces some very good PREMIER CRU wines, the best of which come from the vineyards of **Les Arvelets**, **Clos de la Perrière**, **Clos du Chapitre**, **Clos Napoléon**, and **Les Hervelets**. Wines from these premier cru vineyards and those from the **Fixin AC** are generally ROBUST and full-bodied (*see* BODY) and require several years of AGING before they're really enjoyable. Fixin AC wines are difficult to find because the total vineyard area isn't that large (320 acres, including premier cru vineyards) and because they can also be bottled as CÔTES DE NUITS-VILLAGES AC wines. A number of producers opt for the latter because they have other acreage entitled only to the Côtes de Nuits-Village AC and it's easier to just combine the wines.

flabby *see* Glossary of Wine Tasting Terms, page 655

Flagey-Echézeaux *see* VOSNE-ROMANÉE

flasche [FLAH-shuh] German for "bottle."

flat *see* Glossary of Wine Tasting Terms, page 655

flavonoids A group of PHENOLIC COMPOUNDS that make up a majority of those compounds found in red wine. Flavonoids are responsible for ASTRINGENCY, bitterness, color, some flavors and odors (like VANILLIN), and antioxidant activity (which helps wine AGE well).

fleshy *see* Glossary of Wine Tasting Terms, page 655

Fleurieu Zone *see* SOUTH AUSTRALIA

fliers Tiny visible but tasteless particles that occasionally appear in wine. Usually caused by a cold environment, fliers generally disappear when the wine is warmed.

flight A group of wines served together or in a series. The wines generally have a common theme and are tasted concurrently for comparison purposes. *See also* Types of Wine Tastings in the appendix under Tasting Wine, page 648.

flinty *see* Glossary of Wine Tasting Terms, page 655

Floc de Gascogne [flawk duh gas-KAWN] A FORTIFIED, sweet APÉRITIF made in France's Armagnac region by adding ARMAGNAC to unfermented grape juice to halt any FERMENTATION. Floc de Gascogne is classified as a VIN DE LIQUEUR and is very similar to the much better-known PINEAU DES CHARENTES.

flor [FLAWR] Although this is literally the Spanish word for "flower," in wine terminology *flor* refers to the off-white yeast that develops naturally on certain wines after they're fermented. Usually associated with sherry from the Spanish region of JEREZ DE LA FRONTERA, *flor* is also a factor in Spain's MONTILLA region, as well as France's CHÂTEAU-CHALLON district. In these areas, the wine barrels are not completely filled, so there's enough surface area for air to get to the wine. Assuming reasonable temperature and humidity, this exposure allows flor to grow, creating a gauzy white layer that protects the wine from further air contact and subsequent OXIDATION. Flor also affects the flavor and character of the wine—a sharp pungency or tang is the most notable development. This characteristic is noticeable in the FINO- and AMONTILLADO-style sherries. Flor will not grow on wines FORTIFIED with too much alcohol (above 16.2 percent), as is the case with the OLOROSO-style sherries. In California, Australia, and other areas where flor doesn't grow naturally, flor yeast cultures are introduced to sherry-style wines, thereby creating similar results and improving the quality of such wines.

Flora [FLOR-uh] The fairly rare white-wine grape that is a CROSS of GEWÜRZTRAMINER and SÉMILLON developed in the 1950s by the UNIVERSITY OF CALIFORNIA, DAVIS. As the name suggests, the wines have a floral quality with a high degree of spiciness. They're usually vinified medium-sweet to sweet. Never very popular, Flora plantings are now under a hundred acres.

floraison *see* FLOWERING

floral; flowery *see* Glossary of Wine Tasting Terms, page 655

floral abortion A malady occurring in some grape varieties, such as the Italian PICOLIT, where the flowering buds don't develop properly and often fall off. Floral abortion generally results in a small crop and, therefore, expensive wines.

flowering Viticultural term for the stage when small flowers appear, a critical time in the development of grapes. Flowering (*floraison* in French) occurs about 2½ months after BUD BREAK (when the first tiny leaf buds burst from the vine). After flowering is completed, the tiny green berries (that will eventually become mature grapes) begin to form. Warm, dry, sunny weather is critical during flowering because failure to flower properly can result in COULURE, meaning that some or all of the grapes may not develop adequately. Flowering is also known as *anthesis. See also* VITICULTURE.

flute [FLOOT] 1. In France, a tall, thin, clear glass bottle shaped like the classic green bottle of ALSACE and the brown bottle for RHINE wines. Flutes are also made in clear glass for ROSÉ wines. *See also* Common Wine Bottle Shapes, page 609. 2. A stemmed champagne glass with a tall, slender, cone-shaped bowl. *See also* Glassware, page 647.

Foch *see* MARÉCHAL FOCH

foil *see* CAPSULE

foil cutter Device used to cut through the covering (called CAPSULE or foil) over the top of a wine bottle. Many corkscrews (*see* Wine Openers, page 639) contain a blade that can be used to cut the foil. There are also special foil cutters comprised of two small blades that cut the foil when squeezed and rotated. With either device, the idea is to cut the foil cleanly below the lip of the bottle, not only for cosmetic purposes, but so that wine doesn't touch the capsule as it's being poured.

Folgasão [fool-GAH-sahng] A white-wine grape, known historically as *Terrantez*, grown on the island of Madeira. It was introduced in Madeira in the seventeenth century but today is all but extinct. Currently only about 1,100 pounds of grapes are harvested each year. Aficionados of Madeira lament this, pointing to the highly regarded wines produced from this grape in the past.

Folle Blanche [fawl BLAHNSH] A white-wine grape known for its high YIELDS and high acidity, even in hot growing regions. Folle Blanche was once widely planted in France where it was a principal variety in the production of BRANDY from the COGNAC and ARMAGNAC districts. The PHYLLOXERA epidemic changed all of that because the remedy for phylloxera was to GRAFT vines to American ROOTSTOCK. Unfortunately, the Folle Blanche vines did not perform well after this process. In addition, Folle Blanche is very susceptible to BLACK ROT and GRAY ROT. These frailties resulted in Folle Blanche being replaced by Ugni Blanc (TREBBIANO) in Cognac and by BACO BLANC in Armagnac. Today, the largest growing region for this grape is centered around the mouth of the LOIRE, where Folle Blanche is called *Gros Plant* and VINIFIED into the generally highly acidic VDQS wine *Gros Plant du Pays Nantais*. Small amounts of Folle Blanche are grown in California and Argentina. Folle Blanche is also known as *Camobraque* and *Picpoule* (which translates into "lip-stinger," apparently in reference to its mouth-puckering acidity). Folle Blanche is unrelated to the Piquepoul (or Picpoule) grown in the CHÂTEAUNEUF-DU-PAPE area.

Fondillon *see* ALICANTE DO

F

Forst [FAWRST] Forst, along with the neighboring towns of DEIDESHEIM, RUPPETSBERG, and WACHENHEIM, produce some of the best wines of Germany's Rheinpfalz region (*see* PFALZ). Located southwest of BAD DÜRKHEIM, Forst is acknowledged for its full-bodied (*see* BODY) yet VELVETY wines, which are said to gain extra character from the vein of black, potassium-rich basalt that runs through the area. The best-known EINZELLAGE is the **Jesuitengarten**, but **Freundstück**, **Kirchenstück**, **Pechsten**, and **Ungeheuer** are all highly regarded as well. RIESLING, the dominant grape here, is the variety used to produce the town's most distinguished wines.

fortification; fortified wine Initially used as a method to preserve some wines, **fortification** is the addition of brandy or a neutral spirit in order to boost a wine's ALCOHOL content. **Fortified wines** generally have between 17 and 21 percent alcohol. Many fortified wines are sweet because by adding ALCOHOL to a level (15 to 16 percent) above which the YEAST cannot work, the yeast quits converting the natural sugar. The earlier this fortification process occurs the more RESIDUAL SUGAR is left and the sweeter the wine. Some of the better-known examples are PORT, SHERRY, MADEIRA, MÁLAGA, and MARSALA.

fortified; fortified wine *see* FORTIFICATION

forward *see* Glossary of Wine Tasting Terms, page 655

foudre [foodr] Large oak barrels that vary significantly in size—some over 1,000 gallons. They're used in the south of France, particularly in the RHÔNE valley. Foudres are larger than many other oak barrels such as BARRIQUES, FEUILLETES, and PIÈCES.

foulage [foo-LAHZH] French term for CRUSHING the grapes to extract the juice.

Fourchaume *see* CHABLIS

Les Fourneaux *see* CHABLIS

foxy *see* Glossary of Wine Tasting Terms, page 655

frais [FRAY] French for "cool" or "chilly" but also "fresh." When it appears on a French wine label, it means the bottle should be chilled before serving.

France France is definitely a wine-oriented country. It produces over 20 percent of the world's wines, second only to Italy. It's the top per capita consumer of wines—per person, the French population consumes almost nine times that of the U.S. population. But more than that, in its effort to create the best possible wines, France has set the standard for what wines are meant to be. Except for Portugal's PORTS, Germany's RIESLINGS, and Spain's SHERRIES, the wine-producing world primarily uses French wines as benchmarks for excellence in high-quality wines. France's premier wine-growing regions each contribute extraordinary exemplars: BORDEAUX for the red wines made from CABERNET SAUVIGNON, MERLOT, and CABERNET FRANC, for the rich, sweet SAUTERNES wines made from SAUVIGNON BLANC, SÉMILLON, and MUSCADELLE, and even for the DRY white wines of GRAVES made from Sauvignon Blanc and Sémillon; BURGUNDY for the elegant red wines made from PINOT NOIR, the superb white wines made from CHARDONNAY, and the light, fruity red BEAUJOLAIS wines made from GAMAY; CHAMPAGNE for superior sparkling wines made mainly from Pinot Noir and Chardonnay; the RHÔNE region for its red SYRAH wines and white VIOGNIER wines from the northern Rhône region; the GRENACHE-based red wines from places like CHÂTEAUNEUF-DU-PAPE from the southern region, and the ROSÉ wines of TAVEL; and the LOIRE for the dry, semisweet, and sweet wines made from CHENIN BLANC and Sauvignon Blanc. The wines of ALSACE, another premier growing region, are not as widely imitated by the world's wine producers. However, as winemakers continue to make dry wines from GEWÜRZTRAMINER, RIESLING, SYLVANER, PINOT GRIS, PINOT BLANC, and MUSCAT, they're discovering that such wines are Alsacian specialties. Of course, all this doesn't mean that other countries don't produce superior wines. The Italian wines made from NEBBIOLO and SANGIOVESE or the California ZINFANDELS are superb. But no other country's wines are as widely copied as those of France. From South Africa to the United States to Chile to Australia, winemakers are planting French varieties and making French-influenced wines. In addition to their grape varieties and winemaking acumen, the French have contributed their system of quality control to the winemaking

F

world. Their levels of quality—from lowest to highest—are VIN DE TABLE, VIN DE PAYS, VIN DÉLIMITÉ DE QUALITÉ SUPÉRIEURE, and APPELLATION D'ORIGINE CONTRÔLÉE. France did not achieve its esteemed position in the world of wine overnight. Grapes are thought to have been planted in France at least 2,700 years ago, prior to the Roman occupation. The Romans, however, brought many practices with them that improved French wines, including planting vineyards on the best slopes, pruning and managing the vineyards, and various winemaking techniques. Over the centuries, the French have learned which grape varieties grow best in which locations and have gradually perfected their winemaking craft. This information has been recorded in detail over time and has been a major factor implementing the Appellation d'Origine Contrôlée system that defines the top-quality level for wines. This shouldn't imply that the French drink only top-quality wines. In fact, most of the wine consumed is simple *vin de table* that's produced in huge amounts in southwest France, parts of the Rhône region, the LANGUEDOC-ROUSSILLON and PROVENCE, and in smaller amounts throughout the rest of France. But France is continuing to try to improve even these wines by encouraging practices such as the planting of specific higher-quality grape varieties, lowering YIELDS, and modernizing winemaking procedures.

Franciacorta DOCG; Terre di Franciacorta DOC [frahn-shah-KOR-tah] DOCG area located northwest of Italy's city of Brescia in the eastern part of the LOMBARDY region. This area produces a highly regarded white STILL WINE from Pinot Bianco (PINOT BLANC) and CHARDONNAY and a reasonably good red wine from CABERNET FRANC, CABERNET SAUVIGNON, BARBERA, NEBBIOLO, and MERLOT. But it's the Franciacorta SPUMANTE that's so widely acclaimed. Both the BIANCO and ROSATO sparkling wines are made via MÉTHODE CHAMPENOISE and use a combination of Pinot Bianco, Chardonnay, Pinot Grigio (PINOT GRIS), and Pinot Nero (PINOT NOIR). These sparkling wines achieved DOCG status in 1995. VINTAGE Franciacorta wines must be aged for 30 months in the bottle. The still wines must be designated with the **Terre di Franciacorta DOC**.

Franconia *see* FRANKEN

Francs *see* CÔTES DE FRANCS AC

Franken [FRAHNG-kuhn] One of Germany's thirteen ANBAUGEBIETE (quality-wine regions) that lies just east of the city of Frankfort, along the Main River. The river (and the region) follow a large, shaky-W shape in the northern part of Bavaria, around the university city of

Würzburg (Franken's capital). The climate in Franken (known as **Franconia** in English) can be quite cold, and the approximately 15,000 vineyard acres are planted mainly with white grapes. MÜLLER-THURGAU is the primary grape here, followed by silvaner (*see* SYLVANER) and BACCHUS. RIESLING doesn't perform well in Franken's short growing season. Silvaner produces this region's best wines, which are often compared to white wines from France's BURGUNDY region in terms of richness and BODY (although the flavors are quite different). Most Franken wines, which have a slight EARTHY flavor regardless of the grape used, are different from those in other parts of Germany in that they're DRY rather than sweet. Wines with less than 4 grams of sugar per liter (0.4 percent) are identifed by the term *Fränkisch Trocken* (*see* TROCKEN). Franken wines also differ in that many are bottled in unique, flat-sided flagons called BOCKSBEUTEL. Franken wines are sometimes referred to as **Steinwein**, after the region's most famous vineyard **Würzburger Stein** (*see* WÜRZBURGER), a 210-acre EINZELLAGE. The region has three BEREICHS—**Maindreieck**, **Mainviereck**, and **Steigerwald**. The Bereich names are often found on the region's wine bottles since there are no GROSSLAGEN. Franken wines aren't well known outside the region because most of the production is consumed locally.

Franken Riesling *see* SYLVANER

Frankland *see* GREAT SOUTHERN

Frankovka *see* BLAUFRÄNKISCH

Frans; Fransdruif *see* PALOMINO

Franschhoek WO [FRAHNSH-hoook] This demarcated South African wine ward (*see* SOUTH AFRICA) is part of the larger PAARL district, which is 35 to 40 miles northeast of Cape Town. Franschhoek lies about 15 miles east of the town of Paarl encircled by mountains in the Drakenstein Valley. Franschhoek, which translates to "French Corner," was first settled by French Huguenots in the latter part of the seventeenth century. Although vines were planted then, it was not until recently that the wine era really began. This area's climate is much cooler than the rest of the Paarl area, a drawback when the objective was to produce as large a crop as possible. Now, however, this cooler weather is attracting winegrowers looking to produce higher-quality grapes, a result of the longer growing season. SÉMILLON has historically been quite successful here. Other white VARIETIES that do well are CHARDONNAY and SAUVIGNON BLANC. In recent years, red varieties (CABER-

NET SAUVIGNON, MERLOT, Shiraz (SYRAH), and PINOT NOIR) have also shown promise.

Frascati DOC [frahs-KAH-tee] DOC zone located in the CASTELLI ROMANI area on the southeastern edge of Rome in Italy's LATIUM region. It encircles the town of Frascati and neighboring environs. Frascati produces more wine than any other DOC in Latium, most of it DRY white wine (made from MALVASIA, TREBBIANO, and GRECO), that's a favorite in Rome restaurants for HOUSE WINE. Frascati wines can also be AMABILE, DOLCE, or *cannellino*, the latter a special version using very ripe grapes hopefully infected with BOTRYTIS CINEREA. A SPUMANTE version is also produced.

Fraser Valley VA *see* BRITISH COLUMBIA

Fredericksburg in the Texas Hill Country AVA *see* TEXAS HILL COUNTRY AVA

free-run juice; free-run wine Free-run juice is juice that flows freely from grapes without external pressure, such as that applied by a wine PRESS. This usually occurs simply from the natural weight of the grapes on top of each other or during CRUSHING of the grapes. Free-run juice (usually associated with white-wine grapes) is considered the best because pressing produces **press juice**, which can contain bitter, sometimes unwanted, compounds that are released from the skins and/or seeds. If not overtly astringent or bitter, press juice is sometimes mixed with free-run juice to give the resulting wine STRUCTURE. Similarly, after the fermentation of red wines, the wine that flows freely (without pressing) from the pulp, skins, and seeds is called **free-run wine** (*vin de goutte* in France). **Press wine**, called *vin de presse* by the French, is then pressed from the must. Press wine is darker, more TANNIC, and much coarser than free-run wine. Some winemakers blend some or all of the press wine into the free-run wine to add firmness and structure; those who want more accessible wines don't follow this practice.

free SO$_2$ *see* SULFUR DIOXIDE

free sulfur dioxide *see* SULFUR DIOXIDE

Fréjus *see* CÔTES DE PROVENCE

French Paradox *see* HEALTH CONSEQUENCES OF WINE

Freisa [FRAY-zah] Italian red-wine grape that has been grown in the PIEDMONT region for centuries. After declining in popularity for several decades, Freisa is enjoying a resurgence of interest. It produces highly ACIDIC, pale cherry-red wines whose AROMA and flavor are reminiscent of raspberries. Freisa is VINIFIED in many styles ranging from DRY to sweet, and STILL to FRIZZANTE (lightly sparkling). Freisa has DOC status in *Freisa di Chieri*, *Freisa d'Asti*, and MONFERRATO. It's also known as *Fresa* or *Fresia*.

Fresa *see* FREISA

fresh; freshness *see* Glossary of Wine Tasting Terms, page 655

Fresia *see* FREISA

Freundstück *see* FORST

Friedrich-Wilhelm-Gymnasium [FREET-rikh VL-hehlm jihm-NAH-zee-uhm] A famous secondary school founded in 1563 in the city of TRIER in Germany's MOSEL-SAAR-RUWER region. Its name is well known in wine circles because its endowments include nearly 90 acres of vineyard land located in some of the best villages in the region. The vineyards are planted with about 85 percent RIESLING, and the wines produced are regarded as some of the best of this region.

Friulano *see* SAUVIGNONASSE

Friulara; Friularo *see* RABOSO

Friuli-Venezia Giulia [free-OO-lee veh-NEHT-zee-ah JOO-lee-ah] Wine-producing region located in the northeast corner of Italy, with the former Yugoslavia to the east and Austria to the north. There are just over 45,000 vineyard acres, nine DOCs, and one DOCG (RAMANDOLO) here. DOC wines comprise about 60 percent of this region's total production, which is one of the highest ratios of Italy's twenty winegrowing regions. The most important DOCs in Friuli-Venezia Giulia are COLLIO, COLLI ORIENTALI DEL FRIULI, and GRAVE DEL FRIULI; the others are Annia, AQUILEIA, Carso, ISONZO, LATISANA, and LISON-PRAMAGGIORE (shared with VENETO). A wide variety of different grapes are grown in the region including many nonlocal varieties including CABERNET FRANC, CABERNET SAUVIGNON, MERLOT, Pinot Nero (PINOT NOIR), and CHARDONNAY. White wine DOC production now dominates red wines by two to one. FRIULANO is the most populous white grape, but there are many other varieties including Chardonnay, MALVASIA, Pinot Bianco (PINOT BLANC), Pinot Grigio (PINOT GRIS), RIBOLLA, and SAUVIGNON BLANC.

frizzante *see* Glossary of Wine Tasting Terms, page 655

Fronsac AC [frawn-SAK] APPELLATION centered around the town of Fronsac on the Dordogne River northwest of the SAINT-ÉMILION district in BORDEAUX. Fronsac AC produces only red wines; they're based on CABERNET FRANC plus some CABERNET SAUVIGNON, MERLOT, and small amounts of MALBEC. CANON-FRONSAC AC is a small appellation within Fronsac AC that generally produces better wines, as suggested by its required ½ percent higher minimum ALCOHOL content. Wines from both appellations are known to be BIG and full-flavored (although sometimes somewhat HARD and TANNIC) and require extensive AGING. The improved quality of recent vintages and a new SOFTER style have created renewed interest in the Fronsac area.

Fronteira see BRAZIL

Frontenac [frawn-tee-NAK] This HYBRID was developed at the University of Minnesota by combining a French-American hybrid known as LANDOT with the Native American VITIS RIPARA. The resulting red-wine grape is very cold hardy and is successfully being grown in the upper Midwest and southern Canada. The grapes are fairly high in acid and sugar and have found their way into ROSÉ, DRY red, and PORT-like wines with some agreeable results.

Frontignan see MUSCAT DE FRONTIGNAN AC

Frontonnais see CÔTES DU FRONTONNAIS

fructose [FRUHK-tohs; FROOK-tohs] One of the two main sugars found in grapes (the other being GLUCOSE). Fructose is approximately twice as sweet as glucose.

Frühburgunder see PINOT NOIR

Früher Roter Malvasier see MALVASIA

fruit 1. A general VITICULTURE term for GRAPES. 2. In wine tasting, fruit refers to flavor and aroma characteristics (see FRUITY).

fruit bomb A term applied to wines with high alcohol, big, lush fruit flavors and low acidity. They're usually made from very ripe grapes and are highly EXTRACTED. Some wine lovers adore this style of wine while others deplore it, indicating the wines are excessive and unbalanced. Although California and Australia are most identified with fruit bombs, some areas of Europe are producing this style as well.

fruit set The stage at which fertilized grapevine flowers evolve into tiny green grape berries. See also VITICULTURE.

fruit wines A general term for wines made from fruits other than grapes. Fruit wines can be made with almost any fruit including apples, apricots, blackberries, citrus, cranberries, elderberries, huckleberries, peaches, pears, pineapples, plums, rhubarb (which is actually a vegetable), and strawberries. Such wines are created by FERMENTING fresh fruit, fruit concentrates, or juices and YEAST. Sugar is commonly added to supplement the natural sugars, tea is sometimes used to add TANNIN, and ACIDS are often added to improve the wine's BALANCE. Fruit wines are generally drunk chilled, and while they're still young and FRUITY.

fruity *see* Glossary of Wine Tasting Terms, page 655

full-bodied *see* BODY in the Glossary of Wine Tasting Terms, page 655

F

Fumé Blanc [FOO-may BLAH*N*; BLAH*N*GK] Term originally coined by the Robert Mondavi Winery and another name for sauvignon blanc. Many feel that Mondavi's extensive marketing campaign for its dry, oak-aged style of Sauvignon Blanc is what established this variety as California's second most popular white-wine grape after chardonnay.

Fumin *see* VALLE D'AOSTA

Furmint [FOOR-mint] White-wine grape most renowned for its contribution to the delicious, sweet wines of Hungary's TOKAJI region. Furmint's thin skin makes it susceptible to BOTRYTIS CINEREA, which causes the famous shriveled ASZÚ berries with their concentrated sugars and flavors. The combination of Furmint and HÁRSLEVELÜ creates the rich sweet Tokaji wines that rival—and sometimes surpass—the sweet wines from France's SAUTERNES region. Furmint is also VINIFIED into a strong, high-ALCOHOL, high-ACID, DRY wine, which is widely available throughout Hungary and the rest of eastern Europe. This variety is grown in Hungary and nearby countries. It's thought that *Sipon* and *Posip*, grown in the former Yugoslavia, are actually Furmint. Tokay d'Alsace (PINOT GRIS) and the Italian variety TOCAI (now called FRIULANO) are not related to Furmint.

Furstenberg *see* ERSHERNDORF

fut [FEW] One of the French words for "barrel."

futures A product that's purchased upon agreement of delivery at a specified future date. In the wine world, this equates to buying wine futures prior to the wine's release, which, in many cases, can be as much as two years in advance. Futures can usually be purchased directly from the winery or from wine retailers. Some American wineries, like Château Montelena and Ridge, sell futures for their top CABERNET SAUVIGNON wines at prices lower than what the suggested retail price will be when the wine's released. This practice typically works as a win/win situation for both parties—the winery gets advance payment and can put that money to use, the consumer is assured of getting the desired wine at a lower price (in most instances) than it will be upon release. Occasionally, it's possible to purchase a given wine 18 months after the futures release for less than the futures price. This happens when early hype for a vintage pushes up a futures' price, and then subsequent events moderate the released wine's retail price downward. The practice of selling futures is often associated with French wines like those from BURGUNDY and BORDEAUX, especially highly sought after wines, such as those from FIRST GROWTH châteaux or SUPER SECONDS. In France, buying futures (*en primeur*) is a much more evolved practice than it is in the United States. The individual producers, like the Bordeaux châteaux, set the price they're going to charge for the initial limited portion (*premier tranche*) of a vintage's wines; sometimes additional *tranches* are offered, depending on demand. Then NÉGOCIANTS, who generally sell these wines for the châteaux, pass these futures on through the distribution channels. In the United States, these French-wine futures come to importers, who typically sell to wholesalers and retailers, sometimes directly to individuals. Along every step of the way, each entity adds their cut to the consumer's price (which, of course, is also true for a bottle of wine). When purchasing futures it's important to find a reputable, well-established merchant. There's a significant wait for delivery of this wine bought on futures and you want to ensure that the merchant will still be there when the wine is released. Of course, in transactions like wine futures, there's always a risk of failure by someone in the supply chain or possible fraudulent dealings by disreputable merchants. *Caveat emptor.*

G **Gaglioppo** [gah-LYOHP-poh] The most widely planted red-grape VARIETY in Italy's CALABRIA region, although it's also found in ABRUZZI, CAMPANIA, MARCHES, and UMBRIA. Gaglioppo, also called *Lacrima Nera*, can produce wines with good STRUCTURE and rich, spicy flavors. It is the primary grape in the ROSATO and ROSSO wines of the CIRÒ DOC and is found in the red DOC wines of Donnici, Lamenzia, Melissa, and Savuto.

Gaillac AC [gah-YAHK] This APPELLATION encircles the town of Gaillac in SOUTHWEST FRANCE, northeast of Toulouse. It produces red, white, and ROSÉ wines that can be sweet or DRY, STILL, or SPARKLING. Much of the production goes into the slightly sweet sparkling wines entitled **Gaillac Mousseux AC**, which are made by the MÉTHODE CHAMPENOISE or RURAL METHOD (locally referred to as **méthode gaillacoise**). A PETILLANT (slightly sparkling) wine called **Gaillac Perle AC** is also produced, but not highly regarded. The white grapes used are Mauzac Blanc, Len de L'elh, SAUVIGNON BLANC, and SÉMILLON. **Gaillac Doux AC** is the appellation for sweet white wines. Among the many acceptable red varieties are Duras, FER, GAMAY, NEGRETTE, CABERNET SAUVIGNON, CABERNET FRANC, MERLOT, and SYRAH. The area's red and rosé wines vary greatly in quality, partially due to the number of varieties that can be used.

Gaisböhl *see* RUPPERTSBERG

Galestro [gah-LESS-troh] Name used by a group of CHIANTI producers for a white VINO DA TAVOLA wine made from TREBBIANO, MALVASIA, and VERNACCIA DI SAN GIMIGNANO, plus other varieties such as Pinot Bianco (PINOT BLANC), Pinot Grigio (PINOT GRIS), and CHARDONNAY. Galestro is a LIGHT, CRISP, DRY wine with a maximum of $10\frac{1}{2}$ percent alcohol.

gallo nero *see* CHIANTI DOCG

Gamaret Red-wine grape developed in Switzerland in 1970 by CROSSING Reichensteiner with GAMAY in an attempt to develop an early ripening grape with attributes similar to Gamy and PINOT NOIR. It's grown mainly in the VAUD and VALAIS cantons in Switzerland, but is also being evaluated in Washington State. It's been compared favorably to a light BORDEAUX or Pinot Noir. **Garanoir** was developed at the same time from the same varieties and is similar but ripens earlier and produces lighter wines than Gamaret.

Gamay [ga-MAY] The full name of this French red wine grape is *Gamay Noir a'Jus Blanc*. Gamay wines have gained prominence in France's BEAUJOLAIS region where this grape, which represents 98 percent of all vines planted, reigns supreme. They're so associated with

Beaujolais that winemakers outside of the region often try to imitate the style of immediately drinkable, light- to medium-weight wines with high ACIDITY and low TANNINS. These light purple, fruity wines suggest flavors of bananas, berries, and peaches. Gamay is grown in other parts of BURGUNDY, such as the CÔTE CHALONNAISE, where a blend of PINOT NOIR and not more than two-thirds Gamay is known as BOUR-GOGNE PASSE-TOUT-GRAINS. In the LOIRE, ANJOU produces **Anjou Gamay**, and from TOURAINE comes **Gamay de Touraine**. There is very little true Gamay cultivated in California. For years California vintners grew what they thought was true *Gamay Noir a'Jus Blanc,* calling the result-ing wines GAMAY BEAUJOLAIS. However, this "Gamay" was eventually identified as an unexciting clone of PINOT NOIR. California's NAPA GAMAY is another case of mistaken identity. It too was thought to be a true Gamay but has since been recognized as *Valdiguie,* a variety from Southern France's LANGUEDOC-ROUSSILLON region. The wines produced from both these grapes are light- to medium-bodied and made in a style similar to true Gamay from Beaujolais. Because of historic prac-tice, both California wines are sometimes still called Gamay Beaujolais. BLAUFRÄNKISCH, a variety grown in Austria, is also some-times mistakenly called Gamay. Other names for Gamay include *Bourguignon Noir* and *Petit Gamai.*

Gamay Beaujolais [ga-MAY boh-zhoh-LAY] Grape long thought to be the true GAMAY variety grown in France's BEAUJOLAIS region. Gamay Beaujolais is actually an unexciting clone of PINOT NOIR. The wines pro-duced from this red wine grape are still allowed to be called Gamay Beaujolais, although many wine producers are now labeling them as Pinot Noir. In addition, acreage for this variety has dwindled, making it increasingly difficult to find wines with the Gamay Beaujolais label. These wines are usually light- to medium-bodied (*see* BODY), with pleas-antly fruity flavors and fairly high ACIDITY. They should be drunk young. A small amount of this variety is also cultivated in New Zealand. NAPA GAMAY is unrelated to Gamay Beaujolais or France's Gamay.

Gamay Blanc *see* CHARDONNAY

Gambellara DOC [gahm-bell-AH-rah] A DOC area located in Italy's VENETO region southwest of Venice (Vicenze), next to the SOAVE DOC. Like Soave wines, these use GARGANEGA as the main grape, blended with small amounts of TREBBIANO. The regular white wine is LIGHT, CRISP, and DRY. It is similiar to the Soave wines but generally not outstanding. **Recioto di Gambellara**, a sweet white wine that can be STILL, FRIZZANTE, or SPUMANTE is also made. A tiny amount of **Vin Santo**

di Gambellara, a golden- to amber-colored DESSERT WINE, is produced as well.

Gamé *see* BLAUFRÄNKISCH

gamey; game *see* Glossary of Wine Tasting Terms, page 655

Gamza *see* KADARKA

garage wines Term used used to describe high-quality, extremely expensive wines produced in very small quantities, particularly BOR-DEAUX AC wines from a group of small estates in SAINT-ÉMILION AC. The term derives from the fact that some of these wines are actually made in garages or small buildings and not in the grand châteaux. The prototype "garage" wine came from Chateau Le Pin, a small 5-acre estate in the POMEROL AC next to Saint-Émilion. It became a star in the early 1980s and commanded extremely high prices for its limited wine production. The best-known emulators of this success are Valandraud and La Mondotte of Saint-Émilion. Such wines are sometimes referred to as *vins de garage,* the producers referred to as *microchâteau* and *garagistes.* In the United States, the term garage wines is occasionally but infrequently used for very small production, hard-to-find wines; more often the term CULT WINES is used.

G

garagistes *see* GARAGE WINES

Gargana *see* GARGANEGA

Garganega [gahr-gah-NEH-gah] Prolific white-wine grape that is the principal variety used in Italy's SOAVE wines. Garganega is widely cultivated in Italy's VENETO region where it's been established for several centuries. It's also grown in neighboring LOMBARDY and farther south in UMBRIA. As with many grapes that are allowed high YIELDS, many Garganega-based wines—such as Soave—are generally bland and unexciting. However, controlled yields and careful winemaking can produce delectable, elegant wines that reveal Garganega's notable almond character. This variety is also used in the wines from the DOCS of BIANCO DI CUSTOZA, COLLI BERICI, and GAMBELLARA. Garganega is also known as *Gargana* and *Lizzana.*

Garanoir *see* GAMARET

Garnaccia *see* GRENACHE

Garnacha *see* GRENACHE

Garnacha Blanca *see* GRENACHE

Garnacha Tinta *see* GRENACHE

Garnacha Tintorera *see* ALICANTE BOUSCHET

Garnacho Tinto *see* GRENACHE

Garnatxa *see* EMPORDÀ-COSTA BRAVA DO

garrafeira [gah-rah-FAY-ruh] Portuguese term used on wine labels to suggest a better-quality wine (much like *Reserve* or *Private Reserve* is used in the United States). Red wines using this term must receive 3 years of aging (2 years before bottling and 1 year after). White wines must receive 1 year of aging (6 months before bottling and 6 months after). In addition, these wines must have an alcohol content at least ½ percent higher than the required minimum for regular bottlings.

garrigue *see* Glossary of Wine Tasting Terms, page 655

gassy *see* Glossary of Wine Tasting Terms, page 655

Gattinara DOCG [gah-tee-NAH-rah] Small DOCG zone located in the PIEDMONT region in northwestern Italy, northeast of Turin and northwest of Milan. It's one of the few DOCG areas in Italy and shares this status in the Piedmont region with BARBARESCO and BAROLO. The red wine is made from at least 90 percent Spanna (NEBBIOLO) and the rest BONARDA; it requires 4 years of AGING, two of which must be in wooden barrels. The wines of Gattinara had an excellent reputation from ancient times to the not-so-distant past, but there has been concern about a number of unworthy wines released in more recent VINTAGES. The upgrade to DOCG status in 1990 forced out many second-rate producers and caused a general upgrade in quality. At their best, Gattinara wines can be full-bodied (*see* BODY) and ELEGANT with hints of violets and spice. Some are also long-lived and capable of aging for 10 to 15 years or more.

Les Gaudichots *see* VOSNE-ROMANÉE AC

Gavi DOCG [GAH-vee] Also referred to as *Cortese di Gavi*, this DOCG area is located in the southeastern part of Italy's PIEDMONT region. It encompasses an area southeast of Alexandria and directly north of Genoa and includes the town of Gavi and 12 other small villages. Gavi, which achieved DOCG status in 1998, produces DRY white wine made from the CORTESE grape. A SPUMANTE version may be produced as well. The label term **"Gavi di Gavi"** is only allowed for wine producers with vineyards in the village of Gavi.

gazéifié *see* CARBONATION

GDC *see* TRELLIS SYSTEM

gebiet [geh-BEET] A German term meaning "district" or "territory." Gebiet has no official recognition in the European Economic Community designations, but it is sometimes used in place of ANBAUGEBIET, the official designation. *See also* WEINBAUGEBIET.

Geelong An Australian wine region located in the Port Phillip Zone of VICTORIA. It's situated on Port Phillip Bay about 45 miles southwest of Melbourne around Geelong, Victoria's second largest city. The area has a history going back to the 1860s and 1870s when it was Victoria's most significant wine region. Unfortunately, PHYLLOXERA infected the vineyards, which resulted in the area's demise. It was not until the mid-1960s that recovery began. Although it has not reclaimed its former position, Geelong now has over 600 vineyard acres and 20 wineries. CHARDONNAY and PINOT NOIR are the most successful grapes in this cool, maritime climate. CABERNET SAUVIGNON and Shiraz (SYRAH) are widely planted and can be quite good but require warm, dry years to do well.

Gehrn *see* RAUENTHAL

Geisenheim [GI-zuhn-hime] Prominent village located southwest of Wiesbaden in Germany's RHEINGAU region. It is known equally for its top-quality RIESLING wines and its school of VITICULTURE and ENOLOGY. The best EINZELLAGEN here are **Fuchsberg**, **Mäuerchen**, **Mönchspfad**, and **Rot'tenberg**. The highly regarded wines from Geisenheim have a distinctively EARTHY flavor.

Gelber Muskateller *see* MUSCAT

Gemeinde [ger-MINE-der] A German word for "community" or "village." On German wine labels the name of the Gemeinde (appended with an *er,* which converts it to an adjective) precedes that of the GROSSLAGE or EINZELLAGE. For example, the Einzellage named Mäuerchen associated with the village named Geisenheim appears on the label as "*Geisenheimer Mäuerchen*"; the Grosslage named Auflangen associated with the town of Nierstein appears as "*Niersteiner Auflangen.*"

generic wines [jeh-NEHR-ihk] 1. A general category of wine, such as DESSERT WINE, ROSÉ, SPARKLING WINE, SHERRY (when not specifically from Spain's JEREZ DE LA FRONTERA region), and TABLE WINE. 2. On U.S. labels the broad use of European designations (often specific wine regions) in the name, such as Burgundy, Chablis, Champagne, Chianti, Port, Rhine Wine, Sauterne, and Sherry.

generoso [jeh-neh-ROH-soh] Spanish term referring to wines with high ALCOHOL content (above 15 percent). They can be sweet or DRY and are usually served as an APÉRITIF or DESSERT WINE.

Geneva Double Curtain *see* TRELLIS SYSTEM

Les Genevrières *see* MEURSAULT

Geographe [gee-OH-gra-fee] An Australian wine region located in the South West Australia Zone of WESTERN AUSTRALIA. It's situated around the town of Bunbury, which is about 90 miles south of Perth. The famous MARGARET RIVER region and the Indian Ocean sit on its western border, the BLACKWOOD VALLEY region is to the southeast, and the PEEL region is to the north. There was some viticultural activity in the region in the 1920s and 1930s, but the modern era did not really begin until the 1970s. The climate in the coastal portion of this region is moderated by the ocean breezes and is similar to that of the northern portion of Margaret River. Inland areas are generally hotter during the day and cooler at night. CABERNET SAUVIGNON, CHARDONNAY, MERLOT, RIESLING, SAUVIGNON BLANC, SÉMILLON, and Shiraz (SYRAH) are grown in various areas around the region (Shiraz being the most widely planted).

Geographic Indications This is Australia's answer to the need for an APPELLATION system. It was established in 1993–1994 to fulfill aspects of trade agreements with the European Community and the United States, whereby the place of a wine's origin could be determined. Australia's Geographic Indications are not as restrictive as the French APPELLATION D'ORIGINE CONTRÔLÉE system, which has requirements not only for geographic definition but also for items like permissible grape VARIETIES, YIELDS, and the wine's ALCOHOL level. The Australian Geographic Indications structure is closer to that of the United States AMERICAN VITICULTURAL AREA system, which centers only on defining a geographic area. Like the system used in the United States, the Australian system does not guarantee the quality of the wines. The Australian system follows European labeling requirements regarding label use of geographic location—85 percent of the wine must come from that area. If grapes are sourced from multiple locations identification must be from most important to least important. According to the Australian Wine and Brandy Corporation (AWBC), which administers this system: "A Geographic Indication can be a zone, region, or subregion, terms that are defined in the AWBC Act. A **zone** is an area of land, without any particular qualifying attributes. A **region** must be a single tract of land, comprising at least five independently owned wine grape vineyards of at least five hectares [about 12.35 acres] each and usually produce five hundred tons of wine grapes in a year. A region is required to be discrete from adjoining regions and have measurable homogeneity in grape growing attributes over its area. A **subregion** must also be a single tract of land, comprising at least five independently owned wine grape vineyards of at least five hectares each and usually produce 500 tons of wine grapes in a year. However, a subregion is required to be discrete within the region and have substantial homogeneity in grape growing attributes over the area." Australian states are zones, so a label that says "South Australia" indicates that the wine may come from several locations but all from within the state of SOUTH AUSTRALIA. There are some zones and regions that straddle two states but are one contiguous area. The Big Rivers Zone with the MURRAY DARLING and SWAN HILL regions is an example—the zone and the regions lie in both NEW SOUTH WALES and VICTORIA. MARGARET RIVER is a region that lies in the South West Australia Zone of WESTERN AUSTRALIA—in a single zone and single state. Because Australian winemakers blend a lot of wine from various growing areas, the gigantic SOUTH EASTERN AUSTRALIA zone was approved. It incorporates all producing areas in New South Wales, Tasmania, and Victoria, as well as parts of Queensland and South Australia. It essentially covers 95 percent of Australia's vineyards. It allows wine blended from grapes grown in the various indicated regions to use this name on their label.

geranium *see* Glossary of Wine Tasting Terms, page 655

Germany Germany's approach to wine is somewhat different from that of other European countries like France and Italy because Germans aren't as focused on wine—the simple fact is that Germans prefer beer. In fact, German per capita wine consumption is about one third of that of either France or Italy. Yet Germany is considered a negative producer because it consumes more wine than it makes, whereas Italy and France produce more wine than they drink. The cool climate in Germany makes it overwhelmingly a white-wine producer (and all their best wines are white) because red grapes don't ripen well under such conditions. The main grape varieties for white wines are RIESLING, MÜLLER-THURGAU, and SYLVANER. Other white varieties include BACCHUS, EHRENFELSER, ELBING, FABER, GEWÜRZTRAMINER, Gutedel (CHASSELAS), HUXELREBE, KERNER, MORIO-MUSKAT, OPTIMA, ORTEGA, Rülander (PINOT GRIS), SCHEUREBE, and Weissburgunder (PINOT BLANC). The main red varieties are PORTUGIESER, Spätburgunder (PINOT NOIR), and Trollinger (SCHIAVA). Riesling is by far the star of the German wines.

Germany's approach to promoting wine quality is different from other APPELLATION systems, such as France's APPELLATION D'ORIGINE CONTRÔLÉE and Italy's DENOMINAZIONE DI ORIGINE CONTROLLATA. Appellations in other countries are geographic in nature and have specific regulations controlling each area. Germany, however, chose to base its wine quality on levels of ripeness and sweetness of the grapes. The focus on sugar content embodies the theory that grapes with higher sugar levels are riper and therefore yield richer wines with deep colors, intense flavors, and opulent BOUQUETS. The German wine laws adapted in 1971 set up three categories for defining the quality of German wines. DEUTSCHER TAFELWEIN (DTW) is the lowest-quality level followed by QUALITÄTSWEIN BESTIMMTER ANBAUGEBIET (QbA)—"quality wine from a specified region"—and the top level, QUALITÄTSWEIN MIT PRÄDIKAT (QmP)—"quality wine with distinction." Within the premier QmP category, there are six subcategories that ranked from lowest to highest: KABINETT, SPÄTLESE, AUSLESE, BEERENAUSLESE, EISWEIN, and TROCKENBEERE-NAUSLESE. CHAPTALIZATION (the addition of sugar) is allowed for DTW and QbA wines but not for QmP wines. It's one of the major differences between the quality levels—most grapes with enough natural sugar are reserved for QmP wines. The addition of sugar, which is converted into alcohol during FERMENTATION, allows producers to reach the required minimum alcohol levels for a DTW or QbA wine. If a quality wine (QbA or QmP) passes all its requirements, an AMTLICHE PRÜFUNGSNUMMER (official test number) is assigned. Abbreviated as A.P.Nr., this number is printed on the label, along with name of the ANBAUGEBIET. Additional information may be printed on a quality-wine label if other requirements are met. For instance, the name of the grape variety can be included if 85 percent of the grapes used in the wine are of one variety. Compared to French and Italian wines, those from Germany are generally lower in ALCOHOL (ranging from about 8½ to 11 percent) and usually contain at least some RESIDUAL SUGAR. The higher-quality wines—such as Beerenauslese, Eiswein, and Trockenbeerenauslese—are quite sweet. Recently, there's been a trend toward making more of the DTW, QbA, and Kabinett wines in a less sweet style—either TROCKEN (DRY) or HALBTROCKEN (half-DRY). With the 2000 vintage, Germany introduced two terms associated with DRY VARIETAL wines—"Classic" and "Selection." This effort is meant to simplify information to consumers and encourage the making of higher-quality dry wines. **Classic wines** are above average in quality and dry and are made from a traditional grape variety, such as Riesling, Silvaner, Müller-Thurgau, or Spätburgunder. Classic wines contain a Classic logo and contain the name of the producer and winegrowing region but no vineyard names. **Selection wines** have to meet additional standards like using grapes from vineyards with lower YIELDS, that are hand harvested (instead of mechanically), and that originate from an EINZELLAGE (individual vineyard site), which is used on the label. Selection wines theoretically are of higher quality and less available because of these added criteria. **Erstes Gewächs** is a legal designation used in Rheingau for high-quality DRY wines from an individual vineyard site (einzellage). **Grosses Gewächs** is a designation similar to Erstes Gewächs that's used in other German wine regions (other than Rheingau) although it doesn't have official status under German law. In Mosel, it's used by members in the growers' association, Bernkasteler Ring, and by members in other regions that belong to the prestigious Verband Deutscher Prädikatsweingüter (VDB) growers' association. **Erste Lage**, another designation not recognized by German law, is used by the VDB to indicate vineyard sites that are appropriate for Grosses Gewächs wines. Though Germany's appellation system isn't based on it, geography does come into play. The top two categories, QbA and QmP, must come from specific growing areas. Germany has developed a structure for defining the growing areas—from large general regions to specific vineyard sites. A large general growing region for quality wines is called an ANBAUGEBIET. There are now 13 of these regions, and their regional name is required on labels of quality wines (QbA and QmP). German law established 11 of these Anbaugebiete in 1971 in an effort to meet European Common Market rules. The original eleven Anbaugebiete are AHR, BADEN, FRANKEN, HESSISCHE BERGSTRASSE, MITTELRHEIN, MOSEL-SAAR-RUWER, NAHE, RHEINGAU, RHEINHESSEN, PFALZ, and WÜRTTEMBERG. Two more Anbaugebiete have been added from the former East Germany—SAALE-UNSTRUT and SACHSEN. Except for Saale-Unstrut and Sachsen, all of Germany's primary growing regions are located along the Rhine River or one of its tributaries. Each Anbaugebiet may be further divided into BEREICHE (districts), GROSSLAGEN (general sites), and EINZELLAGEN (individual sites or vineyards). An Einzellage could be compared to a specific GRAND CRU or PREMIER CRU vineyard site in France's BURGUNDY region that's recognized for a history of producing high-quality wines. There are about 2,600 Einzellagen throughout Germany. The names of specific towns and villages with decade-old reputations for wine-producing prowess are also important in the world of German wines. On German wine labels, the name of the town or village (often appended with an *er,* which converts it to an adjective) precedes the name of the GROSSLAGE or EINZELLAGE. For example, the Einzellage named Mäuerchen associated with the village named Geisenheim

G

appears on the label as "*Geisenheimer Mäuerchen*," while the Grosslage named Auflangen associated with the town of Nierstein appears as "*Niersteiner Auflangen.*" If an Einzellage is classified as an ORSTEIL, it doesn't need the nearest village's name.

geropiga [zhih-*r*oo-PEE-guh] Partially fermented grape syrup made by stopping FERMENTATION of grape MUST while it still retains most of the sugar content. It's used in Portugal to sweeten PORT wines during the blending process. It is sometimes spelled *jeropiga.*

Gerümpel *see* WACHENHEIM

Gevrey-Chambertin [zhuh-V*R*UH (zhuh-V*R*AY) shah*m*-beh*r*-TA*N*] Located in France's BURGUNDY region, this famous village is in the northern part (the CÔTE DE NUITS) of the CÔTE D'OR district. It's one of the larger villages in this acclaimed area and contains approximately 1,460 vineyard acres, all focused on producing red wines from PINOT NOIR grapes. At the top-quality level are the village's eight GRAND CRU vineyards—CHAMBERTIN, CHAMBERTIN-CLOS DE BÈZE, CHAPPELLE-CHAMBERTIN, CHARMES-CHAMBERTIN, GRIOTTE-CHAMBERTIN, LATRICIÈRES-CHAMBERTIN, MAZIS-CHAMBERTIN, and RUCHOTTES-CHAMBERTIN. MAZOYÈRES-CHAMBERTIN was sometimes used, but it has the same vineyard area as Charmes-Chambertin, and the latter appellation is generally used. The Chambertin grand cru is so famous that the village, formerly called simply Gevrey, added Chambertin to its name in 1847. Following the grands crus in descending order of quality are the PREMIER CRU vineyards, which are followed by the Gevrey-Chambertin AC and then the Côte de Nuits AC. Several premiers crus are thought to deserve grand cru status (if there's ever a reevaluation) including **Clos Saint-Jacques**, **Combe aux Moines**, **Les Cazetiers**, and **Les Verroilles**. As with much of Burgundy, top producers from premier cru vineyards often turn out better wines than the less-accomplished winemakers from grand cru vineyards. In sharp contrast to the highly rated red wines from the large grouping of grands crus and premiers crus, some critics think that, of all the Côte d'Or villages, **Gevrey-Chambertin AC** produces wines that are the most widely varying in quality. Many of their lower-quality wines are pale and flavorless.

Gewürztraminer [guh-VURTS-trah-mee-ner; geh-VEHRTZ-trah-mee-ner] Cultivated for over a thousand years, this white-wine grape (sometimes referred to simply as *Traminer*) is thought to have originated in the village of Tramin (or Temeno) in Italy's ALTO ADIGE region. Although this variety is not now widely planted in Alto Adige, some of the better Gewürztraminer wines still come from that region.

Gewürztraminer grapes are planted in ALSACE, a French region between Germany and France that specializes in excellent DRY Gewürztraminer wines. They're also cultivated in Germany, Austria, Hungary, Romania, Czechoslovakia, and Ukraine. Because they perform better in cooler climates, Gewürztraminer grapes have not done well in many of California's warmer growing regions. However, they thrive in cooler California areas such as CARNEROS, ANDERSON VALLEY, and MONTEREY COUNTY, as well as in parts of Oregon and Washington. Down under, New Zealand's cooler climate is better than Australia's for this grape. The German word *gewürz* means "spiced," and these wines are known for their CRISP, SPICY attributes. They're highly fragrant, with flavor characteristics of litchis, roses (or flowers in general), and spices such as cloves and nutmeg. Gewürztraminer wines are available in varying degrees of sweetness—DRY, medium-sweet, and LATE HARVEST. Because of the grape's pinkish (sometimes yellow) pigment, Gewurtztraminer wines are some of the more deeply colored of the whites, many have gold or peach tones. The distinctive color and AROMA of these wines make them easily recognizable by those familiar with this VARIETAL WINE. This is a wine that's best drunk fairly young—even VINTAGE Gewürztraminers rarely age well over 5 years. The Gewurtztraminer grape has myriad names, many beginning or ending with "Traminer," such as *Traminer Musqué, Traminer Parfumé, Traminer Aromatique* (or *Aromatico*), and *Roter Traminer.* Gewürztraminer is also called *Edeltraube, Païen, Rousselet, Rusa, Savagnin Rosé, Tramini,* and *Traminac.*

Ghemme DOC [GHEM-meh] A small DOC zone encompassing the town of the same name in the PIEDMONT region in northwestern Italy, northeast of Turin. It's just across the Sesia River from the GATTINARA DOCG. The dominate grape for the red wine made here is Spanna (NEBBIOLO), which must comprise from 65 to 85 percent of the blend. The other grapes used are BONARDA and Vespolina. The wines require 4 years of AGING, 3 of which must be in wooden barrels. Ghemme wines are considered by some to be as good as or better than those of the neighboring Gattinara DOCG. **Collis Breclemae** and **Collis Carellae** are vineyards that belong to one of the high-quality producers, Antichi Vigneti di Cantalupo.

Giaribaldi Dolce (GD) *see* MARSALA DOC

Gigondas AC [zhee-gawn-dah; zhee-gawn-dahss] Gigondas AC was upgraded from CÔTES DU RHÔNE-VILLAGES AC status to its own APPELLATION in 1971. It surrounds the village of the same name, which is located northeast of CHÂTEAUNEUF-DU-PAPE in France's southern RHÔNE region. The wines are mainly red, with a small amount of ROSÉ. The main grape variety is GRENACHE, which is blended with CINSAUT, MOURVÈDRE, and SYRAH. Gigondas wines are generally BIG and ROBUST and require several years of bottle AGING to SOFTEN.

Gippsland A huge Australian wine region that's also a zone (*see* GEOGRAPHIC INDICATIONS) located in VICTORIA. Its western border starts at Bass Strait and includes Phillip Island about 85 miles south of Melbourne and extends northeast to the NEW SOUTH WALES border taking up the Victoria's whole southeast corner. It's divided into three subregions—South Gippsland, West Gippsland, and East Gippsland. As large as it is, this region is still developing; it currently contains less than 400 acres of vineyard. Climate varies across this vast region, with South Gippsland generally the coolest. CHARDONNAY and PINOT NOIR are the principal varieties, although CABERNET SAUVIGNON, CABERNET FRANC, MERLOT, Shiraz (SYRAH), and SAUVIGNON BLANC are also grown.

girasol *see* RIDDLING

Gironde [zhee-*R*AW*N*D] French DÉPARTEMENT in southwestern France that essentially covers the same geographic territory as the BORDEAUX region. Gironde is also the name of the tidal estuary that starts north of the city of Bordeaux where the Garonne and Dordogne Rivers join as they make their way through this area to the Atlantic Ocean. Many of the better MÉDOC wine estates sit on the Gironde's west bank.

Gisborne New Zealand winegrowing region located on the far eastern point of the North Island around the city of Gisborne, about 280 miles southeast of Auckland. Its sits on the edge of **Poverty Bay**, which this region is sometimes called. The Gisborne region lies about 135 miles north of HAWKE'S BAY on the same side of the island, but it has about 30 percent more rainfall and proportionately less sunshine. Although viticultural activity started in the 1920s it wasn't until the 1960s that the area began rapid expansion. It became known for its inexpensive bag-in-a-box wines based primarily on MÜLLER-THURGAU, which was Gisborne's most widely planted VARIETY at the time. In the late 1980s, wineries began to realize that higher-quality wines could be produced here and began to shift away from Müller-Thurgau. During the 1990s, CHARDONNAY began to take over and now comprises about half the vineyards. With this emphasis on high-quality Chardonnay, the region has crowned itself as the "Chardonnay Capital of New Zealand." Of the region's approximately 5,000 acres, most are devoted to white-wine varieties, such as CHENIN BLANC, GEWÜRZTRAMINER, and RIESLING. Only about 10 percent of the vineyards are planted with red varieties.

Givry AC [zhee-VREE] One of the five villages in the CÔTE CHALON-NAISE that has APPELLATION status. Located in France's BURGUNDY region, Givry produces about 90 percent red wine from PINOT NOIR grapes and 10 percent white wine from CHARDONNAY. The red wines are generally made in a lighter style with ripe, fruity flavors—they're comparable to a good CÔTE DE BEAUNE AC wine.

glass stopper *see* CLOSURES

glassware, wine *see* Glassware, page 647

glassy-winged sharpshooter A leafhopper with a mottled-brown body about ½ inch long and grayish translucent, red-veined wings. As with all insects in this family, they feed on plant juices and often transmit diseases between plants via their mouths. The voracious glassy-winged sharpshooter daily consumes about 100 times its body weight in plant material, which makes it particularly destructive. This insect is responsible for the potentially apocalyptic spread of PIERCE'S DISEASE throughout California's vineyards.

Glenrowan *see* RUTHERGLEN

Glera *see* PROSECCO

glögg [GLUHG; GLOEG] Especially popular during Advent, this Swedish spiced-wine punch gets its *punch* from the addition of Aquavit or Brandy. To take the chill off cold winter nights, it's served hot in cups with several almonds and raisins added to each serving.

glucose [GLOO-kohs] One of the two main sugars found in grapes (the other being FRUCTOSE). Glucose is approximately half as sweet as fructose.

Glühwein [GLEW-vine] A popular German MULLED WINE, *Glühwein* ("glow wine") is so named not only because it "glows" with heat but also because it gives those who drink more than one or two a definite glow.

glycerol; glycerine [GLYS-uh-rawl; GLYS-uh-rihn] Also called *glycerine*, glycerol is a colorless, odorless, syrupy substance that, in winemaking, is an incidental by-product of FERMENTATION. It has a slightly sweet taste that gives a palate the impression of smoothness in a wine. Although it has long been thought that glycerol contributes

VISCOSITY and RICHNESS to wine, many experts say that it exists in such minute amounts as to not have such an effect.

Godello *see* VERDELHO

Goldatzel *see* JOHANNISBERG

Goldbächel *see* WACHENHEIM

Golden Chasselas *see* PALOMINO

Golden Hamburg *see* MUSCAT

golden sherry *see* SHERRY

Goldmuskateller *see* MUSCAT

Goldtröpfchen *see* PIESPORT

gönci [GAWN-seh] The traditional casks in which TOKAJI wines are produced. Gönci hold about 140 liters (37 gallons). The name comes from the Hungarian village of Gonc, which is known for its COOPERS.

gooseberry *see* Glossary of Wine Tasting Terms, page 655

Gordo; Gordo Blanco *see* MUSCAT

Goriziano *see* COLLIO DOC

Goron *see* VALAIS

Goulburn Valley An Australian wine region located in the Central Victoria Zone of VICTORIA. It's situated about 90 miles north of Melbourne around the town of Nagambie. Its wine history dates to the 1850s when vines were first planted. In 1860, investors started the Tahbilk Vineyard Proprietary (eventually called Chateau Tahhbilk), which survived the PHYLLOXERA infestation that partially destroyed area vineyards. Chateau Tahbilk, which has continuously produced wines throughout the decades, still has yielding vines that were planted in 1860. Mitchelton, the other major winery, did not arrive on the scene for over a hundred years. The climate of the Goulburn Valley is warm and lends itself to Shiraz (SYRAH) and CABERNET SAUVIGNON. MARSANNE is the other VARIETY with an esteemed reputation; Goulburn Valley is one of the few Australian regions well known for this variety. Other planted varieties are RIESLING, CHARDONNAY, SAUVIGNON BLANC, SÉMILLON, PINOT NOIR, and MERLOT. There are over 1,700 acres planted in the region.

goût; goût de terroir *see* Glossary of Wine Tasting Terms, page 655

Gouveio *see* VERDELHO

governo [goh-VEHR-noh] A VINIFICATION technique used in Italy's TUSCANY area (primarily CHIANTI) whereby the MUST from grapes previously set aside to dry and shrivel is added to the already-fermented wine. This causes a SECONDARY FERMENTATION, creating wines that are SOFTER, higher in ALCOHOL, more deeply colored, and, sometimes, slightly FRIZZANTE. Although not practiced much anymore, some producers desirous of a smooth-drinking wine still use this technique. The more common practice, however, is to use a GRAPE CONCENTRATE instead of semidried grapes.

Graach [GRAHK] Tiny village located between BERNKASTEL and WEHLEN on the Mosel River in Germany's MOSEL-SAAR-RUWER region. It's famous for its rich, intense, fragrant wines, which are considered some of the best in this region. Key EINZELLAGEN, which are located on the well-situated steep slopes surrounding Graach, include **Domprobst**, **Himmelreich**, and JOSEPHSHÖFER.

Graciano [grah-see-YAH-noh (Sp. grah-THYAH-noh)] A high-quality red-wine grape grown in the RIOJA and NAVARRA regions of Spain. Graciano wines are capable of rich color, a lovely fragrant BOUQUET, a hint of spice in the flavor, and long AGING. The high ACIDITY of the Graciano grape makes it a good candidate for blending with low-acid varieties like TEMPRANILLO. Graciano's sparse YIELD is prompting many Spanish growers to replace this quality variety with more productive vines. A similar situation exists in France's LANGUEDOC-ROUSSILLON region where Graciano (known there as *Morrastel*) is also being replaced.

gradazione alcoolica [grah-dah-TSYOH-nay ahl-KAW-lee-kah] Italian term for "ALCOHOL BY VOLUME."

grafting A viticultural (*see* VITICULTURE) technique whereby BUD-WOOD (a bud-bearing shoot) is secured to the ROOTSTOCK. This technique is critical in most vineyards because the rootstock of VITIS VINIFERA vines (CABERNET SAUVIGNON and CHARDONNAY, for example) aren't resistant to PHYLLOXERA, whereas most NATIVE AMERICAN rootstocks are. Phylloxera has attacked vineyards all over Europe and the United States, and there are few places that haven't been infested (CHILE is one). In order to produce the popular VARIETAL WINES, it's necessary to graft the *vitis vinifera* vines to the phylloxera-resistant rootstock. Some believe that grapes from ungrafted vineyards produce the best wines. Most grafting is done in a nursery and is called **bench grafting**. When it's done in the vineyard, it's called **field grafting**. *See also* T-BUDDING.

Grainhübel *see* DEIDESHEIM

Grampians An Australian wine region, formerly known as the **Great Western** region, located in the Western Victoria Zone of VICTORIA. It's situated about 130 miles west and slightly north of Melbourne around the town of Ararat. The region's winemaking history dates back to the 1860s, soon after the short-lived gold boom in the latter 1850s. Seppelt Great Western, established in 1865, became Australia's best-known SPARKLING WINE producer utilizing huge underground caves dug out by unemployed gold miners in the late 1860s. Although still known as a producer of sparkling wines, the Grampians has also gained a reputation for STILL WINES. This is a cool to warm growing region that does well with CHARDONNAY, Shiraz (SYRAH), and CABERNET SAUVIGNON (its most widely planted varieties). Other varieties grown here include SAUVIGNON BLANC, PINOT NOIR, RIESLING, and MERLOT.

Granaccia *see* GRENACHE

Granacha *see* GRENACHE

grand cru; pl. grands crus [grahn KROO] 1. French for "great growth." 2. *Grand cru* is used in BURGUNDY for the top ranking a vineyard can receive. It's only bestowed upon a limited number of vineyards in the CÔTE D'OR and CHABLIS. Because the vineyards of Burgundy are divided among many owners, this top ranking doesn't always guarantee that the very best wines will be produced by the various vintners. The rank just below grand cru is PREMIER CRU. 3. In France's CHAMPAGNE region, villages are classified according to wine quality, and a percentage rating is applied, the very best receiving 100 percent. Seventeen villages in Champagne qualify for this highest (grand cru) status, although it's probably less meaningful in Champagne because the house (producer) is generally considered most important. 4. In ALSACE (as of 1983), the grand cru designation is bestowed upon the top vineyards. To date, 51 have qualified and are allowed to put "Grand Cru" on their labels. 5. In BORDEAUX, the designation grand cru (versus GRAND CRU CLASSÉ) is given to some châteaux (such as those in SAINT-ÉMILION), but it has little real meaning.

grand cru classé; pl. grands crus classés [grahn kroo klah-SAY] 1. French for "great classed growth." 2. *Grand cru classé* is the second highest category for the wines ranked in the SAINT-ÉMILION classification as set forth in 1953 (later revised in 1969 and 1985). As of 1985, the 63 châteaux with this status may label their wines "Grand Cru Classé." These wines do not have the same prestige as the grand cru classé wines of the MÉDOC. 3. The second- through fifth-growth wines of the MÉDOC and SAUTERNES may use "Grand Cru Classé" on their labels.

Grande Marque [grah*n* MAH*R*K] *see* CHAMPAGNE

Les Grandes Loliéres *see* CORTON AC

Les Grandes Ruchottes *see* CHASSAGNE-MONTRACHET AC

Grand River Valley *see* LAKE ERIE AVA

La Grand Rue *see* VOSNE-ROMANÉE AC

La Grand Rue AC [lah GRAH*N* roo] One of the six GRAND CRU vineyards located in the village of VOSNE ROMANÉE in the CÔTE DE NUITS. It was recently promoted from PREMIER CRU status to grand cru status based on its excellent site, which lies between two other famous grand cru vineyards—ROMANÉE-CONTI and LA TÂCHE. La Grand Rue consists of slightly over 4 acres planted with PINOT NOIR. Although the wines from this vineyard are some of the world's most expensive, they're overshadowed by those from the neighboring and more famous grand cru vineyards of Romanée—Conti, RICHEBOURG, and La Tâche.

Grands-Échezeaux AC [grah*n* zay-shuh-ZOH] A prestigious GRAND CRU vineyard located in the CÔTE DE NUITS area of France's BURGUNDY region. Although it's often grouped with the famous grands crus of the neighboring village of VOSNE-ROMANÉE, Grand Échezeaux is physically located in the village of Flagey-Échezeaux. It consists of 22.6 acres, all planted with PINOT NOIR grapes. Grands-Échezeaux red wines don't quite have the acclaim of some of the neighboring grands crus (such as ROMANÉE-CONTI, LA TÂCHE, and RICHEBOURG), but some wine lovers think that makes them a relative bargain. The wines can be very RICH and full-bodied (*see* BODY), with CONCENTRATED aromas and flavors. They're capable of AGING for 10 to 15 years. Grands-Échezeaux AC wines are generally superior to those from the neighboring grand cru, ÉCHEZEAUX.

Grand Siècle *see* CHAMPAGNE

Grand Valley AVA *see* COLORADO

Grand Vidure *see* CARMENÈRE

grand vin [grah*n* VA*N*] French for "grand wine." Although used to distinguish a better wine from other "secondary wines," grand vin has no official definition.

Granja-Amareleja DOC *see* ALENTEJO

gran reserva [grahn ray-SAYR-vah] A Spanish term used for aged, top-quality wines from very good vintages. To use this term on the label, red wines must AGE for 5 years (with 2 of those years in wooden barrels), and white and ROSÉ wines must age for 4 years (with 6 months in wood).

granvas *see* CHARMAT

grape concentrate Grape juice that's concentrated into a very sweet syrup, usually in the range of 60° to 70° BRIX. In California and Italy, adding sugar to wine (CHAPTALIZATION) is illegal, but grape concentrate may be added to boost the alcohol content or increase the sweetness of the final wine.

grapes Although other fruits are vinified, grapes are the basis for most of the world's wine and all of its fine wines. That's because certain grape species (which today have been refined to deliver the utmost in aroma and flavor) comprise the right properties to produce wine naturally—high amounts of fermentable sugar, strong flavors, color in the skins, and TANNINS in the seeds and skins (to assist AGING). It's surmised that over 5,000 years ago someone discovered a naturally created wine—and that it tasted *good*. That prompted grape cultivation, along with winemaking techniques to help nature along. Today, wine production has become relatively sophisticated, and the wine, presumably, has become much better. Grapes belong to the botanical family Ampelidaceae, and of that family's ten genera, the genus *Vitis* is most important to winemakers. There are numerous species within the genus *Vitis*, the most important of which is VITIS VINIFERA, the species that yields over 99 percent of the world's wines. *Vitis vinifera* is native to Europe and East and Central Asia, but it has been planted all over the world. There are estimated to be thousands of varieties of this species, some of the best-known being CABERNET SAUVIGNON, CHARDONNAY, MERLOT, PINOT NOIR, SAUVIGNON BLANC, SYRAH, and ZINFANDEL. Other *Vitis* species that produce grapes suitable for wine include VITIS LABRUSCA, VITIS RIPARIA, and VITIS ROTUNDIFOLIA (all of which are native to the Americas). Even though these species are not the quality of the *Vitis vinifera* grapes, some of them have played a critical role in worldwide grape production. That's because the *Vitis vinifera* roots are susceptible to PHYLLOXERA, and the native American vines, particularly *Vitis riparia*, are resistant to this louse. Most of the world's vineyards now have phylloxera-resistant rootstocks (other than *Vitis vinifera*) that have *Vitis vinifera* vines grafted to them. This resulting marriage allows the roots to survive while still producing the best wine grapes.

grapevine diseases *see* DISEASES, VINEYARD

grapey *see* Glossary of Wine Tasting Terms, page 655

grappa [GRAHP-pah] Made commercially since the eighteenth century, grappa is the Italian counterpart to France's MARC. This colorless, high-alcohol EAU DE VIE is distilled from POMACE—the residue (grape skins and seeds) left in the wine press after the juice is removed for wine. There are hundreds of highly individual, markedly different styles of this fiery distillation, which can have great character and depth. There are also aged grappas, some so complex that they're aged in a series of different woods including acacia, oak, birch, and juniper. The ultimate grappa is spicy, golden-colored Ue [pronounced OO-eh], which is made from grape juice and pomace, and aged in wood.

Grasevina *see* WELSCHRIESLING

grassy; grassiness *see* Glossary of Wine Tasting Terms, page 655

Grauburgunder *see* PINOT GRIS

Grauer Riesling *see* RÜLANDER

Grauvernatsch *see* SCHIAVA

Grave del Friuli DOC [GRAH-veh del free-OO-lee] The largest DOC zone in the FRIULI-VENEZIA GIULIA region in northeastern Italy. It produces over 40 percent of this region's DOC wines. The word *Grave* in the name indicates the presence of gravelly terrain throughout the area. The DOC covers fourteen VARIETAL WINES and a ROSATO. The red varietal wines are Cabernet (made from CABERNET FRANC and CABERNET SAUVIGNON), Cabernet Franc, Cabernet Sauvignon, MERLOT, Pinot Nero (PINOT NOIR), and Refosco del Peduncolo Rosso (REFOSCO). The white varietals are CHARDONNAY, Pinot Bianco (PINOT BLANC), Pinot Grigio (PINOT GRIS), Riesling Italico (WELSCHRIESLING), Sauvignon (SAUVIGNON BLANC), FRIULANO, Traminer Aromatico (GEWÜRZTRAMINER), and VERDUZZO FRIULANO. Varietal wines may contain up to 15 percent of other approved grapes of the same color. The Rosato must be 70 to 80 percent Merlot and 20 to 30 percent other approved red varieties.

gravelly *see* Glossary of Wine Tasting Terms, page 655

Graves [GRAHV] An important wine-producing area in France's BORDEAUX region. It abuts the MÉDOC in the north just above the city of

Bordeaux, extending west and to the south, where it surrounds the appellations of BARSAC, CÉRONS, and SAUTERNES. The Garonne River runs along its eastern border. The word *graves* is French for "gravel," and the area takes its name from its gravelly soil, which is particularly prominent in its northern section. This northern part of Graves contains the best châteaux and, in 1987, was given its own appellation—PESSAC-LEOGNAN AC. Since then, the **Graves AC** covers only red and DRY white wines made in Graves' southern area. This AC doesn't have the quality reputation for wines that the Pessac-Leognan AC does. The **Graves Supérieures AC** is an appellation for DRY, medium-sweet, and sweet white wines with a higher minimum ALCOHOL level (12 percent, versus 11 percent for Graves AC). This rarely used appellation produces primarily sweet wines, which come from southern Graves. The entire region of Graves is rather unique for Bordeaux because it's well known for both white and red wines. In fact, until the mid-1970s the area produced more white wine than red. The white wines, which are made from SAUVIGNON BLANC, SÉMILLON, and MUSCADELLE, have evolved from sweet wines into those with a CRISP, DRY style. One reason the name Graves is often associated with white wines is because white-wine labels specify *Graves AC* (or *Graves Supérieures AC*). Another reason is that the red wines, made predominantly from CABERNET SAUVI-GNON, CABERNET FRANC, and MERLOT, are more apt to display the château's name prominently on the label, with the appellation name in a secondary role. The red wines of Graves are generally credited with being of higher quality than whites, particularly in the northern section (Pessac-Leognan AC). They're often equated to wines of the Médoc, but they have a distinctively EARTHY quality and are SOFTER because a bit more Merlot is used in the blend. The Classification of 1855 (*see* Official Wine Classifications of Bordeaux, page 678) for Bordeaux wines was limited to wines from the Médoc because those from other areas weren't deemed worthy. The only exception was Graves' Château Haut-Brion, which received a PREMIER CRU ranking—one of only four Bordeaux châteaux to receive this honor at that time. Today, Haut-Brion is still consistently one of the top estates of Bordeaux. The châteaux of Graves were classified for red wines in 1953, and again in 1959, when white wines were added and selected châteaux were given CRU CLASSÉ status (but no rankings within this category). Thirteen châteaux were deemed CRUS CLASSÉS for their red wines; six of those thirteen plus two additional estates also received this honor for their white wines. For a list of those châteaux *see* Graves (Pessac-Léognan) Classification of 1959, page 683.

Graves de Vayres AC [grahv duh VEH*R*] Located in the northern part of the ENTRE-DEUX-MERS area of France's BORDEAUX region, this small APPELLATION runs along the Dordogne River across from the SAINT-ÉMIL- ION AC. Graves de Vayres AC is unrelated to the GRAVES region, although it has a similar gravelly soil (from which comes its name). Both the white wines (which are DRY) and the red wines are generally satisfactory. The reds are made from CABERNET SAUVIGNON, CABERNET FRANC, and MERLOT; the whites are made from SAUVIGNON BLANC, SÉMIL- LON, and MUSCADELLE.

Graves-Léognan *see* PESSAC-LÉOGNAN AC

Graves-Pessac *see* PESSAC-LÉOGNAN AC

Gray Riesling; Grey Riesling *see* TROUSSEAU GRIS

gray rot *see* BOTRYTIS CINEREA

Greater Perth Zone *see* WESTERN AUSTRALIA

Great Southern Previously known as **Lower Great Southern**, this Australian wine region is located in the South West Australia Zone of WESTERN AUSTRALIA. It's situated about 240 miles southeast of Perth around the towns of Albany and Mount Barker. This huge area mea- sures approximately 90 miles by 60 miles and is broken up into a num- ber of subregions—**Albany**, **Denmark**, **Mount Barker**, **Frankland**, and **Porongurup**. The climate in the region is moderately warm but varies over this large expanse. Albany and Denmark, which are farther south and close to the Southern Ocean, are influenced by a maritime climate, whereas the other three regions are inland to the north and have a more continental climate. CHARDONNAY is the most widely planted white VARIETY, and the quality of these wines is quite good. But it's RIESLING that's achieved star status here, and the wines made from it rival the best from other parts of Australia. SAUVIGNON BLANC and SÉMIL- LON are also grown in large quantities, followed by VERDELHO and Traminer (GEWÜRZTRAMINER). The most widely planted red varieties are CABERNET SAUVIGNON and Shiraz (SYRAH), and both are gaining excellent reputations. The Cabernet Sauvignon wines have achieved special attention for their BIG, POWERFUL, almost AUSTERE style and long AGING potential. MERLOT, PINOT NOIR, and CABERNET FRANC are also grown in sizeable quantities. There are over 35 wineries scattered throughout the region.

Grechetto; Greghetto [greh-KEH-toh] A white-wine grape grown primarily in Italy's UMBRIA region, where it's a component—

along with TREBBIANO TOSCANO and MALVASIA—in the well-known wines of ORVIETO and TORGIANO. Grechetto has gained a much better reputation by itself, where its delightfully rich, nutty character is showcased—as in the Grechetto di Todi wines. This grape is also used to make excellent VIN SANTO. Although Grechetto is also called *Greco Spoletino* and *Greco Bianco di Perugia*, it's unrelated to the GRECO of southwest Italy.

Greco [GREH-koh] 1. White-wine grape grown in southwestern Italy's CAMPANIA and CALABRIA regions. Greco's origins are certainly Greek, although there are numerous theories as to how this ancient variety was introduced into Italy. If cultivated and VINIFIED carefully, Greco is capable of producing high-quality wines with rich, fruity flavors, as well as hints of smoke and toasted nuts. This variety is best known for the GRECO DI TUFO dry wines and the sweet wines of GRECO DI BIANCO. Greco also plays a principal role in the wines from CIRÒ and FIANO DI AVELLINO. This variety goes by other names—most beginning with Greco—including *Greco delle Torre*, *Greco di Tufo*, and *Greco del Vesuvio*. 2. A name used for the variety ALBANA, which is totally unrelated to the true Greco.

Greco Bianco di Perugia *see* GRECHETTO

Greco delle Torre *see* GRECO

Greco del Vesuvio *see* GRECO

Greco di Ancona *see* ALBANA

Greco di Tufo DOC [GREH-koh dee TOO-foh] DOC area located east of Naples in Italy's CAMPANIA region that includes the vineyards encompassing the village of Tufo. Greco di Tufo wine is made primarily from the GRECO grape, which is thought to have originated in Greece and is quite popular in this region. In addition to the DRY white wine produced, there is a SPUMANTE version that may be made.

Greco Spoletino *see* GRECHETTO

Greece Although ancient Greeks were renowned winemakers, modern Greeks certainly haven't been viewed in the same light until recently. Part of this unenviable contemporary image is attached to Greece's RETSINA wines, which for most outsiders is definitely an acquired taste. Greece started making inroads into modern wine-production techniques and quality control in the 1960s and 1970s as it worked to gain European Economic Community (EEC) membership, which was finalized in 1981. Starting in the early 1970s, the Greeks began implementing an APPELLATION system based on the French model for their quality wines. As with other wine-quality systems, the qualifying categories are determined by several factors including the suitability and history of the grape variety, sugar levels, vineyard elevation, soil composition, yield per *stremma* (¼ acre), and winemaking practices (such as barrel aging). There are four distinct Greek categories. **OPAP (Onomasía Proeléfseos Anotéras Piótitos)**, Greece's "Appellation of Origin of Superior Quality," currently has 20 appellations. **OPE (Onomasía Proeléfseos Eleghoméni)**, or "Controlled Appellation of Origin," has 8 appellations and is for sweet wines made from MUSCAT or MAVRODAPHNE. **Topikos Inos** (local wine), the Greek equivalent to the French VINS DE PAYS, has 139 appellations. This last category has a special designation—"Appellation by Tradition"—which includes RETSINA and Verdea. **Epitrapezios Inos** (table wine) is equivalent to the French VIN DE TABLE and, as in countries like France and Italy, winemakers sometimes choose to make some of their highest-quality wines in this category in order to not be constrained by the restrictions of the higher categories. Three of Greece's top appellations producing red wines are **Neméa**, **Náoussa**, and **Playies Melitona**, the latter allowing the use of CABERNET SAUVIGNON and CABERNET FRANC varieties. Other key OPAP appellations are **Daphnes, Limnos, Patras, Rhodes, Santorini, Sitia**, and **Zitsa**. Top OPE appellations are **Mavrodaphne of Patras** and **Muscat of Samos**. For OPAP and OPE categories, the term **Reserve** means that white wines have been aged for 2 years and red wines for 3 years. **"Grand reserve"** signifies that white wines have aged for 3 years and red wines for 4 years. For table wines, the term **Kava** indicates that white wines have been aged for 2 years and red wines for 3 years. White wines labeled "Reserve," "Grand Reserve," and "Kava" are generally sweet. Greece's principal growing regions include the Peloponnese, the large peninsula in the south of Greece that produces about one-third of the total wines; Macedonia and Epirus in the north; Attica, the second most productive region, which is in the southeastern region around Athens; the Island of Crete, south of the mainland; and Cephalonia and other islands west of the mainland. There are also vineyards south and southeast of the mainland on the islands of Rhodes, Samos, and Santorini. The main white grapes of Greece are Savatiano (the most widely planted of all varieties), ASSYRTIKO, Mavrodaphne, Moscophilero, Robola (RIBOLLA), and Rhoditis. Red varieties include AGIORGITIKO (also called *St. George* and used in the well-known Neméa wines), Liatiko, Limnio, Mandilaria, Romeiko, and the highly respected XINÓMAVRO—used to make Naoussa. Also planted in large quantities are MALVASIA, used to make a MALMSEY-style wine called Monemvasia, and MUSCAT, which makes a delicious DESSERT WINE.

green *see* Glossary of Wine Tasting Terms, page 655

green grafting *see* T-BUDDING

Green Grape *see* SÉMILLON

Green Hungarian A white-wine grape grown in limited amounts in California. Green Hungarian's origin is uncertain, although there are suggested connections to AGOSTON HARASZTHY, a Hungarian count often referred to as the father of California VITICULTURE. Green Hungarian grapes produce pleasant but rather nondescript, neutral wines that are now sold by only a handful of VINTNERS. The best known of these is Weibel Vineyards, where Green Hungarian continues to be one of their leading sellers.

green pruning *see* PRUNING

Green Valley-Solano County AVA The lesser of two AVA named Green Valley, this one is located in Solano County, California, east of the southern end of NAPA COUNTY. This area doesn't receive the cooling ocean breezes, so it's much hotter and has a shorter growing season than the Napa or Sonoma VITICULTURAL AREAS.

Green Valley-Sonoma County AVA *see* SONOMA COUNTY GREEN VALLEY AVA

Grenache [gruh-NAHSH] Grape that comes in both red-wine and white-wine varieties. When used by itself, the word "Grenache" refers to the red version **Grenache Noir**, one of the world's most widely cultivated red grapes. The Grenache grape does well in hot, dry regions, and its strong stalk makes it well suited for windy conditions. It ripens with very high sugar levels and can produce wines with 15 to 16 percent ALCOHOL. Grenache wines are sweet, fruity, and very low in TANNINS. They're usually lacking in color, except in growing areas where YIELDS are low. The vine originated in Spain where it's called *Garnacha* and *Garnacha Tinta* (or *Garnacho Tinto*) and is the most widely cultivated red-wine grape in that country. It's widely planted in NAVARRA and in many of Spain's hotter areas including CARIÑENA, LA MANCHA, PENEDÈS, RIOJA, and UTIEL-REQUENA. In southern France not far from the Spanish border, Grenache is widely cultivated in the areas around LANGUEDOC-ROUSSILLON, PROVENCE, and the southern RHÔNE. It's also extensively grown in Algeria, Australia, Corsica, Israel, Morocco, Sardinia (where it's called *Cannonau*), and California's CENTRAL VALLEY.

Guarnaccia is a Grenache strain native to southern Italy's Ischia island, at the entrance to the Bay of Naples. Red Grenache wines are usually BLENDED with those made from other varieties; 100 percent Grenache wines are rarely found. In Spain Grenache is blended with TEMPRANILLO, and in most of France it's blended with CINSAUT and CARIGNAN. In CHÂTEAUNEUF-DU-PAPE it's used as the primary grape, although it is blended with as many as twelve other VARITIES including CLAIRETTE, MOURVÈDRE, MUSCADINE, and SYRAH. In ROSÉ wines—particularly those from CÔTES-DU-RHÔNE, CÔTES DU VENTOUX, LIRAC, and TAVEL—Grenache is often the dominant grape used. In California and Australia, it's most often used as a blending wine for inexpensive JUG WINES. **Grenache Blanc** [gruh-NAHSH BLAHN; BLAHNGK] Also known as *Garnacha Blanca*, this is the white varient of GRENACHE NOIR. Although not as popular as the red, it's still widely planted in both Spain and France where it is the fifth most planted white grape. The white wines produced are high in ALCOHOL and low ACIDITY. It's used in the CÔTES DU RHÔNE AC and CHÂTEAUNEUF-DU-PAPE AC mainly as a BLENDING WINE. Grenache is known by many different names including *Alicante, Cannonao* (or *Cannonau*), *Carignan Rosso, Granaccia, Granacha,* and *Roussillon*.

G

Grenouilles [gruh-NOO-yuh] One of the seven GRAND CRU vineyards in CHABLIS and, at 23 acres, the smallest. It's situated in the middle of Chablis' grand cru slope, between VAUDÉSIR and VALMUR.

Grés de Montpellier [gray duh mawn-peh-lyay] French APPELLATION created in 2005 as a subzone within the larger CÔTEAUX DU LANGUEDOC AC. It lies around the city of Montpellier and encompasses the communes of **St Drézery**, **Vérargues**, **St Christol**, **La Méjanelle** and **St Georges d'Orques**, which is the most significant of the group. It was approved for red wines consisting of a minimum of 70 percent SYRAH and MOURVÈDRE, a minimum of 20 percent GRENACHE, plus the addition of some CINSAUT or CARIGNAN.

Les Grèves *see* BEAUNE; CORTON

Grignolino [gree-nyoh-LEE-noh] A red-wine grape grown in the southeastern portion of Italy's PIEDMONT region, primarily in the provinces of ASTI and Alessandria. This variety produces unusual wines for this region, which is known for its BIG, bold, long-lived reds. Conversely, Grignolino wines have high ACIDITY and are rust-colored, delicately scented and flavored, and light-bodied (*see* BODY); they are best drunk young. These wines have DOC status in Asti and Monferrato Casalese. Grignolino's sporadic YIELDS have caused it to lose popularity with some growers in recent years. Small amounts of this variety are grown in California, where it's turned into light-bodied red or ROSÉ wines, the best known of which are from Heitz Wine Cellars.

Gringet *see* SAVAGNIN

Griotte-Chambertin AC [gree-AWT shah*m*-behr-TA*N*] Small (less than 7 acres) GRAND CRU vineyard that produces world-class red wines from PINOT NOIR. It's located in the village of GEVREY-CHAMBERTIN in the CÔTE DE NUITS district of France's BURGUNDY region. Only about 800 cases of this hard-to-find wine are produced, all of it generally of high quality. The wines are RICH, PERFUMED, and COMPLEX, although they won't generally AGE as long as wines from some of the area's other grands crus. *See also* CHAMBERTIN.

grip *see* Glossary of Wine Tasting Terms, page 655

Gris Meunier *see* MEUNIER

Groenekloof WO [GRO-neh-klof] Demarcated SOUTH AFRICA wine district located about 40 miles north of Cape Town near the hamlet of Darling on the West Coast. The vineyards are located within 5 miles of the cold Atlantic Ocean. The cool-weather region is becoming known for its SAUVIGNON BLANC wines, although CABERNET SAUVIGNON, PINOTAGE, and SYRAH have also been planted.

Grolleau *see* GROSLOT

Groppello [groh-PEHL-oh] Good-quality red-wine grape grown in Italy's LOMBARDY region, primarily in the DOC of Riviera del Garda Bresciano, where it's used to create appealing ROSÉ (called CHIARETTO) and red wines. Although Groppello is the principal variety in both the reds and rosés from this area, SANGIOVESE and BARBERA grapes are also used in the blend.

Gros Plant *see* FOLLE BLANCHE

Groslot [groh-LOH] Red-wine grape of rather ordinary quality, grown primarily in the ANJOU district of France's LOIRE region. Groslot is the main component in the semisweet, moderately flavored ROSÉ D'ANJOU wines, which generally have low ALCOHOL and high ACIDITY. There are, however, some higher-quality Rosé d'Anjou wines that exhibit a wonderful appley flavor with a hint of nuts. Groslot acreage has been declining in France in favor of higher-quality varieties. This grape is also known as *Grolleau*.

Grosse Roussette *see* MARSANNE

Grosses Gewächs [GROSS guh-VEHKS] *see* GERMANY

Grosse Syrah *see* MONDEUSE

Grosslage; pl. Grosslagen [GROSS-lah-guh; GROSS-lah-gehn] A German term meaning "large vineyard," referring to a collection of individual vineyards (EINZELLAGEN) with similar environmental attributes that produce wines of comparable character and quality. There are about 2,600 Einzellagen and 150 Grosslagen, which are further combined into 34 BEREICHE (districts) and 13 ANBAUGEBIETE (growing regions). Sizes of Grosslagen vary tremendously—from 125 to over 5,000 acres—and contain any number of Einzellagen. The name of an Einselage on a label generally indicates a wine of higher quality than one with the name of a Grosslage. Unfortunately, labels don't indicate whether a name is an Einzellage or a Grosslage, making it difficult to use this information effectively. Moves by various groups to discard the use of Grosslagen have been partially successful. Beginning in September 1994, the German wine law allowed the production of Qualitätswein garantierten Ursprungs (QgU) or a "quality wine of guaranteed origin." A QgU comes from an **Ursprungslage**, which is a specific district, vineyard, or village with a consistent style associated with its site of origin. QgU wines are required to undergo more stringent sensory and analytical evaluations.

Grossriesling *see* ELBLING

Grossvernatsch *see* SCHIAVA

grown, produced, and bottled by Label term that is another way of indicating that a wine is ESTATE BOTTLED, meaning that the grapes are grown at the winery's vineyards or vineyards controlled by the winery and that the wine is VINIFIED and bottled at the winery. *See also* BOTTLED BY; MADE AND BOTTLED BY; PRODUCED AND BOTTLED BY.

Grumello *see* VALTELLINA DOC

Grüner Veltliner [GROO-ner FELT-lih-ner] White-wine grape grown principally in Austria (and that country's most widely planted variety), but also cultivated in Hungary, Czechoslovakia, and Slovenia. This grape produces pale, CRISP, light- to medium-bodied (*see* BODY) slightly SPICY wines of good quality. It's also called *Grünmuskateller* and *Veltlini*, as well as simply *Grüner*.

Grünmuskateller *see* GRÜNER VELTLINER

Guenoc Valley AVA A LAKE COUNTY, California, VITICULTURAL AREA at the northern end of the NAPA VALLEY about 15 miles north of Calistoga. It's unique because it's essentially a single-winery APPELLATION. Guenoc Winery's owner, Orville Magoon, was the designer of the area, which received AVA status in 1981. The valley's growing season swings from warm days to cool nights, making it a Region III (*see* CLIMATE REGIONS OF CALIFORNIA). The main grape varieties are CABERNET SAUVIGNON and CHARDONNAY, with small amounts of SAUVIGNON BLANC.

Guarnaccia *see* GRENACHE

Güldenmorgen *see* DIENHEIM

Gumpoldskirchen [GOOM-pawlts-kirkh-ehn] Celebrated Austrian wine-producing town located just south of Vienna in an area called the Thermenregion district. Gumpoldskirchen produces highly regarded white wines from Rotgipfler and Zierfandler grapes. The Gumpoldskirchener wines are RICH, DRY, full-bodied (*see* BODY), and HEADY.

gunflint *see* FLINTY in the Glossary of Wine Tasting Terms, page 655

Günterslay *see* PIESPORT

Gutedel *see* CHASSELAS

Gutsabfüllung [GOOTS-ab-few-lung] A German term meaning "estate bottled" and comparable to the meaning of ESTATE BOTTLED in the United States. It has a much more restrictive meaning than the term ERZEUGERABFÜLLUNG.

Gutturnio *see* COLLI PIACENTINI

Guyot *see* TRELLIS SYSTEM

gyropallets *see* RIDDLING

Habzó Hungarian for "sparkling."

halbstück [HAHLP-shtook] A round wooden cask holding 600 liters (about 158 U.S. gallons) that's traditionally used by German winemakers along the Rhine River, particularly in the RHEINGAU region. These casks are slowly disappearing because some winemakers no longer use them in wine production for certain grape varieties like MÜLLER-THURGAU.

halbsüss [HAHLP-soos] German for "half sweet," referring to wines with a RESIDUAL SUGAR content of between 1 and 3 percent.

halbtrocken [HAHLP-trahk-en] German for "half-dry" or "medium-dry," pertaining to wines that are sweeter than TROKEN (DRY) wines. In most parts of Germany, halbtrocken applies to wines containing between 9 and 18 grams of RESIDUAL SUGAR per liter (0.9 to 1.8 percent), although the official definition also states that the residual sugar cannot be more than 10 grams greater than the total acidity (*see* ACIDS). For example, if the residual sugar is 18 grams, then the total acidity must be at least 8 grams; if total acidity is only 6 grams, then the residual sugar can't exceed 16 grams. In Austria, halbtrocken has a slightly different meaning, referring to wines with between 4 and 9 grams of residual sugar per liter. **Feinherb** is an unofficial term with no specific definition that's sometimes used in place of halbtrocken and may imply that the wine's slightly sweeter than halbtrocken.

half bottle *see* Wine Bottles, page 609

Hallgarten [HAHL-ga*r*-tuhn] An important village situated in the steep slopes above the Rhine River in Germany's RHEINGAU region. The best vineyard sites (EINZELLAGEN) get good exposure to the sun, which results in RIESLING wines that are RICH, full-bodied (*see* BODY), and capable of longer AGING. The primary Einzellagen are **Hendelberg**, **Jungfer**, **Schönhell**, and **Würzgarten**.

Halloween lady beetle *see* ASIAN LADY BEETLE

Hames Valley AVA This California region is located in the far southern end of the larger MONTEREY AVA just north of the PASO ROBLES AVA. The Hames Valley AVA was established in 1994 and encompasses approximately 10,000 acres just west of the town of Bradley and north of Lake Nacimiento. Currently there are only vineyards here, no wineries. Although this region is cooled by the Monterey Bay, it's protected from the strong winds common in the Salinas Valley and is therefore warmer than many parts of the Monterey County area. The grapes planted here are CABERNET SAUVIGNON, MERLOT, SAUVIGNON BLANC, SYRAH, and ZINFANDEL.

Hamptons, Long Island AVA *see* LONG ISLAND AVA

Hanepoot *see* MUSCAT

hang time The time from VERAISON until the grapes are harvested. The longer the hang time the greater the fruit's depth and complexity—perfectly ripe grapes produce superior, long-aging wines. On the other hand, if the hang time is too long, the grapes will become overripe, which will affect both flavor and aroma of the finished wine.

Haraszthy, Agoston [AG-goo-stawn HAH-rahs-th'ee] A colorful man who played an important part in California's viticultural history. Agoston Haraszthy, sometimes called Count and other times Colonel, was a Hungarian who arrived in California in the mid-1800s. Although he's often called the father of California viticulture, he wasn't the first to bring the VITIS VINIFERA species to the state. He did, however, significantly influence the course of the California wine industry. In 1851, he successfully planted a small sampling of *Vitis vinifera* vines and CUTTINGS in SONOMA COUNTY. Ten years later, he made a trip to Europe and returned with over 100,000 cuttings of 300 different varieties. Some of them were planted at the Buena Vista Winery that he founded in 1857 in Sonoma; others were sold to growers around the state. The large number of cuttings significantly elevated the state's grape-growing and wine-producing industries. In addition to the grape varieties that he brought back, Haraszthy wrote a book, *Grape Culture, Wines and Wine Making*, which contributed immensely to the local knowledge pool. His Buena Vista Winery is also thought to have produced California's first SPARKLING WINE, called *Eclipse*. Unfortunately, Haraszthy was beset with a string of misfortunes, including the loss of financial backing for his Buena Vista Winery. He eventually moved to Nicaragua where, in 1869, he supposedly was eaten by alligators near the plantation on which he lived. Agoston Haraszthy's son, Arpad, in an attempt to increase his own value, made claims about his father that are unsubstantiated and which have, in the long term, damaged the contribution that his father made.

hard *see* Glossary of Wine Tasting Terms, page 655

Harlequin ladybird *see* ASIAN LADY BEETLE

harmonious *see* Glossary of Wine Tasting Terms, page 655

harsh *see* Glossary of Wine Tasting Terms, page 655

Hárslevelü [HARSH-leh-veh-LOO] A white grape grown mainly in Hungary, with some acreage just across the border in Czechoslovakia. Following FURMINT, Hárslevelü is the leading component in Hungary's renowned TOKAJI ASZÚ wines, which are made from grapes infected with BOTRYTIS CINEREA. Although the thick-skinned Hárslevelü grapes aren't as susceptible to botryis as Furmint, they're very AROMATIC and add SUPPLENESS and a strong SPICY, PERFUMED character to Tokaji wines. Good Hárslevelü VARIETAL WINES are produced in Hungary around Baja and Villány in the south and Debrö in the north.

Hasenberg *see* JOHANNISBERG

Hasensprung *see* WINKEL

Hastings River An Australian wine region located in the Northern Rivers Zone of NEW SOUTH WALES. It's situated about 240 miles north of Sydney around the town of Port Macquarie on the Pacific Ocean. Rainfall and humidity are generally abundant in this region, but better vintages occur during dry years. There are just over 400 acres planted in the region. CHARDONNAY is the most popular white variety; CHAMBOURCIN (a HYBRID) is the most popular red because of its resistance to mildew. Other varieties include SÉMILLON, SAUVIGNON BLANC, VERDELHO, PINOT NOIR, CABERNET SAUVIGNON, MERLOT, and Shiraz (SYRAH).

Hattenheim [HAHT-uhn-hime] A well-known wine-producing village located southwest of the city of Wiesbaden in Germany's RHEINGAU region. This beautiful village comprises a number of well-regarded EINZELLAGEN including the famous STEINBERG, considered one of the best in all of Germany. Even though the Einzellage Marcobrunn is partially in Hattenheim, a dispute settled in 1971 produced the result that all wines are attached to the village of Erbach and therefore labeled Erbacher Marcobrunn. Other notable Einzellagen are **Engelsmannberg**, **Mannberg**, **Nussbrunnen**, **Schützenhaus**, and **Wisselbrunnen**.

haut [OH] French term meaning "high," "higher," or "upper," generally used in a geographical sense—as in HAUT-MÉDOC, which is north of (or above) the MÉDOC. Haut does not refer to a higher quality of wine.

Haut-Benauge AC *see* ENTRE-DEUX-MERS

Hautes-Côtes de Beaune AC [oht koht duh BOHN] A separate APPELLATION located in the beautiful hills behind the famous CÔTE DE BEAUNE area in France's BURGUNDY region. Both red wines, made from PINOT NOIR, and white wines, made from CHARDONNAY, are produced by the twenty-nine villages associated with the appellation. The altitude of these vineyards is higher than that of the Côte de Beaune vineyards, but the exposure to the sun is not as good, so the grapes have a more difficult time ripening. The wines are therefore never quite as FRUITY or full-bodied (*see* BODY) as those from the Côte de Beaune area. There are several producers, however, who keep YIELDS down and use new oak barrels to produce some superb wines.

Hautes-Côtes de Nuits [oht koht duh NWEE] Located in the rugged hills directly behind the famous CÔTE DE NUITS area in France's BURGUNDY region, this APPELLATION encompasses the vineyard areas of nineteen different villages. As with the HAUTES-CÔTES DE BEAUNE AC, higher altitude is a problem for both the PINOT NOIR and CHARDONNAY grapes that are grown there. The grapes have a difficult time ripening, which means that both the red and white wines are never quite as FRUITY or full-bodied (*see* BODY) as those from the Côte de Nuits area.

Hautes Mourottes *see* CORTON; CORTON-CHARLEMAGNE

Haut-Médoc [oh may-DAHK] The southern portion of the MÉDOC district located in France's BORDEAUX region. The Haut-Médoc extends north from the GRAVES area just north of the city of Bordeaux, to just above the village of Saint-Seurin-de-Cardourne north of Saint-Estèphe. The Haut-Médoc is where the best and most famous Médoc châteaux are located. The **Haut-Médoc AC** covers all the Haut-Médoc including the six individual village appellations of LISTRAC, MARGAUX, MOULIS, PAUILLAC, SAINT ESTÈPHE, and SAINT-JULIEN, although wine produced from the village appellations tend to use their own appellation labeling and not the Haut-Médoc AC. The Haut-Médoc AC includes five CRU CLASSÉ châteaux not associated with specific village appellations: Belgrave, De Camensac, Cantemerle, La Lagune, and La-Tour Carnet. In general, wines labeled with the "Haut-Médoc AC" are much better than those simply labeled "Médoc AC," but they are not as good as wines from one of the individual COMMUNE appellations like PAUILLAC AC or MARGAUX AC. The main grapes used throughout the Haut-Médoc are CABERNET FRANC, CABERNET SAUVIGNON, and MERLOT, with occasional use of PETIT VERDOT and minute amounts of MALBEC.

Haut-Poitou VDQS [oh-pwah-TOO] VDQS area located north of the city of Poitiers, southwest of Tours, in the central part of France's LOIRE region. A majority of the wines are red or ROSÉ, made mainly from GAMAY and some CABERNET FRANC and CABERNET SAUVIGNON. The CRISP, DRY white wines are made from SAUVIGNON BLANC, CHARDONNAY, or CHENIN BLANC. Some SPARKLING WINE is made as well.

Hautvillers [oh-vee-LEH*R*] A village on the Marne River just north of Epernay in France's CHAMPAGNE region. Hautvillers is where the Benedictine Abbey of Dom Pérignon fame is located. It's here that Dom Pérignon, the seventeenth-century cellarmaster of the abbey, is credited with developing the art of blending wines to create champagnes with superior flavor. He's also known for his work in preventing champagne bottles and corks from exploding. He did this by using thicker bottles and tying the corks down with string.

Hawke's Bay New Zealand winegrowing region located on the east side of the North Island near the city of Napier (known for its Art Deco architecture) and surrounding the beautiful Hawke's Bay. It's about 260 miles southeast of Auckland and 200 miles northeast of Wellington. Vines were planted in the region in the 1850s, but the commercial wine industry didn't really take hold until the 1890s. Hawke's Bay soon developed a reputation for producing high-quality wines from European varieties (VITIS VINIFERA), and by the 1910s it was producing almost one third of New Zealand's wines. After shifting to being a producer of FORTIFIED WINES for a number of decades, the pendulum swung back and Hawke's Bay has again become a region recognized for its excellent TABLE WINES. Its excellent, although moderately cool, climate enables a fairly consistent production of high-quality CABERNET SAUVIGNON, MERLOT, and CHARDONNAY, as well as very good SYRAH, RIESLING, PINOT NOIR, and SAUVIGNON BLANC, although the Sauvignon Blanc wines do not have the CRISPNESS of wines from a cooler area like MARLBOROUGH. Some cooler years may cause problems with proper ripening of varieties such as Cabernet Sauvignon and Syrah. With about 7,600 acres, this region is New Zealand's second largest after Marlborough.

Haw River Valley AVA APPELLATION approved in 2009 in north central North Carolina. It covers about 868 square miles between Durham and Greensboro and includes all of Alamance County and parts of Caswell, Chatham, Guilford, Orange, and Rockingham counties. Currently there are six wineries located in the AVA.

hazy *see* Glossary of Wine Tasting Terms, page 655

head pruned vine A system (with numerous variations) whereby a vine is formed into a small upright shrub that does not use a TRELLIS SYSTEM. A mature head pruned vine consists of short branches or **arms** forming a ring at the top of the shrub that's supported by a trunk. The "head" is where the trunk splits off into the arms. During winter PRUNING, SPURS are left at the ends of the arms. In the growing season, these spurs will produce shoots that will bear the season's grapes. The foliage that grows provides an umbrella-like configuration that shades the grape clusters below.

heady *see* Glossary of Wine Tasting Terms, page 655

health consequences of wine In November 1991, CBS television produced a segment on the "French Paradox." The subject was wine consumption and its importance in protecting the French from coronary heart disease, despite their relatively high-fat diet. Since that program, there have been numerous studies focused on this and other health-related issues linked to wine. Research has confirmed that moderate wine consumption lowers coronary heart disease and strokes. Wine's positive contributing factors are said to be ALCOHOL and PHENOLIC COMPOUNDS. One of the phenolic compounds considered particularly effective is RESVERATROL, which is found in the skin of grapes. Resveratrol (and other phenolic compounds) contribute to lowering bad cholesterol (LDL) and raising good cholesterol (HDL). Red wines contain many more of these beneficial compounds than white wines because they've had longer contact time with grape skins during production. But the health benefits don't stop there. Studies have also indicated that wine drinkers have a lower incidence of ulcers because wine diminishes ulcer-causing bacteria. Other research indicates that moderate wine drinkers may have a lower risk of developing dementia, including Alzheimer's disease. A study from Spain showed that wine's antioxidant properties help ward off colds. Another report proved that moderate wine drinkers had a lower incidence of age-related macular degeneration (AMD). The impact of wine on cancer is mixed. Some studies suggest that resveratrol and other phenolic compounds contain certain antioxidant characteristics that facilitate cancer prevention, while others say that alcohol has a causative effective in increasing certain types of cancers. Other downsides to wine consumption include potential respiratory problems for sulfite-sensitive people. Wine, particularly red wine, is also known to cause headaches in people sensitive to histamines and in migraine sufferers who may react to certain phenolic compounds. Almost all studies involving the positive effects of wine consumption suggest "moderate consumption," which is loosely defined as one to three 4-ounce glasses of wine per day.

hearty *see* Glossary of Wine Tasting Terms, page 655

heat stabilization *see* STABILIZATION

heat summation method *see* CLIMATE REGIONS OF CALIFORNIA

heavy *see* Glossary of Wine Tasting Terms, page 655

hectare [HEHK-tahr] Abbreviated as **ha**, a hectare is a unit of surface or land equivalent to 10,000 square meters or 2.471 acres. In countries using the metric system—such as Europe and South America—vineyard area is expressed in hectares. A European vineyard with 50 hectares is equivalent to a U.S. vineyard with just over 123 acres; a 250-acre U.S. vineyard is tantamount to about a 101-hectare European vineyard.

hectoliter [HEHK-tuh-lee-tuhr] A capacity unit equal to 100 liters, or 26.418 U.S. gallons, or 22 Imperial gallons. In European and South American countries, where metric systems are standard, wine production figures are generally expressed in hectoliters. YIELDS in such countries are expressed in terms of hectoliters per HECTARE. In comparing European yields to those of the United States, a hectoliter is approximately equivalent to 0.183 U.S. tons; 40 hectoliters per hectare would be equivalent to 2.96 tons per acre. Two tons per acre would be the equivalent of 27 hectoliters per hectare. **Hecto** is a shortened form of the word; **hl** is the abbreviated form.

H

Heidsieck, Charles *see* CHAMPAGNE

Heidsieck Monopole *see* CHAMPAGNE

Helfensteiner [HELL-fern-shtigh-ner] A German grape that's a CROSS of Frühburgunder (PINOT NOIR) and Trollinger (SCHIAVA). Helfensteiner is one of the parents of DORNFELDER, another cross that's been much more successful.

Hendelberg *see* HALLGARTEN

Henderson *see* AUCKLAND

Henriot *see* CHAMPAGNE

Henty An Australian wine region located in the Western Victoria Zone of VICTORIA. It's situated a little over 185 miles west of Melbourne around the towns of Hamilton and Portland in the southwest portion of the state (Henty is sometimes referred to as Far South West Victoria). The very cool climate is just right for producing excellent RIESLING and SPARKLING WINES—made from CHARDONNAY, PINOT NOIR, and Pinot Meunier (MEUNIER). Warmer sections of this region produce very good STILL WINES as well, including CABERNET SAUVIGNON during better VINTAGES.

L'Hérault [lay-ROH] A large DÉPARTEMENT on the Mediterranean in southern France. It's part of the LANGUEDOC-ROUSSILLON region, which is often referred to as the Midi. L'Hérault has more vineyards planted than any other French département, but most of the wines produced are very ordinary and make up part of what some call the "European wine lake"—the huge glut of cheap, lackluster wine coming from the warmer regions of France, Spain, and Italy. L'Hérault is undergoing winemaking improvements including implementing stainless steel tanks, using CARBONIC MACERATION, and planting more popular varieties like CABERNET SAUVIGNON, CHARDONNAY, MARSANNE, MERLOT, MOURVÈDRE, SAUVIGNON BLANC, SÉMILLON, and SYRAH. Other grapes grown in the area include BOURBOULENC, CARIGNAN, GRENACH, MACABEO, and MUSCAT. L'Herault has developed popular, quality-winemaking areas in the last 15 years including FAUGERES AC, SAINT CHINIAN AC, and specific villages like LA CLAPE in the CÔTES DU LANGUEDOC. One of the standouts in this region is Mas de Daumas Gassac, a producer of very high-quality red wines based on CABERNET SAUVIGNON and white wines based on CHARDONNAY and VIOGNIER.

herb [HAYRB] German equivalent of BRUT.

herbaceous; herbal *see* Glossary of Wine Tasting Terms, page 655

Hermann AVA A VITICULTURAL AREA located in central Missouri west and southwest of the charming, Germanic town of Hermann, which lies between St. Louis and Jefferson City. This AVA encompasses 51,200 acres south of the Missouri River and west of the Gasconade River in Franklin and Gasconade Counties. Established in 1987, it was the second of Missouri's approved AVAs. German immigrants settled this Missouri River Valley area starting in the 1830s, and set about almost immediately developing hillside vineyards, many of which are in use today. The vineyards are heavily planted with HYBRIDS like CAYUGA, CHAMBOURCIN, CHARDONEL, SEYVAL BLANC, VIDAL BLANC, Vignoles (RAVAT), and the popular Norton (CYNTHIANA), which makes up 20 to 25 percent of the vineyards. VITIS VINIFERA vines are extremely difficult to grow in the area. Stone Hill Winery, established in 1847 and Missouri's largest winery, is located in the Hermann AVA.

Hermannsberg *see* NIEDERHAUSEN

Hermannshöhle *see* NIEDERHAUSEN

Hermitage *see* CINSAUT

Hermitage AC; Hermitage Vin de Paille AC [ehr-mee-TAHZH] 1. Some of France's greatest wines come from the **Hermitage**

AC, which is located in the northern portion of the RHÔNE region south of Lyon. Hermitage, sometimes spelled *Ermitage*, produces both red and white wines, both of excellent repute. The vineyards are thought to have been cultivated as far back as the Roman occupation of this area. The name Hermitage is attributed to a knight, Gaspard de Sterimberg, who, after fighting in the religious wars in the early 1200s, retired to this hill as a *hermit* to tend his vines and meditate. Accolades for Hermitage wines go back centuries, at least to the 1600s, when Louis XIV reigned. The vineyards are planted on the very steep, sun-drenched hillside above the town of Tain-l'Hermitage across the Rhône River from Tournon. The hill itself has three sections, each with a different soil type, and the producers who use grapes from all three of these sections seem to produce the best wines. SYRAH is the red grape of Hermitage. The white varieties MARSANNE and ROUS-SANNE are used both in the white wines and in the blend for the robust red wines. Hermitage red wines, which are deep-colored, full-fla-vored, full-bodied (*see* BODY), and intense, can be brash and TANNIC when young. Those from the best VINTAGES can take up to 15 years to SOFTEN and can AGE for 30 or 40 years or more. The powerful white wines from Hermitage are capable of lengthy aging as well, some as long as the red wines. The **Hermitage Vin de Paille AC** is an APPEL-LATION for the rarely produced, sweet, white VIN DE PAILLE wines. 2. Hermitage is a name used by South Africans for the grape variety CIN-SAUT. 3. In Australia, Hermitage was another name for the grape vari-ety Syrah, which is most often called Shiraz.

Hermitage Blanc *see* MARSANNE

Heroldrebe [HEHR-url-dree-behr] A German grape that's a CROSS of PORTUGIESER and Limberger (BLAUFRÄNKISCH). Heroldrebe is one of the parents of DORNFELDER, another cross that's been much more successful.

Herrenberg *see* ERDEN; KASEL; MAXIMIN GRÜNHAUS; OPPENHEIM

Herrengarten *see* DIENHEIM

Herrgottsacker *see* DEIDESHEIM

Les Hervelets *see* FIXIN

Hessische Bergstrasse [HEH-see-shuh BEHRK-strah-suh] The second smallest of the thirteen German ANBAUGEBIETE (quality-wine regions), with just over 950 acres of vineyards planted. The region starts just north of the city of Darmstadt and extends south to the city of Heidelberg. RIESLING is the most plentiful variety, covering 50 percent of the acreage. There are two BEREICHE, **Starkenburg** and **Umstadt**. The wines from Hessische Bergstrasse are similar in quality and style to those from the better-known RHEINGAU region, with more BODY and flavor than most German wines. Most wines produced here don't make it outside the region.

heurige; pl. heurigen [HOY-rih-guh] 1. Austrian for "new wine," *heurige* refers to wine from the most recent VINTAGE, which is released on November 11. Such wine is officially *heurige* until the following November, when it becomes *alt* wine. Many *heurigen* are produced in the vineyards surrounding Vienna and enjoyed while young by the Viennese. 2. An Austrian wine tavern and cafe that sells these young wines. There are over 1,000 of these *Heurigen* scattered throughout Vienna alone.

Hierro DO *see* CANARY ISLANDS

high toned *see* Glossary of Wine Tasting Terms, page 655

High Valley AVA As its name might indicate, this APPELLATION sits at elevations of 1,600 feet to 3,000 feet with most vineyards located at the 1,800 to 2,200 foot level. The High Valley AVA is located in the eastern section of Lake County, California. Of its 14,000 acres, about 1,000 are planted to red varieties such as CABERNET SAUVIGNON, MERLOT, PETITE SIRAH, PINOT NOIR, SYRAH, TEMPRANILLO, and ZINFANDEL and white varieties such as SAUVIGNON BLANC and PINOT GRIGIO. This AVA was created in August 2005 and is a sub-appellation to the larger LAKE COUNTY AVA and NORTH COAST AVA. Wineries in the area include Brassfield Estate Winery, High Valley Vineyard, Monte Lago, and Shannon Ridge.

Hilltops Australian wine region located in the Southern New South Wales Zone. It's located in NEW SOUTH WALES around the town of Young, approximately 235 miles west of Sydney, between the CANBERRA DISTRICT and COWRA regions. Hilltops has snow in the winter and frost danger in the spring and, although there is rain, it can be dry enough to require irrigation toward the end of the growing season. About 1,000 acres are planted in the Hilltops region. The main varieties are CHARDONNAY, SAUVIGNON BLANC, SHIRAZ, CABERNET SAUVIGNON, SÉMILLON, GEWÜRZTRAMINER, and MERLOT. Like many of the other New South Wales wine regions, much of the grapes are shipped to wineries outside of the area. McWilliams is the biggest presence in the area with its Barwang Vineyard comprising about 250 acres. Area wineries include Chalkers Crossing, Demondrille Vineyards, Grove Estate Vineyard,

Hansen's Hilltops Barwang Ridge Vineyard, and Lindsay's Woodonga Hill Winery.

Himmelreich *see* GRAACH; ZELTINGEN

Hipping *see* NIERSTEIN

hippocras [HIP-uh-kras] A sweet, aromatized wine popular in the Middle Ages. It was made by adding cinnamon, ginger, and other spices and either sugar or honey.

Hitzlay *see* KASEL

Hochgewächs [HOHK-guh-vehks] A German term referring to a QbA (*see* QUALITÄTSWEIN BESTIMMTER ANBAUGEBIET) wine of superior quality made entirely from RIESLING grapes. To qualify, the grapes must be riper and the wines must pass a more rigorous taste test than those for ordinary QbA wines.

Hochheim [HOHKH-hime] Wine-producing town separated from the rest of Germany's RHEINGAU region by the city of Wiesbaden. Hockheim's vineyards actually are situated along the Main River rather than the Rhine River, as are most of the Rheingau's vineyards. Despite the geographic separation, wines from Hochheim have a distinct Rheingau character. The wines are full-bodied (*see* BODY), yet ELEGANT, with a hint of EARTHINESS. The better EINZELLAGEN include **Domdechaney**, **Hölle**, **Kirchenstück**, **Königin Victoriaberg**, and **Stein**. Schloss Schönborn is one of the better Hochheim producers. *See also* HOCK.

H

hock [HOHKH] A term used by the British to refer to wine from the Rhine regions of Germany. The term's a derivation of HOCKHEIM, a town in the RHEINGAU region. Hocks and Moselles still appear as headings on some English wine merchant lists.

hogshead A cask or barrel of varying capacity used to ship wines (and spirits). A hogshead can vary in size from approximately 225 liters to about 275 liters (about 60 to 73 U.S. gallons).

Hoheburg *see* RUPPERTSBERG

Hohenmorgan *see* DEIDESHEIM

Hohnenrain *see* ERBACH

Hölle *see* HOCKHEIM; JOHANNISBERG; NIERSTEIN; WILTINGEN

hollow *see* Glossary of Wine Tasting Terms, page 655

honeyed *see* Glossary of Wine Tasting Terms, page 655

Honigberg *see* ERBACH

horizontal tasting *see* WINE TASTING

Horse Heaven Hills AVA This APPELLATION derives its name from the wild horses that once wandered this area along the Columbia River in south central Washington. It was established in August 2005 as a sub-appellation within the huge COLUMBIA VALLEY AVA and encompasses 570,000 acres in parts of Benton, Klickitat and Yakima counties. There are about 6,000 acres of vineyards planted with a myriad of grape varieties. The most popular are CABERNET SAUVIGNON, CHARDONNAY, MERLOT, RIESLING, SAUVIGNON BLANC, SÉMILLON and SYRAH. The AVA is home to the huge Columbia Crest Winery (owned by Chateau Ste. Michelle) and ten other wineries. Well-known vintners such as Andrew Will, Betz Family, Hogue Cellars, and Woodward Canyon source grapes from Horse Heaven Hills AVA.

Hospices de Beaune [aws-PEES duh BOHN] A famous charitable organization consisting of the Hôtel-Dieu (a charitable hospital) and the Hospices de la Charité. It's located in the town of Beaune in France's BURGUNDY region and was founded in 1443 by Nicolas Rolin, chancellor to the Duke of Burgundy, and his wife Guigone de Salins. The colorfully tiled Hospices building is one of the landmarks in the town of Beaune, and its medieval architecture is often a focus for photographers. The Hospices de Beaune is subsidized by land endowments including some superior vineyard land in the CÔTE DE BEAUNE and CÔTE DE NUITS districts. The total holdings, which include some GRANDS CRUS and PREMIERS CRUS, consist of about 150 acres of vineyards. This land usually produces the equivalent of over 20,000 cases of wine that are sold at a famous auction held on the third Sunday in November. Because these wines are the first to be sold from the new VINTAGE, the auction prices are historically a general indicator of projected prices for this vintage in the rest of the region. After taking delivery of the barrels of wine, the auction buyers are responsible for AGING and bottling it. The wines are named after the major benefactors to the Hospices, appended to that of the APPELLATION—for example, *Corton-Docteur Peste, Beaune-Nicolas Rolin,* and *Mazis-Chambertin-Madeleine Collignon.*

Hospices de Nuits [aws-PEES du NWEE] A charitable foundation established in 1692 in NUIT-SAINT-GEORGES in BURGUNDY'S CÔTE DE NUITS district. This is a much smaller version of the more prominent and neighboring HOSPICES DE BEAUNE. Hospices de Nuits has been endowed with about 22 acres and holds an auction each spring, 2 weeks prior to Easter. Although the Hospices de Nuits auction doesn't elicit the same attention as that of the Hospices de Beaune, it does sell off some very good wines.

hot *see* Glossary of Wine Tasting Terms, page 655

hotte [AWT] A French term for a long basket that's carried on one's back and used to transport grapes during the harvest. The general practice when harvesting grapes manually is to put the freshly cut grapes into hand-held baskets. The grapes are then dumped into the larger hotte, which is then carried to and unloaded into a truck or trailer that will transport the grapes to the winery. A hotte carrier generally works with a group of pickers, taking their grapes from the vineyard to the trailer.

house As used in France's CHAMPAGNE region, the word "house" refers to a company (such as Taittinger or Veuve Clicquot) that produces and sells its Champagne under its brand name.

house wine A wine featured by a restaurant and often served in a CARAFE or by the glass. Sometimes a winery does a special bottling and labels the wines for a restaurant. House wines are usually inexpensive wines that offer the diner an economical option to the more pricey, better-known selections on the wine list. Ask the server what the house wine is—he or she should be able to tell you the variety (Chardonnay, Merlot, etc.), brand name, and VINTAGE (if any).

Howell Mountain AVA This California AVA was approved in 1984 and was the NAPA VALLEY AVA's first subzone. It's located northeast of the town of St. Helena in the Napa Valley, where the hillside vineyards range between 1,600 and 2,200 feet in elevation. The lack of fog at this level allows the vines more hours of sunshine during the day and more warmth at night. The elevation also allows Howell Mountain to remain as much as ten degrees cooler during the day—these reasonably warm temperatures put Howell Mountain AVA into a Region II category (*see* CLIMATE REGIONS OF CALIFORNIA). The area's plentiful sunshine is perfect for CABERNET SAUVIGNON and ZINFANDEL grapes; CHARDONNAY, CABERNET FRANC, and MERLOT are also grown.

Huapai *see* AUCKLAND

Hudson River Region AVA This historic NEW YORK wine area claims both America's oldest vineyard, Benmarl, established in the early 1800s, and its oldest winery, Brotherhood Winery, founded in 1839. Its roots go back to the 1670s when vineyards were first planted. Approved in 1982, this AVA enjoys the moderating influence of the Hudson River much in the same way areas around the Great Lakes take advantage of the LAKE EFFECT. Unfortunately, population growth is pushing wineries away from the river itself where this effect is most beneficial. This region consists of 224,000 acres starting just north of New York City in the northern part of the city of White Plains and runs north until it hits the Columbia County-Rensselaer County line, south of Albany. A majority of the thirty-plus wineries are in the southern part (it's too cold in most northern areas), ending just north of Poughkeepsie and New Paltz. HYBRIDS like SEYVAL BLANC, VIDAL BLANC, and BACO NOIR are the most popular here, although companies like Millbrook Vineyards, Cascade Mountain Winery, and Rivendell Winery are having some success with CABERNET FRANC, CABERNET SAUVIGNON, MERLOT, PINOT NOIR, CHARDONNAY, FIULANO, and RIESLING.

Hungary Hungary produces a wide variety of wines from an equally wide assortment of grapes—some familiar, others a specialty of this eastern European country. Some of the more well-known varieties are CABERNET SAUVIGNON, GEWÜRZTRAMINER, Médoc Noir (MERLOT), Szürkebarát (PINOT GRIS), PINOT NOIR, and SYLVANER. However, the most popular varieties in Hungary are the red KADARKA and the white Olasz Riesling (WELSCHRIESLING). Other white grapes include Ezerjo, FURMINT, HÁRSLEVELÜ, KÉKNYELÜ, and LEÁNYKA. The popular red Kékfrankos is the same as the BLAUFRÄNKISCH grown in Austria, although not related to GAMAY, as some believe. Hungary has two famous wines—TOKAJI, a highly regarded DESSERT WINE, and EGRI BIKAVÉR, the red "bull's blood" wine. Hungary's growing regions include the Great Plain in the south central part of the country, which produces over half the total production (most of it very ordinary); the Lake Balaton area in the western part of the country, which includes the higher-quality-wine districts of Mount Badacsony (see BADACSONYI), Balaton, Balatonfüred-Csopak, Mór, and Somoló; Eger and Tokaji, northeast of Budapest, where Egri Bikavér and Tokaji are made; and Sopron in the northwestern corner. The labels of Hungarian wines include the name of the producing areas to which an *i* is added, making it a possessive form, as in Soproni Kékfrankos—a wine made in the Sopron area from the Kékfrankos variety—or Badacsonyi Szürkebarát—from the Mount Badacsony area and made with Szürkebarát grapes.

Hunter Valley One of Australia's best-known wine-producing regions located in the state of NEW SOUTH WALES, about 100 miles north of Sydney. It's also one of the oldest, with its first vineyards planted in the early 1800s. Although the outside world knows only of Hunter Valley, winemakers in the area distinguish between the **Upper Hunter Valley** and the **Lower Hunter Valley**. The Lower Hunter Valley, which starts around Cessnock in the south and goes toward Branxton in the north, is the older of the two regions and the one most associated with the name. The Upper Hunter Valley, which lies to the northwest of the lower valley near the towns of Denman, Muswellbrook, and Scone, was firmly established in the 1960s when the prestigious wine company Penfolds invested in this area. The Penfolds venture was not successful primarily because of their focus on red wine grapes, which don't grow well here. Rosemount, which purchased the Penfolds property, shifted to white-grape varieties and has been reasonably successful. The grape-growing environment of the Hunter Valley is not the easiest—its soil isn't the best, the weather can be extremely hot, there are often drought conditions, and when it does rain it is often at the most inappropriate time, such as during harvest. Yet the Hunter Valley is known for its unique long-lived SÉMILLON wines, its lush CHARDONNAYS, and its long-aging Shiraz (SYRAH). Chardonnay has passed Sémillon as the most widely planted white variety in Hunter Valley (primarily because of the large acreage devoted to it in the Upper Hunter Valley), and bringing up the rear is VERDELHO. The most popular red grape is Shiraz (SYRAH), formerly called *Hermitage* here, followed by CABERNET SAUVIGNON and PINOT NOIR.

Huxelrebe [HOOK-sehl-reh-buh] A German white-wine grape derived from a CROSS of Weisser Gutedel (CHASSELAS) and Courtillier Musqué. Huxelrebe, grown primarily in the German regions of RHEIN-HESSEN and PFALZ, is named after viticulturist Fritz Huxel, who bred this HYBRID extensively in the late 1920s. Huxelrebe is also grown in England. If carefully pruned, these vines can produce grapes with good ACIDITY and high sugar content, which reward the winemaker with very good AUSLESE wines, even in poor VINTAGES. Conversely, uncontained growth and high YIELDS result in lackluster wines. Huxelrebe is often used as a BLENDING WINE.

hybrid; v. hybridize [HI-brihd; HI-brih-dyz] In a pure sense, the word **hybrid** in the wine world refers to a vine or grape created by breeding two varieties from different species or genuses (such as VITIS VINIFERA and VITIS RIPARIA or VITIS LABRUSCA). It differs from the term, CROSS, which is a vine or grape created by breeding two varieties of the same genus (*Vitis vinifera*, for example). BACO NOIR is a red French-American hybrid created by breeding FOLLE BLANCHE (*Vitis vinifera*) with a native American vine (*Vitis riparia*). MÜLLER-THURGAU is an example of a cross between RIESLING and SYLVANER, both of which are *Vitis vinifera*. Hybrids are created in an effort to produce a plant with the best traits of its parents, such as high productivity, disease resistance, and/or better adaptability to environmental conditions. One who creates hybrids is called a *hybridist* or *hybridizer*. *See also* CLONE.

hydrogen sulfide (H₂S) [HY-druh-jihn SUHL-fyd] Hydrogen sulfide is the result of yeast combining with various forms of SULFUR. It produces an undesirable, rotten-egg smell in wine. Eventually, H_2S in wine transforms into MERCAPTANS (a skunky odor) and disulfides (a sewage smell), both of which ruin a wine.

hydrometer (high-DRAH-mih-ter) Literally meaning "water measurer," a hydrometer is an instrument comprised of a vertical scale inside a sealed glass tube weighted at one end. It's used to measure the ratio (called SPECIFIC GRAVITY) of the density of a liquid (such as grape MUST or wine) to that of pure water. A hydrometer floats upright in liquid; the reading is taken where the liquid's surface hits the scale—and the hydrometer floats higher in denser liquid. In winemaking, a hydrometer has many uses including measuring a must's sugar content and calculating its potential ALCOHOL, determining how FERMENTATION is progressing and indicating when it's finished, gauging effervescence in SPARKLING WINES, and measuring a finished wine's alcohol level.

I **ice bucket** *see* Temperatures for Serving Wine, page 641; Optimum Serving Temperatures by Wine Type, page 642

ice wine *see* EISWEIN

Idaho As with OREGON and WASHINGTON, this northwestern state had vineyards planted in the nineteenth century, and there are indications that Idaho vines preceeded those in the other two states. PROHIBITION killed off the wine industry that existed in 1919 (Idaho had state prohibition a year before the federal government). Like many states, it wasn't until the 1970s that the industry began to revive. Today, Idaho has sixteen wineries and over 1,000 acres of vineyards. While a couple of these are in the Idaho "panhandle," most are along the Snake River in southwestern Idaho, near Boise. Although the climate here is similar to that of Washington's COLUMBIA VALLEY, the vineyards are at a slightly higher altitude, the nights are cooler, and the growing season is shorter. As in other Rocky Mountain states, the long, hot summer days allow the grapes to mature and ripen to proper sugar levels, while the cool nights help set the grape's ACID levels. The northern latitude means longer summer days and more hours of sunlight. The Snake River creates a moderating influence, which mitigates summer heat and winter cold. The most popular varieties here are CHARDONNAY, RIESLING, and CABERNET SAUVIGNON. Other grapes grown here include CABERNET FRANC, CHENIN BLANC, FUMÉ BLANC, GEWÜRZTRAMINER, LEMBERGER, MERLOT, PINOT GRIS, PINOT NOIR, SAUVIGNON BLANC, SEMILLON, and SYRAH. Ste. Chapelle Winery, owned by Canandaigua Wine Company, is Idaho's principal winery, annually producing about 135,000 cases of wine.

Île des Vergelesses *see* PERNAND-VERGELESSES

imbottigliato [ihm-boh-tee-LYAH-toh] An Italian term meaning "bottled." *Imbottigliato da* means "bottled by"; *imbottigliato all'origine* means "bottled at the source (or origin)" and is synonymous with ESTATE BOTTLED; *imbottigliato dal viticoltore* means that the wine was bottled by the grower.

imperial *see* Wine Bottles, page 609

INAO *see* INSTITUT NATIONALE DES APPELLATIONS D'ORIGINE

Indiana Grapes were first planted in this Midwest state in the late 1700s and it became one of the 10 largest grape-producing states in the early to mid-1800s. Vineyard DISEASES destroyed most of the vines in the mid- to late 1800s, and it wasn't until the Small Winery Act passed in the early 1970s that a rebirth took place. Today Indianapolis hosts the annual Indy International Wine Competition, one of the largest U.S. wine competitions outside of California. Currently there are just over twenty-five wineries in the state. A majority of the wines here are made from HYBRID grapes like AURORA, CATAWBA, SEYVAL BLANC, VIDAL BLANC, and VIGNOLES; there are a large number of FRUIT WINES produced. VITIS VINIFERA grapes like CABERNET SAUVIGNON and CHARDONNAY are being planted, particularly near Bloomington and Milan. Some wineries still purchase crushed grapes from areas like California and make the wine at their facility. Areas around the Ohio River are part of the OHIO RIVER VALLEY AVA, which also includes parts of KENTUCKY, OHIO, and WEST VIRGINIA.

Indicação de Proveniencia Regulamentada (IPR) A second-level ranking for Portuguese wines that are striving to achieve Portugal's highest ranking, DENOMINAÇÃO DE ORIGEM CONTROLADA.

Indicazione Geografica Tipica (IGT) Second level of Italian wine classification that ranks between the VINO DA TAVOLA (VDT) and DENOMINAZIONE DI ORIGINE CONTROLLATA (DOC) categories. IGT is similar to France's VIN DE PAYS and Germany's LANDWEIN. IGT wines are officially approved as being representative of their geographic region. Labels may contain the region, the grape variety, and the vintage.

Inferno *see* VALTELLINA DOC

inky *see* Glossary of Wine Tasting Terms, page 655

inoculate A winemaking technique of adding an active yeast culture or malolactic bacteria to juice, MUST, or wine. Winemakers often inoculate their must with known strains of reliable yeasts to activate the primary fermentation (*see* FERMENTATION) and achieve their desired results. Although MALOLACTIC FERMENTATION will sometimes occur naturally, many winemakers prefer to manage this phase by inoculating with a properly prepared malolactic bacteria starter.

insipid *see* Glossary of Wine Tasting Terms, page 655

Institut Nationale des Appellations d'Origine (INAO) [an-stee-tyoo nah-syaw-NAHL dayz ah-pehl-lah-SYOHN daw-ree-ZHEHN] French organization, most often referred to as the INAO, that establishes the broad guidelines for the APPELLATION D'ORIGINE CONTRÔLÉE.

invecchiato [in-veh-chee-YAH-toh] Italian for "aged," *invecchiato* is occasionally used to identify the length of time a DOC wine is aged.

IPR *see* INDICAÇÃO DE PROVENIENCIA REGULAMENTADA

Irancy AC [ee-*rah*n-SEE] A tiny French APPELLATION located around the village of Irancy in northern BURGUNDY just southwest of CHABLIS. Irancy makes red and ROSÉ wines using mainly PINOT NOIR grapes BLENDED with a small amount of two local varieties, César and Tressot. The wines are generally pleasant, LIGHT, and DELICATE.

Irouléguy AC [ee-*r*oo-leh-GEE] An obscure APPELLATION encompassing Irouléguy and eight other villages nestled in the Pyrenees Mountains adjacent to the Spanish border in SOUTHWEST FRANCE. It produces mainly red and ROSÉ wines using the Tannat, CABERNET FRANC, and CABERNET SAUVIGNON varieties. Tiny amounts of white wine are made from Courbu, Gros Manseng, and Petit Manseng.

Isabella [ihz-uh-BELL-uh] HYBRID red-wine grape that is the result of a CROSS between VITIS LABRUSCA and VITIS VINIFERA. Isabella has been essentially replaced by CONCORD in the eastern United States, although small amounts are still grown in New York's FINGER LAKES region, where it's VINIFIED into ROSÉ wine. It's cultivated in areas of the former Soviet Union including Republic of Azerbaijan, Dagestan, Republic of Georgia, Krasnodar, and Republic of Moldavia, as well as in Brazil, Colombia, Madeira, Switzerland, and Uruguay. Isabella has an unattractive FOXY character and is losing its following in most areas. It's also known as *Americano* and *Bellina*.

Ischia DOC [EESS-kyah] Located on the island of Ischia in the Bay of Naples, this DOC is part of Italy's CAMPANIA region. The island produces a BIANCO made primarily from Forastera, along with some Biancolella and other white grapes. The *bianco superiore* allows more Biancolella and requires a higher ALCOHOL level. The ROSSO uses mainly Guarnaccia and Piedirosso along with BARBERA and other red VARIETIES. Ischia wines are generally pretty mediocre but popular with the tourists visiting the island. Varietal wines, which require a minimum of 85 percent of the named variety, include Forastera, Biancolella, and Piedirosso (known locally as *Per e Palummo*).

isinglass [I-zuhn-glas; Izing-glas] Transparent and pure, this form of gelatin comes from the air bladder of certain fish, especially the sturgeon. It's used as a FINING agent to help CLARIFY wine, although today's modern gelatin (made from beef and veal bones, cartilage, tendons, etc.) has replaced isinglass in most instances.

Isle St. George AVA Established on September 20, 1982, this Ohio viticultural area was the first in the state. The island is the northernmost of the Bass Islands very near the Canadian border. Its 640 acres (approximately 350 of which are planted) take up the entire island, which is located in the western section of the LAKE ERIE AVA. Although CATAWBA has been grown here for over 100 years, today the most widely planted are VITIS VINIFERA vines like CABERNET FRANC, CABERNET SAUVIGNON, CHARDONNAY, GEWÜRZTRAMINER, Pinot Grigio (PINOT GRIS), PINOT NOIR, and RIESLING. Firelands Winery and Meier's Wine Cellars (the original petitioner for the island's AVA status) receive most of the grape production.

ISO glass *see* Glassware, page 647

Isonzo DOC [ee-ZOHN-tsoh] DOC, which is also called *Isonzo del Friuli*, that is located in the FRIULI-VENEZIA GIULIA region in northeastern Italy. It's just south of the better-known COLLIO DOC. Twenty different wines are authorized, seventeen VARIETALS plus a BIANCO, a ROSSO, and a Pinot SPUMANTE. The varietal wines are Cabernet (from CABERNET SAUVIGNON and CABERNET FRANC), Cabernet Franc, Cabernet Sauvignon, CHARDONNAY, Franconia, MALVASIA, MERLOT, Pinot Bianco (PINOT BLANC), Pinot Grigio (PINOT GRIS), Pinot Nero (PINOT NOIR), Refosco dal Peduncolo Rosso (REFOSCO), Riesling Italico (WELSCHRIESLING), Riesling Renano (RIESLING), Sauvignon (SAUVIGNON BLANC), FRIULANO, Traminer Aromatico (GEWÜRZTRAMINER), and Verduzzo Friulano. The Bianco is made from Friulano, Malvasia, Pinot Bianco, and Chardonnay; the Rosso is made mainly from Merlot, Cabernet Franc, and Cabernet Sauvignon. The Pinot Spumante is made from Pinot Bianco, Pinot Nero, and Chardonnay. The red wines made from Merlot and Cabernet grapes are highly regarded, and the white wines made from Chardonnay and Sauvignon Blanc grapes are starting to gain a good reputation.

Israel Despite the fact that winemaking is referred to in the Old Testament, modern winemaking wasn't introduced in Israel until the 1880s. That's when Baron Edmond de Rothschild backed the planting of vineyards and the building of two wineries—one in Richon-le-Zion, southeast of Tel Aviv, and the other in Zikhron-Jacob on Mount Carmel, south of Haifa. These vineyards and wineries were donated to Israel in 1906, and the Société Cooperative Vigeronne de Grandes Caves was established as a cooperative to produce the wines. The cooperative still produces a majority of Israeli wines under the brand name Carmel. The main winegrowing areas here are the region around the Sea of Galilee; the Mount Carmel area; the coastal area plains around Tel Aviv; the area around Jerusalem; and the area between Beersheba and Ascalon. The principal grape varieties here are CARIGNAN and GRENACHE, along with CLAIRETTE, MUSCAT, and SÉMILLON. More recently planted grapes include CABERNET SAUVIGNON, MERLOT, PINOT NOIR, CHARDONNAY, CHENIN BLANC, RIESLING, and SAUVIGNON BLANC. Israeli wines have shifted from being primarily sweet and FORTIFIED to mostly DRY TABLE WINES, many of which are VARIETAL.

Italian Riesling *see* WELSCHRIESLING

Italy Italy contends with France as the world's largest wine producer. Each produces between 1.3 and 1.6 billion gallons of wine annually, depending on the year. Together these two countries produce about 40 percent of the world's total. Italy's also the second greatest wine consumer, second only to France—each Italian consumes about eight times the wine of an average American. Italy's a land of vast geographic diversity ranging from its northern cool-temperature vineyards in the foothills of the Alps, to the hot southland. Italy's been making wine for at least 3,500 years in a variety of styles (DRY to sweet, STILL to fully SPARKLING) and in a variety of ways, such as the PASSITO method, from many grape varieties not widely grown outside of Italy. The Italian varieties used for red and rosé wines include AGLIANICO, BARBERA, BONARDA, CANAIOLO, DOLCETTO, FREISA, GRIGNOLINO, LAGREIN, LAMBRUSCO, MONTEPULCIANO, NEBBIOLO, RABOSO, REFOSCO, SANGIOVESE, SCHIAVA, and Teroldego. Those used for white wines are ALBANA, BOMBINO BIANCO, CORTESE, GARGANEGA, GRECO, MALVASIA, Moscato (MUSCAT), PICOLIT, PIGATO, PROSECCO, FRIULANO, TREBBIANO, VERDICCHIO, VERDUZZO, VERNACCIA DI ORISTANO, and VERNACCIA DI SAN GIMIGNANO. Other European (primarily French and German) varieties grown here are CABERNET FRANC, CABERNET SAUVIGNON, MERLOT, Pinot Nero (PINOT NOIR), SYRAH, CHARDONNAY, GEWÜRZTRAMINER, MÜLLER-THURGAU, Pinot Bianco (PINOT BLANC), Pinot Grigio (PINOT GRIS), Riesling Italico (WELSCHRIESLING), Riesling Renano (RIESLING), SAUVIGNON BLANC, and SYLVANER. The Italians have implemented a system similiar to France's for improving the quality of their wines. At the lowest level of this quality ranking are the VINO DA TAVOLA wines, followed by INDICAZIONE GEOGRAFICA TIPICA wines and then the DENOMINAZIONE DI ORIGINE CONTROLLATA (DOC), which is similiar to the French APPELLATION D'ORIGINE CONTRÔLÉE. Parameters for the Italian DOC, however, weren't considered strict enough so another higher level, DENOMINAZIONE DI ORIGINE CONTROLLATA E GARANTITA (DOCG), was added. DOCG status, which requires stricter rules and controls, has been granted to fewer than twenty-five areas since it was implemented in the early 1980s. Italy has twenty large growing regions, the boundaries of which define the area geographically, not by any common wine style, grape variety, or climate. Of these twenty regions, the five largest volume producers (APULIA, SICILY, VENETEO, EMILIA-ROMAGNA, and ABRUZZI) make over 61 percent of the total wine production. The order of these regions (as to whose is first, second, etc.) changes depending on the year. The four top regions producing quality wines (those ranked as DOC or DOCG) are VENETO, PIEDMONT, TUSCANY, and EMILIA-ROMAGNA. These four areas produce over 57 percent of the DOC/DOCG wines. Some of the better known of these wines include CHIANTI from the Tuscany region; ASTI from the Piedmont region; LAMBRUSCO wines from DOC areas like *Lambrusco di Sorbara, Lambrusco Grasparossa di Castelvetro,* and *Lambrusco Salamino di Santa Croce* in the EMILA-ROMAGNA region; and BARDOLINO, VALPOLICELLA, and SOAVE from the Veneto region. High-quality wines also come from DOCGs like BARBARESCO, BAROLO, and GATTINARA in Piedmont; BRUNELLO DI MONTALCINO and VINO NOBILE DI MONTEPULCIANO in Tuscany; and TORGIANO ROSSO RESERVA in UMBRIA.

I

J Jacquère [jah-KEHR] The primary white-wine grape of eastern France's SAVOIE region. Jacquère is the main variety used in the Vin de Savoie APPELLATION wines, which also include ALTESSE grapes. These wines are LIGHT, DRY, and somewhat ACIDIC, with hints of CITRUS and SMOKE. Jacquère is also known as *Buisserate* and *Cugnette*.

Jahant AVA This is currently the smallest of the sub-APPELLATIONS created within larger LODI AVA, which is between Sacramento and Stockton in northern California. The Jahant AVA was established in August 2006 and covers 28,000 acres in the center of Lodi. Of this, some 9,000 acres are planted with a myriad of grape varieties, both red and white, although CARIGNAN and ZINFANDEL have been traditionally grown here and TEMPRANILLO is getting some recognition. The soil here is unique because of its pinkish Rocklin-Jahant loam soils.

jahrgang [YAHR-gahng] The German term for "vintage year."

jammy; jamlike *see* Glossary of Wine Tasting Terms, page 655

Jasnières AC [zhah-NYEH*R*] A tiny APPELLATION 25 miles north of Tours on the smaller Loire River in the central part of France's LOIRE Valley. Jasnières produces delicious DRY white wines from CHENIN BLANC, but because of this grape's high ACID levels, the wines seem SHARP and very, very DRY. Occasionally, the area produces small amounts of semisweet to sweet wines, which better balance the acidity of the Chenin Blanc grape. Occasionally, BOTRYTIS CINEREA infects the grapes and enhance the wines with delightful honey and apple nuances—these wines are produced in both dry and sweet versions.

Jerez; Jerez y Manzanilla [heh-*R*ETH; heh-*R*ETH ee mahn-zuh-NEEL-yuh] Shortened versions of the proper name JEREZ-XÉRÈS-SHERRY Y MANZANILLA DE SANLÚCAR DE BARRAMEDA DO. Jerez may also refer to JEREZ DE LA FRONTERA.

Jerez de la Frontera [heh-*R*ETH day lah f*r*awn-TEH-*r*ah] A city in southwestern Spain's Andulusia region, just inland from the Atlantic Ocean. Jerez de la Frontera (once known as *Xérès*) is the central city in and birthplace of Spain's SHERRY country. *See also* JEREZ-XÉRÈS-SHERRY Y MANZANILLA DE SANLÚCAR DE BARRAMEDA DO.

Jerez-Xérès-Sherry y Manzanilla de Sanlúcar de Barrameda DO [heh-*R*ETH seh-*R*EHS sheh-REE ee mahn-zuh-NEEL-yuh day sah*n*-LOO-kah*r* day bah*r*-*r*ah-MEH-thah] The DO in which true SHERRY is made. It's located in southwestern Spain around the city of JEREZ DE LA FRONTERA. Although the DO zone encompasses a wider area, the core zone, called **Jerez Superior**, forms a rough triangle with Jerez de la Frontera at one corner and the towns of Sanlúcar de Barrameda and El Puerto de Santa Maria at the others. This area is rich with *albariza*, the white, chalky soil that produces the best grapes for fino and manzanilla (*see* SHERRY). This area's clay soil is called *barro*, which isn't quite as good as the albariza for such grapes.

Jeroboam *see* Wine Bottles, page 609

Jessuitengarten *see* WINKEL

Jesuitengarten *see* FORST

Joannes Seyve 26205 *see* CHAMBOURCIN

João de Santarém *see* PERIQUITA

Johannisberg [yoh-HAHN-ihss-be*r*k] Esteemed name in wine circles that is one of Germany's best and most famous estates, Schloss Johannisberg, as well as the famous town where that vineyard is located and the BEREICH covering the entire RHEINGAU region. The town is located in the heart of the Rheingau southwest of the city of Wiesbaden. It's part of a series of towns and villages that are situated in some of Germany's best vineyards. In addition to Schloss Johannisberg, other top EINZELLAGEN include **Goldatzel**, **Hasenberg**, **Hölle**, **Klaus**, and **Vogelsang**. The prestige of the name Johannisberg has crossed the sea where in the United States, the term "Johannisberg Riesling" is often used for RIESLING wine.

Johannisberger *see* RIESLING

Johannisberg Riesling *see* RIESLING

Jonquières *see* TERRASSES DU LARZAC AC

Josephshöf; Josephshöfer [YOH-zehfs-hawf; YOH-zehfs-hawf-uhr] One of Germany's premier EINZELLAGEN, which is located in the township of GRAACH on the Mosel River in Germany's MOSEL-SAAR-RUWER region. The 15-acre RIESLING vineyard, which is situated on a steeply terraced hillside, is owned by Weingut Reichsgraf von Kesselstatt, a respected producer in this area. Josephshöf is famous for RICH, ELEGANT wines that AGE well.

joven [KHOA-bayn] Spanish for "young," referring to LIGHT, FRUITY wines made with little or no AGING and for early consumption. *See also* CRIANZA.

Juan Garcia Spanish red-wine grape native to the area around Fermoselle in Zamora province in the CASTILE AND LEÓN region. Wines with a majority of Juan Garcia in the blend can be found in the TORO and the ARRIBES DOS. The wines produced are generally light and fruity with medium alcohol levels and good acidity.

Juffer *see* BRAUNEBERG

jug wine(s) A term that originated when consumers used to bring their own jugs to wineries to be filled. Today it applies to inexpensive, usually GENERIC WINES, which are customarily (but not always) sold in large 1.5- and 3-liter bottles.

Jujuy *see* ARGENTINA

Juliénas AC [zhoo-lyay-NAH] One of the smaller of the ten CRUS in France's BEAUJOLAIS region. Juliénas wines, made from GAMAY grapes, are some of the more substantial of the Beaujolais wines. They have deeper color, richer fruitiness, and more TANNINS than most. Along with the wines from MOULIN-À-VENT, those from Juliénas' steep hillsides are considered capable of the longest AGING of the ten Beaujolais crus.

Jumilla DO [khoo-MEE-lyah] Located in the Levante region in eastern Spain, northeast of the city of Alicante, this DO has over 100,000 vineyard acres. Jumilla, which has long been associated with BIG, high-ALCOHOL (up to 18 percent) red wines, has been modernizing wine-making techniques in an attempt to produce lower-alcohol wines. In order to achieve a more elegant style of wine, some producers are picking earlier, before grapes get too high in sugar. They're also using modern equipment like cooled, stainless steel tanks. The main grape in this area is Monastrell (MOURVÈDRE), which is planted in about 85 percent of the vineyard area. There are small amounts of Garnacha (GRENACHE) and Cencibel (TEMPRANILLO). The area's white varieties are AIRÉN, MACABEO, Merseguera, and PEDRO XIMÉNEZ. Among those grapes recently planted are CABERNET SAUVIGNON, MERLOT, and SYRAH.

Jungfer *see* HALLGARTEN

Jura *see* ARBOIS AC; CHÂTEAU-CHALON AC; CÔTES DU JURA AC; CRÉMANT DE JURA AC; L'ÉTOILE AC

Jurançon AC [zhoo-*rah*n-SAW*N*] APPELLATION located in the foothills of the Pyrenees near the town of Pau in SOUTHWEST FRANCE. It produces only white wines, which are noted for their distinctive FLORAL and spicy (cinnamon and cloves) nuances. The grape varieties used are the local favorites—Courbu, Gros Manseng, and Petite Manseng. The wines can be DRY or sweet, the latter generally only if the grapes are left on the vine until they are shriveled and sugary, which usually occurs in late November or early December.

K **Kabinett** [kah-bih-NEHT] The first (lowest) of the six subcategories of QUALITÄTSWEIN MIT PRÄDIKAT (QmP)—the highest quality-wine category in Germany. The grapes for Kabinett wines must contain minimum amounts of natural sugar (ranging from 67° to 85° OECHSLE, approximately 17 to 21 percent sugar by weight), depending on the region and the variety. These are the lowest minimums for QmP wines, and these wines are therefore usually the driest (*see* DRY) and least expensive. (QUALITÄTSWEIN BE-STIMMTER ANBAUGEBIET and DEUTSCHER TAFELWEIN are the two quality categories lower than QmP wines.) In Austria, Kabinett is the highest subcategory of QUALITÄTSWEIN and is not included in Austria's highest category, PRÄDIKATSWEIN.

Kadarka [KAH-dahr-kah] Red-wine grape that is Hungary's most widely cultivated variety, although it's thought to have originated in Albania. Kadarka is grown in most other eastern European countries as well, where it's known variously as *Cadarca, Gamza,* and *Skadarska.* This grape produces full-bodied (*see* BODY), TANNIC red wines of medium to deep color. Kadarka wines can be very AROMATIC, with intriguing SPICY characteristics. Along with Kékfrankos and Médoc Noir (MERLOT), Kadarka is one of the varieties used in Hungary's famous EGRI BIKAVÉR.

Kahlenberg *see* BAD KREUZNACH

Kaiserstuhl-Tuniberg [KI-zuhr-shtool TOO-nee-behrg] A prominent BERIECH covering the southern part of Germany's BADEN region, directly across the Rhine River from France's ALSACE region. There are two distinct areas here—Tuniberg and the Kaiserstuhl, which means "emperor's seat." Vineyards for both areas are situated on volcanic hills. The region has undergone FLURBEREINIGUNG, whereby the hillsides have been carefully contoured and replanted into modern, efficient vineyards. The primary grape varieties planted in Beriech Kaiserstuhl-Tuniberg are MÜLLER-THURGAU, Rülander (PINOT GRIS), and SPÄTBURGUNDER (PINOT NOIR).

Kallstadt [KAHL-shtaht] A top German wine-producing village located north of BAD DÜRKHEIM in the middle of the PFALZ region. The vineyards are planted with a high percentage of RIESLING, along with SYLVANER, and SCHEUREBE. The best EINZELLAGEN include **Annaberg, Kronenberg, Saumagen,** and **Steinacker**.

Kalterersee *see* LAGO DI CALDARO

Kamptal DAC *see* DISTRICTUS AUSTRIA CONTROLLATUS

Kanawha River Valley AVA *see* OHIO RIVER VALLEY AVA

Kangaroo Island Australian wine region located on Kangaroo Island (Australia's third–largest) in the Fleurieu Zone of SOUTH AUSTRALIA. It's situated about 70 miles southwest of Adelaide at the mouth of Gulf St. Vincent. The island, which is about 95 miles long and 35 miles wide, understandably has a maritime climate that so far seems suited to CABERNET SAUVIGNON, Shiraz (SYRAH), MERLOT, and CHARDONNAY.

Kanzem [KAHN-tsuhm] A small, picturesque village located on the Saar River in Germany's MOSEL-SAAR-RUWER region. In good vintages, Kanzem produces top-notch RIESLING wines with EARTHY and SPICY characteristics. The best EINZELLAGEN include **Altenberg**, **Schlossberg**, and **Sonnenberg**.

Karthäuserhofberg *see* EITELSBACH

Kasel [KAH-zuhl] Ruwer River village that is the largest and most important in this rustic section of Germany's MOSEL-SAAR-RUWER region. Kasel produces high-quality RIESLING wines that are ELEGANT, yet powerfully fragrant. The best EINZELLAGEN here are **Herrenberg**, **Hitzlay**, **Kehrnagel**, and **Nies'chen**.

Kaseler Romerlay *see* RUWER

Kava *see* GREECE

Kehrnagel *see* KASEL

Kékfrankos *see* BLAUFRÄNKISCH

Kékmedoc *see* MENOIRE

Kéknyelü [KAYK-nyeh-leu; kayk-NYEL-oo] A well-known Hungarian white-wine grape whose name translates to "blue-stalked." Kéknyelü's fame is belied by the fact that today there are very few acres cultivated, and they're limited to the BADACSONY district. Generally, Kéknyelü is VINIFIED into OFF-DRY wines with SPICY flavors, high ALCOHOL, and a color and aroma reminiscent of new-mown hay.

Kékoporto; Kékoportó *see* PORTUGIESER

keller [KEHL-luh*r*] German for "cellar." **Kellerei** is a "wine cellar" and implies a merchant's wine cellar as opposed to a producer's cellar, which is included in the meaning of the term WEINGUT. *See also* WEINKELLEREI.

Kentucky The first commercial vineyard planted in the U.S was located along the Kentucky River just south of Lexington. The vineyard, sponsored by the Kentucky Vineyard Society, was planted in 1799. In the mid-1800s, Kentucky was one of the largest wine producing states in the nation. Unfortunately, the Civil War diminished the state's significance during the latter part of the century and PROHIBITION killed off most wine production in 1920. In 1990, legislation created a more favorable environment for Kentucky wineries and additional laws continued to encourage VITICULTURE. Today there are over a dozen wineries in Kentucky. Like neighboring states, the most widely planted grapes are HYBRIDS like AURORA, CATAWBA, SEYVAL BLANC, VIDAL BLANC, and VIGNOLES. Kentucky produces a large number of FRUIT WINES. In fact, Barker's Blackberry Hill Winery, producer of blackberry and cherry wines, was the first family farm to receive a license under the revised 1990 law. VITIS VINIFERA grapes like CABERNET SAUVIGNON and CHARDONNAY are difficult to grow here and comprise only about 10 percent of total plantings. Areas around the Ohio River are part of the OHIO RIVER VALLEY AVA, which also includes parts of INDIANA, OHIO, and WEST VIRGINIA; wineries in this area can use Ohio River Valley on their labels. Kentucky wineries include Bravard Vineyards and Winery, Broad Run Vineyards and Winery, Century House Winery & Vineyards, Château du Viex Corbeau, Chrisman Mill Vineyards & Winery, Equus Run Vineyards, Highland Winery, Horseshoe Bend Vineyards, Lovers Leap Vineyard & Winery, Rolling Hills Vineyard, Springhill Vineyards Winery, and Stovers Family Vineyard & Winery.

Keppoch *see* PADTHAWAY

Kerner [KEHR-nuhr] Developed in the late 1960s, this very successful German white HYBRID is a combination of a red variety, Trollinger (SCHIAVA), and a white grape, RIESLING. It's most heavily planted in Germany's RHEINHESSEN and PFALZ regions, although it's cultivated to some extent throughout the country. Kerner produces quality, Riesling-like wines with good ACIDITY, FLORAL characteristics, and AGING ability.

K

Kieselberg *see* DEIDESHEIM

Kiewa River Valley *see* ALPINE VALLEYS

King Valley An Australian wine region located in the North East Victoria Zone of VICTORIA. It's situated in the foothills of the Great Dividing Range about 165 miles northeast of Melbourne around the town of Wangaratta. The first commercial vineyards appeared in King Valley in 1882, and the region continued to grow for the next decade. In the 1890s, a depression hit, and PHYLLOXERA in neighboring regions caused a general decline in the local wine industry. Brown Brothers, which was founded in 1885, managed to survive, and today it's the largest producer in the King Valley region. The 1980s saw a general resurgence in this region, which now has nineteen wineries and over 3,700 acres of vineyards. The southern portion sits at higher altitudes and is cooler; the north is lower and warmer. Base wine components for SPARKLING WINE blending come from the south's CHARDONNAY and PINOT NOIR crops. The leading VARIETIES for STILL WINE are Chardonnay and CABERNET SAUVIGNON, followed by RIESLING, Shiraz (SYRAH), MERLOT, SAUVIGNON BLANC, and Pinot Noir.

kir [KEER] White wine that is flavored with a soupçon of crème de cassis, a blackcurrant-flavored liqueur. Kir is typically served as an APÉRITIF. When made with CHAMPAGNE, it's referred to as **kir royale**.

Kirchenstück *see* HOCKHEIM; FORST

Klaus *see* JOHANNISBERG

Kleinberger *see* ELBLING

Klein Karoo Region *see* SOUTH AFRICA

Kleinvernatsch *see* SCHIAVA

Klingelberger *see* RIESLING

Klosterberg *see* AHR; OESTRICH; RÜDESHEIM

Kloster Eberbach [KLAWS-tuh*r* AY-buh*r*-bahkh] Located in the village of HATTENHEIM in Germany's RHEINGAU region, this renowned, ancient monastery is now the home of the German Wine Academy. Kloster Eberbach was founded in the early 1100s and run by the Cistercian monks for nearly seven centuries. Just as they had at France's CLOS DE VOUGEOT, this order established a splendid vineyard next to their monastery and built a stone wall around it. This 79-acre vineyard, which the monks named **Steinberg**, has become world-famous. Because it's classified as an ORTSTEIL, the wines from this vineyard are not required to have the village name (Hattenheim) on the label—only "Steinberger" appears. The vineyard is planted with about 95 percent RIESLING. The highly regarded wines it produces are full-bodied (*see* BODY), full-flavored, and RICH. Kloster Eberbach and the Steinberg vineyard are now controlled by the Staatsweingüter Eltville (*see* STATE DOMAINS).

Knights Valley AVA APPELLATION located in SONOMA COUNTY, California, just north of NAPA VALLEY, southeast of ALEXANDER VALLEY and directly east of the town of Geyserville. Although the APPELLATION designation wasn't approved until 1983, BERINGER VINEYARDS has had vineyards here since the 1970s and has done well with CABERNET SAUVIGNON, MERLOT, SAUVIGNON BLANC, and SÉMILLON. The Peter Michael Winery was completed in 1989 and produces ESTATE-BOTTLED wines from Knights Valley vineyards.

Kocher-Jagst-Tauber, Bereich *see* WÜRTTEMBERG

Königin Victoriaberg *see* HOCKHEIM

Königsfels *see* SCHLOSSBÖCKELHEIM

Koppamurra *see* WRATTONBULLY

kosher wine [KOH-sher] Wine made according to Jewish rabbinical law. The word "kosher" is a derivation of the Hebrew *kasher*, meaning "proper" or "pure." Kosher wine production must follow precise standards of purity under the direction of a rabbi and may be handled only by workers who are orthodox Jews. These wines may be red or white, sweet or DRY, STILL or SPARKLING, but most are sweet and red—made from CONCORD grapes.

Kranzberg *see* NIERSTEIN

Kremstal DAC *see* DISTRICTUS AUSTRIA CONTROLLATUS

Kreuz *see* OPPENHEIM

Kreuznach, Bereich *see* NAHE; BAD KREUZNACH

Krötenbrunnen *see* DIENHEIM

Krötenpfuhl *see* BAD KREUZNACH

Kuhlmann 1882 *see* MARÉCHAL FOCH

Kuhlmann 1942 *see* LEON MILLOT

Kumeu *see* AUCKLAND

Kupfergrube *see* SCHLOSSBOCKELHEIM

Kupp *see* WILTINGEN

Kürfustlay, Grosslage Bernkasteler *see* BERNKASTEL

KWV *see* SOUTH AFRICA

label; labeling *see* Demystifying the Wine Label, page 612

Labrusca *see* VITIS LABRUSCA

Lacrima Nera *see* GAGLIOPPO

Lacryma Christi del Vesuvio (LCV) DOC [LAH-kree-mah KREESS-tee dehl veh-SOO-vee-oh] *see* VESUVIO DOC

lactic acid *see* ACIDS; MALOLACTIC FERMENTATION

Ladoix AC [lah-DWAH seh-ree-NYEE] Little-known APPELLATION that takes its name from the village of Ladoix-Serrigny, which is the northernmost in the CÔTE DE BEAUNE district of France's BURGUNDY region. Most of the wine produced by this area is either entitled to the CORTON GRAND CRU AC, the ALOXE-CORTON PREMIER CRU AC, or the CÔTE DE BEAUNE-VILLAGES AC. This means that only a small amount of wine is actually released as Ladoix AC. Wines from this appellation can be red, made with PINOT NOIR grapes, or white, based on CHARDONNAY. They're generally of satisfactory quality and well priced.

ladybird *see* ASIAN LADY BEETLE

lagar; pl. lagares [lah-GAHR; lah-GAH-resh] The traditional rectangular stone or cement (occasionally wooden) trough used in the production of SHERRY in and around Spain's JEREZ DE LA FRONTERA and of PORT in Portugal's DOURO region. Lagares, which are 3 to 4 feet high and vary in size, are used for treading grapes and/or for fermentation of the juice. Today, most have been replaced by more modern VINIFICATION equipment.

Lagarino *see* LAGREIN

L

lage; pl. lagen [LAH-guh] German for "site," which, in wine parlance, usually refers to a vineyard site. An individual vineyard site is called an EINZELLAGE; an area grouping of einzellagen is called a GROSSLAGE.

Lago di Caldaro DOC [LAH-goh dee kahl-DAH-roh] DOC zone within the larger ALTO ADIGE DOC in northeast Italy's TRENTINO-ALTO ADIGE region. Although located in northern Italy, German is commonly spoken here, and this area is also called *Kalterersee*. The Lago di Caldaro DOC encompasses an area around Lake Caldaro and extends down into northern Trentino. The vineyards right around the lake are also considered a subzone of the ALTO ADIGE DOC, and wines made from grapes grown there may be labeled "Alto Adige Lago di Caldaro

DOC." The area produces light, red wines consisting of at least 85 percent of SCHIAVA, along with small portions of Pinot Nero (PINOT NOIR) and LAGREIN.

Lagrain *see* LAGREIN

Lagrein [lah-GRAYN] A red-wine grape grown mainly in Italy's TRENTINO-ALTO ADIGE region. Lagrein is VINIFIED into deep, dark reds (known as Lagrein Dunkel or Lagrein Scuro) and ROSÉS (called Lagrein Kretzer or Lagrein Rosato). The rosés are considered to be some of Italy's best; the reds can have wonderful CHOCOLATY nuances and rich fruit flavors. A small amount of Lagrein is used to bolster the SCHIAVA grape in the DOC wines of SANTA MADDALENA. This variety is also known as *Lagrain* and *Lagarino*.

lágrima [lah-GREE-mah] Spanish for "tear." In Spain, this term also describes wine made from FREE-RUN JUICE, rather than from grapes that have been mechanically crushed.

Lairén *see* AIRÉN

Lake Chelan AVA AMERICAN VITICULTURAL AREA established in 2009 in the north central part of Washington State, about 112 miles east-north-east of Seattle. Its 24,040 acres are completely within the larger COLUM-BIA VALLEY AVA. The size and depth of the long, slender lake provides a moderating influence on the surrounding area (*see* LAKE EFFECT). Currently there are over a dozen wineries in the area with about 200 acres of vineyards planted to red varieties that include MALBEC, MERLOT, AND SYRAH and white-wine grapes such as CHARDONNAY, GEWÜRZ-TRAMINER, PINOT GRIS, and RIESLING.

Lake County Large California county located north of NAPA COUNTY and east of MENDOCINO COUNTY. The area is dominated by Clear Lake, California's largest lake (which takes up about half of the county's surface area). Lake County is part of the NORTH COAST AVA but has three AVAs of it own—CLEAR LAKE, GUENOC VALLEY, and Benmore Valley, an obscure VITICULTURAL AREA southwest of the town of Lakeport. CABERNET SAUVIGNON, CHARDONNAY, SAUVIGNON BLANC, and ZINFANDEL are the major grape varieties grown in Lake County.

L

Lake Effect A term used by growers around the Great Lakes area and other large lakes in colder regions to describe the environmental influence such lakes have on growing patterns. As the spring growing season for grapevines begins, the lakes' cooling effect (stored from the winter) retards the vines from budding until the spring frost season is over. The lakes store daytime heat as the growing season continues. The effect of the warming water lessens the variation between day and night temperatures, which lengthens the growing season (compared to nearby areas) by as much as four weeks. As summer draws to an end, the stored warmth of the lakes delays frost that might damage vineyards in the fall. In winter, the lakes also cause heavy, moist snowfall, which blankets the vineyards, insulating and protecting the vines from the frigid air. The Lake Effect influences the environment for about 20 to 25 miles inland from the shore, creating a positive viticultural environment that wouldn't exist otherwise in the northern climes. It allows states like MICHIGAN, NEW YORK, PENNSYLVANIA, and OHIO to grow grape VARIETIES that have trouble surviving further south in states like MISSOURI. It is this same effect that allows the FINGER LAKES AVA in New York to provide a hospitable environment for VITICULTURE.

Lake Erie AVA Viticultural area that encompasses 2,236,800 acres in the states of New York, Pennsylvania, and Ohio along the shore, and on the islands of Lake Erie. Although the AVA was established in 1983, the area's history of grape growing and winemaking goes back at least 150 years. This area is broken up into subdistricts—western, central, and eastern. The western subdistrict runs from Toledo, Ohio, to Cleveland, Ohio, and includes the western islands, where the lake's warmth (*see* LAKE EFFECT) provides as many as 206 frost-free days (more than any other area around Lake Erie) on the ISLE ST. GEORGE AVA. The central subdistrict, which runs from Cleveland, Ohio to Erie, Pennsylvania, is the coolest. The **Grand River Valley AVA**, a 125,000-acre area in the northeastern Ohio counties of Lake, Geauga, and Ashtabula along the Grand River, is part of the larger Lake Erie AVA. The eastern subdistrict runs from Erie, Pennsylvania, to Buffalo, New York, and has the next most frost-free days after the western area. There are over 30,000 acres of vineyards in this AVA, a majority of which are in New York's Chautauqua and Erie Counties. A preponderance of these vineyards are planted with CONCORD, which is usually made into grape juice and grape jelly. A very small percentage is planted to HYBRIDS (like CAYUGA, CHAMBOURCIN, SEYVAL BLANC, and VIDAL BLANC) and VITIS VINIFERA vines (like RIESLING CABERNET SAUVIGNON, CABERNET FRANC, CHARDONNAY, GEWÜRZTRAMINER, Pinot Grigio (PINOT GRIS), and PINOT NOIR).

Lake Erie North Shore VA *see* ONTARIO

Lake Michigan Shore AVA *see* MICHIGAN

Lalande-de-Pomerol AC [lah-LAH*N*D duh pawm-uh-*R*AWL] Although it's considered a lesser-known "satellite" APPELLATION of BOR-

DEAUX'S POMEROL district, Lalande-de-Pomerol actually has more acreage. It encompasses the COMMUNES of Lalande-de-Pomerol and Neac on the northeast edge of Pomerol. Even though MERLOT is the dominant grape in Lalande-de-Pomerol wines, they also include CABERNET FRANC, CABERNET SAUVIGNON, and MALBEC. These wines are usually not as BIG and full-bodied (*see* BODY) as the better Pomerol wines, but then they aren't as expensive, either.

Lambrusco [lam-BROOS-koh] A red-wine grape that is grown all over Italy, primarily in the EMILIA-ROMAGNA region. The Lambrusco variety has over sixty subvarieties scattered throughout Italy, the most significant being *Lambrusco Grasparossa, Lambrusco Maestri, Lambrusco Marani, Lambrusco Montericco, Lambrusco Salamino,* and *Lambrusco di Sorbara.* There are a number of Lambrusco wines with DOC status including *Lambrusco di Sorbara, Lambrusco Grasparossa di Castelvetro, Lambrusco Mantovano, Lambrusco Reggiano,* and *Lambrusco Salamino di Santa Croce.* The best of these wines are from the Lambrusco di Sorbara DOC, which come from acreage surrounding the village of Sorbara, believed to be Lambrusco's birthplace. Lambrusco is probably best known, at least by Americans, for the non-DOC, pale red, semisweet, slightly effervescent (FRIZZANTE) wines. It's also made in white (where the skins are quickly separated from the juice) and ROSÉ versions. All three variations are made in two styles—semisweet and DRY, the latter preferred in Italy. Lambrusco wines are not known for their aging capabilities and should be drunk young. This variety is unrelated to the North American vine species VITIS LABRUSCA.

Lancaster Valley AVA Established in 1982, this was Pennsylvania's first AVA. It consists of approximately 225,000 acres in the Lancaster Valley, which measures 12 by 30 miles and is located primarily in southeast Pennsylvania's Lancaster County in and around the city of Lancaster. There were thriving vineyards here as early as the late 1700s, but PROHIBITION brought the industry to a standstill. VITICULTURE didn't reappear on the scene until 1963, when the Conestoga Winery was established. Today there are several hundred acres planted to NATIVE AMERICAN GRAPES, HYBRIDS, and some VITIS VINIFERA varieties. Three wineries are located in this area—Mount Hope Estate & Winery, Nissley Vineyards and Winery Estate, and Twin Brook Winery.

Landot [lahn-DOH] Red-grape variety, also known as *Landot 4511* and *Landot Noir,* that is a French-American HYBRID. Because Landot can withstand moderate winters (to –25°F) and is an early ripener, it has become popular in parts of the midwestern and the northeastern United States. It can make good quality wines capable of aging.

Landwein [LAHNT-vyn] A superior subcategory of DEUTSCHER TAFELWEIN ("German TABLE WINE") that has stricter guidelines than regular Deutscher Tafelwein. For example, the alcohol content must be 0.5 percent higher and the residual sugar shouldn't be over 1.8 percent (which makes it a TROCKEN or HALBTROCKEN in terms of DRYNESS). There are fifteen areas within Germany's broader growing regions authorized to make these wines, and each uses "Landwein" in its name, such as *Ahrtaler Landwein, Landwein der Saar, Frankisher Landwein,* and *Unterbadisher Landwein*. Landweins are equivalent to what the French describe as VIN DE PAYS wines. In Austria, Landwein holds a similar position in the quality hierarchy—slightly above TAFELWEIN, but below QUALITÄTSWEIN. *See also* QUALITÄTSWEIN BESTIMMTER ANBAUGEBIETE; QUALITÄTSWEIN MIT PRÄDIKAT.

Langenmorgen *see* DEIDESHEIM

Langhe DOC [LAHN-gyah] Approved in 1994, this important DOC zone covers a majority of the province of Cuneo around ALBA in northwestern Italy's PIEDMONT region. Much of its area overlaps other demarcated areas, such as BARBARESCO DOCG, BAROLO DOCG, and ROERO DOC. Langhe DOC winemaking rules are less restrictive than those for the Barolo and Barbaresco DOCG wines. Unlike these DOCGs, Langhe can blend other approved grapes with NEBBIOLO. Producers are also allowed to use non-native grapes like CABERNET SAUVIGNON, CHARDONNAY, and SAUVIGNON BLANC. These relaxed rules are allowing area winemakers to be inventive, and some wines produced in the Langhe DOC are gaining a reputation as the Piedmont's equivalent to the SUPER TUSCANS of TUSCANY.

Langhorne Creek An Australian wine region located in the Fleurieu Zone of SOUTH AUSTRALIA. It's situated about 45 miles southeast of Adelaide around the town of Langhorne Creek, which is not far from Lake Alexandrina—the source of its water supply. Although vines were first planted in this region in 1860, the region was largely undiscovered for decades. During the 1970s and 1980s, Wolf Blass saw the potential of the region and promoted it as a good growing area. By the early 1990s, Langhorne Creek had approximately 1,000 acres of vineyards. Since then growth has exploded—at this writing, the vineyard total is nearly 12,000 acres and expanding rapidly, fueled by the likes of Orlando Wyndham, who is investing heavily in the area. Langhorne Creek has a cool, even growing season influenced by

Lake Alexandrina and the Southern Ocean. This is primarily red-wine country, with CABERNET SAUVIGNON and Shiraz (SYRAH) occupying over 75 percent of the vineyards. MERLOT and CHARDONNAY are next, with a variety of other red and white VARIETIES planted in small amounts. Most of the grape crop is shipped out of the Langhorne Creek region to winery facilities in other parts of SOUTH AUSTRALIA where it is blended with grapes from other areas.

Languedoc-Roussillon [lah*n*g-DAWK *r*oo-see-YAW*N*] Also referred to as the *Midi*, this huge region is located in southern France along the Mediterranean. It consists of over 800,000 vineyard acres spread through four French DÉPARTEMENTS—AUDE, Gard, L'HÉRAULT, and Pyrénées-Orientales—which produce about one-third of the total French wine-grape crop, and close to 250 million to 300 million cases of wine. The region is well suited to grape growing, but, unfortunately, the many Languedoc-Roussillon growers have been more concerned with quantity than quality, which means that most of the wines are very ordinary. The majority (almost 90 percent) of the wine here is red, made primarily from CARIGNAN, CINSAULT, and GRENACHE. To improve quality, MOURVÈDRE, SYRAH, and even CABERNET SAUVIGNON and MERLOT are being used as replacements for high-yielding, lower-quality grapes like Carignan. Improved VINIFICATION techniques are also being encouraged. Although most of the wine produced here is VIN ORDINAIRE, there are numerous VIN DE PAYS wines. There are also a growing number of APPEL-LATION D'ORIGINE CONTRÔLÉE areas including BANYULS, BLANQUETTE DE LIMOUX, COLLIOURE, CORBIÈRES, COSTIÈRES DE NÎMES, COTEAUX DU LANGUEDOC, CÔTES DU ROUSSILLON, FAUGÈRES, FITOU, MAURY, MINERVOIS, MUSCAT DE FRON-TIGNAN, MUSCAT DE RIVESALTES, and SAINT-CHINIAN.

Les Languettes *see* CORTON; CORTON-CHARLEMAGNE

Lanson *see* CHAMPAGNE

Lanuvini *see* COLLI LANUVINI DOC

Lanzarote DO *see* CANARY ISLANDS

La Palma DO *see* CANARY ISLANDS

Lardot *see* MACABEO

large format bottles Wine bottles that are larger than the stan-dard 750 milliliters (ml) bottle. *See also* Wine Bottles, page 609.

La Rioja *see* ARGENTINA

Laskiriesling *see* WELSCHRIESLING

Laski Rizling *see* WELSCHRIESLING

late disgorged *see* DISGORGEMENT

late harvest A wine term referring to wines made from grapes picked toward the end of the harvest (usually late fall) when they are very ripe. Such grapes have a higher sugar content (minimum of 24° BRIX), particularly if they've been infected with BOTRYTIS CINEREA, a desirable fungus that shrivels the grape and thereby concentrates the sugar. The terms **Select Late Harvest** and **Special Select Late Harvest** refer to wines made from grapes picked with higher sugar-content minimums—28° and 35° Brix, respectively. A high Brix measurement can translate to a sweet wine, to a wine that's high in ALCOHOL, or to one with both characteristics. **Special Late Harvested** is an Australian labeling term that means the wine must be made from ripe grapes of which a significant proportion has been dehydrated under natural conditions in a manner which favors the concentration of sugars in the berries. Generally, Special Late Harvested, Select Late Harvest and Special Select Late Harvest wines have a RESIDUAL SUGAR content, some ranging as high as 28 percent. Late harvest wines are noted for their rich, deep, honeyed flavors and are customarily served after the main course, often with dessert or with cheeses such as Roquefort. The most popular grapes used for these DESSERT WINES are GEWÜRZTRAMINER, RIESLING, SAUVIGNON BLANC, and SÉMILLON.

Latisana DOC [lah-tee-ZAH-nah] Small DOC zone that is also known as *Latisana del Friuli* and that is located in the southern part of the FRIULI-VENEZIA GIULIA region in northeast Italy. It covers twelve VARIETAL WINES plus a ROSATO, all of which are regarded as fairly ordinary. The varietal wines are Cabernet (from CABERNET SAUVIGNON and CABERNET FRANC), Caberent Franc, Cabernet Sauvignon, CHARDONNAY, MERLOT, Pinot Bianco (PINOT BLANC), Pinot Grigio (PINOT GRIS), Refosco dal Peduncolo Rosso (REFOSCO), Sauvignon (SAUVIGNON BLANC), FRIULANO, Traminer Aromatico (GEWÜRZTRAMINER), and Verduzzo Friulano. The rosé wine is made mainly from Merlot.

Latium [LAH-tyum] A wine-producing region located on central Italy's western coast. Rome is the region's hub, and its 120,000 vineyard acres spread out in all directions. White wines are dominant in Latium (*Lazio* in Italian) and represent about 85 percent of the total production. The most popular white varieties are TREBBIANO and MALVASIA, which are found in some form throughout most of the region. The primary red varieties are Cesanese, SANGIOVESE, MERLOT, and MONTEPULCIANO. Latium contains the following DOC areas: Aleatico di Gradoli,

APRILIA, Atina, Bianco Capena, CASTELLI ROMANI, CERVETERI, Cesanese del Piglio, Cesanese di Affile, Cesanese di Olevano Romano, Circeo, COLLI ALBANI, Colli della Sabina, Colli Etruschi Viterbesi, Colli Lanuvini, Cori, EST! EST!! EST!!! DI MONTEFIASCONE, FRASCATI, Genazzano, MARINO, MONTE-COMPATRI-COLONNA, Tarquinia, VELLETRI, Vignanello, and Zagarolo.

Latour-de-France *see* CÔTE DU ROUSSILLON

Latricières-Chambertin [lah-tree-SYEHR shahm-behr-TAN] An 18-acre GRAND CRU vineyard located in the village of GEVREY-CHAMBERTIN in the CÔTE DE NUITS district of France's BURGUNDY region. The noteworthy red wines (which are made with 100 percent PINOT NOIR) from Latricières-Chambertin are similiar to but LIGHTER than the RICH, CONCENTRATED wines from the adjoining neighbor and well-known grand cru, CHAMBERTIN.

Laudun [loh-DEUHN] One of the best of the villages entitled to the CÔTES DE RHÔNE-VILLAGES AC. Laudun is located northeast of Avignon in the southern portion of France's RHÔNE region. It's known for its white wines, made from BOURBOULENC, CLAIRETTE, and ROUSSANNE, as well as its GRENACHE-based ROSÉ wines.

Lavaux [lah-VOH] Located east of Lausanne on the north shore of Lake Geneva, Lavaux is one of the three premier growing areas in the Swiss canton of VAUD. It produces primarily white wines (some of Switzerland's best) from CHASSELAS grapes, which grow on the terraced vineyards that make up this area.

Les Lavières *see* SAVIGNY-LÈS-BEAUNE

Layon *see* COTEAUX DU LAYON

Lazio *see* LATIUM

LBV *see* PORT

leaf removal *see* PRUNING

L

leaf-roll virus; leaf roll; leafroll A serious grapevine disease that's transmitted by GRAFTING. Some theorize that it may also be disseminated by insects. Leaf-roll virus can be detected visually by downward-curving leaf edges; the leaves of the red-grape varieties turn a brilliant red, while white-grape leaves become golden yellow. The autumnal colors may be wonderful, but this disease is quite the opposite. It impedes the grapes' sugar accumulation, which means that, by the time the grapes reach a sugar level at which they can be harvested, their ACID levels and overall quality is greatly diminished. Such grapes naturally produce wines in which flavor, color and body are attenuated. Leaf-roll virus doesn't kill grapevines but markedly reduces YIELDS. The only treatment currently known for this disease is removal of the vines. Vineyardists can protect against leaf-roll virus by purchasing only vines that are state-certified to be free of known diseases. *See also* DISEASES, VINEYARD.

leafy *see* Glossary of Wine Tasting Terms, page 655

lean *see* Glossary of Wine Tasting Terms, page 655

Leányka [LAY-ahn-kyah] White-wine grape planted in Hungary, Romania (where it's known as *Feteasca, Fetiska, Feteaska,* and *Mädchentraube*), and surrounding areas. The name translates into something on the order of "young girlish," presumably alluding to the wine's soft, delicate traits. Leanyka wines have AROMATIC, SPICY, and apricot characteristics reminiscent of a GEWÜRZTRAMINER-MUSCAT combination. Most are vinified medium-sweet to medium-DRY. Although viewed as a wine that could be AGED, Leányka's moderate ACIDITY generally limits that time to only 2 to 4 years.

leathery *see* Glossary of Wine Tasting Terms, page 655

Leatico *see* ALEATICO

Leelanau Peninsula AVA *see* MICHIGAN

lees [LEEZ] The heavy, coarse sediment that accumulates during FERMENTATION and aging. Lees primarily consists of dead yeast cells and small grape particles that fall to the bottom of the fermentation tank or barrel. In most cases, this sediment is separated from the wine through RACKING. Sometimes the wine is left in contact with the lees in an attempt to develop more flavor. *See also* SUR LIE.

legs *see* Glossary of Wine Tasting Terms, page 655

Lehigh Valley AVA APPELLATION created in April 2008 in the Lehigh Valley of Pennsylvania (west of New York City and north of Philadelphia). It encompasses 1,208,320 acres located in parts of Berks, Carbon, Lehigh, Monroe, Northampton, and Schuylkill counties. There are currently 12 wineries and about 230 acres of vineyards. It's a cool climate in which CHAMBOURCIN, a HYBRID, grows well and is becoming the area's most recognized variety. Also planted are CABERNET SAUVIGNON, CHARDONNAY, PINOT NOIR, RIESLING, and VIDAL BLANC.

Leinhöhle *see* DEIDESHEIM

Lemberger *see* BLAUFRÄNKISCH

Lenchen *see* OESTRICH

length *see* Glossary of Wine Tasting Terms, page 655

Leon Millot [lee-OHN MEE-yoh] A red French-American HYBRID grown in the eastern United States and a few vineyards in England. Officially known as *Kuhlmann 1942*, Leon Millot is the offspring of Goldriesling and an American VITIS RIPARIA–VITIS RUPESTRIS vine—the same parents of the more widely planted MARÉCHAL FOCH. Leon Millot can produce good full-bodied reds with a nuance of chocolate.

Lesquerde *see* CÔTES DU ROUSSILLON AC

Lexia *see* MUSCAT

licoroso [lee-koh-ROH-soh] Portuguese term for a sweet, fortified wine similar to a VIN DE LIQUEUR.

Liebfraumilch; Liebfrauenmilch [LEEP-frow-mihlkh] Germany's most exported wine, which is sweet, inexpensive, and generally looked down upon by connoisseurs. This wine's origins go back to the sixteenth or seventeenth century. The word *Liebfraumilch,* which means "milk of Our Lady," was originally used only for wines produced from the vineyards of the Liebfrauenkirche ("Church of Our Lady"), a church in the city of Worms in Germany's RHEINHESSEN region. Over time, the word *Liebfraumilch* began to be used for any wine made in the Rhine region. In 1971 German law established specifications (which were modified in the 1980s) for calling a wine Liebfraumilch. Today, in order for a wine to be called Liebfraumilch, it must meet the following provisions: be a wine "of pleasant character"; contain a minimum of 18 grams of RESIDUAL SUGAR (1.8 percent); be made only from MÜLLER-THURGAU, SYLVANER, KERNER, or RIESLING grapes; be of QbA quality; not be labeled with Prädikat designations such as SPÄTLESE or AUSLESE; and come from one of the four German regions of RHEINHESSEN, PFALZ, RHEINGAU, and NAHE (in practice, almost all of it comes from the Rheinhessen and the Pfalz). As with most wines, the quality of Liebfraumilch can vary dramatically from producer to producer.

lieblich [lip-LIHK] Term used in Austria and Germany to indicate that a wine has some residual sugar and is moderately sweet. These wines are similar to the French MOELLEUX wines.

light *see* Glossary of Wine Tasting Terms, page 655

Liguria [lee-GOO-*r*yah] Very small wine-producing region located in northwest Italy on the Ligurian Sea. It touches France's PROVENCE region on the west end and TUSCANY on the east. This area is on the Italian Riviera and includes well-known resort areas like Potofino and San Remo, as well as the port city of Genoa. Liguria has only about 12,000 vineyard acres, and its wine production is one of the smallest of the twenty Italian wine-producing regions. It contains the DOCS of CINQUETERRE, Colli di Luni, Colline di Levanto, Golfo del Tigullio, Riviera Ligure di Ponente, ROSSESE DI DOLCEACQUA, and Val Polcevera. The main grapes used for white wines are VERMENTINO and PIGATO; red and ROSÉ wines use DOLCETTO (called *Ormeasco* or *Sciacchetra* locally) and Rossese.

Limberger *see* BLAUFRÄNKISCH

Lime Kiln Valley AVA *see* SAN BENITO COUNTY

Limestone Coast Zone *see* SOUTH AUSTRALIA

limited bottling A wine label term that implies that there's only a small amount of this particular wine. There is no legal definition for this term, however, and it is sometimes misused. Checking the number of cases produced is the only way to determine accurately just how limited a wine really is.

Limnos *see* GREECE

Limousin [lee-moo-ZAN] A forest in south-central France near the city of Limoges that produces oak used in barrels. Limousin oak is prized because it is loosely grained and therefore imparts a more obvious oak flavor and stronger TANNINS. There is some evidence, however, that the cooperage treatment may have as much to do with Limousin's esteemed reputation as the wood itself. Limousin barrels are quite popular for use in making COGNAC. They were once very popular with California winemakers, but many have shifted to the tighter-grained oak produced from the French forests of Allier, Nevers, Tronçais, and Vosges. *See also* OAK.

Limoux AOC [lee-MOO] APPELLATION for still wines made in the hills surrounding the town of Limoux, in Southern France's LANGUEDOC-ROUSSILLON region. Mauzac, also called *Blanquette*, is the traditional grape grown in this region and is the primary VARIETY used in the sparkling wines from the BLANQUETTE DE LIMOUX and CRÉMANT DE LIMOUX ACS. Until 1993, Mauzac was also the only variety that could be used in the appellation's still wines. That changed, and now only a minimum of 15 percent Mauzac is required with the rest made up of CHARDONNAY and/or CHENIN BLANC. (Wines made with 100 percent Chardonnay must be labeled as VIN DE PAYS d'Oc.) The appellation's Chardonnay-based wines have gained an excellent reputation internationally. In 2004, approval was given for a red still wine to be initiated in the 2005 vintage. Appellation rules require a minimum of 50 percent MERLOT with the addition of at least two others, of the following varieties: GRENACHE, MALBEC, SYRAH, and CARIGNAN. Additionally, no two varieties may add up to over 90 percent and if Carignan is used, it must not exceed 10 percent. Carignan is scheduled to be phased out in 2010.

limpid; limpidity *see* Glossary of Wine Tasting Terms, page 655

linalool [lih-NEHL-oh-ahwl] A terpenoid alcohol found in some grapes such as GEWÜRZTRAMINER, MUSCAT, and RIESLING. Linalool helps provide the floral-peachy-spicy character found in some wines made from these grape varieties, particularly Muscat.

Linganore AVA The Linganore VITICULTURAL AREA is located in north-central MARYLAND and encompasses 57,600 acres in parts of Frederick and Carroll Counties. Established in 1983, it is Maryland's first AVA and home to the Berrywine Plantation—Linganore Cellars, Maryland's largest winery. Elk Run Vineyards and Lowe Vineyards are also located there.

Lino Maga *see* BARBACARLO

liqueur de tirage *see* DOSAGE

liqueur d'expédition *see* DOSAGE

Liqueur Muscat *see* RUTHERGLEN

Liqueur Tokay *see* MUSCADELLE; RUTHERGLEN

liquoreux [lee-koh-REUH] A French wine descriptor meaning "rich and sweet," generally used when referring to DESSERT WINES, such as those of SAUTERNES.

liquoroso [lee-kwaw-ROH-soh] An Italian term referring to a wine with a high alcohol content. These wines are usually sweet, and FORTIFIED by the addition of grape alcohol. MARSALA and various wines made from the MALVASIA and MUSCAT (Moscato) varieties are examples of liquoroso-style wines.

Lirac AC [lee-*R*AK] Just north of Tavel in France's southern RHÔNE region is the village of Lirac, surrounded by the vineyards that comprise this APPELLATION. Lirac makes ROSÉ wines similar to those from Tavel. It also produces red wines that are comparable to slightly lighter versions from CHÂTEAUNEUF-DE-PAPE, which is just northeast. These wines, which are improving Lirac's reputation, are made primarily from GRENACHE, with some CINSAUT, MOURVÈDRE, and SYRAH. Tiny amounts of white wine are produced mostly from CLAIRETTE, but BOURBOULENC, Picpoul, and others are also used.

Lison-Pramaggiore DOC [LEE-zawn prah-mahd-JAW-ray] Created in 1986, this DOC includes the old DOCs of Tocai di Lison, Cabernet di Pramaggiore, and Merlot di Pramaggiore. It's located in the eastern part of Italy's VENETO region, with a tiny portion in the FRIULI-VENEZIA GIULIA region. In creating the DOC, the authorities included numerous additional wines. The DOC now covers a total of twelve VARIETAL WINES—Cabernet (made from CABERNET SAUVIGNON and CABERNET FRANC), Cabernet Franc, Cabernet Sauvignon, CHARDONNAY, MERLOT, Pinot Bianco (PINOT BLANC), Pinot Grigio (PINOT GRIS), Refosco dal Peduncolo Rosso (REFOSCO), Riesling Italico (WELSCHRIESLING), Sauvignon (SAUVIGNON BLANC), FRIULANO, and Verduzzo Friulano.

Listán *see* PALOMINO

Listrac AC [lees-T*R*AHK] One of the lesser-known APPELLATIONS in the MÉDOC district of France's BORDEAUX region. The wines from this area aren't quite as good as those from the neighboring COMMUNES of MARGAUX, PAUILLAC, or SAINT-JULIEN, and the Listrac AC (or **Listrac-Medoc AC**) contains no CRUS CLASSÉS (classed growths). The vineyards of this area sit back further from the Gironde estuary and contain less of the desirable gravelly soil than the vineyards of the more famous communes in the area. The area sits northwest of Margaux and southwest of Saint-Julien. The main grapes used are CABERNET FRANC, CABERNET SAUVIGNON, and MERLOT.

liter [LEE-tuhr] A METRIC measure that's equivalent to 33.8 fluid ounces or 0.264 U.S. gallons. *See also* Wine Bottles, page 609.

lively *see* Glossary of Wine Tasting Terms, page 655

Livermore Valley AVA One of California's oldest wine districts, which is located in Alameda County, approximately 50 miles southeast of San Francisco. This AVA, which is about 15 miles long and 10 miles wide, is warm because it is blocked from some of the cooling ocean breezes that some of its neighboring areas receive. For that reason, most of it is ranked a Region III (*see* CLIMATE REGIONS OF CALIFORNIA), although some parts are considered Region II. It is included in the huge CENTRAL COAST AVA and the larger SAN FRANCISCO BAY AVA. SAUVIGNON BLANC and SÉMILLON grapes have always done well here, although CHARDONNAY now accounts for about half the vineyard acreage. CABERNET SAUVIGNON, MERLOT, PETITE SIRAH, RIESLING, SYRAH, and ZINFANDEL, along with numerous other varieties, are planted here as well. Despite the residential influx, vineyard acreage is increasing due to a land-use measure put in place. There are now approximately 4,000 acres planted in this area. The well-known Wente Bros. and Concannon wineries are the oldest in the area, both being established in the 1800s.

Lizzana *see* GARGANEGA

lodge The large warehouses—like those in the town of VILA NOVA DE GAIA in northern Portugal—where PORT matures in wooden vats and barrels. The term was anglicized from the Portuguese word *loja* and is similar to the French CHAI and the Spanish BODEGA.

Lodi AVA [LOH-di] VITICULTURAL AREA in the SAN JOAQUIN VALLEY between Sacramento and Stockton that extends east until it runs into the SIERRA FOOTHILLS AVA. Although this area is part of California's huge, hot CENTRAL VALLEY, cooling breezes from San Francisco Bay and the San Joaquin River Delta can lower temperatures by as much as 10°F compared to areas farther south. Lodi is considered a Region III-Region IV area (*see* CLIMATE REGIONS OF CALIFORNIA), and ZINFANDEL and SAUVIGNON BLANC do well here. The area encompasses approximately 551,000 acres, 90,000 of which are planted. This planted acreage enables Lodi to produce between 17 and 18 percent of California's wine grapes, more than SONOMA COUNTY and the NAPA VALLEY combined. This region now has significant plantings of CHARDONNAY, CABERNET SAUVIGNON, and MERLOT. Robert Mondavi's huge Woodbridge Winery is located here, producing some 5 million to 6 million cases of wine each year. Turner Road Vintners (formerly part of Sebastiani and now part of Canandaigua Wine Company) produces about 7 million cases. The Lodi AVA has been refined even further and currently has the following sub-APPELLATIONS within its confines: ALTA MESA AVA, BORDEN RANCH AVA, CLEMENTS HILLS AVA, COSUMNES RIVER AVA, JAHANT AVA, MOKELUMNE RIVER AVA, and SLOUGHHOUSE AVA.

Loire [LWAHR] The meandering region that follows the beautiful Loire River, which begins its nearly 625-mile journey within 30 miles of the RHÔNE region in the southeastern quarter of France. The river flows northward, angling east toward Orleans and then heads in a southwesterly direction toward the Atlantic Ocean. There are over 85,000 vineyard acres and a multitude of different wine areas along the Loire, producing a number of famous wines. In the upper reaches of the Loire, not too far from its beginning, there are several VDQS and AC areas—CÔTE D'AUVERGNE, CÔTE ROANNAISES, and Saint-Pourçain-Sur-Sioule. As the river nears Orleans, it passes the famous POUILLY-FUMÉ and SANCERRE APPELLATIONS, which are known for FRESH, CRISP white wines made from SAUVIGNON BLANC. After Orleans, the river goes by the TOURAINE province, a region that not only makes white wines from Sauvignon Blanc but also includes two famous areas noted for their CHENIN BLANC wines (VOUVRAY and MONTLOUIS) and two areas with reputations for the best Loire red wines (CHINON and BOURGUEIL). As the river continues to the Atlantic, it passes through ANJOU, noted for its ROSÉ wines—Rosé d'Anjou and the higher-quality CABERNET D'ANJOU. Finally, as the river nears the ocean, it passes through Nantes where the MUSCADET grape reigns. Sparkling wines are made throughout the region with the CRÉMANT DE LOIRE AC designation which identifies those with the highest quality standards.

Lombardy [LOM-buhr-dee] An important wine-producing region in northern Italy, located between PIEDMONT on the western edge and TRENTINO-ALTO ADIGE to the east. Lombardy's capital city is Milan, which is Italy's most populated and industrialized area. Lombardy (*Lombardia*, in Italian) has almost 70,000 vineyard acres, two DOCGS, and fourteen DOCS; it produces over 47 percent of the region's total wine production. The DOCGs are FRANCIACORTA and VALTELLINA SUPERIORE; the DOCs include Botticino, Capriano del Colle, Cellatica, Garda, Garda Colli Mantovani, Lambrusco Mantovano, Lugana, OLTREPO PAVESE, Riviera del Garda Bresciano, San Colombano al Lambro, San Martino della Battaglia, TERRE DI FRANCIACORTA, VALCALEPIO, and VALTELLINA. The grape varieties grown in this region for red and ROSÉ wines include BARBERA, BONARDA, CABERNET FRANC, MERLOT, NEBBIOLO, and Pinot Nero (PINOT NOIR). Those used for white wines are CHARDONNAY, CORTESE, Pinot Bianco (PINOT BLANC), Pinot Gigio (PINOT GRIS), Riesling Renano (RIESLING), and Riesling Italico (WELSCHRIESLING).

London Particular (LP) *see* MARSALA DOC

long *see* Glossary of Wine Tasting Terms, page 655

Long Island AVA A region on the long, slender island that juts into the Atlantic northeast from New York City through Nassau and Suffolk counties. Peconic Bay splits it into the South and North Forks at the eastern end. Although vineyards were planted on Long Island in the

1600s, it wasn't until the last quarter century that this region blossomed into a true quality-wine-producing area. Since Alex and Louisa Hargrave started the first winery (in recent history) on the North Fork in the early 1970s, almost thirty wineries have opened. Long Island has a unique climate that's warmed by the Atlantic to the south, Long Island Sound to the North, and Peconic Bay in the middle. This gives it a longer growing season than might be expected in this part of the United States. In fact, enthusiasts claim that Long Island's climate and well-drained soil is similiar to that of BORDEAUX. With that in mind, wine producers are growing the classic Bordeaux varieties like CABERNET FRANC, CABERNET SAUVIGNON, MERLOT, and SAUVIGNON BLANC, plus other varieties such as CHARDONNAY, PINOT NOIR, RIESLING, and GEWÜRZTRAMINER. There are actually three APPELLATIONS on Long Island. Long Island AVA, which was approved in 2001, encompasses approximately 749,000 acres. Included within its boundaries are two earlier appellations— **North Fork of Long Island AVA** (1986) and **The Hamptons, Long Island AVA** (1985), which is on the island's South Fork. The North Fork, which consists of 101,000 acres, is slightly warmer, has the longest growing season, and contains about 90 percent of the wineries.

long-vatted A winemaker's term for wine made from grape juice that's had extra vat time with the grape skins during FERMENTATION, the end result of which is a deep red color. **Short-vatted** wine has spent little time with the grape skins. *See also* MACERATION.

Loramie Creek AVA *see* OHIO

Los Carneros AVA *see* CARNEROS

lot # 1. Although it has no legal meaning, a lot # most often is used to differentiate wine from the same vintage that was bottled at different times. 2. This term is sometimes used to indicate that wine from the same vintage was processed differently. For instance, part of it could have been barrel-aged longer, aged in different barrels, and so on. 3. Lot # occasionally means that the bottled wine is a blend either of two different vintages or possibly of grapes from two different growing regions.

Louisiana This southern state has one designated VITICULTURAL AREA, the MISSISSIPPI DELTA AVA, and only four wineries. The wines vary from FRUIT WINES made from blueberries and mayhaw (a small fruit resembling a crab apple) to those made from HYBRIDS like SEYVAL BLANC and VIDAL BLANC. One winery brings in CABERNET SAUVIGNON grapes grown in the TEXAS HIGH PLAINS AVA around Lubbock.

Loupiac AC [loo-PYAHK] Sweet white-wine APPELLATION located in France's BORDEAUX region, where it sits on the Garonne River inside the larger PREMIÈRES CÔTES DE BORDEAUX AC, directly across from BARSAC. Made from SÉMILLON, SAUVIGNON BLANC, and MUSCADELLE, Loupiac wines are lighter versions of the famous BOTRYTISED sweet white wines from SAUTERNES and BARSAC.

Loureiro [loh-RAY-roo] Portuguese white-grape variety popular in the VINHO VERDE DOC in northern PORTUGAL. This high yielding, fairly high-ACID grape has a distinctive aroma similar to bay leaves. It's usually blended with Trajadura and sometimes ALVARINHO. In the RÍAS BAIXAS DO in northwestern SPAIN, this grape is known as *Loureira*. In other areas of Portugal, it's called *Branco, Marqués,* and *Redondo.*

Lourinhã DOC [loh-REE-nyah] Located in western Portugal's ESTREMADURA region, this DOC produces high-quality brandy called **aguardente**. Along with COGNAC and ARMAGNAC, Lourinhã is one of the few brandy-making areas to receive APPELLATION status.

Lower Great Southern Region *see* GREAT SOUTHERN

Lower Mosel *see* ZELL

Lower Murray Zone *see* SOUTH AUSTRALIA

Lubéron *see* CÔTES DU LUBÉRON

Luján de Cuyo *see* ARGENTINA

Lump *see* ERSHERNDORF

Lunel *see* MUSCAT DE LUNEL AC

luscious *see* Glossary of Wine Tasting Terms, page 655

lush *see* Glossary of Wine Tasting Terms, page 655

Lussac-Saint-Émilion AC [loo-SAHK sa*n* tay-mee-LYAW*N*] Just northeast of SAINT-ÉMILION sits the village of Lussac and the surrounding vineyards that make up this APPELLATION. It's one of the satellite COMMUNES allowed to append Saint-Émilion to its name. MERLOT dominates the blend, which may also consist of CABERNET FRANC, CABERNET SAUVIGNON, and MALBEC. The wines can be quite good and are best if consumed within 5 to 6 years.

Luxembourg [LUHK-suhm-burg] This tiny country doesn't make much wine, and what is produced is similiar to that of their German neighbors to the east. The vineyards are located along the Moselle

River, which forms the border with Germany. The main varieties are AUXERROIS BLANC, ELBLING, Rivaner (MÜLLER-THURGAU), RIESLING, Rülander (PINOT GRIS), and Traminer (GEWÜRZTRAMINER). Only white wines are produced, and, like their German counterparts, Luxembourg wines are light, fruity, and low in ALCOHOL—some are turned into decent SPARKLING WINES. Luxembourg consumes more wine than it produces, so few of these wines are found outside of Luxembourg or its neighbor Belgium.

lychee *see* Glossary of Wine Tasting Terms, page 655

Lyonnais *see* COTEAUX DU LYONNAIS AC

Lyonnaise Blanche *see* MELON DE BOURGOGNE

Lyre *see* TRELLIS SYSTEM

L

Macabeo [mah-kah-BEH-oh] The most widely cultivated white variety in northern Spain and the most important white grape in the RIOJA region, where it's called *Viura*. It's because of Macabeo's higher yields (and not the quality of its wines) that this variety is pushing out the more traditional white grapes used in Rioja white wines—MALVASIA and Garnacha Blanca (GRENACHE). Macabeo-based wines are generally LIGHT, high in ACIDITY, slightly FLORAL, and fairly fruity. Their AROMA and flavor dissipate very early, however, so they should be drunk quite young. Macabeo is often blended with XAREL-LO and PARELLADA to make SPARKLING WINES. Macabeo is also grown in southern France, where it's the sole variety in the CÔTES DE ROUSSILLON Blanc. This grape is also known as *Maccabeu, Lardot,* and *Alcanol.*

Maccabeu *see* MACABEO

Macedon Ranges One of Australia's coolest growing regions, located in the Port Phillip Zone of VICTORIA. It's situated about 50 miles northwest of Melbourne around this mountain range whose prominent peak is the 3,300-foot Mount Macedon. The region includes portions of the Central Victorian Highlands and the Great Dividing Range. The SUNBURY region, to the south, was once grouped in this region but has now been split off on its own. Vigorous winds and high altitude contribute to the cool climate. The most successfully grown varieties here are the early-ripening CHARDONNAY and PINOT NOIR, which are used both for STILL WINES and SPARKLING WINES. CABERNET SAUVIGNON and Shiraz (SYRAH) can also do well but require the right combination of good vineyard location and warmer years.

maceration [mas-uh-RAY-shun] The period of time grape juice spends in contact with the skins and seeds. **Extended maceration**, which is used only with red wines, takes place after PRIMARY FERMENTATION and prolongs this contact period. The objectives of extended maceration are to increase the wine's depth of color, intensify its aroma, and, according to some winemakers, SOFTEN any harsh, bitter TANNINS so a wine is better suited for aging. In the **cold maceration** process (sometimes called *cold soak)*, the grape juice mixture (MUST) is cooled rapidly and held at a temperature of about 50°F for 5 to 10 days before fermentation is triggered. Some French winemakers add SULFUR DIOXIDE to further control fermentation. Cold-maceration advocates believe this period of pre-fermentation (in the absence of alcohol) favorably extracts PHENOLIC COMPOUNDS, thereby producing wines with increased color intensity and more complex flavors and aromas. *See also* CUVAISON; CARBONIC MACERATION.

M

macération carbonique *see* CARBONIC MACERATION

Mâcon AC; Mâcon Supérieur AC; Mâcon-Villages AC
[mah-KAW*N*; mah-KAW*N* suh-pay-YEU*R*; mah-KAW*N* vee-LAHZH]
These three APPELLATIONS are located in the MÂCONNAIS in the southern
portion of France's BURGUNDY region. The **Mâcon AC** is the basic
appellation for this area and encompasses red, white, and ROSÉ wines.
The main grapes are CHARDONNAY and GAMAY, along with a small
amount of PINOT NOIR. The **Mâcon Supérieur AC** indicates that the
qualifying wines have reached a minimum alcohol level of 1 percent
higher than that for standard Mâcon AC wines. For white wines, the
minimum is increased from 10 to 11 percent; for red wines, from 9 to
10 percent. The **Mâcon-Villages AC**, which produces the highest-
quality wines of the three appellations, is for white wines and encompasses forty-three villages scattered throughout the Mâconnais. These
villages are all allowed to use the term "Mâcon-Villages" on the label
or append their name to the word "Mâcon," as in Mâcon-Lugny. The
better villages include Azé, Clessé, Igé, Lugny, Prissé, Viré, and
Chardonnay, the latter after which the area's most popular white
grape was presumably named. In 1998, two of the villages, Viré and
Clessé, plus two others were given their own appellation.

Maconnais [mah-kawn-NEH] Located in the southern portion of
France's BURGUNDY region, this large grape-growing area takes its name
from the town of Mâcon. It's positioned between BEAUJOLAIS to the
south and the CÔTE CHALONNAISE to the north. White wines, which are
made from CHARDONNAY, make up two-thirds of the area's production.
Red and ROSÉ wines are made primarily from GAMAY, with some PINOT
NOIR. A fair amount of wine is produced under the basic Burgundian
APPELLATIONS of BOURGOGNE, BOURGOGNE PASSE TOUT GRAINS, and the
sparkling wine appellation CRÉMANT DE BOURGOGNE. Other appellations,
in increasing order of quality, are MÂCON AC, MÂCON SUPÉRIEUR AC, and
MÂCON-VILLAGES AC. At the top end of the quality spectrum are a number
of individual villages with their own appellations—POUILLY FUISSÉ,
POUILLY LOCHÉ, POUILLY VINZELLES, and SAINT VÉRAN. Also located in the
Mâconnais are the villages of Chardonnay and CHASSELAS, which presumably gave their names to the grape varieties. *See also* ALTESSE.

macroclimate The general climate of an area or region such as the
NAPA VALLEY, SAUTERNES region, or CHAMPAGNE. Macroclimate pertains to
the largest of areas when discussing climate; MESOCLIMATE relates to a
much smaller area, such as a vineyard or portion of a vineyard; and the

even more restricted MICROCLIMATE typically refers to the climatic conditions near a group of vines or may be even limited to a single vine.

Mädchentraube *see* LÉÁNYKA

made and bottled by Term that means a minimum of 10 percent of the wine was FERMENTED at the winery—the other 90 percent can come from other sources. This designation does not generally indicate the quality implied by the phrase PRODUCED AND BOTTLED BY, where at least 75 percent of the wine must be fermented at the winery. *See also* BOTTLED BY; ESTATE BOTTLED; GROWN, PRODUCED AND BOTTLED BY.

Madeira; madeira [muh-DEER-uh] 1. True madeira comes from Portugal's Madeira island, which is located some 530 miles southwest of Lisbon and 360 miles due west of Morocco. It receives Portugal's highest quality ranking—DENOMINAÇÃO DE ORIGEM CONTROLADA (DOC). Madeira is one of the three best-known FORTIFIED WINES, the others being PORT and SHERRY. Madeira is unique in that it gains its flavor from elements that would ruin most other wines—heat and oxidization (*see* OXIDIZED). The first madeiras evolved from the days when wines were transported by ship. It was discovered that during the lengthy voyage, the air circulation (which caused oxidization) and warm temperatures created wonderful wines. Today this activity is emulated through a process called *estufagem*, during which the wines are placed in hot rooms or heated tanks (*estufas*) for a minimum of 90 days where they're allowed to bake slowly. The finer madeiras are stored in wooden casks and left in attics or other extremely warm areas for years. This wood aging slowly develops the tangy, burnt-caramel, slightly bitter flavor that's unique to this wine. Madeira ranges in color from pale blond to deep tawny. It runs the gamut from quite DRY to very sweet and is usually fortified to the 18 to 20 percent alcohol range. There are four distinct styles of madeira. The pale golden SERCIAL is the lightest, driest style. It's followed by VERDELHO, which is sweeter and stronger, and then by BOAL (or *Bual*), which is fuller and sweeter than either of the previous two. MALMSEY is the richest, darkest, and sweetest of the group. The two lighter wines are generally used as APÉRITIFS, and the heavier, sweeter styles, as DESSERT WINES. **Rainwater** is a SOFT, medium-dry Verdelho. The name, so the story goes, comes from a time when shipments of madeira were left awaiting pickup on one of the island's beaches, during which time the barrels absorbed water during rain showers. This diluted the alcohol and created a less potent wine. The four styles of madeira were originally made from the classic VARIETALS—Sercial, Verdelho, Boal, and MALVASIA (called *Malmsey* on the island of Madeira)—but since the late 1800s, more TINTA NEGRA MOLE and COMPLEXA grapes have been used, especially in the cheaper versions. In 1986, however, Portugal entered the European Common Market, whose regulations require that by 1993 any madeira wine naming a variety on its label must contain at least 85 percent of that grape. This labeling requirement has caused an upsurge in replanting of the four classic vines. Wines labeled "Boal-style" or "Sercial-style" can contain less than the required 85 percent and most likely are made from Tinta Negra Mole and Complexa. 2. A generic name used for dessert wines made in the United States in an attempt to mimic true madeiras. These wines cannot compare with the Portuguese originals, but then they're a fraction of the price. *See also* FOLGASÃO.

Madera AVA [ma-DEHR-uh] Large but obscure APPELLATION in the mid CENTRAL VALLEY, southeast of Merced and northwest of Fresno. The AVA covers most of Madera County and the northern part of Fresno County. Because of the very warm weather, the area is covered with French Colombard (COLOMBARD), followed by CHENIN BLANC and increased planting of CHARDONNAY. The leading red varieties are ZINFANDEL, GRENACHE, and BARBERA. Although this area produces mostly inexpensive JUG WINES, there are two well-known PORT-style winemakers here—Ficklin Vineyards and Quady Winery.

maderisé [mad-DEHR-ee-zay] French for MADERIZED.

maderized *see* Glossary of Wine Tasting Terms, page 655

Made Wine *see* BRITISH WINE

Madiran AC [mah-dee-RAHN] The AC that encompasses the area around the village of Madiran, which is located in the Pyrenees foothills along the Adour River south of ARMAGNAC in southwestern France. Tannat is the principal grape of this APPELLATION'S red wines, which are generally TANNIC and ROUGH. CABERNET FRANC and CABERNET SAUVIGNON are sometimes used to SOFTEN the area's reds. White wines from this same geographic area are labeled with the PACHERENC DU VIC BILH AC.

M

Madrid *see* VINOS DE MADRID

magnum; double magnum *see* Wine Bottles, page 609

Maindreieck, Bereich *see* FRANKEN

Maindviereck, Bereich *see* FRANKEN

Maipo Valley [mah-EE-poa] Also called *Valle del Maipo*, this is Chile's oldest and most famous growing area. It's a subregion within the larger CENTRAL VALLEY region and lies just south of Santiago, Chile's capital city. Although Maipo isn't the largest area, it contains a considerable concentration of vineyards and a large representation of important producers, largely due to its close proximity to Santiago. Ocean breezes and elevation provide a number of cool growing areas within the region. The official areas within the Maipo Valley are Buin, Isla de Maipo, Melipilla, Pirque, Pueto Alto, Santiago, and Talagante. For the most part, this is red-wine country, with CABERNET SAUVIGNON the most celebrated and widely planted VARIETY. There are also good examples of CHARDONNAY, MERLOT, PINOT NOIR, SAUVIGNON BLANC, and SÉMILLON being produced.

Maipú *see* ARGENTINA

maître de chai [MEH-truh duh SHAY] French for "cellarmaster." This term is used in BORDEAUX to refer to the person in charge of the VINIFICATION and AGING of wines. The *maître de chai* needs to be a proficient winemaker and have a good palate.

Malaga *see* CINSAUT

Málaga DO [MA-luh-guh] A DO located in southern Spain, east of JEREZ and south of MONTILLA-MORILES. In the nineteenth century, there was a time that Málaga's sweet, FORTIFIED WINES were more famous than the acclaimed SHERRY from Jerez. But in the 1870s, PHYLLOXERA devastated the area, which has never recovered its glorious past. Today, Málaga has less than 1 percent of the vineyard land that it did in the nineteenth century. There are four subzones here, but *Zona Norte*, which is north of the city of Málaga, is the most important. The wines, which are made from PEDRO XIMÉNEZ or Moscatel (MUSCAT) and other white varieties like AIRÉN, come in a variety of styles ranging from DRY to sweet; most are FORTIFIED. Production of the sweeter versions consists of adding various elements such as **arrope** (cooked MUST that's been reduced by about two-thirds), **pantomina** or **vino de color** (an even more concentrated cooked must than arrope), and **vino maestro** and **vino borracho** (differing blends of grape juice and ALCOHOL). The label of a Málaga wine identifies its style—sweetness ranges from SECO to DULCE and colors are *blanco* (white), *dorado* (golden), *rojo-dorado* (tawny), *osuro* (dark), and *negro* (black). Other labeling information may indicate a VARIETAL WINE made entirely from either Pedro Ximénez or Moscatel. The term "Lagrima" on a label specifies a wine made purely from FREE RUN JUICE. Málaga's *Dulce Color* is the most popular style—dark and sweet with about 10 percent arrope added, which gives it a slight molasses characteristic. Better

M

Málaga wines come from a SOLERA SYSTEM like those used for making the best sherry wines. To qualify as Málaga DO wine, the wine must be shipped to and matured in the city of Málaga. *See also* SIERRAS DE MÁLAGA DO.

Malbec [mahl-BEHK] A French red-wine grape grown in BORDEAUX, in parts of the LOIRE VALLEY, and in CAHORS and that has risen to prominence in Argentina. In Bordeaux, where Malbec is called *Cot* or *Pressac*, it plays a subordinate role to and is usually BLENDED with CABERNET FRANC, CABERNET SAUVIGNON, and MERLOT. In the Loire Valley, Malbec again plays a lesser role because it's blended with GAMAY and Cabernet Franc. However, in Cahors it's a key variety, where dark-colored, full-flavored, TANNIC wines are produced, Malbec is the prominent variety, usually blended with small amounts of Merlot and Tannat. In Cahors, Malbec is called *Auxerrois*, which causes some confusion because it's unrelated to an entirely different variety—AUXERROIS BLANC. Malbec has gained international notice for the wines coming out of Argentina (where it is sometimes called FER) and it's now a key variety, especially in the Mendoza region. It's gaining in popularity in Chile, as well, but has only modest acreage in Australia and the United States.

Les Malconsort *see* VOSNE-ROMANÉE AC

Malepère *see* CÔTES DE LA MALEPÈRE AC

Malibu-Newton Canyon AVA Tiny 850-acre AVA located in Los Angeles County's Malibu area. Approved in 1996, this region is situated in Newton Canyon, a small area in the Santa Monica Mountains above Malibu. There is only one vineyard, Rosenthal, with 14 acres planted to CABERNET SAUVIGNON, 3 acres to CHARDONNAY, and a small amount of CABERNET FRANC and MERLOT. Wines from this area are currently produced in San Luis Obispo and sold under the Rosenthal-The Malibu Estate label.

malic acid *see* ACIDS; MALOLACTIC FERMENTATION

M

Malmsey [MAHM-zee] 1. The richest, darkest, and sweetest (though rarely cloying) of the MADEIRA wines. Originally made primarily with the MALVASIA grape (called *Malmsey* on the island of Madeira), this style of Madeira has recently included more TINTA NEGRA MOLE (which is considered a *good,* but not classic grape). This use is particularly prominent in the cheaper versions of Madeira. However, in 1986, Portugal entered the Common Market, whose regulations required that by 1993 any Madeira wine naming a grape variety on its label must contain at least 85 percent of that grape. This labeling requirement has caused an upsurge in replanting of the classic vines like Malvasia. Wines labeled "Malmsey-style" can contain less than the required 85 percent of Malvasia grapes and can be counted on to include more Tinta Negra Mole. 2. On the island of Madeira, Malmsey is another name for the MALVASIA grape. 3. Extremely sweet, strongly flavored wine popular in ancient Greece.

malolactic fermentation [ma-loh-LAK-tihk] A biochemical reaction, sometimes called SECONDARY FERMENTATION, where bacteria converts malic acid into lactic acid and carbon dioxide—no alcohol is produced. Because lactic acid is milder than malic acid, wines that undergo this process become softer and smoother. In addition, malolactic fermentation produces diacetyl (or biacetyl), which resembles the smell of heated butter and adds complexity to wine. Malolactic fermentation is a positive event in some cases, and most high-quality red wines and some white wines (including white Burgundies and California Chardonnays) undergo it. On the downside, the fruitiness of wines undergoing this process is diminished, and sometimes off-odors can result. Many white wines need malic acid's higher acidity to retain their crisp, lively character, and some are too delicate to withstand the potential off-odors that might be introduced. Many winemakers now encourage malolactic fermentation for some batches of their Chardonnay while inhibiting the process in others, thereby giving the final blend improved complexity while retaining fruitiness and higher acidity.

La Maltroie *see* CHASSANGE-MONTRACHET AC

Malvasia [mal-vah-SEE-ah; mal-VAH-zha] Grape that has existed for about 2,000 years. It's believed to have come from the area around the Aegean Sea, possibly from what is now the southwestern area of Turkey and the islands between Turkey and Greece. Malvasia is primarily a white-wine grape, but it has many known subvarieties, including a red version called **Malvasia Nera**. The red grape is chiefly grown in Italy—around Piedmont in the north and Puglia in the south. It produces very PERFUMY wines and lends a delightful fragrance to some Italian red wines. The white variations are better known, the most recognized strains being **Malvasia Bianca del Chianti**, **Malvasia del Lazio**, **Malvasia delle Lipari**, **Malvasia di Candia**, **Malvasia di Sardegna,** and **Malvasia Istiana** (or **Malvasia Friulana**). These white varieties are grown all around the Mediterranean in one form or another. They produce golden, perfumy, flavorful wines with hints of apricots, musk, and almonds. Unfortunately, Malvasia is not an extremely high-yielding vine and is being replaced by better-producing but less-flavorful grapes such as TREBBIANO in Italy and Viura (MACABEO) in Spain. Malvasia is made into a variety of finished wines—DRY, sweet, FORTIFIED, and SPARKLING—but probably is best known for its sweet fortified products. On the island of MADEIRA, the Malvasia variety is called *Malmsey* and is combined with TINTA NEGRA MOLE and VERDELHO. The sweetest and richest style of Madeira wine is also often referred to as MALMSEY. In Portugal, some port makers use Malvasia grapes in their WHITE PORT. The VERMENTINO grape, grown on CORSICA and SARDINIA, is thought to be related to Malvasia as well. **Malvasia Bianca** is also grown in California, mostly in the CENTRAL VALLEY, and is used primarily in sweet fortified wines. Malvasia is also called *Blanca-Roja, Früher Roter Malvasier,* and *Malvoisie* (although most French Malvoisie is not Malvasia), as well as a host of other names beginning with "Malvasia."

Malvoisie *see* MALVASIA

Malvoisie du Languedoc *see* BOURBOULENC

La Mancha DO [lah MAHN-chah] Spain's and Europe's largest designated quality-wine area, with around 420,000 acres of designated vineyard land (vineyards in La Mancha but not designated as part of the DO more than double the acreage). Ninety percent of it is planted with AIRÉN. La Mancha DO was once known for producing dull, yellowish, high-ALCOHOL, somewhat OXIDIZED wines. Now, however, thanks to earlier harvesting and new modern equipment and winemaking techniques, La Mancha is producing light, crisp, fruity, and slightly aromatic white wines that are gaining in image. The small amount of red wine from this area comes chiefly from the Cencibel (TEMPRANILLO) grape. Smaller amounts are made from Garnacha Tinta (GRENACHE) and Moravia. The new winemaking approaches are improving the La Mancha red-wine image as well. CABERNET SAUVIGNON, CHARDONNAY, and MERLOT are among the nonlocal varieties being introduced here.

M

Manchega *see* AIRÉN

Manchuela DO [MAHN-choo-lah] APPELLATION created in the Castile-La Mancha region in central Spain in 2000. It includes vineyards in both the Albacete and Cuenca provinces. Some of the area vineyards were previously a part of the huge LA MANCHA DO. Manchuela borders La Mancha along with the DOS of ALMANSA and UIEL-REQUENA. Red and ROSÉ wines can be made from BOBAL, CABERNET SAUVIGNON, TEMPRANILLO, Garnacha (GRENACHE), MERLOT, Monastrell (MOURVÈDRE), Moravia, and

SYRAH. ALCOHOL BY VOLUME must be a minimum of 12 percent for red wines and a minimum of 11.5 percent for rosé wines. White wines can be made from Albillo, CHARDONNAY, MACABEO, and SAUVIGNON BLANC. Their alcohol content must be a minimum of 11 percent.

Mandelaria; Mandelari [mahn-dee-layr-YAH] Popular red-grape variety, also called *Amorgiano*, that's grown on various Greek islands but mainly on Crete and Rhodes. It produces dark colored, TANNIC wines and is usually blended with other grape varieties to produce softer wines, except on Rhodes, where a VARIETAL WINE is produced.

Manjimup *see* PEMBERTON

Mannberg *see* HATTENHEIM

manzanilla *see* SHERRY

Maranges AC [mah-RAHNGzh] A small APPELLATION southwest of Santenay that's part of the CÔTE DE BEAUNE area of France's BURGUNDY region. In 1989, the Maranges AC replaced three former appellations—Cheilly-lès-Maranges, Dezize-lès-Maranges, and Sampigny-lès-Maranges. This area produces good, medium-bodied (*see* BODY) PINOT NOIR wines. There are a number of PREMIER CRU vineyards in the Maranges appellation, which may label their wines "Maranges," "Maranges Premier Cru," or "Maranges" plus the name of the premier cru vineyard. Prior to AC approval, many producers labeled their wines as CÔTE DE BEAUNE-VILLAGES, which they may still use along with Maranges Côte de Beaune. Red wines dominate the area's production, although white wines made from CHARDONNAY are also allowed.

marc [MARK; MAHR] 1. A French term (known as POMACE in English) for the residue (skins, pips, seeds, etc.) remaining after the juice has been PRESSED from the grapes. 2. A potent EAU DE VIE distilled (*see* DISTILLATION) from this mixture. It's the French counterpart to GRAPPA (the name used in Italy and California).

Marches; It. Marche [MAHR-kay] A region in central Italy running along the east coast on the Adriatic Sea between EMILIA-ROMAGNA and ABRUZZI. The Marches has about 60,000 vineyard acres and contains twelve DOC areas that produce about 20 percent of the region's total wine. The DOCs include Bianchello del Metauro, Colli Maceratesi, Colli Pesaresi, Esino, Falerio dei Colli Ascolani or Falerio, Lacrima di Morro d'Alba, Offida, ROSSO CONERO, ROSSO PICENO, VERDICCHIO DEI CASTELLI DI JESI, VERDICCHIO DI MATELICA, and Vernaccia di Serrapetrona. Lacrima,

MONTEPULCIANO, and SANGIOVESE are the primary red grapes, and MALVA-
SIA, TREBBIANO, and VERDICCHIO are the main white varieties.

Marchigiano *see* VERDICCHIO

Marcillac AC [mahr-see-LYAHK] A small APPELLATION located in
SOUTHWEST FRANCE east of the CAHORS AC. The area produces RED and
ROSÉ wines from at least 90 percent of the FER grape, blended with
small amounts of CABERNET SAUVIGNON, CABERNET FRANC, and/or MERLOT.
Young wines can be TANNIC with good amounts of ACIDITY but as they
AGE and SOFTEN have a PEPPERY, PERFUMED quality.

Marcobrunn [MAHR-koh-bruhn] A famous EINZELLAGE located in
Germany's RHEINGAU region between the villages of ERBACH and HATTEN-
HEIM. Marcobrunn's 13 acres are actually situated partly in both of these
villages. In 1971, however, a dispute was settled to the effect that all
wines produced are attached to the village of Erbach and therefore
labeled "Erbacher Marcobrunn." Wines from the Marcobrunn site are
generally full-bodied (*see* BODY), fragrant, and long-lived.

Les Marconnets *see* BEAUNE

Maréchal Foch [MAH-ray-shahl FOHSH] This red grape, officially
known as *Kuhlmann 1882*, is a widely grown French-American
HYBRID. It's a CROSS of Goldriesling and an American VITIS RIPARIA–VITIS
RUPESTRIS vine, the same parents of LEON MILLOT. Maréchal Foch is cultivated in the eastern United States and Canada (where it is often simply called *Foch*), but it is rarely found in France today. It produces
light, BEAUJOLAIS-like red wines.

Les Maréchaudes *see* CORTON

Margaret River An Australian wine region located about 200
miles south of the city of Perth in the South West Australia Zone of
WESTERN AUSTRALIA. Although vineyards were first planted in the nineteenth century, this is considered a relatively new area because major
vineyards weren't reestablished until the late 1960s. The red wines,
which attracted considerable attention, didn't reach the market until
the mid-1970s. The Margaret River wines are known for their elegance
in contrast to the FRUIT BOMBS produced throughout much of Australia.
This beautiful region is uniquely bounded on three sides by water—
to the south is the Southern Ocean, to the west is the Indian Ocean,
and to the north is Geographe Bay. This results in a maritime-influ-
enced climate that, when combined with the area's Mediterranean
environment, produces a setting of only small temperature fluctua-

M

tions. Margaret River has about 7,500 acres of vineyards. Grape varieties grown in this region include CABERNET SAUVIGNON, Shiraz (SYRAH), MERLOT, PINOT NOIR, CHARDONNAY, SÉMILLON, SAUVIGNON BLANC, CHENIN BLANC, and RIESLING.

Margaux AC [mahr-GOH] APPELLATION considered one of the best areas within the MÉDOC district of France's BORDEAUX region. It not only encompasses vineyards around the village of Margaux but also includes those of the villages of Arsac, Cantenac, Issan, Labarde, and Soussans. The Margaux AC has twenty-one CRU CLASSÉ châteaux, more than any of the other Médoc COMMUNE appellations. Heading the list is the PREMIER CRU Château Margaux, followed by other top châteaux including d'Issan, Malescot-St.-Exupéry, Palmer, and Rausan-Segla. The wines from the Margaux AC can be very PERFUMY and exhibit a wonderful silkiness (see SILKY) and ELEGANCE. They're made from CABERNET FRANC, CABERNET SAUVIGNON, MERLOT, and PETIT VERDOT.

Maria Gomes see FERNÃO PIRES

Marino DOC [mah-REE-noh] DOC area that sits in the CASTELLI ROMANI area southeast of Rome in Italy's LATIUM region. The wines are made from MALVASIA, TREBBIANO, Bonvino, and Cacchione. Most of the wines produced are STILL and DRY, although AMABILE and SPUMANTE are also permitted. Marino's wines are very similiar to those from its better-known neighbor FRASCATI DOC.

Markgräflerland, Bereich [MARK-grehf-luhr-lahnt] A large BEREICH (subregion) located in the southern part of Germany's BADEN region. It runs along the Rhine River, south from the University city of Freiburg to Basel on the Swiss border. The wines from this area are generally mild and rather neutral but quite pleasant. Gutedel (CHASSELAS) is the most popular grape variety, along with MÜLLER-THURGAU and Spätburgunder (PINOT NOIR).

M

Marlborough New Zealand's most important winegrowing region, located around Cloudy Bay on the north end of the South Island right across Cook's Strait from New Zealand's capital city Wellington. It was named Cloudy Bay in 1770, by Captain Cook because of its murky look (caused by silt from the Wairau River). Vines were first planted in this area in the 1870s, but it took over a hundred years before the region truly blossomed. This occurred in 1973, when Montana (New Zealand's largest wine company) planted vines at their Brancott Estate vineyard. Additional wineries were slow to come, and it wasn't until the 1980s and 1990s that this region took off like a rocket because of one grape—SAUVIGNON BLANC. There were many who thought this cool maritime climate would be unsuitable for premium grape varieties. But for Sauvignon Blanc, the moderately warm days, cool nights, light rainfall, and plentiful sunshine have proven magical. In 2002, Marlborough was New Zealand's largest growing area with nearly 13,000 acres, about 40 percent of the country's total vineyards. Marlborough Sauvignon Blancs, especially those from Cloudy Bay Vineyards, have received worldwide recognition. Because of this, Sauvignon Blanc is now planted in about half the vineyards. Also planted here are CHARDONNAY, PINOT NOIR, RIESLING, and CABERNET SAUVIGNON. This cool climate lends itself to producing high-quality SPARKLING WINES—a large amount of Pinot Noir and some Chardonnay is used for such wines. There are also high hopes for Pinot Noir (for which this region may yet develop a reputation) to be used in STILL WINES. Riesling also produces very good wines here.

Marmajuelo [mahr-mah-HWAY-lah] White-grape variety, also referred to as *Bermejuela*, that's adapted well to the TERRIOR of the CANARY ISLANDS, the Spanish islands off the coast of Morocco. Although still not widely planted, Marmajuelo is gaining recognition for its ability to create high-quality wines in this region.

Marmandais *see* CÔTES DU MARMANDAIS AC

Marqués *see* LOUREIRO

Marsala DOC [mahr-SAH-lah] DOC that produces Italy's most famous FORTIFIED WINES. The DOC vineyards are located around the old seaside port city of Marsala on the western tip of SICILY. This area has a long history of making this style of fortified wine, going back to Roman times and later, during Spanish rule, when sherrylike wines were made here. In the late 1700s, however, an Englishman by the name of John Woodhouse devised today's conventional techniques for making Marsala and subsequently developed its following in England. As with other fortified wines, like SHERRY and MADEIRA, much of a Marsala's flavor comes from OXIDATION during aging. Marsala wines come in various styles—secco (DRY), semisecco (semisweet), and dolce (sweet). The wines are initially VINIFIED completely dry and must reach a minimum of 12 percent ALCOHOL. Depending on the quality level, this dry wine may be supplemented with a concentrated MUST; a cooked, reduced must (called **cotto** or **musto cotto**) that acquires a carmelized flavor; and/or a mixture of grape alcohol and sweet must known as **sifone** (sometimes called **mistella** and similar to the French MISTELLE). The various quality levels for Marsala are *Fine,*

M

Superiore, Superiore Riserva, Vergine, and *Vergine Stravecchio* or *Vergine Riserva.* **Fine**, which is the lowest level and the most commonly found, has a minimum alcohol level of 17 percent and requires 1 year of AGING. **Superiore** must have a minimum of 18 percent alcohol and 2 years aging in wood, and **Superiore Riserva** must have a minimum of 4 years of wood aging. Superiore may also be called *Giaribaldi Dolce (GD), London Particular (LP),* or *Superior Old Marsala (SOM).* The highest-quality Marsala is **Vergine**, which may be fortified with grape alcohol but cannot have any concentrated must, cotto, or sifone added; it requires aging in wood for a minimum of 5 years. Vergine can be **stravecchio** or RISERVA, which must be aged in wood for a minimum of 10 years. Vergine wines are dry and austere with a distinctive caramel or toffee flavor and hints of smoked wood. Dry Marsalas, especially the Vergine styles, are best served as APÉRITIFS, whereas many of the semisweet and sweet styles are best as DESSERT WINES. In 1984, the official terms of **ambra** (amber), **oro** (gold), and **rubino** (ruby) became optional additional descriptions for any of the Marsala wine's quality levels. Ambra and oro describe Marsala wines made from white grapes—CATARRATTO, Inzolia, GRILLO, and Damaschino. The addition of cotto is not allowed in the ambra versions. Ambra wines darken as they age, turning from the paler yellowish hues, to gold, to amber. The term rubino describes Marsala wines made from red grapes—Perricone, Calabrese, and NERELLO (though up to 30 percent of any of the aforementioned white grapes can also be used). **Cremevo** (*Cremevo Zabaione Vino Aromatizzato*) is a wine made from 80 percent Marsala and other flavorings like coffee or egg and was once called **Marsala Speciali**.

Marsana *see* MARSANNE

Marsannay AC [mahr-sah-NAY] In 1987, this became the first new village APPELLATION to be established in the CÔTE D'OR area since the 1930s. The village of Marsannay, also called *Marsannay-la-Côte*, is located at the northern end of the CÔTE DE NUITS (the northern portion of the Côte d'Or) in France's BURGUNDY region. The Marsannay AC covers all three categories of wine (red, white, and ROSÉ), which is unique for this area. Prior to receiving their own AC status, red wines from this area were sold as **Bourgogne Marsannay-la-Côte AC**, and rosé wines, as **Bourgogne Marsannay-la-Côte Rosé AC**. Marsanny AC wines are generally considered comparable to those from the CÔTE DE NUITS-VILLAGES.

Marsanne [mahr-SAHN] White-wine grape that is widely grown in France's northern RHÔNE region and that is the principal grape in the white wines of CROZES-HERMITAGE, HERMITAGE, SAINT JOSEPH, and SAINT PÉRAY. Small amounts of Marsanne are also grown in Australia, Switzerland, and the United States. Marsanne, which is usually BLENDED with ROUSSANNE in the Rhône whites, is also officially sanctioned in the Hermitage red wines. Traditionally made white wines can be full-bodied (*see* BODY), heavy, and somewhat dull when young but can develop magnificently with age. Wines made with more modern methods can be lighter and fruitier, with a perfumy fragrance; they should be drunk young. Marsanne is also known as *Ermitage, Hermitage Blanc, Marsana,* and *Grosse Roussette.*

Marselan [mahr-say-lahn] Red-grape variety created by the French National Institute for Agricultural Research (INRA) in the early 1960s by CROSSING CABERNET SAUVIGNON with GRENACHE. After being disregarded for over 30 years because growers didn't think it produced a large enough crop, Marselan began to be planted in the LANGUEDOC-ROUSSILON region in France. Early results indicate Marselan can produce good quality wines.

Martha's Vineyard; Martha's Vineyard AVA 1. A famous 40-acre vineyard located south of the town of Oakville in the western part of California's NAPA VALLEY. The vineyard is planted with CABERNET SAUVIGNON and produces (under the Heitz Cellars label) one of the most sought-after California red wines. These RICH, full-bodied (*see* BODY), long-lived wines are known for their minty/eucalyptus character, noticeable in most VINTAGES. The eucalyptus flavor is thought by some to come from the grove of eucalyptus trees that surround the vineyard. 2. Also a Massachusetts AVA, which encompasses 64,000 acres on the islands of Martha's Vineyard and Chappaquiddick. It has only one winery, Chicama Vineyards, which grows CABERNET SAUVIGNON, CHARDONNAY, CHENIN BLANC, GEWÜRZTRAMINER, MERLOT, PINOT NOIR, and RIESLING.

M

Martinborough *see* WELLINGTON

Maryland Grape growing and winemaking in this Mid-Atlantic state appear to have started as early as the mid-1600s when both native American vines and European varieties (VITIS VINIFERA) were grown and made into wine. The European varieties were not successful because of their susceptibility to local pests and disease—elements to which the local varieties had adapted. On the other hand, wines from local varieties didn't taste that good. Over the centuries, numerous attempts were made with hybrids, *Vitis vinifera,* and with GRAFTING of *Vitis vinifera* to native vine rootstocks (to solve the PHYLLOXERA problems)—all with limited success. In the 1940s, Phillip Wagner made a concerted effort to obtain as many hybrid vines as possible, which he then propagated and sold to other grape growers. This boosted the viticulture industry not only in Maryland but all around the eastern seaboard. Today, Maryland has three VITICULTURAL AREAS—the CATOCTIN AVA, the LINGANORE AVA, and the CUMBERLAND AVA (which it shares with PENNSYLVANIA). As in most of the eastern and midwestern states, hybrids like CHAMBOURCIN, CHARDONEL, SEYVAL BLANC, and VIDAL BLANC play a major role. But good *Vitis vinifera* wines are made from CABERNET SAUVIGNON, CHARDONNAY, MERLOT, and RIESLING. Maryland has over a dozen wineries—Boordy Vineyards is one of the best-known (given that it was started in 1945 by Phillip Wagner) and is the state's second largest winery behind Berrywine Plantation–Linganore Cellars.

Marzemina Bianca *see* CHASSELAS

mas [mahs] The word used in southern France for DOMAINE.

masculine *see* MUSCULAR in the *see* Glossary of Wine Tasting Terms, page 655

Massachusetts This New England state has two VITICULTURAL AREAS—the SOUTHEASTERN NEW ENGLAND AVA, which it shares with RHODE ISLAND and CONNECTICUT, and MARTHA'S VINEYARD AVA. The area wineries make a number of wines from HYBRIDS like VIDAL BLANC, SEYVAL BLANC, CHANCELLOR, CAYUGA, MARÉCHAL FOCH, and AURORA. VITIS VINIFERA varieties here include CHARDONNAY, CABERNET SAUVIGNON, PINOT NOIR, MERLOT, CABERNET FRANC, and RIESLING. Some grapes are also brought in from LONG ISLAND and CALIFORNIA. FRUIT WINES play an import role at some of the wineries. Westport River Vineyard and Winery, producer of SPARKLING WINES, is probably the best known winery. Chicama Vineyards on Martha's Vineyard was the first BONDED winery in the state.

masseria [mahs-suh-REE-uh] A term used mainly in southern Italy, referring to a wine-producing farm or estate. *See also* FATTORIA.

massive *see* Glossary of Wine Tasting Terms, page 655

mass selection *see* CLONAL SELECTION

Master of Wine A title earned by passing extensive tasting and written examinations given by the Institute of Masters of Wine, a British organization established in the 1950s. The examinations include BLIND TASTINGS of about three dozen wines and written tests on

VITICULTURE, VINIFICATION, and various aspects of the wine trade. The Master of Wine title was available only to British citizens until 1988, when non-British citizens were allowed to apply. Taking and passing the test culminates intensive schooling and at least 5 years experience working in the wine trade. A Master of Wine may put the initials M. W. after his or her name.

master sommelier *see* SOMMELIER

Matakana *see* AUCKLAND

Mataro *see* MOURVÈDRE

maturation of wine *see* AGING

mature; maturity *see* Glossary of Wine Tasting Terms, page 655

Mäuerchen *see* GEISENHEIM

Maule Valley [MAO-lay] Known locally as *Valle del Maule,* this important Chilean wine area is the southernmost subregion within the larger CENTRAL VALLEY region. It's located around the town of Talca, which lies about 170 miles south of Santiago, CHILE's capital city. There are three principal zones within the Maule Valley: Del Claro Valley, within which are three areas (Pencahue, San Clemente, and Talca); Loncomilla Valley, which includes four areas (Linares, Parral, San Javier, and Villa Alegre); and Tutuvén Valley, with its one area of Cauquenes. Maule Valley's weather is cool and wet, and though irrigation isn't required, it's sometimes used. The dominant grape here is *Pais* (MISSION), although higher-quality grapes like CABERNET FRANC, CABERNET SAUVIGNON, CARMENÈRE, MERLOT, SAUVIGNON BLANC, and SÉMILLON are making inroads.

Maury AC [moh-*R*EE] A little village located northwest of Perpignan in the southern part of France's vast LANGUEDOC-ROUSSILLON region. The vineyards surrounding Maury make up this AC, which makes both ROSÉ and red VIN DOUX NATUREL from the GRENACHE grape. The wines are available in both a young, fresh style and a RANCIO style, which has an OXIDIZED character.

Mavrodaphne [mahv-rroh-DAHF-nee] Popular Greek red-wine grape grown along the Gulf of Corinth. It is generally made into a sweet, full-bodied, AROMATIC, lightly FORTIFIED WINE. The name, which translates to "black laurel," comes from the resemblance this grape has to the laurel berry. The celebrated Mavrodaphne wines spend their first summer in oak barrels outside, basking in the sunshine. This technique allows the wine to SOFTEN into a pleasant DESSERT WINE.

Mavrodaphne of Patras *see* GREECE

Maximin Grünhaus [MAHK-sih-mihn GRYOON-howss] A tiny village located on the Ruwer River in Germany's MOSEL-SAAR-RUWER region. It's actually classified as an ORSTEIL that's part of the village of Mertesdorf. Maximin Grünhaus has approximately 80 acres that have been owned by the von Schubert family since 1882. The vineyards are broken into three EINZELLAGEN (individual vineyard sites)—**Bruderberg** at the bottom, **Herrenberg** in the upper section, and **Abtsberg**, the steep middle section that produces the best grapes. The wines from each Einzellagen are labeled separately, using the village's name. The wines are highly regarded, and those from good VINTAGES are capable of AGING for around 20 years.

May wine Originally a German specialty, this is a punch made from sweet, light wine infused with aromatic woodruff leaves. It's served cold with fruit (usually strawberries) floating in it.

Mazis-Chambertin AC [mah-ZEE shah*m*-behr-TAN] A 22½-acre GRAND CRU vineyard that adjoins that of the better-known CHAMBERTIN-CLOS DE BÈZE. Mazis-Chambertin is located in the village of GEVREY-CHAMBERTIN in the CÔTE DE NUITS district of France's BURGUNDY region. The general quality of its red (PINOT NOIR) wines is extremely high, and they're considered some of the best in the world. These wines are deep-colored, RICH, CONCENTRATED, and TANNIC, which makes them prime candidates for long aging (15 to 25 years for the best ones). *See also* CHAMBERTIN.

Mazoyères-Chambertin AC *see* CHARMES-CHAMBERTIN

Mazuela *see* CARIGNAN

Mazuelo *see* CARIGNAN

MCC *see* METHODE CAPE CLASSIQUE

McDowell Valley AVA Small California VITICULTURAL AREA in MENDOCINO COUNTY between the town of Hopland on the west and the large CLEAR LAKE AVA on the east. It's a subregion of the larger MENDOCINO and NORTHCOAST AVAS. The only winery here is McDowell Valley Vineyards and, although the winemaking facility itself has been sold and turned into a custom crush facility run by Associated Vintage Group, the wines are still made there. McDowell specializes in RHÔNE varieties like SYRAH, GRENACHE, MOURVÈDRE, CINSAULT, and VIOGNIER.

McLaren Vale An Australian wine region located in the Fleurieu Zone of SOUTH AUSTRALIA. It's situated on the coast a little over 20 miles south of Adelaide around the town of McLaren Vale. Vines were first planted in this region in 1838 at Reynella, but the wine industry was slow to develop until the late 1870s. Then there was expansion for several decades, and by the early 1900s McLaren Vale had established itself as one of Australia's important wine-producing regions—an identity it maintained throughout the twentieth century. Today there are over fifty wineries and about 13,000 acres of vineyards. McLaren Vale is known for its BIG, FULL-BODIED red wines—Shiraz (SYRAH), CABERNET SAUVIGNON, MERLOT, and GRENACHE. This region's CHARDONNAY, SAUVIGNON BLANC, and SÉMILLON also enjoy excellent reputations.

McMinnville AVA APPELLATION created in March 2005 within the larger WILLAMETTE VALLEY AVA. Its 40,500 acres are located in the foothills of Yamhill County in northwestern Oregon about 40 miles southwest of Portland, just west of the city of McMinnville (home of the annual International Pinot Noir Celebration). Currently there are 14 wineries in this APPELLATION and about 600 acres planted mainly to PINOT NOIR but also to CHARDONNAY, PINOT BLANC, PINOT GRIS, and RIESLING.

mead [MEED] A beverage made by fermenting (*see* FERMENTATION) honey, water, and yeast with flavorings such as herbs, spices, or flowers. Mead dates back to Biblical times and was popular in early England. Although not widely distributed today, it is still bottled.

meaty *see* Glossary of Wine Tasting Terms, page 655

mechanical pruning *see* PRUNING

Médoc [may-DAWK] BORDEAUX's largest and best-known wine region. It's located on the triangular piece of land between the Atlantic Ocean and the Gironde estuary in western France. It stretches some 50 miles, from just below the Pointe de Grave at the peninsula's northern point, to south of the village of Blanquefort just outside the northern suburbs of the city of Bordeaux. The Médoc region is broken into the Bas-Médoc ("lower" Médoc) and the HAUT-MÉDOC ("upper" Médoc) and, in addition to the standard Bordeaux APPELLATIONS, includes two area and six village appellations. The **Bas-Médoc** is the area from the northern point down to just above the village of Saint-Seurin-de-Cardourne north of SAINT-ESTÈPHE. This area, which has the least desirable soil, produces good-quality wines but generally not great ones. The Bas-Médoc red wines are covered under the **Médoc AC**, one of the two area appellations—the other being the **Haut-Médoc AC**, which is also only for red wines. (White wines throughout the Médoc are simply

M

labeled BORDEAUX AC or BORDEAUX SUPÉRIEUR AC.) The **Haut-Médoc** area, which covers the southern portion of the Médoc, extending from just north of the city of Bordeaux to the Bas-Médoc, is where the best and most famous Médoc châteaux are located. The Haut-Médoc AC encompasses all of this area except for the six village appellations of LISTRAC, MARGAUX, MOULIS, PAUILLAC, Saint-Estèphe, and SAINT-JULIEN. In general, wines labeled with the individual village appellations are better than those with the "Haut-Médoc AC," which are better than those labeled "Médoc AC." The main red grapes used throughout the Médoc are CABERNET FRANC, CABERNET SAUVIGNON, and MERLOT, with occasional use of PETIT VERDOT and minute amounts of MALBEC. The Classification of 1855 (*see* Official Wine Classifications of Bordeaux, page 678), which created five tiers of CRUS CLASSÉS (Classed Growths) for red wines, was limited to sixty-one châteaux—all in the Médoc with the exception of GRAVES' Château Haut-Brion. Included in this classification's top category of PREMIER CRU (first growth) are the châteaux of Lafite-Rothschild, Latour, and Mouton-Rothschild (all from Pauillac AC); Margaux from Margaux AC; and Haut-Brion from Graves. Just below the cru classé category is that of CRU BOURGEOIS, which was established for the better châteaux that didn't qualify for the top grouping. There are numerous cru bourgeois châteaux in the Médoc, and a majority of these are in the Haut-Médoc area. The classification system provides some guidance to the quality of wines from the Médoc, although many feel it's outdated and needs revision. *See also* Summary of the 1855 Classification page 679.

Médoc Noir *see* MERLOT, MENOIRE

meio-seco [may-oo-SAY-koo] Portuguese term meaning "half-DRY," referring to wine that is slightly sweet.

La Méjanelle *see* GRÉS DE MONTPELLIER

Mélinots *see* CHABLIS

mellow *see* Glossary of Wine Tasting Terms, page 655

Melon d'Arbois *see* CHARDONNAY

Melon de Bourgogne [meh-loh*n* duh boor-GAWN-yuh] Although this French white-wine grape originated in BURGUNDY, it has now all but vanished from that region. Those that are still grown in Burgundy go into the BOURGOGNE GRAND ORDINAIRE wines. Melon de Bourgogne, however, is widely planted in the LOIRE, particularly in the Pays Nantais region where the grape and the wine is known as **Muscadet**. The grape's popularity in this part of the Loire is related to its ability to withstand cold weather and to its tendency to ripen early and produce a large crop. Unfortunately, most wines produced from this grape are viewed as insipid in flavor. The best wines are those from the APPELLATION of MUSCADET DE SÈVRE-ET-MAINE and are labeled *mise en bouteille sur lie,* which means that they're bottled directly off the LEES without filtering. This process can produce flavorful wines that are SOFT and CREAMY with hints of CITRUS. It was discovered that a variety growing on the grounds of the UNIVERSITY OF CALIFORNIA, DAVIS, which was thought to be PINOT BLANC, was actually Melon de Bourgogne. It's now believed that many of the wines called Pinot Blanc in California are really Melon de Bourgogne. This grape is also known as *Lyonnaise Blanche* and *Weisserburgunder.*

Mencía [mehn-THEE-ah; mehn-SEE-ah] Red-wine grape grown mainly in Spain's northwest region, particularly the BIERZO, RIBEIRA SACRA, and VALDEORRAS DOS. It's indigenous to this region, but it's only been in the last decade that Mencía has developed an international following. This is mainly due to the discovery of hillside vineyards of OLD VINE Mencía and the high EXTRACT, complex wines being produced. Until then light, delicate, and fruity wines were the norm. Long thought to be related to CABERNET FRANC, DNA FINGERPRINTING indicates that Mencía is not related. Descriptors commonly used to describe the Mencía wines include FLORAL, licorice, EARTHY, plum, black cherry, MEATY, and RUSTIC.

Mendocino County; Mendocino AVA [mihn-doh-SEE-noh] **Mendocino County** is north of San Francisco and is the northernmost county in the NORTH COAST AVA. In addition to proposed (but not approved) non-AVA areas like Sanel Valley and Ukiah Valley, the county contains nine approved AVAs—ANDERSON VALLEY, COLE RANCH, DOS RIOS, MCDOWELL VALLEY, Mendocino, MENDOCINO RIDGE, POTTER VALLEY, REDWOOD VALLEY, and YORKVILLE HIGHLANDS. The **Mendocino AVA** is situated in the county's southern portion and encompasses all the other AVAs, as well as the Sanal and Ukiah Valleys. The climate varies throughout this area, ranging from a cool Region I (*see* CLIMATE REGIONS OF CALIFORNIA) rating for the Anderson Valley to a Region III for most other parts of Mendocino. CHARDONNAY is the most widely planted variety, followed by ZINFANDEL, CABERNET SAUVIGNON, CARIGNANE, and SAUVIGNON BLANC. Other grapes grown here are COLOMBARD, RIESLING, GEWÜRZTRAMINER, PINOT NOIR, and PETITE SIRAH.

M

Mendocino Ridge AVA Because it covers only the areas at or above an elevation of 1,200 feet in the Mendocino Range, this is the only AVA in the United States with noncontiguous areas. It's located

west of the ANDERSON VALLEY (although it includes some higher elevations of the Anderson Valley), from the Sonoma-Mendocino County
line near Gualala in the south to where the Navarro River spills into
the Pacific Ocean near Albion in the north. The 1,200-foot level was
chosen for this AVA because the fog that's sucked in off the Pacific
during the summer growing season seldom climbs that high. The
ridges above this level receive more sunshine and some but not all of
the cooling effect. Mendocino Ridge encompasses some 262,000 acres
but only about 87,000 are high enough to qualify as part of the AVA;
of these, less than 2,000 acres are considered plantable. At this writing, there are less than 100 acres planted. Greenwood Ridge
Vineyards (whose tasting room is in the Anderson Valley) grows
CABERNET SAUVIGNON, MERLOT, PINOT NOIR, and RIESLING on Greenwood
Ridge, one of the many named ridges in this APPELLATION.

Mendoza *see* ARGENTINA

Menetou-Salon AC [meh-neh-TOO sah-LOHN] APPELLATION located
near the more famous SANCERRE AC in western France's upper LOIRE
Valley. There are ten small villages whose wines are covered by this
appellation. Although the white wines, which are made from SAUVI-
GNON BLANC, are compared to those of Sancerre, they're not equal to
Sancerre's best. On the other hand, the red and ROSÉ wines, made from
PINOT NOIR, are as good or better than Sancerre's.

meniscus *see* Glossary of Wine Tasting Terms, page 655

Menoire [mehm-WAH] This red-wine grape, also sometimes called
Kékmedoc, Morne Noir, and *Medoc Noir,* is grown in various parts of
Hungary, including around Eger, and is an allowed grape in the
famous EGRI BIKAVÉR. It's thought to be related to ALEATICO or Mornen
Noir.

M

Méntrida DO [mayn-TRREE-dah] This large but obscure DO is
located southwest of Madrid in Spain's CASTILLA-LA MANCHA region.
Because most of the wine produced is sold in BULK, not much of what
is bottled is seen outside of central Spain. This DO produces red and
ROSÉ wines. The main grape used is Garnacha Tinta (GRENACHE), along
with some Cencibel (TEMPRANILLO) and Tinto Madrid. Most of these
wines are mediocre in quality and high in ALCOHOL (ranging from 13 to
18 percent). Méntrida is slowly modernizing and adopting new winemaking approaches in an effort to improve wine quality. COOPERATIVES
dominate the area's winemaking and have joined in this effort.

mercaptans [mer-KAP-tuhns] The result of HYDROGEN SULFIDE combining with wine components like yeast and producing a pungently offensive, sour odor that can smell like garlic, stale sweat, skunk, or rubber. Mercaptan characteristics in a wine are often a sign of careless winemaking and signal the wine's deterioration. However, mercaptans (also called *thiols*) aren't always foul smelling. Some have positive traits such as those providing SAUVIGNON BLANC'S varietal character, while others provide hints of black currant, grapefruit, passion fruit and smoke. Toasted oak barrels may release a mercaptan reminiscent of coffee during barrel AGING.

Mercier *see* CHAMPAGNE

Mercurey AC [meh*r*-kyoo-*R*EH] The biggest and the most important of the five villages with individual APPELLATION status in the CÔTE CHALONNAISE in France's BURGUNDY region. About 95 percent of the wine produced is red, made from PINOT NOIR. The red wines are thought to be the best of the Côte Chalonnaise, comparable to a good CÔTE-DE-BEAUNE-VILLAGES AC wine from the better-known neighboring area to the north. The area produces a small amount of white wine, made from CHARDONNAY. These flavorful, LIGHT, CRISP white wines are meant to be drunk young. A number of major wine firms from other parts of Burgundy own land in Mercurey. This gives these wines better representation than other Côte Chalonnaise wines, both in France and internationally. The Mercurey wines have such presence that the Côte Chalonnaise is occasionally referred to as *Région de Mercurey,* and there is pressure to change the name formally.

Meritage [MEHR-ih-tihj] Instituted in 1989, the term *Meritage* is a certification mark registered with the U.S. Department of Trademarks and Patents. It was coined in 1988 by a group of vintners who sought to establish standards of identification for a category of American blended wines made with traditional BORDEAUX grape varieties. The name Meritage (a compound of the words *merit* and *heritage*) was chosen from over 6,000 entries in an international contest held by these vintners. The purpose of The Meritage Association is to help identify quality American wine blends that, because they're not made with at least 75 percent of a single variety, can't use the variety name on the label. This forced many producers of excellent wines to either use generic names (like CLARET or Red TABLE WINE) or PROPRIETARY names (like *Insignia* from Joseph Phelps Vineyards). Both practices caused great confusion in the marketplace. To be designated as Meritage, a wine must meet the following standards: 1. It must be a blend of two

M

or more Bordeaux grape varieties—for red wines these are CABERNET FRANC, CABERNET SAUVIGNON, Carmenere, Gros Verdot, MALBEC, MERLOT, PETIT VERDOT, and St. Macaire; and for whites they're SAUVIGNON BLANC, MUSCADELLE, and SÉMILLON (no more than 90 percent of any single variety may go into a Meritage wine); 2. It must be the winery's best wine of its type; 3. It must be produced and bottled by a U.S. winery from grapes that carry a U.S. APPELLATION; and 4. Its production is limited to a maximum 25,000 cases per VINTAGE. Wineries that are approved for the Meritage designation may use it in various ways on the label. They may simply use the term "Meritage" or use "Meritage" in conjunction with their own PROPRIETARY name (as with *Cardinale* from Kendall-Jackson Vineyards), or they may use only their proprietary name.

Merlau *see* MERLOT

Merlau Blanc *see* MERLOT BLANC

Merlot [mehr-LOH; mer-LOH] Though commonly referrred to as simply *Merlot*, this red-wine grape is really **Merlot Noir** (there's also a MERLOT BLANC variety). Merlot is the primary grape in SAINT-ÉMILION and POMEROL and one of two primaries (the other being CABERNET SAUVIGNON) of BORDEAUX. Merlot acreage in the DÉPARTEMENT of GIRONDE, which encompasses most of Bordeaux, is almost twice that of Cabernet Sauvignon. However, Merlot has never been as highly regarded as Cabernet Sauvignon, which dominates in the MÉDOC and GRAVES—growing areas that produce wines traditionally viewed as Bordeaux's most important. Much of the wine world views Merlot as simply a grape to be blended with Cabernet Sauvignon or CABERNET FRANC. Still, Merlot can produce great wines like those of Pomerol's Château Pétrus, which makes one of the world's most expensive red wines, most of which are 100 percent Merlot. Merlot is also widely planted in other areas of France. Growers in the LANGUEDOC-ROUSSILLON region, for instance, are being encouraged to plant this grape to improve the vast quantities of wine produced there. Merlot is grown extensively throughout the world but has developed a tarnished reputation from overproduction in areas like northeastern Italy. It's an extremely important grape in Italy's FRIULI-VENEZIA GIULIA and VENETO regions, which produce some great Merlots. This grape is widely grown in eastern Europe with sizable plantings in Bulgaria, Hungary, and Romania. Australians have been slow to adopt Merlot because their dominate grape SHIRAZ is often used for blending with Cabernet Sauvignon. In California and Washington, Merlot was initially planted as a blending grape, but in the late 1970s it began to stand on its own as a variety and has been continually gaining popularity. California Merlot acreage has continued to increase, as have the number of wineries producing Merlot VARIETAL wines. This state's Merlot plantings have grown from several thousand acres in the mid-1980s to almost 50,000 acres by the end of the twentieth century. California's Duckhorn Vineyards, generally regarded as a leading producer of quality Merlot wines, has been producing them since the late 1970s. In French, the word *Merlot* means "young blackbird," probably alluding to the grape's beautiful dark-blue color. Compared to Cabernet Sauvignon, Merlot grapes ripen fairly early and have lower TANNINS and higher sugar levels. They produce wines that are generally SOFTER and with slightly higher ALCOHOL content. High-quality Merlot wines are medium to dark red in color, rich, and FRUITY, with characteristics of BLACKCURRANT, CHERRY, and MINT. Merlot wines are ROUNDER and more SUPPLE than Cabernet Sauvignons and usually can be enjoyed much earlier. Generally, Merlot wines do not AGE as long as Cabernet Sauvignons. A small amount of Cabernet Sauvignon or Cabernet Franc is often blended with Merlot grapes to give the wine a bit more STRUC-TURE. Merlot is also called *Bigney, Crabutet, Médoc Noir,* and *Merlau.*

Merlot Blanc [mehr-LOH BLAH*N*; mer-LOH BLAH*N*GK] Also called *Merlau Blanc,* this white-wine grape is not related to MERLOT (Noir). It's presumed that the name comes from the simple fact that the leaves of this variety resemble those of Merlot Noir. Merlot Blanc is an unimportant variety grown mainly in France's districts of Blaye, Bourg, and Fronsac, northeast of the city of Bordeaux. It generally produces low-quality wines.

Merritt Island AVA [MEHR-riht] Tiny VITICULTURAL AREA that is a sub-zone to the CLARKSBURG AVA and home of Bogle Vineyards and Winery. Merritt Island, a 5,000-acre man-made island, is south of Clarksburg in Yolo County. It's cooled by San Francisco Bay breezes and is generally considered a Region II growing area (*see* CLIMATE REGIONS OF CALIFORNIA). The variety that's done the best here is CHENIN BLANC.

M

Mesilla Valley AVA This APPELLATION contains approximately 284,800 acres beginning at the far west tip of the TEXAS border, near El Paso, and flowing into southern NEW MEXICO, ending slightly north of Las Cruces. Much of the area is over the 4,000-foot level, which offers a hospitable environment for grape growing because of its hot dry days and cool nights. It's believed that this may be one of the oldest winegrowing regions in the U.S., dating back to the late 1500s.

Area wineries include Blue Teal Vineyards, La Vina Winery, and Mademoiselle de Sante Fe.

Mesnil, Le [meh-neel, luh] GRAND CRU village in the Côte des Blancs district in the CHAMPAGNE region. Its full name is Le Mesnil-sur-Oger, but it is usually referred to simply as Le Mesnil or Mesnil. The vineyards surrounding the village are renowned for the CHARDONNAY grapes that are grown here; a special clone is grown that gives the SPARKLING WINES of the village their special style. The Champagnes of this area can be RACY when young, but evolve with age to become COMPLEX with hints of almond, toffee, and vanilla. The village includes the famous Clos du Mesnil vineyard, which encompasses 4½ acres planted with grapes in 1698 and is completely surrounded by stone walls. The Champagne house of Charles Krug owns the vineyard and the grapes go into their top cuvee, aptly named "Clos du Mesnil."

mesoclimate The discrete climatic conditions of a specific localized area, usually measured in terms of tens of yards, sometimes hundreds of yards if there is a consistent set of traits for a larger area. Mesoclimate falls between the larger MACROCLIMATE and the smaller MICROCLIMATE. It's often used to refer to a specific vineyard site or portion of a site that is unique.

meta *see* POTASSIUM METABISULFITE

metallic *see* Glossary of Wine Tasting Terms, page 655

méthode ancestrale *see* RURAL METHOD

méthode artisnale *see* RURAL METHOD

Methode Cape Classique (MCC) Term created in South Africa in 1992 for sparkling wine made in the MÉTHODE CHAMPENOISE. Also known by the acronym "MCC."

M

méthode champenoise [may-TOHD shahm-peh-NWAHZ; may-TOD shahm-peh-NWAHZ] The traditional method of making SPARKLING WINE developed in France's CHAMPAGNE region. This process, referred to as the "champagne method," consists of taking various STILL WINES and blending them to make a CUVÉE that represents the style of a winery or champagne house. A complex cuvée can consist of as many as thirty to forty different wines. Once the various wines are blended in large blending vats, a bottling DOSAGE (also known as *dosage d'tirage* or *liqueur d'tirage*), a syrupy mixture of sugar and wine (and sometimes BRANDY and/or citric acid), is added along with special yeasts. The cuvée is then immediately bottled and corked (or often capped with a

CROWN CAP, which is much less expensive and just as effective). The sugar (in the bottling dosage) and the yeast cells cause a SECONDARY FERMENTATION to take place in the bottle. This results in the creation of additional alcohol and CARBON DIOXIDE gas, which gives the wine its effervescence or "sparkle." During this secondary fermentation, pressure in the bottle builds up to 90 to 110 pounds per square inch (psi). If less bottling dosage is used in the cuvée, there will be less pressure, which will result in a lightly sparkling wine style called CRÉMANT. Such wines have slightly more than half the pressure of a regular bottling. SEDIMENT is also thrown off during the second fermentation and is removed through the steps of RIDDLING (or *rémuage*) and DISGORGING (or *dégorgement*). Just before final bottling, a shipping dosage (*dosage d'expédition* or *liqueur d'expédition*), sugar, and some of the same cuvée (reserved for this purpose) is added. The percentage of sugar in the shipping dosage determines the degree of sweetness in the final wine. From driest (*see* DRY) to sweetest, sparkling wines are classified as BRUT, EXTRA DRY (or *extra-sec*), SEC, DEMI-SEC, or DOUX. Once the final handling is complete and the bottles are recorked, the final pressure in a standard bottle ranges from 60 to 90 psi (approximately 6 ATMO-SPHERES). The words "méthode champenoise" are used only on labels of wines that use this method. *See also* CHARMAT.

méthode classique [may-TOHD klah-SEEK] A term approved by the EUROPEAN UNION for SPARKING WINE made by the traditional method (often referred to as MÉTHODE CHAMPENOISE). The English term is "classical method."

méthode dioise *see* CLAIRETTE DE DIE

méthode gaillaçoise *see* GAILLAC; RURAL METHOD

méthode rurale *see* RURAL METHOD

méthode tradition *see* CLAIRETTE DE DIE

methoxy-dimethylpyrazine [meh-THOX-ee di-meh-thahl-HI-drah-zeen] A compound found in corks that taints them with an unpleasant woody, musty, and moldy aroma that's transferred to wine. Technically it's identified as 2-methoxy-3, 5-dimethylprazine with an acronym of MDMP. It's different than TCA or 2,4,6-Trichloroanisole which is usually associated with CORKED WINES. MDMP is now thought to be the second most common cause of wines ruined by cork taint after TCA.

M

Methuselah *see* Wine Bottles, page 609

metodo champenois [MEH-toh-doh shahm-peh-NWAHZ] Italian phrase for the French MÉTHODE CHAMPENOISE. However, because EEC regulations restrict the term "MÉTHODE CHAMPENOISE" and its translations to French sparkling wines, Italy more commonly uses the terms "METODO TRADIZIONALE" or "METODO CLASSICO."

metodo charmat [MEH-toh-doh shar-MAHT] An Italian phrase for the CHARMAT PROCESS.

metodo classico [MEH-toh-doh CLAH-see-coh] *see* MÉTODO TRADIZIONALE

método continuo *see* CHARMAT

método tradicional [MAY-toh-doh trah-dhee-thyoh-NAHL] The Spanish term for SPARKLING WINE (such as CAVA) made by MÉTHODE CHAMPENOISE.

metodo tradizionale [MEH-toh-doh trah-dee-tsyoh-NAH-lay] The Italian term for SPARKLING WINE made in the French manner by MÉTHODE CHAMPENOISE. Also referred to as *metodo classico.*

metric A decimal-based measurement system used throughout much of the world. For volume, the **liter** is the standard measurement and is equivalent to 33.8 fluid ounces. A **milliliter** is equal to one thousandth of a liter or 0.338 ounces; a **centiliter** is equal to one hundredth of a liter. A HECTOLITER is equal to 100 liters and is a common measurement of wine production in most European and South American countries. BATF (now the TAX AND TRADE BUREAU) implemented the metric system for wine bottles in 1975, with mandatory compliance beginning in January of 1979. The size of a standard wine bottle is 750 milliliters or 75 centiliters or 0.75 liters. Other bottles both larger and smaller are based on this metric measurement. *See also* Wine Bottles, page 609

Meunier [muh-NYAY] French red grape that is the most widely cultivated variety in France's CHAMPAGNE region, even though its relative, PINOT NOIR, and CHARDONNAY get most of the attention. Meunier is used extensively in the region's SPARKLING WINES, usually blended with these other two varieties. The name for this grape is French for "miller," derived from the fact that the white underside of its leaves looks like sifted flour. This variety's positive properties include more fruitiness and higher ACIDITY than Pinot Noir or Chardonnay, an ability to better survive in the coolest areas of the Champagne region, and higher yields than Pinot Noir. Australia, which produces limited amounts of

100-percent Meunier STILL WINE, and Germany are the only other areas to grow Meunier in any quantity, although California's sparkling wine-makers have emulated French producers by planting it in the cooler growing regions like CARNEROS. Meunier is also known as *Gris Meunier, Plant Meunier, Pinot Meunier, Müllerrebe,* and *Schwarzriesling.*

Meursault AC [meh*r*-SOH] APPELLATION that surrounds the village of Meursault, which is one of the largest of the CÔTE DE BEAUNE. Although it has no GRAND CRU vineyards, Meursault is quite famous for its white wines. Its reputation comes from its PREMIER CRU vineyards, the best known of which are **Les Charmes**, **Les Genevrières**, and **Les Perrières**. This last vineyard is often touted as a grand cru candidate, and its wines are favorably compared to those of LE MONTRACHET, considered by many as the very best white-wine grand cru vineyard. The *premier cru* vineyards can append their name on the label, as in Meursault-Perriers or Mersault-Charmes.

Mexico Even though vineyards were planted as early as the 1500s, Mexico does not produce much TABLE WINE. That's primarily because the climate isn't particularly suited for wine grapes and Mexicans don't drink much wine—beer is the beverage of choice. The majority of the vineyard crop is used for table grapes. Most Mexico-made wine undergoes either FORTIFICATION or further DISTILLATION to make BRANDY. Table wines are made with European grape VARIETIES along with some HYBRIDS. The main wine-producing vineyards are in Mexico's northern portion in Baja California, in Parras Valley (north of Mexico City), and in the Zacatecas Plateau, northwest of Mexico City.

Michelmark *see* ERBACH

Michigan Although Michigan's grape-growing history goes back to the mid-1800s, its chronicle of fine winemaking didn't start until the end of the 1960s. During the nineteenth and early twentieth centuries, CONCORD was the primary grape variety here, and because Concord grapes are used primarily for juice and jelly, many vineyards survived PROHIBITION. Today Michigan has over 13,000 vineyard acres, mostly planted with Concord and NIAGARA. There are only about 1500 acres of wine grapes (primarily HYBRIDS and some VITIS VINIFERA) and over thirty wineries scattered around the state. Michigan has four AVAs, all of which (particularly the northern two), benefit from the distinctive climate brought about by the LAKE EFFECT, which provides a moderated environment and longer growing season. The majority of the vineyards are in the state's southwest corner along Lake Michigan. Two AVAs are located here—Lake Michigan Shore and Fennville. **Lake**

Michigan Shore AVA encompasses 1,280,000 acres along a 72-mile section running from where the Kalamazoo River intersects with Lake Michigan (about 10 miles south of Holland) in the north, down to the Michigan–Indiana state line in the south, and inland approximately 35 miles. The **Fennville AVA** (Michigan's first) was established in 1981, a little over 2 years before the Lake Michigan Shore AVA. It takes up the 75,000 acres of the northern portion of the Lake Michigan Shore AVA, from the Kalamazoo River down to the City of South Haven—about a 20-mile section. Michigan's northwest portion contains Leelanau Peninsula AVA and Old Mission Peninsula AVA. **Old Mission Peninsula AVA** is the northernmost, encompassing 19,200 acres on the narrow 19-mile peninsula surrounded by Grand Traverse Bay near Traverse City. Area wineries produce mostly *Vitis vinifera* wines from the area's 200 vineyard acres. The **Leelanau Peninsula AVA**, approved in 1982, is the second oldest Michigan AVA. It's just south and west of the Old Mission Peninsula AVA, with Lake Michigan on the western side and Grand Traverse Bay on the eastern side. This AVA, which covers approximately 211,000 acres and takes in all of Leelanau County except for the offshore islands, has only about 200 acres planted to vineyards. Although hybrids were once dominant, *Vitis vinifera* grapes now make up almost half of the acreage. Michigan's oldest and largest winery is the **St. Julian Wine Company**, established in 1921 in Ontario, Canada, and relocated to Michigan in 1934.

microbullage *see* MICRO OXYGENATING; MICRO OXYGENATION

microchâteau *see* GARAGE WINES

microclimate The climate that exists in a very small area in and around a specific grapevine or group of grapevines. Microclimate depicts an area that is usually a few yards or smaller and often as small as around a particular vine's canopy or even a particular cluster of grapes. MESOCLIMATE and MACROCLIMATE depict successively larger areas. Microclimate is affected by the traits of the larger mesoclimate but has many elements that can be controlled by the vineyard manager through techniques like CANOPY MANAGEMENT. Microclimate is used to conceptualize the impact that slight changes in temperature, soil, exposure to sunlight, and so on, can have on vines and grapes, and therefore on the resulting wine.

micro oxygenating; micro oxygenation Sometimes called MOX, micro oxygenation is a method of adding small amounts of oxygen to wine in a controlled environment. It's a technique that introduces oxygen to wine much as an oak barrel does, except MOX does it in a shorter period of time and at less cost. The process usually takes place in stainless steel tanks and is used mostly on red wines, although use with white wines is increasing. Initially, it was used with low- to medium-priced wines but its use is increasing with slightly more expensive wines. Properly done, MOX will add oxygen at just the correct rate. But it's still an evolving science and requires careful monitoring since wines differ and therefore the effects of MOX differ. Some of the benefits of MOX can be to modify tannins for a softer finish, reduce unpleasant SULFITE characters, stabilize color, improve the aroma profile, and increase potential longevity. The French, who call it *microbullage*, are one of the leading users of this technology.

Middle Rio Grande Valley AVA An APPELLATION in NEW MEXICO covering 278,400 acres in the center of the state between Santa Fe and Belen (just south of Albuquerque). Established in 1988, this area is high (in the 4,000- to 6,500-foot range), dry—warm during the day, and cool during the night (particularly in the higher elevations). The colder northern portion has a shorter growing season, requiring some wineries to purchase grapes from southern New Mexico vineyards. The area is home to five wineries.

Midi *see* LANGUEDOC-ROUSSILLON

mildew Various fungi that can cause severe damage to vineyards if not treated for prevention. There are two main types—powdery mildew and downy mildew, both of which are partial to VITIS VINIFERA vines (NATIVE AMERICAN GRAPES are resistant). **Downy mildew** (*Plasmopara viticola*), also called *peronospera*, is a major disease in wet, humid grape-growing areas. Native to North America, this fungal disease was first detailed in the early 1800s. By the middle of that century, France (and other European winegrowing regions) were besieged by downy mildew, which caused widespread vineyard damage almost as serious as the PHYLLOXERA epidimic that followed shortly thereafter. The symptoms of this fungus first appear as yellow-green spots on a grape leaf's upper surface, followed by a fuzzy white growth on the underside. Infected shoots, petioles, or cluster stems become distorted or curled and, under warm, humid conditions, may be covered with a downy growth. Eventually the affected segments wither and brown. Berries are vulnerable until they are pea-size; mature berries are resistant to infection. **Powdery mildew** (*Uncinula necator*), also known as *oidium*, isn't dependent on moisture like other fungi. It's found in dryer climates, like California, where most fungi don't do well, and spreads most rapidly at temperatures

M

between 70 to 86°F. Powdery mildew favors dense canopies (*see* CANOPY) and attacks all portions of the grapevine, causing young leaves to curl and wither and mature leaves to develop a dark surface stain; the berries can discolor, split, or drop off the vine. When the gray powdery growth is rubbed off of CANES, it reveals dark brown, weblike markings. Most mildews can be controlled by using copper sulfate sprays (*see* BORDEAUX MIXTURE) or ground or powdered sulfur. *See also* DISEASES, VINEYARD.

Les Millandes *see* MOREY-SAINT-DENIS

millésime [mee-lay-ZEEM] French for "vintage" or "year." Often used to indicate a vintage Champagne.

milliliter *see* METRIC

Mimbres Valley AVA This VITICULTURAL AREA, approved in 1985, encompasses 636,800 acres within Grant and Luna Counties in southwestern New Mexico not far from the Mexican border. St. Clair Winery is the area's only winery and, with a capacity of 100,000 gallons, New Mexico's largest. It sits at the 4,500-foot level where warm days and cool nights provide a good environment for growing grapes.

minerally; mineral *see* Glossary of Wine Tasting Terms, page 655

Minervois AC [mee-neh*r*-VWAH] APPELLATION that produces some of the best red wines in France's LANGUEDOC-ROUSSILON region. It's located north of CORBIÈRES, inland from the Mediterranean coast. The vineyards begin around the village of Minerve on a high plateau and run south and west down to the river Aude. Minervois wines, which are generally good and fairly full-bodied (*see* BODY), are made from CARIGNAN, CINSAUT, GRENACHE, and, in an effort to improve quality, increasingly from MOURVÈDRE and SYRAH. Most of the production comes from area cooperatives, which generally produce agreeable wines.

minty; mint *see* Glossary of Wine Tasting Terms, page 655

Mireval *see* MUSCAT DE MIREVAL

mirin *see* SAKE

Mis au Domaine *see* MIS EN BOUTEILLE

Mis en Bouteille [mee zahn boo-TEH-yuh (boo-TAY)] A French phrase meaning "bottled." *Mis en Bouteille au Domaine* (or *Mis au Domaine*) means "bottled at the estate" (ESTATE BOTTLED); *Mis en Bouteille au Château* (or *Mis du Château*) means "bottled at the château" (CHÂTEAU BOTTLED). *Mis en Bouteille a la Propriete* ("bottled at the property") and *Mis par le Propriétaire* ("bottled by the proprietor") have the same meaning as estate bottled. *Mis en Bouteille dans nos Caves* and *Mis en Bouteille dans nos Chais* mean "bottled in our cellars" and usually suggest that the grapes were grown elsewhere and that the wine is not the quality of one that is estate bottled.

Mis par le Propriétaire *see* MIS EN BOUTEILLE

Mission [MISH-uhn] The red-wine grape that the Franciscan missionaries planted during the eighteenth century as they migrated from Mexico up through southern and northern California. Although Mission was California's prevailing grape through the 1870s, its popularity and acreage have since diminished. Most of the remaining plantings are in the CENTRAL VALLEY and southern California. The Mission grape, which is closely related to Chile's *Pais* variety and Argentina's *Criolla*, is still extensively grown in Argentina as well as Mexico. Although definitely a VITIS VINIFERA grape, its European connection has never been clearly established, although recent theories suggest that it is the same as the Monica grape variety grown in Sardinia. Mission wines are generally poor to medium quality; they're primarily used in BLENDING.

Mississippi Delta AVA Large AVA encompassing 3,840,000 acres along the Mississippi River Delta in the states of Mississippi, Louisiana, and Tennessee. The native MUSCADINE is the grape of choice in this area.

Missouri Missouri has a rich winemaking history that dates back to the mid-1800s. Although settlers in the 1700s tried their hand at winemaking, Missouri wine production did not accelerate until the 1830s and 1840s, thanks to German immigrants. Settling west of St. Louis in the areas around Hermann and Augusta (hillside locales similar to grape-growing regions in Germany), they began planting vineyards. In fact, their efforts were so successful that the region eventually became known as the "Missouri Rhineland." Throughout the latter 1800s, Missouri rivaled Ohio and then California for top wine-producing state. California's ability to grow the more popular VITIS VINIFERA wine grapes (CABERNET SAUVIGNON, CHARDONNAY, etc.) and Missouri's difficulty with these varieties, gave California the lead. But Missouri was still second moving into the twentieth century. During this period, Missouri's NORTON wines became famous. PROHIBITION ended most wine production from 1920 until 1933. Even after Prohibition ended, Missouri's legal environment did not encourage winery development for several decades. In the mid-1960s things started to change with

M

several old wineries reopening and new ones launching. Currently, there are over thirty-five wineries in the state, most of which produce wines from Norton or HYBRIDS like CHAMBOURCIN, SEYVAL BLANC, VIDAL BLANC, and Vignoles (RAVAT). Few *Vitis vinifera* vines are planted. Mount Pleasant Winery is one of the few that produces BORDEAUX-style wines. Missouri has four AVAS—AUGUSTA (established in 1980 and the first AVA in the United States), HERMANN AVA, the large OZARK HIGHLANDS AVA, and the huge OZARK MOUNTAIN AVA, which Missouri shares with ARKANSAS and Oklahoma.

mistella *see* MARSALA DOC; MISTELLE

mistelle [mees-TEHL] French term for grape juice in which FERMENTATION has been stopped by the addition of ALCOHOL. Because only small amounts of the grape sugars have usually been converted to alcohol, mistelle is very sweet. It's used mainly as a base for APÉRITIFS, particularly VERMOUTH. The Spanish equivalent is *Mistella* or *Mistela*.

Mittelburgenland DAC *see* DISTRICTUS AUSTRIA CONTROLLATUS

Mittelhaardt/Deutsche Weinstrasse, Bereich *see* PFALZ

Mittelmosel [MIHT-uhl-MOH-zuhl] One of Germany's best wine-producing areas. Its name, which means "middle Mosel," refers to its location in the central portion of German's MOSEL-SAAR-RUWER region. Its boundaries closely approximate those of the BEREICH BERNKASTEL and include villages such as BRAUNEBERG, BERNKASTEL, GRAACH, PIESPORT, WEHLEN, and ZELTINGEN. The RIESLINGS of Mittelmosel are highly regarded.

Mittelrhein [MIHT-uhl-rine] With less than 1,700 acres of vineyards planted, Mittelrhein is the fifth smallest of the thirteen German ANBAUGEBIETE (quality-wine regions). The region follows the path of the Rhine River from the bend in the river near the villages of Lorch and Bingen stretching northward about 60 miles to Konigswinter, just south of Bonn. RIESLING grapevines cover nearly 75 percent of the thin strand of vineyards running along both sides of the Rhine. The wines are of high quality, and most are consumed within the region. High-quality SEKT is made as well. The Mittelrhein region is noted for its spectacular, picturesque scenery as the Rhine twists and turns its way north. There are three BEREICHE—**Siebengebirge**, **Rheinburgengau**, and **Bacharach**—and eleven GROSSLAGEN in the region.

Mittervernatsch *see* SCHIAVA

moelleux [mwah-LEUH] A French term used to describe white wines that have at least some RESIDUAL SUGAR. A single-word translation is difficult because the meaning for *moelleux* is a complex compound meaning "soft-smooth-mellow-velvety-lush."

Mokelumne River AVA [moh-KUHL-uh-mee] This VITICULTURAL AREA was established in August 2006. Its 85,700 acres are located in the southwestern portion of the larger LODI AVA, which is between Sacramento and Stockton in northern California. Of these, almost half (42,000 acres) is planted with vines. It was the first area with the Lodi AVA to be planted and features sources for OLD VINE ZINFANDEL, along with ALBARIÑO, CABERNET SAUVIGNON, and CHARDONNAY.

moldy *see* Glossary of Wine Tasting Terms, page 655

Molette Noire *see* MONDEUSE

Molise; Molise DOC [moh-LEE-seh] Small mountainous region in southern Italy, located along the Adriatic Sea south of ABRUZZI and north of APULIA. This region has about 19,000 vineyard acres and three DOCs— Molise (or Del Molise), **Pentro d'Isernia**, and **Biferno** (which is so far the most important of the three). The main grape variety used for its white wines is TREBBIANO, but there are other white grapes used including BOMBINO BIANCO and MALVASIA. The primary grape used for ROSSO and ROSATO wines is MONTEPULCIANO, followed by Trebbiano and AGLIANICO. Many of the area's better wines haven't used any of the DOCs on their label but rather are sold simply as VINO DA TAVOLA. This may soon change because the Molise DOC, which was approved in 1998, allows a variety of white wines from grapes like CHARDONNAY, Falanghina, Moscato, (MUSCAT), Pinot Bianco (PINOT BLANC), and SAUVIGNON BLANC, and red wines from varieties like Aglianico, CABERNET SAUVIGNON, MONTEPULCIANO, and SANGIOVESE. Such wines can be made without required percentages for the varieties used, as Biferno and Pentro d'Isernia do. The best-known producer here is Alessio Di Majo Norante.

Monastrell [maw-nahs-TRRELL] *see* MOURVÈDRE

Monbazillac AC [mawn-bah-zee-YAHK] APPELLATION for semisweet and sweet wines that is located in France's BERGERAC area, east of the city of Bordeaux. The wines, made mainly from SÉMILLON with some MUSCADELLE and SAUVIGNON BLANC, rely on BOTRYTIS CINEREA-infected grapes. This infection is important for the grapes to have the CONCENTRATED sweetness and flavor necessary for the best DESSERT WINES. If botrytis doesn't develop, some growers—not wanting to risk losing their crop to the late autumn weather—get nervous and pick the grapes before it does. Those who lack tenacity for the waiting game produce LIGHT, semisweet wines of average quality. In good years, however, the wines can assume the character of a SAUTERNES, although usually not with the same richness and finesse. Wines not qualifying for Monbazillac AC status may be downgraded to Côtes de Bergerac AC (*see* BERGERAC) status.

Mönchspfad *see* GEISENHEIM

Mondéjar DO [mohn-day-HAR] DO in Spain's Castilla-La Mancha region. It's located east of Madrid and lies on the eastern border of the VINOS DE MADRID DO. There are two primary growing areas situated around the towns of Mondéjar and Sacedón. Although winemaking has been practiced here for over four centuries, the Mondéjar area is just now starting to innovate with more modern winemaking practices, moving away from the bulk wine market that has been its mainstay for decades. The primary grapes are the white VARIETIES MACABEO, Malvar and TORRONTÉS, plus some AIRÉN. Principal red varieties are Cencibel (TEMPRANILLO) and CABERNET SAUVIGNON. Bodegas Mariscal is the best-known winery in the area.

Mondeuse [mohn-DEUHZ] Although commonly referred to as Mondeuse, this red-wine grape is really **Mondeuse Noir**. There's also an obscure white variety called **Mondeuse Blanche**. Mondeuse is primarily grown in France's SAVOIE. It can produce high-quality, deeply colored wines with CONCENTRATED flavors reminiscent of tart plums and a FINISH that's slightly bitter. In France, the MUSCULAR Mondeuse is often lightened slightly by BLENDING in PINOT NOIR and/or GAMAY. Other names for Mondeuse Noire include *Grosse Syrah, Molette Noire,* and *Savoyance.* There are theories that Mondeuse and the Italian REFOSCO are the same variety, but this has not been proven, and some evidence suggests that it may not be true. In California, there is a variety called *Refosco* that's related to Mondeuse but not to samples of the Italian Refosco that were available for DNA testing.

M

Monestel *see* CARIGNAN

Monferrato DOC [mohn-fayr-RAH-toh] DOC zone located in Italy's southeastern PIEDMONT region in the hills of the provinces of Asti and Alessandria. Established in 1994, this DOC allows a range of different native and non-native grape varieties to be used in the Monferrato ROSSO. These red wines may also be bottled as VARIETAL wines as long as they contain 85 percent of the named grape. Such wines include BARBERA, BONARDA, CABERNET FRANC, CABERNET SAUVIGNON, FREISA, GRIGNOLINO, Pinot Nero (PINOT NOIR), and NEBBIOLO. Monferrato BIANCO can contain non-native white varieties like CHARDONNAY and SAUVIGNON BLANC.

Monforte d'Alba [mohn-fo*rr*-teh DAHL-bah] *see* BAROLO

monolithic *see* Glossary of Wine Tasting Terms, page 655

monopole [maw-naw-PAWL] French for "monopoly," this word on a French wine label refers to sole ownership of a name. It is usually associated with BURGUNDY where it's used to indicate that a classified vineyard is wholly owned by a single proprietor. LE TÂCHE AC and ROMANÉE-CONTI AC owned by Domaine de la Romanée-Conti are two of the most famous.

monoterpenes [mah-noh-TER-peens] A subgroup of terpenoids that impart fruity and floral aspects to wine. They are associated with the MUSCAT family, which fully exhibits these traits, but also to VARIETIES like GEWÜRZTRAMINER and RIESLING.

Montagne de Reims *see* CHAMPAGNE

Montagne-Saint-Émilion AC [mawn-TAHN-yuh sa*n* tay-mee-LYAW*N*] APPELLATION that is considered a satellite of and is located northeast of the better-known SAINT-ÉMILION AC in the eastern part of France's BORDEAUX region. As in Saint-Émilion and neighboring POMEROL, MERLOT is the dominant grape. It's usually blended with CABERNET FRANC, CABERNET SAUVIGNON, and MALBEC. Montagne-Saint-Émilion AC wines are generally quite good, with the top ones compared to better Saint-Émilion wines.

Montagny AC [mawn-tah-NYEE] One of the five villages in the CÔTE CHALONNAISE in France's BURGUNDY region that has an individual APPELLATION. It produces only white wines from CHARDONNAY. Unlike the rest of Burgundy, where only specific vineyards are designated PREMIER CRU, Montagny AC allows any wine with a minimum of 11½ percent ALCOHOL to be labeled premier cru.

Montalbano *see* CHIANTI DOCG

Montalcino *see* BRUNELLO DI MONTALCINO DOCG; ROSSO DI MONTALCINO DOC

M

Mont de Milieu *see* CHABLIS

Montecarlo DOC [mawn-teh-KAR-loh] A DOC zone surrounding the hilltop town of Montecarlo, west of Florence in the northwestern part of Italy's TUSCANY region. Montecarlo DOC makes a BIANCO, a ROSSO (it has the best reputation), and VIN SANTO. The white wine uses mainly TREBBIANO, but a host of other grapes are allowed—Pinot Bianco (PINOT BLANC), Pinot Grigio (PINOT GRIS), ROUSSANNE, Sauvignon

(SAUVIGNON BLANC), SÉMILLON, and VERMENTINO. The red wine uses from 50 to 75 percent SANGIOVESE, plus CANAIOLO, Cilegiolo, COLORINO, MALVASIA, and SYRAH.

Montecompatri-Colonna DOC [mawn-teh-kawm-PAH-tree koh-LOHN-uh] DOC that encompasses vineyards surrounding the villages of Montecompatri and Colonna and that is located in the CASTELLI ROMANI area southeast of Rome in Italy's LATIUM region. The DRY white wine is made from MALVASIA, TREBBIANO, Bonvino, and Bellone. Montecompatri-Colonna DOC wines are very similiar to those from its better-known neighbor FRASCATI DOC. An AMABILE version is also allowed. Labels may contain both village names or either one individually.

Montée de Tonnerre see CHABLIS

Montefalco DOC; Montefalco Sagrantino DOCG [mawn-teh-FAHL-koh sah-grahn-TEE-noh] A small hilltop town located southeast of Perugia in Italy's UMBRIA region. The DOC zone covers the vineyards on the slopes around Montefalco, plus those of several neighboring villages. Montefalco makes a good-quality, full-flavored ROSSO out of SANGIOVESE, TREBBIANO, and SAGRANTINO plus small amounts of BARBERA, Cilegiolo, MERLOT, MALVASIA, and MONTEPULCIANO. However, the **Montefalco Sagrantino** (or **Sagrantino di Montefalco**) wines— made in both DRY and PASSITO versions from Sagrantino grapes—are creating this area's reputation. These wines are RICH and full-bodied (see BODY) with adequate TANNINS to let them AGE for a while. In recognition of its high-quality wines, the Sagrantino di Montefalco zone was upgraded to DOCG status in the mid-1990s.

Montefiascone see EST! EST!! EST!!! DI MONTEFIASCONE DOC

Montepulciano [mohn-teh-pool-CHAH-noh; mawn-teh-pool-CHAH-naw] 1. A red-wine grape widely cultivated throughout Italy, with the most concentrated plantings in the southeastern regions from the MARCHES down to APULIA. Some argue that Montepulciano originated in the ABRUZZI region, with which it's still most closely associated, mainly because of the DOC wines of MONTEPULCIANO D'ABRUSSO. This grape variety is capable of creating deeply colored, rich red wines with blackberry fruit flavors and SPICY, PEPPERY qualities. Because of its moderate ACID levels, Montepulciano generally produces wines that are smooth and MELLOW, but sometimes TANNIC enough to be AGED. This variety is also made into a cherry-pink ROSÉ called CERASUOLO. Other red wines based on Montepulciano grapes (but usually blended with local grapes) include the ROSSO CONERO DOC wines from the Marches region and the DOC wines of CERVETERI and VELLETRI from the LATIUM region. Montepulciano is also known as *Cordisco, Morellone, Primaticcio,* and *Uva Abruzzi.* 2. A town in western Italy's TUSCANY region that lends its name to VINO NOBILE DI MONTEPULCIANO, a wine based on the SANGIOVESE, not the Montepulciano, grape.

Montepulciano d'Abruzzo DOC [mawn-teh-pool-CHAH-noh dah-B*R*OOD-dzoh] DOC that is located in central Italy's ABRUZZI region and that isn't related to the VINO NOBILE DI MONTEPULCIANO DOCG, which is named after a town in the TUSCANY region. Montepulciano d'Abruzzo is named after the grape variety MONTEPULCIANO, which must make up at least 85 percent of this DOC's wine (the rest is SANGIOVESE). Montepulciano d'Abruzzo DOC wines are generally ordinary, although several producers who keep YIELDS low take care to produce good, full-bodied (*see* BODY) wines capable of long AGING. Wines with "VECCHIO" on the label have been AGED for a minimum of 2 years. The same grapes go into a CERASUOLO (DRY ROSATO), which is considered quite good.

Monteregio di Mass Marittima DOC [mohn-tay-RAY-zhee-oh dee mahss mah-REET-tee-mah] Approved in 1994, this DOC is located near the coast in the western part of Italy's TUSCANY region, south of the BOLGHERI and VAL DI CORNIA DOCS and north of the city of Grosseto. Along with other areas along the Tuscan coast, it is attracting attention as a desirable growing area. SANGIOVESE is the main red variety; the primary whites are VERMENTINO, TREBBIANO, and MALVASIA. In addition to BIANCO, ROSSO, and ROSATO wines, a VARIETAL WINE is made from Vermentino (requires a minimum 90 percent). Also white and red VIN SANTO wines are made. The red, called *Vin Santo Occhio di Pernice*, requires 50 to 70 percent Sangiovese.

Monterey County; Monterey AVA Located on the California coast south of San Francisco. Most of the growing area is centered in the 84-mile long Salinas Valley which, though inland, is subject to cooling breezes off Monterey Bay and the Pacific Ocean. The climate, which is very cool at the northern end of the valley, is ranked a Region I growing area (*see* CLIMATE REGIONS OF CALIFORNIA). Heading south, it gets warmer, changing to a Region II, then a Region III, and finally a Region IV around San Lucas at the valley's southern end. CHARDONNAY is by far the most widely planted variety in Monterey County. CABERNET SAUVIGNON is second, followed by MERLOT, PINOT NOIR, RIESLING, SAUVIGNON BLANC, CHENIN BLANC, ZINFANDEL, GEWÜRZTRAMINER, PINOT BLANC, and others. The **Monterey AVA** encompasses approximately 36,000 acres, which is essentially the Salinas Valley. Other

M

Monterey County APPELLATIONS are ARROYO SECO, CARMEL VALLEY, CHALONE, HAMES VALLEY, SAN ANTONIO VALLEY, and SAN LUCAS.

Monterey Riesling *see* SYLVANER

Monterosso Val d'Arda *see* COLLI PIACENTINI

Monthélie AC [maw*n*-tay-LEE] Small APPELLATION that surrounds the tiny, picturesque village of Monthélie, located in the CÔTE DE BEAUNE district of France's BURGUNDY region. It's situated on a hill just north of MEURSAULT and southwest of VOLNAY. The wines, predominantly red and made from PINOT NOIR, used to be sold under the better-known Volnay AC label. They're similar in style to the Volnay wines but are not as well known, which means that they're not as expensive and, therefore, are a good value. The best wines usually come from the two PREMIER CRU vineyards closest to Volnay, **Les Champs Fulliot** and **Sur la Velle**. Small amounts of CHARDONNAY-based white wines are also produced.

Monticello AVA A VITICULTURAL AREA encompassing approximately 800,000 acres around the city of Charlottesville, Virginia. It's located mostly in Albermarle County but extends into the counties of Greene, Nelson, and Orange. The Monticello AVA, established in 1984, takes its name from Monticello Mountain, part of the Southwest Mountain Ridge in central Virginia. This is the area where Thomas Jefferson resided and planted vineyards (with little success) in the late 1700s. Today's vineyards are planted in both HYBRID and VITIS VINIFERA vines. In 2002, almost half of Virginia's wineries were in this area.

Montillia-Moriles DO [mawn-TEE-lyah maw-*R*EE-lehs] DO area located northeast of JEREZ in southern Spain. The designated area includes vineyards around the town of Montillia and the village of Moriles. The dominant grape is the PEDRO XIMÉNEZ, which develops best when grown in the white chalky soil that's similiar to Jerez's better vineyard areas. The Montillia-Moriles DO produces wines similiar to the SHERRY wines made in Jerez. Until the 1960s, large amounts of BULK WINE were shipped from Montillia and Moriles to Jerez to be used for blending. Today, the sherrylike wines are FERMENTED in stainless steel tanks, although some of the large earthenware vessels called *tinjas* are still used. The wines are then matured in a SOLERA SYSTEM like that used in sherrymaking. Unlike sherry, not all Montillia-Moriles wines need to be FORTIFIED. That's because the high natural sugar levels of the grapes can usually produce wines with 15 percent or more ALCOHOL. Although there are some excellent wines from this DO, most of what's available are blends of *finos* and *olorosos* (*see* SHERRY) with sweet concentrated MUST added. Owing to legal hassles with the Jerez producers, the terms *fino, oloroso,* and *amontillado* couldn't be used by Montillia-Moriles for a period of time (even though *amontillado* means "made in the style of Montilla"). Many of the wines are simply labeled Dry, Medium, Cream, or Sweet. Today, *fino* wines with over 15 percent alcohol and *oloroso* and *amontillado* wines with over 16 percent can use these terms on the labels. In recent years, Montillia producers have been producing JOVEN wines, which are young, fresh, and fruity and meant to be consumed early. The wines are usually made from Baladi or Torrontés grapes but sometimes from PEDRO XIMÉNEZ or MUSCAT.

Montlouis AC [mawn-LWEE] APPELLATION that surrounds the village of Montlouis, which is located in the TOURAINE area of France's LOIRE region, directly across the Loire River from VOUVRAY. The wines are similar to those from Vouvray, although they are usually not quite as rich. CHENIN BLANC is the only grape allowed in the wines of this AC. The wines can range from DRY to sweet, and be STILL, PÉTILLANT, or SPARKLING (MOUSSEUX).

Montmains *see* CHABLIS

Montonec *see* PARELLADA

Montpellier *see* GRÉS DE MONTPELLIER

Montpeyroux *see* CÔTEAUX DU LANGUEDOC; TERRASSES DU LARZAC AC

Montrachet AC (Le Montrachet) [luh mawn-rah-SHAY] Famous GRAND CRU vineyard that produces one of the most sought after and expensive white wines in the world. The 20 acres of CHARDONNAY grapes are situated on a slope in the CÔTE D'BEAUNE district in France's BURGUNDY region. Half the acreage is in the village of PULIGNY-MONTRACHET, the other half in CHASSAGNE-MONTRACHET. The vineyard is so famous that both villages added its name to their own, as did several adjacent *grand cru* vineyards—BÂTARD-MONTRACHET, BIEN-VENUES-BÂTARD-MONTRACHET, CHEVALIER-MONTRACHET, and CRIOTS-BÂTARD-MONTRACHET. There are various theories on why this particular vineyard is so special including the angle of the slope, the chalky soil on top of a bed of limestone; the excellent drainage; the just-right, maximum sun exposure; or the combination of all these. The result is a RICH, luscious wine that, though DRY, seems to be full of sweet, HONEYED fruit. All these qualities produce another result—Montrachet wines are among the most expensive white wines in the world. These wonderful wines are generally best when aged for 10 years or longer.

M

Montravel [mawn-rah-VEHL] Located on the west side of the BER-GERAC area close to France's BORDEAUX region, Montravel produces white wines from SÉMILLON, SAUVIGNON BLANC, and MUSCADELLE. Wines labeled **Montravel AC** are almost DRY, whereas those designated **Côtes de Montravel AC** or **Haut-Montravel AC** are semisweet to sweet. The wines are not outstanding, and, because they don't fall into today's popular catagories of fully DRY or richly sweet, they're declining in popularity.

Montsant [MOHN-sahnt] Spanish APPELATION located in the southern part of Spain's CATALONIA region. It was carved out of the TARRAGONA DO in 2001 because of the high-quality wines produced in this subregion (formerly known as **La Comarca de Falset**). Montsant encompasses 12 villages and practically encircles its famous neighbor, PRIORAT DOCA. Its wines have not achieved the fame that Priorat wines have but many think they are almost as good, especially the powerful reds made from the OLD VINE Garnacha (GRENACHE) and Cariñena (CARIGNAN). Other allowed red varieties are CABERNET SAUVIGNON, MERLOT, Monastrell (MOURVÈDRE), SYRAH AND TEMPRANILLO. White wines can be made from CHARDONNAY, Garnacha Blanca (GRENACHE), MACABEO, Moscatel (MUSCAT), and PARELLADA.

Les Monts Luisants *see* MOREY-SAINT-DENIS

Morastel *see* MOURVÈDRE

Morellino di Scansano DOC [maw-reh-LEE-noh dee skahn-SAH-noh] DOC zone located in the southern portion of Italy's TUSCANY region southeast of Grosseto. It encompasses the vineyards around the hilltop town of Scansano. The wine, which is developing a very good reputation among Sangiovese fans, is made from at least 85 percent SANGIOVESE grapes. This DOC is one of only a few that may use 100 percent of this grape. "Riserva" on the label means that the wine's been AGED for 2 years, one of which must be in wooden barrels.

Morellone *see* MONTEPULCIANO

Morey-Saint-Denis [maw-ray san duh-NEE] The vineyards surrounding the small village of Morey-Saint-Denis include all or part of five GRAND CRU vineyards and twenty PREMIER CRU vineyards. Even so, this village is not as well known as its neighboring villages, GEVREY-CHAMBERTIN and CHAMBOLLE-MUSIGNY, in the CÔTE DE NUITS area of France's BURGUNDY region. This is largely because, until the 1950s, most wines were sold under the labels of these two neighboring villages. The grands crus located in Morey-Saint-Denis are BONNES-MARES,

CLOS DE LA ROCHE, CLOS DE TART, CLOS DES LAMBRAYS, and CLOS SAINT-DENIS. The village of Morey added the name of this last grand cru to its own in 1927. The better premier cru vineyards include **Clos des Ormes**, **Les Monts Luisants**, **Les Millandes**, and **La Bussière**. Because of the high number of quality producers, the village wines (labeled **Morey-Saint-Denis AC**) can generally be relied on to be of very high quality. Almost all the Morey-Saint-Denis wines are red and made from PINOT NOIR, although a few hundred cases of white wine are produced each year.

Morgeot *see* CHASSANGE-MONTRACHET AC

Morgon AC [mawr-GAWN] One of the best of the ten CRUS in France's BEAUJOLAIS region. These GAMAY-based wines are full-bodied and CONCENTRATED. They have a more intense color but less fruitiness than wines from other crus. Their flavors are reminiscent of cherries and plums, as opposed to the lighter, fresher, strawberry nuances of the other cru wines. Unlike most Beaujolais wines, those from Morgon AC are generally bottled later. They're better after a little BOTTLE AGING and do well for 2 to 5 years. The best wines come from the slopes of Mont du Py, whereas those from the flatlands have a much lighter style.

Morio-Muskat [MOH-ree-oh MEWS-kat] German white-wine grape—a CROSS of SYLVANER and Weissburgunder (PINOT BLANC)—that was created by Peter Morio. Morio-Muskat produces such exotically perfumed wines that only small amounts are needed to enrich the flavor and aroma of a blander wine. It's grown mostly in Germany's PFALZ and RHEINHESSEN regions and is used mainly in the production of less-expensive wines.

Morne Noir *see* MENOIRE

Mornington Peninsula An Australian wine region located in the Port Phillip Zone of VICTORIA. It's situated about 50 miles south of Melbourne on the peninsula that lies between the Port Phillip Bay and Bass Strait, around the towns of Mornington and Red Hill. The surrounding waters make this a cool climate region and, not surprisingly, CHARDONNAY and PINOT NOIR are the most widely planted and consistently successful VARIETIES. Following these varieties are CABERNET SAUVIGNON, PINOT GRIS, SAUVIGNON BLANC, Shiraz (SYRAH), MERLOT, CABERNET FRANC, and RIESLING. Although there have been scattered vineyards over the years, this region didn't really start to blossom until the mid-1970s.

M

Today, the Mornington Peninsula has almost 2,000 vineyard acres and over thirty-five wineries, most of them small.

Morocco [muh-RAHK-oh] The population of this North African country is predominately Muslim, a religion that prohibits the consumption of alcoholic beverages. It wasn't until the French took control and French settlers began arriving in the late 1920s and early 1930s that vineyards were planted in large numbers. As a French protectorate, Morocco produced substantial quantities of wine. When Morocco regained its independence in 1956, however, wine production began to decline. Although the wines don't compare with the quality of the French wines, Morocco has a quality system, *appellation d'origine garantie*, that is similiar to the French AC system. Most Moroccan wines are red and are usually ROUGH and ALCOHOLIC. They're generally exported in BULK to be used as BLENDING WINES by European countries. Morocco's main grape varieties are ALICANTE BOUSHET, CARIGNAN, CINSAUT, and GRENACHE. MOURVÈDRE and SYRAH are grown in small quantites for higher-quality wines. Some ROSÉ wines and a small amount of white wine are also made. The main growing areas are near the coastal cities of Casablanca and Rabat and inland around Meknès and Fes at the base of the Atlas Mountains.

Morra, La [lah MOHR*R*-ah] *see* BAROLO

Morrastal *see* GRACIANO

Mortágua *see* TOURIGA NACIONAL

Moscadello di Montalcino DOC [moss-kah-DELL-oh dee mawn-tahl-TCHEE-noh] DOC zone that is in the southern portion of Italy's TUSCANY region and is exactly the same zone as that for the BRUNELLO DI MONTALCINO DOCG. Moscadello di Montalcino DOC produces a sweet white wine, made mainly from Moscato Bianco (MUSCAT), which can be STILL or FRIZZANTE. There's also a LIQUOROSO, which is a FORTIFIED version. There was a similiar wine made in the Middle Ages, but the grape used is thought to have been the Moscadelletto, a Muscat mutant not quite the same as today's variety.

Moscatel *see* MUSCAT

Moscatel de Málaga *see* MUSCAT

Moscatel de Setúbal DOC [maws-kah-TEHL deh sih-TOO-bawl] *see* SETÚBAL DOC

Moscatel Gordo *see* MUSCAT

M

Moscatello *see* ALEATICO

Moscatel Rosé *see* MUSCAT

Moscato Bianco *see* MUSCAT

Moscato d'Asti DOCG *see* ASTI DOCG

Moscato di Amburgo *see* MUSCAT

Moscato di Pantelleria DOC; Moscato Passito di Pantelleria DOC [maws-KAH-toh (pah-SEE-toh) dee pahn-tehl-LEH-*r*yah] Two DOCs that are located on the small Italian island of Pantelleria, which is southwest of Sicily, close to North Africa. They produce sweet wines of varying styles—PASSITO and non-passito (*naturale*), some are FORTIFIED and some are SPARKLING. The variety used is the Zibibbo, one of the MUSCAT grapes. The best Moscato di Pantelleria wines make lusciously sweet dessert wines.

Moscato Giallo *see* MUSCAT

Moscato Rosa *see* MUSCAT

Mosel; Moselle [MOH-zuhl; moh-ZELL] A famous river that winds through one of Germany's important ANBAUGEBIETE (quality-wine regions), MOSEL-SAAR-RUWER. The river actually starts in eastern France's Vosges Mountains, flows along the Luxembourg border into western Germany, and finally joins the Rhine River in western Germany at the city of Koblenz. There are vineyards along the river in France and Luxembourg, but wines from the German vineyards are the most widely recognized. *Mosel* is the German spelling; *Moselle* is the English and French spelling.

Mosel-Saar-Ruwer [MOH-zuhl sahr ROO-vay*r*] The official all-encompassing name of the German ANBAUGEBIET (quality-wine region) that encompasses the vineyards surrounding the Mosel River and its two tributaries, the Saar and the Ruwer. The region stretches from the French border to the point where the Mosel joins with the Rhine. Internationally, this Anbaugebiete is the best known of the thirteen German regions. RIESLING grapes cover over 50 percent of the 31,000 vineyard acres, followed by MÜLLER-THURGAU and ELBLING. Many of the vineyards are on steep, difficult, slate-based terrain, which produces excellent, STEELY Riesling wines, the best of which are capable of AGING for many years. The region consists of 4 BEREICHE—ZELL/MOSEL, BERNKASTEL, SAAR-RUWER, and **Obermosel**—19 GROSSLAGEN, and 525 EINZELLAGEN. The Zell/Mosel is the northernmost part of this Anbaugebiet.

M

Bernkastel, the most prolific of the Bereiche, covers the midsection of the Mosel River called the MITTELMOSEL. Saar-Ruwer covers the two tributaries, and Obermosel, which means "Upper Mosel," is the farthest south. Well-known Grosslagen include Bernkasteler Badstube, Bernkasteler Kurfürstlay, Kröver Nacktarsch, Michelsberg, Piesporter, Wiltinger Scharzberg, and Zeller Schwarze Katz.

Moseltaler [MOH-zuhl-TAH-luh*r*] Created in 1986, Moseltaler is a category for wines produced in Germany's MOSEL-SAAR-RUWER region. These wines are similar to the LIEBFRAUMILCH wines produced along the Rhine. Moseltaler must be made from ELBLING, KERN, MÜLLER-THURGAU, or RIESLING grapes, contain between 1.5 and 3 percent RESIDUAL SUGAR and a minimum of 0.7 percent total acidity (*see* ACIDS), and be of QUAL-ITÄTSWEIN BESTIMMTER ANBAUGEBIET (QbA) quality.

mosto [MAWSH-toh] Italian for "MUST" or "grape juice."

Moulin-à-Vent AC [moo-la*n*-nah-VAH*N*] APPELLATION that gets its name from the windmill (moulin-à-vent) that sits in the area's vineyards. Moulin-à-Vent is considered by many to be the best of the ten CRUS in France's BEAUJOLAIS region and is sometimes called the King of Beaujolais wines. The full-bodied (*see* BODY), CONCENTRATED wines—some of Beaujolais' most expensive—are made from GAMAY and have abundant TANNINS. Unlike the common perception of Beaujolais wines, these should not be drunk young but rather AGED—some can last ten years or more. Moulin-à-Vent AC wines are so uncharacteristic of the region that many wine aficionados compare them to the lighter style, PINOT NOIR-based red Burgundies from the CÔTE D'OR.

Moulin-Riche *see* LÉOVILLE-POYFERRÉ

Moulis AC [moo-LEE] The smallest of the village APPELLATIONS in the HAUT-MÉDOC area. Its center is the village of Moulis, which is located a few miles northwest of the Margaux AC. None of the Moulis AC châteaux were included in the Classification of 1855 (*see* Official Wine Classifications of Bordeaux, page 678), which helps explain why it's not as well known as other village appellations such as MARGAUX, PAUIL-LAC, SAINT-ESTÈPHE, and SAINT-JULIEN. There are some excellent red wines (made with the BORDEAUX varieties) produced in the Moulis AC, however, and they've proven to be some of the longest lived. The best wines usually come from Château Chasse-Spleen, followed by those from Châteaux Gressier Grand-Poujeaux, Maucaillou, and Poujeaux.

Mount Barker *see* GREAT SOUTHERN

Mount Benson New Australian wine-producing region located about 180 miles southeast of the city of Adelaide in SOUTH AUSTRALIA'S Limestone Coast Zone. It's situated between the coastal towns of Kingston and Robe. Vines weren't planted here until 1989, but there's excitement about the area because its soil (terra rossa over limestone) is similar to that of the famous COONAWARRA region, about 65 miles inland to the east. The primary difference between the two areas is that Mount Benson is on the coast and has a slightly longer growing season. The climate and soils are very similar to the ROBE RANGES region about 25 miles south. Mount Benson grows CABERNET SAUVIGNON, SHIRAZ, MERLOT, PINOT NOIR, CHARDONNAY, SÉMILLON, and SAUVIGNON BLANC.

Mount Gambier Wine-producing region located about 270 miles southeast of the city of Adelaide in the Limestone Coast Zone of SOUTH AUSTRALIA. It's situated around the city of Mount Gambier in the far southeast corner of the state, near the coast. This setting provides it with the coolest climate of the Limestone Coast regions. Vines were first planted in 1982, and today there are between 200 and 300 vineyard acres. The most popular varieties are the earlier maturing PINOT NOIR, CHARDONNAY, and SAUVIGNON BLANC, along with CABERNET SAUVIGNON and CABERNET FRANC. Haig Vineyard and Winters Vineyard are area wineries.

Mount Harlan *see* SAN BENITO COUNTY; CALERA

Mount Lofty Ranges Zone *see* SOUTH AUSTRALIA

Mount Veeder AVA This APPELLATION is part of the larger NAPA VALLEY AVA and encompasses 15,000 acres on 2,677-foot Mount Veeder, which is west of the town of Yountville and is part of the Mayacamas Mountains that divide the Napa Valley and SONOMA VALLEY. The appellation was approved in 1990. The climate in this area differs from the floor of the Napa Valley because of the fog on the valley floor, the thermal layers created, and the altitude of the vineyards. The result is more sunshine but generally cooler daytime temperatures and warmer nighttime conditions. Mount Veeder AVA straddles the Region I-Region II growing areas (*see* CLIMATE REGIONS OF CALIFORNIA), depending on the atmospheric conditions of a particular year. CABERNET SAUVIGNON and CHARDONNAY do well and are widely planted, along with small amounts of ZINFANDEL, SAUVIGNON BLANC, MERLOT, SYRAH, and VIOGNIER.

M

Moura DOC *see* ALENTEJO

Les Mourottes *see* CORTON; CORTON-CHARLEMAGNE

La Moutonne *see* CHABLIS

Mourvèdre [moo*r*-VEH-d*r*uh] Though best known today for its presence in southern France, this red-wine grape is Spain's second most widely planted red variety after GRENACHE, and is called both *Monastrell* and *Mataro* in that country. Mourvèdre produces good-quality, garnet-colored wines with SPICY, PEPPERY characteristics. They can, however, be a bit TANNIC and HARD and are at their best when blended with other grape varieties. Mourvèdre is the principal component in the BANDOL red and ROSÉ wines of France's PROVENCE region. In other red wines—such as those from CÔTES DU RHÔNE, CHÂTEAUNEUF-DE-PAPE, and CÔTES DE PROVENCE—Mourvèdre is used to improve color and STRUCTURE. In Spain, Mourvèdre is grown in the regions of RIOJA, PENEDÈS, ALICANTE, and Murcia (especially the Jumilla and Yecla DOS). It's typically blended with Grenache (*Garnacha Tinta*) for red wines and is sometimes processed similarly to SHERRY to produce FORTIFIED, RANCIO-style wines. Although there's recently been renewed interest in California, only small amounts of this variety are currently grown in California and Australia, where it's also known as *Mataro*. Mourvèdre is also called *Morastel* (or *Morrastal*), although it's unrelated to the *Morrastel* of southern France (which is actually GRACIANO).

mousse [MOOSS] A French term meaning "froth" or "foam," which, when applied to wine, refers to the foam that forms on the surface of SPARKLING WINE when it's first poured. Mousse is analogous to the term "head," which is the foam on a freshly poured glass of beer.

mousseux [moo-SEUH*R*; moo-SUR] A French term that means "sparkling" or "frothy." It's used to refer to all SPARKLING WINES except those produced in the CHAMPAGNE region, which are the only ones allowed to be called *Champagne*. Sometimes referred to as *vins mousseux*, these sparkling wines are produced all over France, and there are some twenty that have achieved AC status. The ACs of BLAN-QUETTE DE LIMOUX, CLAIRETTE DE DIE TRADITION, CRÉMANT D'ALSACE, CRÉMANT DE BOURGOGNE, CREMANT DE LOIRE, GAILLAC, MONTLOUIS, SEYSSEL, and VOU-VRAY all produce good vins mousseux. Most of these sparkling wines are made by MÉTHODE CHAMPENOISE, although some are still made by *méthode rurale* (RURAL METHOD).

mousy; mousey *see* Glossary of Wine Tasting Terms, page 655

mouthfeel *see* Glossary of Wine Tasting Terms, page 655

mouth-filling *see* Glossary of Wine Tasting Terms, page 655

MOX *see* MICRO OXYGENATING; MICRO OXYGENATION

Mudgee A small Australian wine-producing area located about 160 miles northwest of Sydney and 100 miles west of the better-known HUNTER VALLEY region. It's part of the Central Ranges Zone in NEW SOUTH WALES. Mudgee is called Nest in the Hills by the Aborigines because it's nestled in the western hills of the Great Dividing Range. This area's cooler and drier than the Hunter Valley to the east. There are approximately 11,000 vineyards in the Mudgee area, with red VARIETIES in the majority. Shiraz (SYRAH) is the most widely planted, but CABERNET SAUVIGNON consistently produces the best wines. CHARDONNAY is the most widely planted white variety and does quite well in the area. SÉMILLON, RIESLING, VERELHO, SAUVIGNON BLANC, MARSANNE, MERLOT, CABERNET FRANC, and PINOT NOIR are also grown here.

muffa nobile [MOOF-fah NAW-bee-lay] Italian for "noble mold," which in the wine world refers to BOTRYTIS CINEREA, the beneficial mold that contributes to some of the world's great DESSERT WINES.

mulled wine Red or white wine that's heated with various citrus fruits and spices such as cinnamon, cloves, allspice, or nutmeg. Mulled wine is generally sweetened with sugar and often fortified with a spirit, usually brandy. Some recipes call for stirring the hot wine mixture into beaten eggs, which gives the beverage flavor and body. GLÜHWEIN is a popular German mulled wine.

Müllerrebe *see* MEUNIER

Müller-Thurgau [MEW-luhr TOOR-gow; MOO-lehr TOOR-gow] Dr. Hermann Müller, who created the Müller-Thurgau variety in the late 1800s, indicated that this grape was a RIESLING-SYLVANER hybrid, and this was thought to be the case for many decades. Then some ENOLOGISTS believed this grape was a CROSS of two strains of RIESLING. Most recent DNA analysis indicates that Riesling is one parent but that the other is CHASSELAS. Regardless of its beginnings, this white-wine grape is now one of the most widely cultivated grapes in Germany, especially in the regions of BADEN, RHEINHESSEN, and PFALZ. Although not extensively grown in the United States, this prolific vine is planted in Austria, Switzerland, England, New Zealand, Italy's northern mountain regions, and Hungary (the world's second largest grower after Germany). Müller-Thurgau grapes produce smooth, low-ACIDITY, medium-sweet wines with a hint of MUSCAT character. Unfortunately, because of high YIELDS, these wines generally lack flavor, and most don't age well. The best wines come from Germany's MOSEL region

M

and Italy's ALTO ADIGE. They're made with grapes grown in yield-restricted vineyards, which produce grapes with concentrated flavor. Müller-Thurgau is also a heavy contributor to the flood of inexpensive LIEBFRAUMILCH coming out of Germany. In New Zealand, the wines—often referred to as *Riesling-Sylvaner*—have higher acidity and are more flavorful than most German examples. Müller-Thurgau is also known as *Rivaner* and *Rizlingszilvani.*

multivintage *see* VINTAGE

Aux Murgers *see* NUITS-SAINT-GEORGES

Murray Darling Large, productive Australian wine region straddling the Murray River with vineyards in both the Big Rivers Zone of NEW SOUTH WALES and the North West Victoria Zone of VICTORIA. It's situated about 270 miles northwest of Melbourne; the main town in the area is Mildura. The climate in this region is hot and dry and vineyards require constant irrigation, which is provided by an irrigation system developed in the late 1800s. This system has turned the vast, dry, arid area into a garden spot not only for grapes but also for lots of other produce. Vines in this hot, well-irrigated area are very vigorous, producing high YIELDS and generally less than the highest quality wines. Most of the production is destined for Australia's inexpensive and popular bag-in-box (or cask) wines. The wine regions along the Murray River—Murray Darling, the SWAN HILL region, and the RIVERLAND region—generate 50 percent of Australia's wine production. SULTANA, MUSCAT, CHARDONNAY, and COLOMBARD are the most widely planted wine grapes. There is also considerable acreage of Shiraz (SYRAH) and CABERNET SAUVIGNON.

Muscadel *see* MUSCAT

Muscadelle [mus-kuh-DEHL] A highly productive white-wine grape grown in France's BORDEAUX region, mostly in sweet-wine-producing areas such as BARSAC, SAUTERNES, and PREMIERES CÔTES DE BORDEAUX. Muscadelle has an intense, perfumy character and is used in small quantities to add bouquet to sweet wines, usually those based on SÉMILLON and/or SAUVIGNON BLANC grapes. Because of Muscadelle's intensity, no more than 5 percent is added to the higher-quality wines of Barsac and Sauternes. A larger percentage often finds its way into the wines of Premieres Côtes de Bordeaux. Some Muscadelle is grown in Australia, where it's known as *Tokay* and often used in DESSERT WINES called *Liqueur Tokays.* Muscadelle is also called *Musquette, Muscadet Doux,* and *Raisinotte.*

Muscadet; Muscadet AC [meuhs-kah-DAY] A popular LIGHT, DRY wine produced in western portion of France's LOIRE region. Unlike most other wines in France, the name is not taken from a town or geographic area but rather from a grape known locally as Muscadet (although its proper name is MELON DE BOURGOGNE). The area where Muscadet is produced is centered around Nantes, not far from where the Loire River empties into the Atlantic Ocean. Four APPELLATIONS produce these wines—Muscadet AC, Muscadet de Sèvre-et-Maine AC, Muscadet des Coteaux de la Loire AC, and Muscadet Côtes de Grandlieu AC. The **Muscadet AC** produces the lowest-quality wines, which are usually inexpensive and ordinary. One unusual requirement of this appellation is that the ALCOHOL level has a *maximum* (rather than minimum) strength of 12.3 percent. The best Muscadet wines come from **Muscadet de Sèvre-et-Maine AC**, an area southeast of Nantes that produces 85 percent of the Muscadet wines. Because of the large amount produced, some of these wines are also fairly ordinary. Wines labeled *mise en bouteille sur lie,* meaning they're bottled directly off their LEES without filtering, are considered best. This process produces more flavorful wines that are SOFT and CREAMY and have citrus nuances. Only a small amount of wine is produced in the third appellation, **Muscadet des Coteaux de la Loire AC**, which is located northeast of Nantes. Another appellation, **Muscadet Côtes de Grandlieu AC**, was approved in the mid-1990s for the area southwest of Nantes around Lac de Grandlieu. Most Muscadet should be drunk young, although the SUR LIE versions can sometimes AGE for several years.

Muscadet Doux [meuhs-kah-DAY DOO] *see* MUSCADELLE

Muscadine [MUHS-kuh-dihn] Found in the southeastern United States, the Muscadine grape family has at least eleven important varieties. The best-known species of this family is VITIS ROTUNDIFOLIA, a name attributed to the vines' round leaves. The thick-skinned Muscadine grapes have a strong, musky flavor and can range in color from bronze to deep purple. Even though these NATIVE AMERICAN GRAPES are primarily grown for table grapes, they're also used to make limited quantities of wine. In fact, some of the very first American wines were made from Muscadine grapes. One variety—the bronze-colored SCUPPERNONG—is used to make sweet wines that are still popular in some parts of the South.

M

Muscat [MUHS-kat; MUHS-kuht] Grape family used for winemaking, table grapes, and raisins. It is comprised of hundreds of varieties that range in color from white to almost black. Muscat grapes are grown in temperate climates around the world in Italy, France, Greece, Spain, Australia, and California. This category of grapes has existed for centuries and is one of the oldest known to man. Muscat wines are noted for their musky, fresh-grape flavors and range from fine, light whites (often SPARKLING) to sweet, dark versions (often FORTIFIED). **Muscat Blanc à Petits Grains** ("white Muscat with little berries") is generally regarded as the best of the Muscat grape family. It varies in color from white to pink to dark reddish-brown. This grape has a limited YIELD, which produces concentrated flavors. It's responsible for the lovely, sweet, fortified MUSCAT DE BEAUMES-DE-VENISE wines from the southern RHÔNE. It also makes the dark, fortified liqueur wines of Australia, where their Muscat Blanc à Petits Grains is called *Brown Muscat* or *Frontignan*. In the northern Rhône, this grape is blended with CLAIRETTE to produce the CLAIRETTE DE DIE wines. In Italy, it forms the basis for the sparkling ASTI wines. In California, Muscat Blanc à Petits Grains is called *Muscat Blanc, Muscat Canelli,* or *Muscat Frontignan. Moscato Giallo* (or *Goldmuskateller*) and *Moscato Rosa* (or *Rosenmuskateller*) are thought to be colored versions of Muscat Blanc à Petits Grains. Although also VINIFIED DRY, these colored grapes are best known for making the fragrant sweet wines from Italy's ALTO ADIGE region. Regardless of where Muscat grapes are grown or what types of wines they're used to produce, the PERFUMY, MUSKY, ripe-grape characteristics persist. Muscat Blanc à Petits Grains has many names around the world including *Gelber Muskateller, Moscato Bianco, Muscat de Frontignan, Muscat d'Alsace, Muscadel, Muskadel, Muskateller, Muscatel de Grano Menudo, Moscatel Rosé,* and *Tamyanka*. Although not as well regarded as the Muscat Blanc à Petits Grains, another strain—**Muscat of Alexandria** (also known as *Moscatel Romano* or *Roman Muscat*)—is very ancient and thought to go back to Egyptian times. These high-yield grapes have low ACID and high sugar content, which generally produces low-quality wines with raisiny characteristics. A majority of the cultivated Muscat of Alexandria end up as table grapes or raisins. This grape is grown in warmer climates throughout the world. It's most widely cultivated in Spain, where it's known as *Moscatel de Málaga* and made into heavy, sweet, golden- to dark-brown wines. In Portugal, it's the basis for the sweet, fortified MOSCATEL DE SETÚBAL wines. Muscat of Alexandria is also known as *Gordo Blanco, Hanepoot, Lexia, Moscatel, Moscatel Gordo,* and *Zibibbo*. Another variety is **Muscat Ottonel**, which is thought to be a cross between an unknown strain of Muscat and CHASSELAS. This much lighter flavored grape is not as overpoweringly "Muscat" as the other variations. It grows in cooler climates, and its most notable wines come from ALSACE, which produces

M

DRY, perfumy wines, and Austria, where rich DESSERT WINES are the result. Muscat Ottonel is also known as *Muskotaly*. The dark-colored **Muscat Hamburg** variety is used mainly as a table grape but also produces thin, red wines—mainly from eastern European countries. DNA PROFILING indicates the Mustcat Hamburg is a cross of Muscat of Alexandria and SCHIAVA. In Australia and the United States, where it's called *Black Muscat,* this grape seldom finds its way into wine. Muscat Hamburg is called *Moscato di Amburgo* in Italy. Other synonyms include *Black Hamburg* and *Golden Hamburg*. The ORANGE MUSCAT variety is apparently unrelated to the Muscat family.

Muscat Blanc *see* MUSCAT

Muscat Blanc à Petits Grains *see* MUSCAT

Muscat Canelli *see* MUSCAT

Muscat d'Alsace *see* MUSCAT

Muscat de Beaumes-de-Venise AC [mews-KAH (muhs-KAT) duh bohm duh vuh-NEEZ] APPELLATION located in France's southern RHÔNE region. The wine, made from Muscat à Petits Grains (MUSCAT) grapes, is a VIN DOUX NATUREL. This is a category of sweet, FORTIFIED WINE made from grapes that are high in natural sugar (capable of reaching 15 percent ALCOHOL) and whose FERMENTATION is stopped by the addition of alcohol (no more than 10 percent of the volume). Muscat de Beaumes-de-Venise has blossomed from a little-known local potable enjoyed by BEAUMES-DE-VENISE residents to an extremely popular, high-priced wine. It's rich, honeyed, and full of floral and fruit aromas and flavors like peaches, apples, oranges, roses, and the ever-present GRAPEY character of Muscat. Good ACIDITY stops it from being CLOYING.

Muscat de Frontignan AC [mews-KAH (muhs-KAT) duh frawn-tee-NYAHN] APPELLATION that is centered around the town of Frontignan, southwest of Montpellier on the Mediterranean in France's LANGUEDOC-ROUSSILLON region. It produces a well-known VIN DOUX NATUREL (sweet, FORTIFIED WINE) made from the Muscat Blanc à Petits Grains variety, also referred to locally as *Muscat de Frontignan* (*see* MUSCAT). These wines are deep golden to almost orange in color and have a distinctive Muscat aroma and flavor.

M

Muscat de Lunel AC [mews-KAH (muhs-KAT) duh lew-NEHL] Lunel is a little town northeast of Montpellier in southern France. It's the heart of an AC that produces FORTIFIED WINES (both VIN DOUX NATUREL and VIN DE LIQUEUR) made from the MUSCAT variety.

Muscat de Mireval AC [mews-KAH (muhs-KAT) duh mee-ray-VAHL] APPELLATION centered around the town of Mireval, southwest of Montpellier on the Mediterranean in France's LANGUEDOC-ROUSSILLON region. It produces a well-known VIN DOUX NATUREL (sweet FORTIFIED WINE) made from the Muscat Blanc à Petits Grains variety (*see* MUSCAT). The wines from Mireval are similar to those from the neighboring Frontignan (*see* MUSCAT DE FRONTIGNAN), although they are slightly BIGGER and RICHER.

Muscat de Rivesaltes AC [mews-KAH (muhs-KAT) reev-SAHLT] APPELLATION that surrounds the small town of Rivesaltes, which is located north of Perpignan in France's LANGUEDOC-ROUSSILLON region. It produces a well-known VIN DOUX NATUREL (sweet FORTIFIED WINE) using the primary grapes of Muscat Blanc à Petits Grains and Muscat of Alexandria (*see* MUSCAT). The resulting wines are deeply colored, alcoholic, and sweet. The RIVESALTES AC also produces Vin Doux Naturel in which GRENACHE, MALVOISIE, MACABEO, and Muscat grapes can be used.

Muscat Du Cap Corse AC *see* CORSICA

Muscatel de Grano Menudo *see* MUSCAT

Muscateller *see* ALEATICO

Muscat Frontignan *see* MUSCAT

Muscat Hamburg *see* MUSCAT

Muscat of Alexandria *see* MUSCAT

Muscat of Samos *see* GREECE

Muscat Ottenel *see* MUSCAT

muscular *see* Glossary of Wine Tasting Terms, page 655

muselet [mew-zeh-LAY] Invented in France by Adolphe Jacqueson in 1844, a *muselet* is the wire cage that secures a cork in a bottle of Champagne or other sparkling wine.

Musigny AC [myoo-zee-NYEE] A distinguished GRAND CRU vineyard located in the village of CHAMBOLLE-MUSIGNY in the CÔTE DE NUITS district of France's BURGUNDY region. The 26½-acre site, which sits just above the famous CLOS DE VOUGEOT *grand cru* vineyard, is planted entirely with PINOT NOIR grapes (except for a small ¾-acre plot that grows CHARDONNAY). Known for their magnificent PERFUMED fragrance, Musigny red wines are LIGHTER and have more ELEGANCE and FINESSE than many of the other grands crus (such as CHAMBERTIN or BONNES

MARES). They generally MATURE more quickly and can be drunk relatively YOUNG. Even though the small plot of Chardonnay produces very good white wines, their quantity is limited, which makes them very expensive. They're generally not deemed as good as white wines from other top grands crus, nor are they as highly regarded as the Musigny red wines.

Muskadel *see* MUSCAT

Muskateller *see* MUSCAT

Muskotaly *see* MUSCAT

musky *see* Glossary of Wine Tasting Terms, page 655

Musquette *see* MUSCADELLE

must The juice of freshly crushed grapes that will be FERMENTED into wine. Must can include pulp, skins, and seeds. *See also* MUST WEIGHT.

musto cotto *see* MARSALA DOC

must weight A measurement of the sugar content of unfermented grape MUST. Knowing the must weight helps winemakers forecast the finished wine's POTENTIAL ALCOHOL. The must weight is usually measured by using either a REFRACTOMETER or a HYDROMETER. The three scales used to quantify the must weight are BAUMÉ, BRIX, and OECHSLE. *See also* SPECIFIC GRAVITY.

musty *see* Glossary of Wine Tasting Terms, page 655

mutage [meu-TAZH] A French term for the process of stopping FERMENTATION either by using SULFUR DIOXIDE and sterile FILTERING or by adding grape alcohol or brandy. The latter technique is how PORT wines or VINS DOUX NATURELS are made.

muté [mew-TAY] Completely unfermented or partially fermented grape juice whose FERMENTATION was stopped. This can happen either by adding SULFUR DIOXIDE, followed by sterile FILTERING to extract any yeast, or by adding grape alcohol or brandy. The resulting juice retains all or most of its natural grape sugars and is used to blend with other wines that need BODY or sweetness or to make APÉRITIFS.

M

mycoderma [my-koh-DER-muh] A class of bacteria that converts ethyl alcohol (*see* ALCOHOL) into acetic acid (*see* ACIDS) and ETHYL ACETATE and spoils wine with a vinegary flavor and odor. Wine affected by mycoderma is sometimes referred to as PIQUÉ.

N

Nackenheim [NAHK-ehn-hime] One of the better wine-producing villages in Germany's RHEINHESSE region. It's located in the area of excellent vineyards known as the RHEINTERRASSE, which is south of the city of Mainz. The red sandstone, which runs through the area, yields grapes that produce high-quality wines with unique CHARACTER. RIESLING and SYLVANER grapes can both produce great wines. **Engelsberg** and **Rothenberg** are the top EINZELLAGEN.

Nagyburgundi *see* PINOT NOIR

Nahe [NAH-uh] Although the Nahe is one of the smaller of Germany's ANBAUGEBIETE (quality-wine regions), it's well known to connoisseurs as a producer of high-quality RIESLING wines. The Nahe River is a tributary of the Rhine River, flowing into it at Bingen. The 12,000 vineyard acres, which are spread out along both banks and part of the surrounding areas, are planted primarily with white varieties. MÜLLER-THURGAU is the most widely planted grape, followed by Riesling and SYLVANER. Riesling grapes, however, occupy most of the prime vineyard sites. The Nahe is divided into two BEREICHE, **Kreuznach** and SCHLOSSBÖCKELHEIM, and has seven GROSSLAGEN. Of the Grosslagen, **Burgweg** is considered the best, but the best known is **Rüdesheimer Rosengarten** (not to be confused with the more famous village of RÜDESHEIM in the RHEINGAU region).

naked *see* Glossary of Wine Tasting Terms, page 655

Náoussa *see* GREECE

Napa County; Napa Valley AVA The Napa Valley is the most famous wine region in California and the United States. Its winemaking history started in 1838 when MISSION grapes were planted by George C. Yount, who made his first wines in the early 1840s. The earliest commercial winery was established by Charles Krug in 1861. This was followed by Schramsberg (1862), Beringer (1876), Inglenook (1879) and Beaulieu Vineyard (1900). After growing to over 160 wineries in the 1880s, the Napa Valley was devastated by PHYLLOXERA, which had attacked vineyards in Europe and now began to ravage the Napa vineyards. Napa's next major setback was PROHIBITION, instituted from 1920 to 1933, which severely curtailed the growth of the winemaking industry. A few wineries survived Prohibition by making sacramental wines and selling grapes to home winemakers. By the end of the 1950s, only a dozen or so wineries had survived the dual devastation of phylloxera and Prohibition. Viticultural activity began to revive in the 1960s when Joe Heitz started Heitz Wine Cellars in

1961, the Davies' reestablished Schramsberg in 1966, and Robert Mondavi left the family winery (Charles Krug Winery) and established his own winery in 1966. Others were getting the same idea, and wineries began appearing in quick succession all over the Napa Valley. Today there are over 300 wineries and over 43,000 acres of vineyards. The terms *Napa County* and *Napa Valley* are almost synonymous because the Napa Valley AVA lies totally within Napa County and includes almost all of Napa County except for a small portion northeast of Lake Berryessa and a region to the south where the city of American Canyon lies. Almost all wines produced in the county are eligible for and use the Napa Valley AVA designation. Few wines use the county designation and those that do are usually wines made with grapes from Sonoma County and Napa County and their labels must show the grape percentage used from each county. The **Napa Valley AVA**, approved in 1983, is located northeast of San Francisco, beginning on the south end at San Pablo Bay, which is connected to and just north of San Francisco Bay. The Napa Valley ranges in width from about 1 to 5 miles and extends north and slightly west for just over 30 miles to Mount St. Helena. From south to north, it encompasses the towns of Napa, Yountville, Oakville, Rutherford, St. Helena, and Calistoga. The Napa Valley AVA climate ranges from a cool Region I (*see* CLIMATE REGIONS OF CALIFORNIA) in the south to a warm Region III in the north. This VITICULTURAL AREA encompasses numerous smaller subzones that, although they have their own AVA status, must use "Napa Valley" on the label. Wines from the CARNEROS AVA, which is partly in the Napa Valley and partly in SONOMA COUNTY, are not required to label their wines "Napa Valley." Within the large Napa Valley AVA there are many notable and distinct growing areas. At this writing, 14 AVAs have been approved: ATLAS PEAK, CARNEROS, CHILES VALLEY DISTRICT, DIAMOND MOUNTAIN DISTRICT, HOWELL MOUNTAIN, MOUNT VEEDER, OAK KNOLL DISTRICT, OAKVILLE, RUTHERFORD, SPRING MOUNTAIN DISTRICT, ST. HELENA, STAGS LEAP DISTRICT, WILD HORSE VALLEY, and YOUNTVILLE. Only about 30 percent of the Napa acreage is planted to white-grape varieties, over 70 percent of which are CHARDONNAY. Other white varieties in order of popularity include SAUVIGNON BLANC, RIESLING, SÉMILLON, CHENIN BLANC, and VIOGNIER. The dominant red variety is CABERNET SAUVIGNON, with just under 50 percent of the vineyard acreage. Other red varieties include MERLOT, PINOT NOIR, ZINFANDEL, CABERNET FRANC, SANGIOVESE, SYRAH, and PETITE SIRAH.

Napa Gamay *see* GAMAY

Naracoorte Ranges *see* WRATTONBULLY

native American grapes Grape varieties indigenous to the Americas. Four main species are related to wine production—VITIS AESTIVALIS, VITIS LABRUSCA, VITIS RIPARIA, and VITIS ROTUNDIFOLIA—none of which produce grapes used to make the world's fine wines. That honor goes to VITIS VINIFERA (which includes CABERNET SAUVIGNON, CHARDONNAY, and SAUVIGNON BLANC grapes), an Asian and European species used in over 99 percent of the world's wines. Native American varieties have made an important contribution to the wine world in that they are PHYLLOXERA-resistant, particularly the *Vitis riparia* species. After European vineyards were devastated by the phylloxera infestation in the 1800s, it was discovered that GRAFTING *Vitis vinifera* BUDWOOD to native American ROOTSTOCKS produced phylloxera-resistant *Vitis vinifera* grapes.

native yeast fermentation *see* YEAST

natur; naturrein; naturwein [nah-TOOR] Old German terms referring to wines that don't have added sugar. These terms have been outdated by the QUALITÄTSWEIN MIT PRADIKÄT (QmP) category, established in 1971, which defines the finest German wines.

nature; naturel [nah-TEWR; nah-tew-REHL] 1. French words meaning "nature" and "natural," referring to wine to which nothing (usually meaning sugar or ALCOHOL) has been added. 2. On CHAMPAGNE or SPARKLING WINE labels, these terms typically refer to wines that don't have *liqueur d'expédition* (DOSAGE) added, which would contribute to sweetness. Such wines are sometimes called *Brut Nature*. 3. On some sparkling wine labels, *naturel* may mean that the wine is not totally DRY but simply the driest style of that producer. 4. In the Champagne region, the terms *Vin Nature* or *Vin Nature de la Champagne* were once used when referring to still wines from this area. Since 1974, however, the CÔTEAUX CHAMPENOIS AC name appears on the labels of these wines.

naturrein; naturwein *see* NATUR

Navarra DO [nah-VAH*R*-*R*AH] A DO located south of Pamplona in the southern part of the Navarra province in north-central Spain. This region's winemaking history dates back to the Roman occupation and its wines were long well regarded. At the end of the nineteenth century, PHYLLOXERA took its toll, shrinking the vineyard acreage from an estimated 120,000+ acres to less than 2,000 acres. Today there are about 35,000 acres. Garnacha (GRENACHE) is grown in over half the vineyards and is the dominant grape, although TEMPRANILLO is gaining in popularity. Historically Navarra is best known for its *rosado* (ROSÉ) wines, but red wine now makes up half of the production. CABERNET SAUVIGNON, GRACIANO, Mazuelo (CARIGNAN), and MERLOT are also allowed in Navarra's red wines. The area produces a small amount of white wine from CHARDONNAY, Garnach Blanca (GRENACHE), MALVASIA, and Viura (MACABEO).

Néac *see* LALANDE-DE-POMEROL

Nebbiolo [neh-b'YOH-loh] The fog (*nebbia* in Italian) that rolls over the hills of northern PIEDMONT and the regions nearby, helps the Nebbiolo grape ripen properly, thereby creating some of Italy's finest red wines. Wines made from Nebbiolo grapes are associated with a variety of DOC and DOCG names including BAROLO, BARBARESCO, GATTI-NARA, GHEMME, and SPANNA. They're characterized as being RICH, full-bodied (*see* BODY), and CHEWY. These wines often have a high ALCOHOL content (13 percent and above), as well as fairly substantial TANNINS, both of which are easily supported by the wine's hefty fruit flavors. The aroma and flavor of these dark-colored wines are suggestive of chocolate, licorice, raspberries, truffles, and violets. Nebbiolo wines generally are long-lived and require significant aging to develop and SOFTEN. Although recognized as one of the world's great wine grapes, Nebbiolo has not been planted in significant amounts outside of northwest Italy. Very few have been planted in California or other U.S. growing regions. The Nebbiolo grape is also known as *Chiavennasca, Picotener* or *Picutener, Pugent,* and *Spanna* or *Spana.*

Nebbiolo d'Alba DOC [nehb-BYOH-loh DAHL-bah] DOC zone that covers a large area around the town of Alba extending on both sides of the Tanaro River in the southeastern part of Italy's PIEDMONT region. These wines are made from the NEBBIOLO grape, which is the same one used in the famous neighboring DOCGs of BAROLO and BAR-BERESCO. Nebbiolo d'Alba DOC red wines, however, require only 1 year of AGING, compared to a minimum of 3 years for Barolo and 2 years for Barbersco wines. Nebbiolo d'Alba wines are well regarded and viewed as lighter versions of those from Barolo and Barbersco. Although most of the wines produced here are STILL and DRY, DOC rules permit sweet and SPUMANTE versions as well.

Nebuchadnezzar *see* Wine Bottles, page 609

négociant [nay-goh-SYAHN] French for "merchant" or "dealer," used in the wine world to refer to a person or firm that sells and ships wine as a wholesaler. The extent of the role played by this intermediary has expanded over time. Traditionally, négociants bought, matured, sometimes blended, and then bottled and shipped wine. Over time, the role expanded to include purchasing grapes and making wine. Some labels may contain the phrase *négociant-éleveur* (*see* ÉLEVEUR), indicating that the merchant played a more extensive role in producing the wine. In some transactions, there is another intermediary—a COURTIER or "wine broker," who helps establish the price paid by a négociant to a small producer. Some of the better-known French négociants are Barton & Guestier, Calvet, Cordier, Moueix, and Sichel.

Negra Mole; Tinta Negra Mole [NAY-gruh MOH-leh; TEEN-tuh NAY-gruh MOH-leh] A red-wine grape grown on the island of MADEIRA and in the Portuguese regions of Algrave and CARCAVELOS. After the PHYLLOXERA invasion in the 1870s, Negra Mole replaced many of Madeira's classic varieties including BOAL, MALVASIA, SERCIAL, and VERDELHO. Although Negra Mole is considered only a *good* variety, it's important today in the production of the long-lived FORTIFIED WINES of Madeira. In 1986, Portugal entered the Common Market, whose regulations stipulated that by 1993 any Madeira wine naming a variety on its label would have to contain at least 85 percent of that grape. This new requirement stimulated replanting of the more classic varieties as already mentioned and will probably lessen the importance of Negra Mole in the future. In Spain, this variety is called *Negramoll.*

Negramoll *see* NEGRA MOLE

Négrette [neh-GREHT] A red-wine grape cultivated mainly in southwestern France. Négrette is the main grape in the wines of CÔTES DU FRONTONNAIS, which can be very SMOOTH and SUPPLE, have flavor aspects of strawberry and raspberry, and be capable of medium-term AGING. Limited amounts of this variety are grown in California, where it's known as *Pinot St. George* because it was long thought to be a member of the Pinot family. Negrette is also known as *Petit Noir.*

Negron *see* RABOSO

Nelson New Zealand wine-growing region that shares the northern end of the South Island with its more famous neighbor MARLBOROUGH. German settlers first planted vines in this region in the 1840s; however, many became disheartened and moved on to the more hospitable climate of Australia's BAROSSA VALLEY. Over the decades other VITICULTURE attempts were made in the Nelson region, but it was not until the 1970s that the modern era began. Nelson sits to the west of Marlborough across the Richmond and Bryant Mountain Ranges. It's sheltered on the west by the Tasman Mountains and Mount Arthur Range. The sheltering effect of the mountains makes the Waimea Plains, where most vineyards are planted, one of the sunniest places in New Zealand. Still, this area is cooler and wetter than Marlborough, though fortunately rains don't generally hamper efforts late in the growing season. CHARDONNAY, SAUVIGNON BLANC, RIESLING, and PINOT NOIR account for a large majority of the planted varieties and are the most successful. With less than 800 acres, Nelson is one of New Zealand's smallest growing regions.

Neméa *see* AGHIORGHITIKO; GREECE

Nerello [nay-RAY-loh] Grown in Sicily, this red-grape VARIETY comes in two versions—**Nerello Cappuccio** and **Nerello Mascalese**. The latter appears to have the most potential and is the most widely cultivated. Nerello Mascalese is used primarily as a blending wine, providing a spicy, AROMATIC character that helps add complexity to wines. In the wines of the Faro DOC, Nerello Mascalese grapes make up from 45 to 60 percent, whereas Nerello Cappuccio grapes account for from 15 to 30 percent. They make up even higher proportions in the ETNA DOC reds.

Neretto *see* CROATINA

nero [NAY-roh] Italian for "black," used in the world of wine as to describe dark red grapes and wines.

Nero d'Avola [NAY-roh DAH-voh-lah] Important Italian red-grape VARIETY grown in Sicily. Nero d' Avola has the ability to produce dark-red, RICH, CHEWY wines with AGING potential. However, it can be low in ACIDITY and is often BLENDED with other varieties to give the resulting wine more BALANCE. It's also called *Calabrese*.

nerveux *see* Glossary of Wine Tasting Terms, page 655

nervy *see* Glossary of Wine Tasting Terms, page 655

Neuburger *see* AUSTRIA

Neuchâtel [neuh-shah-TEHL] Located north of Geneva, this Swiss canton is well known for its white wines made from CHASSELAS grapes. These Chasselas wines are LIGHT and DRY, with a touch of effervescence, the latter the result of being bottled SUR LIE, which produces a second fermentation in the bottle. The vineyards, located on the north shore of Lake Neuchâtel, are planted mainly with Chasselas, although some PINOT NOIR is grown as well. The Pinot Noir wines, which are

N

considered some of the best Swiss reds, are often produced in a pale ROSÉ style known as ŒIL DE PERDRIX ("eye of the partridge").

Neuguén *see* ARGENTINA

neutral *see* Glossary of Wine Tasting Terms, page 655

New Jersey Although New Jersey's winemaking tradition goes back over 200 years, it has yet to become a major wine-producing state, in part because New Jersey law restricted winery development until 1981. Renault Winery, started in 1864 and still around today, survived PROHIBITION by selling sacramental and medicinal wines—their curative tonic (at 22% alcohol) was sold throughout the United States. Today, area wineries use HYBRIDS like CHAMBOURCIN, CHANCELLOR, LEON MILLOT, MARÉCHAL FOCH, SEYVAL BLANC, and VIDAL BLANC. VITIS VINIFERA grapes grown here include CHARDONNAY, RIESLING, CABERNET SAUVIGNON, PINOT NOIR, and VIOGNIER. New Jersey has two VITICULTURAL AREAS—the CENTRAL DELAWARE VALLEY AVA (which it shares with PENNSYLVANIA) and the 144,640-acre **Warren Hills AVA**, established in 1988 in Warren County.

New Mexico This southwestern state is the oldest known VITIS VINIFERA growing region in the United States. History tells us that in 1629 monks successfully planted MISSION vines in Senecu, an Indian pueblo south of the city of Socorro (about 80 miles south of Albuquerque). But it's thought that there may have been earlier plantings in southern New Mexico, dating as far back as the late 1500s, over a century before the Spanish missionaries in California began planting. The viticultural area along the Rio Grande River was so successful that by the 1880s, it was the fifth largest wine-producing region in the United States with an annual output of about one million gallons of wine. Floods, crop disease, and PROHIBITION curtailed this copious production, finally bringing it to a halt in 1920. It wasn't until the late 1970s and early 1980s that New Mexico's wine industry began to revive. Winemakers realized that the high-desert climate's long hot days (which allow grapes to mature and ripen to proper sugar levels) and cool nights (which help set good ACID levels) was favorable to the production of good wines. There are three approved AVAs in New Mexico—southern New Mexico has MESILLA VALLEY AVA and the MIMBRES VALLEY AVA; MIDDLE RIO GRANDE VALLEY AVA is in the middle of the state. Today there are nearly 25 wineries throughout the state. The best known is probably Gruet Winery—partially because the owners are French and partially because it produces great sparkling wine. Luarent Gruet and Farid Himeur started the winery in 1987. They came to New

Mexico from the CHAMPANGE region in FRANCE where their families had produced sparkling wines since 1952 at Gruet Champagne.

New South Wales A state located along the Pacific Ocean in southeastern Australia, bordered by the state of Queensland on the north, and the state of Victoria on the south. New South Wales is Australia's most populous state thanks to Sydney, the country's largest city. It's the birthplace of Australian winemaking. Settlers in the 1780s planted the first vineyards in the Sydney area. During the 1800s the HUNTER VALLEY became Australia's most important wine region. The zones and regions established under the Australian GEOGRAPHIC INDICATIONS system paint a picture of the New South Wales wine landscape. Farthest north is the **Northern Rivers Zone** that currently contains the small HASTINGS RIVER region. Heading south toward Sydney lies the Hunter Valley, known for unique, long-lived SÉMILLON wines, lush CHARDONNAYS, and long-aging Shiraz (SYRAH). West of Sydney on the other side of the Great Dividing Range are a number of emerging growing areas that have the humidity problems prevalent on the eastern side. Farthest north of these is the **Central Ranges Zone** that includes (from north to south) the regions of MUDGEE, ORANGE, and COWRA. Farther south is the **Southern New South Wales Zone** that includes (from north to south) the HILLTOPS, CANBERRA DISTRICT, and TUMBARUMBA regions. Farther west in the southernmost section of New South Wales is the **Big Rivers Zone**, the result of the giant irrigation projects implemented in this dry, arid region. This zone includes the huge RIVERENA region, which produces 65 percent of New South Wales wine production, the Pericoota region, and parts of the highly productive MURRAY DARLING and SWAN HILL regions. Additionally, New South Wales grapes can make their way into wines under the designation of SOUTH EASTERN AUSTRALIA, a gigantic zone that covers three full states and parts of two others.

New World Wine; techniques A reference to non-European wine-producing countries such as ARGENTINA, AUSTRALIA, CHILE, NEW ZEALAND, SOUTH AFRICA, and the UNITED STATES. New World wine techniques are modern, science-based VITICULTURE and VINICULTURE methods, although the differences are rapidly disappearing. *See also* OLD WORLD WINE.

New York This state is the United States' third-largest premium wine-producing state after California and Washington. A majority of the state's vineyards are planted with native VITIS LABRUSCA or HYBRID vines. Because of this, New York wasn't considered a producer of high-quality wines until recently. Acreage devoted to VITIS VINIFERA grapes (like

CABERNET SAUVIGNON, CHARDONNAY, PINOT NOIR, and RIESLING) is slowly increasing, but these varieties account for only about 10 percent of New York's total vineyard land. On the other hand, NATIVE AMERICAN GRAPES (like CATAWBA, CONCORD, DELAWARE, and NIAGARA) comprise over 70 percent of the vineyard acreage. HYBRIDS like AURORA, BACO NOIR, CHELOIS, DE CHAUNAC, and SEYVAL BLANC account for the remaining vineyard acreage. New York's most important premium wine-producing region (in which 45 percent of the state's 160 wineries reside) is the FINGER LAKES AVA and its subzone CAYUGA LAKE AVA. Other regions include the HUDSON RIVER VALLEY REGION AVA, LAKE ERIE AVA (which extends into PENNSYLVANIA and OHIO), and LONG ISLAND AVA, with its VITICULTURAL AREAS of North Fork of Long Island and The Hamptons. Much of New York's production goes into GENERIC WINES (labeled BURGUNDY, CHABLIS, RHINE WINE, or SAUTERNE) or into SPARKLING WINES. Wines labeled with an AVA designation must contain a minimum of 85 percent of that area's wine. "New York State" on the label tells you that a minimum of 75 percent of the wine came from within the state. Wines labeled with the name of a *Vitis labrusca* grape must comprise 51 percent of that grape. Other VARIETAL WINES must contain 75 percent of a particular grape.

New Zealand Although New Zealand had vineyards and produced wines as far back as 1819, it didn't have a reputation for making high-quality TABLE WINES until recently. It's essentially been a nation of beer drinkers, and the wine it did produce was usually FORTIFIED. Many of New Zealand's grapes were HYBRIDS but, starting in the mid-1960s, winemakers gradually began to experiment with European varieties like CHARDONNAY. What resulted was a rapid expansion of vineyards producing VITIS VINIFERA wines, with New Zealand winemakers determining they had better success with white wines. The clincher, and what put New Zealand on wine consumers' radar, was the success with SAUVIGNON BLANC—first from Montana, New Zealand's largest wine company, and then, on an even more dramatic scale, from Cloudy Bay Vineyards. About two-thirds of the country's vineyards are planted to white varieties. MÜLLER-THURGAU, which was the most widely planted white grape a decade ago, has been surpassed by a number of higher-quality grape varieties. Chardonnay is the most widely planted followed by SAUVIGNON BLANC, PINOT NOIR, MERLOT, CABERNET SAUVIGNON, and RIESLING. New Zealand's most highly regarded wines are Sauvignon Blancs, followed by Chardonnay, sweet DESSERT WINES (from BOTRITISED Riesling grapes), and SPARKLING WINES from Pinot Noir and Chardonnay. Because of New Zealand's cool climate, Cabernet Sauvignon and Cabernet Sauvignon/Merlot blends lean toward being slightly HERBA-

CEOUS. Pinot Noir is gaining ground as producers discover that it's not only good for SPARKLING WINES, but also as STILL WINE. There are currently ten recognized growing areas. New Zealand's North Island—the first of the islands to produce wines—has growing regions in AUCKLAND, GISBORNE, HAWKE'S BAY, NORTHLAND, WAIKATO, and WELLINGTON. The South Island has growing areas in MARLBOROUGH, CANTERBURY, CENTRAL OTAGO, and NELSON. Marlborough surpassed the North Island's Hawke's Bay as the largest growing area primarily owing to its successful Sauvignon Blanc cultivation. Gisborne is the third-largest producing area in the country. These three growing regions comprise 80 percent of New Zealand's vineyard acreage. Although New Zealand has attained a certain stature in the wine world, it's still a fairly small producer in the global picture. It has yet to move into being one of the top 30 wine-producing nations in the world—but it's a country with fewer than four million people.

Niagara [ni-AG-ruh] An American white-wine grape created by CROSSING the CONCORD and Cassady varieties. Niagara is grown primarily in the eastern United States (with the heaviest concentration in New York) and, to some extent, in the Midwest. It's also found in Canada, Brazil, and New Zealand. Niagara is generally vinified into sweet or medium-sweet wines that have GRAPEY and FOXY properties.

Niagara Escarpment AVA This VITICULTURAL AREA takes its name from a 650-mile long limestone ridge that runs though New York, Ontario, Michigan, Wisconsin, and Illinois. The AVA, which was established in October 2005, only covers an area in Niagara County in northern New York State. The Niagara River forms its western border just above Buffalo and runs for about 30 miles to the east and is only about half a mile wide. It encompasses 18,000 acres; of these, only about 50 acres are planted with wine grapes, mostly PINOT NOIR. Another 350 acres are planted with CONCORD meant for juice, jams, and jellies. There are currently 13 wineries located within the APPELLATION.

Niagara Peninsula VA *see* ONTARIO

Nieddera [nee-EHD-deh-rah] Ancient red-grape VARIETY grown in Sardinia in the Tirso River Valley. Nieddera, also called *Bovale*, is being rediscovered as a source for interesting red and ROSÉ wines.

Niederhausen [NEE-duhr-how-zuhn] A small, highly regarded wine-producing village located southwest of BAD KREUZNACH in Germany's NAHE region. It has a reputation for producing some of the region's finest RIESLING wines. The top EINZELLAGEN are **Hermannshöhle** and **Hermannsberg**.

N

Niederösterreich *see* AUSTRIA

Nielluccio *see* SANGIOVESE

Nierstein [NEE*R*-SHTINE] The premier wine-producing village of Germany's RHEINHESSE region. It's located in an area of excellent vineyards known as the RHEINTERRASSE, south of the city of Mainz. Nierstein also lends its name to the BEREICH that covers this area and to the three GROSSLAGEN that cover its vineyards—Niersteiner **Auflangen**, Niersteiner **Rehbach**, and Niersteiner **Spiegelberg**. In addition, it's used in the name of the Grosslage Niersteiner Gutes Domtal, which covers vineyards for other area villages. Nierstein has many fine vineyards including **Bildstock**, **Hipping**, **Hölle**, **Kranzberg**, **Ölberg**, **Paterberg**, and **Pettenthal**. The finest wines generally come from vineyard sites (EINZELLAGEN) like these and, because the Bereich Nierstein annually produces a tremendous amount of wine (12 million cases in some years), it's important for consumers to check the label for the Einzellagen name (such as Niersteiner *Olberg*). Many estates also produce fine wines under the three Niersteiner Grosslagen.

Nies'chen *see* KASEL

noble *see* Glossary of Wine Tasting Terms, page 655

noble grapes A term that in the past has been used for the grape varieties once acknowledged to produce the world's great wines: CABERNET SAUVIGNON, CHARDONNAY, MERLOT, PINOT NOIR, SAUVIGNON BLANC, and RIESLING. In French, the term is *cépages nobles*.

noble mold *see* BOTRYTIS CINEREA

noble rot *see* BOTRYTIS CINEREA

node Swollen, evenly spaced areas on a CANE or SPUR where buds, leaves, and fruit clusters form.

nonalcoholic wine *see* DEALCOHOLIZED WINE

Nonnenberg *see* RAUENTHAL

non-vintage *see* VINTAGE

North Carolina This southern state is home to the SCUPPERNONG, a white-wine grape that belongs to the MUSCADINE family. Europeans found Muscadine vines growing wild here as early as 1524. During the nineteenth and early twentieth centuries, Scuppernong wines from North Carolina were quite well known, particularly the Virginia Dare brand. At this writing, North Carolina's 22 wineries produce 550,000 gallons of wine from approximately 900 acres of vineyard. Although Muscadine grapes are still popular, the planting of HYBRIDS and European (VITIS VINIFERA) vines is increasing. More than half the wineries produce wines from these grape varieties. North Carolina is home to the **Biltmore Estate Winery**, one of the largest in the southern United States and the former country retreat of the Vanderbilts. This winery produces over 75,000 cases of STILL WINES (RED, WHITE, and RÓSE), as well as SPARKING WINES from an area that was originally the estate's dairy complex.

North Coast AVA APPELLATION comprised of the counties north of San Franciso including LAKE, Marin, MENDOCINO, NAPA, SONOMA, and Solano. Previously, the North Coast region included counties south of San Francisco, which are now in the CENTRAL COAST region. It encompasses over 3,000,000 acres and includes many smaller AVAS like NAPA VALLEY AVA, the various Sonoma County AVAs and those in Mendocino and Lake Counties. The North Coast AVA is a leader in acreage producing high-quality wine grapes including CABERNET FRANC, CABERNET SAUVIGNON, CHARDONNAY, MERLOT, PINOT NOIR, and SAUVIGNON BLANC.

North East Victoria Zone *see* VICTORIA

Northern Neck George Washington Birthplace AVA This 590,080-acre VITICULTURAL AREA takes up the VIRGINIA peninsula that extends south and east from Fredericksburg between the Potomac and Rappahannock Rivers. It encompasses the counties of Westmoreland (where George Washington was born), King George, Northumberland, Lancaster, and Richmond. Ingleside Plantation Vineyards, the only winery in the area, has about 70 acres of vineyards and produces a variety of SPARKLING WINES and STILL WINES.

Northern Rivers Zone *see* NEW SOUTH WALES

Northern Sonoma AVA *see* SONOMA COUNTY

North Fork of Long Island AVA *see* LONG ISLAND

North Fork of Roanoke AVA Small southern Virginia AVA located southwest of the city of Roanoke on the north fork of the Roanoke River in parts of Roanoke and Montgomery Counties. It received approval as a designated area in 1987.

Northland New Zealand winegrowing region located in the far north of the North Island near the towns of Kaitaia and Whangarei. The southernmost point at Whangarei is about 115 miles north of the city of Auckland. Although vines were planted here in 1819, making

N

Northland the birthplace of New Zealand viticulture, the region's winemaking nearly vanished until a strong VITICULTURE resurgence in the 1980s and 1990s. The region's warmth, humidity (from heavy rains), and rich soils encourage large yields. Careful site selection and good crop management programs are required to produce excellent wines. When managed properly CABERNET SAUVIGNON, MERLOT, Shiraz (SYRAH), and CHARDONNAY can produce high-quality wines.

North West Victoria Zone *see* VICTORIA

North Yuba AVA A 22,400-acre California AVA located in the larger SIERRA FOOTHILLS AVA, northwest of the towns of Grass Valley and Nevada City. Small amounts of CABERNET SAUVIGNON, RIESLING, and SAUVIGNON BLANC are planted here. The Renaissance Vineyard and Winery is the only one in the area.

Norton Many winemakers think this is the best indigenous American grape variety for making TABLE WINES. Also sometimes called *Virginia Seedling,* this red variety is thought to be part of the VITIS AESTIVALIS family, although some conjecture that it is a cross between *Vitis aestivalis* and another North American species. Its origins are controversial, including the theory that Dr. D. N. Norton of Richmond, Virginia, propogated this grape in the 1830s, hence its name. Norton wines don't exhibit the undesireable FOXY character usually associated with North American grape varieties. It's also disease-resistant and extremely hardy, which makes it popular in a number of growing regions east of the Rocky Mountains. Norton grapes produce wines that are rich, full-bodied, and flavorful. Occasionally these wines have a "grapey" flavor similar to that of the CONCORD grape. Although some growers believe there are slight differences, most believe that the Norton grape is the same as the **Cynthiana**. In Missouri, which made popular Norton wines from the mid-1800s to the early 1900s, Cynthiana and Norton are used interchangeably.

nose *see* Glossary of Wine Tasting Terms, page 655

Nostrano *see* TICINO

nouveau; pl. nouveaux [noo-VOH] French for "new" that, when applied to wine, refers to one that is very young. Because of the influence of France's BEAUJOLAIS NOUVEAU wines, this word has taken on a meaning relating to this particular wine's style—light, fruity, youthful, and lacking aging potential. These nouveau wines are almost always released shortly after harvest. Many of them are made using CARBONIC MACERATION, a FERMENTATION technique designed to enhance their intensely fruity yet light-bodied (*see* BODY) characteristics. The term *nouveau* is also used in the United States. Italians call this style of wine *novello* or VINO NOVELLO.

Nova Scotia *see* CANADA

novello *see* NOUVEAU; VINO NOVELLO

nu [NEUH] French for "naked," which in the wine trade refers to the price of wine without cask or bottles.

Nuits-Saint-Georges AC [nwee sa*n* ZHAW*R*ZH] After BEAUNE, the town of Nuits-Saint-Georges is the second most important commercial center in France's CÔTE D'OR section of BURGUNDY. The town contains a significant number of NÉGOCIANTS and has given its name to the northern half of the Côte d'Or—the CÔTE DE NUITS. The town is the center of the Nuits-Saint-Georges AC, which lies between the villages of VOSNE-ROMANÉE and Prémeaux-Prissey. Prémeaux-Prissey wines are allowed to use the Nuits-Saint-Georges AC and usually do. There are no GRAND CRU vineyards in this APPELLATION, but there are 38 PREMIERS CRUS—more than in any other appellation. The best of these are **Les Saint-Georges**, **Les Vaucrains**, and **Les Cailles**, followed by **Les Damodes**, **Aux Boudots**, **Aux Murgers**, **Les Pruliers**, and **Les Perrières**. Red wines made from PINOT NOIR grapes dominate the production, although tiny amounts of white wine are also made. The wines from the best producers can be quite good with richly CONCENTRATED flavors and good TANNIC structure. They're best when aged for 5 years or more. Current critiques indicate that the presence of many mediocre producers results in varying levels of quality, which makes the selection of Nuits-Saint-Georges AC wines difficult.

Nuragus di Cagliari DOC [noo-RAH-goos dee kah-LYAH-ree] The largest DOC on the island of SARDINIA (except for those DOCs covering the entire island), Nuragus di Cagliari covers the southern third of the landmass and is centered in the province of Cagliari. The wines, which are made mainly from Nuragus grapes, are DRY, LIGHT, and CRISP thirst quenchers that are mediocre, at best. AMABILE and FRIZZANTE versions are also permitted.

Nussbien *see* RUPPERTSBERG

Nussbrunnen *see* HATTENHEIM

nutty *see* Glossary of Wine Tasting Terms, page 655

NV *see* VINTAGE

oak The preferred wood for making the barrels and casks in which wine is AGED. Oak barrels impart flavors and TANNINS, both of which are desirable for most red wine as well as some white wines. Oak is slightly porous, which creates an environment ideal for aging wines. Redwood and chestnut are distant second choices to oak, and neither do the job as well. Sometimes these woods are used for larger casks because the expense of using oak is a luxury. Despite oak's unique capabilities, more delicate wines do not do well with oak aging of any length, and some wines can easily become over-oaked. In either case, oak flavors and tannins can overpower a wine's VARIETAL CHARACTER, which results in a poorly BALANCED wine. Oak is also a matter of personal taste. For instance, some wine lovers prefer big, oaky CHARDONNAYS, while others prefer leaner, cleaner styles where the oak character isn't so prominent. Choosing the right barrel requires some knowledge of and experience with various types of oak, as well as the COOPERS who make the barrels. The favorite wood for wine barrels is **white oak** (red oak is too porous), with the U.S. species differing slightly from European. In Europe, the primary sources of oak are France and the former Yugoslavia. The best-known French sources are LIMOUSIN, a forest in south-central France; central France's forests of Allier, Nevers, and Troncais; and Vosges, a forest in northeastern France. The leading sources of white oak in the United States are Kentucky, Minnesota, Missouri, Ohio, Tennessee, and Wisconsin. There's a great deal of discussion about how the oak from different locations affects various types of wines. Some believe that Limousin oak, which has a looser grain, imparts more oak flavor, while others say that it delivers less. Most agree that American oak imparts a slightly sweeter character than European oak. However, it's also argued that the cooper's barrel-making technique has as much to do with the barrel's effect on wine as the wood from which it's made. Barrel making in America (which was primarily for the distilled spirit industry) was much different than that found in Europe. This is now changing, with many European barrel makers opening COOPERAGES in California to handle the expanded demand from California winemakers. Oak barrels lose their ability to impart flavor in 4 to 5 years, and most high-quality wine estates and CHÂTEAUX replace all or part of their oak barrels with new ones each year so a high level of new oak character is imparted to each new VINTAGE.

oaking The process of imbuing wine with oak flavors either by barrel AGING, soaking oak chips in the wine, or by inserting special oak staves into stainless steel tanks.

Oak Knoll District AVA Established in 2002, this VITICULTURAL AREA is located at the southern end of the NAPA VALLEY AVA. It encompasses 9,940 acres and is bordered by the YOUNTVILLE AVA to the north, the MOUNT VEEDER AVA to the west, the CARNEROS AVA to the south, and the Silverado Trail to the east. It excludes most of the City of Napa south of Trancas Street. The area gets its name from the Oak Knoll Ranch that was located in the area and quite well known in the mid-1800s. This area is one of the coolest in the Napa Valley. The only cooler AVA is Carneros AVA, which is farther south. This climate allows some parts of the Oak Knoll District to excel with cooler weather grapes like PINOT NOIR and CHARDONNAY; other portions succeed with CABERNET SAUVIGNON and MERLOT.

Oakville AVA This VITICULTURAL AREA is located in the center of the NAPA VALLEY. It begins north of the town of Yountville and extends northwest about a mile past the town of Oakville just before Cakebread Cellars winery. It abuts the RUTHERFORD AVA on its northwest boundary and the YOUNTVILLE AVA along the southeastern side. The Oakville AVA extends across the valley floor and, although it encompasses less than 6,000 acres, includes many esteemed Napa Valley wineries. This region also hosts several distinguished vineyards, including the famous MARTHA'S VINEYARD (whose CABERNET SAUVIGNON grapes go into the esteemed VINEYARD DESIGNATED bottling by Heitz Wine Cellars), Franciscan Oakville Estate vineyards, Beringer's State Lane Vineyard, and Robert Mondavi's famous To Kalon Vineyard. Although other grape varieties like SAUVIGNON BLANC, SEMILLON, MERLOT, CABERNET FRANC, MALBEC, and PETIT VERDOT are grown, the Oakville AVA is prime CABERNET SAUVIGNON country.

oaky; oakiness *see* Glossary of Wine Tasting Terms, page 655

Obermosel, Bereich *see* MOSEL-SAAR-RUWER

Obidos *see* ESTREMADURA

Ockfen [AWK-fuhn] A highly regarded wine-producing village located south of Konz along the Saar River in Germany's MOSEL-SAAR-RUWER region. The village owes its reputation to the extremely steep hillside vineyards, which include the well-known EINZELLAGE **Bockstein**. In good growing years, Ockfen's STEELY, yet ELEGANT and intensely fragrant RIESLING wines can rival any produced in Germany.

Oechsle [UHK-sluh] A German method of measuring the SPECIFIC GRAVITY (therefore, the sugar content) of MUST or grape juice prior to FERMENTATION. Developed in the nineteenth century by Germany's

Christian Ferdinand Oechsle, this method is similar to the BRIX system used in the United States and the BAUMÉ scale used in France. Germany employs the Oechsle scale to establish the quality levels of wines (*see* QUALITÄTSWEIN BESTIMMTER ANBAUGEBIET (QbA) and QUALITÄTSWEIN MIT PRÄDIKAT (QmP)). The required Oechsle reading varies for a given quality level, depending on the grape varieties and the German region. For example, KABINETT wines (the lowest quality level within QmP—the highest quality category) require an Oechsle reading of 73° for RIESLING in the RHEINGAU region, but only 67° in Germany's AHR region. TROCKENBEERENAUSLESE, the highest quality level of all German wine, requires an Oechsle reading of 150° (equivalent to a 35° Brix reading) for Riesling in all regions.

œil de perdrix [uh-yuh deuh peh*r*-D*R*EE] A French term meaning "partridge eye," used in the past to describe white wines that are made from red grapes and have a pinkish hue—similar to the pinkish tint of a partridge's eye. Today the terms VIN GRIS or VIN ROSÉ usually appear on labels of such wines.

Œillade *see* CINSAUT

oenologist *see* ENOLOGY

oenology *see* ENOLOGY

oenophile *see* ENOPHILE

Oestrich [UH-st*r*ihch] A large village located along the Rhine River southwest of the city of Wiesbaden in Germany's RHEINGAU region. The wines from this area are generally of high quality and occasionally superior. RIESLING is the grape of choice, and it produces FIRM, full-bodied (*see* BODY) wines. The best EINZELLAGEN include **Doosberg**, **Klosterberg**, **Lenchen**, and **Schloss Reichartshausen** (the latter, which is classified as an ORTSEIL, isn't required to use Oestrich's name on the label).

off *see* Glossary of Wine Tasting Terms, page 655

off dry *see* Glossary of Wine Tasting Terms, page 655

Official Wine Classifications of Bordeaux *see* page 678

Ohio Throughout the years, Ohio has been one of the important Midwestern wine-producing states. There was a period during the mid-1800s when Ohio was the largest wine producer in the nation, but vineyard DISEASES impeded industry growth; then, PROHIBITION killed it. Attempts at rejuvenating Ohio's wine industry didn't really take hold until the late 1960s. Today the state has six AVAS, and the number of wineries is over 65 and growing. The LAKE ERIE AVA includes growing areas near the shores of Lake Erie in Ohio, New York, and Pennsylvania and includes two Ohio subzones—ISLE ST. GEORGE and Grand River Valley. The OHIO RIVER VALLEY AVA is the largest VITICULTURAL AREA in the United States, comprising a total of 16,640,000 acres in portions of INDIANA, KENTUCKY, WEST VIRGINIA, and Ohio. It also contains a small subzone, the Kanawha River Valley AVA. The sixth AVA is **Loramie Creek**, a small 3,600-acre area in west central Ohio's Shelby County, surrounded by Loramie and Tuttle Creeks and State Route 47. It currently has no operating winery. Almost 45 percent of the state's wineries are located around Lake Erie in the northeastern section of Ohio. The vineyards are planted primarily with native vines like CATAWBA, CONCORD, and NIAGARA. HYBRIDS like SEYVAL BLANC and VIDAL BLANC are also very popular. VITIS VINIFERA vines (including CABERNET SAUVIGNON, CABERNET FRANC, CHARDONNAY, GEWÜRZTRAMINER, MERLOT, PINOT GRIS, PINOT NOIR, and RIESLING) are growing in popularity but still make up less than 10 percent of the total vineyards.

Ohio River Valley AVA Established in 1987, this is the largest VITICULTURAL AREA in the United States. It covers parts of four states (INDIANA, KENTUCKY, OHIO, and WEST VIRGINIA) along the Ohio River and encompasses a total of 16,640,000 acres. For all its size, the acreage planted in wine grapes is quite small—less than 600 acres. The **Kanawha River Valley AVA** is a 64,000-acre subzone located in the southeastern corner of Ohio and the southwestern part of West Virginia. It has approximately 100 acres of vineyards. This AVA is home to a large number of wineries that produce FRUIT WINES. VITIS VINIFERA (such as CABERNET SAUVIGNON and CHARDONNAY) are difficult to grow here so HYBRID grapes like AURORA, CATAWBA, SEYVAL BLANC, VIDAL BLANC, and VIGNOLES are the most widely planted. Some wineries that wish to make Cabernet Sauvignon, Chardonnay, or MERLOT wines purchase crushed grapes from other areas, such as California. Such crushed grapes are typically shipped in containers chilled to just above freezing in order to keep the grape MUST as fresh as possible on its cross-country journey.

oidium *see* MILDEW

oily *see* Glossary of Wine Tasting Terms, page 655

Ojo de Liebre *see* TEMPRANILLO

Okanagan Valley VA *see* BRITISH COLUMBIA

Olaszriesling *see* WELSCHRIESLING

Ölberg *see* NIERSTEIN

Old Mission Peninsula AVA *see* MICHIGAN

old vine A term frequently used on wine labels to indicate that grapes from old vines were used to produce the wine. It's thought that the quality of these grapes is superior. There is no legal definition for "old vine," and there is no true consensus about its use. The terms **vieilles vignes** on French labels and **alte reben** on German wines mean the same thing.

Old World wine; techniques Wine from European countries, as opposed to NEW WORLD WINE from countries like AUSTRALIA, SOUTH AFRICA, and the UNITED STATES. Old World winemaking and VITICULTURAL techniques are customarily based on tradition, rather than science, although the differences are rapidly disappearing.

Olifants River Region *see* SOUTH AFRICA

oloroso *see* SHERRY

Oltrepò Pavese DOC [ohl-TRAY-poh pah-VEH-zuh] Large DOC zone located in the southwestern corner of Italy's LOMBARDY region, south of Pavia. Two of the designated wines—**Buttafuoco** (which means "sparks like fire") and **Sangue di Giuda** ("blood of Judas")—can only be produced in a smaller subzone located in the northeastern part. These two red wines are made from BARBERA, CROATINA, Pinot Nero (PINOT NOIR), Uva Rara, and Ughetta (Vespolina). They both can be STILL but are usually FRIZZANTE. The Buttafuoco is DRY; the Sangue di Giuda ranges from dry to sweet. These same grapes are used for the Oltrepò Pavese ROSSO and ROSATO. Other wines made include the red VARIETALS Barbera, Bonarda (CROATINA), and Pinot Nero and the white varietals CORTESE, Moscato (MUSCAT), Pinot Grigio (PINOT GRIS), Riesling Italico (WELSHRIESLING), and Riesling Renano (RIESLING). Many of these are allowed to be frizzante (some SPUMANTE) and can range from dry to sweet.

Onomasía Proeléfseos Anotéras Piótitos *see* GREECE

Onomasía Proeléfseos Eleghoméni *see* GREECE

Ontario Ontario is Canada's second largest and most populous province, and its most productive wine-producing area. It's Canada's southmost province, and portions of it extend south of much of the United States' northern border, down to the Great Lakes and the St.

Lawrence River; the northern section abuts the huge Hudson Bay. There are about 12,000 acres of wine grapes planted in Ontario. The majority of the grape growing and winemaking is centered in the southernmost section in an area called the Niagara Peninsula, which lies south of Toronto, Ontario, and west of Buffalo, New York. The northern portion of the peninsula has been designated an appellation—**Niagara Peninsula VA**. It's bordered on the north by Lake Ontario, on the east by the Niagara River, on the south by the Welland River, and on the west by Highways 20 and 56. The environment of this extremely southern (for Canada) area is moderated by Lake Ontario (*see* LAKE EFFECT). Another positive feature of this area is the Niagara Escarpment—a 575- to 600-foot ridge (at the eastern end of which is the world-famous Niagara Falls) that runs east to west and holds back winds coming off Lake Ontario. This produces good air circulation and helps protect the vineyards from frost and vineyard DISEASES. All these geographical and environmental factors combine to create an area that produces over 80 percent of Canada's grapes. Other approved appellations in Ontario include the Pelee Island VA and the Lake Erie North Shore VA. The **Pelee Island VA** is located in the western portion of Lake Erie some 15 miles from the Canadian mainland about halfway between Toledo and Cleveland, Ohio, and southeast of Windsor, Ontario. It is Canada's most southerly area and comes within 6 or 7 miles of ISLE ST. GEOGE AVA, a U.S. appellation. Canada's first commercial winery, Vin Villa, was established here in 1866. Pelee Island's southern location combined with the moderate temperatures provided by being surrounded by Lake Erie, gives it the longest growing season in Canada. Pelee Island Winery has 500 vineyard acres planted on the island. **Lake Erie North Shore VA** is located along Lake Erie in the southwestern part of Ontario, south of the City of Windsor, running from the city of Amherstburg to Leamington. The approximately 300 acres of wine grapes here also benefit from the southern location and the lake effect from Lake Erie. Growers compare this growing climate to that of BORDEAUX, although winters here are certainly more severe. The vineyards on Pelee Island and in the Lake Erie area are now planted to about 60 percent VITIS VINIFERA. Ontario vineyards include the following *Vitis vinifera* varieties: CABERNET FRANC, CABERNET SAUVIGNON, CHARDONNAY, GAMAY NOIR, GEWÜRZTRAMINER, MERLOT, PINOT GRIS, PINOT NOIR, RIESLING, and SAUVIGNON BLANC. The planted HYBRIDS include BACO NOIR, MARÉCHAL FOCH, SEYVAL BLANC, and VIDAL. *See also* CANADA; VQA.

OPAP *see* GREECE

OPE *see* GREECE

open *see* Glossary of Wine Tasting Terms, page 655

opening *see* Glossary of Wine Tasting Terms, page 655

opening wine *see* Opening and Serving Wine at Home, page 636

Oporto *see* PORT; PORTUGIESER

Oppenheim [AHP-uhn-hime] An important wine-producing village in Germany's RHEINHESSEN region, south of the city of Mainz near NIERSTEIN. Oppenheim, along with towns like Nierstein, NACKENHEIM, and DIENHEIM, is part of area of excellent vineyards known as the RHEINTERRASSE. Its wines, which are generally rated just a fraction below Nierstein in terms of overall quality, are some of the Rheinhessen's finest. RIESLING, which is planted on over half of the available vineyard land, produces the best wines—ELEGANT, with CONCENTRATED flavors. The best Oppenheimer wines come from EINZELLAGEN such as **Herrenberg**, **Kreuz**, and **Sackträger**.

Optima [OP-tee-muh] German white-wine variety created in the 1970s that is a cross of MÜLLER-THURGAU and a SYLVANER-RIESLING hybrid. Optima grapes, which tend to grow in less than choice conditions, are low in ACID and high in sugar. The wines they produce can be very sweet and are generally used to boost the sugar content of other wines.

Orange Australian wine region located in the Central Ranges Zone of NEW SOUTH WALES. It's situated approximately 165 miles west of Sydney, between the COWRA and MUDGEE regions around the slopes of Mount Canobolas. This emerging area offers a diversity of climatic conditions unavailable in most of the other New South Wales regions. High-quality SAUVIGNON BLANC, RIESLING, and PINOT NOIR grapes are grown at the higher, cooler elevations. Memorable wines from here are made from CHARDONNAY, and the red varieties (which are grown on the lower, warmer plains) include Shiraz (SYRAH), CABERNET SAUVIGNON, MERLOT, and CABERNET FRANC. Like the Cowra region to the south, much of the grape harvest is trucked to out-of-the-area wineries. Bloodwood Estate was a pioneer in the Orange area and has since been joined by Brangayne, Canobolas-Smith, Highland Heritage, Ibis, and Reynolds Orange. Carbonne, with its huge 1,200-acre Little Boomey Vineyard, is the big player in this region.

Orange Muscat Apparently unrelated to the MUSCAT family, the orange muscat grape is not well known and is believed to have been grown in the south of France around the village of Orange. There are small plantings in Italy, Australia, and California, where Quady Winery pioneered this variety in its proprietary brand, *Essencia*.

Orange River Region *see* SOUTH AFRICA

ordinaire [ohr-dee-NAY*R*] French term meaning "plain" or "ordinary." *Vin ordinaire* refers to inexpensive, everyday wines.

Oregon Along with Washington and Idaho, Oregon makes up the region known as the Pacific Northwest. Although grapes were planted here in the nineteenth century, most of the vineyards were abandoned during PROHIBITION. It wasn't until the early 1960s that Oregon was viewed as a promising site for vineyards, particularly for cooler climate varieties like RIESLING, which Richard Sommer planted at his Hillcrest Vineyard in 1961, and PINOT NOIR, which has become this state's most celebrated grape. David Lett of Eyrie Vineyard first demonstrated the promising marriage of Oregon and Pinot Noir with his 1975 vintage, which showed extremely well in a 1979 BLIND TASTING with a number of wines from BURGUNDY. Today, Pinot Noir, Riesling, and CHARDONNAY are Oregon's most popular grape varieties, followed by PINOT GRIS. Other grapes planted in smaller amounts include CABERNET SAUVIGNON, GEWÜRZTRAMINER, MÜLLER-THURGAU, SÉMILLON, SYRAH, and ZINFANDEL. The best growing areas are situated between the coastal range to the west and the Cascade Mountains to the east, running from north of the city of Portland to the south. There are six approved AVAS in Oregon. The WILLAMETTE VALLEY AVA is in the northern portion, starting north of Portland and stretching to just south of Eugene. The UMPQUA VALLEY AVA is just south of the Willamette Valley and encompasses the towns of Umpqua and Roseburg. Just before the California border and west of Medford and Ashland is a smaller area, ROGUE VALLEY AVA and its subzone, APPLEGATE VALLEY AVA. Although primarily associated with the state of Washington, the COLUMBIA VALLEY AVA and WALLA WALLA AVA both have portions that extend into northern Oregon. By 2005 Oregon had over 14,000 acres of vineyards and is adding wineries at a rapid pace. Now it has more than 300. A majority of these are located in the northern part of the Willamette Valley, where Pinot Noir is king. In Oregon, a VARIETAL WINE must contain at least 90 percent of the named variety, except for Cabernet Sauvignon, which requires only 75 percent. Wines labeled with a named region must contain 100 percent of the wine from that region.

Oremasco *see* DOLCETTO

organic wine [or-GAN-ihk] The definition of an organic wine is continually in flux, changing as various organizations study the subject in detail. In the United States, these organizations include the TAX AND TRADE BUREAU (previously the BATF), the USDA (their National Organic Program (NOP)) and the California Certified Organic Farmers (CCOF)). **Organically grown grapes** are those that have been grown without the use of synthetic or chemically altered pesticides or fertilizers. **Organically processed wines** cannot contain any SULFUR DIOXIDE added during winemaking. If a wine contains less than 10 parts per million (ppm) of sulfur dioxide, it's not required to print the "Contains Sulfites" warning on the label. The Tax and Trade Bureau does not allow the term "organic wine" to be used on wine labels, so the label must carry phrases such as "grapes organically grown" and "wine organically processed." Wines made from organically grown grapes can use sulphur dioxide in the winemaking process (up to 100 ppm) and be labeled "made from organic grapes." However, a winery wishing to use this phrase and a vineyard choosing to claim that its grapes have been grown organically must be certified by one of the USDA's approved organic certifying organizations. The Organic Grapes Into Wine Alliance (OGWA) is also exploring other winemaking aspects such as FINING, FILTERING, and clarifying (*see* CLARIFY) materials, storage tanks, barrel sterilizing materials, bottle CAPSULE materials, and CORKS (the chemicals used to bleach them) to determine how such elements fit into the organic winemaking concept. There are a number of similar organic endeavors going on around the globe, with France being a leader in this area.

organoleptic [or-guh-nl-EHP-tihk; or-ga-nl-EHP-tihk] In the wine world, this term—which fundamentally means "perceived by a sense organ"—is used in relation to evaluating wine with the senses of sight, smell, and taste, rather than by a scientific or chemical examination. Although winemakers rely on precise technical evaluations of their wines, the final outcome usually depends on an expert's organoleptic determination.

Orientali del Friuli *see* COLLI ORIENTALI DEL FRIULI DOC

originalabfüllung [oh-RIHG-ih-nahl-AHB-foo-lung] A German term once used to indicate that a wine was ESTATE BOTTLED. In 1971 the term **Originalabfüllung** was legally replaced by ERZEUGERABFÜLLUNG, which means "bottled by the proprietor" and has a denotation similar to estate bottled. More recently, the term GUTSABFÜLLUNG was introduced—it's more restrictive and even closer to the U.S. definition of estate bottled.

Ormeasco *see* DOLCETTO

Ornellaia *see* BOLGHERI DOC

Ortega [or-TAY-guh] White-wine grape named after the Spanish philosopher José Ortega y Gasset. It is a cross of MÜLLER-THURGAU and Siegerrebe (which is a GEWÜRZTRAMINER–Madeleine Angevine hybrid). The low-ACID, high-sugar Ortega grape produces wines with delightful FLORAL characteristics and hints of peach in both aroma and flavor. Ortega VARIETAL WINES are popular in Germany where they've won numerous medals in wine competitions. Ortega is primarily used for BLENDING; however, it is usually combined with grapes that have lower sugar content and higher acid.

Ortsteil [OHRTS-tile] A German term referring to an area that's part of a larger commuity (as a suburb is of a city), yet is independent of that larger community. For example, the village of ERBACH is an *Ortsteil* of Eltville. Esteemed vineyards like Schloss Johannisberg and Steinberg are classified as Ortsteil; therefore, unlike other vineyards, they aren't required to put the name of their village (the larger community) on bottle labels. For example, wines from the Steinberg vineyard, which is part of HATTENHEIM, are labeled simply "Steinberg," whereas wines from the neighboring Schützenhaus vineyard are labeled "Hattenheimer Schützenhaus."

Orvieto DOC [ohr-VYAY-toh] Well-known DOC area that is located in the southwestern part of Italy's UMBRIA region. It covers a large area surrounding the hilltop town of Orvieto, with a CLASSICO zone covering a smaller area at the center. Wines from this classico area are generally better. Orvieto produces mostly DRY, ordinary white wines from TREBBIANO, MALVASIA, Verdello, GRECHETTO, and Drupeggio grapes. The sweeter wines of this DOC (ABBOCCATO, AMABILE, or DOLCE) are better, especially those made from grapes infected with BOTRYTIS CINEREA, which engenders a RICH, honeyed flavor. It's thought that Orvieto's *abboccato*-style wines were favored in the Middle Ages; they were also prized by Pope Gregory XVI in the nineteenth century.

Otago *see* CENTRAL OTAGO

Ottavianello *see* CINSAUT

ouillage *see* TOPPING

Outer Coastal Plain AVA APPELLATION established in March 2007 that encompasses 2,255,400 acres in southeastern New Jersey. This area has grown wine grapes since the mid-1700s. Renault Winery, located in the AVA, was established in 1864 in Egg Harbor City. It is the oldest winery in the United States to operate on a continuous basis. VITIS VINIFERA grapes that would not survive in many parts of the East Coast will grow in the region because of the tempering influence of the Atlantic Ocean and Delaware Bay (*see also* LAKE EFFECT). Therefore, in addition to NATIVE AMERICAN GRAPES and HYBRIDS such as CAYUGA, CHAMBOURCIN, NIAGARA, SEYVAL BLANC, VIDAL BLANC, and VIGNOLES, one can find CABERNET FRANC, CABERNET SAUVIGNON, CHARDONNAY, MERLOT, PINOT GRIS, SANGIOVESE, and TREBBIANO planted in the region. There are currently 18 wineries located throughout the region.

ouvrée [OO-vray] An old French measure used in Burgundy for area. An ouvrée is equal to about one-tenth of an acre.

Ovens Valley *see* ALPINE VALLEYS

Overberg WO A demarcated SOUTH AFRICA wine district located south and east of Cape Town along the continent's southernmost tip. It's one of the coolest due to the maritime climate. Two wards, **Elgin** and **Walker Bay**, have been gaining particular fame for their endeavors with cool-climate varieties—CHARDONNAY, PINOT NOIR, and SAUVIGNON BLANC. Elgin sits up in the hills and is known for its Granny Smith apples. Walker Bay is on the coast close to the seaside town of Hermanus.

overcropping A VITICULTURE practice where too many buds are left on the vine during winter PRUNING. This produces a very large crop, which produces lower-quality grapes. The large grape crop has trouble ripening and will be lower in desirable attributes such as color, sugar, and flavor. Quality growers use crop management programs to develop the optimum balance of YIELD and quality.

overripe *see* Glossary of Wine Tasting Terms, page 655

oxidation A wine that's been exposed to air undergoes oxidation, which causes chemical changes and deterioration. An oxidized wine has a stale, dull, sherrylike smell and flavor; its color takes on a brownish cast. Although oxidation is an asset in wines like SHERRY and MADEIRA, it's undesirable in a TABLE WINE and can render it undrinkable. *See also* PREMATURE OXIDATION.

oxidized *see* Glossary of Wine Tasting Terms, page 655

Ozark Highlands AVA A very large (1,280,000 acres) AVA located in south-central Missouri, southwest of St. Louis, covering portions of eleven Missouri counties. It starts in the north in Osage, Gasconade, and Franklin Counties; runs south through Maries, Pulaski, Crawford, Phelps, and Dent Counties; and finally ends in the south in the counties of Texas, Reynolds, and Shannon. Although the designated area was approved in 1987, the grape-growing tradition here goes back to the 1870s. Vineyards are planted to HYBRIDS and NATIVE AMERICAN GRAPE varieties.

Ozark Mountain AVA Established in 1986, this huge AMERICAN VITICULTURAL AREA covers some 3,500,000 acres in portions of three states—southern MISSOURI, northwestern ARKANSAS, and northeastern Oklahoma. A number of smaller AVAs reside within its boundaries—ALTUS and Arkansas Mountain in Arkansas and AUGUSTA, HERMANN, and OZARK HIGHLANDS in Missouri. The area is so large that there is no representative wine style for the varied climatic and soil conditions that exist.

P

Paarl Riesling *see* CROUCHEN

Paarl WO [PAH-rool] An important demarcated SOUTH AFRICA wine district that is part of the Coastal Region. It's located around the town of Paarl, 35 to 40 miles northeast of Cape Town. Paarl (Dutch and Afrikaans for "pearl") has long been one of the country's largest growing regions, although its share is down slightly and is now between 16 and 17 percent of the nation's total. It's also considered the home of the South African wine industry and headquarters of the giant Cooperative Wine Growers' Association (known as the KWV—*Kooperatieve Wijnbouwers Vereniging van Zuid-Africa*). Paarl is a diverse growing area with a variety of climates—hotter on the lower plains, cooler on the mountain sites. Almost one-quarter of Paarl's 43,000 acres is planted to CHENIN BLANC (called *Steen* locally). However, this percentage is dwindling as the area shifts to other VARIETIES, primarily red grapes like CABERNET SAUVIGNON, Shiraz (SYRAH), MERLOT, PINOTAGE, and RUBY CABERNET. Whereas this was once white-wine country, the vineyards are now evenly split between red and white varieties. Other primary white varieties grown here are SAUVIGNON BLANC, CHARDONNAY, Columbar (COLUMBARD), and Cape or Paarl Riesling (CROUCHEN). The Paarl district includes the ward of FRANSCHHOEK, which produces excellent white and red wines.

Pacheco Pass AVA Established in 1984, this small 3,200-acre VITICULTURAL AREA straddles the Pacheco Pass Highway (California Highway 152) in parts of Santa Clara and San Benito Counties. It's just north of the city of Hollister, California, about 35 to 45 miles southeast of San Jose. Although the area is not yet very developed, several small wineries are located in the area.

Pacherenc du Vic Bilh AC [pah-shuh-RAH/VK doo veek BEEL] In this part of SOUTHWEST FRANCE, the local dialect uses the word *pacherenc* for "posts in a row." This refers to the modern method of planting vineyards in regular rows, using a post to support each vine. Vic Blih is the name for the local hills in this area, which are part the Pyrenees foothills, along the Adour River south of ARMAGNAC. This APPELLATION produces only white wines and shares the same geographic area as the MADIRAN AC, which produces only red wines. The grapes used for these white wines are Arrufiat (or *Ruffiac*), Gros Manseng, and Petit Manseng, with some SAUVIGNON BLANC and SÉMILLON. These wines are similiar to those from the JURANCON AC (SPICY and FLORAL) and should be drunk young.

Padthaway [PAD-thuh-way] An Australian wine-producing region located in the Limestone Coast Zone in the southeastern corner of

SOUTH AUSTRALIA around the town of Padthaway near the New South Wales border. Early on, this region was called **Keppoch**, but after a struggle over the name it was changed to Padthaway. Although not far from COONAWARRA, which is known for red wines, Padthaway's reputation is for its white wines. CHARDONNAY is the superstar of this region; RIESLING and SÉMILLON are also grown in quantity. Although Padthaway is most recognized for Chardonnay, it also produces quality wines from CABERNET SAUVIGNON and Shiraz (SYRAH). However, in the Australian fashion, such wines are most often blended with wines produced in other growing regions. There are about 8,000 acres of vineyard in the Padthaway region.

Pagadebit; Pagadebito *see* BOMBINO BIANCO

pago [PAH-goh] A term for "vineyard" that's used in some parts of Spain. *See also* VINO DE PAGO.

Paicines AVA *see* SAN BENITO COUNTY

Païen *see* GEWÜRZTRAMINER

Pais *see* MISSION

Palatinate *see* PFALZ

pale cream *see* SHERRY

Palette AC [pah-LEHT] A tiny APPELLATION located east of Aix-en-Provence in the western part of France's PROVENCE region. The majority of the wines are red and ROSÉ, produced from CINSAUT, GRENACHE, MOURVÈDRE, and SYRAH. White wines use CLAIRETTE, Grenache Blanc, MUSCAT, Picpoul, and Ugni Blanc (TREBBIANO). The dominant producer is **Château Simone**.

Pálido *see* RUEDA DO

La Palma DO *see* CANARY ISLANDS

Palmela DOC [pahl-MEH-lah] A DOC covering parts of the municipalities of Palmela and SETÚBAL in southern Portugal, which includes the former IPR, **Arrábida**. Palmela is known mainly for its deep full-bodied red wines made from the PERIQUITA grape, but it also produces some interesting white wines from the FERNÃO PIRES grape. *See also* TERRAS DO SADO.

palo cortado [PAH-loh koh-TAH-doh] *see* SHERRY

Palomino [pah-loh-MEE-noh] The grape that makes the great Spanish SHERRIES. Palomino is not distinctive when used to make standard white TABLE WINES, but when it's processed to make sherry, it can turn into something special. It's heavily grown in and around JEREZ DE LA FRONTERA in the ANDALUCIA region of Spain. *Palomino Fino* is actually the strain that now represents about 90 percent of the planting in the Jerez area, as opposed to the previously favored *Palomino Basto* (or *Palomino de Jerez*) grape. Palomino is also cultivated in the hotter growing areas of Australia, California, France, and South Africa, where its Afrikaans name is *Fransdruif* or simply *Frans*. Attempts to make sherry in these regions has produced some good versions of this FOR-TIFIED WINE, but they're not the quality of the top Spanish wines. Palomino is also called *Ablan, Listán,* and *Tempranilla*; in California, it's mistakenly called *Golden Chasselas*. Australia's *Common Palomino* is not the same grape as Palomino.

pantomina *see* MÁLAGA DO

Paradiesgarten *see* DEIDESHEIM

Parellada [par-eh-LYAH-duh] Spanish white-wine grape that is one of the main varieties in Spain's CATALONIA region. Parellada produces light, fruity, good-quality STILL wines with floral BOUQUETS. These wines don't AGE well, however, and should be drunk young. The best-known single-variety Parellada wine is the Vina Sol from TORRES. This producer also blends Parellada with CHARDONNAY to produce Gran Vina Sol and with SAUVIGNON BLANC to produce Fransola. Parellada is one of the three main varieties used in SPARKLING WINE production as well. It's also known as *Montonec*.

parent vine A grapevine from which a CUTTING to propagate another vine is made.

Parsac *see* PUISSEGUIN-SAINT-ÉMILION AC

Paso Robles AVA [PAH-soh ROH-blays] A large APPELLATION established in 1983 and located around the town of Paso Robles in the northern part of California's SAN LUIS OBISPO COUNTY. Its northern boundary is the MONTEREY COUNTY line, and it extends south of the town of Santa Margarita. The eastern boundary is parallel to the Kern County line, and the western boundary used to be the San Lucia Mountains, west of Paso Robles. The western boundary was extended in late 1995 to include an area east of the mountain range in the northern portion above the YORK MOUNTAIN AVA. Most of the growing area is classified as Region III (*see* CLIMATE REGIONS OF CALIFORNIA), although portions in the east are hotter and fall into Region IV. Some MESOCLI-MATES that receive more cooling ocean breezes fall into the cooler

Region II category. As of 2002, there were over 18,000 acres of vineyards. CABERNET SAUVIGNON, MERLOT, ZINFANDEL, SYRAH, CHARDONNAY, and SAUVIGNON BLANC are the top six grape varieties grown in the Paso Robles AVA. Other red varieties include PETITE SIRAH, PINOT NOIR, GAMAY, and CABERNET FRANC. Other whites grapes are CHENIN BLANC, MUSCAT, and SÉMILLON. The area's best known for its red wines such as Cabernet Sauvignon and Zinfandel.

passerillage; passerillé [pah-seh-ree-LAHZH; pah-seh-ree-LAY] *Passerillage* is the French term for the process of drying grapes so their flavors and sugar become concentrated. *Passerillé* is the descriptor for dried, shriveled grapes used in DRIED-GRAPE WINES. This is similar to the Italian PASSITO.

passe-tout-grains *see* BOURGOGNE PASSE-TOUT-GRAIN AC

passito [pah-SEE-toh] An Italian term used both for a method of making sweet wines and for the sweet wines made this way. Passito wines begin by laying freshly picked grapes on mats (or hanging them in bunches) so that they can partially dry. This process eliminates much of the grape's water and concentrates its sugar and flavor components. Depending on the technique used, the drying time can vary from several weeks (in the hot sun) to several months (in a cool ventilated room). When the grapes are crushed and FERMENTATION begins, the sugar content is usually high enough to take the wine to a reasonable alcohol level (*see* ALCOHOL BY VOLUME) and still end up with enough RESIDUAL SUGAR to make these wines fairly sweet.

passive wine cellar *see* WINE CELLAR

pasteurization [PAS-chuh-rize; PAS-tuh-rize] The killing of bacteria by heating wine or other liquid to moderately high temperatures for a short period of time and then rapidly cooling it to 40°F or lower. The process was discovered by the famous French scientist Louis Pasteur while he was researching the cause of beer and wine spoilage. Although pasteurization is used in beer processing and for some wines meant for early consumption, it's not used for fine wines because it kills off the bacteria that contribute to AGING.

pastoso [pahs-TOH-soh] Italian for "medium-DRY."

Paterberg *see* NIERSTEIN

Patras *see* GREECE

Patrimonio AC [pah-tree-MOH-nee-oh] An APPELLATION that encompasses the wines made in the area west of the city of Bastia on the northwestern coast of the French island of CORSICA. The appellation designation covers red and ROSÉ wines made primarily from the local Nielluccio grape (SANGIOVESE) and white wines from VERMENTINO.

P

Pauillac AC [poh-YAK] The town of Pauillac, located in HAUT-MÉDOC that is probably the most noteworthy in France's BORDEAUX region. The APPELLATION surrounding Pauillac contains three of the five PREMIER CRU (first-growth) châteaux—Latour, Lafite-Rothschild, and Mouton-Rothschild—along with fifteen other CRU CLASSÉ châteaux including Lynch-Bages, Pichon-Longueville-Baron, and Pichon-Lalande. Because cru classé châteaux own much of the approximately 2,700 acres in the appellation, there are few well-known CRU BOURGEOIS châteaux. The dominant grape in Pauillac is CABERNET SAUVIGNON, which is blended with CABERNET FRANC, MERLOT, and, occasionally, small amounts of MALBEC and PETIT VERDOT. Pauillac AC wines from the best VINTAGES are generally powerful, full-flavored, and ELEGANT. When young, they're a bit ROUGH, but they AGE magnificently.

Les Paulands *see* CORTON

pays *see* VIN DE PAYS

P.D. *see* PIERCE'S DISEASE

Pécharmant AC [pay-shar-MAHN] A small area east of the town of BERGERAC that produces red wines from MERLOT, CABERNET SAUVIGNON, CABERNET FRANC, and MALBEC. The wines, which are some of the better ones in the Bergerac region, resemble those from nearby SAINT-ÉMILION in the BORDEAUX region.

Pechsten *see* FORST

Pedernão *see* ARINTO

Pedro Domecq *see* DOMECQ, PEDRO

Pedro Jiménez *see* PEDRO XIMÉNEZ

Pedro Ximénez [PEH-droh hee-MEH-nihs; PAY-droh hee-MAY-nays] A white-wine grape grown in southern Spain whose name is the Hispanic transliteration of Peter Siemens, the man who brought the vine from Germany to Spain's sherrymaking region, Jerez (JEREZ Y MANZANILLA). Although usually associated with sherry, Pedro Ximénez (or PX, as it's commonly called) has been heavily supplanted by palomino in Jerez and is now used mainly for sweetening and darkening the

Palomino-based blends. Pedro Ximénez is still widely planted in Spain's MONTILLIA-MORILES area where it's often processed to make a sherry-style wine. It's also a major grape of Spain's MÁLAGA region where it's made into high-alcohol, medium- to very-sweet wines. In much of Spain, a light, rather bland, dry white table wine is also made from this variety. Pedro Ximénez is the most widely planted white variety in Argentina and is widely grown in Australia as well. In the United States, small amounts of sherry-style PX wines are used to soften blended whiskeys. Pedro Ximénez is also known as Pedro Jiménez and Pero Ximen.

Peel Australian wine region located in the Greater Perth Zone of WESTERN AUSTRALIA. It's situated around the town of Mandurah, which is about 50 miles south of Perth. The GEOGRAPHE region borders it to the south, with the Indian Ocean to the west. This area is part of what was once called the **South West Coast**. Vines were first planted in this region in the 1850s and there was sporadic dabbling with VITICULTURE over the years. The modern era didn't really begin until the 1970s. The breezes off of the Indian Ocean moderate the climate in this area and the soil conditions of sand over limestone necessitate some irrigation in the summer. Primary varieties here are CHARDONNAY, CHENIN BLANC, SEMILLON, CABERNET SAUVIGNON, and Shiraz (SYRAH).

Pelaverga [peh-lah-VEH*RR*-gah] A red-wine grape grown in the VERDUNO PELAVERGA DOC in Piedmont in northern Italy near the BAROLO DOCG. It's also referred to as *Pelaverga Piccolo*. This grape is thin-skinned and produces non-tannic wines that are ruby-red in color and light and spicy with floral and red fruit aromas. They are best drunk young. It's not the same variety as the Pelaverga di Pagno variety grown around Saluzzo to the west.

Pelee Island VA *see* ONTARIO

pelure d'oignon *see* Glossary of Wine Tasting Terms, page 655

Pemberton An Australian wine region located in the South West Australia Zone of WESTERN AUSTRALIA. It's situated a little over 200 miles southeast of Perth around the towns of Manjimup and Pemberton. This region is relatively new—the first commercial vineyards didn't appear until the early 1980s. The climate of this region's southern portion around the town of Pemberton (and farther south) is quite cool. It does best with cool-climate VARIETIES like CHARDONNAY and PINOT NOIR, some of which finds its way into SPARKLING WINES. In the north around **Manjimup** (which may one day be split into its own region), the climate is warmer with occasional hot days and cool nights. This makes it better suited to red grapes like CABERNET SAUVIGNON, CABERNET FRANC, MERLOT, PETIT VERDOT, and Shiraz (SYRAH). Whites that excel here include SAUVIGNON BLANC and SÉMILLON, although Chardonnay also does quite well.

Penedès DO [pay-NAY-dahss] A DO area located southwest of the city of Barcelona in northeast Spain's CATALONIA region. The area is also the center of the SPARKLING WINE industry, which has its own DO, CAVA. Penedès has approximately 65,000 vineyard acres, which are spread throughout three subzones—Bajo (or Lower) Penedès, Medio (or Middle) Penedès, and Penedès Superior (Upper). Each subzone has different growing conditions, making each one best for specific grape varieties. The Penedès DO makes STILL WINES, which are predominantly white because of the large amount of white varieties planted for the sparkling wine industry. The predominant grapes are PAREL-LADA, MACABEO, and XAREL-LO, though there is a growing interest in CHARDONNAY. The smaller amount of red and ROSÉ wine that's produced here is made primarily from Garnacha Tinta (GRENACHE), Carinena (CARIGNAN), and TEMPRANILLO. The best red wines come from CABERNET SAUVIGNON, an approved variety. Compared to most of Spain's wine industry, the Penedès DO is very modern. It was the first region in Spain to introduce international varieties like CABERNET FRANC, Cabernet Sauvignon, Chardonnay, GEWÜRZTRAMINER, MERLOT, PINOT NOIR, RIESLING, and SAUVIGNON BLANC—all sanctioned by DO rules. Penedès is a leader in STILL WINE innovations, led by the wine estates of Torres, Jean León, and Masía Bach.

penetrating *see* Glossary of Wine Tasting Terms, page 655

Pennsylvania Located in the Middle Atlantic states, Pennsylvania is one of the thirteen original states of the United States. Grape growing and winemaking appear to have started here as early as the mid-1600s, when members of the New Sweden Company planted VITIS VINIFERA vines in the state's southeastern portion (with little success). In 1684, William Penn tried VITICULTURE again in Philadelphia in the area that is now Fairmont Park. Again, no success. In 1793, The Pennsylvania Wine Company, the first commercial winery in Pennsylvania and the United States, was established along the Schuylkill River near Philadelphia. In the 1800s, grape-growing centers sprang up around the Susquehanna River in York County and around the Ohio River near Pittsburgh. Around the middle of the nineteenth century, shortly after the Erie Canal project was finished, the Lake Erie area in Erie County became another major wine-producing area. The wine industry in Pennsylvania continued to grow into the twentieth century. Of course, PROHIBITION brought wine production to a halt in 1920. Even after Prohibition ended in 1933, wine production was inhibited by the state liquor monopoly. Although the Conestoga Winery was established in 1963, it wasn't until the 1968 Farm Winery Act was put in place that the number of wineries started to expand. Today Pennsylvania has approximately seventy wineries, none of them very large. The largest of these is Chaddsford Winery, in the state's southeastern portion, which annually produces approximately 30,000 cases. Pennsylvania has four AVA's—CENTRAL DELAWARE VALLEY AVA, which it shares with NEW JERSEY; CUMBERLAND VALLEY AVA, which it shares with MARYLAND; LAKE ERIE AVA, which it shares with OHIO and NEW YORK; and LANCASTER VALLEY AVA. Pennsylvania is the fourth-largest grape grower in the United States but only ranks in the top fifteenth in wine production. A large majority of the vineyards (especially around Lake Erie) are planted with CONCORD, which is usually made into juice and jelly. A very small percentage of vineyards (mostly located in southeastern Pennsylvania) are planted with HYBRIDS like CAYUGA, CHAMBOURCIN, SEYVAL BLANC, and VIDAL BLANC, and VITIS VINIFERA vines like RIESLING, CABERNET SAUVIGNON, CABERNET FRANC, CHARDONNAY, GEWÜRZTRAMINER, Pinot Grigio (PINOT GRIS), and PINOT NOIR—all of which are used for wine production.

peppery *see* Glossary of Wine Tasting Terms, page 655

perfume   The perfume of a wine is simply its smell. *See also* BOUQUET; Glossary of Wine Tasting Terms (perfumed), page 655.

Periquita [peh-ree-KEE-tah] A red-wine grape grown throughout southern Portugal, especially in the coastal areas. Periquita produces full-bodied (*see* BODY) wines that can be quite HARSH when young. They AGE well, however, and SOFTEN in the bottle, developing into firm-STRUCTURED wines with a hint of fig in the flavor. In Portugal's Algrave region, Periquita is often BLENDED with TINTA NEGRA MOLE, producing a much lighter style of wine. Periquita is also known as *Castelão, Castelão Francês, Castelhão Frances* and *João de Santarém.*

Perlan *see* CHASSELAS

perlant *see* Glossary of Wine Tasting Terms, page 655

perlwein [PEHRL-vine] A German term for a slightly SPARKLING WINE, usually artificially carbonated and of TAFELWEIN (the lowest) quality. SEKT is a finer-quality German sparkling wine.

Pernand-Vergelesses AC [peh*r*-NAH*N* veh*r*-zhuh-LEHSS] A lesser-known wine-producing village at the northern end of the CÔTE DE BEAUNE district in France's BURGUNDY region. The most celebrated wines come from the vineyards on Montagne de Corton, a vast hill rising above the village. The area's red wines, made from PINOT NOIR grapes, and white wines, made from CHARDONNAY grapes (and a small amount from ALIGOTÉ grapes), are both highly regarded—the reds slightly more than the whites. Pernand-Vergelesses shares two GRANDS CRUS—CORTON (red wines) and CORTON-CHARLEMAGNE (white wines)—with the villages of ALOXE-CORTON and LADOIX-SERRIGNY. Wines from these two grands crus are ranked among the world's finest. The red wines from Corton are considered some of the best and longest aging in Burgundy, and Corton-Charlemagne's whites are compared to other top white wines from the region. Pernand Vergelesses also has a number of fine PREMIER CRU vineyards including **En Caradeux**, **Île des Vergelesses**, **Les Vergelesses**, and **Les Fichots**. The wines produced under the general village appellation of **Pernand Vergelesses AC** are generally of good quality and usually less expensive than some of Burgundy's other village wines. Wine produced from the *premier cru* vineyards can append "Premier Cru" to the label or the name of the vineyard as in Pernand-Vergelesses Île des Vergelesses.

peronospera *see* MILDEW

Pero Ximen *see* PEDRO XIMÉNEZ

Les Perrières *see* CORTON; MEURSAULT; NUITS-SAINT-GEORGES

persistence *see* Glossary of Wine Tasting Terms, page 655

Perth Hills An Australian wine region located in the Greater Perth Zone of WESTERN AUSTRALIA. It's situated just east of Perth running north and south in the Darling Range around the towns of Kalamunda and Mundaring. The SWAN DISTRICT region runs along much of the Perth Hills' western border; the PEEL region lies just south. Vines were first planted in this region in the 1880s. There were intermittent VITICULTURE efforts over the years, but the modern winemaking era didn't begin until the 1970s. The climate here is moderately hot but varies depending on the location—both altitude and the Indian Ocean breezes can moderate the temperature. CHARDONNAY can do well in this region, and is the most widely grown. Other white varieties include CHENIN BLANC, SÉMILLON, VERDEHO, and SAUVIGNON BLANC. Shiraz (SYRAH) is the leading red variety, followed by CABERNET SAUVIGNON, GRENACHE, PINOT NOIR, and MERLOT.

Pessac-Léognan AC [peh-SAK leh-oh-NYAH/V] An APPELLATION created in 1987 out of the northern part of the GRAVES area in France's BORDEAUX region. Wines in this area were formerly part of the Graves AC, although the use of **"Graves-Pessac"** or **"Graves-Léognan"** had been allowed on labels for several years prior to the appellation's approval. This northern part of Graves contains more of the desirable gravelly soil than the southern portion and generally makes superior wines. The Pessac-Léognan AC takes in all the CRU CLASSÉ châteaux of Graves. It encompasses ten northerly COMMUNES, two of which—Pessac and Léognan—contribute to the appellation's name. This appellation's roster of CHÂTEAUX is led by Haut-Brion, the only non-MÉDOC château to be included in the Classification of 1855 (*see* Official Wine Classifications of Bordeaux, page 678) and one of only four Bordeaux châteaux to receive a PREMIER CRU ranking at that time. Other noteworthy châteaux include La Mission Haut-Brion, Les Carmes Haut-Brion, Domain De Chevalier, Pape-Clément, Haut-Bailly, Haut-Bergey, La Louvière, and Smith-Haut-Lafitte. The area's white wines, which are produced from SAUVIGNON BLANC, SÉMILLON and MUSCADELLE, are made in a CRISP, DRY style. Pessac-Léognan AC's distinctive, EARTHY red wines—made predominantly from CABERNET SAUVIGNON, CABERNET FRANC, and MERLOT—have a reputation for being of higher quality than the whites.

pétillant; pétillance *see* Glossary of Wine Tasting Terms, page 655

Petit Chablis AC *see* CHABLIS

Petite-Cabernet *see* CABERNET SAUVIGNON

Petite Sirah; Petite Syrah [peh-TEET sih-RAH; peh-TEET see-RAH] 1. Grown mainly in California, this red-wine grape was initially thought to be related to the renowned SYRAH of France's RHÔNE region. Then the belief shifted—Petite Sirah was not related to Syrah; it was actually a variety called DURIF, which was also grown in the Rhône but is now almost extinct. However, in the late 1990s, DNA analysis indicated that Durif was in fact a CROSS between Syrah and a variety called Peloursin—so the original perception that Petite Sirah was related to Syrah is once again viewed as true. To further complicate matters, it was also discovered that while a majority of the Petite Sirah plantings in California are Durif, a few are actually Peloursin. Add to this confusion the fact that Petite Sirah was mentioned as early as the 1880s in California, just as Durif was beginning to be propagated. All of which leads to the suspicion that Petite Sirah may not actually have been a true Durif at the time. Over the years various vines thought to be

P

Petite Sirah have turned out to actually be different varieties including true Syrah, CARIGNANE, MOURVÈDRE, and GRENACHE. True Petite Sirah grapes produce deep-colored, ROBUST, PEPPERY wine that packs plenty of TANNIN, giving it good AGING ability. While Petit Sirah may not be as popular as CABERNET SAUVIGNON, PINOT NOIR, or ZINFANDEL and enjoys wider esteem in California than in France, it has a following among those who like BIG, full-bodied wines. Although Petit Sirah was in vogue during the 1970s (and is currently enjoying renewed interest), its diminished popularity during the century's last two decades produced a decline in the acreage devoted to it. In addition to being bottled as a VARIETAL WINE, Petite Sirah is often blended with other varietals (ZINFANDEL, for example) to add zest and complexity. It is also planted in ARGENTINA, BRAZIL, and MEXICO. Petite Sirah is sometimes spelled *Petite Syrah* or *Petit Sirah* 2. The term "Petite Syrah" is also used by some French producers for a small-berried version of Syrah.

Petit Gamai *see* GAMAY

Petit Gris *see* PINOT GRIS

Petit Noir *see* NÉGRETTE

Petit Rhin *see* RIESLING

Les Petits Vougeots *see* VOUGEOT

Petit Verdau *see* PETIT VERDOT

Petit Verdot [puh-TEE veh*r*-DOH] A high-quality red-wine grape grown mainly in France's BORDEAUX region. Petit Verdot produces full-bodied, extremely deep-colored wines with peppery, spicy flavor characteristics, and high TANNINS and ALCOHOL. It's traditionally been used to add flavor, color, and tannins to the BORDEAUX blend. This is particularly true in the southern MÉDOC where, because of the soils, lighter wines are generally produced from the basic grapes CABERNET SAUVIGNON, MERLOT, and CABERNET FRANC. Petit Verdot ripens very late and sometimes doesn't mature at all, a trait that's prompted a number of CHÂTEAUX in Bordeaux to eliminate it from their vineyards. Recently, there's been a minor planting revival by some of the more quality-conscious producers. Small amounts of Petit Verdot are planted in Chile and California. It's also called *Carmelin, Petit Verdau,* and *Verdot Rouge.*

petrol; petroleum *see* Glossary of Wine Tasting Terms, page 655

Pettenthal *see* NIERSTEIN

Pfalz [FAHLTS] With about 59,000 vineyard acres, this is the second largest of Germany's thirteen ANBAUGEBIETE (quality-wine regions). However, it's often Germany's largest volume producer, averaging over 25 percent of the country's total wine production. The region's English name, *Palatinate,* is derived from the Latin *palatium,* meaning "palace." It refers to the first palace built by the Holy Roman Empire for its governors, who became known as Counts Palatine. The region was previously called the **Rheinpfalz**, but this was shortened in 1992 to Pfalz, the German transliteration of *palatium.* Pfalz borders France's ALSACE region in the south and RHEINHESSEN in the north, with the Rhine River forming its eastern boundary. There are two BEREICHE covering the Pfalz—**Südliche Weinstrasse**, which is the southern half of the region, and **Mittelhaardt/Deutsche Weinstrasse**, which takes in the north. The southern half is extremely sunny and fertile and produces large quantities of wine—almost as much inexpensive LIEBFRAU-MILCH as the Rheinhessen region. Most of the best wines produced in the Bereich Südliche Weinstrasse are consumed locally. The northern section produces the better wines, and the best area of that section is called the Mittelhaardt, which lies between Neustadt and Bad Dürkheim. Great wines, primarily RIESLING, are made in the villages of Deidesheim, Forst, Ruppertsberg, and Wachenhem. MÜLLER-THURGAU is the most widely planted variety, followed by Riesling and a host of others including GEWÜRZTRAMINER, KERNER, MARIO-MUSKAT, Rülander (PINOT GRIS), SCHEUREBE, SYLVANER, and the red PORTUGIESER.

pH A standard used to measure a liquid's acidity or alkalinity on a scale of 0 to 14. A pH greater than 7 represents alkalinity, 7 denotes neutrality, and less than 7 indicates acidity (the lower the number, the higher the acidity). The pH measurement represents the *intensity* of the acid, whereas titratable (total) acidity measures the *volume* of acid. The desirable pH range for TABLE WINES is approximately 3.0 to 3.6. As the pH level drops below 3.0, the wine becomes unpleasantly SHARP; above 3.6 and it becomes FLAT and FLABBY. Even though the volume of acidity might be in the proper range, if the pH is too high or too low, the wine won't be well BALANCED. Low pH also deters bacterial growth (which translates to better AGING) and helps wine keep its color. Winemakers use pH, along with other factors such as grape ripeness and volume of acid, to help determine the resulting wine's potential quality. *See also* ACIDITY; ACIDS; MALOLACTIC FERMENTATION.

phenolic compounds [fee-NAHL-ihk] Naturally occurring compounds present in grape stems, skins and seeds and extracted from oak barrels. Phenolic compounds, sometimes called *phenols, pheno-*

lics or *polyphenols*, include TANNINS and PIGMENTS and are responsible for ASTRINGENCY, bitterness, color, some flavors and odors (like VANILLIN), and antioxidant activity (which helps wines AGE well). These compounds are present in all wine in small amounts, with red wines containing more because of the extended contact with skins and seeds and, in many cases, longer oak barrel aging.

phenolics; phenols *see* PHENOLIC COMPOUNDS

Phomopsis *see* DEAD ARM

phylloxera [fihl-LOX-er-uh] A tiny aphidlike insect that attacks the roots of grapevines. Phylloxera sucks the nutrients from the roots and slowly starves the vine, creating a dramatic decrease in fruit. It doesn't affect the taste of the resulting wine but, eventually, replanting is required. Unfortunately, new vines do not produce the same quality fruit until they mature, which can take 8 to 10 years or more. *Phylloxera vastatrix* (its Latin name) is thought to be indigenous to the eastern United States, and the thick, strong, native American ROOT-STOCKS are reasonably resistant to this parasite. Much more vulnerable to phylloxera is the VITIS VINIFERA rootstock—a species native to Europe and Central Asia and responsible for a majority of the world's wine production. In the 1860s, vine CUTTINGS from the eastern United States transmitted phylloxera to Europe, and eventually most of the vineyards in France and many in other parts of Europe were totally devastated. The parasite eventually spread, causing grave problems in California and other parts of the world including Australia, New Zealand, and South Africa. The solution was to graft *Vitis vinifera* vines to native American rootstocks, a remedy that worked for the better part of a century. However, in the early 1980s a new strain of phylloxera—Biotype B—attacked California vineyards. It appears that a rootstock called AxR #1, used primarily throughout California's NAPA and SONOMA COUNTIES (and in other parts of California) wasn't resistant to this new phylloxera strain. Although AxR #1 had some *Vitis vinifera* in its makeup, experts at the UNIVERSITY OF CALIFORNIA, DAVIS originally recommended it because it produced much higher yields than other rootstocks and appeared to be phylloxera-resistant. There are a few places around the world that phylloxera has never invaded either because of the remote location of the vineyards or the inhospitable soil makeup. Many of these vineyards are planted on *Vitis vinifera* rootstock. Some parts of AUSTRALIA, ARGENTINA, CHILE are phylloxera free as are island vineyards on Crete, CYPRUS, and Rhodes and a few isolated areas like Spain's COLARES DOC. *See also* DISEASES, VINEYARD.

Picardan Noir *see* CINSAUT

Picolit [PEEK-oh-lee] Thought to have been cultivated since Roman times, Picolit is a rather scarce and unique white-wine grape found in Italy's FRIULI-VENEZIA GIULIA region. The only DOC in which it is designated is COLLI ORIENTALI DEL FRIULI. Picolit was once more widely planted than it is now and had gained a reputation as this region's most exalted DESSERT WINE. However, because of FLORAL ABORTION, Picolit is an extremely low-yielding vine, and plantings are very limited today. The historic reputation and the scarce supply has created exorbitant prices for these sweet, flowery wines.

Picotener; Picutener *see* NEBBIOLO

Picpoule *see* FOLLE BLANCHE

Pic Saint-Loup *see* COTEAUX DU LANGUEDOC

pièce [pee-YESS] The French name for an oak barrel used in the CÔTE D'OR, BEAUJOLAIS, and MACON regions of BURGUNDY to age and store wine. A pièce can vary in size from 215 to 228 liters (approximately 56 to 60 U.S. gallons). It's similar in size to the BARRIQUE used in BORDEAUX.

Piedmont; It. Piemonte [PEED-mawnt (It. pay-MAWN-tay)] An important wine-producing region in northwestern Italy. Its name, which means "foot of the mountain," refers to its place at the base of the Alps, which create the natural boundary between Italy and its two neighbors, France and Switzerland. A majority of the region's 142,000 acres of vineyards are southeast of Turin, the capital of Piedmont, although there are a few vineyards to the north and northeast. Piedmont contains seven DOCG areas—ASTI, BAROLO, BARBARESCO, BRACHETTO D'ACQUI, GATTINARA, GAVI, and GHEMME. It also has over forty-four DOCS including BARBERA D'ALBA, BARBERA D'ASTI, CAREMA, DOLCETTO D'ALBA, ERBULANCE DI CALUSO, LANGHE, MONFERRATO, and NEBBIOLO D'ALBA. These DOCGs and DOCs produce over 50 percent of Piedmont's wines. Red wines are the favorites in this region, and the premier grape variety is NEBBIOLO, which is used in four of the DOCG wines and in a number of the DOC wines. However, BARBERA is the most widely planted variety, taking up over half the available vineyard space. Other popular red varieties include DOLCETTO, BONARDA, FREISA, GRIGNOLINO, CROATINA, and Vespolina. White wines are made from CORTESE, Moscato Bianco, Moscato di Caneli (*see* MUSCAT), ARNEIS, ERBALUCE, and Favorita. Also very popular in this region are the Muscat-based SPUMANTE (sparkling) wines from the DOCGs of ASTI and MOSCATO D'ASTI (*see* ASTI).

P

Pierce's disease (P.D.) A bacterial disease that attacks and kills grapevines and other crops including almonds, citrus, and stone fruits. It's named for Newton Pierce, a plant pathologist who investigated the first outbreak of the disease in California vineyards in the late nineteenth century. Pierce's disease is a bacterium (*Xylella fastidiosa*) that lives and multiplies in a plant's xylem, its pipelike water-transportation system. It takes a year for symptoms of the disease to begin appearing. Within 2 to 3 years from infection, bacteria levels become so concentrated that they clog the plant's vascular system, preventing transfer of moisture and nutrients and killing the plant. Infected vines exhibit stunted growth, discolored, underdeveloped leaves, and dried, shriveled grapes. A vine killed by the disease is withered and black. California winemakers have been battling this fatal disease on and off for well over a century. It decimated southern California vineyards in the 1880s, struck again in the 1930s and 1940s, and returned in full force at the approach of the new century. Normally, Pierce's disease is transmitted by the blue-green sharpshooter, a tiny leafhopper that feeds on plant juices. The disease is spread by the insect's mouth, which transfers bacteria from an infected grapevine to a healthy one. Although the blue-green sharpshooter has long been a bane to the California wine industry, it's an insect that breeds and does most of its damage within 100 yards of rivers and streams, which meant that there was some degree of control. All that changed in 1989, however, when nursery stock from the southern United States carried an uninvited and much more powerful predator—the **glassy-winged sharpshooter**. Most leafhoppers are weak flyers, but the glassy-winged sharpshooter is the exception. Called the "pterodactyl of sharpshooters," this insect is an aggressive flyer with a voracious appetite; it has spread Pierce's disease with astonishing speed. At this writing, most of the area infested by the glassy-winged sharpshooter is in Southern California and Southern San Joaquin Valley. However, the fact that there is currently no known cure for this dreaded disease has California winemakers worried that it could potentially wipe out the entire industry. For this reason, hundreds of people are frantically searching for an answer, and a statewide program has been initiated to find either a cure for or a way to control Pierce's disease. Currently, the best hope for controlling the glassy-winged sharpshooter is through detection and inspection and through targeted vineyard ground spraying in heavily infested areas. Biocontrol methods are introducing parasitic wasps that lay eggs in the glassy-winged sharpshooter eggs, thereby killing their host. Scientists are trying to decipher the disease's DNA in order to develop a way to kill the bacterium without harming the vine. Grapevines are being bred in hopes of identifying disease-resistant characteristics. A "chemotherapy" method using natural zinc, manganese, copper, and iron compounds is being tested with the goal of inhibiting in vitro growth of Pierce's disease. Unfortunately, nothing has helped, and the dreaded Pierce's disease continues to threaten California's wine industry. About the only good news about this disease is that it doesn't affect wine quality or pose a health risk to humans. Furthermore, it seems to thrive only in southern U.S. climes, from Florida to California, and hasn't been seen north of California or the equivalent latitude. All of which is little consolation to VINTERS who are in jeopardy of losing their livelihoods. *See also* DISEASES, VINEYARD.

pierre-à-fusil *see* Glossary of Wine Tasting Terms, page 655

Piesport [PEEZ-port] A famous wine-producing village located along the Mosel River southwest of BERNKASTEL in Germany's MOSEL-SAAR-RUWER region. It's situated in the middle of a huge horseshoe-shaped bend in the river, where its steep hillside vineyards get the best southerly exposure. Piesporter wines, which are usually RIPE yet ELEGANT, with powerful BOUQUETS, can be some of the best of this region. The most famous EINZELLAGE is the 300-acre **Goldtröpfchen**, followed by **Falkenberg**, **Günterslay**, and **Treppchen**.

Pigato [pee-GAH-toh] A white-wine grape grown primarily in Italy's LIGURIA region. Pigato, whose name refers to its blotchy (oddly pigmented) skin, is thought to have originated in Greece. It produces attractive, full-bodied dry wines with floral and peach characteristics.

pigéage [pee-zhay-AHZH] French term for PUNCHING DOWN the CAP (the mass of grape solids that floats on the surface of the juice during FERMENTATION).

pigments Substances that impart color to wine. ANTHOCYANINS, along with compounds within TANNINS, help determine the color of red wines. Nonflavonoids provide the primary color for white wines, although this process is less well understood than it is for red wine.

Pignolo [peen-YOH-loh] A red-wine grape, also known as *Pignul*, grown primarily in Italy's FRIULI-VENEZIA GIULIA region. Pignolo, whose name means "fussy" or "finicky," refers to the difficulty in cultivating consistent and productive yields. Although it's thought to date back to at least the twelfth century, production is very small. In the COLLI ORIENTALI DEL FRIULI DOC Pignolo is gaining some prominence. It produces deep red, medium-bodied (*see* BODY) wines with attractive, PERFUMY aromas and flavors of dark fruits such as blackberries, raspberries, and plums. Some highly EXTRACTED versions are very full-bodied with rich, jam-like characteristics.

Pignul *see* PIGNOLO

Pineau *see* PINOT NOIR

Pineau d'Anjou *see* CHENIN BLANC

Pineau de la Loire *see* CHENIN BLANC

Pineau des Charentes [pee-NOH day shah-*RAHN*T] A FORTIFIED sweet APÉRITIF made in France's Cognac region by adding COGNAC to unfermented grape juice to halt any FERMENTATION activity. The result is sweet (12 to 15 percent RESIDUAL SUGAR) and potent (from 16 to 22 percent ALCOHOL). Pineau des Charentes can be found in white, ROSÉ, and red versions. Because it's made with cognac instead of a neutral alcoholic spirit, it's not classified as a VIN DOUX NATUREL but rather as a VIN DE LIQUEUR. Pineau des Charentes is similar to the RATAFIA from the CHAMPAGNE region and the FLOC DE GASCOGNE from the ARMAGNAC region, although it is better known than either. All are drunk chilled or on ice.

pink champagne A generic term used in the United States for inexpensive, pink-hued, usually sweet, SPARKLING WINE. Pink champagne is generally made via the CHARMAT process or with artificially induced CARBONATION. *See also* CHAMPAGNE.

Pinotage [pee-noh-TAHJ] A South African CROSS of PINOT NOIR and CINSAUT (which the South Africans call *Hermitage,* thus the derived name Pinotage). This red-wine grape was bred in 1925, but it wasn't until wines made from Pinotage won awards in 1959 that it became popular. Pinotage is now extensively grown in South Africa with small amounts in California and New Zealand. The best examples of Pinotage wines are medium-bodied and subtly flavored—better than most Cinsaut wines but not as good as Pinot Noir.

Pinot Beurot *see* PINOT GRIS

Pinot Bianco *see* PINOT BLANC

Pinot Blanc [PEE-noh BLAH*N* (BLAH*N*GK)] There is much confusion about this white-wine grape. Pinot Blanc is not related to CHARDONNAY as once believed. Adding to the confusion about Pinot Blanc is that much of what is called Pinot Blanc in Australia is really Chardonnay, and some of the Pinot Blanc vines in California have been identified as MELON DE BOURGOGNE. Pinot Blanc grapes produce comely DRY white wines that are often compared to Chardonnay. They are, however, generally not as COMPLEX or flavorful as Chardonnay. Pinot Blanc's most noted growing area is the ALSACE region in France. However, some of the best Pinot Blanc wines come from California (Chalone Vineyards does an excellent job) and the ALTO ADIGE region in Italy. Pinot Blanc wines are noted for their FRESH, YEASTY, appley aroma, sometimes with hints of spice. Although not considered to AGE as well as Chardonnay, better Pinot Blancs that are aged for a few years take on delicious honey overtones. Because of the crisp fresh flavors and the grape's high ACIDS, Pinot Blanc is finding its way into more and more SPARKLING WINE. Pinot Blanc is also known as *Beli Pinot, Clevner, Pinot Bianco, Weissburgunder, Weisserburgunder,* and *Weisser Klevner.*

Pinot Blanco *see* CHENIN BLANC

Pinot Buot *see* PINOT GRIS

Pinot Chardonnay *see* CHARDONNAY

Pinot de l'Ermitage *see* DURIF

Pinot de Romans *see* DURIF

Pinot Grigio *see* PINOT GRIS

Pinot Gris [PEE-noh GREE] *Gris* is French for "gray," which presumably refers to the grayish hue of this member of the Pinot family. Pinot Gris grapes can vary widely in color from silvery blue to grayish violet to ashen yellow. The grapes' varying colors produce wines that range from white to slightly pink. The style of wines ranges from CRISP, LIGHT, and DRY—such as those produced in northern Italy (where Pinot Gris is called *Pinot Grigio*), to the RICH, FAT, HONEYED versions from France's ALSACE region (where Pinot Gris is called *Tokay d'Alsace*). Limited amounts of this grape are grown in other parts of France, as well as in Austria, Germany, Hungary, and Romania. Other than a small group of producers in Oregon and minor plantings in the NAPA VALLEY and MONTERREY, there aren't substantial Pinot Gris plantings in the United States. The Okanagan Valley in BRITISH COLUMBIA, Canada, also grows small amounts of this VARIETY, as do AUSTRALIA and NEW ZEALAND. Pinot Gris is also known as *Auxerrois Gris, Grauburgunder, Petit Gris, Pinot Beurot, Pinot Buot, Rülander,* and *Szükerbarát.*

Pinot Meunier *see* MEUNIER

Pinot Nero *see* PINOT NOIR

Pinot Noir [PEE-noh NWAHR] *The* red grape of France's BURGUNDY region. It's responsible for the great (and expensive) red wines from Burgundy's CÔTE D'OR region, which include those from BEAUNE, BONNES MARES, CHAMBERTIN, CORTON, MUSIGNY, POMMARD, RICHEBOURG, ROMANÉE-CONTI, and VOLNAY. Pinot Noir is thought to have been grown in France for over 2,000 years, perhaps even prior to the Roman invasion of this area. The Pinot vine is described as "genetically unstable," meaning that it mutates very easily, which makes consistency from this vine extremely difficult. There are estimates of over 1,000 different types or clones belonging to the Pinot family. Some, such as PINOT BLANC, PINOT GRIS, and PINOT MEUNIER, have become well-known varieties in their own right. The combination of Pinot Noir's mutating characteristic and difficult growing requirements (a long, cool growing season) makes this variety a frustrating grape from which to make wine, even for Burgundians. This situation is aggravating for Pinot Noir lovers as well because the gap between the high and low quality of this wine is broader than any of the other important reds. The flavor of Pinot Noir is chameleon-like. When young, good wines exhibit the simpler fruity characteristics of cherries, plums, raspberries, and strawberries. As these wines mature, they display a variety of COMPLEX characteristics including chocolate, game, figs, prunes, SMOKINESS, truffles, and violets. France is the largest cultivator of the Pinot Noir grape, but few areas outside of Burgundy make really *great* Pinot Noir wines. The regions of ALSACE, IRANCY, Jura, Lorraine, SANCERRE, and SAVOIE all use Pinot Noir to produce lighter red and rosé wines. In the CHAMPAGNE region, Pinot Noir is one of the three grape varieties (along with CHARDONNAY and MEUNIER) allowed in the region's sparkling wine. Here, care must be taken in pressing the grapes so that the juice does not pick up the indigo color of the grape's skin. Pinot Noir is also an important red grape in Germany (where an early-ripening version is known as *Frühburgunder* and a late-ripening form, as *Spätburgunder*), but it has a hard time fully ripening there and produces pale, light-bodied wines. In northern Italy, Pinot Noir is known as *Blauburgunder* in some areas and *Pinot Nero* in others. Italy's mountainous areas produce some very good Pinot Noirs. This grape is also grown in Switzerland, as well as some of the eastern European countries. There's been a great deal of effort in the United States to emulate the great Burgundy Pinots, but vintners are still experimenting to come up with the right formula. Some of California's better Pinot Noir wines come from the state's cooler regions such as CARNEROS, the RUSSIAN RIVER VALLEY, and parts of MONTEREY, SAN LUIS OBISPO, and SANTA BARBARA counties. Oregon's long, cool growing season is conducive to the production of some acclaimed

Pinot Noir wines. In various parts of the world, Pinot Noir is also known as *Blauer Klevner, Blauer Spätburgunder, Burgundac Crni, Clevner, Nagyburgundi, Pineau,* and *Savagnin Noir.*

Pinot St. George *see* NÉGRETTE

pipe The Portuguese word for barrel is *pipa.* A pipe is, in fact, a large, lengthy barrel or cask with tapered ends. It's used for aging and shipping wine and is used extensively for PORT and also for MARSALA and MADEIRA. Pipes range in capacity from 418 to 630 liters (110½ to 166½ U.S. gallons). In Portugal's DOURO region where most port is made, the standard pipe measures 550 liters (145 U.S. gallons). In VILA NOVA DE GAIA where much of the port wine is aged, pipes vary in size, although the standard pipe measure is 534 liters (141 U.S. gallons). For madeira wines, the standard is 418 liters (110½ U.S. gallons).

pips Another term for grapeseeds that, if broken during CRUSHING, can impart a bitterness to the wine.

piqué *see* Glossary of Wine Tasting Terms, page 655

Piquepoul de Pays *see* BACO BLANC

Pisse-vin *see* ARAMON

Pla del Bages DO [plah dehl BAHZH] Small DO that's located around the town of Manresa about 45 miles northwest of the city of Barcelona in northeast Spain. Many vineyards in the area grow grapes for the SPARKLING WINES of the CAVA DO. As the quality of STILL WINES improved, the DO status was given, encouraging others to join in producing quality still wines. The primary white VARIETIES are MACABEO, PARELLADA, CHARDONNAY, and Picapoll; the reds are TEMPRANILLO, Garnacha (GRENACHE), MERLOT, and CABERNET SAUVIGNON.

Pla i Llevant DO [PLAH ee YEH-vahnt] Spanish wine region located on the southeast part of the island of Mallorca that's gaining some recognition. It shares the island with the BINISSALEM DO. The Pla i Llevant DO makes red, ROSÉ, white, SPARKLING, and FORTIFIED wines. Red and rosé wines dominate the region's production; they're made primarily from the local Manto Negro often blended with Callet. But other red grapes are planted, including CABERNET SAUVIGNON, Fogoneu, MERLOT, Monastrell (MOURVÈDRE), PINOT NOIR, and Ull de Llebre (TEMPRANILLO). The main white variety is Moll, also called Prensal Blanc. Other white varieties include CHARDONNAY, MACABEO, MOSCATEL, PAREL-LADA, and RIESLING.

Planalto Mirandes IPR *see* TRÁS-OS-MONTES

Plante Riche *see* ARAMON

Plant Gris *see* ALIGOTÉ

Plant Meunier *see* MEUNIER

plastering In winemaking, this term refers to an archaic practice of adding gypsum or calcium sulfate (plaster of Paris) to improve the ACID level of a low-acid grape juice. As a side benefit, plastering also helps to CLARIFY the wine. In Spain, where gypsum is called *yeso*, plastering has been popular in the making of SHERRY. In recent years, however, the addition of tartaric acid (*see* ACIDS) is replacing this process. Today, plastering is not used in making most higher-quality wines.

Plavac Mali A red grape VARIETY grown in Croatia along the Dalmatian coast and the nearby Adriatic islands. In late 2001, DNA FINGERPRINTING determined that Plavac Mali was a descendant of Crljenak Kastelanski, a Croatian variety determined to be identical to ZINFANDEL. So as many have speculated, there is a relationship between Zinfandel and Plavac Mali, but they are not identical. The wines produced from Plavac Mali can be deeply colored, full-bodied (*see* BODY), and high in ALCOHOL and TANNINS.

Playies Melitona *see* GREECE

plonk [PLONGK] Slang for ordinary low-quality wine, referring to any cheap wine, red or white. Over the years plonk has had various meanings, at one time referring specifically to cheap, strong, FORTIFIED WINE. The term was coined by Australians during World War I as they drank French VIN BLANC, continuing to massacre and abbreviate the words "vin blanc," which ended up as "plonk." The word plonk is commonly used in Australia and Great Britain and, to some extent, in the United States.

plump *see* Glossary of Wine Tasting Terms, page 655

podere [poh-DAY-reh] Italian for a "farm" or "estate."

pointe [PWANT] A French word synonymous with PUNT, the indentation in the bottom of a wine or CHAMPAGNE bottle.

Poitou *see* HAUT-POITOU VDQS

polyphenols *see* PHENOLIC COMPOUNDS

pomace [PAH-muss] The residue (skins, pips, seeds, and pulp) that remains after the juice has been PRESSED from the grapes. Sometimes the pomace is further processed to make a brandy variously known as pomace brandy, EAU DE VIE, MARC, GRAPPA, or SUGAR WINE.

Pomerol AC [paw-muh-RAWL] Located on the east side of France's Dordogne River, this is the smallest of the fine-wine-producing districts of the BORDEAUX region. It's also the only district not to have rated its CHÂTEAUX in some official classification. Because it's not near the better-known districts of MÉDOC and GRAVES, Pomerol didn't gain much of an international following until the 1960s. Now its wines, led by those from the famous Château Pétrus, bring some of the highest prices in all of Bordeaux. The Pomerol area's 1,900 acres are planted predominantly with MERLOT, which does extremely well in the region's clay soil. Merlot, blended with some CABERNET FRANC and small amounts of CABERNET SAUVIGNON, produces wines that are generally SOFTER and less TANNIC than those from the Cabernet Sauvignon-dominated Médoc, yet Pomerol wines are still RICH and LUSH. The general perception is that these wines don't AGE as well as those from the Médoc, but there are great Pomerol wines from outstanding VINTAGES that have aged beautifully for 40 years and more. Château Pétrus, which is favorably compared to the PREMIERS CRUS (first growths) of the Médoc, is first among many superb châteaux including Certan De May, Clos l'Eglise, La Conseillante, L'Eglise-Clinet, L'Evangile, Lafeur, Lafeur-Pétrus, Latour à Pomerol, Le Pin, Trotanoy, and Vieux-Château-Certan.

Pomino DOC [paw-MEE-noh] A small DOC area located east of Florence in Italy's TUSCANY region. The area encircles the town of Pomino and includes vineyards that are within the CHIANTI Rufina subzone as well. Pomino produces BIANCO, ROSSO, VIN SANTO Bianco, and Vin Santo Rosso. The BIANCO wines are made mainly from Pinot Bianco (PINOT BLANC), CHARDONNAY, and TREBBIANO but can also include up to 15 percent of other white grapes. SANGIOVESE is the dominant grape in the ROSSO wines, which can also include CANAIOLO, CABERNET FRANC, CABERNET SAUVIGNON, MERLOT, and others. Standard Rosso must be AGED for 1 year; the RISERVA, for 3 years. The *vin santo* wines can range from DRY to sweet and must be aged for 3 years in small oak barrels called *caratelli*. The wine estate of Marchesi de'Frescobaldi dominates the area's production.

Pommard AC [paw-MAHR] The vineyards of this APPELLATION encircle the village of Pommard, which sits between BEAUNE and VOLNEY in the CÔTE DE BEAUNE area of France's BURGUNDY region. The fact that the wines are quite well known is somewhat the result of the pronounceability of its name. In fact, it's well known enough for unscrupulous producers to pass non-area wines off as Pommard. Even though this deceitful practice is seemingly over, it's still best to know the producer for any wines bearing "Pommard AC" on the label. Although this AC has no GRAND CRU vineyards, there are two excellent PREMIER CRU vineyards that many feel are of grand cru caliber—**Les Epenots** (also spelled *Epeneaux*) and **Les Rugiens**. The better wines from this appellation can be ROBUST and full-bodied (*see* BODY), with perfumed BOUQUETS.

Pommery and Greno *see* CHAMPAGNE

Pope Valley Located east of Calistoga, California, this small Napa County growing area is somewhat hotter than the Napa Valley. The grape it does best with is SAUVIGNON BLANC, with SANGIOVESE on the rise. Other varieties planted here are CHARDONNAY, CABERNET SAUVIGNON, and MERLOT. Although not physically in the Napa Valley, Pope Valley wines are entitled to use "NAPA VALLEY AVA" on their labels.

porron [paw*r*-*R*AWN] A Spanish glass wine container with a narrow, pointed spout that shoots a stream of wine directly into a drinker's mouth. The concept is similar to that of the goatskin BOTA bag from Spain. The use of a *porron* takes skill and good guzzling ability to keep up with the steady stream of wine.

port; Porto; Port DOC A sweet FORTIFIED WINE most often served after a meal. Port originated in northern Portugal's Douro Valley, and the best ports still come from that area. The name port derives from the fact that these wines are shipped out of the Portugese city of Oporto; in fact, such wines (true ports) are labeled "*Porto*" rather than *port*. Today there's a specific demarcated region (**Port DOC**) in the Douro Valley. This region has established rules for producing quality port wines. To make port, a neutral grape alcohol is added to the wine partway through FERMENTATION. This stops the fermentation process while the wine still has plenty of natural sweetness (9 to 10 percent RESIDUAL SUGAR) and boosts the alcohol level to 18 to 20 percent. The wines are then generally shipped from the Douro Valley across the river to the town of Vila Nova de Gaia, which is replete with LODGES (warehouses) for AGING the wines. Wines left to age in the Douro often develop what's called the *Douro bake*, a baked character that's a result of the hotter climate there. Although there are many types of port wine (which can make labels confusing), there are four basic categories—vintage, ruby, tawny, and white. **Vintage ports** are regarded by many as the best; they're also the most expensive. They are made from grapes of a single VINTAGE and bottled within 2 years. Vintage ports are made only with grapes from the best sites and from the best vintages, and not every year is *declared*—a port firm won't produce a traditional vintage port in undeclared years (those not considered the best). Wines from years that aren't declared go into other types of port wine. The very best vintage ports can age 50 years or more. **Ruby ports** are made from lower-quality batches of wine, which are aged in wood for about 2 years. The wine is bottled while it still exhibits youth, fruitiness, and a bright red color. Ruby ports are generally the least expensive. **Tawny ports** are made from a blend of grapes from several different years; they can be aged in wood for as long as 40 years. They're tawny in color and ready to drink when bottled. The labels on the best tawny ports stipulate the time that they've matured—10, 20, 30, or 40 years. Inexpensive tawny ports are created by blending white port and ruby port. Ruby and tawny ports are sometimes called *wood ports* or *wood-aged ports*. Many grapes can be used for red (vintage, ruby, and tawny) ports, but the main ones are Tinta Barroca, TINTO CÃO, Tinta Roriz (TEMPRANILLO), TOURIGA FRANCESA, and TOURIGA NACIONAL. **White ports** are produced the same way that red ports are produced except that they use white grapes—Esgana Cão (SERCIAL), Folgasão, MALVASIA, Rabigato, VERDELHO, and Viosinho. If the producer wants a drier (*see* DRY) style of white port, a longer fermentation is allowed. The subsequent wine is generally consumed as an APÉRITIF. Within the four basic categories of port are many types. **Single-quinta ports** are essentially vintage ports produced from a single high-quality wine estate. They're usually made in years when a port firm doesn't declare a traditional vintage port; however, some port producers have started to make them in declared years. In many cases, these single-quinta ports are not quite as rich or intense as the standard vintage ports. On the other hand, some port firms believe that single-quinta bottlings should be even better and consider them comparable to RESERVE wines. The Quinta de Vargellas from Taylor, Fladgate & Yeatman is an example of a single-quinta port. **Second label vintage ports** are produced when a port firm thinks that a traditional vintage port should not be declared but that the vintage is still quite good. A second label vintage port, like a traditional one, is made from the better wines from various sites. Graham's Malvedos is an example of a second label vintage port. **Late-bottled vintage ports (LBV)** and **colheita ports** (also called *single-vintage ports* or *dated ports*) are made from grapes of a single vintage, even though the quality of the grapes is not as high as that for vintage ports. LBVs are aged in wood from 4 to 6 years and are considered high-quality ruby ports;

colheita ports have been wood-aged at least 7 years and fall into the tawny port category. Both are ready to drink when bottled and do not have the aging potential of vintage ports. **Crusted ports**—a blend of two or three wines from different vintages—are aged for 3 or 4 years before being bottled. Like vintage port, crusted port improves with age in the bottle. It derives its name from the deposit or CRUST that is thrown during this aging process. Crusted port is not often made today and has been replaced primarily by late-bottled vintage port. **Vintage character ports** are essentially high-quality ruby ports. They're blended from several vintages and wood-aged, but not nearly as long as tawny port. They're the lightest and fruitiest in flavor and are ready to drink when bottled. In countries outside of Portugal, port is a generic name for wines modeled after the Portuguese originals. Inexpensive "ports" will usually simply use names like Ruby or Tawny. The better ones will be vintage ports and may possibly be a VARIETAL WINE either made from native Portuguese varieties or perhaps ZINFANDEL or CABERNET SAUVIGNON.

Portalegre DOC *see* ALENTEJO

Portimão DOC [poor-teh-MAWN (-MERN)] APPELLATION located in southern Portugal's Algarve region. White wines are made from a minimum of 70 percent ARINTO and Roupeiro, plus the addition of MUSCAT and SAUVIGNON BLANC. Red wines must contain at least 70 percent NEGRA MOLE and Trincaderia and may include Aragonez, ALICANTE BOUSCHET, CABERNET SAUVIGNON, and PERIQUITA.

porto *see* PORT

Port Phillip Zone *see* VICTORIA

Portugais Bleu *see* PORTUGIESER

Portugal Although Portugal may be best known internationally for its two FORTIFIED WINES (PORT and MADEIRA) and its ROSÉS (such as Lancer's and Mateus), it produces a large amount of red and white TABLE WINE. In fact, it ranks as one of the world's top ten wine-producing nations, even though it only has a population of around 10 million. Most of Portugal's wine is consumed within its borders—it usually ranks in the world's top five for per capita consumption. As a wine-producing country, Portugal's somewhat of an enigma. In one sense it's innovative—it was the first country to implement an APPELLATION system with its REGIÃO DEMARCADA (RD), now called DENOMINAÇÃO DE ORIGEM CONTROLADA (DOC). It instituted this "demarcated region" system in 1756, almost 180 years before the French adopted their APPEL-

LATION D'ORIGINE CONTRÔLÉE system. Yet Portugal has been so steeped in tradition that, in general, its winemaking techniques are far from progressive by today's standards. Those producers who have kept up with modern methods have done so outside Portugal's appellation system. To do so, they've adopted proprietary brand names and dropped the use of regional names. This means, of course, that there's no sense of regional identification as there is with French and Italian wines. Neither do the Portuguese have a labeling procedure to identify their wines by grape varieties, as is popular in some countries like Australia, Chile, and the United States. Portugal began to sharpen its image only after joining the European Economic Community in 1987 (which made European countries more accessible) and realizing that their table wines have tremendous export potential. It reviewed the structure of the *Região Demarcada* (now DOC) system, adding a few regions to increase the number of DOCs. The areas currently entitled to DOC status include **Alenquer**, ALENTEJO, **Arruda**, BAIRRADA, **Bucelas** (which produces full-bodied white wines), CARCAVELOS, COLARES, DÃO, DOURO, **Lagoa**, **Lagos**, LOURINHA, MADEIRA, **Obidoos**, PALMELA, PORT, PORTIMÃO, RIBATEJO, SETÚBAL, **Tavora-Varosa**, and VINHO VERDE. Portugal has also established INDICAÇÃO DE PROVENIENCIA REGULAMENTADA (IPR) system to denote regions that are striving to become DOCs. A third tier that addresses regional wines is the VINHO REGIONAL wines like those from BEIRAS, ESTREMADURA, and RIBATEJANO. These designations are for wines that either are made outside the DOC or IPR areas or don't satisfy the requirements for these demarcated areas. Some producers in the DOC or IPR areas think that they can produce better wines by avoiding various DOC and IPR restrictions, such as by using prohibited grape varieties. These vintners get around such confines by labeling their wines "vinho regional." A big problem for Portuguese DOC wines is the continued requirement for extensive AGING, which causes some of the wines to become dull and lifeless. In addition, cooperatives, many of which often lacked the modern equipment necessary to produce fresh fruity wines, make a majority of the Portuguese wines. However, this has been changing since the 1980s, and many producers are updating their winemaking equipment and methods and are producing good high-quality wines. As Portugal continues to make improvements, its wines continue to gain acceptance, offering international markets new and interesting wines made from the many local varieties. Portuguese white wines are made from a wide variety of grapes including ARINTO, Assario, BICAL, BOAL, Cerceal do Douro (SERCIAL), ENCRUZADO, FERNÃO PIRES, Galego Dourado, LOUREIRO, MALVASIA, Moscatel (MUSCAT), Rabo de Ovelha, Roupeiro (also called *Codega*), TREBBIANO, and VERDELHO. Red wines are made from Alfrocheiro Preto, Azal Tinto, Bastardo (TROUSSEAU), Borraçal, Espadeiro, NEGRA MOLE (also called *Tinta Negra Mole*), Parreira Matias, PERIQUITA, Ramisco, TINTA AMARELA, Tinta Bairrada (BAGA), Tinta Pinheira, Tinta Roriz (TEMPRANILLO), TOURIGA FRANCESA, TOURIGA NACIONAL, and Trajadura.

Portugieser [por-chuh-GHEE-zer; por-too-GHEE-zer] This variety (whose full name is *Blauer Portugieser*) is the most widely planted red-wine grape in Austria, second behind Spätburgunder (PINOT NOIR) in Germany. Despite its name, Portugieser seems to have no connection to Portugal and appears, in fact, to have originated in Austria. It is a high-yielding vine that produces slightly sweet but rather ordinary light red and ROSÉ wines. Moderate amounts are planted in France, where it's called *Portugais Bleu*. Small quantities are also grown in Hungary, where it's known as *Kékoporto* or *Kékoportó and Oporto* and is used as a minor component in their "bull's blood" (EGRI BIKAVÉR) wines.

pot [POH] A small French bottle that holds about 50 centiliters (500 milliliters or just under 17 ounces). It is used in and around BEAUJOLAIS for serving wine in restaurants and cafés. This size bottle is slowly beginning to make an appearance in the U.S. market. A *pot* is generally filled from a cask.

potassium bitartrate *see* TARTRATES

potassium metabisulfite [puh-TAS-ee-uhm meht-uh-bi-SUHL-fite] A white powder or salt containing approximately 57 percent SULFUR DIOXIDE. Potassium metabisulfite also comes in tablet form, known as **Campden tablets**. *Meta*, as it's also called, is dissolved in warm water before being used. When stirred into wine or MUST, it reacts with natural ACIDS to release sulfur dioxide, which protects wines from unwanted bacteria and OXIDATION.

potential alcohol The ALCOHOL level that could be achieved if grape MUST is fully fermented (*see* FERMENTATION) and the resulting wine is completely DRY. Winemakers measure the MUST WEIGHT or SPECIFIC GRAVITY (generally with a REFRACTOMETER or HYDROMETER) to calculate the potential alcohol—it's one way to determine the quality of the must. The three scales used in this analysis are BAUMÉ, BRIX, and OECHSLE. From 40 to 45 percent of the grapes' sugar content is converted into carbon dioxide and from 55 to 60 percent is converted into ethyl alcohol (the only alcohol suitable for drinking). Therefore, a wine whose grapes were picked at 23° Brix will have a potential alcohol level of between 12.6 to 13.8 percent if VINIFIED completely DRY.

Potter Valley AVA Small 27,500-acre AVA that is part of California's larger MENDOCINO AVA. It's located on the eastern side of Mendocino County, northeast of CLEAR LAKE AVA, and shares its western border with the adjoining REDWOOD VALLEY AVA. The growing season here is characterized by warm days and very cool nights. SAUVIGNON BLANC, SÉMILLON, and RIESLING do well in this climate; CHARDONNAY and PINOT NOIR are also grown. There are no wineries here, only vineyards.

Les Pougets *see* CORTON; CORTON-CHARLEMAGNE

Pouilly-Fuissé AC [poo-yee fwee-SAY] Located in the MÂCONNAIS area of France's BURGUNDY region, this well-known APPELLATION controls the white wines from five villages—Chaintré, Fuissé, Pouilly, Solutré, and Vergisson. The CHARDONNAY wines can be quite good when made by diligent producers. Unfortunately, much of the Pouilly-Fuissé wine is made by the large cooperative in Chaintré from grapes picked from vineyards that are allowed huge YIELDS. Although these wines have a large international audience, many wine reviewers think they're mediocre and overpriced. Pouilly-Fuissé should not be confused with POUILLY-FUMÉ wines from the LOIRE region, which are made from SAUVIGNON BLANC grapes. As an historical note, the rock of Solutré, which towers over the scenic Pouilly-Fuissé area, is commemorated as the site where early man drove thousands of wild horses off the cliffs to their deaths.

Pouilly-Fumé AC [poo-yee few-MAY] APPELLATION that produces some of the better-known wines in the central part of France's LOIRE region. The vineyards are scattered around seven villages including Pouilly-Sur-Loire, which lends its name to the appellation. The word *fumée* is French for "smoke," and it's said the name comes from the SMOKY or FLINTY quality of these wines. The only grape allowed in the Pouilly-Fumé AC is SAUVIGNON BLANC, which produces wines that are generally CRISP, TART, and somewhat GRASSY. There's some criticism that Pouilly-Fumé wines have become too well known and are now overpriced. Occasionally, Pouilly-Fumé wines also are labeled **"Pouilly-Blanc-Fumé AC"** or **"Blanc Fumé de Pouilly AC."** Pouilly-Fumé wines should not be confused with the BURGUNDY region's POUILLY-FUISSÉ wines, which are made from CHARDONNAY. *See also* POUILLY-SUR-LOIRE AC.

Pouilly-Loché AC [poo-yee law-SHAY] APPELLATION that is located next to the better-known POUILLY-FUISSÉ AC in the MÂCONNAIS area of France's BURGUNDY region. Its vineyards surround the village of Loché, which is near the village of Fuissé. Much of the Pouilly-Loché AC

CHARDONNAY-based wine is produced by the cooperative at Loché. It's considered a cheaper alternative to Pouilly-Fuissé wine, although some wine critics believe that the use of "Pouilly" in its name allows Pouilly-Loché to be a bit overpriced. Pouilly-Loché wines may also be sold under the better-known "POUILLY-VINZELLES AC" label.

Pouilly-Sur-Loire AC [poo-yee syoo*r* LWAH*R*] The small French town of Pouilly-Sur-Loire is the center not only for the APPELLATION of the same name but also for POUILLY-FUMÉ AC wines. The Pouilly-Sur-Loire AC produces white wines from the area's traditional grape, CHASSELAS. Because Chasselas is considered a better table grape than a winemaking grape, its allotted acreage has dwindled tremendously. SAUVIGNON BLANC is now planted everywhere possible, leaving Chasselas only with whatever acreage is least desirable for Sauvignon Blanc. Pouilly-Sur-Loire AC wines are considered fairly mediocre and should be drunk young.

Pouilly-Vinzelles AC [poo-yee va*n*-ZEHL] APPELLATION that adjoins the better-known POUILLY-FUISSÉ AC in the MÂCONNAIS area of France's BURGUNDY region. Its vineyards encompass the village of Vinzelles, which is southeast of the village of Fuissé. The wines are similar to but a bit LIGHTER (and less expensive) than those from the neighboring Pouilly-Fuissé AC. The nearby POUILLY-LOCHÉ AC may also sell its wines under the "Pouilly-Vinzelles AC" label.

pourriture gris; pourriture noble [poo-ree-TYUR GREE; NOH-bl] French for "gray rot" and "noble rot," respectively. *See also* BOTRYTIS CINEREA.

Poverty Bay *see* GISBORNE

powdery mildew *see* MILDEW

powerful *see* Glossary of Wine Tasting Terms, page 655

Prädikat *see* QUALITÄTSWEIN MIT PRÄDIKAT

Prädikatswein [preh-dih-KAHTS-vine] The highest general quality category for wine in Austria, similar to the German QUALITÄTSWEIN MIT PRÄDIKAT. Austria differs from Germany in that Kabinett is not included in this highest category. Prädikatswein includes the following subcategories, from lowest to highest quality—SPÄTLESE, AUSLESE, STROHWEIN, EISWEIN, BEERENAUSLESE, AUSBRUCH, and TROCKENBEERENAUSLESE. Below Prädikatswein are the wine quality levels of QUALITÄTSWEIN (with its subcategory of KABINETT), below which is TAFELWEIN (with its subcategory of LANDWEIN).

Pralat *see* ERDEN

Pramaggiore *see* LISON-PRAMAGGIORE

premature oxidation OXIDATION that takes place in wine before it should—usually within a few years after the vintage. This trend was noticed in some white BURGUNDIES in the mid-1990s. Usually capable of graceful AGING, some quickly darkened in color and took on the stale, dull, sherrylike smell and flavor that's characteristic of oxidized wine. Blame for this premature oxidation is being placed on use of less SULFUR DIOXIDE (which helps protect wines from oxidation) and different corks (used in an attempt to eliminate the issue of CORKED wines).

Prémeaux [pray-MOH] A small village just south of NUITS-SAINT-GEORGES in the CÔTE DE NUITS area of France's BURGUNDY region. The PINOT NOIR-based red wines produced here are entitled to be bottled as NUITS-SAINT-GEORGES AC or Côte de Nuits-Villages AC. There are several PREMIER CRU vineyards, the best known being **Clos de la Maréchale**.

premier cru; pl. premiers crus [preh-MYAY (preh-MEER) KROO] 1. A French phrase meaning "first growth." 2. In BORDEAUX'S regions of the MÉDOC and SAUTERNES, premier cru is the highest subcategory of CRU CLASSÉ (classed growth), which was established in the Classification of 1855. Bordeaux wines that achieve this ultimate ranking may put "Premier Grand Cru Classé" on their labels. In 1855, four red-wine-producing châteaux were given this top ranking: Lafite-Rothschild, Latour, Margaux, and Haut-Brion. In 1973, Château Mouton-Rothschild was upgraded to *premier cru* status. There are eleven châteaux in Sauternes with the premier cru designation, plus Château d'Yquem, with its elevated status of premier grand cru (first great growth). *See also* PREMIER GRAND CRU CLASSÉ; FIRST GROWTH. 3. In BURGUNDY, where premier cru vineyards are some of the best, there is one higher category—GRAND CRU.

premier grand cru; pl. premiers grands crus [preh-MYAY (preh-MEER) grah*n* KROO] The French phrase for "first great growth."

premier grand cru classé; pl. premiers grands crus classés [preh-MYAY (preh-MEER) grah*n* kroo klah-SAY] 1. The French phrase for "first great classed growth." 2. Premier grand cru classé is the highest category for French wines classified in the APPELLATION of SAINT-ÉMILION as set forth in the 1953 classification (and later revised in 1969 and 1985). As of 1985, this status was given to eleven châteaux, which may label their wines "Premier Grand Cru Classé." 3.

France's first-growth (PREMIER CRU) wines of the MÉDOC and SAUTERNES may use "Premier Grand Cru Classé" on their labels.

Premières Côtes de Blaye AC *see* BLAYE

Premières Côtes de Bordeaux AC [pruh-MYEHR koht duh bohr-DOH] Located in France's BORDEAUX region, this AC extends for about 38 miles along the right bank of the Garonne River, across from the better-known APPELLATIONS of GRAVES and SAUTERNES. The Premières Côtes de Bordeaux AC applies to red, ROSÉ, and slightly sweet white wines. Because slightly sweet wines are no longer popular, the white wines are moving toward a drier style, but DRY wines can qualify only as BORDEAUX AC or BORDEAUX SUPÉRIEUR AC wines. The area is shifting to more red-wine production, which now accounts for about two-thirds of the total. Generally, red wines come from the appellation's northern portion, and whites come from the southern part (particularly around the sweet-wine villages of CADILLAC and LOUPIAC). As with the rest of Bordeaux, the white-wine grapes are MUSCADELLE, SAUVIGNON BLANC, and SÉMILLON; red-wine grapes are primarily CABERNET FRANC, CABERNET SAUVI-GNON, and MERLOT. Premières Côtes de Bordeaux AC wines are considered to be of good quality and improving as newly planted vineyards mature. Prices for these wines are relatively inexpensive.

première taille *see* TAILLE

premier tranche *see* FUTURES

press *n.* A device used to squeeze juice from grapes. Of the many types of presses in use today, the **basket press**, designed to squeeze out as much juice as possible, is one of the earliest. It uses a plate to push down on the grapes in the basket, forcing out juice through small slots. Numerous versions of this press have evolved over time and many are still used today. A **bladder press** uses an inflatable bladder that forces the grapes against a perforated outer shell through which the juice drains into a container. The most recent generation is the **tank press**, which uses an airtight tank lined with a membrane that lightly presses the grapes. The tank press is currently thought to be one of the best because the gentle pressure and lack of air exposure produces high-quality juice. **press**. *v.* To extract juice from grapes using one of several various presses. Pressing usually follows CRUSHING and precedes FERMENTATION of white wines, but it follows the fermenting of red wines.

Pressac *see* MALBEC

press juice; press wine *see* FREE-RUN JUICE

Les Preuses [lay PREWZ] One of the seven GRAND CRU vineyards in CHABLIS. Positioned between BOUGROS and VAUDÉSIR, Les Preuses consists of just under 29 acres. The land benefits from being higher up the grand cru slope and therefore receiving more sun.

pricked *see* Glossary of Wine Tasting Terms, page 655

prickly; prickle *see* Glossary of Wine Tasting Terms, page 655

primary fermentation *see* FERMENTATION

Primaticcio *see* MONTEPULCIANO

de primeur [day pree-MUR] French term for wine that's sold and drunk young, such as BEAUJOLAIS NOUVEAU.

Primitivo *see* ZINFANDEL

Primitivo di Manduria DOC [pree-mee-TEE-voh dee mahn-doo-REE-uh] DOC located in the APULIA region in southern Italy. It's part way down the Salento peninsula, which is the "heel" on the Italian boot. The wines are made from Primitivo, a variety that's related to California's ZINFANDEL grape. In addition to making a DRY red wine, producers make other styles including AMABILE, DOLCE NATURALE (a sweet wine with a minimum of 16 percent ALCOHOL), LIQUOROSO SECCO (a dry FORTIFIED WINE with a minimum of 18 percent alcohol), and *liquoroso secco naturale* (a sweet, fortified wine with a minimum of $17\frac{1}{2}$ percent alcohol).

Priorat; Priorato DOCa [pree-oh-RAHT; pree-oh-RAH-toh] This DOCA is located next to the larger TARRAGONA DO in the southern part of Spain's CATALONIA region. Priorat, which gained DO status in 1975, has only about 2,500 vineyard acres. In the 1980s and 1990s, a new group of producers, called the "Gratallops pioneers," transformed this region and put Priorat on the map when they began producing very high-quality wines that gained international fame. In the year 2000, Priorat was raised from a DO to a DOCa (DENOMINACIÓN DE ORIGEN CALIFICADA), Spain's top classification. Priorat is only the second DO (after the RIOJA DOCA) to be so honored. The area's mountainous region finds terraced vineyards clinging to steep hillsides. The climate produces low YIELDS, which allows winemakers to create intense, full-flavored, full-bodied (*see* BODY) wines that are generally high in ALCOHOL (from 13.5 percent to 18 percent). Most of the wines are red, made from Garnacha Tinta (GRENACHE), Carinena (CARIGNAN), and a variant of Garnacha Tinta called Garnacha Peluda. A small amount of white wine is made from Garnacha Blanca (Grenache), MACABEO, and PEDRO XIMÉNEZ. This area also produces FORTIFIED WINES ranging from DRY to sweet. Non-native grape VARIETIES have been introduced into the area including CABERNET SAUVIGNON, CHENIN BLANC, MERLOT, and SYRAH.

Private Reserve *see* RESERVE

produced and bottled by This phrase indicates that the named winery CRUSHED, FERMENTED, and bottled a minimum of 75 percent of the wine in that particular bottling. The phrase, however, does not mean that the winery *grew* the grapes. *See also* BOTTLED BY; ESTATE BOTTLED; GROWN, PRODUCED AND BOTTLED BY; MADE AND BOTTLED BY.

production *see* Principal Wine Producing Countries, page 686

produttore [proh-doot-TOH-ray] Italian for "producer."

Prohibition In January 1920, the U.S. Federal Prohibition Law was enacted through the Eighteenth Amendment to the Constitution. This law prohibited the manufacture, transportation, or sale of alcoholic beverages. It wasn't until almost 14 years later, in December 1933, that Prohibition was repealed by the Twenty-First Amendment. During Prohibition, certain activities were sanctioned, including home winemaking and wineries being allowed to make sacramental wines. During this period, wine consumption actually increased. Many wineries did not survive Prohibition, however. Those that did had converted their vineyards from high-quality wine grapes to varieties like THOMPSON SEEDLESS (which could be used for table grapes, raisins, or very ordinary wines) or ALICANTE BOUSCHET (which could survive the cross-country trip for home winemakers in the east). As the close of Prohibition drew near, resourceful wineries stockpiled wines and had ample stocks to sell a thirsty nation. The conversion of vineyards back to high-quality grapes happened slowly over the next several decades.

Prongurup *see* GREAT SOUTHERN

propriétaire [proh-pree-ay-TEHR] French for "proprietor," "owner," or "grower." *See also* MIS EN BOUTEILLE.

proprietary wine A wine that's name-branded, as opposed to one that's sold with the primary identifiers being the winery or varietal. For example, Sassicaia (*see* BOLGHERI DOC) is the proprietary name for a CABERNET SAUVIGNON/CABERNET FRANC blend produced by Italy's Marchesi Incisa della Rocchetta estate.

Proprietor's Reserve *see* RESERVE

Prosecco [praw-SEHK-koh; proh-SEHK-koh] A white-wine grape that's grown primarily in the eastern part of Italy's VENETO region. Prosecco's made into lightly sparkling (FRIZZANTE), fully sparkling (SPUMANTE), and STILL WINES. Its fine reputation, however, comes from the sparkling versions. The wines are CRISP and appley and, though they can be sweet, are more often found DRY. The best-known wines made principally from Prosecco come from the DOC of Prosecco di Conegliano-Valdobbiadene and are generally sold with either the name of Conegliano or Valdobbiadene attached. The very best Prosecco wines are labeled "Superiore di Cartizze" and come from a subzone within Valdobbiadene. Prosecco is also known as *Balbi, Glera, Serprina,* and *Tondo.*

Prosecco di Conegliano-Valdobbiadene DOC *see* CONEGLIANO

Provence [praw-VAH*N*SS] It's thought that winemaking has existed in this beautiful area of southern France since about 600 B.C. Although Provence, which sits on the Mediterranean just east of the RHÔNE region, has never been known for fine wine, it's now undergoing an upgrading process. The largest APPELLATION in this area is CÔTES DE PROVENCE. Other appellations are BANDOL, BELLET, CASSIS, PALETTE, COTEAUX D'AIX-EN-PROVENCE, and LES BAUX DE PROVENCE AC. Red-wine grapes grown in this area include CARIGNAN, CINSAUT, GRENACHE, MOURVÈDRE, SYRAH, and, increasingly, CABERNET SAUVIGNON. BOURBOULENC, CLAIRETTE, SAUVIGNON BLANC, SÉMILON, and Ugni Blanc (TREBBIANO) are some of the white-wine grapes used.

Prugnolo *see* SANGIOVESE

Les Pruliers *see* NUITS-SAINT-GEORGES

Prunella *see* CINSAUT

pruney *see* Glossary of Wine Tasting Terms, page 655

pruning A critical viticultural practice involving the cutting back of grapevines, usually during the dormant season. Pruning helps properly maintain the vines to produce a good crop of high-quality grapes. It's done for any of several objectives including controlling the YIELD, strengthening the vines, improving grape quality, and making the grapes easier to harvest. The generally agreed upon wisdom is that superior wines come from vines that don't overproduce—when a vine's productivity exceeds its optimum level the fruit's flavor is diluted. In the past, most pruning has been done by hand by skilled pruners. Today, some areas are utilizing **mechanical pruning**, done by a group of small circular power saws that encircle the upper part of the vine and cut all wood extending beyond the perimeter of the saws. Although this mechanical method isn't particularly aesthetic and may require some secondary hand pruning, it costs a fraction of hand pruning. **Summer pruning**, also called **green pruning**, is usually performed in May and June (in the northern hemisphere) to remove excess growth and foliage. It consists of removing suckers, excess shoots, and the foliage around the grapes so that they receive more nutrients and sunshine (the latter technique is sometimes referred to simply as **leaf removal**).

puckery *see* Glossary of Wine Tasting Terms, page 655

Pugent *see* NEBBIOLO

Puget Sound AVA Located in the northwestern portion of Washington State, this AVA was approved in 1995. It comprises a total of 5,536,000 acres—4,576,000 of which is land, the rest is water. It is approximately 190 miles long and 45 to 60 miles wide. Currently, less than 100 acres are planted—PINOT NOIR and PINOT GRIS are the most popular, followed by cool-weather varieties like CHASSELAS and MÜLLER-THURGAU. Despite the small acreage, there are numerous wineries in the area, some of which get their grapes from eastern Washington's growing areas of COLUMBIA VALLEY AVA, YAKIMA VALLEY AVA, and WALLA WALLA AVA. A few also make wines with estate-grown grapes.

Puglia *see* APULIA

Puisseguin-Saint-Émilion AC [pwees-GA*N* sa*n* tay-mee-LYAW*N*] The easternmost of the six small APPELLATIONS surrounding the famous SAINT-ÉMILION AC in France's BORDEAUX region. Its vineyards encompass the village of Puisseguin and the neighboring village of **Parsac**. (Parsac essentially dissolved its appellation, preferring to market its wines as Puisseguin-Saint-Émilion AC.) It's said that the word Puisseguin is Celtic in origin and means "hill with the powerful wine." The red wines, made primarily from MERLOT and CABERNET FRANC, with some CABERNET SAUVIGNON and MALBEC, are generally SOFT yet full-bodied (*see* BODY) and can represent good values for Bordeaux wines.

Puligny-Montrachet AC [pew-lee-NYEH (pew-lee-NYEE) maw*n*-rah-SHAY] Puligny-Montrachet is a famous village in the CÔTE DE BEAUNE section of the CÔTE D'OR in France's BURGUNDY region. The village itself is rather unexciting, but it is regarded as *the* home of

CHARDONNAY, a reputation based on the general consensus that the world's best DRY white wines are produced here. Puligny-Montrachet AC contains two GRAND CRU vineyards—CHEVALIER-MONTRACHET and BIEN-VENUES-BÂTARD-MONTRACHET—and nearly half of each of two others—LE MONTRACHET and BÂTARD-MONTRACHET. The best wines from Le Montrachet are viewed by many as the best DRY white wines in the world, although the wines from Chevalier-Montrachet have supporters who have the same opinion. The other two grand cru aren't far behind, and the village's fourteen PREMIER CRU vineyards also produce superb wines. The best of these premier cru vineyards are **Le Cailleret**, **Les Combettes**, **Les Folatières**, **Les Pucelles**, and **Les Referts**. Wines from other vineyards are bottled under the designation of **Puligny-Montrachet AC** or CÔTE-DE-BEAUNE VILLAGES AC. This area produces small amounts of red wine (from PINOT NOIR), which don't have the stature of the great whites.

pulp The soft, fleshy, juice-laden part of the grape.

pumping over A process of pumping juice over the CAP during FERMENTATION to expedite extraction of color, flavor, and TANNINS and to ensure that the cap doesn't dry out and develop unwanted bacteria.

puncheon [PUNCH-uhn] A large oak barrel that can vary in capacity from about 80 to about 133 gallons.

punching down A process of pushing the CAP down into the juice during FERMENTATION to facilitate extraction of color, flavor, and TANNINS and to ensure that the cap doesn't dry out and develop unwanted bacteria. Workers use a long paddle to punch the cap down.

punt The indentation in the bottom of a wine or champagne bottle. The punt's design serves two purposes—catching sediment and reinforcing the bottle.

pupitres *see* RIDDLING

puttonyos *see* TOKAJI

Pyrenees An Australian wine region located in the Western Victoria Zone of VICTORIA. It's situated a little over 100 miles north of Melbourne in the heart of Victoria's gold country around the town of Avoca in the foothills of the Great Dividing Range. Its wine history ties to the discovery of gold in this region in the mid-1800s. Wine production was spotty until the 1960s and 1970s when interest in the Pyrenees began to revive. Today there are about 1,000 acres of vineyards and thirteen wineries in the region. Although Chardonnay is the most widely planted variety, this is red-wine country, and the Pyrenees Shiraz (SYRAH) and CABERNET SAUVIGNON wines have very good reputations. Other planted varieties include CABERNET FRANC, MERLOT, PINOT NOIR, RIESLING, SAUVIGNON BLANC, and SÉMILLON. The region produces some SPARKLING WINE from Pinot Meunier (MEUNIER), Chardonnay, and Pinot Noir.

PX *see* PEDRO XIMÉNEZ

QbA *see* QUALITÄTSWEIN BESTIMMTER ANBAUGEBIET

QgU *see* QUALITÄTSWEIN BESTIMMTER ANBAUGEBIET

QmP *see* QUALITÄTSWEIN MIT PRÄDIKAT

Qualitätschaumwein *see* SEKT

Qualitätswein [kvah-lih-TAYTS-vine] Term used for "quality wine" in Germany and Austria. Qualitätswein is the middle wine-quality level, above TAFELWEIN and LANDWEIN. In Germany Qualitätswein is further divided into QUALITÄTSWEIN BESTIMMTER ANBAUGEBIET (QbA) and QUALITÄTSWEIN MIT PRÄDIKAT (QmP). In Austria, Qualitätswein includes a subcategory called KABINETT, which in Germany is in the higher Qualitätswein Mit Prädikat category. Austria's highest general category is PRÄDIKATSWEIN, which is similar to the German Qualitätswein Mit Prädikat.

Qualitätswein bestimmter Anbaugebiet (QbA) [kvah-lih-TAYTS-vine beh*r*-SHTIHMT-tuhr ahn-BOW-geh-beet] The German wine laws adapted in 1971 set up three categories defining the quality of German wines. *Qualitätswein bestimmter Anbaugebiet* ("quality wine from a specified region") is the middle quality category in between DEUTSCHER TAFELWEIN (DTW), the lowest quality, and QUAL-ITÄTSWEIN MIT PRÄDIKAT (QmP), the highest. To qualify for Qualitätswein bestimmter Anbaugebiet (QbA) status, a wine must be tested by a local panel to ensure that it shows the typical character of an approved grape variety and of the region. In addition, the MUST (unfermented grape juice) needs to be a certain sugar level, and the wine must have a minimum ALCOHOL content. The required sugar and alcohol levels vary from region to region and from variety to variety. QbA wines must come from one of the thirteen ANBAUGEBIETE (quality-wine regions) and cannot contain wine from any other region. The thirteen Anbaugebiete are AHR, BADEN, FRANKEN, HESSISCHE BERGSTRASSE, MITTEL-RHEIN, MOSEL-SAAR-RUWER, NAHE, RHEINGAU, RHEINHESSEN, PFALZ, and WÜRT-TEMBERG—plus SAALE-UNSTRUT and SACHSEN, additions from the former East Germany. CHAPTALIZATION (the addition of sugar) is allowed for QbA wines and is one of the major differences between these wines and higher-quality QmP wines (most grapes with enough natural sugar go into QmP wines). The addition of sugar, which is converted into alcohol during FERMENTATION, allows the wines to reach the required minimum alcohol levels for a QbA rating. If a wine passes all the QbA requirements, an AMTLICHE PRÜFUNGSNUMMER (official test number) is assigned. Abbreviated as A.P.Nr., this number is printed on the label, along with the name of the Anbaugebiet. Additional information may be printed on a QbA wine label if other requirements are met. For instance, the name of the grape variety can be included if it comprises 85 percent of the grapes used to make the wine. Beginning in September 1994, the German wine law allowed the production of a special type of QbA—**Qualitätswein garantierten Ursprungs (QgU)**, or "quality wine of guaranteed origin." A QgU is a QbA from an Ursprungslage—a specific district, vineyard or village with a consistent style associated with its site of origin. These wines are required to undergo more stringent sensory and analytical evaluations.

Qualitätswein garantierten Ursprungs *see* QUALITÄTSWEIN BESTIMMTER ANBAUGEBIET

Qualitätswein mit Prädikat (QmP) [kvah-lih-TAYTS-vine mitt PRAY-dee-kaht] The highest quality category defined by the German wine laws adapted in 1971. DEUTSCHER TAFELWEIN (DTW) and QUALITÄTSWEIN BESTIMMTER ANBAUGEBIET (QbA) are the two lower quality categories. Qualitätswein mit Prädikat translates crudely to "quality wine with distinction" or "quality wine with special attributes." In addition to meeting the rules for QbA wines, QmP wines cannot have any sugar added (*see* CHAPTALIZATION); must be ESTATE BOTTLED (*erzeugerabfüllung*), and must come from a defined BEREICH (district). There are six subcategories within the QmP category, ranked from lowest to highest: KABINETT, SPÄTLESE, AUSLESE, BEERENAUSLESE, EISWEIN, and TROCKENBEERENAUSLESE. Each category is defined by a minimum sugar content of the grapes, which varies from region to region and from variety to variety. The focus on sugar content embodies the theory that grapes with higher sugar levels are riper and therefore yield richer wines with deep colors, intense flavors, and opulent BOUQUETS.

Quarts de Chaume AC [kah*r* duh SHOHM] APPELLATION that encompasses the village of Chaume in the ANJOU area of France's LOIRE region. As the story goes, its name stems from the fact that a former landowner required a quarter (*quart*) of the vintage be turned over to him as a form of payment. The climate in this area is perfect for CHENIN BLANC grapes to ripen to their fullest. The environment also creates the conditions necessary to attract the desirable mold BOTRYTIS CINEREA, which shrivels the grapes and concentrates the flavors and sugar. The YIELDS from the Quarts de Chaume AC vineyards are some of the lowest in France, and the crop is harvested several times so that individual grapes are picked at their ripest. The combination of climate and low yields produces RICH, HONEYED, golden wines that, thanks to the Chenin Blanc grape's good ACIDS, can AGE for 30 to 40 years or more. These wines are generally at their best after 10 years of bottle aging.

quatrième cru [kah-tryehm KROO] A French phrase meaning "fourth growth," referring to the fourth-highest subcategory of the MÉDOC area's CRUS CLASSÉS (classed growths), which were established in the Classification of 1855 (*see* Official Wine Classifications of Bordeaux, page 678). Ten châteaux were ranked as quatrième cru in 1855, and this hasn't changed.

Quebec *see* CANADA

Quincy AC [kan-SEE] A tiny APPELLATION surrounding the village of Quincy in the central LOIRE region southwest of SANCERRE AC and POUILLY-FUMÉ AC. Quincy produces white wines from the SAUVIGNON BLANC grape that are similar in style to those from these other two appellations—generally CRISP and TART, with a somewhat GRASSY characteristic.

quinta [KEEN-tah] Portuguese for "farm," used to refer to a vineyard site or estate. Quintas, which are similar in connotation to the CHÂTEAUX of BORDEAUX, grow grapes for port, as well as for other wines. They're often connected with one of the well-known port houses, such as Dow, Fonseca, or Graham. Many of the wines end up in house blends, but the concept of single-quinta wine, including single-quinta vintage port (*see* PORT), is becoming more popular.

Rablay-sur-Layon *see* COTEAUX DU LAYON

Raboso [ruh-BOH-soh] A red-wine grape grown primarily in Italy's VENETO region, where it's thought to have originated. Raboso's known for its heavy TANNINS, high ACID, and deep color. There are two distinct clones of this variety—*Raboso Veronese* and *Raboso del Piave*. Raboso Veronese produces greater YIELDS and is more widely planted. Raboso del Piave, also known as *Friularo* or *Friulara,* produces a more AUSTERE wine than does the Raboso Veronese grape. Raboso is often BLENDED with much softer wines to improve their STRUCTURE, COMPLEXITY, and smoothness. The Raboso VARIETAL WINES from the Piave DOC are usually HARSH and austere in their youth but can SOFTEN nicely with AGE. This variety is also called *Negron*.

race *see* Glossary of Wine Tasting Terms, page 655

racking The process of siphoning off the clear juice from the SEDIMENT that has fallen to the bottom of the container either naturally or with the help of FINING agents. During the winemaking process, racking can occur three or four times before the wine is clear. After racking, some wines are also FILTERED prior to bottling to remove any remaining miniscule particles.

racy *see* Glossary of Wine Tasting Terms, page 655

Rainwater *see* MADEIRA

Raisinotte *see* MUSCADELLE

raisiny *see* Glossary of Wine Tasting Terms, page 655

Rajinski Rizling *see* RIESLING

Rajnai Rizling *see* RIESLING

Ramandolo DOCG [rah-mahn-DOH-loh] DOCG zone located in the FRIULI-VENEZIA GIULIA region in northeast Italy, north of Udine around the village of Ramandolo. It's a COLLI ORIENTALI DEL FRIULI DOC subzone that achieved DOCG status in 2001. The DOCG covers the famous sweet DESSERT WINES made from the VERDUZZO grape (called the Ramandolo grape in this region).

Ramona Valley AVA VITICULTURAL AREA established in January 2006 that's located in San Diego County, California, northeast of the city of San Diego. It encompasses 89,000 acres around the town of Ramona and is a sub-zone within the larger SOUTH COAST AVA. Currently there are just over 60 acres of vineyards planted mainly with CABERNET SAUVI-

GNON, MOURVÈDRE, and SYRAH, but also with smaller amounts of CABERNET FRANC, CHARDONNAY, MERLOT, MUSCAT, SAUVIGNON BLANC, TEMPRANILLO, and ZINFANDEL. There are twelve wineries in the area led by Schwaesdall Winery and Ramona Vintners.

rancio [Fr. *r*ah*n*-SYOH; Sp. *R*AHN-thyoh] A style of wine made by purposefully OXIDIZING or MADERIZING it by placing small barrels of wine in the hot summer sun. This procedure gives the wine a tawny color and a rich, unique flavor. Rancio wines are usually either naturally very high in alcohol or FORTIFIED. The results are similar to MADEIRA, tawny PORT, or MARSALA. Rancio wines are made throughout Spain, as well as in southern France. They're usually sipped as an APÉRITIF.

Rapel Valley [rah-PELL] Known locally as *Valle del Rapel,* this important Chilean wine region is a subregion within the larger CENTRAL VALLEY. It's located south of the MAIPO VALLEY around the towns of Rancagua and San Fernando. Within the Rapel Valley are two principal zones: Cachapoal Valley, which has four areas (Peumo, Rancagua, Rengo, and Requinoa); and Colchagua Valley, which has six areas (Chimbarongo, Nancagua, Palmilla, Peralillo, San Fernando, and Santa Cruz). Rapel Valley weather consists of warm summer days and cooler nights, which makes it an ideal growing area. Red VARIETIES hold the majority acreage here and have an excellent reputation. CABERNET SAUVIGNON is the most widely planted red grape, although MERLOT is making a good showing. The white varieties of CHARDONNAY and SAUVIGNON BLANC are also grown in quantity. *See also* CHILE.

Rasteau [rass-TOH] A village in the southern portion of France's RHÔNE region, northeast of CHÂTEAUNEUF-DU-PAPE. It's one of the seventeen villages entitled to use the CÔTES DU RHÔNE-VILLAGES AC, and the label usually also includes the village's name. These wines generally exhibit dark color, spicy fruit, and enough TANNINS to age well. The main grapes used for red wines are GRENACHE, SYRAH, CINSAUT, and MOURVÈDRE. A specialty of Rasteau is a VIN DOUX NATUREL, a category of sweet, FORTIFIED WINE (red or white) made from Grenache grapes.

ratafia [rat-uh-FEE-uh] 1. A sweet French APÉRITIF made from a mixture of unfermented grape juice and BRANDY or other spirit. The best known are Ratafia de Bourgogne and Ratafia de Champagne. Ratafia is similar to the better-known PINEAU DES CHARENTES. 2. A sweet cordial flavored with various fruits, fruit pits, citrus peels, or almonds.

Rattlesnake Hills AVA APPELLATION established in March 2006 that encompasses 68,500 acres in the northern part of the large YAKIMA VALLEY AVA (which is part of the even larger COLUMBIA VALLEY AVA). The town of Zillah, which is southeast of the city of Yakima, sits at the center of the VITICULTURAL AREA. The elevation in these hills ranges from 850 feet to just over 3,000 feet. Some controversy surrounded its approval as a separate sub-appellation, with detractors feeling the area was not different enough from the rest of the Yakima Valley to warrant special treatment. The boundary lines are also in question since some vineyards located in the Rattlesnake Hills actually fall outside the AVA. Nonetheless, there are some very good vineyards located in the appellation. CABERNET FRANC, CABERNET SAUVIGNON, CHARDONNAY, CHENIN BLANC, GEWÜRTRAMINER, MALBEC, MERLOT, MUSCAT, PETITE SIRAH, RIESLING, SEMILLON, SYRAH, and VIOGNIER are popular varieties grown here.

Rauenthal [ROW-uhn-tahl] A small wine-producing village situated in the foothills of the Taunas Mountains, set back from the Rhine River in Germany's RHEINGAU region. Rauenthal produces highly regarded wines that are known for their spiciness, excellent ACIDITY, and age-worthiness. **Steinmächer** is the GROSSLAGE that covers Rauenthal's vineyards, but the better wines are labeled with the names of the individual EINZELLAGEN—**Baiken**, **Gehrn**, **Nonnenberg**, **Rothenberg**, and **Wülfen**.

Ravat [ra-VA] In the late nineteenth century, J. F. Ravat, a French HYBRIDIZER, created numerous successful HYBRIDS by combining VITUS VINIFERA vines with NATIVE AMERICAN VINES. The best known of these are *Ravat 262* (popularly known as *Ravat Noir*), which produces light fruity red wines; *Ravat 6* (better known as *Ravat Blanc*), which produces good-quality white wines; and *Ravat 51* (or *Vignoles*), another white-wine grape. The latter has become the more widely planted of the Ravats, with acreage in New York, Pennsylvania, and Michigan. When BOTRYTIS CINEREA forms on the high-ACID Vignoles grapes, the result is a rich, HONEYED wine. Vignoles grapes are also made into DRY and semisweet wines.

raw *see* Glossary of Wine Tasting Terms, page 655

RD *see* DENOMINAÇÃO DE ORIGEM CONTROLADA

rebêche *see* VIN DE CUVÉE

Rebula *see* RIBOLLA

Rechbächel *see* WACHENHEIM

recioto [reh-CHAW-toh] An Italian wine made in the VENETO region using the PASSITO method. In this method, grapes are dried in a cool, airy room for up to 4 months until semidry, which produces concentrated sugars and flavors. Occasionally, the grapes develop BOTRYTIS CINEREA, which gives them added richness. If during VINIFICATION, FERMENTATION stops either naturally or because of human intervention, the wine's left with RESIDUAL SUGAR, and it's simply a *recioto*. If fermentation continues until the wine is completely DRY, then the term *amarone,* which means "strongly bitter," is added to the name. RECIOTO DELLA VALPOLICELLA and RECIOTO DELLA VALPOLICELLA AMARONE are examples of these two different types of wines. Recioto's name is derived from a local dialect term *recie* meaning "ears." A grape bunch often has two small clusters—called ears—branching out of the main bunch. The ears are thought to be of better quality because they stick out and catch more sun. Because of this, ears were always used in recioto wines. Today, although this approach isn't consistently employed, the grapes used are always of high quality. *See also* RECIOTO DI SOAVE DOC.

Recioto della Valpolicella DOC; Recioto della Valpolicella Amarone DOC [*r*eh-CHAW-toh deh-lah vahl-paw-lee-CHEHL-lah (ah-mah-ROH-neh)] These wines are made primarily from the red CORVINA grape, but also with Rondinella, Molinara, and others. They are not like other VALPOLICELLA wines because of the special process that RECIOTO wines go through, such as the use of semi-dried grapes. The *Recioto della Valpolicella,* with its cherry and plum flavors, can be sweet and quite pleasant. The *Recioto della Valpolicella Amarone* (also called *Amarone della Valpolicella*) is the DRY version, which is essentially the same as the sweet except that it's allowed to FERMENT fully. It too can be quite good, with similar flavors but a bittersweet essence. There are FORTIFIED and SPARKLING versions also, although they're not as highly regarded.

Recioto di Gambellara *see* GAMBELLARA DOC

Recioto di Soave DOCG [*r*eh-CHAW-toh dee SWAH-veh] A sweet wine made using the PASSITO process whereby grapes are dried to concentrate the sugar and flavors. Made primarily from GARGANEGA with smaller amounts of CHARDONNAY, Pinot Bianco (PINOT BLANC), and/or TREBBIANO grapes, in the same designated area as SOAVE DOC wines, *Recioto di Soave* can be an excellent ABBOCCATO (lightly sweet) wine, with more richness and lushness than most Soave wines. It can be found in SPUMANTE and LIQUOROSO styles as well. In 1992 Recioto di Soave was upgraded to DOCG status, the first zone in the VENETO region to be upgraded to Italy's highest quality category.

recólte [ray-KAWLT] French for "harvest," "crop," or "vintage."

redcurrant *see* Glossary of Wine Tasting Terms, page 655

Red Hill Douglas County, Oregon AVA This APPELLATION is located in southwestern Oregon and is a sub-zone within the larger UMPQUA VALLEY AVA, which is part of the even larger SOUTHERN OREGON AVA. Red Hill Douglas County was created in November 2005 and encompasses 5,500 acres near the town of Yoncalla. Currently, there are about 220 acres planted primarily with PINOT NOIR. Sienna Ridge Winery is currently the only winery in the AVA. Red Hill Douglas County should not be confused with the RED HILLS OF LAKE COUNTY AVA or RED MOUNTAIN AVA.

Red Hills Lake County AVA This APPELLATION, established in 2004, is located in Lake County in northern California and is a sub-zone within the larger CLEAR LAKE AVA and the huge NORTH COAST AVA. The AVA encompasses 31,250 acres that have the Coast Range Mountains as its southern border and Clear Lake on its northern border. About 3,000 acres are planted mainly with CABERNET SAUVIGNON. There are 10 wineries located within the area and a number of other wineries that source grapes from here. Red Hills of Lake County should not be confused with RED HILL DOUGLAS COUNTY, OREGON AVA.

Red Mountain AVA *see* YAKIMA VALLEY AVA

Redondo DOC *see* ALENTEJO

redox Term formed by combining REDUCTION and OXIDATION and used to indicate a change in the amount of oxygen—oxidation indicating an increase and reduction indicating a decrease.

reduced; reduction; reductive This refers to an environment lacking oxygen. Since OXIDATION is undesirable in TABLE WINES, some winemakers try to achieve this limited oxygen environment after fermentation through a variety of techniques, including introducing inert gases such as nitrogen, argon, and carbon dioxide into wine containers. Once bottled, SCREW CAP closures such as Stelvin limit oxygen in a bottle more than corks. Because the lack of oxygen may make sulfur compounds more pronounced, some descriptions use the terms reduced or reductive to mean a wine that has sulfur characteristics (*see* SULFUR; SULPHUR in Glossary of Wine Tasting Terms, page 655). In many cases AERATION will help these characteristics dissipate.

reducing sugar *see* RESIDUAL SUGAR

red wine A wine made from crushed dark-skinned grapes (red, purple, black, blue), which remain in contact with the grape skins (from which color is extracted) during FERMENTATION. The grapes used for red wine don't typically have a red flesh, the rare exceptions being TEINTURIER grapes like ALICANTE BOUSCHET. Blush and rosé wines are a lighter color because they're not kept in contact with the skins as long.

Redwood Valley AVA This California VITICULTURAL AREA was established in 1997 and is part of the larger MENDOCINO and NORTH COAST AVAS. It encompasses about 22,400 acres beginning at the northern end of Lake Mendocino just north of Ukiah in Mendocino County and stretching for approximately 12 miles north along the Russian River. Its eastern border is shared with the adjoining POTTER VALLEY AVA. The area is somewhat cooler than the Ukiah and Sanel Valleys to the south. Red varieties dominate, and the most popular are CABERNET SAUVIGNON, PETITE SIRAH, and ZINFANDEL. There are also plantings of BARBERA, CHARBONO, CARIGNANE, MERLOT, PINOT NOIR, SYRAH, and SANGIOVESE. The top white grapes by far are CHARDONNAY and SAUVIGNON BLANC, but a little MUSCAT and PINOT BLANC are also found here.

refined *see* Glossary of Wine Tasting Terms, page 655

Refosco [ray-FOHS-koh] Red-grape variety heavily planted in Italy's FRIULI-VENEZIA GIULIA. Refosco (also known as *Cagnina* and *Terrano*) can produce high-quality, deeply colored wines with CONCENTRATED flavors reminiscent of tart plums and a slightly bitter FINISH. But it can also have high ACIDITY if grapes aren't fully ripened. Italy has several Refosco CLONES, with the one known as *Refosco del Peduncolo Rosso* considered superior to the *Refosco Nostrano*. There are theories that Refosco and the French MONDEUSE are the same variety, but this hasn't been proven, and some evidence suggests that it may not be true. In California, there is a variety called *Refosco* that is related to Mondeuse but not to samples of the Italian Refosco that were available for DNA testing.

refractometer [ree-frak-TOM-ih-tuhr] An instrument used in winemaking to measure the sugar content of grapes and MUST. A refractometer, which can be used right in the vineyard, works by placing a drop of juice between the refractometer's prisms and reading the angle at which the light bends. The angle will vary depending on the juice's sugar content. This refractometer reading is described in terms of BRIX in the United States, BAUMÉ in France, and OECHSLE in Germany.

Região Demarcada (RD) *see* DENOMINAÇÃO DE ORIGEM CONTROLADA

region *see* GEOGRAPHIC INDICATIONS

regional A regional wine is generally one that's a blend of several wines from different parts of a region or district instead of from a single vineyard or proximate vineyards. The use of a term such as NAPA VALLEY, SONOMA VALLEY, CALIFORNIA, MÉDOC, BORDEAUX, or RIOJA indicates that the wine is regional.

Regions I-V *see* CLIMATE REGIONS OF CALIFORNIA

régisseur [ray-zhee-SEU*R*] The manager in charge of a CHÂTEAU'S vineyard and cellar operations in France's BORDEAUX region.

Régnié AC [ray-NYAY] The newest of the ten CRUS in France's BEAU-JOLAIS region. In 1988, its status was upgraded from BEAUJOLAIS-VILLAGES AC. Régnié AC wines, which are made from GAMAY grapes, vary depending on the locale. The northern and eastern portions of the APPELLATION abut the MORGON AC, and the Régnié AC wines there are similar—BIG and RICH. In the southern portion, the wines are much more like its southern neighbors, the BROUILLY AC and the CÔTES DE BROUILLY AC—LIGHT and FRUITY.

Reguengos DOC *see* ALENTEJO

Rehbach *see* NIERSTEIN

Rehoboam *see* Wine Bottles, page 609

reid Austrian for "vineyard." When the name of a reid is used on a label, 100 percent of the wine must be from the named site.

Reiterpfad *see* RUPPERTSBERG

Remstal-Stuttgart, Bereich *see* WÜRTTEMBERG

remuage *see* RIDDLING

remuer *see* RIDDLING

Les Renardes *see* CORTON; CORTON-CHARLEMAGNE

Renault Winery *see* NEW JERSEY

Requena *see* BOBAL

reserva [ray-ZEHR-vah] A Spanish and Portuguese term referring to quality wine from a good VINTAGE that has satisfied specific AGING requirements. To be labeled "reserva," red wines must have a minimum of 3 years of aging with at least 1 year in OAK barrels; ROSÉ and white reservas require a minimum aging of 2 years with no less than 6 months in oak. *See also* GRAN RESERVA.

reserve Even though this term is found on U.S. wine labels, it has no legal definition, which means it can't be relied on to have any special meaning. Reserve appears on labels in a number of ways—*Private Reserve, Proprietor's Reserve, Special Reserve, Vintner's Reserve,* or simply *Reserve.* For some producers—like Beaulieu Vineyards and Beringer Vineyards—the term *Private Reserve* means the wines are their top quality. These wines are either produced from grapes coming from special vineyards or blended from superior batches of grapes. But the terms do not always indicate high quality and are often used simply as a marketing ploy. The bottom line is that wines using any of these terms should be judged on their own merit and not on the labeling.

R

residual sugar (RS) The natural grape sugar that is either unfermented at the end of the FERMENTATION process or added back into the wine, as with a DOSAGE added to a SPARKLING WINE. In some cases, there is so much natural sugar that fermentation can't complete its process, as is the case with some DESSERT WINES like Germany's TROKENBEER-ENAUSLESE. In other instances, fermentation is purposefully arrested by adding a soupçon of SULFUR DIOXIDE, which inhibits the yeast, or by adding ALCOHOL (as is done with FORTIFIED WINES), which raises the alcohol to a level (15 to 16 percent) above which the YEAST cannot work. DRY wines may have little residual sugar (0.1 to 0.2 percent), semisweet wines usually range from 1 to 3 percent, and LATE HARVEST wines may range as high as 28 to 30 percent. Residual sugar is sometimes referred to as **reducing sugar** or by the initials **RS**.

residuo [ray-SEE-dwoh] The Italian term used for "RESIDUAL SUGAR."

resinous *see* Glossary of Wine Tasting Terms, page 655

restzucker [REHST-tsoo-kehr] German for "RESIDUAL SUGAR." *Restsüsse* means "residual sweetness" and is also used to refer to residual sugar.

resveratrol [rez-VEHR-ah-trawl] One of the PHENOLIC COMPOUNDS in wine that is thought to reduce serum cholesterol levels when wine is consumed in moderate amounts. Resveratrol is produced in plants during times of environmental stress such as adverse weather or ecological attack. It's been identified in numerous plant species, including mulberries, peanuts, and grapes. Resveratrol is not found in the flesh but in the skin of grapes. Which is why red wines, which stay in contact with the skins much longer than white or ROSÉ wines, are associated with reduced risk of heart disease. It's also believed the processes such as FILTERING or FINING result in the loss of resveratrol. Recently resveratrol has been shown to have a positive effect on lipid levels and a preventative quality against certain cancers. *See also* HEALTH CONSEQUENCES OF WINE.

retsina [reht-SEE-nah] Made for more than 3,000 years, this traditional Greek wine is resinated—treated with pine-tree resin. This process gives the wine a distinctively sappy, turpentine-like flavor, which, according to most non-Greeks, is an acquired taste. In Greece, the word *retsina* (Greek for "resin") is synonymous with wine. Retsinas can be either white (labeled "Retsina") or ROSÉ (labeled "Kokineli"); both should be served very cold. The Savatiano grape is the main variety used in retsina, although it's usually blended with either Rhoditis or Assyrtiko grapes.

Reuilly AC [reuh-YEE] Located southwest of the SANCERRE AC and POUILLY-FUMÉ AC, this tiny APPELLATION surrounds the village of Reuilly near the QUINCY AC in the central LOIRE region. Reuilly produces white wines from the SAUVIGNON BLANC grape that are similar in style to those from these three neighboring appellations—generally CRISP and TART with a somewhat GRASSY characteristic. It also produces light red wines from PINOT NOIR and ROSÉ wines from Pinot Noir and PINOT GRIS.

reverse osmosis A filtration process that works by forcing wine through an extremely dense membrane by using pressure. The technique allows only water, alcohol, and volatile elements through the membrane. After reverse osmosis, additional steps can lower VOLATILE ACIDITY, lower ALCOHOL levels (*see* DEALCOHOLIZATION), increase alcohol levels by removing water and/or remove some of the byproducts of BRETTANOMYCES spoilage. *See also* SPINNING CONE; WATERING BACK.

Rhein [RINE] The German name for the Rhine River, which appears in many of the country's regional names.

Rheinburgengau, Bereich *see* MITTELRHEIN

Rheinelbe *see* ELBLING

Rheingau [RINE-gow] The wines of this German ANBAUGEBIET (quality-wine region) are considered by many to be some of the finest in Germany and among the world's great wines. Over 80 percent of the 8,000 vineyard acres are planted with RIESLING, Germany's premier variety. The Rheingau, whose vineyards cover the right (northerly) bank of the Rhine River, starts just east of Hochheim and extends north to Lorch, with the principal portion situated between the villages of RAUENTHAL and RÜDESHEIM. The climate and soil of this stretch of vineyards is ideal for Riesling. It's from this area that the Rheingau gets its reputation for wines that are generally RICH, FRUITY, and full-bodied (*see* BODY) with a STEELY character. The better VINTAGES can produce AUSLESE, BEERENAUSLESE, and occasionally TROCKENBEERENAUSLESE wines of remarkable quality. Even though these wines are very RICH, they're balanced with good ACIDITY and are capable of very long AGING. The Rheingau's only BEREICH is JOHANNISBERG, which covers the entire region and includes ten GROSSLAGEN—Burgweg, Daubhaus, Deutelsberg, Erntebringer, Gottesthal, Heiligensotck, Honigberg, Mehrhölzchen, Steil, and Steinmächer. Some of Germany's best-known wine estates are located here, including Schloss Johannisberg, Schloss Schönborn, Schloss Rheinhartshausen, and Schloss Vollrads. *See also* ERSTES GEWACHS.

Rheinhell *see* ERBACH

Rheinhessen [RINE-hehs-uhn] With nearly 65,000 acres of vineyards, this is the largest of Germany's thirteen ANBAUGEBIETE (quality-wine regions). It's in the center of the winegrowing regions located along the Rhine, with RHEINGAU to the north, PFALZ to the south, NAHE to the west, and HESSISCHE BERGSTRASSE to the east. Rheinhessen is divided into just three BEREICHE—BINGEN, NIERSTEIN, and Wonnegau— and twenty-four GROSSLAGEN. Despite the large number of vineyards, only a small percentage produce high-quality wines. Many of the vineyards in the fertile land away from the Rhine have large YIELDS and are major providers of vast quantities of LIEBFRAUMILCH. In fact, over 50 percent of Germany's production of this simple, inexpensive wine come from Rheinhessen. The best wines come from the vineyards located closest to the Rhine, starting near Bingen in the north, east to Mainz, and then south to around Worms. In particular, the vineyards near Bingen and Ingelheim and the RHEINTERRASSE near Nierstein produce excellent wines. MÜLLER-THURGAU, which accounts for about 25 percent of Rheinhessen's total planted acreage, is the most widely planted variety. It's followed by SYLVANER and SCHEUREBE, as well as myriad others like BACCHUS, Faberebe (FABER), HUXELREBE, and KERNER.

Rheinpfalz *see* PFALZ

Rheinterrasse [RIN-tehr-ah-suh] This German term, which means "Rhine terrace," refers to a strip of vineyards situated along the Rhine River from the village of Bodenheim south to the village of Mettenheim. These vineyards are part of the RHEINHESSEN region and are noted for producing superb wines, particularly those made from

RIESLING, but also SYLVANER. The very best of the Rheinterrasse vineyards are around the villages of NACKENHEIM, NIERSTEIN, and OPPENHEIM.

Rhine Riesling *see* RIESLING

Rhine wine [RINE] A generic name in the United States for white, usually somewhat sweet, TABLE WINES. Such wines shouldn't be confused with German wines from the Rhine region.

Rhode Island This New England state has one VITICULTURAL AREA—the SOUTHEASTERN NEW ENGLAND AVA—which covers not only Rhode Island but also parts of CONNECTICUT and MASSACHUSETTS. The area wineries make a number of wines from HYBRIDS like VIDAL BLANC, SEYVAL BLANC, CAYUGA, and MARÉCHAL FOCH and from VITIS VINIFERA varieties like CHARDONNAY, CABERNET SAUVIGNON, PINOT NOIR, MERLOT, CABERNET FRANC, and RIESLING. FRUIT WINES also play an important role at some wineries. **Sakonnet Vineyards** is the largest winery in New England with over 50 planted acres and production of over 50,000 cases per year.

Rhodes *see* GREECE

Rhône [ROHN] The Rhône River actually starts high in the Swiss Alps, tumbling down the mountains into Lake Geneva and then exiting the lake to begin its journey through France. The vineyards of the Rhône form one of France's great wine regions, which follows the river for approximately 125 miles from just below Vienne in the north, to south of Avignon. The Rhône region has over 170,000 vineyard acres and breaks up into two distinct north and south portions. The northern part contains many great individual APPELLATIONS like CÔTE RÔTIE, CONDRIEU, CHÂTEAU GRILLET, SAINT-JOSEPH, and HERMITAGE. Many of these vineyards are planted on small steep terraces with breathtaking views of the Rhône River. The dominant grapes here are SYRAH for red wines and MARSANNE, ROUSSANNE, and VIOGNIER for whites. As one heads south, there is a gap in the vineyards around Montélimar and then the valley widens to form the southern portion. The most famous appellation in the south is CHÂTEAUNEUF-DU-PAPE. Other well-known ACs are GIGONDAS, LIRAC, MUSCAT DE BEAUMES-DE-VENISE, and TAVEL. Most of the vineyards in the southern Rhône produce wines covered by the ACs of CÔTES DU RHÔNE and CÔTES DU RHÔNE-VILLAGES. In the southern Rhône, the principal red grape is GRENACHE, but others include CARIGNAN, Counoise, MOURVÈDRE, Terret Noir, and SYRAH. The white grapes used include BOURBOULENC, CLAIRETTE, Marsanne, Muscardine, Picardan, Roussanne, and Piquepoul (or *Picpoule*). More blends of different grapes are used in the south than in the north.

Rhone Rangers Nonprofit, educational organization established in the United States to promote wines made from the RHÔNE VARIETY grapes. To qualify as a "Rhone Ranger" wine, it must be made of at least 75 percent of any single variety or a combination of approved varieties. Although the accepted list includes the twenty-one varieties approved for the CÔTES DU RHÔNE AC, plus PETITE SIRAH (also known as Durif), only about half of these varieties are currently grown in the United States. In addition to Petite Sirah, approved grapes include CARIGNANE, CINSAULT, COUNOISE, GRENACHE, MARSANNE, MOURVÈDRE (also called Mataro), ROUSSANNE, SYRAH, and VIOGNIER. The organization was started informally in the 1980s by some of the pioneers of Rhône-style wines and formalized in 1997. Today the Rhône Rangers includes over 130 member wineries.

R

Rías Baixas DO; Rías Bajas DO [REE-ahs bi-SHAHS (BAH-hahs)] A DO area in northwestern Spain's Galicia region, adjacent to Portugal's northern border. The word *Rías* refers to this region's numerous estuaries, similiar to fjords, that reach inland from the Atlantic Ocean. Rías Baixas (also called *Rías Bajas*) refers to the lower or southern part of the region. This area consists of five distinct districts: the Condado de Tea, O Rosal, Ribeira del Ulla, Soutomaior, and Val do Salnés. The best-known white wines are made from Albariño (ALVARINHO), although other white varieties grown include Caiño Blanco, LOUREIRA, Torrontés, and Treixadura. The Albariño vines are low yielding; the grapes are thick-skinned and don't produce a lot of juice. This combination produces somewhat expensive wines that not only are highly prized by Spaniards but have gained considerable international recognition as well. Wines labeled "Albariño" must contain 100 percent of this variety. Wines labeled with one of the district names but not the variety name must contain some Albariño (in most cases 70 percent), which can be blended with one of the other white grapes. The area's red wines are made from a variety of local grapes and are not at all highly regarded.

Ribatejano *see* RIBATEJO

Ribatejo; Ribatejo DOC [rree-bher-TAY-yoh] A VINHO REGIONAL and DOC located in the south central part of Portugal just northeast of Lisbon. Within the Ribatejo DOC are now a number of village areas that have been given DOC status, which means they may add their name to that of Ribatejo on labels. These DOC areas are **Ribatejo/Almerim**, **Ribatejo/Cartaxo**, **Ribatejo/Chamusca**, **Ribatejo/Coruche**, **Ribatejo/Santarém**, and **Ribatejo/Tomar**. The most common native white-grape varieties found in the Ribatejo DOC are ARINTO, FERNÃO PIRES, and Talia (TREBBIANO). Castelão Frances (PERIQUITA) is the principal red grape and is used along with BAGA, Camarate, and Trincadeira (TINTA AMARELA). Quality DRY red wines are starting to gain a decent reputation; white wines (which make up the majority) are light-bodied, fruity, and drinkable but not very complex. Wines made according to the standards established for the DOC may use "DOC" on the label. Wines that don't (such as those using unauthorized DOC grape varieties) must use the vinho regional designation **Ribatejano**. Plantings of these nonlocal grapes—CABERNET SAUVIGNON, MERLOT, SYRAH, SAUVIGNON BLANC, and CHARDONNAY—are expanding, perhaps more so than any other vinho regional.

Ribbon Ridge AVA APPELLATION created in July 2005 within the larger WILLAMETTE VALLEY AVA and is sub-appellation of the CHEHALEM MOUNTAINS AVA. At only 3,350 acres, it's Oregon's smallest VITICULTURAL AREA. The ridge itself is about 3½ miles long by 1¾ miles wide. There are currently 5 wineries and about 500 acres planted mainly to PINOT NOIR, PINOT GRIS, and MUSCAT, but also CHARDONNAY, GAMAY, GEWÜRZTRAMINER, RIESLING, and SAUVIGNON BLANC. Top producers include Beaux Frères and Brick House.

Ribeira Sacra DO [ree-BAY-rah SAH-krah] This beautiful DO zone is located in the Galacia region in northwestern Spain and covers the area where the Miño and Sil Rivers converge. It's situated around the town of Monforte de Lemos with the VALDEORRAS DO on its eastern border. Ribeira Sacra is cooler and wetter than most Spanish growing regions, although not more so than the coastal DO of RÍAS BAIXAS. Over a dozen grape VARIETIES are grown in this area. The most important red is MENCÍA, while the significant white varieties are Albariño (ALVARINHO) and Godello (VERDELHO).

Ribeiro DO [ree-BAY-roh] A DO area of about 7,000 vineyard acres located in the Galicia region in northwest Spain, inland from the RÍAS BAIXAS DO. Two-thirds of the wines produced here are white. The primary white grape here is PALOMINO, the principal variety used in making Spanish SHERRY. Because it's too neutral for the DRY, fresh wine that the area produces, Palomino is being replaced with varieties like Albariño (ALVARINHO) Godello (VERDELHO), LOUREIRO, Treixadura, and Torrontés. These grapes are known to produce more exciting wines, similiar to the fresh, crisp wines from Portugal's VINHO VERDE DOC. The generally undistinguished red wines here are made from Garnacha (GRENACHE) and local varieties like Caiño, Ferrón, and MENCÍA.

Ribera del Duero DO [ree-BEHR-ah del DWAY-roh] Significant DO area located along the Duero River in northern Spain, halfway between Madrid and the Atlantic Ocean (Bay of Biscay). The Duero River becomes the Douro (the famous PORT river) in Portugal. A small amount of ROSÉ wine is produced here; white wines are not included as part of the DO. What Ribera del Duero is famous for is its excellent red wines, which are full-bodied, deeply colored, and flavorful. This area's prominent red-wine position is principally due to Vega Sicilia, a premier wine estate over a century old. This estate uses about 60 percent Tinta del Pais (TEMPRANILLO) blended with CABERNET SAUVIGNON, MERLOT, and MALBEC. Since the 1980s, several other area wine estates have attracted vintners interested in producing high-quality red wines. One of these estates is Alejandro Fernández, world famous for their Tinto Pesquera wines made primarily from Tinta del Pais with some Garnacha (GRENACHE). Today, the internationally recognized Ribera del Duero comprises over fifty wine producers.

Ribera del Guadiana DO [ree-BEHR-ah del gwah-dee-AH-nah] DO zone located in the Extremadura region in western Spain on the Portuguese border. In 1998, six VINO DE LA TIERRA areas were combined to form this DO—Cañamero, Montánchez, Ribera Alta, Ribera Baja, Matanegra, and **Tierra de Barros** (the best known of the six). This zone takes its name from the Guadiana River, which flows through the area and eventually into Portugal. There is a broad assortment of grapes grown throughout the region. White varieties include Alarije, Borba, Cayetana Blanca, Pardina, Viura (MACABEO), CHARDONNAY, Montúa, Malvar, PARELLADA, PEDRO XIMÉNEZ, and VERDEJO. Red varieties include Garnacha (GRENACHE), TEMPRANILLO, BOBAL, CABERNET SAUVIGNON, GRACIANO, Mazuela (CARIGNAN), MERLOT, Monastrell (MOURVÈDRE), and SYRAH. A number of these grapes are of lesser quality, and a movement is underway to reduce their use and focus on the higher-quality varieties.

Ribera del Júcar DO [ree-BEHR-ah del khoo-KAHR] Rising APPELLATION located in southern part of Cuenca province of the CASTILLA-LA MANCHA region in central Spain. The area is made up of approximately 22,500 acres, encompassing the municipalities of Casas de Benítez, Casas de Fernando Alonso, Casas de Guijarro, Casas de Haro, El Picazo, Pozoamargo, and Sisante. Red wines are made from the traditional varieties, Cencibel (TEMPRANILLO) and BOBAL, along with CABERNET FRANC, CABERNET SAUVIGNON, MERLOT, PETIT VERDOT, and SYRAH. Moscatel (MUSCAT) and SAUVIGNON BLANC are the authorized white grapes.

La Ribera d'Erbe *see* TARRAGONA DO

Ribolla [ree-BOH-lah] White-wine grape, whose full name is *Ribolla Gialla,* that is grown in Italy's FRIULI-VENEZIA GIULIA, in Slovenia, where it's known as *Rebula,* and in Greece, where it's called *Robola.* Ribolla's been grown in Friuli since the twelfth century and is thought to be a native of this region, although there's some speculation that it has Greek origins. This variety produces DRY, CRISP, citrus-flavored wines that are medium-bodied and deeply colored. Ribolla will stand some aging, during which time it becomes richer and SOFTER. There's also a red version, *Ribolla Nera,* more popularly known as SCHIOPPETTINO.

rice wine A sweet, golden wine made from fermenting freshly steamed glutinous rice. Most rice wines are low in alcohol. The most well-known Japanese rice wines are SAKE and MIRIN, while Chinese renditions include Chia Fan, Hsiang Hsueh, Shan Niang, and Yen Hung.

rich *see* Glossary of Wine Tasting Terms, page 655

Richebourg AC [*r*eesh-BOO*R*] Located at the northern end of the village of VOSNE-ROMANÉE in the CÔTE DE NUITS, Richebourg is one of the great Burgundian GRAND CRU vineyards. Its 19.8 acres are planted with PINOT NOIR, and the red wines that are produced here are some of the best in the world. The largest and most famous of the twelve different parcel owners is the Domaine de la Romanée-Conti. The wines from the Richebourg vineyards are said to be richer and more deeply colored than those from the famous neighboring vineyards ROMANÉE-CONTI and LA TÂCHE, although they are not quite as PERFUMED or elegant.

riddling [RIHD-ling] Madame Clicquot, a young French widow who took over her dead husband's CHAMPAGNE house in 1805, was the visionary who developed the important riddling procedure—a way to remove dead yeast cells from bottles of SPARKLING WINE made by the MÉTHODE CHAMPENOISE. In the step just before riddling, a BOTTLING DOSAGE (*dosage de tirage* or *liqueur de tirage*) and yeast are added to a CUVÉE (a blend of still wines) to produce a SECONDARY FERMENTATION in the bottle. The SEDIMENT that forms during this secondary fermentation is maneuvered into the neck of the bottle and up against the CORK or CROWN CAP through riddling (called *remuage* in France). The riddling process consists of positioning the bottles upside down at a 45° angle in specially built racks called *pupitres.* Every 3 or 4 days, a trained worker (called a *remuer* in France) gives the bottles a shake and a slight turn, gradually increasing the angle of tilt and dropping the bottle back in the rack with a slight whack. In 6 to 8 weeks, all the bottles are positioned straight downward and the sediment has collected in the neck. The sediment is then removed by another step called DIS-GORGEMENT. A skilled *remuer* can handle over 30,000 bottles per day. Although riddling was once done entirely by hand, today many wine-makers are employing large metal racks (pioneered in Spain) that hold over 500 bottles. These racks—called *girasols* in Spain, *gyropallets* in France, and *VLMs* (very large machines) in the United States—mechanically perform the riddling process and have dramatically shortened the procedure. Another process being tried is the place-ment of yeast in **calcium alginate beads** (also called **encapsulated yeasts**), which fall to the neck of the bottle immediately when it is turned upside down. If successful, this technique could eliminate the need for riddling altogether.

Riesling [REEZ-ling; REES-ling] Riesling is considered to be one of the world's great white-wine grapes and produces some of the very best white wines. It's a native of Germany, where it's believed to have been cultivated for at least 500 years, possibly as long as 2,000 years. This grape's balance of good ACID and high sugar levels produces wines with considerable aging potential. The DELICATE but COMPLEX Riesling wines are characterized by a SPICY, FRUITY flavor (that's some-times reminiscent of peaches and apricots), a flower-scented BOUQUET, and a long FINISH. Riesling is vinified in a variety of styles ranging from DRY to very sweet. In Germany, these sweet wines, which are usually affected by BOTRYTIS CINEREA, are graded in ascending order of sweet-ness as AUSLESE, BEERENAUSLESE, and TROCKENBEERENAUSLESE. There are extensive Riesling plantings in California where early wines were made in a DRY, OAKY style. California winemakers now produce high-quality, German-style Rieslings, which are lighter, more delicate, and slightly to medium sweet. They also make some excellent LATE HARVEST wines from botrytis-infected grapes. Other states that have had success with Riesling wines include Oregon, Washington, and New York. Australia has extensive plantings of this grape and produces high-quality Riesling wines, particularly from the Eden and Clare Valleys. France's ALSACE region and Italy's ALTO ADIGE also produce excellent Rieslings. Because the name "Riesling" is used in many ways, it's sometimes dif-ficult to find wines truly made from this variety. In California, for instance, **Johannisberg Riesling** is the true Riesling, whereas GRAY RIESLING and EMERALD RIESLING are actually other varieties. Californians also call the variety SYLVANER such names as *Sylvaner Riesling, Franken Riesling, Monterey Riesling,* and *Sonoma Riesling.* A bottle of California wine labeled simply "Riesling" usually means that the wine's made from one of the lesser varieties, not Johannisberg Riesling. In parts of

Europe, there is also WELSCHRIESLING (or Italian Riesling), which is a different variety. In Australia, the word *Riesling* often refers to any type of white wine, whereas **Rhine Riesling** refers to the real thing. South Africans have *Cape Riesling, Clare Riesling, Paarl Riesling,* and *South African Riesling,* all of which refer to a variety officially known as CRUCHEN BLANC. **Weisser Riesling** is the name South Africans (and some Germans) use for the true Riesling. The confusion is perpetuated even in Germany, where the variety Müllerrebe (MEUNIER) is called *Schwarzriesling* and the variety RÜLANDER is called *Grauer Riesling.* The Germans have also bred a number of Riesling crosses, the most famous being the MÜLLER-THURGAU, a CROSS of two strains of RIESLING. Riesling is also known as *Johannisberger, Klingelberger, Petit Rhin*, *Rajinski Rizling, Rajnai Rizling, Riesling Renano,* and *White Riesling.*

Riesling Italico *see* WELSCHRIESLING

Riesling Renano *see* RIESLING

Riesling-Sylvaner *see* MÜLLER-THURGAU

rim color *see* MENISCUS in the Glossary of Wine Tasting Terms, page 655

Rio Grande do Sul *see* BRAZIL

Rioja DOCa [ree-OH-hah] One of Spain's most important wine regions, this DOCA is in northern Spain around the town of Logroño and along the Ebro River. The name comes from Río Oja, a tributary of the Ebro River. Established in 1926, Rioja was the first DO, and in 1991 it became the first DOCa (Spain's top category). Wine has been made in this region for over 2,500 years—prior to the Roman occupation. The TABLE WINES from the Rioja DOCa are some of Spain's best and most famous. The area comprises about 135,000 vineyard acres situated in the provinces of Alava and Navarra, as well as La Rioja. This DOCa is divided into three subzones—**La Rioja Alavesa** is the northwestern portion, **La Rioja Alta** in the southwestern section, and **La Rioja Baja** in the eastern segment. The cooler, wetter climate of the two western subzones produces more delicate wines. La Rioja Alta generally produces the best wines, followed by those from La Rioja Alavesa. The hotter, drier easterly La Rioja Baja produces bigger, more ALCOHOLIC wines. Rioja wines, which tend to be made very much in a BORDEAUX style, are greatly influenced by winemaking practices introduced by French families who migrated to Rioja in the late 1800s after PHYLLOXERA struck the Bordeaux vineyards. The extensive use of American oak BARRIQUES (called *barricas* locally) for AGING still exists, although somewhat less aggressively than in the past; French oak use is now on the rise. The American OAK imparts the familiar vanilla characteristic that's associated with Rioja wines. Red wines make up 75 to 80 percent of the total production, and TEMPRANILLO is the primary red grape used. Garnacha Tinta (GRENACHE), Mazuelo (CARIGNAN), and GRACIANO are also allowed. In Rioja, CRIANZA wines must have 2 years of aging, with 1 year in oak; RESERVA wines must have 3 years of aging, with 1 year in oak; and GRAN RESERVA must have 5 years of aging, with 2 years in oak. There's a small quantity of ROSÉ wine made from these same grapes. A limited amount of white wine is made from Viura (MACABEO), Garnacha Blanca (GRENACHE), and MALVASIA. In the past, the white wines from Rioja have also been heavily oaked, but fresher, crisper wines are now the style.

La Rioja *see* ARGENTINA

Rio Negro *see* ARGENTINA

riparia *see* VITIS RIPARIA

ripasso process [ree-PAH-soh] A process used in producing some VALPOLICELLA wines to give them richness and BODY. After the wine is FERMENTED in the usual way, it's placed in casks containing the LEES from a prior batch of RECIOTO or RECIOTO AMARONE, a CONCENTRATED wine made from PASSITO grapes. This process, which lasts from 2 to 3 weeks, adds color, TANNINS, and complex flavors. Unfortunately, the term *ripasso* is not allowed on the label, so you need to know producers who make this style of wine. Boscaini's Le Canne, Masi's CAMPO FIORIN, and Santi's Castello are some of the wines made this way.

ripe *see* Glossary of Wine Tasting Terms, page 655

riserva [ree-ZEHR-vah] Italian for "reserve," which in the wine world can be applied only to DOC or DOCG wines that have been AGED longer than regular wines. The better wines are usually chosen to become riservas. The total aging time varies from wine to wine. For instance, CHIANTI Riserva receives a minimum of 2 years and 3 months aging, BARBARESCO Riserva gets 4 years, and BAROLO and BRUNELLO DI MONTALCINO Riservas each get 5 years of aging. Sometimes, but not always, part of the additional aging time occurs in wood. *Riserva speciale* denotes even longer aging, usually an additional year.

riserva speciale *see* RISERVA

Rivaner *see* MÜLLER-THURGAU

Riverina Huge Australian wine region located in the Big Rivers Zone of NEW SOUTH WALES. It's situated in a hot dry area of the state around the town of Griffith, 350 miles west of Sydney and 270 miles north of Melbourne. Riverina requires irrigation and is the beneficiary of the Murrumbidgee Irrigation Area, which allows this region to be not only the largest growing area in New South Wales (generating 65 percent of the production) but one of the largest in Australia (20 percent of the production). Riverina is often criticized for excessive YIELDS and large quantities of BULK wines. This wine region has over 35,000 acres of vineyards. SÉMILLON is the leading variety followed closely by Shiraz (SYRAH). Other white varieties include CHARDONNAY, COLOMBARD, MARSANNE, MUSCAT, SAUVIGNON BLANC, TREBBIANO, and VERDELHO; other reds include CABERNET SAUVIGNON, MERLOT, and MOURVÈDRE. The stars of the region are the BOTRYTISED Sémillon wines—those from family-owned De Bortoli Wines are particularly well thought of.

River Junction AVA A 1,300-acre (of which over 300 acres are currently planted), California VITICULTURAL AREA situated in southern San Joaquin County south of Stockton and west of Modesto where the San Joaquin and Stanislaus Rivers converge. Vineyeards adjacent to the rivers enjoy a cooling influence of 3 to 5 degrees from those areas not near the river.

Riverland An Australian wine region located in the Lower Murray Zone of SOUTH AUSTRALIA. It's situated about 145 miles northeast of Adelaide around the towns of Renmark and Berri. It is just east of the huge MURRAY DARLING region that lies in the states of NEW SOUTH WALES and VICTORIA. Like the Murray Darling region, Riverland is the product of the irrigation systems implemented on the Murray River beginning in the 1890s. The Riverland is hot and dry, and vineyards require irrigation water from the Murray River. This region also resembles Murray Darling with regard to the huge quantities of reliable quality wine it churns out—much of it going into Australia's inexpensive and popular bag-in-box (or cask) wines. The over 45,000 vineyard acres here produced 48 percent of South Australia's total production in 2001. The most widely planted varieties from largest to smallest are Shiraz (SYRAH), CABERNET SAUVIGNON, CHARDONNAY, MUSCAT, MERLOT, RUBY CABERNET, SULTANA, COLOMBARD, GRENACHE, PETIT VERDOT, and Mataro (MOURVÈDRE), plus a dozen other varieties. Riverland has several large wineries; however, much of the crop is sent south to the BAROSSA VALLEY for FERMENTATION.

Rivesaltes AC [reev-ZALT] Small town located just north of Perpignan in France's LANGUEDOC-ROUSSILLON region. The APPELLATION that surrounds the town produces VIN DOUX NATUREL (VDN), a category of sweet, FORTIFIED WINE. Rivesaltes AC produces red, white, and ROSÉ wines from GRENACHE, MALVOISIE, MACABEO, and MUSCAT. A more celebrated VDN from this same area is MUSCAT DE RIVESALTES AC, which is made from 100 percent MUSCAT.

Riviera Ligure di Ponente *see* VERMENTINO

Rizlingszilvani *see* MÜLLER-THURGAU

Rkatsiteli [ruh-KAT-see-TELL-ee] White-wine grape that is the most widely planted variety in what was formerly the Soviet Union—it's extensively grown in Russia and Georgia. Rkatsiteli is also widely grown in Bulgaria and is now thought to be the world's second most planted white grape after Spain's AIRÉN. There are even a few acres in California and New York. Rkatsiteli produces good-quality wines with high ACIDITY, good sugar levels, and pleasantly SPICY, FLORAL characteristics. It's vinified in a variety of styles ranging from DRY to very sweet, used in sparkling wine production, and even processed into SHERRY-like wines and COGNAC-style spirits.

Roaix *see* CÔTES DU RHÔNE

Roannaises *see* CÔTE ROANNAISES AC

Robe Ranges Australian wine-producing region located about 200 miles southeast of the city of Adelaide in the Limestone Coast Zone of SOUTH AUSTRALIA. It's situated between the coastal towns of Robe and Beachport. Vines weren't planted until 1994, so this area doesn't have a long wine history. There's excitement about Robe Ranges because its soil—terra rossa over limestone—is similar to the famous COONAWARRA region, which is approximately 60 miles inland and eastward. The primary difference is that Robe's coastal location gives it a slightly longer growing season. The climate is very similar to the MOUNT BENSON region about 25 miles north. Varieties grown here are CABERNET SAUVIGNON, SHIRAZ, MERLOT, PINOT NOIR, CHARDONNAY, SÉMILLON, and SAUVIGNON BLANC. Southcorp is the big player in this region.

Robertson WO A demarcated SOUTH AFRICA wine district that is part of the Breede River Valley Region and located about 110 miles east of Cape Town around the town of Robertson. This is a hot, dry area that requires irrigation. Water comes from the Breede River, but VITICULTURE wasn't feasible until the Brandvlei Dam was constructed in the early 1900s. Today, this district has 12,000 acres of vineyards, about 12 percent of the nation's total. White varieties still dominate the vineyards with Columbar (COLUMBARD), CHENIN BLANC (called *Steen* locally), CHARDONNAY, and SAUVIGNON BLANC the leaders. Recent plantings have been mostly red varieties—CABERNET SAUVIGNON, Shiraz (SYRAH), MERLOT, PINOTAGE, and RUBY CABERNET. The region was traditionally a producer of FORTIFIED WINES and BRANDY but is shifting rapidly to higher-quality TABLE WINES, as evidenced by the shift in grapes being planted (and those being uprooted).

Robola *see* RIBOLLA

robe *see* Glossary of Wine Tasting Terms, page 655

robust *see* Glossary of Wine Tasting Terms, page 655

Rochegude *see* CÔTES DU RHÔNE

Rockpile AVA Established in April 2002, this California VITICULTURAL AREA is located in northwestern Sonoma County. It covers 15,400 rugged, rock-strewn acres that must be at or above the 800-foot level. About 2,500 acres overlap the northwestern corner of DRY CREEK AVA. Rockpile currently has approximately 160 acres of vines planted mainly to ZINFANDEL and PETITE SIRAH, with some CABERNET SAUVIGNON. The name of this region dates back to 1858 when the Rock Pile Ranch (cattle) was operating. Currently no wineries exist in the AVA, but some wineries outside the area purchase grapes from the Rockpile AVA.

Rocky Knob AVA A small (9,000 acre) VITICULTURAL AREA in parts of southern Virginia's Floyd and Patrick Counties around the towns of Woolwine and Meadows of Dan. Established in 1987, it was named after the eponymous recreational area located in this area of the Blue Ridge Mountains. Château Morrisette's wines are the best known from this region.

Roero DOC; Roero Arneis DOC [roh-EHR-oh ahr-NAYZ] DOC located in the Roero hills north and east of Alba in southeastern PIED-MONT. This zone lies within the larger NEBBIOLO D'ALBA DOC and was granted its own DOC designation in 1985 at the request of the area's producers. The wines from the two DOCs are similiar. **Roero** makes red wine primarily from NEBBIOLO grapes, although small amounts of ARNEIS and other grapes are allowed. The *Roero Superiore* has a higher ALCOHOL content and is AGED for 8 months. The right to make DOC white wine was granted in 1989. The white wine called **Roero Arneis** (or *Arneis di Roero*) is made from 100 percent Arneis grapes. The *Superiore* version has a higher alcohol content and is aged for 1 year. A SPUMANTE rendition of the Roero Arneis may be made as well.

Le Rognet et Corton *see* CORTON; CORTON-CHARLEMAGNE

Rogue Valley AVA Located in southern Oregon near the California border, this AVA encompasses the towns of Medford and Ashland. This area is warmer than most parts of Oregon and is best known for its CABERNET SAUVIGNON and CHARDONNAY. It has several valleys with varying climatic conditions—Illinois Valley, the westernmost, is cooler; Bear Creek Valley is the warmest. Between the two in climate is APPLEGATE VALLEY.

Rolle *see* VERMENTINO

La Romanée AC [lah raw-ma-NAY] The tiniest GRAND CRU vineyard in France's BURGUNDY region and also the smallest APPELLATION in France (not CHÂTEAU-GRILLET, as is often indicated). La Romanée is located in the village VOSNE-ROMANÉE next to two other famous grands crus of this village—ROMANÉE-CONTI AC and RICHEBOURG AC. La Romanée consists of slightly more than 2 acres planted in PINOT NOIR. The miniscule amount of red wine that it produces is ranked as some of the best in the world, as is that of its neighbors. These wines are usually considered more like those from Richebourg AC than Romanée-Conti, which is more deeply colored and more intense but not as elegant or PERFUMED as Romanée-Conti.

Romanée-Conti AC [raw-ma-NAY kawn-TEE] A 4½-acre GRAND CRU vineyard that's wholly owned by the Domaine de la Romanée-Conti. It's located in the village of VOSNE-ROMANÉE in the CÔTE DE NUITS area of France's BURGUNDY region. The wines are considered the ultimate in PINOT NOIRS and so sought after that they are some of the world's most expensive wines—destined only for the very wealthy. Romanée-Conti wines, although usually not as RICH and intense in their youth as those from the neighboring RICHEBOURG AC and LA TÂCHE AC, are considered to be the perfect example of what a red Burgundy should be. They're RICH, with a seeming sweetness and have enough TANNINS to AGE gracefully. Their most distinguishing trademark is an exotic spiciness reminiscent of cinnamon and cloves.

Romanée-Saint-Vivant AC [raw-ma-NAY san vee-VAHN] The largest of the six GRAND CRU vineyards located in the village of VOSNE ROMANÉE in the CÔTE DE NUITS. It consists of slightly over 23 acres planted with PINOT NOIR. Although the wines from this vineyard are some of the world's best and most expensive, they're often overshadowed by those from the neighboring and more famous grand cru vineyards of ROMANÉE-CONTI, RICHEBOURG, and LA TÂCHE. The Romanée-

Saint-Vivant AC wines are somewhat lighter in style than the wines from these other famous vineyards, but they possess much of the elegance and spiciness found in the celebrated Romanée-Conti AC wines.

Romania Romania ranks as one of the top ten wine-producing countries, yet few Romanian wines are seen in Western countries. With the fall of the communist regime, however, this is slowly changing. Romania grows many international as well local grape varieties and produces a wide assortment of wines. In general, the white wines are better than the reds. Some of the white grapes grown here are Banat Riesling, CHARDONNAY, Fetească Albă, GEWÜRZTRAMINER, Grasă, MUSCAT, RIESLING, Rülander (PINOT GRIS), and Tamîîoasă Romaneasca. The red varieties used include CABERNET SAUVIGNON, Babeasca Neagra, Fetească Negră, MERLOT, and PINOT NOIR. The Tîrnave area in the northern part of the country (Transylvania) is thought to produce Romania's best wines. By most accounts, however, the sweet SAUTERNES-style wines from Cotnari in the northeast (Moldavia) are really the only ones worth seeking. Other growing areas include Stefănesti, Dragăsăni, and Segarcea, all in the southern part of the country; Odobești, Nicorești, and Cotești in the eastern portion; Murfatlar near the Black Sea; the Banat Plain in the west; and Dealul Mare in the southeast where Pinot Noir and other international varieties are grown.

Roman Muscat *see* MUSCAT

römer [RUH-muhr] A traditional German wine glass with a long green or amber stem. The bowl, which is made of clear glass and is sometimes engraved, holds from 6½ to 8½ ounces.

room temperature *see* CHAMBRER

rootstock The lower portion of a root and its corresponding growth buds, used for plant propagation. In grape growing, the rootstock should be resistant to pests like PHYLLOXERA and nematodes. In addition, rootstock is chosen based on environmental factors like soil salinity or potential drought conditions. American rootstock often has European (VITIS VINIFERA) vines GRAFTED to it.

Roriz *see* TEMPRANILLO

rosado [roh-SAH-thoh] Spanish and Portuguese for ROSÉ.

Rosana *see* ROUSSANNE

rosato; Rosato [roh-ZAH-toh] Italian for "rosé," the capitalized *Rosato* is used to indicate a ROSÉ wine that's made from specific, approved grape varieties, which can differ depending on the DOC and region.

rosé [roh-ZAY] French for "pink" or "rose-colored," rosé is used in the wine world to refer to wines of this color. Except for rosé CHAMPAGNES, rosé wines are typically made from red grapes. However, whereas the normal process for making red wine leaves the juice in contact with the grape skins during FERMENTATION, for rosés the juice is drained off from the skins within 2 to 3 days and allowed to ferment in another vessel. This comparatively brief skin contact gives rosé its pale pink color—it's also the reason rosés don't have the BODY and CHARACTER of most red wines. In addition to being lighter-bodied, rosés are typically low- to medium-alcohol and slightly sweet. They have lively ACIDITY and perfumy, fruity aromas and flavors. In France's rosé CHAMPAGNES, a small amount of red wine can be added to the white-wine CUVÉE prior to the SECONDARY FERMENTATION. In the United States, rosé SPARKLING WINES are usually a blend of red- and white-grape varieties. Excellent French rosé wines come from TAVEL and ANJOU. In the United States the term BLUSH WINE is sometimes used in place of rosé. *See also* BLANC DE NOIR; SAIGNÉE.

Rosé d'Anjou AC [roh-ZAY dah*n*-ZHOO] An APPELLATION for ROSÉ wines from the ANJOU region, which is in the central part of France's LOIRE Valley. These sweetish, pale pink wines are produced from the Cot (MALBEC), GAMAY, GROSLOT, and Pineau d'Aunis grapes. Although this appellation's production is one of the largest in the region, the wines don't have a great reputation. The CABERNET FRANC-based rosé wines of the CABERNET D'ANJOU AC from this same geographic area are more highly regarded.

Rosé de Loire AC [ro-ZAY duh LWAH*R*] An APPELLATION that covers a wide area in France's LOIRE Valley including the subregions of ANJOU, SAUMUR, and TOURAINE. The Rosé de Loir AC is for wines made from a minimum of 30 percent Cabernet (usually CABERNET FRANC) blended with GAMAY, GROSLOT, Pineau d'Aunis, and PINOT NOIR. The wines are drier (*see* DRY) than the ROSÉ D'ANJOU AC wines produced throughout much of the same region.

Rosé des Riceys AC *see* CHAMPAGNE

Rosenberg *see* WILTINGEN

Roseneck *see* RÜDESHEIM

Rosengarten *see* RÜDESHEIM

Rosenmuskateller *see* MUSCAT

Rosette AC [raw-ZEHT] A tiny APPELLATION in the BERGERAC area, located in southwestern France not far from BORDEAUX. It produces semisweet white wines of mediocre quality from MUSCADELLE, SAUVIGNON BLANC, and SÉMILLON. As the popularity of semisweet wines has dwindled, so has this appellation's production.

Rossese di Dolceacqua DOC [raw-SEH-zeh dee dawl-cheh-AHK-wah] Small DOC zone, also known simply as *Dolceacqua,* located in the western part of Italy's LIGURIA region, close to the French border. The area, which encircles the town of Dolceacqua, overlaps in some areas with the **Riviera Ligure di Ponente DOC**. The Rossese di Dolceacqua wines must include 95 percent of the Rossese grape. These red wines are very fruity and reminiscent of French BEAUJOLAIS wines. The *superiore* has 1 percent higher ALCOHOL (13 percent) and is AGED for 1 year.

rosso; Rosso [RAWS-soh] 1. Italian for "red" 2. *Rosso* is also used to indicate a red wine that's made from specific, approved grape varieties, which can differ depending on the DOC and region. *"Rosso"* is added to the name of several Italian DOC wines including ROSSO CONERO, ROSSO DI MONTALCINO, ROSSO DI MONTEPULCIANO, and ROSSO PICENO. 3. *Vino rosso* is usually a DRY wine in Italy, whereas in the United States it's often an inexpensive sweet wine.

Rosso Conero DOC [RAWS-soh KAW-neh-roh] The full-flavored red wines from this area are considered the best from central Italy's MARCHES region. Rosso Conero is a small zone located on the Adriatic Sea surrounding the seaside town of Ancona. The wines are made from at least 85 percent MONTEPULCIANO and the rest SANGIOVESE.

Rosso di Montalcino DOC [RAWS-soh dee mawn-tahl-CHEE-noh] DOC that was established after BRUNELLO DI MONTALCINO was upgraded to DOCG status. Rosso di Montalcino encompasses the same area as Brunello di Montalcino (around the town of Montalcino in southern TUSCANY) and uses the same SANGIOVESE clone, Brunello. Rosso di Montalcino wines require only 1 year of AGING, compared to the 4 years necessary for Brunello di Montalcino. The reduced aging time allows this area's producers to release a less-expensive version of the Brunello di Montalcino, which is lighter and less intense, but has a younger, fresher character to it. It also enables producers to make better Brunello di Montalcino wines because the best grapes can be selected for them, with the rest of the grapes going into the Rosso di Montalcino.

Rosso di Montepulciano DOC [RAWS-soh dee mohn-teh-pool-CHAH-noh] DOC located in the hilly area around the town of Montepulciano, southeast of Siena in the eastern portion of Italy's TUS-CANY region. Its designated zone is precisely the same as the one for VINO NOBILE DI MONTEPULCIANO DOCG. The exact same grapes are used as well—minimum 70 percent Prugnolo (SANGIOVESE), maximum 20 percent CANAIOLO, and up to 20 percent of other varieties, although no more than 10 percent white grapes. One of the other red varieties most often used is the Mammolo, which contributes the fragrance of violets to the BOUQUET. The AGING requirement is only 6 months instead of the 2 years required for Vino Nobile di Montepulciano wines. The result is that Rosso di Montepulciano wines are fruitier, less intense mimics of their big brothers.

Rosso Piceno DOC [RAWS-soh pee-CHEH-noh] Rosso Piceno is located in the southern half of (and is the largest DOC in) the MARCHES region. This DOC's DRY red wines are made from 35–70 percent Montepulciano, 30–50 percent Sangiovese, and 15 percent other local red varieties. The wines labeled "Superiore" (which are usually the best) are from a special area at this region's southern end around Ascoli Piceno. They're more like a CLASSICO and require an additional ½ percent minimum ALCOHOL and 1 year of AGING. A VARIETAL Sangiovese is also made and must contain 85 percent of this variety.

rotary fermentor; rotofermenter A horizontal, automated FERMENTATION and CAP management container that replaces more traditional PUMPING OVER or PUNCHING DOWN techniques. Because the tank of a rotary fermentor lies horizontally, there's greater contact between the cap (the mass of grape solids that floats on the surface of the juice during FERMENTATION) and the juice it floats on. The tank either rotates or contains paddles that rotate inside the tank. This rotation mixes the cap with the juice, achieving what occurs with pumping over or punching down. In most cases the rotary fermentor produces wines with higher EXTRACT.

ROTE *see* SCREW CAPS

Roter Raushcer *see* FEDERWEISSER

Roter Traminer *see* GEWÜRZTRAMINER

Rothenberg *see* GESENHEIM; NACKENHEIM; RAUENTHAL

rotling [ROHT-ling] A rose-colored wine made from a mixture of red and white grapes (not wines). *Rotling* is produced in limited quantities in Germany.

rotofermenter *see* ROTARY FERMENTOR

rotten eggs *see* SULFUR in the Glossary of Wine Tasting Terms, page 655

Rottland *see* RÜDESHEIM

rotundifolia *see* VITIS ROTUNDIFOLIA

rotwein [RAWT-vine] German for "red wine."

Rouchefort-sur-Loire *see* CÔTEAUX DU LAYON

rouge [*R*OOZH] French for "red."

Rougeon [*R*OOZH-uhn] French-American HYBRID, also called *Seibel 5898*, grown in New York's FINGER LAKES AVA as well as other parts of the Northeast and as far south as Virginia. It has a deep red color that's valued for its ability to add color to many blends. It's highly productive but its somewhat inconsistent yields are a drawback. Rougeon is appreciated for cold weather tolerance although it's prone to various mildews.

rough; roughness *see* Glossary of Wine Tasting Terms, page 655

round; rounded *see* Glossary of Wine Tasting Terms, page 655

Roussanne [roo-SAHN] A white-wine grape grown mainly in the northern portion of France's RHÔNE region. Roussanne can produce delicate, refined wines and is best known for its use in the white wines of CHÂTEAUNEUF-DU-PAPE, CROZES-HERMITAGE, HERMITAGE, and SAINT-JOSEPH. It's also one of the four white grapes allowed in the red wines of Châteauneuf-du-Pape. Since the 1950s, Roussanne has been steadily replaced by the more productive MARSANNE, which produces full-bodied (*see* BODY), somewhat FAT wines. Small amounts of Roussanne are also grown in Italy's TUSCANY region and are allowed in the white wines of the MONTECARLO DOC. There's also a pink variation known as *Roussanne du Var* that's used in many of the Rhône's lesser wines. This grape is also called *Bergeron* and *Rosana*.

Rousselet *see* GEWÜRZTRAMINER

Rousset-les-Vignes *see* CÔTES DU RHÔNE

Roussette [roo-SEHT] Another name for the ALTESSE grape that's cultivated in southeastern France, particularly in the SAVOIE and BUGEY districts where the wines are, respectively, entitled to the APPELLATIONS Roussette de Savoie and Rousette de Bugey. Roussette is unrelated to ROUSSANNE with which it's sometimes erroneously associated.

Roussette de Bugey VDQS *see* BUGEY VDQS

Roussette de Savoie AC *see* SAVOIE

Roussillon *see* CÔTES DU ROUSSILLON; GRENACHE; LANGUEDOC-ROUSSILLON

Roussillonen *see* CARIGNAN

Royalty Created from the varieties Trousseau and Alicante Ganzin, this HYBRID is a red grape that yields red juice (instead of white). It's used mainly to add color to BLENDS. Royalty was developed by the UNIVERSITY OF CALIFORNIA, DAVIS and released in 1958. It's grown primarily in California's CENTRAL VALLEY, although its acreage is declining owing to lack of popularity.

RS Abbreviation for RESIDUAL SUGAR.

rubbery *see* Glossary of Wine Tasting Terms, page 655

Rubesco *see* TORGIANO DOC

Rubienne Australian red-wine grape created by crossing CABERNET SAUVIGNON with Sumool, a Spanish variety. It was developed to produce high-quality wine and be productive in Australia's growing environments, particularly in hot irrigated regions. It compares favorably with and in some of the evaluations scored as well or better than Cabernet Sauvignon. Rubienne derives its name from rubient, which is a purplish color. *See also* CIENNA and TYRIAN.

Rubin Bulgarian grape variety created by the Wine and Vine Institute in Pleven in 1944 but not recognized as a VARIETY until 1961. It's a CROSS between NEBBIOLO and SYRAH. It's made into single VARIETAL wines (both TABLE and DESSERT) and is also a component in blended wines often combined with CABERNET SAUVIGNON.

rubino *see* MARSALA DOC

Rubired [ROO-bee-red] Introduced in 1958, this HYBRID was developed by the UNIVERSITY OF CALIFORNIA, DAVIS by crossing Alicante Ganzin and Tinta Cão. *Alicante Ganzin* is also a hybrid, whose parentage is traceable to ALICANTE BOUSHCHET; TINTO CÃO is a good-quality PORT variety. Rubired is an easy-to-grow, prolific red grape that produces red juice instead of white. Grown primarily in California's CENTRAL VALLEY, it's used to add color to port-style and JUG WINES.

Ruby Cabernet [ROO-bee ka-behr-NAY] This CROSS between CARIGNAN and CABERNET SAUVIGNON was developed in the 1940s by Dr. Harold Olmo at the UNIVERSITY OF CALIFORNIA, DAVIS. His goal was to combine the Carignan's ability to withstand hot weather and produce high YIELDS with the excellent quality of Cabernet Sauvignon. Disappointingly, Ruby Cabernet takes on Cabernet Sauvignon characteristics only in the very best of its wines. Most Ruby Cabernet grapes are grown in California's hot CENTRAL VALLEY, although the best results have been achieved in cooler climates and where yields have been kept down. Generally the wines from the Central Valley have few Cabernet Sauvignon characteristics and are used mainly in JUG WINES.

ruby port *see* PORT

Ruchottes-Chambertin AC [ryoo-SHAWT shah*m*-behr-TA*N*] A small, 8-acre GRAND CRU vineyard that adjoins the grand cru MAZIS-CHAMBERTIN in the village of GEVREY-CHAMBERTIN. It's located in the CÔTE DE NUITS district of France's BURGUNDY region. These PINOT NOIR-based wines are deeply colored, RICH, intense, TANNIC, and generally good candidates for long AGING. They're considered to be some of the best red wines in the world and, with production of only about 1,000 cases per year, very difficult to find. *See also* CHAMBERTIN.

Rüdesheim [*R*OO-duhs-hime] An important wine-producing village located in Germany's RHEINGAU region, southwest of the city of Wiesbaden and across the Rhine River from BINGEN (which is in the NAHE region). Rüdesheim is the last of a string of villages (including ERBACH, OESTRICH, WINKEL, and GEISENHEIM) that have some of the best vineyards in the Rheingau. Of the numerous good EINZELLAGEN (vineyard sites), those carrying the designation **"Berg"** as well as the site name are generally the best. Rüdesheimer Berg **Roseneck**, Rüdesheimer Berg **Rottland**, and Rüdesheimer Berg **Schlossberg** for example, are all situated on the prime steepest section called the Rüdesheimer Berg. Other quality vineyard sites are **Bischofsberg**, **Drachenstein**, **Klosterberg**, and **Rosengarten**. The wines of Rüdesheim are generally full-bodied (*see* BODY) and rich with RIPE, CONCENTRATED flavors. In years with exceptionally good weather, however, these wines can become a bit too BIG and ALCOHOLIC. This famous Rüdesheim shouldn't be confused with the small village of Rüdesheim in the Nahe region, the wines of which are not in the same class.

Rüdesheimer Rosengarten *see* NAHE

Rueda DO [roo-AY-dah] An important DO northwest of Madrid near Portugal's northeast corner, not far from the city of Valladolid. The winemaking history of this area goes back hundreds of years, at least to the eleventh century after the Moors were driven out. During the seventeenth and eighteenth centuries, Rueda was well known for its SHERRY-style FORTIFIED WINES. At the end of the nineteenth century, PHYLLOXERA devastated the winemaking industry, and it wasn't until the 1970s that the area was revitalized; it achieved DO status for white wines in 1980. Today, this area is best known for its high-quality white wines made from VERDEJO, although other varieties like Viaura (MACABEO), PALOMINO, and SAUVIGNON BLANC are used. Rueda's climate and altitude create an environment that enables the Verdejo grapes to develop favorably, producing AROMATIC, FRESH, yet full-bodied (*see* BODY) wines. Basic Rueda wines require a minimum of 25 percent Verdejo; **Rueda Superior** wines require a minimum of 60 percent (SAUVIGNON BLANC is also allowed in the Superiors). This DO also produces sherrylike wines—**Pálido**, which is like a fino (*see* SHERRY), and **Dorado**, which is like an amontillado (*see* SHERRY). **Rueda Espumoso**, a DO category for quality SPARKLING WINE, was recently added. Red wines were not allowed under DO rules until 2001. Until then, producers experimented with TEMPRANILLO as well as CABERNET SAUVIGNON and MERLOT, but the wines were categorized as VINOS DE MESA until the Rueda DO red wine category was approved.

Rufete [roo-FEH-tee] Red-wine grape grown mainly in Salamanca province in the CASTILE AND LEÓN region of Spain and across the border in northern Portugal. Rufete produces light, fruity wines, although some examples of heavier, more rustic versions can be found. It is often blended with TEMPRANILLO and the combination produces some interesting wines. In Portugal it's sometimes used in making PORT as well as red TABLE wine. Rufete is replacing *Tinta Pinheira* as the name used for this variety.

Rufina *see* CHIANTI DOCG

Les Rugiens *see* POMMARD

Rulander *see* PINOT GRIS

Rully AC [ryoo-YEE] One of the five villages in the CÔTE CHALONNAISE in France's BURGUNDY region that has APPELLATION status. It produces FRESH, CRISP white wines from CHARDONNAY and LIGHT, fruity reds from PINOT NOIR. Production is about equally divided between the red and white wines. About 25 percent of the 1,200 acres is allocated to the 25 premier cru vineyards that produce higher-quality wines. They are allowed to append their name to the label.

Rumania *see* ROMANIA

Ruppertsberg [*R*OOP-uh*r*ts-be*r*k] One of several adjoining towns, including DEIDESHEIM, Forst, and WACHENHEIM, that produce some of the best wines of Germany's PFALZ region. These appealing wines are made from RIESLING, SCHEUREBE, and SYLVANER. The top wines come from the EINZELLAGEN of **Gaisböhl**, **Hoheburg**, **Nussbien**, **Reiterpfad**, and **Spiess**.

rural method Known in France as *méthode rurale, méthode artisnale, méthode ancestrale,* or *méthode gaillacois,* the rural method is an old technique for making SPARKLING WINE. It's generally been replaced by MÉTHODE CHAMPENOISE for higher-quality wines or by the CHARMAT PROCESS for less-expensive wines. To create effervescence using the rural method, FERMENTATION is slowed or stopped, sometimes by chilling the MUST to a very cold temperature. The must is then bottled, and the fermentation process is restarted, often by warming the bottles. As with the *méthode champenoise,* the by-product of this fermentation is carbon dioxide, which creates bubbles in the bottled wine. Sparkling wines produced by the rural method are often cloudy unless they undergo a filtering process. Only a few wines are still made this way, including some from the GAILLAC AC and Limoux. The CLAIRETTE DE DIE TRADITION AC uses a variation of the rural method called *méthode dioise,* which is unique to this APPELLATION. This technique removes sediment by RACKING and FILTERING the wines under pressure, which eliminates the sediment while retaining as much effervescence as possible. The wines are then rebottled.

Rusa *see* GEWÜRZTRAMINER

Russia There are three main wine-producing regions in Russia—the area along the Caspian Sea just north of Azerbaijan, which is known for its DESSERT WINES; the area south of the city of Krasnodar, along the Black Sea and somewhat inland; and the area surrounding the city of Rostov, north of the Black Sea on the Sea of Azov. The two latter regions make red, white, and SPARKLING WINES. Although most Russian wines are made from indigenous grape varieties like RKATSITELI, Black Tsimlyansky, Pletchistik, and Saperavi, some western European grapes are now being cultivated.

Russian River Valley; Russian River Valley AVA The Russian River basin starts in MENDOCINO COUNTY, runs south into SONOMA COUNTY, and then west as the river turns toward the Pacific Ocean just north of Forestville, California. Along the way it encompasses the Ukiah and Alexander Valleys. The area comprising the **Russian River AVA** starts around Healdsburg (in Sonoma County) and goes in a southerly direction toward Sebastopol. The eastern section includes the CHALK HILL AVA, which is located just east of the town of Windsor; the western section extends to the coastal hills and includes the GREEN VALLEY-SONOMA AVA. The climate is quite cool, mostly Region I (*see* CLIMATE REGIONS OF CALIFORNIA), and does well with CHARDONNAY, GEWÜRZTRAMINER, PINOT NOIR, and SAUVIGNON BLANC grapes. Occasionally, good ZINFANDEL grapes are produced as well. Cabernet Sauvignon doesn't usually peform too well here, although in the warmer growing areas it can produce good wines. The Russian River AVA has more than fifty wineries.

rustic *see* Glossary of Wine Tasting Terms, page 655

Rutherford AVA VITICULTURAL AREA located in the central part of the NAPA VALLEY. Its southeastern boundary is adjacent to that of the OAKVILLE AVA (just south of CAKEBREAD CELLARS), and its northwestern boundary parallels Zinfandel Lane. The Rutherford AVA was established in 1993 and extends from the foothills of the western hills across the valley floor to just the other side of the Silverado Trail, covering just under 6,700 acres. The Rutherford area produces some of the best CABERNET SAUVIGNON wines in the world. The vineyards consist of almost 60 percent of that variety followed by MERLOT, CABERNET FRANC, CHARDONNAY, and SAUVIGNON BLANC.

Rutherford Bench A California growing area with a reputation for producing some of the best CABERNET SAUVIGNON grapes in the world. At this writing, the Rutherford Bench is not an official AMERICAN VITICULTURAL AREA (AVA), and the area it covers isn't fully defined. However, the term generally refers to about a 6-mile stretch of land in the NAPA VALLEY that runs along the west side of Highway 29 from just north of Yountville to north of Rutherford and includes a small section east of the freeway between Oakville and Rutherford. Some argue, however, that the term Rutherford Bench should also include the land between Highway 29 and the Napa River, a mile or so to the east. Whatever the final resolution (if there is one) for a designated Rutherford Bench AVA, the bottom line is that this area contains deep, alluvial soils that drain well and are capable of producing remarkable Cabernet Sauvignon grapes (some CHARDONNAY grapes also grow here).

Rutherglen An Australian wine region located in the North East Victoria Zone of VICTORIA. It's situated about 170 miles northeast of Melbourne around the town of Rutherglen. The 1850s gold boom brought settlers into this area and vines followed shortly thereafter in 1851. As the gold played out, grapes took on a more important role and the Rutherglen region became Victoria's most significant wine region during the latter 1800s. PHYLLOXERA and finances pulled the industry down toward the end of the nineteenth century, but it continued to endure into the twentieth century. This area is known for its BIG, MEATY red wines made from Shiraz (SYRAH) and CABERNET SAUVIGNON. But it's also known for its FORTIFIED WINES, particularly *Liqueur Tokay* made from MUSCADELLE and *Liqueur Muscat* (Brown Muscat) made from Muscat Blanc á Petits Grains (*see* MUSCAT). CHARDONNAY and RIESLING grapes are also grown, but the wines are not as consistently well received as the others. **Glenrowan**, a neighboring region to the southwest that's pending approval, has a similar profile.

Ruwer [*R*OO-vay*r*] Located in Germany's MOSEL-SAAR-RUWER region, Ruwer is a small tributary of the Mosel River and host to a number of fine vineyards in the surrounding valley. Although the wines from this area aren't considered quite as superb as those from the SAAR River area, they can rank as some of Germany's best. The main wine-producing villages are EITELSBACH, KASEL, and Waldrach. The GROSSLAGE **Kaseler Römerlay** covers this area.

Saale-Unstrut [ZAHL oon-shtruht] With about 1,500 acres of vineyards, this is the third smallest of Germany's thirteen ANBAUGEBIETE (quality-wine regions). Its vineyards are situated around the Saale and Unstrut Rivers in eastern Germany. Naumburg and Weissenfels are the main towns in the region. Because Saale-Unstrut was part of the former East Germany, wine producers are still in the process of working their way out from under the problems left by the former communist regime. The wines are similar to those of FRANKEN, but the true quality potential won't be known for several more years until vineyards and winemaking facilities are upgraded. The main variety planted in this region is MÜLLER-THURGAU, with 37 percent of the total acreage, followed by SYLVANER, with about 28 percent. Other varieties include BACCHUS, Gutedel (CHASSELAS), PORTUGIESER, and Spätburgunder (PINOT NOIR).

Saar [ZAHR; SAHR] Starting high in the Vosges Mountains in France, this tributary of the Mosel River joins the Mosel at the German town of Konz, southwest of the city of Trier. The vineyards, which begin around the tiny German village of Serrig in the south, are part of the Bereich SAAR-RUWER and Germany's MOSEL-SAAR-RUWER region. This is a cold growing region, and in good growing years, the wines of the Saar area can be magnificent—some of Germany's best. In the cooler years when grapes don't fully ripen, much of the crop is used in SEKT. The main villages are Ayl, Seerig, Ockfen, and WILTINGEN, which has SCHARZHOFBERG, the best vineyard in the area. The GROSSLAGE **Wiltinger Scharzberg** covers the vineyards in this area.

Saar-Ruwer, Bereich [ZAHR (SAHR) ROO-vayr] One of four BEREICHE (subregions) in Germany's MOSEL-SAAR-RUWER region. It covers all the vineyards surrounding the two tributaries of the MOSEL—the RUWER and SAAR Rivers. The Bereich has two GROSSLAGEN—Wiltinger Scharzberg for the Saar area and Kaseler Römerlay for the Ruwer area.

Sablet *see* CÔTES DU RHÔNE

Sachsen [ZAHKH-zuhn] The smallest of Germany's thirteen ANBAUGEBIETE (quality-wine regions), with about 1,000 acres of vineyards. Its vineyards are situated around the Elbe River area in eastern Germany; Dresden is the region's main city. The primary variety planted in this region is MÜLLER-THURGAU, which has 38 percent of the total acreage. Traminer (GEWÜRZTRAMINER) and Weissburgunder (PINOT BLANC) follow, each with about 15 percent of the acreage. Other varieties include Gutedel (CHASSELAS), RIESLING, and PORTUGIESER. Like SAALE-UNSTRUT, the Sachsen region was part of the former East Germany, which means its area producers are still in the process of working out from under the problems left by the former communist regime. The true potential quality of this region's wines won't be known for several more years as vineyards and winemaking facilities are upgraded.

sack The name used in the sixteenth century during the reign of Elizabeth I for SHERRY or other FORTIFIED WINES from MÁLAGA or the Canary Islands. Such wines were known as Málaga Sack and Canary Sack. The word comes from the Spanish *sacar,* meaning "to take out" or "to export."

Sackträger *see* OPPENHEIM

Sacramento Valley *see* CENTRAL VALLEY

Saddle Rock Malibu AVA Small APPELLATION (2,100 acres) created in August 2006 in Los Angeles County in southern California. Malibu Family Wines, located on the 1,000-acre Saddlerock Ranch in the Santa Monica Mountains, is the only winery in the AVA. There are about 65 acres of vineyards planted to CABERNET SAUVIGNON, MERLOT, SAUVIGNON BLANC, SYRAH, MALBEC, GRENACHE, MOUVÈDRE, and VIOGNIER.

Sagrantino [sah-grahn-TEE-noh] An Italian red-grape variety grown in central Italy's UMBRIA region. It produces dark, inky wines with plenty of tannins and rich, dark red fruit flavors. Sagrantino has gained famed for the wines produced in and around the village of Montefalco. It's blended with other red varities to produced the MONTEFALCO DOC but reaches its full potential in the MONTEFALCO SAGRANTINO DOC wines where it's produced in both DRY and PASSITO versions.

Sagrantino di Montefalco DOCG *see* MONTEFALCO DOC

saignée [say-NAY] From the French *saigner* ("bleed"), *saignée* refers in the wine world to a process used to make ROSÉ wines by which a blend of dark-skinned red grapes are crushed and left to stand in a stainless-steel tank or vat for several hours. A certain amount of juice is then "bled" out of the tank or vat and used for making rosé. The remaining juice stays with the skins until ready to be utilized for red wine. This juice (and the wine it produces) becomes more concentrated in both flavor and color because the ratio of skins to juice is higher.

Saint-Amour AC [sa*n* tah-MOOR] The northernmost of the ten CRUS in France's BEAUJOLAIS region. Saint-Amour sits far enough north that it's the only Beaujolais cru extending into the MÂCONNAIS area. White wines from this area are entitled to the SAINT-VÉRAN AC, a Mâconnais APPELLATION. Saint-Amour is one of the smaller Beaujolais crus, making its wines more difficult to find. The wines, made from GAMAY grapes, are LIGHT, delicate, and fruity (strawberries, bananas, and peaches).

Saint-Aubin AC [sa*n* toh-BA*N*] APPELLATION that consists of the vineyards surrounding the villages of Gamay (the village that gave its name to the grape variety) and Saint-Aubin. It's located in the CÔTE DE BEAUNE section of France's BURGUNDY region. The Saint-Aubin AC sits between CHASSAGNE-MONTRACHET AC and PULIGNY-MONTRACHET AC, wedged into a small valley higher up the hill. Although there are a fair amount of GAMAY grapes grown in this geographic area, only PINOT NOIR can go into this appellation's red wines. Compared to many of the neighboring villages, Saint-Aubin AC reds are of a lighter, more elegant style. The white wines, which make up over half of the production, are considered better than the reds. There are twenty-nine PREMIER CRU vineyards that are allowed to append their names to the label. The better premier cru vineyards include **Les Murgers des Dents de Chien** and **En Remilly**. The best of these CHARDONNAY wines are often compared to good-quality Chassagne-Montrachet or MEURSAULT AC wines. The Saint-Aubin AC wines are regarded as relatively good values.

Saint-Aubin-de-Luigné *see* CÔTEAUX DU LAYON

Saint-Bris *see* SAUVIGNON DE SAINT BRIS VDQS

Saint-Chinian AC [sa*n* shee-NYAH*N*] The village of Saint-Chinian is located in the hills above Beziers, southwest of FAUGÈRES AC in France's LANGUEDOC-ROUSSILLON region. Like the Faugères AC, the Saint-Chinian AC makes red wines of a much higher quality than most of the rest of this huge region. The grapes used are CARIGNAN, CINSAUT, GRENACHE, and, recently, increasing amounts of MOURVÈDRE and SYRAH. The wines, which are full-bodied (*see* BODY) and SPICY, are generally slightly lighter than those from the Faugères AC.

St. Christol *see* GRÉS DE MONTPELLIER

St. Drézery *see* GRÉS DE MONTPELLIER

Sainte-Croix-du-Mont AC [sah*n*t krwah dew MAW*N*] A small APPELLATION located in the area around the picturesque little town of Sainte-Croix-du-Mont in the southern end of the PREMIÈRES CÔTES DE BORDEAUX in France's BORDEAUX region. It sits on the Garonne River across from SAUTERNES and BARSAC. The appellation is only for white wines made from SÉMILLON, SAUVIGNON BLANC, and MUSCADELLE, which must be semisweet or sweet. Although some of the grapes in the

Sainte-Croix-du-Mont AC are infected by BOTRYTIS CINEREA, the resulting wines aren't generally as intense or luscious (nor are the prices as high) as those from Sauternes and Barsac.

Saint-Émilion [sah*n* tay-mee-LYAW*N*] The village of Saint-Émilion is exceedingly picturesque with its medieval walls and buildings, undulating hills, and the vineyards that grow right up to the ancient walls. Saint-Émilion is northeast of the city of Bordeaux and sits on the east side of the Dordogne River next to the smaller, but well-known, POMEROL AC. Grapes have been cultivated here since at least the second century. Saint-Émilion is the second most important growing area in BORDEAUX after the MÉDOC, and because it's not broken up into smaller APPELLATIONS like the Médoc (such as MARGAUX AC, PAUILLAC AC, SAINT-ESTÈPHE AC, and SAINT-JULIEN AC), more fine wine is sold under the Saint-Émilion appellation than any other. Unlike the Médoc where CABERNET SAUVIGNON reigns, MERLOT is the dominant grape in Saint-Émilion because of the clay soil. CABERNET FRANC is the next most popular grape, followed by Cabernet Sauvignon and some MALBEC. Because of the prevalent use of Merlot, the Saint-Émilion wines are generally SOFTER and more drinkable at an earlier age than those from the Médoc. However, wines from good VINTAGES of top CHÂTEAUX like Ausone and Cheval Blanc have considerable AGING ability. Saint-Émilion was passed over in the Classification of 1855 (*see* Official Wine Classifications of Bordeaux, page 678), which established the CRU CLASSÉ châteaux of the Médoc, and it wasn't until 1955 that an official classification for Saint-Émilion estates was developed. Unlike the Médoc, Saint-Émilion's classification system was set up so that it could be revised every 10 years, at which time châteaux could be elevated or downgraded. Another review was completed in 1996. It listed thirteen châteaux as PREMIERS GRANDS CRUS CLASSÉS (the highest level). Two of the thirteen, Château Ausone and Château Cheval Blanc, were set above all the rest into Category A; they're both generally considered comparable in quality to the Médoc FIRST GROWTHS. The other eleven châteaux, which are in Category B, are Angélus, Beau-Séjour Bécot, Beauséjour-Duffau-Lagarrosse, Belair, Canon, Clos Fourtet, Figeac, La Gaffelière, Magdelaine, Pavie, and Trottevieille. Fifty-five estates are classified at the next level, GRANDS CRUS CLASSÉS, and there is a third level called simply GRANDS CRUS. The number in this last category (usually 150 to 200) varies because châteaux must apply each year and qualify by submitting their wines for tastings. The aforementioned three levels of châteaux receive the **Saint-Émilion Grand Cru AC**. Other wines in the area may qualify for the simpler **Saint-Émilion AC**, while those below that may receive the designation BORDEAUX SUPÉRIEUR AC or BOR-DEAUX AC. From 2006 through 2009 there was another classification review and a number of ensuing court skirmishes. The result of all the legal haggling was a law passed in 2009 that promoted eight châteaux; it allows Châteaus Pavie-Macquin and Troplong-Mondot to use Premier Grand Cru Classé on their labels and six other châteaux to put Grand Cru Classé on theirs (at least through 2011). In the 1990s the area attracted additional attention as very small wineries, not part of the traditional structure and sometimes called *microchâteau* or *garagistes* (*see* GARAGE WINES), began producing very high quality wines. Best-known of this group are Valandraud and La Mondotte. Saint-Émilion is surrounded by six "satellite" COMMUNES, which once sold their wines as Saint-Émilion AC but now are part of separate appellations that may append the name Saint-Émilion to their own (as in PUISSEGUIN-SAINT-ÉMILION AC). The communes are LUSSAC, MONTAGNE, Parsac, Puisseguin, Sables, and SAINT-GEORGES, although separate appellations for Parsac and Sables no longer exist. *See also* TREBBIANO.

Saint-Estèphe AC [sa*n* teh-STEHF] The northernmost of the communal APPELLATIONS in the HAUT-MÉDOC area of France's BORDEAUX region. Of the wines from the well-known COMMUNES in the Haut-Médoc, those from Saint-Estèphe AC are usually ranked fourth in quality after those of MARGAUX, PAUILLAC, and SAINT-JULIEN. This ranking is because Saint-Estèphe contains fewer (only five) GRAND CRU CLASSÉ châteaux and more CRUS BOURGEOIS. The grand cru classé CHÂTEAUX are Calon-Ségur, Cos d'Estournel, Cos Labory, Lafon-Rochet, and Montrose. Saint-Estèphe AC wines are made from CABERNET SAUVIGNON, MERLOT, CABERNET FRANC, and PETIT VERDOT. They're often described as being full-bodied (*see* BODY), the most TANNIC, and requiring the longest period to mature. Many producers are now using more Merlot to produce suppler (*see* SUPPLE), SOFTER wines.

Ste. Genevieve *see* ESCONDIDO VALLEY AVA

Sainte-Victoire *see* CÔTES DE PROVENCE

Les Saint-Georges *see* NUITS-SAINT-GEORGES

St. George *see* AGHIORGHITIKO

St. Georges d'Orques *see* GRÉS DE MONTPELLIER

Saint-Georges-Saint-Émilion AC [sa*n* ZHOR*R*ZH ay-mee-LYAW*N*] One of the SAINT-ÉMILION AC satellite APPELLATIONS that's allowed to append the name Saint-Émilion to its own. Some feel that the wines from this AC are the best of those from the appellations surrounding Saint-Émilion. Like Saint-Émilion itself, the dominant grape here is MERLOT. Since 1972, wines from this appellation have been allowed to be labeled with the MONTAGNE-SAINT ÉMILION AC—the larger, neighboring appellation. Some producers still prefer to use the Saint-Georges-Saint-Émilion AC, however.

Saint Gervais *see* CÔTES DU RHÔNE

Saint Helena AVA A California VITICULTURAL AREA established in 1995 in the northern part of the NAPA VALLEY AVA in and around the town of St. Helena. Its southeastern boundary aligns with the RUTHERFORD AVA along Zinfandel Lane, and its northern boundary is set about halfway between the towns of Calistoga and St. Helena at Bale Lane running up into the foothills on each side. SPRING MOUNTAIN AVA runs along the northern two thirds of the Saint Helena AVA's western flank. There are just over 9,000 acres in this area, a substantial portion of which are planted with vineyards—over 70 percent to BORDEAUX VARITIES. The Napa Valley climate becomes warmer as one moves northwest from the southeastern portion (nearest to San Pablo Bay). Therefore the Saint Helena AVA is warmer than the OAKVILLE KNOLL DISTRICT and the YOUNTVILLE AVAS. The Saint Helena area has a rich wine history—Charles Krug established the first winery in 1861, and the Beringer brothers started their winery in 1876. Today there are over thirty wineries in this APPELLATION.

Saint-Joseph AC [sa*n* zhoh-ZEHF] Located south of the CHÂTEAU-GRILLET AC in the northern portion of France's RHÔNE Valley, this APPELLATION was established in 1956. It ecompasses six villages clustered around the village of Mauves. In 1969, the Saint-Joseph AC was expanded to include another twenty small COMMUNES farther south, creating an appellation that extends for over 35 miles along the west bank of the Rhône River, stopping in the south at the CORNAS AC. The Saint-Joseph AC produces both red and white wines. White wines are made from MARSANNE and ROUSSANNE grapes; reds use mainly SYRAH, sometimes blended with a small amount of the two white grapes. The red wines are similar to but lighter than those from neighboring appellations of HERMITAGE and Cornas—deep-colored, full-flavored, full-bodied (*see* BODY), and intense. White wines are usually lighter versions of the powerful, long-aging whites from Hermitage AC.

St. Julian Wine Company *see* MICHIGAN

Saint-Julien AC [sa*n* zhoo-LYA*N*] Many people think that the Saint-Julien AC produces the most consistently high-quality wines of any APPELLATION in France's BORDEAUX region. It's the smallest of four main COMMUNES in the MÉDOC and is located just south of PAUILLAC. It contains eleven CRU CLASSÉ châteaux (which use about 75 percent of the available vineyard land) and a number of very good CRU BOURGEOIS châteaux. This leaves very little land for low-quality wine producers. Heading the list of cru classé CHÂTEAUX are Ducru-Beaucaillou, Gruaud-Larose, and Léoville-Las Cases—DEUXIÈMES CRUS (second growths). They're followed by other excellent châteaux including Lagrange, Léoville-Barton, Léoville-Poyferré, and Talbot. CABERNET SAUVIGNON is the dominant grape, which is blended with CABERNET FRANC, MERLOT, and, occasionally, small amounts of PETIT VERDOT.

Saint-Lambert-du-Lattay *see* COTEAUX DU LAYON

Saint Maurice-sur-Eygues *see* CÔTES DU RHÔNE

Saint-Mont *see* CÔTES DE SAINT-MONT VDQS

Saint-Nicolas-de-Bourgueil AC [sa*n* nee-koh-lah duh boor-GUH-yuh] A village located in the TOURAINE region of France's LOIRE Valley. Like its neighbors the CHINON AC and the BOURGUEIL AC, the Saint-Nicolas-de-Bourgueil AC is one of the few village APPELLATIONS in the area focused on red wines. Its dry climate allows it to grow CABERNET FRANC and limited quantities of CABERNET SAUVIGNON. Generally, the wines are light and fruity, with raspberry overtones. Better vintages can be AGED for 8 to 10 years.

Saint-Pantaléon-les-Vignes *see* CÔTES DU RHÔNE

Saint-Péray AC [sa*n* pay-*R*EH] The village that lies just below the CORNAS AC and that is the farthest south of the wine-producing villages in the northern RHÔNE. There are two APPELLATIONS here—**Saint-Péray AC** for white STILL WINES and **Saint-Péray Mousseux AC** for SPARKLING WINES. In both types of wine, MARSANNE is the dominant grape, usually blended with some ROUSSANNE. The sparkling wines make up about 75 to 80 percent of the production.

Saint-Romain AC [sa*n* raw-MA*N*] Tiny APPELLATION that surrounds the village of Saint-Romain, which is located in the CÔTE DE BEAUNE area of France's BURGUNDY region. It consists of only 350 acres and is wedged in a valley up behind the better-known villages of MEURSAULT and AUXEY-DURESSES. Saint-Romain AC produces both red wines from PINOT NOIR and white wines from CHARDONNAY.

Saint-Saturnin-de-Lucian *see* TERRASSES DU LARZAC AC

Saint-Véran AC [san vay-RAHN] This APPELLATION, which surrounds the village of Saint-Vérand (the *d* is correct) and six other villages, is located in the MÂCONNAIS subregion in BURGUNDY. The Saint-Véran AC is located next to the well-known POUILLY-FUISSÉ AC and produces white CHARDONNAY wines of a similar style. Although it only received appellation status in 1971, the wines have long been thought to be the equal of those from Pouilly-Fuissé, and because they're not as well known, they're available at much lower prices.

sake [SAH-kee; SAH-kay] Although sake is often called Japanese rice wine, it's difficult to categorize as wine because it's not made from fruit—in fact, some consider it a beer because it's made from grain. The TAX AND TRADE BUREAU (previously BATF), however, settles any dispute by categorizing sake in Class 6—wine from other agricultural products. Sake is made in several steps, during which the starch of specially selected, steamed rice is converted to sugar and then to ALCOHOL and CARBON DIOXIDE through FERMENTATION. Once fermentation is complete, the liquid is drawn off, filtered, heated, and placed in casks for maturing. None of the carbon dioxide is retained so there's no effervescence. Sake's alcohol ranges from 12 to 16 percent—high for beer, low for most grain-based spirits, but in the range for most wines. Sake, which is colorless (or very pale yellow) and slightly sweet, is traditionally served warm in small porcelain cups called *sakazuki*. Another popular Japanese rice wine is *Mirin*.

Sakonnet Vineyards *see* RHODE ISLAND

Salado Creek AVA APPELLATION created in August 2004 near the town of Patterson in western Stanislaus County, about 80 miles southeast of San Francisco and 20 miles southwest of Modesto. The area encompasses 2,940 acres with less than 50 planted with grapes (CABERNET SAUVIGNON, SAUVIGNON BLANC, SYRAH, and VIOGNIER). KitFox Vineyard is currently the only winery based in the area.

Salice Salento DOC [SAH-lih-chay sah-LEHN-toh] A DOC zone located around the COMMUNE of Salice Salento on the Salentine peninsula in southeastern Italy (the "heel of the boot"). It's in the APULIA region and produces some of the regions better wines. The Negroamaro grape makes up at least 80 percent of both the ROSSO and ROSATO wines. CHARDONNAY makes up at least 70 percent of the BIANCO wines. VARIETAL wines from Pinot Bianco (PINOT BLANC) and ALEATICO also are made—both require 85 percent minimums of these varieties.

Salmanazar *see* Wine Bottles, page 609

Salon *see* CHAMPAGNE

Salta *see* ARGENTINA

Salvagnin *see* VAUD

Sampigny-lès-Maranges *see* MARANGES AC

Samsó *see* CARIGNAN

San Antonio Valley AVA California VITICULTURAL AREA established in July 2006 that encompasses 150,400 acres in the southern portion of the MONTEREY AVA, which is part of the even larger CENTRAL COAST AVA. Grape growing dates back to the 1770s in the region. The San Antonio Valley is shaped like a bowl that's surrounded by the Santa Lucia range. It has a warm, dry environment similar to the PASO ROBLES AVA. About 800 acres are planted to over 20 different grape varieties and, because of the climate, a majority are red grapes such as CABERNET SAUVIGNON, CABERNET FRANC, SYRAH, and ZINFANDEL. There are currently ten wineries in the area.

San Benito County; San Benito AVA [san beh-NEE-toh] California's San Benito County lies just east of MONTEREY COUNTY and is known for the vineyards planted by Almaden Vineyards during the 1970s. The county has five AVAs but less than 2,000 acres of vines. Most of the potential vineyard area is covered by the 45,000-acre **San Benito AVA**, which encompasses two smaller AVAs—CIENEGA VALLEY and **Paicines**. The other two AVAs are the 2,300-acre **Lime Kiln Valley AVA** and the 7,500-acre **Mount Harlan AVA**. Because it's positioned in one of the openings that draws air off the Pacific through the mountain ranges into the CENTRAL VALLEY, some areas of San Benito County are fairly cool and are classified as a Region II (*see* CLIMATE REGIONS OF CALIFORNIA). Mount Harlan is the highest and therefore the coolest; it hosts CALERA WINE COMPANY, the best-known winery in the area.

San Bernabe AVA California APPELLATION established in August 2004. It's just south of King City, which is about 145 miles south of San Francisco. It encompasses 24,796 acres and resides within the larger MONTEREY AVA and CENTRAL COAST AVA. The AVA is dominated by the huge San Bernabe Vineyard owned by the Indelicato family. Their estate is over 13,000 acres with more than 5,500 acres planted with over 22 different grape varieties. It's considered the world's largest single vineyard. The nearby SAN LUCAS AVA had 1,281 acres taken from it and assigned to the San Bernabe AVA so the giant vineyard would not be broken up and end up in two different appellations.

Sancerre AC [sah*n*-SEH*R*] The Sancerre AC surrounds the village of Sancerre and thirteen others in the upper portion of France's LOIRE Valley. It's located 120 miles south and slightly west of Paris, where Sancerre white wines first gained a huge following before becoming international favorites. SAUVIGNON BLANC is the grape used for the white wines, which are generally CRISP and high in ACIDITY with herb and gooseberry characteristics—very similar to those from the neighboring POUILLY-FUMÉ AC. The best white Sancerre AC wines come from the better producers in the villages of Bué, Chavigno, Ménétréol, and Verdigny and not from the village of Sancerre itself. Small amounts of red and ROSÉ wines are made from PINOT NOIR grapes, but most of these are rather LIGHT and not nearly as highly regarded as the white wines.

San Francisco Bay AVA Created in 1999, this large AVA encompasses approximately 1,566,000 acres in seven California counties— San Francisco, San Mateo, Santa Clara, Alameda, Contra Costa, Santa Cruz, and San Benito. All these counties except Santa Cruz and San Benito actually border on the bay, but portions of these two counties were included because of their long association with the San Francisco Bay area. This AVA is included in the larger CENTRAL COAST AVA, which was expanded to include areas not already encompassed by its boundaries. There are nearly 6,000 planted acres, most of which are in the smaller LIVERMORE VALLEY AVA that is now included in the San Francisco Bay AVA boundaries.

Sangiovese [san-joh-VAY-zeh; san-jaw-VAY-zeh] Etymologists believe this red grape's name is derived from *sanguis Jovis* meaning "the blood of Jove (Jupiter)." Its beginnings are thought to predate Roman times. Sangiovese is one of the top two red grapes (the other being NEBBIOLO) in Italy, where it's extensively planted—particularly in the central and southern regions. Sangiovese is Italy's most widely planted variety; it's planted in over 10 percent of all vineyards. It's believed to have originated in TUSCANY, where it dominates today. Sangiovese wines vary immensely depending on where the grapes are grown, how they're grown (the YIELD allowed), and which of the many subvarieties they're made from. Generally, Sangiovese wines have high ACIDITY, moderate to high TANNINS, and medium ALCOHOL levels. The flavors have a hint of EARTHINESS and are usually not boldly FRUITY. Sangiovese wines are not deeply colored and often have a slightly orange tint around the edges. Most are not long-lived and will last for less than 10 years. Of the numerous strains of this grape, *Sangiovese Grosso* and *Sangiovese Piccolo* have taken the lead. Compared to Sangiovese Piccolo's smaller grape clusters, Sangiovese Grosso has larger, more loosely bunched grapes. It's also more widely cultivated and yields a larger crop. One strain of Sangiovese Grosso is *Brunello* ("little dark one"), so named for the brown hue of its skin. It's the grape responsible for the potent and long-lived BRUNELLO DI MONTAL-CINO wines, which are made totally from this variety. *Prugnolo* is MON-TEPULCIANO'S local name for the Sangiovese Grosso grape, which produces the VINO NOBILE DI MONTEPULCIANO wines. Though Sangiovese is the dominant grape in Italy's well-known CHIANTI wines, it must offi-cially (for DOC qualification) be BLENDED with other varieties, including a percentage of white grapes. Fortunately, the maximum allowable Sangiovese (also known as *Sangioveto* in Chianti) went from 80 to 90 percent in 1984 and is now 100 percent, which allows Chianti wines to have a more robust character. Some producers, particularly in Tuscany, are now making non-DOC wines either using only Sangiovese grapes or blending them with small amounts of CABERNET SAUVIGNON, although more and more DOC regulations are allowing Cabernet Sauvignon and CABERNET FRANC in the BLEND—Chianti now allows up to 15 percent. The CARMIGNANO DOCG officially allows 20 percent Cabernet Sauvignon to be blended with their elegant Sangiovese-based wines. Cabernet is a particularly complimentary partner that lends BOUQUET, STRUCTURE, and longevity. Outside of Italy, Sangiovese is almost a stranger to the vineyard, although this has been changing during the 1990s. California has small amounts of Sangiovese planted—the best-known producer is Napa Valley's Atlas Peak Vineyards, which drew attention when it released its 1989 Sangiovese. It's showing up in the NAPA VALLEY, SONOMA COUNTY, and in some CENTRAL COAST locations. In South America, ARGENTINA is showing some interest in this variety. Sangiovese is known by several different names including *Nielluccio, Sanvicetro,* and *San Gioveto,* as well as many beginning with "Sangiovese," such as *Sangiovese di Romagna* and *Sangiovese Dolce.*

Sangioveto; San Gioveto *see* SANGIOVESE

sangria [san-GREE-uh] The blood-red color of this beverage inspired its name, which is Spanish for "bleeding." Sangria is made with red wine, fruit juices, soda water, fruit, and sometimes liqueurs, and BRANDY or COGNAC. Sangria *blanco* (white sangria) is made with white wine. Both are served cold over ice.

Sangue di Giuda *see* OLTREPO PAVESE DOC

San Joaquin Valley *see* CENTRAL VALLEY

San Juan *see* ARGENTINA

Sanlúcar de Barramdea *see* SHERRY; JEREZ-XÉRÈS-SHERRY Y MAN-ZANILLA DE SANLÚCAR DE BARRAMEDA DO

San Lucas AVA VITICULTURAL AREA established in 1987 at the southern end of the Salinas Valley between King City and San Ardo around the town of San Lucas in MONTEREY COUNTY. Daytime temperatures can get quite warm (110° F), while nights are cool. Of the approximately 34,000 acres in this AVA some 8,000 are planted in vineyards. Most of the region comprises vine farms (like the 1,850-acre Lockwood Vineyards) that sell grapes to out-of-the-area wineries. Lockwood built a winery and began making its own well-regarded wines in the early 1990s. The most popular varieties planted in the San Lucas AVA are CHARDONNAY, CABERNET SAUVIGNON, MERLOT, and SAUVIGNON BLANC.

San Luis Obispo County [san LOO-ihs uh-BIHS-poh] Located just south of MONTEREY COUNTY, this area is part of California's CENTRAL COAST AVA. San Luis Obispo County has over twenty-five wineries centered in the three main growing areas—PASO ROBLES AVA, EDNA VALLEY AVA, and ARROYO GRANDE AVA. The YORK MOUNTAIN AVA is also located in the county. The most popular varieties grown in this county are CHARDONNAY, CABERNET SAUVIGNON, ZINFANDEL, MERLOT, SAUVIGNON BLANC, and CHENIN BLANC.

San Pasqual Valley AVA Small 9,000-acre California AVA located north of San Diego and southeast of Escondido in the San Pasqual Valley. It's situated 10 to 15 miles inland from the Pacific Ocean, from which it receives maritime breezes that moderate the temperatures (although it sustains occasional winter freezes). San Pasqual Valley AVA is part of the larger SOUTH COAST AVA. It was approved in 1981 and has only one winery in the area, Orfila Vineyards.

San Rafael *see* ARGENTINA

San Severo *see* APULIA DOC

Santa Barbara County California area just south of SAN LUIS OBISPO COUNTY and north of Ventura County. This county's vineyard land has grown enormously during the last two decades. There are now over twenty-five wineries, located in the two major growing areas—SANTA MARIA VALLEY AVA and SANTA YNEZ VALLEY AVA, both of which are north of Santa Barbara. The Santa Maria Valley AVA is the farthest north and actually starts in San Luis Obispo County. The dominant variety is CHARDONNAY, which takes up over 50 percent of the planted vineyard land. It's followed by CABERNET SAUVIGNON, PINOT NOIR, RIESLING, SAUVIGNON BLANC, and CHENIN BLANC.

Santa Clara County; Santa Clara Valley AVA County located at the south end of the San Francisco Bay that includes the cities of San Jose, Sunnyvale, and Santa Clara. The population expansion has pushed out most of the vineyard area, and the majority of what's left is in the **Santa Clara Valley AVA**. This AVA encompasses over 330,000 acres in the southern end of Alameda County around Pleasanton plus the vineyard areas in the Santa Clara Valley—those around Gilroy, Hecker Pass, and Morgan Hill. The western boundary runs along the SANTA CRUZ MOUNTAINS AVA. The dominant variety in the Santa Clara area is CHARDONNAY followed by CABERNET SAUVIGNON, MERLOT, and ZINFANDEL. There are over twenty-five wineries in Santa Clara County, but most get their grapes from other areas.

Santa Cruz Mountains AVA A region in California's Santa Cruz mountains, starting in northern San Mateo County and extending south to about the MONTEREY COUNTY line. To the east, the AVA extends down to the lower levels of the foothills to the 800-foot contour line; to the west, some portions reach almost to the Pacific Ocean stopping at the 400-foot level. A majority of this area is cool and therefore classified as a Region I (*see* CLIMATE REGIONS OF CALIFORNIA). Portions on the inland valley side are warmer and classified as Region II areas. The primary grapes grown in this VITICULTURAL AREA are CHARDONNAY, CABERNET SAUVIGNON, and PINOT NOIR.

Santa Lucia Highlands AVA This California AVA was established in 1992 on the western edge of the Salinas Valley. It encompasses 22,000 acres along an 18-mile stretch of benchland that runs between Gonzales and the AROYO SECO AVA. This area sits above the normal Salinas Valley fog level at the 200- to 1000-foot level facing southeast. This position allows long sunlit days for optimum ripening without the afternoon heat that hits the valley. This cool area has a long growing season where varieties like CHARDONNAY (the most widely planted) and PINOT NOIR (the area's rising star) do extremely well. Other varieties here are CABERNET SAUVIGNON, MERLOT, PINOT BLANC, and RIESLING. A number of area growers sell grapes to out-of-the-area wineries that bottle wines labeled with the Santa Lucia Highlands APPELLATION.

Santa Maddalena DOC [SAHN-tah mahd-dah-LEH-nah] A DOC located in the larger ALTO ADIGE DOC area of Italy's TRENTINO-ALTO ADIGE region. Although it is in northern Italy, German is commonly spoken here, and this area is also called *St. Magdalener.* The vineyards are located just minutes above the city of Bolzano, the capital city of the Alto Adige area. Santa Maddalena DOC wine has had an excellent reputation since the 1920s and was considered one of the top three or four wines by Mussolini's regime. These red wines are made primarily from SCHIAVA grapes, although small amounts of LAGREIN and Pinot Nero (PINOT NOIR) may be added. The result is a light red wine with fresh, fruity flavors and a slightly smoky character—it's not TANNIC and should be drunk young.

Santa Maria Valley AVA APPELLATION located in SANTA BARBARA COUNTY, except for a tiny northern section in SAN LUIS OBISPO COUNTY. It's situated east of the town of Santa Maria in both northerly and southerly directions and encompasses 80,000 acres. Its cool climate is classified mostly as Region I, although there are a few warmer Region II areas (*see* CLIMATE REGIONS OF CALIFORNIA). Approximately 7,500 acres are planted. CHARDONNAY is the dominant variety followed by PINOT NOIR, CABERNET SAUVIGNON, SAUVIGNON BLANC, RIESLING, CHENIN BLANC, and MERLOT. Two large vineyards in the area, Bien Nacido and Sierra Madre, provide grapes to wineries both inside and outside the Santa Maria Valley AVA.

Santa Rita Hills AVA California VITICULTURAL AREA established in 2001 between the towns of Buellton and Lompoc in northern Santa Barbara County. It encompasses almost 31,000 acres in the western section of the existing SANTA YNEZ VALLEY AVA, although the western ends of the two zones don't align exactly. The hills in this western section of the Santa Rita Hills AVA are directly exposed to the Pacific Ocean breezes and fog, making them cooler than the eastern section of the Santa Ynez Valley AVA. The Santa Rita Hills AVA is particularly well suited for CHARDONNAY and PINOT NOIR. The area has only two wineries. The seventeen different vineyard properties include the well-known Sanford and Benedict Vineyard, planted in the 1970s.

Santa Ynez Valley AVA [SAN-tuh ee-NEHZ] A VITICULTURAL AREA approved in 1983 and located in California's SANTA BARBARA COUNTY, north of the city of Santa Barbara and south of the SANTA MARIA VALLEY AVA. Its 76,800 acres are bounded on the east by Los Padres National Forest and on the west by the Pacific Ocean. The AVA is cooled by the ocean breezes and is considered a Region II (*see* CLIMATE REGIONS OF

CALIFORNIA) area. Approximately 1,500 acres of vineyards are planted. In 2001, a subzone, the SANTA RITA HILLS AVA, was created in the western end of this AVA. CHARDONNAY is by far the dominant grape variety, followed by CABERNET SAUVIGNON, RIESLING, PINOT NOIR, CHENIN BLANC, SAUVIGNON BLANC, and GEWÜRZTRAMINER. This area produces very good wines from the white varieties and Pinot Noir. Cabernet Sauvignon can be quite good but has been inconsistent. Very good examples of Rhône-style wines are now being produced from SYRAH, VIOGNIER, ROUSSANNE, GRENACHE, MOURVÈDRE, and MARSANNE.

Santenay AC [sah*n*-tuh-NEH] The last major village in the southern part of the famous CÔTE D'OR in BURGUNDY. It's just north of the next major Burgundian subregion, the CÔTE CHALONNAIS. Because the Santenay AC is not nearly as well known as most of the neighboring village APPELLATIONS to the north (CHASSAGNE-MONTRACHET, PULIGNY-MONTRACHET, and MEURSAULT), the prices of the wines are usually lower. Almost all the wines produced are red, made from PINOT NOIR. The red wines are similar in style to those from CHASSAGNE-MONTRACHET but usually are not quite as good. Miniscule amounts of white wines are produced from CHARDONNAY. There are no GRAND CRU vineyards, but there are several fine PREMIER CRU vineyards including **Clos de Tavannes**, **La Comme**, **Les Gravières**, and **Le Passe Temps**.

Santerém *see* RIBATEJO DOC

Santorini *see* GREECE

Sanvicetro *see* SANGIOVESE

San Ysidro District AVA Small 2,340-acre California AVA located southeast of the town of Gilroy in Santa Clara County. Cool air from Monterey Bay keeps this area much more temperate than the warmer surrounding SANTA CLARA VALLEY AVA. Established in 1990, it has a single vineyard, which is best known for the CHARDONNAY grapes.

Sardinia; It. Sardegna [sahr-DIHN-ee-uh (It. sahr-DIHN-yuh)] An Italian island and wine-producing region located off Italy's west coast just south of the French island of CORSICA. Sardinia makes a wide variety of wines, most of them quite ordinary. The area has over 100,000 vineyard acres, one DOCG (Vermentino di Gallura), and nineteen DOCS, which comprise about 16 percent of Sardinia's total wine production. This percentage has increased over the last decade primarily because of the dramatically decreasing production of non-DOC wines. Sardinia's main DOC is NURAGUS DI CAGLIARI. Other popular DOCs include Cannonau di Sardegna and Monica di Sardegna. The principal red-grape varieties are Cannonau (GRENACHE), Monica, Carignano (CARIGNAN), and Giro. White wines are made from the widely planted Nuragus plus VERMENTINO, Torbato, and VERNACCIA DI ORISTANO.

SAREP *see* SUSTAINABLE VITICULTURE

Sassella *see* VALTELLINA DOC

Sassicaia DOC [sahs-see-KAH-yah] *see* BOLGHERI DOC; BOLGHERI SAS-SICAIA DOC.

Saumagen *see* KALLSTADT

Saumur [soh-MYOOR] An attractive town located on the LOIRE River not far from the city of Angers in the central Loire. The surrounding area is part of a larger growing region known as Anjou-Saumur. There are a number of appellations in the area including Saumur, Cabernet de Saumur, Saumur Mousseux, and Saumur-Champigny. The **Saumur AC** is for red, white, and ROSÉ wines. The white wines are made mainly from CHENIN BLANC, although some CHARDONNAY and SAUVIGNON BLANC are sometimes added. The wines are usually quite ACIDIC, and many of them end up in the SPARKLING WINES of the **Saumur Mousseux AC**. These sparkling wines, which are made via MÉTHODE CHAMPENOISE, have been produced in this area since 1811. They're allowed to use Chenin Blanc, Chardonnay, and Sauvignon Blanc, as well as other varieties like CABERNET FRANC, CABERNET SAUVIGNON, GAMAY, and PINOT NOIR. Some of the area producers are shifting production to a higher-quality CRÉMANT DE LOIRE AC sparkling wine. **Saumur AC** red and rosé wines are made mainly from Cabernet Franc, occasionally with the addition of Cabernet Sauvignon and Pineau d'Aunis. The **Saumur-Champigny AC** is an appellation with higher standards for red wines made from these same grapes. Qualifying rosé wines from this area can also, and usually do, use the **Cabernet de Saumur AC**.

Sauser *see* FEDERWEISSER

Saussignac AC [sohs-see-NYAHK] A small sweet-wine APPELLATION located in France's BERGERAC area, east of the city of Bordeaux. The wines are made primarily from SÉMILLON, along with some MUSCADELLE and SAUVIGNON BLANC grapes that have either been partially raisined or infected with BOTRYTIS CINEREA (noble rot). The botrytis-infected grapes have the concentrated sweetness and flavor necessary for the best DESSERT WINES. In good years, Saussignac wines can assume the character of a SAUTERNES, although usually not with the same richness and finesse.

sauterne [soh-TERN; saw-TERN] A generic name used in the United States for inexpensive white wines ranging from DRY to semisweet. Such wines aren't anything like the famous French SAUTERNES (spelled with a final *s*) and are often simply JUG WINES made from a variety of mediocre grapes.

Sauternes AC [soh-TEHRN] Famous APPELLATION that produces some of the most outstanding sweet wines in the world. The Sauternes AC lies within the GRAVES district of France's BORDEAUX region, approximately 25 miles southeast of the city of Bordeaux. The designated area includes the five COMMUNES of Barsac, Bommes, Fargues, Preignac, and Sauternes. Barsac is unusual in that it has its own appellation and its wines can be labeled either "BARSAC AC" or "Sauternes AC"; however, none of the other wines can be labeled "Barsac AC." The dominant grape in Sauternes is SÉMILLON, although the final blend generally includes some SAUVIGNON BLANC and, occasionally, small amounts of MUSCADELLE. In good VINTAGES, this appellation is the lucky recipient of the right climatic conditions to infect the grapes with BOTRYTIS CINEREA. This beneficial mold causes the grapes to shrivel, leaving sugar-laden fruit full of rich, CONCENTRATED flavors. *Botrytis cinerea* doesn't always develop and, when it does, it's sometimes very late, rewarding only those daring vineyard owners who haven't picked their grapes (but who have risked losing the entire crop due to inclement weather). The best Sauternes wines come from low-yielding vines that have been hand-picked (some as many as twelve separate times) to ensure that the grapes are not culled before reaching the perfect degree of required ripeness. The resulting classic Sauternes wine is rich and sweet—the *botrytis cinerea* contributes a desirable HONEYED and COMPLEX nature to both the aroma and flavor. Châteaux don't produce sweet Sauternes AC wines every vintage. If the grapes do not progress properly—through suitable ripening and botrytis infection—a château may make fully DRY wines and sell them as BORDEAUX AC or BORDEAUX SUPÉRIER AC wines. Some Sauternes properties started using CRYOEXTRACTION in the late 1980s in an effort to produce good sweet wines from poorer vintages. The Sauternes châteaux were ranked in the Classification of 1855 (*see* Official Wine Classifications of Bordeaux, page 678). Château d'Yquem was elevated to a class all by itself—known variously as PREMIER GRAND CRU, grand premier cru, and premier cru superieur—and is allowed to put PREMIER GRAND CRU CLASSÉ on its label (although it doesn't). It undisputedly makes the best wines in the area and some feel they're the best in all Bordeaux. The classification also named eleven PREMIERS CRUS and fifteen DEUXIÈMES CRUS. Some of the other châteaux producing excellent wines are Climens,

Coutet, Doisy-Daëne, de Fargues, Gillette, Guiraud, Lafaurie-Peyraguey, Rabaud-Promis, Raymond-Lafon, Rieussec, Suduiraut, and La Tour Blance. *See also* SAUTERNE.

sauvage [SOH-vahzh] French term for "savage," "wild," or "uncultivated." On wine labels it sometimes refers to the use of native (wild) YEAST (versus cultivated yeast). Using native yeasts is thought to provide more complexity, since there are often multiple strains of yeast around, each with a different set of characteristics. It occasionally appears in tasting notes and can refer to a wine that's GAMEY or has other animal traits such as smoked meat.

Sauvignon *see* SAUVIGNONASSE

Sauvignonasse [soh-vihn-yoh-NAH-say] White-wine grape, also known as *Sauvignon Vert,* that's widely planted in various parts of the world. In Italy's FRIULI-VENEZIA GIULIA region it's been called *Tocai* or *Tocai Friulano* until recently. After the Hungarians won a court battle to protect the name of their TOKAJI wines, the Italians have chosen simply *Friulano* to replace the prior name. In neighboring Slovenia, where it was called Tocaj, they've decided to call the wines Sauvignonasse. This variety is widely planted in Chilean vineyards and was, for some time, thought to be SAUVIGNON BLANC. Although Sauvignonasse and Sauvignon Blanc grapes look somewhat alike, they produce distinctively different wines, with Sauvignon Blanc wines generally far superior. In Chile, vineyards often plant both varieties side-by-side so they have a FIELD BLEND that goes into the wine, which is often just called "Sauvignon." In California, the variety known as as Sauvignon Vert is actually MUSCADELLE. Sauvignonasse is unrelated to Tokay d'Alsace (which is actually PINOT GRIS) or to Hungary's famous TOKAJI wines (which are made primarily from the FURMINT grape). When Sauvignonasse vines are pruned back and the YIELDS held down, this variety can produce ELEGANT yet LIVELY full-bodied (*see* BODY) wines. Otherwise, it produces rather bland juice, most of which finds its way into JUG WINES.

Sauvignon Blanc [SOH-vihn-yoh*n* BLAH*N*; SOH-vee-nyaw*n* BLAH*N*GK] White-wine grape that is widely cultivated in France and California. It's also grown in Italy, eastern Europe, Australia, New Zealand, and South America. Sauvignon Blanc wines have noticeable ACIDITY and a GRASSY, HERBACEOUS aroma and flavor. They are CRISP, flavorful, and generally best when drunk young. The best of the French wines made from 100 percent Sauvignon Blanc grapes are produced in the LOIRE Valley at SANCERRE and POUILLY-FUMÉ. They're crisp and TART and sometimes have a noticeable FLINTY characteristic. A classic aroma reference for some of the Loire Valley wines is CAT PEE. The elegant DRY wines from BORDEAUX—primarily from GRAVES—are a blend of Sauvignon Blanc and SÉMILLON that's been AGED in oak barrels. The Sémillon rounds out the flavor and provides additional STRUCTURE, enabling these wines to age for decades. Some of the best and most expensive of these Bordeaux wines come from Château Haut-Brion and Domaine De Chevalier. Although Sémillon is, in most cases, the primary grape used in the great SAUTERNES wines, Sauvignon Blanc plays an important role in these rich, sweet wines. In California, Robert Mondavi gave Sauvignon Blanc a push when he introduced an oaky-styled Sauvignon Blanc VARIETAL WINE he called FUMÉ BLANC. Now the second best-selling varietal in California after CHARDONNAY, Sauvignon Blanc wines are made in a variety of additional styles, from those that are crisp and unoaked to Sémillon blends. Steps have been taken over the last decade to lessen the pronounced grassy characteristic of California's Sauvignon Blancs. New Zealand jumped into the international wine scene during the 1980s and 1990s with its renowned Sauvignon Blancs, which continue to have a tremendous following. In 1997, researchers at UNIVERSITY OF CALIFORNIA, DAVIS determined that Sauvignon Blanc and CABERNET FRANC were the likely parents of the renowned CABERNET SAUVIGNON grape. This grape is also known as *Blanc Fumé, Sauvignon Jaune,* and *Sauvignon Musqué.* There are mutations of Sauvignon Blanc that have darker pink or grayish skins and which produce slightly different results from the standard Sauvignon Blanc variety. Known variously as **Sauvignon Rosé**, **Sauvignon Rouge**, or **Sauvignon Gris**, these darker versions produce wines with somewhat more BODY and a spicier character. There appear to be differences in what is called Sauvignon Rosé and Sauvignon Gris, but current evidence is inconclusive. Some Sauvignon Rosé is planted in the Loire and Sauvignon Gris is planted in Bordeaux, Chile, and, more recently, California.

Sauvignon De Saint-Bris VDQS [SOH-vihn-yoh*n* day sa*n* BREES] A small APPELLATION located in the north of BURGUNDY southwest of CHABLIS. It produces SAUVIGNON BLANC wines rather than CHARDONNAY, which is the usual VARIETY seen in this region. Plans are underway to upgrade this appellation to AC status.

Sauvignon Gris *see* SAUVIGNON BLANC

Sauvignon Jaune *see* SAUVIGNON BLANC

Sauvignon Musqué *see* SAUVIGNON BLANC

Sauvignon Rose *see* SAUVIGNON BLANC

Sauvignon Rouge *see* CABERNET SAUVIGNON; SAUVIGNON BLANC

Sauvignon Vert *see* SAUVIGNONASSE

Savagnin [sah-vah-NYA*N*] A rather rare, high-quality white-wine grape grown primarily in France's Jura region. Savagnin is best known as the variety used in the VIN JAUNE (yellow wine) of Château-Chalon. AGED for 6 years, vin jaune undergoes a process similar to SHERRY, whereby a film of YEAST covers the surface, thereby preventing OXIDATION but allowing evaporation and the subsequent concentration of the wine. The result is a sherrylike wine with a delicate, nutty richness that can age for decades. Savagnin is also blended—most often with CHARDONNAY—as in the white wines of ARBOIS, CÔTES DU JURA, and L'ETOILE. It's also known as *Gringet, Savagnin Blanc,* and *Savagnin Jaune.* The term *Savagnin Noir* is a synonym for PINOT NOIR.

Savagnin Noir *see* PINOT NOIR

Savagnin Rosé *see* GEWÜRZTRAMINER

Savennières AC [sa-veh-NYEH*R*] Consisting of only 150 acres, Savennières AC is one of the smallest APPELLATIONS in the Anjou area of France's LOIRE region. The grape used is CHENIN BLANC, and the white wines produced are considered some of the area's best. Because of Chenin Blanc's high ACID levels, Savennières wines are capable of long AGING; in their youth they can be quite ROUGH. This AC's wines are required to have an unusually high minimum ALCOHOL content of 12 percent. There are two GRAND CRU vineyards here with their own appellations—**Coulée de Serrant** and **LaRoche aux Moines**.

Savigny-lès-Beaune AC [sa-vee-nyee lay BOH*N*] The village of Savigny-lès-Beaune is located between BEAUNE and ALOXE-CORTON. The Savigny-lès-Beaune AC, which surrounds this village, is the third largest producing APPELLATION in the CÔTE DE BEAUNE section of BURGUNDY. Red wines are made from PINOT NOIR, and white wines are made from CHARDONNAY. The reputation of the wines from Savigny-lès-Beaune is that they're generally LIGHTER and less full-bodied (and therefore not considered as good) as that of many of its neighbors, which means prices are lower. **Aux Vergelesses**, **Aux Guettes**, **Les Lavières**, and **Aux Serpentières** are some of the better PREMIER CRU vineyards. They are allowed to append after the appellation name.

Savoie [sa-VWAH] Wine district located in eastern France very close to the Swiss border near Lake Geneva. Vineyards are scattered throughout the area, stretching south toward Grenoble. The main APPELLATIONS in the area are Vin de Savoie, Vin de Savoie Mousseux, CRÉPY, Roussette de Savoie, and SEYSSEL. **Vin de Savoie**, the area's main appellation, is for DRY wines—white, red, and ROSÉ. The grapes for red wines are GAMAY, MONDEUSE, and PINOT NOIR. Many wine aficionados prefer the Mondeuse-based wines. White wines make up 75 percent of the production. They're made primarily from JACQUÈRE, but ALIGOTÉ, ALTESSE, CHARDONNAY, and CHASSELAS are also used. The **Vin de Savoie Mousseux AC** is for SPARKLING WINES made from Altesse, Molette, and Chardonnay. The **Roussette de Savoie AC** is for DRY white wines made mainly from the Altesse variety (locally called *Roussette*), with small amounts of Chardonnay and Mondeuse Blanche. There are sixteen CRU villages in the Savoie, all of which have higher standards than those of the Vin de Savoie AC and Roussette de Savoie AC and may append their name to either of these appellations if their wines meet these higher criteria.

savory *see* Glossary of Wine Tasting Terms, page 655

Savoyance *see* MONDEUSE

Scharlachberg *see* BINGEN

Scharzhofberg [SHAH*R*TS-hoff-be*r*k] One of Germany's premier vineyards, which is located near the village of Wiltingen along the SAAR River in the MOSEL-SAAR-RUWER region. RIESLING wines from this vineyard are often rated in the top echelon of all German wines. The Scharzhofberg vineyard consists of approximately 67 acres planted almost entirely with Riesling vines. There are a half-dozen growers, but the largest and best parcel is owned by the Müller family. Scharzhofberg is classified as an ORTSTEIL, which means its wines don't use Wiltingen in the name—they're simply labeled "Scharzhofberg." Wines from the GROSSLAGE that covers this area are labeled "Wiltinger Scharzberg," which can cause some confusion.

Schaumwein [SHOUM-vine] *Schaum* means "froth" or "foam," and *Schaumwein* refers to the lowest category of SPARKLING WINE in Germany. The highest category is called *Qualitätschaumwein* and is popularly known as SEKT.

Scheurebe [SHEWR-uhb] The most widely grown grape in Germany's RHEINHESSEN and PFALZ regions, this CROSS of RIESLING and SYLVANER was created in 1916 by botanist George Scheu (*Rebe* means "vine"). Even though this white-wine grape is one of the higher-quality Riesling crossings, it must be fully ripe to achieve its potential. This feature is a drawback for Scheurebe because it requires this variety to be planted on prime vineyard land, which is most often reserved for Riesling. This grape is susceptible to BOTRYTIS CINEREA, making it attractive for the production of DESSERT WINES. Compared to Riesling, Scheurebe produces higher sugar levels, greater YIELDS, and strong ACID levels. Scheurebe wines can be similiar to Rieslings, with an added BLACKCURRANT characteristic. Small amounts of this grape are cultivated in California where it's used to make VARIETAL WINES.

Schiava [SKYAH-vah] A red-wine grape thought to be native to Italy's ALTO ADIGE region, where it's extensively grown. It's also widely cultivated in neighboring TRENTINO. These regions are heavily populated with German-speaking citizens who call this grape *Vernatsch*. This variety produces light-colored, fruity wines that are low in ACID-ITY, TANNINS, and ALCOHOL; they should be drunk young. There are several varieties of Schiava: *Schiava Grossa* (in German, *Grossvernatsch*), which is the most common; *Schiava Grigia* (or *Grauvernatsch*), which is more difficult to grow but produces better wines; and the low-yielding *Schiava Gentile* (also called *Kleinvernatsch* and *Mittervernatsch*). Another clone called *Tschaggel* (or *Tschaggelevernatsch*) produces good wines but isn't widely planted because it's an inconsistent ripener. The best Schiava-based wines come from the DOCS LAGO DI CALDARO (*Kalterersee,* in German) and SANTA MADDALENA (or *St. Magdalener*). This variety is also cultivated in Germany's WÜRTTEMBERG region where it's called *Trollinger.*

Schilcher [SHEEL-shyuh] A specialty wine of western Styria, which is in the most southern part of Austria. Schilcher is made from Blauer (blue) Wildbacher grapes and vinified DRY and can be found in both STILL and SPARKLING styles. This wine's color is described by many as shimmeringly iridescent, oscillating between white, pink, and red. Indeed, the Middle High German word for such a change of colors is "schillern" or "schilchen." Although Schilcher is often called a ROSÉ, many Styrians object to such a label for this unique wine. Schilcher has a lively ACIDITY; a fresh, fruity flavor; and a spicy BOUQUET reminiscent of strawberries. It should be drunk young.

Schillerwein [SHEEL-luh*r*-vine] A ROSÉ wine that's a specialty in Germany's WÜRTTEMBERG region. It's made from a mix of red and white grapes that are FERMENTED together. In the past, these grapes were also sometimes planted and harvested together. *Schillern* means "to change color" and refers to the varying shades of pink found in the wines.

Schioppettino [skyaw-peh-TEE-noh] A red-wine grape grown in Italy's FRIULI-VENEZIA GIULIA region, particularly in the DOC of COLLI ORIENTALI DEL FRIULI. Schioppettino, also known as *Ribolla Nera,* was on the verge of extinction when it was resurrected by the Ronchi di Cialla estate. Since then other producers have followed suit, and this variety has slowly been gaining a following. Schioppettino produces DRY, intense wines with a flavor suggestive of wild blackberries.

schloss [SHLAWSS] German for "castle." When the name of a schloss is used on a wine label, the meaning is similar to ESTATE GROWN, meaning the wine must be made from grapes grown in its own vineyards. The word *schloss* can also appear as part of the name of a BEREICH—as in Bereich Schloss Bockelheim—or of a GROSSLAGE—as in Grosslage Schloss Rodeck.

Schlossberg *see* ERBACH; KANZEM; RÜDESHEIM; ZELTINGEN

Schlossböckelheim [SHLAWSS BUH-kuhl-hime] A prime wine-producing village located southwest of BAD KREUZNACH in Germany's NAHE region. The village produces top-quality RIESLINGS from its top vineyard sites, which include **Kupfergrube**, **Felsenberg**, and **Königsfels**. The name Schlossböckelheim is also used in the name of the BEREICH that covers this area (the southern part of the Nahe region), in which case it's usually split into two words—Bereich Shloss Böckelheim. The area's GROSSLAGE, which covers other surrounding villages as well, also uses this village's name—Grosslage Schlossböckelheimer Burweg.

Schloss Reichartshausen *see* OESTRICH

Schönhell *see* HALLGARTEN

Schützenhaus *see* HATTENHEIM

Schwarze Katz *see* ZELL

Schwarzriesling *see* MEUNIER

Sciacchetra *see* CINQUETERRE DOC

scion [SI-uhn] Another name for a CUTTING taken from a vine and grafted onto a root system from another vine.

Scott Henry *see* TRELLIS SYSTEM

screw caps One of the alternative types of CLOSURES that quality-wine producers are exploring in an effort to overcome the problems caused by faulty corks (*see* corked wines). The screw cap closure (sometimes called ROTE for roll-on, tamper evident) generally has an outer layer of aluminum alloy with a liner of expanded polyethylene which, when compressed against the bottle top, forms an airtight seal. Wine bottles, of course, must have a threaded lip to accept the cap. One of the best known screw cap closures is the brand Stelvin, which was developed in the 1960s and is now part of Rio Tinto Alcan. Although often associated with less-expensive JUG WINES, screw caps have recently been successfully used by a number of high-quality NEW WORLD wine concerns. Two California producers lead the way— Plumpjack Winery used the screw cap for portions of its $125-plus 1997 Reserve CABERNET SAUVIGNON and in 2002 Bonny Doon Vineyard released 80,000 cases of screw-capped wine, accompanied by several "Death of the Cork" events. In Australia's Clare Valley, many RIESLING producers have begun using screw caps, and a large number of New Zealand winemakers used them for their vintage 2002 wines. Although many producers are still concerned about consumer acceptance, the idea of screw caps as a viable wine-closure alternative is taking hold.

Scuppernong [SKUHP-uhr-nawng] White-wine grape that is indigenous to the southeastern United States and is probably the most important member of the MUSCADINE family. Scuppernong is one of the first grapes the colonists used to make wine. It's now cultivated primarily in the southeastern United States and is well known for its high YIELD. Scuppernong produces an unusual, rather sweet, aromatic wine that takes some getting used to by those more familiar with wines made from European-type (VITIS VINIFERA) grapes.

sec [SEHK] This French word literally means "DRY," which in the wine world means "not sweet." When used to describe STILL (non-SPARKLING) wines, *sec* indicates that the wine has little if any RESIDUAL SUGAR left after FERMENTATION. In sparkling wines like CHAMPAGNE, however, the word takes on quite another meaning: sec indicates a relatively sweet wine, whereas DEMI-SEC is even sweeter. Drier sparkling wines are referred to as BRUT and the very driest as *Extra Brut* or *Brut Nature*.

secco [SHE-koh] Italian for DRY. *Semisecco* is the term for "semi-dry." *See also* ASCIUTTO.

seco [SAY-koh] Spanish and Portuguese for DRY. *Semiseco* means "semi-dry."

secondary fermentation 1. When making SPARKLING WINE via MÉTHODE CHAMPENOISE, the FERMENTATION that takes place in the bottle once the *liqueur d'tirage* (*see* DOSAGE) is added is called the secondary (or second) fermentation. 2. When making still wines, MALOLACTIC FERMENTATION is sometimes called secondary fermentation.

second crop Grapes from clusters where FLOWERING took place noticeably after the main flowering. This group of grapes will not mature with the first group and will still be unripe during the initial harvest. If growers are willing to wait until this second crop matures, the quality can be excellent, but it is often so small that it's not cost-effective to pick.

second growth *see* DEUXIÈME CRU

second label A term used for winery- or CHÂTEAU-produced wines that aren't the quality necessary to be bottled under the primary label. Such wines are generally made from grapes that are either from new vineyards or below top quality because of a substandard growing season. Although not usually as wonderful as primary-label wines, second labels can be surprisingly good. Some examples of second labels in California include Liberty School from Caymus Vineyards and Hawk Crest from Stag's Leap Wine Cellars. Examples in BORDEAUX, where such wines are sometimes referred to as **second wines**, are Les Forts de Latour from Château Latour and Moulin-des-Carruades from Château Lafite-Rothschild.

second wine *see* SECOND LABEL; SUGAR WINE

sediment The grainy, bitter-tasting deposit sometimes found in wine bottles, most often with older wines. Sediment is not a bad sign but in fact may indicate a superior wine. It's the natural separation of bitartrates (*see* ACIDS, tartaric acid), TANNINS, and color pigments that occurs as wines AGE. Although generally associated with finer red wines, sediment occasionally appears in white wines, usually in the form of nearly colorless crystals. For PORT drinkers, the term CRUST, synonymous with sediment, is often used. Sediment should be allowed to settle completely before the wine is DECANTED into another container so that when the wine is served none of the deposit will transfer to the glass.

seepage *see* WEEPER

Séguret *see* CÔTES DU RHÔNE

Seibel, Albert A well-known French hybridist (*see* HYBRID) who lived from 1844 to 1936. Albert Seibel was responsible for creating numerous new grape varieties including Plantet and Rayon d'Or and the French-American hybrids AURORA, Cascade, CHANCELLOR, CHELOIS, Colobel, DE CHAUNAC, Rougeon, and Verdelet.

Seibel 5279 *see* AURORA

Siebel 5898 *see* ROUGEON

Seibel 7053 *see* CHANCELLOR

Seibel 9549 *see* DE CHAUNAC

Seibel 10878 *see* CHELOIS

Sekt [ZEHKT] A German term that's the popular shortened substitute for *Qualitätschaumwein*—"quality sparkling wine." It's the top-quality category for sparkling wine, the lowest being SCHAUMWEIN. The term **Deutscher Sekt** may be used for sparkling wine made entirely from grapes cultivated in Germany, whereas other countries simply use *Sekt* in their German-speaking regions. If a wine is from one of Germany's thirteen ANBAUGEBIETE (official growing regions), its label can state "Deutscher Sekt bA" and may contain the name of a BEREICH (district) and GROSSLAGE (general site). The label may also include the EINZELLAGE (individual site or vineyard) if 85 percent of the grapes are from the named vineyard and the rest of the grapes are from the Anbaugebiet. If a Sekt is made from a single variety (usually RIESLING), the label may include the name of the variety and would read *Rieslingsekt*. Sekt is fruity and traditionally somewhat sweeter than the better sparkling wines from France, Spain, and the United States.

select A label term that, though not legally defined, is used often as a marketing term to infer there's something special about the wine. Such a conclusion, however, may not be true.

Sélection de Grains Nobles *see* ALSACE

Selection wines *see* GERMANY

Select Late Harvest *see* LATE HARVEST

Sémillon [say-mee-YOHN; seh-mee-YOHN (Fr. say-mee-YAW*N*)] White-wine grape that is planted around the world—Argentina, Australia, Chile, France, South Africa, eastern Europe, and the United States—and, in most cases, turns out neutral-flavored, mediocre wines. By itself, Sémillon generally produces wines that are not well-ROUNDED. Combine Sémillon with SAUVIGNON BLANC, however, and the resulting wines can be quite extraordinary. Sémillon marries well with oak and tends to produce high-ALCOHOL, low-ACIDITY wines that have good

EXTRACT and TEXTURE but pale AROMA. Sauvignon Blanc adds the missing acidity and aroma, while Sémillon tempers Sauvignon Blanc's tendency toward GRASSINESS. Blending the two grapes creates a richer, more COMPLEX wine than either can create alone. Indicative of this style are the white wines from BORDEAUX, which often use from 50 to 80 percent Sémillon in the BLEND, producing DRY, marvelously complex wines with great AGING ability. Bordeaux also produces the world-famous sweet wines from SAUTERNES, which capitalize on Sémillon's susceptibility to BOTRYTIS CINEREA, a mold that shrivels the grapes, intensifying the levels of sugar and ACIDS. The resulting wines are RICH, HONEYED, CONCENTRATED, and expensive. In Australia, the image of this grape's inability to stand alone is blurred by the world-class, dry Sémillon wines from HUNTER VALLEY (which are sometimes called *Hunter Valley Riesling*) and—to some extent—the dry, oaked wines produced in the Barossa Valley. Tremendous recognition is also going to Australia's De Bortoli Wines for their botrytised, Sauternes-style Sémillon wine. In the United States, Sémillon grapes have not been extensively grown. There are elegant Sémillon wines coming out of the Pacific Northwest (like those from Washington's Hogue Cellars), but much of the west coast Sémillon is used simply for blending. In the United States and Australia, there are now Sémillon/Chardonnay blends appearing on retail shelves. Sémillon is also known as *Chevrier, Green Grape,* and *Wyndruif.*

semisecco *see* SECCO

Sercial [SER-shuhl] 1. Also called *Cerceal do Douro*, this white-wine grape is grown primarily in Portugal's DÃO DOC. Although associated historically with the island of MADEIRA, Sercial is now found there only in limited quantities. When PHYLLOXERA attacked the Madeira vineyards in the 1870s, the vineyards were eventually replanted, replacing the classic Madeira varieties like Sercial with TINTA NEGRA MOLE. Because of Common Market labeling regulations (see the following discussion), Sercial is making a comeback. These wines are very PERFUMY, yet so ASTRINGENT that they take 6 to 8 years to mellow into drinkability. The word "Sercial" is the Anglicized form of *Cerceal*. 2. The driest and lightest style of the Madeira wines. Although originally associated with the Sercial grape, a lot of Tinta Negra Mole has been used in this style of Madeira in the recent past (especially in the cheaper versions). However, in 1986 Portugal entered the Common Market, whose regulations required that by 1993 any Madeira wine naming a variety on its label must contain at least 85 percent of that grape. This labeling requirement caused an upsurge in replanting the classic vines such as Sercial. Wines labeled "Sercial-style" can contain less than the required

85 percent, and most likely contain more Tinta Negra Mole. Sercial is also called *Cerceal* (Portuguese spelling) and *Esgana Cão*, which means "dog strangler" and refers to its astringent character.

Aux Serpentières *see* SAVIGNY-LÈS-BEAUNE

Serprina *see* PROSECCO

Serra Gaúcha *see* BRAZIL

Serralunga d'Alba [seh*r*-ah-LOON-gah DAHL-bah] *see* BAROLO

serre *see* VIN DE CUVÉE

serving wine *see* Opening and Serving Wine at Home, page 636

set *see* FRUIT SET

Setúbal DOC [sih-TOO-bawl] This area, located south of Lisbon on the Setúbal peninsula, has had RD (now called DOC) status since 1907. It is the most important DOC in the larger VINHO REGIONAL of TERRAS DO SADO. Moscatel (MUSCAT) grapes (with ARINTO sometimes added for ACIDITY) are used for the area's strong FORTIFIED WINES, which are produced by halting FERMENTATION partway through the process by adding grape alcohol. The fortified wine then goes through a period of MACERATION where it's left in contact with the skins for 5 or 6 months. The wines are then AGED for 5 years or more in large vats and small barrels. The wines are categorized by the amount of time spent in oak—5 years, 20 years, 25 years, and 50 years (this last one is usually labeled "Setúbal Apoteca"). Younger wines are deep golden colored, grapey-flavored, high-ALCOHOL, and capable of aging for many years. The older wines become much darker and take on nutty, molasses characteristics. If the wines contain 85 percent Moscatel, they may be labeled "Moscatel de Setúbal." Otherwise, they must contain 70 percent Moscatel to be called simply "Setúbal."

Sèvre-et-Maine *see* MUSCADET

Seyre-Villard 5276 *see* SEYVAL BLANC

Seyssel [seh-SEHL] One of the best-known villages in France's SAVOIE region, Seyssel is located just southwest of Lake Geneva on the Rhône River, not far from the Swiss border. Seyssel produces white STILL WINES under the **Seyssel AC** and SPARKLING WINES under the **Seyssel Mousseux AC**. The grapes used are ALTESSE (locally called *Roussette*) and a local variety Molette, which lends an interesting peppery character. Most of these wines should be drunk young.

Seyval Blanc [say-vahl BLAH*N*; BLAH*N*GK] A French-American HYBRID created by the French hybridizers Seyve and Villard by crossing two other hybrids—Seibel 5656 and Seibel 4986 (Rayon d'Or). Officially known as *Seyre-Villard 5276*, Seyval Blanc is widely grown in the eastern United States, England, and parts of northern France. Wines produced from this variety are high in ACIDITY and therefore CRISP and LEAN, with a hint of grapefruit in the flavor. This is particularly characteristic of the wines from the northern areas like Michigan and New York. Wines produced from the more southern areas such as Virginia and Maryland are somewhat softer and fuller. Some producers are aging their Seyval Blanc wines in oak barrels to SOFTEN and enrich the wine, as well as increase the bottle life.

Seyve Villard 12.375 *see* VILLARD BLANC

Seyve Villard 18.315 *see* VILLARD NOIR

Sforzato; Sfursat; Sfurzat *see* VALTELLINA DOC

shallow *see* Glossary of Wine Tasting Terms, page 655

sharp *see* Glossary of Wine Tasting Terms, page 655

sharpshooter *see* GLASSY-WINGED SHARPSHOOTER

shatter The stage following bloom when unfertilized green berries fall or are cut from the CLUSTER.

Shawnee Hills AVA Southern Illinois APPELLATION established in December 2006. It consists of 1,369,600 acres that lie between the Ohio River and the Mississippi River, largely within the Shawnee National Forest and around the city of Carbondale. This cool region does best with HYBRIDS or NATIVE AMERICAN GRAPES. White varieties include CHARDONEL, SEYVAL BLANC, Traminette, and VIDAL BLANC; for red grapes the most popular are CHAMBOURCIN, CHANCELLOR, and NORTON. Some vintners think CABERNET FRANC will do well since it performs ably in cool weather climates and ripens early. There are currently 18 wineries and about 300 acres of vineyards.

sheets *see* Glossary of Wine Tasting Terms, page 655

shelling When berries fall off a grape cluster, typically due to DISEASE, stress, or overripeness.

Shenandoah Valley AVA Large AVA that starts in the north in West Virginia above Martinsburg in the far eastern corner of the state and runs southwest through Berkeley and Jefferson Counties, then into

VIRGINIA down through Frederick, Clarke, Warren, Shenandoah, Page, Rockingham, Augusta, Rockbridge, Botetourt, and Amherst counties. It was established in 1987 and encompasses approximately 2,400,000 acres in the Blue Ridge Mountains. *See also* CALIFORNIA SHENANDOAH VALLEY AVA.

sherrified *see* Glossary of Wine Tasting Terms, page 655

sherry A FORTIFIED WINE made in the JEREZ-XÉRÈS-SHERRY Y MANZANILLA DE SANLÚCAR DE BARRAMEDA DO, a designated area located around the town of JEREZ DE LA FRONTERA in southern Spain's Analucía region. Along with PORT and MADEIRA, sherry is considered one of the three great fortified wines. Sherries range broadly in color, flavor, and sweetness, but there are fundamentally only two types—*fino* and *oloroso*. The difference between these two originates with a peculiar yeast called FLOR and relates to the level of ALCOHOL. **Fino**: Flor develops only on fino-type wines and imparts a sharp, tangy characteristic. It also forms an insulating layer on the wine's surface that protects the wine from OXIDATION and keeps the wine's pale color. Flor won't develop in wines with over 15½ percent alcohol, so *fino*-style wines are generally lower in alcohol than olorosos, which are fortified up to 18 percent alcohol. **Oloroso**: Since all sherry barrels are only filled about five-sixths full, air gets to the *olorosos* and—because they're not protected by a layer of flor—causes them to oxidize. This oxidation turns the wine's color from deep gold to deep brown and endows the aroma and flavor with rich, nutty-raisiny characteristics. Because olorosos are usually aged longer than most sherries, they're also more expensive. In Spain, most olorosos are DRY. **Cream sherries** are usually lower-grade olorosos that have been heavily sweetened. **Amoroso** (also called *East India*) is also a sweetened oloroso, as is the very dark, extremely sweet **brown sherry**. **Rayas** are also lower-grade olorosos. Because of their color, lighter olorosos are sometimes called **golden sherries**. There are several different variations of fino-style sherries. **Fino**: This pale, delicate, very dry, tangy wine is considered by many to be the world's finest sherry. Finos are excellent when young and should not be aged because they don't improve and may lose some of their vitality. A **fino amontillado** occurs when a fino has lost its flor (at about 6 years) and begins to turn amber-colored and gain a little of the nutty flavor found in an oloroso. **Amontillado**, still a fino-style wine, is aged longer and is darker and softer than a fino amontillado. It should have a distinctively nutty flavor and retain some of the pungent tang. **Manzanilla** is the lightest, most delicate, and most pungent of the fino-style sherries. It's made in

Sanlúcar de Barrameda, a seaside town whose location is said to give the wine a hint of saltiness. A **manzanilla pasada** occurs when the flor fades (at about 7 years) and the wine takes on some of the characteristics of an amontillado—nutty flavor and darker color—while still retaining its pungent character. **Pale cream sherry** is a fino that has been sweetened. **Palo cortado** is a cross between an oloroso and a fino and varies from producer to producer. Supposedly, a palo cortado starts life as a fino—developing and gaining a tangy character from flor. At some point in its evolution, it deviates and evolves as an oloroso would by oxidizing and developing rich, nutty characteristics and a darker color—all while retaining some of a fino's tanginess. This style is very rare and greatly sought after by sherry connoisseurs. Generally sherries are non-vintage (*see* VINTAGE), and the quality is consistent year after year because the Spanish use the SOLERA SYSTEM of topping off older wines with the more recently made sherry. Simply described, the solera system consists of a number of tiers of sherry casks from oldest to the most recently made. Usually one-quarter to one-third of the oldest wine is drawn off for bottling and then replaced by wine from the next oldest tier and so on up through the solera system. This process lets the old wines infuse the younger wines with character, while the younger wines give their nutrients to the older wines. In fino-style wines, this latter activity gives the flor something to live on. In 1994, sherry producer Gonzales Bypass introduced two unusual vintage-dated sherries, a 1963 and a 1966. Both sherries bypassed the normal solera system aging process and were aged separately in their own oak casks. In 2000, two additional categories were approved for high-quality sherry: VOS and VORS. **VOS** stands for Very Old Sherry (or *Vinum Optimu Signatum*) and applies to sherries with an average age of at least 20 years. **VORS** stands for Very Old Rare Sherry (or *Vinum Optimu Rare Signatum*) and applies to sherries with an average age of at least 30 years. The VOS and VORS categories only apply to the oxidatively aged sherry—amontillado, oloroso, palo cortado, and Pedro Ximénez. To qualify, each sherry is tasted by an independent tasting committee, which determines an average age and verifies that the sherry meets the necessary quality level. The age may also be analyzed by the use of carbon dating. Spanish sherry is made primarily from the PALAMINO grape along with small amounts of PEDRO XIMÉNEZ and Moscatel (MUSCAT). Sherry-style wines are now also made in the United States, as well as in other parts of the world including Australia and South Africa. Many wines that call themselves sherry are inexpensive potables that aren't produced anything like the Spanish originals. A few, however, attain a close approximation by using flor inoculations and the solera system. Sherries can be drunk before or after dinner. Dry sherries are usually served chilled; sweet sherries are served at room temperature.

shipping dosage *see* DOSAGE

shiraz *see* SYRAH

Shoalhaven An Australian wine region located in the South Coast Zone of NEW SOUTH WALES. It's situated along the Pacific Ocean about 95 miles south of Sydney around the town of Nowra. This area is not as warm as the HASTING RIVER region north of Sydney, where the weather is more subtropical but still humid and where summer rains can be problematic. Slightly over 500 acres are planted with CABERNET SAUVIGNON, CHARDONNAY, GEWURTZTRAMINER, MERLOT, PINOT NOIR, SAUVIGNON BLANC, SEMILLON, SHIRAZ, and VERDELHO. The HYBRID, CHAMBOURCIN, is also grown here because of its resistance to humidity-related diseases like mildew.

shoot A grapevine's new growth, which develops from a bud as a bright green stem and eventually sprouts leaves, then flowers, then clusters of minuscule green grape berries. *See also* VITICULTURE.

short *see* Glossary of Wine Tasting Terms, page 655

short-vatted *see* LONG-VATTED

Sicily [SIHS-uh-lee] Sicily (*Sicilia* in Italian) is located right off the tip of the "toe" of Italy's boot-shaped land mass. It's the biggest island in the Mediterranean and, with over 325,000 vineyard acres, Italy's largest wine-producing region (both in vineyard acreage and overall size). Sicily usually competes with APULIA or VENETO for the largest wine production out of Italy's twenty wine regions. As with Apulia's production, much of Sicily's wine is distilled (*see* DISTILLATION) into spirits. Even though there are twenty DOC areas in Sicily, less than 2½ percent of the total wine production is covered by DOCs. Some of the better-known DOCs are ALCAMO, ETNA, MOSCATO DI PANTELLERIA, and the historically well-known MARSALA. Many of the best wines are VINO DA TAVOLA (VdT), made by better producers like Corvo and Regaleali. Sicily has developed its own regional method of identifying quality wines, establishing its own standards and allowing wines that qualify to place a *Q* for "quality" on the label or CAPSULE. The most widely planted white grape is CATARRATTO, followed by TREBBIANO. Other white grapes include GRILLO, Inzolia, Carricante (also called *Catanese Bianco*), and MUSCAT (the local subvariety is called *Zibibbo*). The most widely planted red grape is NERO D'AVOLA (also called *Calabrese*), followed by NERELLO, Mascalse, and Perricone (also called *Pignatello*). The red varieties, BARBERA and SANGIOVESE, are starting to make some inroads.

Siebengebirge, Bereich *see* MITTELRHEIN

Siegelsberg *see* ERBACH

Sierra Foothills AVA [see-EHR-ruh] Large APPELLATION that runs through California's "gold country." It's about 160 miles long and covers approximately 2,600,000 acres in parts of Yuba, Nevada, Placer, EL DORADO, AMADOR, Calaveras, Tuolumne, and Mariposa Counties. There are more than sixty wineries scattered throughout the region, mostly in El Dorado and Amador Counties. The Sierra Foothills AVA includes the smaller AVAs of El Dorado, FIDDLETOWN, NORTH YUBA, and SHENANDOAH VALLEY. The most widely planted grape variety by a very wide margin is ZINFANDEL. It's followed by SAUVIGNON BLANC, CABERNET SAUVIGNON, CHARDONNAY, and an assortment of other grapes.

Sierras de Málaga DO [see-EHR-uhs deh MA-luh-guh] A DO located in southern Spain, east of JEREZ and south of MONTILLA-MORILES. It covers essentially the same area as the MÁLAGA DO. The difference is the Málaga DO is primarily associated with its famous sweet, FORTIFIED WINES and naturally sweet but unfortified wines with at least 13 percent alcohol. The Sierras de Málaga DO produces white, rosé, and red wines that are unfortified and usually DRY with alcohol levels under 15 percent. White wines are made from PEDRO XIMÉNEZ, Moscatel (MUSCAT), CHARDONNAY, MACEBEO, and SAUVIGNON BLANC. Rosé and red wines use CABERNET SUAVIGNON, MERLOT, SYRAH, and TEMPRANILLO.

sifone *see* MARSALA DOC

silky *see* Glossary of Wine Tasting Terms, page 655

Silvaner *see* SYLVANER

Similkameen Valley VA *see* BRITISH COLUMBIA

simple *see* Glossary of Wine Tasting Terms, page 655

sinewy *see* Glossary of Wine Tasting Terms, page 655

Sitia *see* GREECE

Skadarska *see* KADARKA

skin contact; skin contact time A process associated with making white wines that is the step between CRUSHING and FERMENTATION. Unlike red wine, white wine isn't fermented with the skins and seeds so it doesn't extract any of the skins' flavors and aromas. However, winemakers get favorable results by leaving the freshly expressed juice in contact with the skins and seeds for a short period—2 hours to 2 days. The major concerns are that the white wine would extract too much color from the grape skins and/or extract some bitterness from the skins or seeds. These factors can be controlled by keeping the juice at a cooler temperature during the skin contact time. *See also* MACERATION.

skunky *see* Glossary of Wine Tasting Terms, page 655

Sloughhouse AVA This VITICULTURAL AREA was established in August 2006. Its 78,800 acres are located in the northeastern portion of the larger LODI AVA, which is between Sacramento and Stockton in northern California. It's the warmest of the Lodi sub-zones and as such, the 7,000 acres currently planted have a majority of red-grape varieties such as CABERNET SAUVIGNON, CABERNET FRANC, MERLOT, and ZINFANDEL.

Smaragd [smah-RAHG] Austrian for "emerald," Smaragd is a specialty wine category of Lower Austria's Wachau area. Smaragd wines are made from the ripest grapes and must have an alcohol content of at least 12 percent. These full-bodied wines have excellent aging potential, sometimes of 20 years or more.

Smart Dyson *see* TRELLIS SYSTEM

smell *see* AROMA and BOUQUET

smoky *see* Glossary of Wine Tasting Terms, page 655

smooth *see* Glossary of Wine Tasting Terms, page 655

Snake River Valley AVA This VITICULTURAL AREA was established in April 2007 and is Idaho's first AVA (although it extends into eastern Oregon). It contains 5,288,320 acres, located in southwestern Idaho—Ada, Adams, Boise, Canyon, Elmore, Gem, Gooding, Jerome, Owyhee, Payette, Twin Falls, and Washington counties—and Baker and Malheur counties in Oregon. Currently there are about 1,800 acres planted. The region is cool and grape varieties that do well in this climate such as CHARDONNAY, GEWÜRZTRAMINER, and RIESLING, are popular. But there are warmer microclimates that perform well with varieties such as CABERNET SAUVIGNON and MERLOT. CABERNET FRANC, CHENIN BLANC, CINSAULT, GRENACHE, MALBEC, MOURVÈDRE, and SYRAH are also planted. Top producers include Ste. Chapelle Winery, Sawtooth Winery, and Bitner Vineyards.

Snipes Mountain AVA AMERICAN VITICULTURAL AREA established in 2009 in Washington State in the southeast part of the Yakima Valley between the towns of Granger and Sunnyside. The small, 4,145 acre area is a sub-region within the larger YAKIMA VALLEY AVA and the huge COLUMBIA VALLEY AVA. Growers first planted grapes on this modest-size hill as early as 1917, making it one of the earliest to plant European varieties (VITIS VINIFERA). Today the grapes planted include CABERNET SAUVIGNON, PINOT NOIR, SEMILLON, and SYRAH on about 700 acres of vineyards. Over 25 different wineries use grapes grown in the area.

soapy *see* Glossary of Wine Tasting Terms, page 655

Soave DOC; Soave Superiore DOCG [SWAH-veh] Located in the western part of Italy's VENETO area east of Verona around the town of Soave, this demarcated zone produces Italy's most popular DRY white wine. There's a smaller CLASSICO zone that encompasses the hilly areas that are mostly north and east of the town. Soave wines are made from a minimum 70 percent GARGANEGA plus other varieties like CHARDONNAY, Pinot Bianco (PINOT BLANC), and TREBBIANO grapes. Most Soave wine is regarded as undistinguished, but the wines from the Classico area are generally of higher quality. There are also a few producers that make very high quality single-vineyard wines. In 2001, the SUPERIORE version was elevated to DOCG status. Superiore on the label indicates that the wine is 1 percent higher in ALCOHOL and is AGED for a minimum of 6 months (RISERVA wines for 24 months). The Superiore designation only allows wines from about 80 percent of the vineyards in the full Soave DOC. It also requires that these vineyards lower allowable YIELDS by about 30 percent. This same area also makes a SPUMANTE version and a RECIOTO DI SOAVE DOCG (a sweet wine). Bolla, the Verona-based wine firm, is closely associated with Soave, so much so that many consumers have thought that Soave is a proprietary brand name of Bolla.

soft; softening *see* Glossary of Wine Tasting Terms, page 655

Solano County Green Valley AVA The lesser of two California AVAS named Green Valley (the other is in SONOMA COUNTY), located in Solano County, west of SUISUN VALLEY AVA and east of the southern end of NAPA COUNTY. This 2,560-acre area doesn't receive the cooling ocean breezes, so it's much hotter and has a shorter growing season than the Napa or Sonoma VITICULTURAL AREAS—it's rated a Region III category (*see* CLIMATE REGIONS OF CALIFORNIA). Quail Creek is the lone winery in the area.

solera system [soh-LEH-rah] Spain's age-old blending and maturation system, used to maintain quality and style consistency in some FORTIFIED WINES. It's used most notably for Spain's SHERRY, although producers of such wines in other countries have also established soleras. The solera system is based on the maturity levels of several wines, ranging in tiers from the oldest to the most recently produced. It consists of drawing off one-quarter to one-third of the oldest wine for bottling. The wine that was drawn off is replaced with wine from the next oldest tier, which is replaced with a younger wine from the next level, and so on up through the levels of the solera. With this process, the old wines infuse the younger ones with character, while the youngsters endow their older counterparts with nutrients, which—in *fino*-style sherries—gives the FLOR something to live on. A solera is generally pictured as tiers of wine casks stacked on top of each other—the oldest wines being the bottom level, the next oldest on the tier above that, and on up, with the youngest wine at the top. In actuality, however, the various age levels or scales (*escalas*) of wine may be kept in separate BODEGAS (storage areas). The oldest wines in a solera depend on when it was established—some are 40 to 50 years old. In practice, soleras are very complex, with numerous casks and levels involved. Young wines are managed in a CRIADERA (nursery) prior to being selected to go into a particular solera. To be precise, only the oldest level of wines is referred to as the solera; the successive (next oldest) tier up is referred to as the **first criadera**, followed by the **second criadera**, and so forth. Some producers have up to fourteen levels in their solera systems. The final wine that's bottled is often a blend of the output of various soleras—the result of the integrated solera system.

solid *see* Glossary of Wine Tasting Terms, page 655

sommelier [saw-muh-LYAY] The French term for a wine steward or waiter in charge of wine. For hundreds of years, sommeliers were responsible for the cellaring and serving of wines for royalty. Eventually, the tradition of the sommelier spread to restaurants, where such an individual is expected to have extensive knowledge of wines, their suitability with various dishes, and how to serve and DECANT them. **Master Sommeliers** are individuals who have advanced training in this area and have passed rigorous testing. The first exam for Master Sommeliers was held in 1969 in the United Kingdom and over the years the testing has been enhanced and refined. Individuals who take this higher level of training and pass the difficult exams are entitled to use the prestigious MS initials. *See also* TASTEVIN.

Somontano DO [saw-mon-TAH-noh] Centered around the city of Barbastro in the province of Huesca, this DO is in the ARAGON autonomous region in northeast Spain. Much of Aragon suffers from high temperatures, which produce overripe, high-alcohol wines. Somontano (a contraction meaning "under the mountains") is showing the most promise of Aragon's wine zones. With vineyards in the Pyrenees foothills, Somontano winemakers take advantage of the cooler environment to produce lower-alcohol, higher-quality wines. The more traditional red wines here are made from Moristel, the primary red variety, along with Parraleta and Ganarcha (GRENACHE). Among the red varieties being planted are TEMPRANILLO, CABERNET SAUVIGNON, MERLOT, and PINOT NOIR. New white varieties (CHARDONNAY, CHENIN BLANC, and GEWÜRZTRAMINER) are showing up along side the traditional white grapes Alcañón and Viura (MACABEO). COVISA (Compañia Vitivinicola del Somontano SA), established in the mid-1980s with modern facilities, is producing some of the most interesting wines in this region.

Sonnenberg *see* KANZEM

Sonnenuhr *see* WEHLEN; ZELTINGEN

Sonoita AVA *see* ARIZONA

Sonoma Coast AVA A large 480,000-acre AVA designed to identify specific SONOMA COUNTY, cooler-climate areas, which can be classified as Region I or Region II (*see* CLIMATE REGIONS OF CALIFORNIA). This APPELLATION is thus an odd-shaped area that runs from near the Mendocino County line in the north to the Marin County border in the south. It includes part of other AVAs like CHALK HILL, GREEN VALLEY-SONOMA, LOS CARNEROS, SONOMA VALLEY, and RUSSIAN RIVER, while excluding warmer areas like the ALEXANDER VALLEY AVA and the DRY CREEK AVA. This region was originally created at the bequest of Sonoma-Cutrer winery so that it could maintain ESTATE-BOTTLED labeling for its Les Pierres Vineyard. There are now several firms who have started wineries and vineyards very close to the coast and can truly be considered "Sonoma Coast."

Sonoma County; Northern Sonoma AVA Sonoma County is a very important California wine-producing county situated north of San Francisco and west of the NAPA VALLEY. Although the neighboring Napa Valley has dominated the region in terms of recognition and attracting many major wineries, Sonoma has made tremendous progress since the early 1970s and has now carved out significant recognition in its own right. Sonoma's winemaking history goes back to the 1820s, when the Sonoma Mission's vineyards were planted by

Franciscan monks. Unfortunately, they planted MISSION grapes, which don't produce high-quality TABLE WINES. In the 1850s and 1860s, AGOSTON HARASZTHY (who established the original Buena Vista Winery in 1857) expanded the effort by trying to determine which varieties did best in various California areas. To this end, he imported thousands of CUTTINGS of about 300 different grape varieties. He planted many of these in SONOMA COUNTY and sold the rest to others around the state. Like much of California, the influx of PHYLLOXERA in the 1890s and PROHIBITION from 1920 to 1933 severely curtailed the growth of Sonoma County's wine business. It wasn't until the Napa Valley boom started in the mid- to late-1960s that Sonoma County was reenergized as a top winemaking region. It began converting from grapes that had been used primarily for JUG WINES—like ALICANTE BOUSCHET, CARIGNANE, and PETITE SIRAH—and now leads Napa County in acreage for CHARDONNAY, PINOT NOIR, and ZINFANDEL. Sonoma has built a solid reputation for wines made from CABERNET SAUVIGNON, Chardonnay, GEWÜRZTRAMINER, Pinot Noir, SAUVIGNON BLANC, and Zinfandel. In 2000, there were over 55,000 planted acres, almost 65 percent to red varieties. Cabernet Sauvignon is the most widely planted red followed by Pinot Noir, Merlot, and Zinfandel. Chardonnay makes up over 80 percent of the white variety acreage. Sonoma County is quite large and has diverse climate areas ranging from Region I to Region III (*see* CLIMATE REGIONS OF CALIFORNIA). Numerous AVAs have been established here since 1978, some sharing the same geographic area. In addition to belonging to the huge NORTH COAST AVA and having its own APPELLATION, Sonoma County contains the following AVAs: ALEXANDER VALLEY, CARNEROS, CHALK HILL, DRY CREEK, KNIGHTS VALLEY, Northern Sonoma, RUSSIAN RIVER VALLEY, SONOMA COAST, SONOMA COUNTY GREEN VALLEY, SONOMA MOUNTAIN, and SONOMA VALLEY. A number of wineries are permitted to use any of five or six different AVA designations for the same wine. The **Northern Sonoma AVA** begins around the city of Sebastopol in the south and goes up to the Mendocino County line in the north and covers the smaller VITICULTURAL AREAS of Alexander Valley, Chalk Hill, Dry Creek, Green Valley-Sonoma, Knight's Valley, and Russian River Valley. Sonoma County has over 175 wineries, which ranks it second only to Napa County in the United States for number of wineries.

Sonoma County Green Valley AVA A 32,000-acre California APPELLATION that's a subregion within the southwest portion of the larger RUSSIAN RIVER VALLEY AVA. It's located between the towns of Sebastopol and Occidental and extends north of Forestville to the Russian River. Because this area's closer to the ocean, it's cooler than many other parts of the Russian River Valley, making it a Region I growing area (*see* CLIMATE REGIONS OF CALIFORNIA). This makes it ideal for CHARDONNAY and PINOT NOIR, which are used for both STILL WINES and SPARKLING WINES.

Sonoma Mountain AVA A small 5,000-acre subzone of the SONOMA VALLEY AVA in SONOMA COUNTY, California. The Sonoma Mountain AVA is situated in the Sonoma Mountain range, west of the town of Glen Ellen. The area covers much of the east-facing hills and then curves around the northern end and includes some western-facing slopes—most of the vineyards are on the eastern side. Elevation levels for Sonoma Mountain vineyards are 400 to 600 feet on the east and 1,200 to 1,600 feet on the west. At these elevations, the vineyards receive more precipitation. They're also warmer and less susceptible to temperature changes than the valley floor because they're above the fog line. The area is best known for STURDY yet elegant CABERNET SAUVIGNON wines; ZINFANDEL also does very well here.

Sonoma Riesling *see* SYLVANER

Sonoma Valley AVA California's Sonoma Valley, also known as *Valley of the Moon,* is situated between the Mayacamas Mountains (which separate it from the NAPA VALLEY to the east) and the Sonoma Mountain range on the west. The northern end of the Sonoma Valley AVA starts just southeast of Santa Rosa and extends in a southeasterly direction to San Pablo Bay; it includes the Sonoma portion of the CARNEROS AVA. The smaller SONOMA MOUNTAIN AVA is part of the Sonoma Valley AVA. The southern end of the valley (Carneros) is cooler, and CHARDONNAY, GEWÜRZTRAMINER, PINOT NOIR, and MERLOT do better there. CABERNET SAUVIGNON and ZINFANDEL do well in various warmer locations around the valley and in the mountains. There are about thirty wineries in the Sonoma Valley AVA. including the valley's first winery—the original Buena Vista Winery, established by AGOSTON HARASZTHY.

sori [SOHR-ree] Piedmontese for a hill or slope that has the best exposure to the sun and therefore produces riper grapes and the best wines. Sori is often used with the vineyard names, like *Sori San Lorenzo* and *Sori Vigna Riunda. See also* BRICCO.

sound *see* Glossary of Wine Tasting Terms, page 655

sour *see* Glossary of Wine Tasting Terms, page 655

Sousão *see* SOUZÃO

Sousón *see* SOUZÃO

South Africa This country's wine industry began in the mid-1600s when Jan van Riebeck planted the first grapevines. In 1685, Simon van der Stel established Groot Constantia (which still exists), a winery that developed a worldwide reputation for its DESSERT WINES called *Constantia*. In 1688, South Africa's wine industry was given a boost with the arrival of the French Huguenots, who brought with them many winemaking skills. Over the years South African wines had many ups and downs, including serious problems with overproduction in the early 1900s. This dilemma resulted in the formation of the Cooperative Wine Growers' Association known as the **KWV** (*Kooperatieve Wijnbouwers Vereniging van Zuid-Africa*). The KWV, which controls the supply and demand of grapes and establishes consistent pricing, remains a powerful force today. In addition to KWV, which markets a wide range of wines and distilled (*see* DISTILLATION) spirits, the other two major producers are Oude Meester and the Stellenbosch Farmers' Winery (known as *SFW* or *Farmers*). The primary South Africa growing areas are all in the southwestern part of the country near the Cape of Good Hope. In 1973, an APPELLATION system, **Wine of Origin (WO)**, was established along the lines of the European Economic Community rules. On wine labels, the appellation name is appended with "WO." In the Wine of Origin system, the smallest demarcated area is an **estate**, which consists of one or more contiguous vineyards (called farms) that are farmed as a single unit. The next largest is a **ward**, which consists of multiple vineyards within a geographical area. Wards are usually part of a district, but not necessarily. Next in size is a **district** (which is usually, but not necessarily, part of a region); the largest area is called a **region**. South Africa's Wine of Origin system is slightly confusing because boundaries of smaller areas don't always align with the larger areas of which they're a part, and because smaller units don't necessarily belong to the next largest designation. Some demarcated areas are identified for specific wine types. One of these is the **Boberg Region**, an area identified for the production of FORTIFIED WINES. The PAARL and Tulbagh districts may be included in the Boberg Region for fortified wines only. The **Coastal Region** contains many of the premium winegrowing areas and a mix of districts and wards. Paarl (which contains FRANSCHHOEK, a highly regarded ward) and STELLENBOSCH are two of this region's most prominent and esteemed districts. The Coastal Region also contains the famous CONSTANTIA ward (birthplace of the South African wine industry), the DURBANVILLE ward, and the Swartland District. The **Breede River Valley Region** includes two heavily irrigated districts, ROBERTSON and WORCESTER. These districts have over 25 percent of the country's vineyard acreage and provide an even larger portion of the country's wine production, most of which ends up in BRANDY or fortified wine. The **Orange River Region**, **Klein Karoo Region,** and **Olifants River Region** are all hot and dry, require irrigation, and produce wine similar to the Robertson and Worcester districts. As the market for brandy and fortified wines has fallen, these regions have all begun moving toward TABLE WINE production with plantings of higher-quality VARIETIES (called *cultivars* here) in the cooler areas. Other WOs are Analusia, Benede-Orange, Cederburg, Douglas, OVERBERG (with its wards Elgin and Walker Bay), Piketberg, Ruiterbosch, and Swellendam. White varieties occupy twice as much vineyard areas as red. The most widely planted white grape here is CHENIN BLANC (called *Steen* locally). However, its signifigance is diminishing, dropping from over 30 percent of the total vineyard acreage in 1990 to under 20 percent in 2001. Other white varieties include Colombar (COLOMBARD), CHARDONNAY, and SAUVIGNON BLANC. Of the red-grape varieties, CABERNET SAUVIGNON pushed CINSAUT (called *Hermitage* locally) into fifth place in the mid-1990s. Following the most widely planted Cabernet Sauvignon are Shiraz (SYRAH), PINOTAGE (a Cinsaut-PINOT NOIR CROSS that's a South African specialty), and MERLOT. During much of this century, fortified wines (SHERRY and PORT styles) dominated South African wine production. In the 1970s, semisweet white table wines, influenced by Germany, became popular. Now South Africa is producing a wide range of red and white DRY table wines and SPARKLING WINES.

South African Riesling *see* CROUCHEN

South Australia Australia's most important wine state, South Australia is located in the south central part of the country. It's bounded on the south by the Southern Ocean; on the east by the states of Queensland, NEW SOUTH WALES, and VICTORIA; on the west by the state of WESTERN AUSTRALIA; and on the north by the Northern Territories. Its capital city is Adelaide, which contains more than two thirds of the state's population. South Australia's wine industry started in the late 1830s, and by the beginning of the twentieth century, it was becoming the dominant wine-producing state. Today, it produces between 45 and 55 percent of the nation's wines. It has over 150,000 acres of vineyards and is continuing to plant more each year, although recently the growth rate has slowed slightly. One distinct advantage for South Australia's wine industry is the fact that PHYLLOXERA hasn't infested the vineyards here as it has in some other states. And South Australia has an ongoing quarantine system to ensure that the vineyards remain phylloxera free. About two-thirds of the state's production is red wine. Using the Australian GEOGRAPHIC INDICATIONS system, South Australia officially has eight major ZONES and fifteen REGIONS (although more are being approved all the time). Some 145 miles northeast of Adelaide lies the **Lower Murray Zone**, which contains the RIVERLAND region. This hot, irrigated region produces about 50 percent of South Australia's wines. The other remote zone (farthest from Adelaide in the state's southeast corner) is the **Limestone Coast Zone**. It contains well-known regions like COONAWARRA and PADTHAWAY, as well as some other regions (some quite new) like BORDERTOWN, MOUNT BENSON, MOUNT GAMBIER, ROBE RANGES, and WRATTONBULLY. Some of Australia's best CABERNET SAUVIGNON wines come from Coonawarra. A number of other zones surround Adelaide. Just to the northeast is the **Barossa Zone**, which includes the BAROSSA VALLEY and EDEN VALLEY regions. The Barossa Valley, along with the HUNTER VALLEY in New South Wales, is Australia's most famous wine region. Just south and slightly west of the Barossa Zone is the **Mount Lofty Ranges Zone**, which includes the CLARE VALLEY, ADELAIDE HILLS, and Adelaide Plains regions. North of the Clare Valley and running northwest to the Spender Gulf is the **Southern Flinder Ranges**, the most northerly of South Australia's wine regions. Father south is the **Fleurieu Zone**, which includes the regions of CURRENCY CREEK, MCLAREN VALE, LANGHORNE CREEK, and **Southern Fleurieu** (all of which are located on the Fleurieu Peninsula), as well as the KANGAROO ISLAND region, which lies 10 miles off the coast. Two other zones, The Peninsulas and Far North, do not have much VITICULTURAL activity at this point. The ADELAIDE zone name can be used on labels for wines that include grapes from the following wine regions in the Adelaide area: Adelaide Hills, Barossa Valley, Clare Valley, Eden Valley, Langhorne Creek, and McLaren Vale. In addition, South Australia grapes can make their way into wines under the gigantic region called SOUTH EASTERN AUSTRALIA that covers three states and parts of two others.

South Coast AVA California VITICULTURAL AREA that includes parts of Orange, Riverside, and San Diego Counties. There are two smaller AVAS (subzones) here—TEMECULA and SAN PASQUAL. The South Coast AVA covers about 115,000 acres with slightly over 3,000 acres of vines, most of which are in the Temecula AVA. The main grape varieties are CHARDONNAY and SAUVIGNON BLANC. Other varieties are CHENIN BLANC, CABERNET SAUVIGNON, RIESLING, MERLOT, ZINFANDEL, PINOT BLANC, and VIOGNIER. There are about twenty wineries in this area.

South Eastern Australia A gigantic Australian zone that incorporates all producing areas in New South Wales, Tasmania, Victoria, and parts of Queensland and South Australia. It essentially covers 95 percent of Australia's vineyards. It allows wine blended from grapes grown in the various indicated regions to use this name on their label.

Southeastern New England AVA Large VITICULTURAL AREA established in 1984 covering 1,875,200 acres in CONNECTICUT, MASSACHUSETTS, and RHODE ISLAND. It starts around Plymouth, Massachusetts, and spreads south and west through Rhode Island and into Connecticut, ending around New Haven. The various bodies of water (like Long Island Sound and Rhode Island Sound) that run along the southern edge of the AVA moderate the region's temperatures, making the climate comparable to the cooler growing regions in France, such as BURGUNDY and the LOIRE. There are over twenty-five wineries in the region growing HYBRIDS like VIDAL BLANC, SEYVAL BLANC, CHANCELLOR, CAYUGA, MARÉCHAL FOCH, and AURORA. VITIS VINIFERA varieties grown here include CHARDONNAY, CABERNET SAUVIGNON, PINOT NOIR, MERLOT, CABERNET FRANC, and RIESLING.

Southern Fleurieu *see* SOUTH AUSTRALIA

Southern Flinder Ranges *see* SOUTH AUSTRALIA

Southern New South Wales Zone *see* NEW SOUTH WALES

Southern Oregon AVA APPELLATION established in February 2005 that encompasses 2,001,430 acres in southwestern Oregon. It extends from about 25 miles south of Eugene for about 125 miles to the California border and includes the APPLEGATE VALLEY, RED HILL DOUGLAS COUNTY, ROGUE VALLEY, and UMPQUA VALLEY sub-appellations. This area is warmer and drier than Oregon's well-known WILLAMETTE VALLEY AVA and although it grows PINOT NOIR, a range of other grape varieties are grown as well. These include CABERNET FRANC, CABERNET SAUVIGNON, CHARDONNAY, GEWÜRZTRAMINER, MERLOT, PINOT GRIS, RIESLING, SYRAH, TEMPRANILLO, and VIOGNIER. There are currently 45 wineries in the AVA and over 3,000 acres of vineyards.

South Tyrol *see* TRENTINO-ALTO ADIGE

South West Coast *see* PEEL

South West Australia Zone *see* WESTERN AUSTRLIA

Southwest France French wine region with about 32,000 vineyard acres located in the country's southwestern quadrant between

BORDEAUX and the Pyrenees. Although technically Bordeaux and COGNAC lie in this quadrant, they are excluded from the description of this area. The Southwest France region, however, does include many other well-known APPELLATIONS. On Bordeaux's eastern flank are BERGERAC AC and the smaller ACS within its boundaries (MONBAZILLAC, MONTRAVEL, PÉCHARMANT, ROSETTE, and SAUSSIGGION), along with the CÔTES DE DURAS AC and the CÔTES DU MARMANDAIS AC. To the southeast of these areas and right next to ARMAGNAC is BUZET AC. To the northeast of Buzet is CAHORS AC and MARCILLAC AC. Heading southeast is GAILLAC AC, which is northeast of Toulouse. Just southwest of it is CÔTES DU FRONTONNAIS AC. In the southwest part of this region are the ACs of PACHERENC DU VIC BILH, MADIRAN, JURANÇON, and BÉARN, and in the far southwest corner, nestled in the Pyrenees Mountains adjacent to the Spanish border, is the IROULÉGUY AC. Joining these ACs are a number of areas with VDQS status. Southwest France is a large area, and there are a variety of climatic conditions, grape VARIETIES, and wine styles produced. Growing areas near Bordeaux grow varieties similar to those cultivated there— CABERNET SAUVIGNON, CABERNET FRANC, MERLOT, MALBEC, PETIT VERDOT, SAUVIGNON BLANC, SÉMILLON, and MUSCADELLE. In other parts of the region, you'll find a unique collection of local varieties including Arrufiac, Baroque, Courbu, Duras, FER, Jurançon, Len de L'elh, Petit and Gros Manseng, Mauzac, Négrette, and Tannat. In general, the red wines are full-bodied (*see* BODY) and slightly ROUGH and TANNIC. White wines range from dry to sweet; some areas produce wines from BOTRYTIS CINEREA-infected grapes that are decent imitations of SAUTERNES wines in good years.

Souzão; Sousão [suh-ZAH-oh; shuh-ZAH-oh] Red-wine grape indigenous to northern Portugal and grown—because of its high acidity, deep color, and concentrated flavors—in the PORT DOC for blending into that region's port wines and in the VINHO VERDE DOC for TABLE WINES. Souzào has also met with great success in California and South Africa, where it's more highly regarded for port production. The official name in Portugal is *Vinhão*; in parts of Spain it's called *Sousón*.

Spain Spain has more vineyard acreage than any other country, but comes in third behind Italy and France in terms of volume of wine produced. The vineyard land is extremely arid in many areas and can't be densely planted because the vines won't get enough moisture. This, plus rather antiquated VITICULTURAL practices, limits YIELDS in most parts of the country. The exception is the area around JEREZ where yields are very high. In the past, aside from SHERRY, the RIOJA DOCA red wines, and the SPARKLING WINES from the CAVA DO (mainly from Penedès in CATALONIA), most of Spain's wines didn't have a following outside the country. This is partially because the old style of many Spanish wines—such as high-ALCOHOL, full-bodied (*see* BODY) reds and neutral, low-ACIDITY whites—weren't popular internationally. But Spain is changing this image. It began by revamping its APPELLATION system, DENOMINACIÓN DE ORIGEN (DO), after criticism that many areas with DO status didn't produce wines of acceptably high quality. A higher classification, DENOMINACIÓN DE ORIGEN CALIFICADA (DOCa), has more exacting standards than those established for DOs. While there are over fifty regions with DO status, only two—RIOJA and PRIORAT—are classified as DOCa. Tighter DO regulations, plus planting in cooler regions, modernizing winery equipment, and improving winemaking techniques have all contributed to improving the overall quality of Spain's wines. Additionally, both red and white wines have benefited because long AGING requirements have been lowered. In the case of white wines, such requirements have been eliminated altogether because extensive oak aging tended to eradicate their freshness and make many seem dull. Conversely, some aged red Riojas are quite highly regarded. Many DOs throughout Spain are notable in their own right. SHERRY is by far Spain's most famous wine and one of the world's classic FORTIFIED WINES. It's produced in Jerez (JEREZ-XÉRÈS-SHERRY Y MANZANILLA DE SANLÚCAR DE BARRAMEDA DO) in a variety of styles. The nearby DOs of MÁLAGA and MONTILLA-MORILES also produce similarly styled fortified wines, which usually sell at lower prices. The Rioja DOCa is still best known for its red wines but is now producing improved white wines, for which it's attaining a good reputation. The white wines from the GALICIA and RUEDA DOs are also gaining stature. Spain's Catalonia area—particularly with the Priorat DOCa, which attracted international attention in the 1990s; the PENEDÈS DO; and potentially with DOs like TARRAGONA—is gaining a reputation for high-quality red and white STILL WINES, in addition to their MÉTHODE CHAMPENOISE sparkling wines. The red wines from the RIBERA DEL DUERO DO have a solid reputation based on the historically renowned Vega Sicilia wine estate and the more recently acclaimed Tinto Pesquera wines from Alejandro Fernandez. Other high-quality wine estates are now also in place in this region. The TORO DO in the Castile and León region is viewed as one of the country's rising stars. Although improvements are underway, large amounts of ordinary wine are still produced from the vast central plains south of Madrid. This includes the wine-producing region of LA MANCHA and the neighboring ALICANTE, JUMILLA, UTIEL-REQUENA, and YECLA regions, as well as CARIÑENA farther north. Some of the other Spanish DOs are ALELLA, ALMANSA, CAMPO DE BORJA,

CONCA DE BARBERÀ, CONDADO DE HUELVA, COSTERS DEL SEGRE, EMPORDÀ-COSTA BRAVA, MENTRIDA, NAVARRA, RÍAS BAIXAS, RIBEIRO, TARRAGONA, TERRA ALTA, VALDEORRAS, VALDEPEÑAS, VALENCIA, and VINOS DE MADRID. A large number of grape varieties are used throughout Spain for the diverse styles of wine. Red varieties include Azal Tinto, Baga, Borracal, Caiño, Cariñena (CARIGNAN), Espadeiro, Ferron, Garnacha Tinta (GRENACHE), GRACIANO, Mazuelo (Carignan), MENCÍA, Monastrell (MOURVÈDRE), Moreto, Pansá Rosado, TEMPRANILLO (also called *Cencibel, Ull de Llebre,* and *Tinto del Pais*), and Tinta Pinheira. The most widely planted white variety in Spain and, in fact, the world is AIRÉN. Other white varieties in this country include Albariño (ALVARINHO), Garnacha Blanca (Grenache), Godello (VERDELHO), LOUREIRO, Malvar, MALVASIA, Merseguera, Moscatel (MUSCAT), PALOMINO, PARELLADA, PEDRO XIMÉNEZ, Planta Nova, Torrontés, Trajadura, Treixadura, Verdil, Viura (MACABEO), and XAREL-LO (also called *Pansá Blanca*). In addition, there are some plantings of French favorites including CABERNET SAUVIGNON, CABERNET FRANC, CHARDONNAY, MALBEC, MERLOT, PINOT NOIR, and SAUVIGNON BLANC.

Spanna *see* NEBBIOLO

sparkling *see* SPARKLING WINE

sparkling Burgundy In France, sparkling Burgundies are always the lower-quality wines—red, white or rosé—that are processed by either MÉTHODE CHAMPENOISE or the CHARMAT PROCESS. In the United States, this term usually describes an inexpensive, lower-quality red wine made by the charmat process.

sparkling wine Wine that contains bubbles of CARBON DIOXIDE gas. There are generally four methods to infuse wine with gas. MÉTHODE CHAMPENOISE is the traditional method used in France's CHAMPAGNE region and other countries that make fine sparkling wine. With this method, a second fermentation takes place in the bottle, thereby creating carbon dioxide that permeates the wine. The TRANSFER METHOD is similar to *méthode champenoise* except the RIDDLING and DISGORGEMENT processes are replaced by conveying the wine through a pressurized filtration system and then rebottling it. The CHARMAT PROCESS, also called *bulk process* or *cuve close,* uses large pressurized tanks throughout production. These interconnecting tanks retain the pressure created during a second fermentation throughout the entire process. A fourth method, called CARBONATION, injects carbon dioxide directly into the wine. This last method is the least successful in creating effervescence and is used only for very inexpensive wines. Sparkling wines are measured for pressure in ATMOSPHERES (atm). Technically, an atm is the normal air pressure at sea level, approximately 14.7 pounds per square inch. Sparkling wines such as champagne or SPUMANTE should have 6 atm of pressure. A CRÉMANT-style sparkling wine has about half that pressure, and some FRIZZANTE-style Italian wines may have only 2 atm of pressure. *See also* Opening and Serving Wine at Home, page 636.

Spätburgunder *see* PINOT NOIR

Spätlese [SHPAYT-lay-zuh] German for "late picking," this wine term refers to grapes that are selectively picked at least 7 days after the main harvest starts for that specific variety. Because such fruit is riper than the grapes from the main harvest, it contains more sugar and produces wines that are richer. Spätlese is one of the six subcategories of QUALITÄTSWEIN MIT PRÄDIKAT (QmP) and ranks above KABINETT but below AUSLESE, BEERENAUSLESE, EISWEIN, and TROCKENBEERENAUSLESE. To attain the Spätlese category, the natural sugar content of the grapes must reach a certain minimum—76° to 95° OECHSLE, approximately 19 to 23 percent sugar by weight, depending on the region and the variety. The selective picking process makes Spätlese wines quite expensive. AUSTRIA has a Spätlese category that's similar and requires a minimum 94° OECHSLE.

Special Late Harvested *see* LATE HARVEST

Special Reserve *see* RESERVE

specific gravity The ratio of the density of a substance (such as MUST or wine) to the density of pure water, measured by an instrument called a HYDROMETER. A liquid with precisely the same density as water has a specific gravity (s.g.) reading of 1.000. If it's denser than water (as would be the case if sugar is present), its reading will be over 1.000. When grape juice begins to ferment—converting the sugar into alcohol—the specific gravity drops because the s.g. of pure ALCOHOL is 0.792—lower than that of water. Therefore, a DRY wine, which contains little or no sugar, would have a specific gravity reading below 1.000. In the United States, specific gravity is measured on the BRIX scale, in Germany on the OECHSLE scale, and in France on the BAUMÉ scale.

spicy *see* Glossary of Wine Tasting Terms, page 655

Spiegelberg *see* NIERSTEIN

Spielberg *see* BAD DÜRKHEIM

Spiess *see* RUPPERTSBERG

spinning cone; spinning cone column A process for lowering the alcohol level in wine that utilizes a stainless steel column with alternating rotating and stationary cones. It uses a form of vacuum distillation whereby the spinning column creates centrifugal force that forces the wine into a very thin layer. As this is happening an inert gas such as nitrogen is released in the bottom of the column and as it passes by this thin layer the gas strips the wine of volatile compounds which are then condensed and stored. A second pass is made during which alcohol is removed. Then the volatile compounds (which contain flavor and aroma elements) are added back to the wine. The spinning cone process is said to allow alcohol removal at lower temperatures, thus limiting heat-related damage to the wine. *See also* REVERSE OSMOSIS; WATERING BACK.

spitzenwein [SHPIHTS-ehn-vine] The Austrian term for "top-quality wine."

split *see* Wine Bottles, page 609

Spring Mountain District AVA This APPELLATION is situated on Spring Mountain in NAPA VALLEY just west of the town of St. Helena. Although Spring Mountain (part of the Mayacamas Range that separates Napa from SONOMA COUNTY) was a fashionable growing area prior to PROHIBITION, it's only been in the last 25 to 30 years that some of these vineyards and wineries have been reestablished. The 8,600-acre area has a diversity of MESOCLIMATES, which allow CABERNET SAUVIGNON, CHARDONNAY, MERLOT, PETITE SIRAH, PINOT NOIR, SYRAH, and ZINFANDEL to do well here.

spritzer [SPRIHT-ser] A tall, chilled drink, customarily made with wine and soda water.

spritzig *see* Glossary of Wine Tasting Terms, page 655

spritzy *see* Glossary of Wine Tasting Terms, page 655

spumante; pl. spumanti [spoo-MAHN-tay; spoo-MAHN-tee] Italian for "sparkling," "foamy," or "frothy," referring to fully sparkling wines, as opposed to those that are slightly sparkling (FRIZZANTE). Spumante is made throughout Italy from a variety of different grapes either by the Metodo Classico (MÉTHODE CHAMPENOISE) or by using an AUTOCLAVE (sealed tanks). The most renowned of the spumanti are the sweet ASTI DOCG wines from the PIEDMONT region, which are made from the MUSCAT grape and the FRANCIACORTA DOCG wines from the LOMBARDY region, which are made from combinations of Pinot Bianco (PINOT

BLANC), CHARDONNAY, Pinot Grigio (PINOT GRIS), and Pinot Nero (PINOT NOIR).

spur Viticulture term referring to a CANE that's pruned back so that it has less than 5 NODES (usually just two or three). A spur-trained vine will have several spurs, some of which are multiple years old. This contrasts to the cane-trained vine where the canes are never more than one year old. The spurs are somewhat permanent (although they may be pruned if they are interfering with the proper growth of the vine) and these permanent branches are called CORDONS.

St. *see listings under* SAINT

staatliche weinbaudomänen *see* STATE DOMAINS

staatsweingüter *see* STATE DOMAINS

stabilization A process that clears a wine of tartrates and small protein particles that might cause it to be cloudy or contain small crystals and may also elimitate problematic microorganisms that cause difficulties once the wine is bottled. **Heat stabilization** is a process for ensuring that wine doesn't develop a haziness or cloudiness when stored at warm temperatures. It's usually accomplished by FINING with an agent such as BENTONITE just prior to bottling. Fining collects the minute particles that cause cloudiness and settles them to the bottom of the storage vessel. The wine is then RACKED to separate the clear wine from the SEDIMENT. **Cold stabilization** is a method of removing tartrates by storing wine at a very low temperature (26 to 32°F) for up to 3 weeks. The flavorless tartrates, which are removed only for aesthetic purposes, fall to the bottom at such cool temperatures, leaving the wine clear. Sterile filtration (*see* FILTERING), using extremely fine membrane filters, helps eliminate problematic microorganisms.

Stags Leap District AVA Situated north of the town of Napa along the Silverado Trail, this California AVA WAS established in 1989 within the NAPA VALLEY AVA. It runs from the Yountville Crossing south for about 3 miles. Its name comes from an outcropping of red rocks at the area's eastern end, where a stag supposedly escaped his pursuers by leaping across the treacherous gap. This 2,700-acre area comprises the right soil and climate to make superb CABERNET SAUVIGNON wines. MERLOT is planted here as well, but CHARDONNAY is losing acreage as growers increasingly turn to Cabernet Sauvignon.

stainless steel tanks Large, enclosed containers used by modern wineries for the FERMENTATION and AGING of wine. Stainless steel tanks are extremely efficient and cost-effective. Most are double-jacketed, circulating coolant between the inner and outer walls. This allows winemakers to adjust the tank's temperature so that they can manage the fermentation speed. Stainless steel tanks are extremely easy to clean and very sanitary, both desirable attributes in winemaking. Because stainless steel is a relatively neutral material that doesn't impart flavors, the tanks preserve the fruit's fresh flavors. Some tanks have automated pump-over systems or mechanical punch-down devices that enhance the winemaking process. Wineries rely on these tanks not only for the fermentation process but also for bulk storage and blending. Wines that don't receive oak AGING (such as many whites and some fruity reds) are typically kept in stainless steel tanks until bottling.

stale *see* Glossary of Wine Tasting Terms, page 655

stalky *see* STEMMY in the Glossary of Wine Tasting Terms, page 655

Starkenburg, Bereich *see* HESSISCHE BERGSTRASSE

starter A term used for a YEAST culture added to fresh grape MUST to "start" the FERMENTATION process. Many winemakers use commercially developed yeast cultures with specific characteristics to ensure that fermentation proceeds in a desired fashion.

state domains Scattered throughout Germany are a number of state-owned wine estates, which, in addition to conducting research, produce commerically available wines. State domains (called a *Staatsweingüter* or *Staatlichen Weinbaudomänen*) were established by the King of Prussia in the late 1800s and early 1900s. The best known are **Staatsweingüter Eltville** (with acreage in the RHEINGAU and HESSICHE BERGSTRASSE regions), **Staatliche Weinbaudomäne Trier** (which owns vineyards in the MOSEL-SAAR-RUWER region), and **Staatliche Weinbaudomäne Niderhausen-Schlossböckelheim** (which is in the NAHE region). The quality of the wines from the state domains is quite high, a surprise to those wary of government-run operations. The gold-rimmed state-domain labels display a black and gold eagle.

steely *see* Glossary of Wine Tasting Terms, page 655

Steen *see* CHENIN BLANC

Steigerwald, Bereich *see* FRANKEN

Stein *see* CHENIN BLANC; HOCKHEIM; WÜRZBURG

Steinacker *see* KALLSTADT

Steinberg *see* KLOSTER EBERBACH

Steinfeder [SHTINE-fee-duh] A specialty wine category of Lower Austria's Wachau area. Steinfeder wines are light-bodied and fruity and have an alcohol content of between 10 and 10.7 percent. They should be drunk young.

Steinmächer *see* RAUENTHAL

Steinmorgen *see* ERBACH

Steinweg *see* BAD KREUZNACH

Steinwein *see* FRANKEN

Stellenbosch WO An important demarcated wine district in SOUTH AFRICA that is part of the Coastal Region. It's located about 30 miles east of Cape Town around the beautiful college town of Stellenbosch. In addition to being one of the premier grape-growing areas, it contains several wine-related research and teaching institutions. The climate in the Stellenbosch WO varies considerably—the ocean cools those areas close to False Bay, while inland locales are warmer because they're protected from ocean breezes. Stellenbosch has long held an excellent reputation for red wines, and red varieties make up about 60 percent of the vineyard acreage. The best in this category are CABERNET SAUVIGNON, MERLOT, Shiraz (SYRAH), and PINOTAGE. The most widely planted white variety is CHENIN BLANC, followed closely by SAUVIGNON BLANC, and then CHARDONNAY. In addition to creating some of South Africa's top reds, Stellenbosch WO also produces first-class Chardonnays and Sauvignon Blancs. This area contains almost 42,000 acres, just under 16 percent of the nation's total. A large number of important wine estates are located here. Some, like Meerlust Estate, Rustenberg Wines, and Spier Cellars, date back to the late 1600s.

stemmer A device for separating grape stems from the crushed grapes. *See also* CRUSHER.

Stelvin *see* SCREW CAPS

stemmy *see* Glossary of Wine Tasting Terms, page 655

stem retention A technique used by some winemakers in the making of red wine (particularly PINOT NOIR) where some of the grape stems are added back into the MUST in order to make the wine richer, as well as more TANNIC and VISCOUS. The risk with this process is in making the wine too ASTRINGENT.

stemware *see* Glassware, page 647

sterile filtering *see* FILTERING

steward, wine *see* SOMMELIER

stickie *see* Glossary of Wine Tasting Terms, page 655

still wine A descriptor for wine that contains no CARBON DIOXIDE, which would make it sparkling or effervescent.

stoppers *see* CLOSURES

storing wine *see* WINE CELLAR

Strathbogie Ranges *see* CENTRAL VICTORIAN HIGH COUNTRY

Stravecchia *see* MARSALA DOC

straw wine *see* VIN DE PAILLE; STROHWEIN

Strohwein Austrian for "straw wine," referring to a subcategory in their highest wine category, PRÄDIKATSWEIN. Wines are made from grapes reaching a minimum natural sugar level of 127° OECHSLE. This is achieved by drying the grapes on straw mats or trays. The dried grapes are full of sweet, concentrated juice.

strong *see* POWERFUL in the Glossary of Wine Tasting Terms, page 655

structure *see* Glossary of Wine Tasting Terms, page 655

stuck fermentation *see* FERMENTATION

sturdy *see* Glossary of Wine Tasting Terms, page 655

Sturm *see* FEDERWEISSER

Styria *see* AUSTRIA

Les Suchots *see* VOSNE-ROMANÉE AC

Südlich Weinstrasse *see* PFALZ

Südtirol *see* ALTO ADIGE

sugaring *see* CHAPTALIZATION

sugar measurement *see* MUST WEIGHT; SPECIFIC GRAVITY

sugar wine A "wine"—sometimes called **false** or **second wine**—made by adding sugar, water, and tartaric acid (*see* ACIDS) to the POMACE after the true wine has all been PRESSED from it. The pomace still contains yeasts, which cause FERMENTATION to begin. The result is a much lighter version of the real wine. It's illegal for commercial wineries to make and sell sugar wines.

Suisun Valley AVA A 15,360-acre VITICULTURAL AREA established in 1982 in Solano County, California. Its western border runs along the GREEN VALLEY SOLANO COUNTY AVA border, the western part of its northern border runs along the NAPA COUNTY-Solano County line, and in the south it goes to the Suisun Bay marshlands. Although the area has some coastal cooling, it is fairly hot here, which classifies it a mid-Region III rating (*see* CLIMATE REGIONS OF CALIFORNIA). There are a number of growers here and one winery, Wooden Valley Winery.

sulfites; sulfiting [SUHL-fites] Sulfites, the salts of sulfurous acid, have been used to preserve food and drink for eons. Today sulfites can be found in everything from beer to cookies to pickles. All but a tiny fraction of wines made today contain sulfites, small amounts of which are a natural by-product of FERMENTATION. Additionally, winemakers around the world prevent spoilage and OXIDATION by adding controlled amounts of SULFUR DIOXIDE in a process called **sulfiting**. In the United States, the words "Contains Sulfites" are mandatory on wine labels if the wine contains 10 ppm (parts per million) or more of sulfites. The upper limit is 350 ppm, but most wines contain less than 150 ppm. Sulfites can cause allergic reactions in certain sulfite-sensitive individuals. The number of individuals affected is small and the allergic reaction will probably be a breathing problem. It's unlikely that sulfites are the cause of headaches that some people get from drinking red wine. Although not fully understood, headaches are thought to result from either the histamines or tannins that are more prevalent in red wines than white wines.

sulfur; sulphur *see* Glossary of Wine Tasting Terms, page 655

sulfur dioxide (SO₂) A colorless, water-soluble, nonflammable gas used viticulturally in small, controlled amounts through a process called sulfiting. Winemakers use sulfur dioxide in a variety of ways. Grapevines can be sprayed with it to deter many insects and diseases. After the grapes are crushed, sulfur dioxide is used to inhibit the growth of bacteria, mold, and wild yeasts in MUST. It's also used to prevent spoilage or OXIDATION in the finished wine. There are several ways to introduce sulfur dioxide. It can be added to wine as a gas or as POTASSIUM METABISULFITE, often in the form of Campden tablets. It reacts with the natural acids in grapes to create sulfur dioxide gas. **Sulfur wicks** can be burned to create sulfur dioxide in empty or partially filled wine barrels to prevent the growth of mold. During such processes, some sulfur dioxide combines with the wine, in which case it's called **fixed** (or **bound**) **sulfur dioxide;** it has no odor so isn't noticeable. **Free sulfur dioxide** is that which doesn't combine with wine. Excessive amounts of it can produce an undesirable trait indicated by a slight biting sensation at the back of the throat and in the upper part of the nose. **Total sulfur dioxide** includes all bound and free sulfur dioxide in wine, the allowed amounts of which are regulated by law. *See also* HYDROGEN SULFIDE; ORGANIC WINE; SULFITES.

Sultana [suhl-TAN-uh] Originating in Smyrna, Turkey, this small, pale golden-green grape is the most widely planted variety in California. There it's known as *Thompson Seedless,* after William Thompson, the first commercial Sultana grower in California. In the United States, during the white-wine boom of the 1970s, Sultana was widely used for winemaking. Today, however, varieties like FRENCH COLOMBARD and CHENIN BLANC have diminished Sultana's role. In California, Sultana's use for winemaking ranks third behind its demand first as a raisin and then as a table grape. Sultana is also widely grown in Australia and Chile. It produces a neutral-flavored wine used in JUG WINES and inexpensive SPARKLING WINES.

Sumarello *see* UVA DI TROIA

summer pruning *see* PRUNING

Sunbury An Australian wine region located in the Port Phillip Zone of VICTORIA. It's situated about 20 to 25 miles northwest of Melbourne around the town of Sunbury. This region is just south of the MACEDON RANGES region and was once grouped with that region. It is much flatter than the Macedon Ranges but is similarly affected by strong winds and is therefore a cool growing region (but not as cool as the Macedon Ranges). This allows Shiraz (SYRAH) to do very well as evidenced by the wines from Craiglee. CHARDONNAY, PINOT NOIR, and CABERNET FRANC also like the cool weather, although there's not much of the latter two VARIETIES planted. Although CABERNET SAUVIGNON grapes are planted here, to be successful they require a good vineyard location and warmer years. SAUVIGNON BLANC and SÉMILLON are also grown in this area. There are just over 200 acres of vineyards in the Sunbury region.

supérieur [soo-pehr-YUR] A French term indicating a somewhat higher-quality wine than the standard. This ranking is generally expressed as a requirement for a slightly higher ALCOHOL content and slightly lower maximum vineyard YIELDS (the latter produces more intense flavors). For example, the BORDEAUX SUPÉRIEUR AC requires a minimum alcohol level of 10½ percent, versus 10 percent for BOR-DEAUX AC, and BEAJOLAIS-SUPÉRIEUR AC wines must be 1 percent higher in alcohol than those of BEAJOLAIS AC. The maximum vineyard yield for Bordeaux Supérieur AC is set about 20 percent lower than that for the Bordeaux AC.

Superior Old Marsala (SOM) *see* MARSALA DOC

superiore [soo-payr-YOH-reh] Italian for "superior." On an Italian wine label, "superiore" indicates a DOC wine that has a slightly higher alcoholic strength and, sometimes, longer aging capabilities than other DOC wines. The higher alcohol content is due to riper grapes, which results in a fuller flavored and, therefore, superior wine.

super seconds An unofficial term referring to some of BORDEAUX'S most lauded DEUXIÈME CRUS (second growths), some of which are so highly regarded that they're considered as good as (sometimes better than) the PREMIER CRUS (first growths). Most times, the prices of the super seconds are less than that of their higher-ranking relatives. Some of the most highly sought after super seconds Châteaux are Cos d'Estournel, Pichon-Longueville Comtesse de Lalande, Pichon Longueville Baron, Leoville-Las-Cases, Ducru-Beaucaillou, and Palmer (although the latter is actually a third growth, it's usually included in this group). *See also* Official Wine Classifications of Bordeaux, page 678.

super Tuscan Term that came into vogue in the late 1980s when several red wines from TUSCANY began attracting international attention. These superlative wines had to be labeled VINO DA TAVOLA (table wines), though in some cases they were superior to DOCG and DOC wines and able to command higher prices. But such wines were ineligible for Italy's top classifications because they were produced using either unauthorized varieties (like CABERNET SAUVIGNON and MERLOT), an unapproved composition (such as 100 percent SANGIOVESE in areas where it wasn't approved), or unsanctioned methods (like using small, nontraditional oak barrels for aging). And so the problem became what to call wines of superior quality that didn't meet official premium wine designations—"super Tuscans" fit the bill. Although most super Tuscans are still sold as "vino da tavola," in the mid-1990s, the Italian government granted some of the top super Tuscans their own DOC status. For example, Sassicaia may now be labeled "Bolgheri Sassicaia DOC" (*see* BOLGHERI DOC). Other super Tuscans are La Brancaia, Camartina, Casalferro, Cepparello, Felciaia, Fontalloro, Grattamacco Rosso, Guado al Tasso, Luce, Lupicaia, Olmaia, Ornellaia, Paleo Rosso, Saffredi, Sassello, Solaia, Summus, and Tignanello.

supple *see* Glossary of Wine Tasting Terms, page 655

surdo [SOOR-dhoo] Surdo, sometimes called *vinho surdo,* is the Portuguese term for grape juice that has been prevented from FERMENTING by the addition of ALCOHOL. None of the grape sugar has been converted to alcohol, so surdo is very sweet. It's used to sweeten other wines, particularly MADEIRA. The French MISTELLE is a similar solution.

Sur la Velle *see* MONTHÉLIE

sur lie [soor LEE] The French expression for "on the lees." LEES is the coarse sediment, which consists mainly of dead yeast cells and small grape particles that accumulate during fermentation. Winemakers believe that certain wines benefit from being aged *sur lie.* CHARDONNAY or SAUVIGNON BLANC wines are thought to gain complexity if aged in this way for a few months. This happens as a matter of course with SPARKLING WINES made via MÉTHODE CHAMPENOISE because the second fermentation occurs in the bottle where the wine is aged (sometimes for up to 10 years) until the lees are DISGORGED. MUSCADET wines from France's LOIRE region occasionally have the phrase "*mis en bouteille sur lie*" on the label, which means the wine was bottled from barrels where the lees were not drained (although the sediment has fallen to the bottom of the barrel). These wines have a creamy, yeasty flavor and a touch of CARBON DIOXIDE, which gives a slight prickling sensation on the tongue. *See also* AUTOLYSIS.

surmaturité; sur maturité *see* Glossary of Wine Tasting Terms, page 655

Suser *see* FEDERWEISSER

Süssreserve; Süss-Reserve [sooss-ray-ZEHR-veh] German for "sweet reserve," referring to unfermented grape juice that's set aside to be added later to fully fermented (DRY) wines in order to achieve the desired level of sweetness. The Germans developed this technique so that winemakers don't have to be so exacting about arresting FERMENTATION in order to control RESIDUAL SUGAR. The procedure also lowers the use of SULFUR DIOXIDE, which is often employed to stop fermentation. There are strict rules about using *Süssreserve,* including limiting its volume to 15 percent of the final wine and ensuring that its origin and quality are the same as the wine to which it's added.

sustainable viticulture A system of growing wine grapes that is still evolving. Simply put, viticulture is economically viable, socially supportive, and ecologically sound. Sustainable agriculture evolved out of several movements, including organic farming. The American Agronomy Society adopted the following definition for sustainable agriculture in 1989: "A sustainable agriculture is one that, over the long term, enhances environmental quality and the resource base on which agriculture depends; provides for basic human food and fiber needs; is economically viable and enhances the quality of life for farmers and society as a whole." At UC Davis, the Sustainable Agriculture Research and Education Program (UC SAREP) emphasizes that sustainable agriculture integrates three major goals—environmental health, economic profitability, and social and economic equity. Congress passed a farm bill in 1990 that defined sustainable agriculture as "an integrated system of plant and animal production practices having a site-specific application that will, over the long term: 1) satisfy human food and fiber needs, 2) enhance environmental quality and the natural resource base upon which the agricultural economy depends, 3) make the most efficient use of nonrenewable resources and on-farm resources and integrate, where appropriate, natural biological cycles and controls, 4) sustain the economic viability of farm operations, and 5) enhance the quality of life for farmers and society as a whole." The practices that meet these objectives are still evolving and have many different interpretations but take into account issues such as irrigation management, soil management, nutrition management, pest management, weed management, pesticide use, disease control, and pruning practices.

Suvereto *see* VAL DI CORNIA DOC

Swan District An Australian wine region located in the Greater Perth Zone of WESTERN AUSTRALIA, situated just north of Perth around the Swan River and its tributaries, primarily in the Swan Valley. This area's VITICULTURAL history dates back to the 1830s with the establishment of Olive Farm, believed to be Australia's oldest continuous use winery. The very hot climate and the valley's flat plain provide an ideal grape-growing environment. In fact, the Swan Valley was the most important winegrowing area in Western Australia over a hundred years, growing both table grapes and grapes for FORTIFIED WINES. Unfortunately, as the demand for fortified wines waned, so did the demand for the region's other wines. Today the Swan District is adapting to the changing times, choosing grapes that thrive in this environment and sourcing fruit from other areas like MARGARET RIVER. Almost 75 percent of the grapes grown here are white VARIETIES—CHENIN BLANC leads production with about half of that total. It's followed by VERDELHO, CHARDONNAY, SÉMILLON, MUS-

CADELLE, and SAUVIGNON BLANC. The top red grape is Shiraz (SYRAH), followed by CABERNET SAUVIGNON, GRENACHE, and MERLOT. Area wineries produce some very interesting Chenin Blanc wines, even though the climate is far different from that of the cool LOIRE, home to the grape. Dominating this region's winemaking in both quantity and quality is Houghton, owned by BRL Hardy.

Swan Hill Large, productive Australian wine region situated about 235 miles northwest of Melbourne; the main town in the area is Swan Hill. It straddles the Murray River, with vineyards in both the Big Rivers Zone of NEW SOUTH WALES and the North West Victoria Zone of VICTORIA. The climate in this region is hot and dry, which means vineyards require constant irrigation, which is provided by a system first developed in the late 1800s. Irrigation's turned this vast, hot, arid area into a garden spot not only for grapes but also for lots of other produce. Vines here are vigorous, producing high YIELDS and generally less than the highest-quality wines. Most grapes are destined for Australia's inexpensive and popular bag-in-box (or cask) wines. The wine regions along the Murray River—Swan Hill; the MURRAY DARLING region, just northwest; and the RIVERLAND region, west of Murray Darling in SOUTH AUSTRALIA—generate 50 percent of Australia's wine production. SULTANA, MUSCAT, CHARDONNAY, and COLUMBARD are the most widely planted varieties. There is considerable Shiraz (SYRAH) acreage, as well as CABERNET SAUVIGNON.

sweet *see* Glossary of Wine Tasting Terms, page 655

sweetness Sweetness is detected on the very tip of the tongue and, in wine, comes from RESIDUAL SUGAR or, occasionally, from GLYCEROL, a by-product of FERMENTATION. The sugar may be intrinsic (from the grapes) or supplemental (as by adding GRAPE CONCENTRATE) or both. Some fine sweet wines (such as BEERENAUSLESE) are made from grapes that have been left on the vine until they're so overripe that the fruit is sugar-laden and full of rich, concentrated flavors. The juice from such grapes contains more sugar than can be fermented out. Whether or not sweetness in a wine is pleasant or cloying depends on the balance between ACIDITY and sugar. Though the term *sweet* generally applies to the sense of taste, certain components—such as oakiness, which contributes a sweet vanilla essence, or intense fruitiness—can give wine a seemingly sweet smell. *See also* SWEET in Glossary of Wine Tasting Terms, page 655.

sweet reserve *see* SÜSSRESERVE

Switzerland Although Switzerland produces a reasonable amount of wine and ranks as one of the top twenty wine-producing countries, few Swiss wines are seen outside the country. There are several reasons for this including the fact that the Swiss consume between 2½ and 3 times what they produce. Their wines are also generally expensive by international standards, and they produce many wines that are specialized for the Swiss market and not widely accepted elsewhere. Like its culture, Switzerland's growing areas can be segmented into French-, German-, and Italian-speaking cantons. The French-speaking cantons include the primary vineyard areas of VAUD and VALAIS, and Geneva, the only canton to introduce a comprehensive APPELLATION system. (Vaud has introduced a less-strict version.) The most productive German-speaking cantons are Zürich and Schaffhausen. The most notable Italian-speaking canton is the TICINO or *Tessin.* CHASSELAS (also known as *Dorin, Fendant,* and *Perlan* in various parts of Switzerland) is Switzerland's most widely planted white grape. Generally, it produces neutral, low-ACIDITY, low-ALCOHOL wines that reflect the flavor of the soil in which they're grown. The Swiss like Chasselas wines, although they're not popular outside the country. Red wines are made predominantly with PINOT NOIR and GAMAY grapes, which are often blended together into a wine called Dôle (*see* VALAIS). In the Italian areas, MERLOT is the most popular red grape. Other varieties grown in Switzerland include Amigne, Arvine, BARBERA, FREISA, Humagne, Johannisberger (RIESLING), Malvoisie de Valais (PINOT GRIS), PINOT BLANC, and Riesling-Sylvaner (MÜLLER-THURGAU).

Sylvaner; Silvaner [sihl-VAN-uhr; sihl-VAH-ner; Ger. zihl-vah-nehr] This productive white-wine grape was once the most widely planted vine in Germany (where it's spelled *Silvaner*) but has now been replaced by the prolific MÜLLER-THURGAU (long thought to be a Riesling/Sylvaner HYBRID but recently found to be unrelated to Sylvaner). However, Sylvaner is still extensively cultivated in Germany, particularly in RHEINHESSEN, PFALZ, and FRANKEN. Although this grape is believed to have originated in Austria, very little is planted there now. The extensive plantings once found in France's ALSACE region have now also dwindled, and only small amounts of Sylvaner come out of Switzerland and northern Italy. California—where Sylvaner is variously called *Sylvaner Riesling, Franken Riesling, Monterey Riesling,* and *Sonoma Riesling*—has all but abandoned this variety. Sylvaner grapes generally produce LIGHT, SOFT wines with noticeable ACIDITY and pleasant but not pronounced AROMA and flavor. Some of today's best Sylvaner wines derive from Alsace, Franken (where this variety is often called *Franken Riesling*), northern Italy, and Switzerland (where it's also called *Johannisberger*). The correct name for this grape is actually *Grüner Sylvaner,* differentiating it from the rarely grown, pale-red strain called *Blauer Sylvaner.* Other names for Sylvaner include *Osterreicher* and *Gentil Vert.*

Sylvos *see* TRELLIS SYSTEM

Symphony [SIHM-fuh-nee] A CROSS between Muscat of Alexandria (MUSCAT) and Grenache Gris, Symphony was developed by the UNIVERSITY OF CALIFORNIA, DAVIS and introduced in 1981. Symphony has met with limited acceptance and is therefore planted in limited amounts. Symphony wines have a hint of spiciness and sometimes show apricot and peach characteristics. Château de Baun in SONOMA is the best-known producer of a variety of Symphony wines—from DRY to sweet and from STILL to SPARKLING. This winery's known for the musical names of their various Symphony wines such as *Finale, Rhapsody Rosé,* and *Jazz.*

synthetic closures *see* CLOSURES

Syrah [see-RAH] This high-quality red-wine grape gained its reputation in France's RHÔNE region. The ancient Syrah grape has been grown in the Rhône valley at least since Roman times. In 1998, DNA testing indicated that Syrah's parents were the Dureza and the MONDEUSE BLANCHE varieties (both from southeastern France) and analysts deduced that Syrah originated in the northern Rhône instead of the Middle East as had long been thought. In the northern Rhône, Syrah is the principal grape of the esteemed wines from CORNAS, CÔTE-RÔTIE, CROZES-HERMITAGE, HERMITAGE, and SAINT-JOSEPH. When young, these wines are deep-colored and TANNIC, with strong TAR, SPICE, and PEPPER qualities. Syrahs are long-lived, and as they slowly mature, they take on characteristics of sweet blackberries, blackcurrants, and plums, with hints of SMOKINESS. In the southern Rhône, Syrah is used to contribute flavor and STRUCTURE to the multivariety WINES from CHÂTEAUNEUF-DU-PAPE and CÔTES-DU-RHÔNE. France's LANGUEDOC ROUSSILLON region has been planting large amounts of new Syrah acreage because it's one of the grapes recommended for improving the quality of that region's wines. *Shiraz,* as Syrah is called in Australia, made its way there in the 1830s and is now that country's most widely planted red grape. Because this grape's so widely cultivated in Australia, an extensive variety of wine styles are produced there—from JUG WINES to very serious wines of international renown. The best of these auspicious wines come from COONAWARRA and the BAROSSA and

HUNTER VALLEYS. The most famous Shiraz is the incredibly rich and complex GRANGE HERMITAGE, produced by Penfolds. In California, the PETITE SIRAH grape was long thought to be Syrah, but some ENOLOGISTS now believe it actually may be the DURIF variety (a CROSS between Syrah and a variety called Peloursin). True Syrah has been increasingly planted in California over the years, and there are now many more Syrah wines and Rhône-style blends appearing on retail shelves. Syrah has not significantly established itself in other parts of the world. It's also known as *Hermitage, Marsanne Noir, Petite Syrah,* and *Sirac.*

syrupy *see* Glossary of Wine Tasting Terms, page 655

szamorodni [sah-moh-RAHD-nee] Hungarian label term meaning "as it comes." It refers to the fact that nothing is added to the wine—usually only ASZÚ paste (*see* TOKAJI) is used for sweetening. These wines are therefore generally DRY or semisweet rather than sweet.

száras [sah-RAHSS] Hungarian for "DRY."

Szekszárd [SEHK-sahrd] Wine region in southern HUNGARY with a winemaking tradition that goes back to at least the ninth century. KADARKA was long the most popular red-grape variety, but it is no longer as other red varieties such as BLAUFRÄNKISCH, CABERNET FRANC, CABERNET SAUVIGNON, MERLOT, PINOT NOIR, and Zweigelt have been planted. White varieties include CHARDONNAY, Italian Riesling (WELSCHRIESLING), PINOT BLANC, PINOT GRIS, RIESLING, Rizlingszilváni (MÜLLER-THURGAU), SAUVIGNON BLANC, and Tramini (GEWÜRZTRAMINER).

Szükerbarát *see* PINOT GRIS

T **table wine** 1. Any wine that isn't FORTIFIED or SPARKLING. 2. In the United States, the official definition for table wine is a wine that contains a minimum of 7 percent alcohol and a maximum of 14 percent. This definition does not define quality in any way, although some connote table wine with lower-quality, inexpensive wine. That's a mistake because many wines that simply say "Red Table Wine" or "White Table Wine" are excellent and not at all inexpensive. 3. The EUROPEAN UNION has developed a meaning that indentifies table wine as something that doesn't qualify as a quality wine under the various APPELLATION rules. In most cases, this means that table wine is probably of lower quality, but some independent producers feel the appellation rules are too restrictive. They produce some very high-quality wines labeled as table wine that just don't happen to be made exactly as the rules dictate. European synonyms for table wine include Germany's DEUTSCHER TAFELWEIN, France's VIN DE TABLE, Italy's VINO DA TAVOLA, Portugal's VINHO DE MESA, and Spain's VINO DE MESA.

La Tâche AC [lah TAHSH] A GRAND CRU vineyard that produces what some consider to be the epitome of a red BURGUNDY wine. Some even rank it ahead of that of the neighboring ROMANÉE-CONTI. The nearly 15-acre vineyard is located in the village of VOSNE-ROMANÉE in the CÔTE DE NUITS. La Tache produces more wine than the $4\frac{1}{2}$-acre Romanée-Conti, and its prices are not quite as high (although they're still some of the most expensive wines in the world). Like Romanée-Conti, La Tâche is wholly owned by the Domaine de la Romanée-Conti. When young, La Tâche AC wines are RICHER, more intense, and more deeply colored than those from the Romanée-Conti vineyard, and they possess some of the latter's exotic spiciness.

Tacoronte-Acentejo DO *see* CANARY ISLANDS

Tafelstein *see* DIENHEIM

Tafelwein [TAH-fuhl-vyn] Lowest category of wine in countries like AUSTRIA and GERMANY. *See also* DEUTSCHER TAFELWEIN.

taglio [TAH-lyoh] Italian for "cut." A *vino da taglio* is a "cutting wine"—one with high ALCOHOL, deep color, and/or good BODY. Such wines are added in small quantities to other wines either to correct their deficiencies or to enhance them in some way.

taille [TI] A term used in France's CHAMPAGNE region to describe the juice produced from the second and third PRESSING of the grapes. The juice from the second pressing is called *premiere taille;* the third pressing is *deuxieme taille*. Both are considered lower quality than VIN DE CUVÉE (the juice from the first pressing) and are either used in lower-quality wines or sold off.

Talia *see* TREBBIANO

Tamyanka *see* MUSCAT

Tannat [tah-nah] Red-wine grape thought to have originated in the Basque region of France. It's the principal VARIETY used in the ROUGH, TANNIC wines of MADIRAN AC. Tannat's also grown in other French regions such as the BÉARN and IROULÉGUY ACS, and the Tursan VDQS. It's very TANNIC (hence it's name) and is usually blended with CABERNET FRANC, CABERNET SAUVIGNON, and FER to SOFTEN the resulting wines. Efforts to soften the tannins in this grape led to the development of *microbullage* (*see* MICRO OXYGENATING) by a winemaker in the Madiran area. Tannat has found a prominent place in Uruguay where it's widely planted and the wines are lower in tannins and lighter bodied.

tannic *see* Glossary of Wine Tasting Terms, page 655

tannins [TAN-ihns] Any of a group of astringent substances found in the seeds, skins, and stems of grapes, as well as in oak barrels, particularly new ones. Tannins are part of a grouping technically called PHENOLIC COMPOUNDS. They are important in the production of good red wines because they provide flavor, STRUCTURE, and TEXTURE and, because their antioxidant traits contribute to long and graceful AGING. Tannins often give young wines a noticeable astringency, a quality that diminishes as the wine ages, mellows, and develops character. Wines with excessive tannins are referred to as *tannic*. *See* Glossary of Wine Tasting Terms, page 655.

tar *see* Glossary of Wine Tasting Terms, page 655

Tarragona DO [tah-rah-GAW-nuh] A large DO located in the southern part of Spain's CATALONIA region. There are about 28,000 vineyard acres spread throughout three subzones—**El Campo de Tarragona**, **La Comarca de Falset**, and **La Ribera d'Erbe**. El Campo de Tarragona, the largest subzone, produces mainly white wines from MACABEO, PARELLADA, and XAREL-LO grapes. La Comarca de Falset adjoins the PRIORAT DOCA to the north and produces intense red wines from Garnacha Tinta (GRENACHE) and Cariñena (CARIGNAN). La Ribera d'Erbe produces both red and white wines using the aforementioned grapes. Historically, most of the area's wine, much of which is mediocre, is produced by the numerous cooperatives in the region. Producers in the Falset subzone in particular are watching the success of their neighbors in Priorat and are imitating the fresh, intense red wines made there. They are also planting nonlocal VARIETIES like CABERNET SAUVIGNON and MERLOT. Tarragona Clasico is a rich, sweet DESSERT WINE that is sometimes FORTIFIED up to 23 percent ALCOHOL.

tart *see* Glossary of Wine Tasting Terms, page 655

tartar *see* TARTRATES

tartaric acid *see* ACIDS

tartrates [TAR-trayts] One of the by-products of tartaric acid (*see* ACIDS), tartrates are also called *potassium bitartrate, cream of tartar,* and *tartar.* These small, innocuous crystals can appear in wine unless removed through the COLD STABILIZATION process. Tartrates aren't harmful and only impact the wine visually. In Germany, tartrates are called *weinsteins* ("wine stones").

Tasmania This beautiful Australian island state is about the size of Ireland. It sits roughly 150 miles off the southeast corner of the mainland, directly south of Melbourne. Tasmania is Australia's southernmost area and the closest to Antarctica, which is about 1675 miles across the Southern Ocean. Hobart is its capital and most populous city. Although Tasmania's wine history goes back to 1823, when vines were first planted near Hobart, within two decades most commercial winemaking had been abandoned. There wasn't much interest in Tasmanian VITICULTURE until the 1950s and even then the wine industry grew sporadically over the next several decades. Today its vineyard acreage makes up less than 1 percent of Australia's total, its wine production less than 0.5 percent. Under the Australian GEOGRAPHIC INDICATIONS rulings, Tasmania is a zone but doesn't have any officially recognized regions. Unofficially, there are a number of areas that are distinct. Around Hobart in the southeastern corner of the state are the Derwent, Coal River, and Huon Valleys; along the east coast are various isolated growing areas grouped under the East Coast designation; near the city of Launceston in northern Tasmania are the Tamar Valley and the Pipers Brook-Pipers River areas; and to the west of Launceston is an area called simply Northwest. There are about 2,300 vineyard acres in Tasmania. This far south the climate is very cool (although some areas can be warmer than parts of VICTORIA on the mainland), so cool-climate varieties of PINOT NOIR and CHARDONNAY are the most popular. They're used for both STILL WINES and SPARKLING WINES, while some grapes are shipped to the mainland for the winemaking process. Other grapes grown here include CABERNET SAUVIGNON, RIESLING, SAUVIGNON BLANC, PINOT GRIS, and GEWÜRZTRAMINER. The state's largest producing area is Pipers Brook-Pipers River, one of the cooler regions, which hosts the state's dominant winery, Pipers Brook Vineyard.

tastevin [taht-VAH*N*; tahst-VAH*M*] Used in Burgundian cellars for analyzing and tasting wine, a tastevin is a small, shallow silver cup with raised indentations that help reflect the wine's color and exhibit its clarity. It's become customary for a SOMMELIER to wear a tastevin on a chain or ribbon around his or her neck. The Burgundian wine tasting fraternity, Chevaliers du Tastevin, was named after the tasting cup. A tastevin is sometimes referred to as a *wine taster*.

tasting *see* WINE TASTING

tasting terms *see* Glossary of Wine Tasting Terms, page 655

tasting wine *see* Glossary of Wine Tasting Terms, page 655

Taurasi DOCG [tow-RAH-zee] Located east and slightly north of Naples in Italy's CAMPANIA region, this highly regarded DOCG is situated in the hilly area surrounding the village of Taurasi, northeast of Avellino. The red wine is made primarily from AGLIANICO grapes. When young, Taurasi wines are noted for their ROUGHNESS owing to high TANNINS, noticeable ACIDITY, and a dense concentration of flavors; they're definitely built for AGING. As these wines mature, they can show great BALANCE, with subtle fruit flavors and EARTHY, TARRY, and CHOCOLATY characteristics. Prior to release, Taurasi wines are aged for a minimum of 3 years, one of which must be in wood barrels. The RISERVA has been aged for 4 years.

Tautavel *see* CÔTES DU ROUSSILLON AC

Tavel AC [ta-VEHL] An AC located just southwest of CHÂTEAUNEUF-DU-PAPE in the southern part of France's RHÔNE region. It makes only ROSÉ wines, which some believe are France's best. Tavel wines, which are generally DRY and more full-bodied (*see* BODY) than most rosés, have an international reputation and are probably the best-known rosés from France. They're made primarily from GRENACHE (although this variety can't comprise more than 60 percent of the total) and CINSAUT, even though seven other grapes are allowed.

tawny port *see* PORT

TBA; T.B.A. *see* TROCKENBEERENAUSLESE

T-budding A technique for converting a vine from one specific variety to another, such as from ZINFANDEL to SAUVIGNON BLANC. This process is done by cutting off the fruit-bearing part of the vine and GRAFTING the new variety to a T-shaped incision made in the top portion of the ROOTSTOCK. This process speeds up the time in which the new variety is productive by 2 to 3 years. A newly planted vine might take 3 years or more to become fully productive, whereas a variety created by T-budding can be fully productive in the second year. This process is widely used in California and Australia, where it's called *green grafting*.

TCA *see* CORKED WINE

tears *see* LEGS in the Glossary of Wine Tasting Terms, page 655

Teinturier [ta*n*-tew*r*-EH*R*] Dark-skinned grapes that have red (rather than white) pulp and juice. (Most grapes have white pulp and juice and get their coloring from being in contact with the skins during FERMENTATION.) Teinturier grapes are often planted to be used as a BLENDING WINE to add color to such wines. Examples of Teinturier grapes are ALICANTE BOUSCHET, ROYALTY, and RUBIRED. Most Teinturier grapes have some connection to Alicante Bouschet.

Temecula AVA [teh-MEH-kyoo-luh] An AVA located in southern California's Riverside County between the cities of Riverside and San Diego. The area encompasses about 30,000 acres, 3,000 of which are planted. At this writing, Temecula has lost several hundred acres of vineyards to the ravages of PIERCE'S DISEASE, which is spread by the GLASSY-WINGED SHARPSHOOTER. The main grape varieties here are CHARDONNAY, SAUVIGNON BLANC, MERLOT, VIOGNIER, SYRAH, and PINOT GRIS. There are about fifteen wineries in the area.

temperatures, wine storing and serving *see* WINE CELLAR; Temperatures for Serving Wine, page 641; Optimum Serving Temperatures by Wine Type, page 642

Tempranilla *see* TEMPRANILLO

Tempranillo [tem-prah-NEE-yoh; tem-prah-NEE-lyoh] An important red-wine grape native to northern Spain and widely cultivated in the northern and central parts of that country. Tempranillo produces its best results in the cooler growing regions of Rioja Alavesa, Rioja Alta, RIBERA DEL DUERO, and parts of PENÈDES. In these areas, Tempranillo can generate deep-colored wines with characteristics of strawberry, SPICE, and fresh TOBACCO. Because of its lower ACIDITY and ALCOHOL levels, Tempranillo is usually blended with other grape varieties. It's a principal component in the famous RIOJA wines, which are usually blended with Garnacha (GRENACHE), Mazuelo, and GRACIANO. It's also the dominant red variety of VALDEPEÑAS and LA MANCHA; both areas call the grape *Cencibel*. In different regions of Spain, Tempranillo goes by various names including *Ojo de Liebre, Tinto Fino, Tinto del Pais, Tinto de Toro,* and *Ull de Llebre*. Argentina is one of the few places outside of Spain where Tempranillo is widely planted. In the Portugese regions of Alentejo (where this grape's called *Aragonêz*) and DOURO (where it's known as *Roriz* or *Tinta Roriz*), Tempranillo's a minor grape used in PORT production. There's speculation that *Valdepeñas,* a secondary grape used for JUG WINES in California, might actually be Tempranillo.

tent An old English word (probably derived from the Spanish word TINTO, which means "red") that referred to POWERFUL red wines from Spain, particularly from the area in and around ALICANTE.

tenuta [teh-NOO-tah] An Italian term meaning "holding," which applies to land, and in wine parlance refers to an estate that grows its own grapes and bottles the wine.

Termeno Aromatico *see* GEWÜRZTRAMINER

Teroldego Rotaliano DOC [teh-*r*awl-DEH-goh roh-tahl-YAH-noh] DOC located in the Campo Rotaliano area in the Trentino province, which is part of the TRENTINO-ALTO ADIGE region in northeastern Italy. Its specialties are ROSSO and ROSATO wines produced in a DRY style from Teroldego grapes.

Terra Alta DO [TEHR-ruh AHL-tah] A rising DO zone of about 20,000 vineyard acres located around the town of Gandesa west of the TARRAGONA DO in the southwestern portion of Spain's CATALONIA region. The name means "high land," and the area is hilly and hot with low grape YIELDS. Traditionally about 75 percent of the wine produced has been white, made from Garnacha Blanc (GRENACHE) and MACABEO; the red and ROSÉ wines are made from Cariñena (CARIGNAN) and Garnacha Tinta (Grenache). But things are beginning to change—small producers have begun modernizing winemaking methods and producing wines of much higher quality, much in the same way as the PRIORAT DOCA and Tarragona DO zones are reinventing themselves. To help boost wine quality, several VARIETIES have been added to the allowable DO grapes—white varieties now include Moscatel (MUSCAT) and PARELLEDA, and reds include CABERNET SAUVIGNON, MERLOT, and TEMPRANILLO. As of this writing, however, local cooperatives produce the majority of the region's wines, which are generally high in ALCOHOL and of mediocre quality.

Terrano *see* REFOSCO

Terrantez *see* FOLGASÃO

Terras do Sado [tehr-REHSH doh SAH-doh] A VINHO REGIONAL area in southern Portugal between the Tagus and Sado Rivers surrounding the Setúbal Peninsula just south of Lisbon. The Terras do Sado region includes the PALMELA and SETÚBAL DOCs in its borders. PERIQUITA is this area's primary red grape; MUSCAT OF ALEXANDRIA, the most common white.

Terrasses du Larzac AC [teh-RAHSS deu LAHR-zak] French APPELLATION created in 2005 as a subzone in the north central part of the larger CÔTEAUX DU LANGUEDOC AC. It was created for red wines consisting of a minimum of 60 percent GRENACHE and/or MOURVÈDRE (but no more than 75 percent of either one) and a minimum of 20 percent Mourvèdre and/or SYRAH, plus the addition of up to 30 percent CINSAUT or CARIGNAN. ALCOHOL BY VOLUME must be a minimum of 12 percent. The appellation encompasses a number of villages, including two with excellent reputations, **Montpeyroux** and **Saint-Saturnin-de-Lucian**, and also the villages of **Aniane** and **Jonquières**, which contain the well-known producers, Mas de Daumas Gassac and Mas Jullien, respectively.

Terre di Franciacorta DOC *see* FRANCIACORTA DOCG

terroir [tehr-WAH*R*] French for "soil," but in the wine world *terroir* encompasses much more than that. When French wine producers use the term *terroir,* it not only includes reference to the type of soil (chalky, claylike, gravelly, sandy) but also to other environmental factors that might influence the quality of the finished wine, such as altitude, position relative to the sun, angle of incline, and water drainage. The French and many other OLD WORLD traditionalists are emphatic about the impact of terroir on wine, insisting that one can taste the difference. NEW WORLD producers have not been as quick to embrace this idea, believing that VITICULTURE and VINICULTURE practices are what make the wine. Of course there is always the middle ground. It has become evident that the grapes from some vineyards in the New World result in better and more distinctive wines, and those grapes are sought after by winemakers. It's also true that from the same terroir some French producers create much higher quality wines and that there are stylistic differences introduced by winemakers even in wines of similar quality. *See also* GOÛT in Glossary of Wine Tasting Terms, page 655. *See also* CLIMAT.

Tessin *see* TICINO

tête de cuvée *see* CUVÉE

Les Teurons *see* BEAUNE

Texas Since the 1970s, this state has grown from one to over fifty wineries, even though growth slowed during the economic trials of the late 1980s. Texas has become the fifth largest wine-producing state and the fifth largest wine consumer in the United States. The history of Texas grape growing goes back at least to the 1660s, when Franciscan monks planted MISSION grapes adjacent to their missions. In the 1880s, a Texan by the name of Thomas Volney Munson became a hero to the French when he shipped thousands of ROOTSTOCKS to European vineyards after they'd been attacked by PHYLLOXERA. Texan vineyards initially used native American varieties and HYBRIDS like CHANCELLOR, CHAMBOURCIN, and VIDAL BLANC. In the late 1970s, however, wineries began to move toward European varieties. Today a majority of Texan vineyards grow VITIS VINIFERA grapes including CABERNET FRANC, CABERNET SAUVIGNON, CHARDONNAY, CHENIN BLANC, COLOMBARD, GEWÜRZTRAMINER, MERLOT, MUSCAT, PINOT NOIR, RIESLING, RUBY CABERNET, SAUVIGNON BLANC, and SÉMILLON. Texas now has a number of AVAs including BELL MOUNTAIN, ESCONDIDO VALLEY, MESILLA VALLEY (which it shares with NEW MEXICO), FREDERICKSBURG, TEXAS DAVIS MOUNTAINS, TEXAS HIGH PLAINS, and TEXAS HILL COUNTRY. Wineries are scattered throughout the state, but the biggest concentrations are around the city of Lubbock in northwestern Texas (Texas High Plains) and west of Austin in central Texas (Texas Hill Country). There are also wineries near Fort Stockton in western Texas (Texas Davis Mountains) and some north of the Dallas-Fort Worth area.

Texas Davis Mountains AVA A VITICULTURAL AREA approved in 1998 in the Trans-Pecos region of west TEXAS, southwest of Fort Stockton. It contains approximately 270,000 acres spread out north and northwest of Fort Davis, the "highest town in Texas." Blue Mountain Vineyard is the only commercial winery.

Texas High Plains AVA Approved in 1993, this huge viticultural area encompasses 7,680,000 acres in the central and western Texas Panhandle region around Lubbock. Although it covers all or parts of twenty-four Texas counties, its size takes second place to the TEXAS HILL COUNTRY AVA near Austin. The Texas High Plains AVA is located on a huge high plateau, the height of which ranges from 2,800 to 4,000 feet above sea level. This positioning provides an environment of long, hot, dry summer days, which allow the grapes to mature and ripen to proper sugar levels, and cool evenings, which help set the grape's ACID levels. Currently, this region has over 3,500 planted acres—the most popular grapes are CABERNET SAUVIGNON and CHARDONNAY, followed by SAUVIGNON BLANC and CHENIN BLANC.

Texas Hill Country AVA A huge (9,600,000-acre) viticultural area established in 1991 in central Texas. Next to the OHIO RIVER VALLEY AVA, this is the United States' second-largest AVA; it's the largest AVA within a single state. Although this AVA is massive, there are currently less than 1,000 vineyard acres planted. The favorite grapes here are CABERNET SAUVIGNON, MERLOT, and CHARDONNAY; CHENIN BLANC, SAUVIGNON BLANC, SEMILLON, PINOT NOIR, and RIESLING are also planted. Within its boundaries are two smaller AVAs that were actually approved prior to this huge region. **Bell Mountain AVA**, the first Texas AVA (approved in 1986), is located in northeastern Gillespie County about 15 miles north of Fredericksburg. The **Fredericksburg in the Texas Hill Country AVA** is located approximately 80 miles west of Austin near Fredericksburg.

Texoma AVA North central Texas APPELLATION established in January 2006. It consists of 2,336,000 acres south of Lake Texoma and the Red River along the Texas-Oklahoma border in Montague, Cooke, Grayson, and Fannin Counties. This area lies north of the Dallas-Fort Worth metroplex. Although the area has only 55 acres of vineyards and six wineries, it has historical significance because of Thomas Volney Munson. It was in his experimental vineyards in this area that he discovered VINIFERA VINES could be grafted to native American rootstock, which are resistant to PHYLLOXERA. This essentially saved the French wine industry in the 1880s when it was going through a huge phylloxera epidemic. Some CABERNET SAUVIGNON is grown here, but the vineyards contain mostly NATIVE AMERICAN GRAPES and HYBRIDS.

texture *see* Glossary of Wine Tasting Terms, page 655

Thalia *see* TREBBIANO

thick *see* Glossary of Wine Tasting Terms, page 655

thief *see* WINE THIEF

thin *see* BODY in the Glossary of Wine Tasting Terms, page 655

thiols *see* MERCAPTANS

third growth *see* TROISIÈME CRU

Thompson Seedless *see* SULTANA

Ticino [tee-CHEE-noh] This Italian-speaking Swiss canton, also known as *Tessin,* is located in the southern Alps. There are four main wine-producing areas in Ticino—around Lake Lugano and Mendrisiotto and in the areas north and south of Monte Céneri, Sopraceneri, and Sottoceneri. Ticino produces mostly red wines, with MERLOT the dominant variety. These wines are usually labeled *Merlot del Ticino.* Lower-quality wines made from a mix of red grapes such as BARBERA and FREISA are often labeled *Nostrano* (Italian for "ours"). The word *Nostrano* was once used for VITIS VINIFERA grapes to set them apart from Americano grapes, the latter alluding to NATIVE AMERICAN vines used in this area after PHYLLOXERA wiped out most of the European varieties.

Tierra de Madrid *see* VINOS DE MADRID

tight; tightly knit *see* Glossary of Wine Tasting Terms, page 655

Tindilloro *see* CANAIOLO

tinta; tinto [TEEN-tah; TEEN-toh] Spanish and Portuguese for "red." *Tinta* is the feminine form; *tinto,* the masculine. Both words are often used in the name of red-grape varieties like TINTA AMARELA and TINTA MADEIRA.

Tinta *see* GRENACHE

Tinta Amarela [TEEN-tah er-mah-REH-lah] Also called *Trincadeira* or *Trincadeira Preta,* this red Portuguese grape is grown in the DOURO DOC to be used in making PORT and in the DOCS of DÃO and ALENTEJO for rich, full-bodied, DRY red wines.

Tinta Barroca; Tinta Barocca [TEEN-tah behr-RROH-kehr] A red Portuguese grape primarily used in the DOURO DOC in PORT, to which it contributes a softening effect and fruity aromas. In South Africa, Tinta Barroca is used both for rich, powerful DRY red wines and for PORTlike FORTIFIED WINES.

Tinta Caiada [TEEN-tah kah-EE-ah-duh] Also called *Tinta Lameira,* this red Portuguese grape is grown in the ALENTEJO region. It likes hot, dry climates and produces wines with deep color and good acidity.

Tinta de Toro *see* TEMPRANILLO

Tinta Lameira *see* TINTA CAIADA

Tinta Madeira [TEEN-tah muh-DEH-ruh] A minor red-wine grape grown in limited amounts on the Portuguese island of MADEIRA, where plantings are now slightly on the increase. In California, a small amount of Tinta Madeira is grown (mostly in the CENTRAL VALLEY) and used in the production of PORT.

Tinta Miúda [TEEN-tah MYOO-der] The Portuguese name for the GRACIANO grape.

Tinta Negra Mole *see* NEGRA MOLE

Tinta Pinheira *see* RUFETE

Tinta Roriz *see* TEMPRANILLO

tinto *see* TINTA

Tinto *see* GRENACHE

Tinto Cão [TEEN-toh keng] High-quality red Portuguese grape variety grown in the DOCS of DOURO and DÃO. Tinto Cão, which means "red dog," is thought to have been planted in the Douro Valley for over 300 years. It gradually faded from use because of its low yields. However, growers striving to improve their PORT wines have begun planting this grape. *See also* RUBIRED.

Tinto del Pais *see* TEMPRANILLO

Tinto de Requena *see* BOBAL

Tinto de Toro *see* TEMPRANILLO

Tinto Fino *see* TEMPRANILLO

tirage [tee-RAHZH] French for "to pull" or "to draw." In France's wine industry, it means "to draw from the barrel," referring to bottling wine; a **tireuse** is a bottling machine. In the CHAMPAGNE region, a *liqueur de tirage* (*see* DOSAGE) is added when the wine is bottled to cause a SECONDARY FERMENTATION in the bottle. *En tirage* refers to the time SPARKLING WINE stays in the bottle to AGE, both during this secondary fermentation and after it's complete.

tired *see* Glossary of Wine Tasting Terms, page 655

tireuse *see* TIRAGE

tischwein [TIHSH-vine] German for TABLE WINE, but referring to common, ordinary wine. It shouldn't be confused with DEUTSCHER

TAFELWEIN, which has certain quality requirements. *Tischwein* is similar to France's VIN ORDINAIRE.

titratable acidity *see* ACIDS

titration *see* ACIDS

toast; toasted; toasted barrels One of the processes in barrel making is to toast the insides of the staves before the heads (barrel ends) are fitted. Toasted barrels greatly affect the final flavor of a wine, and winemakers can order the level of toast they want. As a rule, the lighter the toast, the more a wine reflects the oak flavors and accompanying TANNINS. The level of toast can range from light to medium to heavy. A **light toast** produces wine that tastes of the wood—OAKY, sometimes TANNIC. A **medium toast** generates a browner wood—the wine has vanilla aromas and fewer tannins. A **heavy toast** turns the wood very dark, and wine aged in such barrels has spicy, smoky flavors that can be reminiscent of roasted coffee or toasted bread.

toasty *see* Glossary of Wine Tasting Terms, page 655

tobacco *see* Glossary of Wine Tasting Terms, page 655

Tocai; Tocai Friulano Former name for the variety SAUVIGNONASSE now called Friulano in the FRIULI-VENEZIA GIULIA region.

toe curler *see* Glossary of Wine Tasting Terms, page 655

Tokai *see* TOCAI

Tokaji; Tokaji Aszú; Tokaji Essencia [toh-KAY ah-SOO; ehs-SIHN-see-uh] 1. This esteemed Hungarian wine ranks as one of the world's best sweet white wines. It comes from the area around the town of Tokaj. Hungarian wine labels include the name of the originating area by adding an *i,* which makes it a possessive form. Therefore, labels for this wine display *Tokaji* or *Tokaji Aszú,* though the wines are sometimes referred to as Tokay or Tokay Aszú in English-speaking countries. Tokaji-area wines are made primarily from FURMINT grapes, although a small amount of HÁRSLEVELŰ is used and, occasionally, some MUSCAT. The Tokaji area is located in the foothills of the Carpathian Mountains in northeastern Hungary. Warm summers combined with the humidity from the area's streams and rivers can create an environment where BOTRYTIS CINEREA (which Hungarians call ASZÚ) develops. The shriveled, botrytis-infected grapes are picked separately and set aside in large vats. **Tokaji Essencia**, the rarest and most expensive of the Tokaji wines, is made from the small amount of juice that is squeezed out naturally by the weight of the grapes on top of each other. Over a period of years, this syrupy juice slowly ferments in casks called *gönci* (which are approximately 140 liters or 37 gallons in size). This extremely slow process produces a liquid so sweet that the ALCOHOL level rarely exceeds 2 percent. There are numerous stories of the restorative powers of Tokaji Essencia, including the fact that it was once reserved principally for dying monarchs. **Tokaji Aszú** is made from those same botrytis-infected grapes that gave up much of their juice to make Tokaji Essencia. These grapes are kneaded into a paste, which is measured in traditional *puttonyos* (baskets or hods that hold about 25 kilograms or 55 pounds). The sweetness and RICHNESS of a Tokaji Aszú depends on how many puttonyos go into a gönci (along with regular MUST from uninfected grapes). The more puttonyos, the sweeter and richer the wine. Tokaji Aszú labels indicate how many puttonyos have been used—three, four, or five are the norm, and six on rare occasions. Even sweeter and richer than a six-puttonyos Tokaji Aszú is the **Tokaji Aszú Essensia**, which is made without any regular must. A Tokaji Aszú Essencia is not too far removed from a Tokaji Essensia and is likened to a German TROKENBEERENAUSLESE. The sugar content of a Tokaji Aszú Essencia is so high that it takes several years and the use of a special yeast for it to ferment. **Tokaji Szamorodni**, which means "as it comes," is a basic wine made from uninfected grapes without the intentional addition of any aszú grapes. It can range from sweet (*édes*) to DRY (*száras*), depending on whether or not and, if so, how many aszú grapes were picked along with the uninfected grapes.

Tokay In Australia, the MUSCADELLE grape is called Tokay, as are the FORTIFIED WINES made from this grape. *See also* TOKAJI

Tokay d'Alsace *see* PINOT GRIS

Tomar *see* RIBATEJO DOC

Tondo *see* PROSECCO

tonneau [taw-NOH] A volume measurement that was once used in BORDEAUX for selling wine. A *tonneau* is equal to 900 liters (about 238 gallons), which represents the capacity of four French BARRIQUES (225 liters each). Although the tonneau isn't a real barrel or container, it was an old method for pricing wine. It was intially equivalent to 96 cases of wine, a figure that was adjusted to 100 cases in 1977. Today, however, most Bordeaux CHÂTEAUX price their wine by the bottle, not the tonneau.

Topikos Inos *see* GREECE

La Toppe au Vert *see* CORTON

topping; topping-up A term that refers to adding wine to containers, such as oak barrels, to replace liquid that has evaporated. Topping is necessary to ensure there's no airspace (ULLAGE) that would allow air contact with the wine (*see* OXIDIZED). The French term for this procedure is *ouillage*.

Torgiano DOC; Torgiano Rosso Reserva DOCG [tohr-jee-AH-noh] Demarcated zone that encircles the town of Torgiano, which is just south of Perugia in the center of Italy's UMBRIA region. The Torgiano DOC covers ROSSO wines made from SANGIOVESE, CANAIOLO, TREBBIANO, Ciliegiolo, and MONTEPULCIANO grapes. The area's BIANCO wines are made from Trebbiano, GRECHETTO, MALVASIA, and Verdello. The DOC also allows varietal wines made with a minimum 85 percent of the variety to be made from grapes such as CABERNET SAUVIGNON, CHARDONNAY, Pinot Grigio (PINOT GRIS), Pinot Nero (PINOT NOIR), and Riesling Italico (WELSCHRIESLING). The **Torgiano Rosso Riserva**, which was upgraded to DOCG status in 1990, has a higher ALCOHOL content and 3 years of AGING. This area's production is so dominated by the Lungarotti firm's production that the DOCG is closely associated with Lungarotti's proprietary brand names—**Rubesco** for the red wines and **Torre di Giano** for the whites. The very best wines are the Rubesco Riserva from the Monticchio vineyard and the Torre di Giano Riserva from the Il Pino vineyard. The other well-known producer is Castello di Antignano.

Toro DO [TOH-roh] Small DO zone located around the town of Toro in the western part of Spain's Castile and León region. It sits on the northwestern boundary of the better-known RUEDA DO. During the sixteenth through eighteenth centuries, this region was an extremely important wine area known for its bold red wines. In the late nineteenth century, however, PHYLLOXERA devastated the area and it wasn't until the mid-1980s that the wine industry began to revitalize. Today Toro is viewed as one of the country's rising stars. About 9,000 acres sit on Spain's central plateau—most vineyards are at the 2,000- to 2,500-foot level. At this altitude, they enjoy hot, sunny days and cool nights. Red wines still dominate, and Tinto de Toro (TEMPRANILLO) is the most widely planted VARIETY. Granacha (GRENACHE) and CABERNET SAUVIGNON are also grown here, though the latter isn't permitted in the DO wines. Toro is attracting more attention as producers move away from the dull, heavy red wines to styles that are still powerful but in a fresh, fruity style. Small amounts of white wine are produced, mainly from MALVASÍA and VERDEJO.

Torre di Giano *see* TORGIANO DOC

Torres Vedras *see* ESTREMADURA

Toscana *see* TUSCANY

total acidity *see* ACIDS

total SO₂ *see* SULFUR DIOXIDE

tough *see* Glossary of Wine Tasting Terms, page 655

Touraine [too-REHN] A large, picturesque, wine-producing provence surrounding the city of Tours in the middle of France's LOIRE Valley, an area commonly known as the château country. Red, white, and ROSÉ wines are produced throughout the region. The grapes used for red wines include CABERNET SAUVIGNON, CABERNET FRANC, GAMAY, MALBEC, and PINOT NOIR. These grapes, plus the local grapes of Grolleau and Pineau d'Aunis, are also used for rosé wines. The two white-wine grapes are CHENIN BLANC and SAUVIGNON BLANC—wines made from this latter grape are usually the best. **Touraine AC** is a general APPELLATION that encompasses most of the surrounding region. Three villages—Amboise, Azay-le-Rideau, and Mesland—make higher-quality wines and can therefore append their name to the Touraine AC. In addition, there are a number of smaller appellations scattered throughout the area, some of which are quite well known. These include BOURGUEIL, CHINON, and SAINT-NICOLAS DE BOURGUEIL (all known for their red wines), and JASNIÈRES, MONTLOUIS, and VOUVRAY, which are known for their white wines. Appellations making fully SPARKLING WINES include **Touraine Mousseux AC**, **Montlouis Mousseux AC**, and **Vouvray Mousseux AC**. Those making lightly sparkling wine include **Touraine Pétillant AC**, **Montlouis Pétillant AC**, and **Vouvray Pétillant AC**.

Touriga Francesa [too-REE-gah fran-SAY-zer] Portuguese red-wine grape that is important in the production of PORT. Although Touriga Francesa is lighter and more delicate in body, color, and flavor than TOURIGA NACIONAL, it has a wonderful perfumy character that makes it perfect for port blends.

Touriga Nacional [too-REE-gah nah-syoo-NAHL] This high-quality Portuguese red-wine grape is thought to be the preeminent variety for making PORT. The very best VINTAGE ports are based on this grape.

Touriga Nacional is widely grown in Portugal's DOURO region. It's also highly prized in the DÃO region, where it's known simply as *Touriga,* and where it must represent 20 percent of that region's red-wine blends. This vine yields very small, concentrated berries that produce wines that are very dark, fruity, aromatic, and TANNIC. Touriga Nacional is also known as *Mortagua.* Related subvarieties include *Touriga Fina, Touriga Foiufeira,* and *Touriga Macho.*

Tracy Hills AVA Northern California APPELLATION established in December 2006. It consists of 39,200 acres in San Joaquin and Stanislaus Counties. It's southwest of the town of Tracy and about 55 miles southeast of San Francisco. There are 2 wineries (La Bonne Vie Cellars and Windmill Ridge Winery) and 5 vineyards planted with CABERNET SAUVIGNON, CHARDONNAY, MERLOT, NERO D'AVOLA, SANGIOVESE, and SYRAH.

traditional method Name adopted by the EUROPEAN UNION as the official name for MÉTHODE CHAMPENOISE.

Traisen [TRI-zen] A small wine-producing village located southwest of BAD KREUZNACH in Germany's NAHE region. It's best known for superb RIESLING wines produced from two EINZELLAGEN—**Bastei** and **Rotenfels**.

Traisental DAC *see* DISTRICTUS AUSTRIA CONTROLLATUS

Traminac *see* GEWÜRZTRAMINER

Traminer *see* GEWÜRZTRAMINER

Traminer Aromatico *see* GEWÜRZTRAMINER

Traminer Aromatique *see* GEWÜRZTRAMINER

Traminer Musqué *see* GEWÜRZTRAMINER

Traminer Parfumé *see* GEWÜRZTRAMINER

Tramini *see* GEWÜRZTRAMINER

Trás-Os-Montes [TREH-zoos MAHNGN-tehsh] VINHO REGIONAL located in northern Portugal on the Spanish border. It's a very mountainous region with a diversity of growing environments from very hot to cool. The Douro River flows through the area and the valley around the river is home to the vineyards of the DOURO DOC and the PORT DOC. In addition, Trás-Os-Montes encompasses four IPRS that are working toward DOC status. **Chaves IPR** is located around the town of Chaves and is best known for its light-bodied reds. **Planalto Mirandes IPR** is located on Spain's western border. The red wines are light and fruity and the whites are fresh with good acidity and a slight effervescence. **Valpaços IPR** is located around several municipalities, including Valpaços, and is known for its light, fruity, dry red wines. **Varosa IPR** is located around the towns of Armamar, Lamego, and Tarouce and is known for the fresh, fruity reds and crisp, acidic whites. Varieties grown in the Trás-Os-Montes region include Bastardo, CABERNET FRANC, CABERNET SAUVIGNON, CHARDONNAY, GEWURZTRAMINER, Gouveio, MALVASIA, MERLOT, Mourisco Tinto, PINOT NOIR, Rabo de Ovelha, SAUVIGNON BLANC, SEMILLON, TEMPRANILLO, TINTA AMARELA, TINTA BARROCA, TINTA CAO, TOURIGA FRANCESA, TOURIGA NACIONAL, and Viosinho.

Trinity Lakes AVA An APPELLATION established in April 2005 that's located in northern California's Trinity County, just north of MENDOCINO COUNTY. Its 96,000 acres surround two man-made lakes, Trinity and Lewiston, northwest of the city of Redding. There's one winery, Alpen Cellars, with about 30 acres planted with CHARDONNAY, GEWÜRZTRAMINER, PINOT NOIR, and RIESLING.

transfer method A method of making SPARKLING WINE that's similar to MÉTHODE CHAMPENOISE. The major difference is that—instead of the RIDDLING and DISGORGEMENT steps—the wine, after a second fermentation in the bottle, is transferred to a pressurized tank where it passes through a filtration system to remove sediment. Sparkling wines made this way may be labeled "bottle fermented," "fermented in the bottle," or "transfer method."

Trebbianino Val d'Arda *see* COLLI PIACENTINI

Trebbiano [treb-BYAH-noh; treh-bee-AH-noh] A very important white-wine grape, not because it produces great wines, but because it's so extensively planted. Estimates indicate that Trebbiano produces more wine than any other variety in the world even though the AIRÉN is planted on more acreage. However, these rather neutral wines have high ACIDITY, medium ALCOHOL, and very little discernible aroma or flavor. The Trebbiano grape is most often blended with varieties exhibiting more dominant traits. Originating in central Italy, Trebbiano spread throughout that country and across the border to become France's most important white variety as well. In Italy, it's so extensively grown that, in some areas, it's difficult to find a bottle of white wine that doesn't contain some Trebbiano. In TUSCANY, the laws controlling wine production specify that a certain amount of Trebbiano and MALVASIA (another white-wine grape) be blended into their red-wine CHIANTI. There are many different Trebbiano clones, *Trebbiano Toscano* and *Trebbiano Romagnolo* being the most important.

Trebbiano Abruzzo, however, is actually a different variety—BOMBINO BIANCO. In France, where this grape is known by various names including *Ugni Blanc* and *Saint-Émilion,* large amounts of Trebbiano wine is processed into brandy, including the finest from COGNAC and ARMAGNAC. Other French names for this grape include *Clairette Ronde* and *Clairette Rose*—sometimes confusing because there's an entirely different variety called CLAIRETTE. Trebbiano is also planted in eastern Europe, Australia, South America, and Portugal, where it's called *Thalia* or *Talia*. It's known as *Saint-Emilion* in California and planted mainly in the SAN JOAQUIN VALLEY, where its primary use is in the production of brandy.

Trebbiano Abruzzo; Trebbiano d'Abruzzo   *see* BOMBINO BIANCO

Trebbiano d'Abruzzo DOC [treh-BYAH-noh dah-BROOD-zoh] DOC located in Italy's ABRUZZI region and covering a number of vineyard areas throughout the region. It's one of the two DOCs to use the name of the TREBBIANO grape (the other is *Trebbiano di Romagna* in Italy's EMILIA-ROMAGNA region). The odd thing is that this DOC adopted this name because the main grape variety used is the *Trebbiano Abruzzo,* which actually appears not to be Trebbiano, but an entirely different variety—BOMBINO BIANCO. The wines of this DOC can use Trebbiano Toscano (*see* TREBBIANO) grapes instead, but the better wines generally come from Bombino Bianco grapes. Up to 15 percent of other white grapes can be used as well. Generally the quality of the Trebbiano d'Abruzzo DOC wines is not very high, but a few producers keep YIELDS down and produce some very good wines.

Trebbiano Romagnolo *see* TREBBIANO

Trebbiano Toscano *see* TREBBIANO

trellis system; trellising A trellis system is simply a framework that supports grapevines as they grow, training them upward rather than letting them grow outward along the ground. Trellising not only keeps the vines off the ground but exposes both CANOPY and grape clusters to more sunlight and better air circulation. In the most basic terms, a trellising system consists of a row of posts or stakes anchored in the ground at various intervals and typically connected by taut wires on which the vines can be trained. Trellising is customized according to the vineyard site and grape variety. Here are just a few of the trellis styles. **Geneva Double Curtain** or **GDC** trellises consist of a pair of parallel wires designed to train two CORDONS from the same trunk to grow on each side of it. This approach allows for good sun and wind exposure. Occasionally, a third wire is positioned between the other two wires and a bit higher to further open up the canopy. The fruiting vines are trained to grow downward. **Guyot** trellises are used in both single and double systems. The single Guyot system uses a single, vertically grown CANE trained horizontally after the prior year's harvest is finished. Other vertically grown canes are pruned. A double Guyot is similar, except that two canes are kept from the prior year and trained horizontally. The Guyot systems are less complicated than many of the other trellis options, yet provide the grape clusters with good sun and wind exposure. They're used extensively in Bordeaux in part because yields are easily restricted. Fruiting vines grow upward on Guyot trellises. **Sylvos** trellises are variations of the Guyot trellises where the trunks of the vines are about twice as high. **Lyre** trellis systems are designed for vines of moderate vigor. They fall into a category called split canopy, or open center, because they are designed with one fruit wire and four foliage wires attached to two end posts on each end. From the end of the row these two posts look like a "V," or are sometimes attached to a single post making it look like a "Y." By spreading the canopy apart, light penetration and air movement are improved. The Lyre trellis is mostly used for SPUR-trained vines but occasionally for cane-trained. Fruiting vines grow upward. **Scott Henry** trellis systems were developed by Scott Henry of Henry Estate Winery in Oregon's Umpqua Valley. They draw on the VSP and the Guyot Double trellis systems. The big difference is the canes are trained to grow both up and down, which spreads out the canopy. This allows the grape clusters to receive maximum sun exposure, which lends itself to earlier ripening—helpful in the Oregon climate. All vine shoots are actually allowed to grow upward during most of the growing season; then a wire supporting about half the vines is moved downward about two to three weeks prior to harvest. These systems are harder to maintain but are noted for producing more fruit than either VSP or Guyot Double trellis systems and the fruit is of very high quality. **Smart Dyson** is a version of the Scott Henry system that uses spurs instead of canes. **VSP** or **Vertical Shoot Positioning** trellis systems are designed for vines of low to moderate vigor (high vigor vines may be too vigorous). VSP trellises consist of one fruit wire and four foliage (or catch) wires attached to a single vertical end post on each end. They're fairly widely used since they're well suited for mechanization and handle both CANE-trained and SPUR-trained vines. Fruiting vines grow upward. *See also* VITICULTURE; HEAD PRUNED VINE.

Trentino-Alto Adige [trehn-TEE-noh AHL-toh AH-dee-jeh] Wine-producing region with about 32,000 vineyard acres located in north-eastern Italy and bordered by LOMBARDY on the west, VENETO on the east, and Austria on the north. It consists of two provinces—Alto Adige in the north and Trentino in the south—which, although linked together into one region, are quite different. **Alto Adige**, also known as *South Tyrol* or *Südtirol,* is officially bilingual. It has a German-speaking majority that still has strong ties to Austria, which ceded this area to Italy in 1918. Alto Adige wines reflect this bilingual approach on their labels—a wine made from the PINOT BLANC grape might be referred to as both *Weissburgunder* and *Pinot Bianco* (both synonyms for Pinot Blanc). In addition to the ALTO ADIGE DOC, which covers this whole provence, there are a number of smaller DOCs such as Colli di Bolzano, LAGO DI CALDARO, Meranese di Collina, SANTA MADDALENA, Terlano, and Valle Isarco. **Trentino**, the southern portion of this region, begins north of the city of Trento and continues south. This part of Trentino-Alto Adige is much more Italian. The TRENTINO DOC covers the whole southern portion and includes a number of VARIETAL WINES like CABERNET SAUVIGNON and MERLOT. In addition, there are several indi-vidual DOCs such as CASTELLER, Sorni, TEROLDEGO ROTALIANO, and VAL-DADIGE. Over 75 percent of the total wine production of Trentino-Alto Adige is DOC wine (the highest percentage of Italy's twenty wine-producing regions), and a majority is red. The dominant red grapes are the local varieties LAGREIN, SCHIAVA (also called *Vernatsch*), and Lambrusco a Foglia Frastagliata (which is apparently unrelated to the other LAMBRUSCO varieties found throughout Italy). There are also wines made from CABERNET SAUVIGNON, MERLOT, Marzemino, and Pinot Nero (PINOT NOIR) grapes. There are many well-known white-grape varieties grown in the region including CHARDONNAY, MÜLLER-THURGAU, Pinot Bianco (Pinot Blanc), Pinot Grigio (PINOT GRIS), RIESLING, SAUVIGNON BLANC, SYLVANER, and GEWÜRZTRAMINER—the latter is thought to have orig-inated in the Alto Adige village of Tramin (*Temeno*).

Trentino DOC [trehn-TEE-noh] A large DOC that covers the Trentino province—the southern portion of Italy's TRENTINO-ALTO ADIGE region. Most of the vineyards are scattered around the Adige River Valley that meanders from north to south. The northern third of this area is much like its northern neighbor ALTO ADIGE, both in the Austrian culture and in the wine. From the city of Trento south, the region becomes much more Italian. The Trentino DOC authorizes a number of VARIETAL WINES—Cabernet (from Cabernet Sauvignon and Cabernet Franc), CABERNET SAUVIGNON, CABERNET FRANC, CHARDONNAY, LAGREIN, Marzemino,

MERLOT, MUSCAT (both Moscato Giallo and Moscato Rosa), MÜLLER-THUR-
GAU, Noisiola, Pinot Bianco (PINOT BLANC), Pinot Grigio (PINOT GRIS),
Pinot Nero (PINOT NOIR), Rebo, Riesling Italico (WELSCHRIESLING), Riesling
Renano (RIESLING), Sauvignon (SAUVINGON BLANC), and Traminer
Aromatico (GEWÜRZTRAMINER). There's also BIANCO (made from a blend
of white grapes), ROSSO (made from a red-grape mixture), and VIN SANTO
(made from Noisiola grapes). The Trentino province also has several
individual DOCs including CASTELLER, LAGO DI CALDARO, TEROLDEGO ROTAL-
IANO, and VALDADIGE. Sorni is a subzone of the Trentino DOC.

Treppchen *see* ERDEN; PIESPORT

Tricastin *see* CORTEAUX DU TRICASTIN

trichloroanisole; trichloro anisole *see* CORKED WINE

Trier [TREER] A city that has existed for over 2,000 years, with its
wine-producing origins dating back to Roman times. It's located in
Germany's MOSEL-SAAR-RUWER region along the Mosel River north of
where the Saar River joins the Mosel. Trier, which is the largest and
most important city in this region, is where many of the leading wine
estates, like Bischöflichen Weingüter and Friedrich-Wilhelm-
Gymnasium, keep their cellars. The city has nearly 1,000 acres of vineyards, which are included in the BEREICH of SAAR-RUWER and the
GROSSLAGE of Römerlay.

Trincadeira; Trincadeira Preta *see* TINTA AMARELA

trocken [TRAWK-uhn] German for "DRY." Officially, a wine labeled
"trocken" must meet the following requirements: RESIDUAL SUGAR may
not exceed 4 grams per liter (0.4 percent), but it may go up to 9 grams
per liter (0.9 percent) as long as the total acidity (*see* ACIDS) is within 2
grams per liter of the residual sugar. For example, if residual sugar is
9 grams, then total acidity must be at least 7; if total acidity is only 6
grams, then the residual sugar can't exceed 8 grams.

Trockenbeerenauslese (TBA) [TRAWK-uhn-bay-ruhn-OWS-
lay-zuh] The German term for "dry selected berries," used to describe
wines made from specially selected, overripe grapes that are left on the
vine until nearly dry. Because these grapes—picked one by one at
fullest maturity—are very concentrated in flavor and sugar, they produce extremely rich, nectarous wines. Trockenbeerenauslese is the
highest subcategory of QUALITÄTSWEIN MIT PRÄDIKAT and ranks above
KABINETT, SPÄTLESE, AUSLESE, BEERENAUSLESE, and EISWEIN. To attain the
Trockenbeerenauslese category, the natural sugar content of the grapes

must reach a certain minimum (150 OECHSLE, approximately 35 percent sugar by weight), depending on the region and the variety. The grapes are usually infected with BOTRYTIS CINEREA (*Edelfäule* in German), which shrivels them and thereby concentrates the sugar. The superior wines made from these grapes are extremely sweet but have enough ACIDITY for proper BALANCE. Because of the extraordinarily high sugar content, these wines frequently have trouble FERMENTING and often contain only 5.5 to 6 percent alcohol (from a potential of 21.5 percent or more if fermented DRY). Trockenbeerenauslese wines are exceptionally rare and extremely expensive (even more than Beerenauslese wines) and are considered to be one of the world's premier DESSERT WINES. They will AGE for many years, during which time they'll develop even more complexity. AUSTRIA has a Trockenbeerenauslese category that's similar and requires a minimum 156° OECHSLE.

troisième cru [twah-zyem KROO] The French phrase for "third growth," referring to the third-highest subcategory of the MÉDOC area's CRUS CLASSÉS (classed growths), which were established in the Classification of 1855 (*see* Official Wine Classifications of Bordeaux, page 678). Fourteen CHÂTEAUX were ranked as *troisièmes crus* in 1855, and this hasn't changed.

Trollinger *see* SCHIAVA

Trouchet Noir *see* CABERNET FRANC

Trousseau Gris [troo-soh GREE] Gray mutation of the red Trousseau grape that is used to make white wines. It's grown principally in France's Jura region and in California, where it's called *Gray* or *Grey Riesling*. It's not as popular in California as it once was. Small amounts are also grown in New Zealand where it's also called *Grey Riesling*. The wines produced from Trousseau Gris are generally mild and have muted aromas and flavors and light ACIDITY. The styles can range from DRY to medium-sweet. In California, small amounts of CHENIN BLANC or SYLVANER are often blended with Trousseau Gris to enhance the resulting wines. Another name for Trousseau Gris is *Chauche Gris*.

truffles *see* Glossary of Wine Tasting Terms, page 655

Tschaggel; Tschaggelevernatsch *see* SCHIAVA

TTB *see* ALCOHOL AND TOBACCO TAX AND TRADE BUREAU

Tulum Valley *see* ARGENTINA

Tumbarumba [tum-brr-UHM-bah] A remote Australian wine region located in the Southern New South Wales Zone of NEW SOUTH WALES. It's situated around the former gold mining town of Tombarumba in the western foothills of the Snowy Mountains, about 300 miles southwest of Sydney. Growth has increased here in recent years as this cool weather area gained a reputation for good sparkling wines made from CHARDONNAY, PINOT NOIR, and Pinot Meunier (MEUNIER), and for STILL WINES from Chardonnay, Pinot Noir, and SAUVIGNON BLANC. Small amounts of CABERNET SAUVIGNON, MERLOT, and Shiraz (SYRAH) are also grown in the region. Southcorp and BRL Hardy both buy grapes and make wines from this area.

Tunisia [too-NEE-zhuh] Like its neighbor ALGERIA, this north African country was greatly influenced by French winemaking traditions. Its modern vineyards were originally planted by the French, although they were nearly wiped out by the PHYLLOXERA epidemic that spread to this area in the 1930s. Tunisia produces mainly red and ROSÉ wines from French-style grapes—ALICANTE BOUCHET, CABERNET SAUVIGNON, CARIGNAN, GRENACHE, MOURVÈDRE, and PINOT NOIR. Tunisia is also recognized for its MUSCAT wines, particularly the sweet FORTIFIED WINES. Its main vineyards are all located around the Gulf of Tunis.

Tupungato *see* ARGENTINA

Turkey It's conjectured that Turkey's winemaking history may go back as far as 6,000 years. The modern wine industry was reborn in the 1920s after being essentially shut down by Islamic traditionalists. Today the main growing areas are central and eastern Anatolia, Trakya, and the area around Izmir on the Aegean coast. Many of the vines are native, and a number of European varieties are grown in Trakya. Native red varieties include Adakarasi, Karasakiz, and Papazkarasi; native white grapes include Apincak (or Yapincak), Beylerce, Emir, and Narince. Imported vines include CABERNET SAUVIGNON, CARIGNAN, CHARDONNAY, CINSAUT, CLAIRETTE, GAMAY, MERLOT, MUSCAT, PINOT NOIR, RIESLING, SÉMILLON, and SYLVANER. Tekal, the state-run monopoly, dominates wine production and has over twenty wine-producing facilities scattered throughout the country. Turkey also has over 100 private wineries.

Tuscany [TUHS-kuh-nee] A region in central Italy, east of the Ligurian Sea and the Tyrrhenian Sea; its capital city is Florence. Tuscany (*Toscana* in Italian) has almost 160,000 vineyard acres and six DOCGS: BRUNELLO DI MONTALCINO, CARMIGNANO, CHIANTI, CHIANTI CLASSICO, VINO NOBILE DI MONTEPULCIANO, and VERNACCIA DI SAN GIMIGNANO, all of which are red-wine areas. The area also comprises numerous DOCS including CORTONA, ELBA, MONTECARLO, MONTEREGIO DI MASS MARITTIMA, MORELLINO DI SCANSANO, MOSCADELLO DI MONTALCINO, POMINO, ROSSO DI MONTALCINO, ROSSO DI MONTEPULCIANO, and VAL DI CORNIA. For centuries, Tuscany has been producing its famous CHIANTI wine; it's also well known for its VIN SANTO. And this area is also at the vanguard of producing superlative wines that break the rules by using unapproved winemaking methods, grape VARIETIES, or percentage of varieties. These exceptional wines—known as SUPER TUSCANS—haven't been given Italy's approved wine categories of DOC or DOCG, so must be labled VINO DA TAVOLA (TABLE WINE). Thanks to the success of these super Tuscan wines, Italy's wine laws are changing, and grapes like CABERNET FRANC, CABERNET SAUVIGNON, and MERLOT are now being approved for some DOC areas. The dominant red grape grown in Tuscany is SANGIOVESE, but Cabernet Franc, Cabernet Sauvignon, and Merlot are also important. CANAIOLO, which historically played a meaningful role in Chianti production, is diminishing in importance. Tuscany's most important white grape is TREBBIANO. Other white grapes include MALVASIA, VERNACCIA DI SAN GIMIGNANO, CHARDONNAY, GRECHETTO, Pinot Gigio (PINOT GRIS), Pinot Bianco (PINOT BLANC), SAUVIGNON BLANC, and VERMENTINO.

typicity *see* Glossary of Wine Tasting Terms, page 655

Tyrian [teer-ee-uhn] Australian red-wine grape created by crossing CABERNET SAUVIGNON with Sumool, a Spanish variety. It was developed to produce high-quality wine and be productive in the Australian drier, warmer growing environment. It compares favorably with Cabernet Sauvignon and in some of the evaluations it scored as well or better. Tyrian, which is also a shade of purple, derives its name from its color. *See also* CIENNA and RUBIENNE.

U**Uclés DO** [eu-KLAYS] Promising Spanish APPELLATION established in 2005 in the CASTILLA-LA MANCHA region. Uclés is situated around the town of Uclés at the base of the Altomira Mountain range in the western part of the province of Cuenca, and the northeast section of the province of Toledo. Although the DO encompasses over 400,000 acres, less than 5,000 are planted with wine grapes. The area was initially approved for red wines made from CABERNET SAUVIGNON, Garnacha (GRENACHE), MERLOT, SYRAH, and Cencibel (TEMPRANILLO). Since then ROSÉ, white, and SPARKLING wines have been added. Approved white-wine grapes are CHARDONNAY, MACABEO, Moscatel (MUSCAT), SAUVIGNON BLANC, and VERDEJO.

Uco Valley *see* ARGENTINA

Ue *see* grappa

Ugni Blanc *see* TREBBIANO

Ugni Noir *see* ARAMON

ullage [UHL-ihj] The empty space that develops in bottles, barrels, or casks as wine evaporates. It's important for the ullage in casks or barrels to be kept to a minimum by TOPPING so that the air exposure won't cause OXIDATION. Older bottles of wine may have a larger space between the CORK and the wine owing to slow leakage or evaporation over time. However, a young bottle of wine with a large ullage could indicate a faulty cork. *See also* FILL LEVEL.

Ull de Llebre *see* TEMPRANILLO

Ullum Valley *see* ARGENTINA

umami [oo-MAH-mee] In the Western world, it's long been accepted that there are four elements of taste—sweet, salty, sour, and bitter, all of which are identified on various parts of the tongue. For centuries, Asian cultures have included a fifth taste—hot. However, in 1908, Tokyo Imperial University researcher Kikunae Ikeda identified a fifth taste that was decidedly more complex than "hot." He called this fifth taste sensation "umami," a word that has no exact English translation, but which may be loosely interpreted as "delicious" or "savory"—the essence of flavor, another dimension. Ikeda concluded that, of the five tastes, umami and sweetness were the only two the palate perceives as singularly pleasant. He also determined that foods exhibiting this umami sensation had one common denominator—the amino acid L-glutamate—monosodium glutamate, better known as MSG. The fifth taste was recently legitimized when University of Miami scientists Charles Zuker and Charles Ryber discovered specific taste-bud receptors that identify amino acids. L-glutamate can be found in high-protein foods such as consommés, aged meats, shitake mushrooms, dried seaweed, shellfish (clams, scallops, shrimp), soy sauce, and tomatoes. But, compared to the other four tastes, umami is exceedingly subtle, personifying more as an overall distinctive palate sensation than a taste. As with the other four tastes of sweet, salty, sour, and bitter, umami in food can affect a wine's flavor elements. According to Master of Wine Tim Hanni, who conducted food and wine pairing classes at Beringer Vineyards for over a decade, a dish that adversely affects a wine's taste is typically high in either sweetness or umami, both of which heighten a wine's TANNIN, bringing out bitterness and sometimes a metallic quality. For example, a marinara-sauced shrimp dish is high in both sweetness (from the tomatoes) and umami (from the shrimp). But adding salt and lemon juice to the sauce (to balance the umami and sweetness respectively) puts the entire dish in the right perspective for a moderately tannic red wine. In the end, a few simple adjustments is all it takes to bring a high-umami dish and the wine into harmony.

U

Umbria [UHM-bree-uh; OOM-bree-uh] Wine-producing region located in central Italy, bordered on the west by TUSCANY and on the east by the MARCHES. Some of Italy's most famous wines—like the whites from the ORVIETO DOC—come from Umbria. The two DOCGs in the area, MONTEFALCO SANGRANTINO and TORGIANO ROSSO RESERVA, are both for red wines. There are ten other DOCs in this hilly region including Assisi, Colli Altotiberini, Colli Amerini, Colli del Trasimeno, Colli Martani, Colli Perugini, Lago di Corbara, MONTEFALCO, Rosso Orvietano (or Orvietano Rosso), and TORGIANO. As in Tuscany, a fair amount of VIN SANTO is also made here. About 30 percent of the wines have DOC or DOCG status. There are about 40,000 vineyard acres in the region. Umbria's most popular white-wine grapes are TREBBIANO, GRECHETTO, and Verdello. Red and ROSÉ wines use CANAIOLO, Cilegiolo, SANGIOVESE, and Sagrantino. Non-local grapes like CABERNET SAUVIGNON, CHARDONNAY, and MERLOT are making inroads in this region.

Umpqua Valley AVA [UHMP-kwah] Approved in 1984, this Oregon AVA encompasses 768,000 acres around the towns of Umpqua and Roseburg, about 180 miles south of Portland, and just south of the WILLAMETTE VALLEY AVA. This 70-mile long area is located in the prime growing region between the coastal range to the west and the Cascade Mountains. It's classified as a Region I growing area (*see* CLIMATE REGIONS OF CALIFORNIA) because it's cool, although slightly warmer and drier than the Willamette Valley. This allows growers some success with warmer-climate grape varieties, although the cooler-weather varities of BURGUNDY—PINOT NOIR and CHARDONNAY—are the most popular. Other planted varieties include CABERNET SAUVIGNON, GEWÜRZTRAMINER, MERLOT, MÜLLER-THURGAU, PINOT GRIS, RIESLING, and ZINFANDEL. There are even small amounts of DOLCETTO, GRENACHE, MALBEC, SYRAH, and TEMPRANILLO being cultivated at Abacela Vineyards. In 2005, the RED HILL DOUGLAS COUNTY, OREGON AVA was established as a sub-appellation.

Umstadt, Bereich *see* HESSISCHE BERGSTRASSE

unctuous *see* Glossary of Wine Tasting Terms, page 655

unfiltered A term for wine that has not been filtered (*see* FILTERING), a process that, according to some winemakers, removes some of a wine's flavor and body along with any SEDIMENT. An unfiltered wine has undergone other processes such as CENTRIFUGING, COLD STABILIZATION, FINING, or RACKING to remove particles from the wine. Unfiltered wines, which are usually labeled as such, often leave a small deposit of sediment in the bottle.

unfined Some winemakers believe that FINING takes too much flavor and body out of wines, so they rely on other processes (CENTRIFUGING, COLD STABILIZATION, FILTERING, RACKING) to remove the particles from wine. Wines bottled without fining are sometimes labeled "Unfined" to point out that the wine should be more flavorful. Unfined wines may throw off a small amount of SEDIMENT in the bottle.

Ungeheuer *see* FORST

United States The United States ranks as the world's fourth largest wine-producing nation after France, Italy, and Spain. U.S. wine consumption has increased about 400 percent over the last 25 years. Even so, on a per capita basis, Americans consume only about one-seventh the wine that the French, Italians, or Portuguese do. In 1999, the United States ranked thirty-fourth in per capita consumption, but its large population allowed this country to finish third in total consumption. About 90 percent of U.S. wines are produced in CALIFORNIA, which would rank California in fourth place if it were a nation. California's CENTRAL VALLEY provides over 70 percent of the state's wine, and although the quality of Central Valley wine is improving, most of it is still considered rather ordinary. On the other hand, most higher-quality U.S. wine comes from California, although it's not the only state producing first-rate wine. WASHINGTON is now viewed as being the second-largest producer of fine wine. Wine is now produced in all fifty states—that is to say that all fifty have at least one federally bonded winery. The resurgence in quality-wine production, which started in California in the mid-1960s (decades after PROHIBITION almost decimated the wine industry), has triggered a similar rally in other parts of country. At this writing, there are over 2,200 wineries scattered throughout the nation. California has the most with over 900, but there are over 200 in WASHINGTON, almost that many in OREGON, over 160 in NEW YORK, and more than 70 in both OHIO and VIRGINIA. States like ARIZONA, COLORADO, NEW MEXICO, and TEXAS are all finding ideal grape-growing locales where warm days and cool nights create just the right combination. In 1983, the United States implemented the AMERICAN VITICULTURAL AREA (AVA) system, designed to identify U.S. wines in a fashion similar to France's APPELLATION D'ORIGINE CONTRÔLÉE for their wines. Unlike the French regulations, however, AVA rules (under the jurisdiction of TAX AND TRADE BUREAU, previously BATF) are extremely lax and must be strengthened before they become truly meaningful. There are many AVAs that do reflect a sense of quality because the winemakers in that area want it to be meaningful; unfortunately that isn't always true. Currently, there are about 150 AVAs throughout the United States. *See also* ARIZONA, CALIFORNIA, COLORADO, CONNECTICUT, IDAHO, INDIANA, KENTUCKY, LOUISIANA, MASSACHUSETTS, MARYLAND, MICHIGAN, MISSOURI, NEW JERSEY, NEW MEXICO, NEW YORK, OHIO, NORTH CAROLINA, OREGON, PENNSYLVANIA, RHODE ISLAND, TEXAS, VIRGINIA, and WASHINGTON.

University of California, Davis The small town of Davis is located in northern California just west of Sacramento. It's home to the UNIVERSITY OF CALIFORNIA, DAVIS, and its well-known Viticulture and Enology Department. In addition to training a mulitude of today's top winemakers, this department is a leader in many areas of research and development including grape varieties and their CLONES, ROOTSTOCKS, vineyard diseases (*see* DISEASES, VINEYARD), and winemaking techniques.

unripe; underripe *see* Glossary of Wine Tasting Terms, page 655

Untermosel *see* ZELL

Ursprungslage *see* GROSSLAGE

Ürzig [UHR-tsikh] A tiny village situated on the Mosel River in Germany's MOSEL-SAAR-RUWER region. Its highly regarded wines are known for their distinctive spicy character, which comes from the area's red clay soil. Ürzig's best-known vineyard is **Würzgarten**, which means "spice garden."

Utiel-Requena DO [oo-TYEHL *r*eh-KEH-nah] A DO located west of the city of Valencia in the Levante region of eastern Spain. There are almost 100,000 vineyard acres in the region, which encompasses the towns of Utiel and Requena and touches the Valencia DO on its eastern boundary. This area produces good ROSÉ wines and full-bodied (*see* BODY) reds, mainly from the BOBAL grape, with minor use of TEMPRANILLO and Garnacha (GRENACHE). Utiel-Requena's rather ordinary white wines are made from MACABEO, Merseguera, and Planta Nova. Among the grapes currently being tested are CABERNET SAUVIGNON, CHARDONNAY, and MERLOT.

uva [OO-vah] Italian for "grapes."

Uva Abruzzi *see* MONTEPULCIANO

Uva Canina *see* CANAIOLO

Uva della Marina *see* UVA DI TROIA

Uva di Troia [OO-vah dee TROY-uh] A high-quality red-wine grape grown primarily in the Italian region of APULIA. Uva di Troia is one of the basic grapes of several DOCS, most notably that of CASTEL DEL MONTE. This grape makes rich, CONCENTRATED wines with good aging potential. Uva di Troia, also known as *Sumarello* and *Uva della Marina,* is usually blended with other varieties such as BOMBINO NERO, MONTEPULCIANO, and SANGIOVESE.

Uva Merla *see* CANAIOLO

Uva Vermiglia *see* CROATINA

V **VA** 1. VA is the Canadian abbreviation for an approved VITICULTURAL AREA, which is a region that has been approved by Canada's VINTNERS QUALITY ALLIANCE (VQA). Wines using VA designations on their labels must meet strict standards and pass certification tests. Currently there are four VAs in BRITISH COLUMBIA and three in ONTARIO. 2. Also an abbreviation for VOLATILE ACIDITY.

Vacqueyras AC [va-keh-*R*AS] One of France's better winemaking villages, located northeast of CHÂTEAUNEUF-DU-PAPE in the southern portion of the RHÔNE region. Vacqueyras was one of the villages entitled to use the CÔTES DU RHÔNE-VILLAGES AC but was given its own AC status in 1990. This gave it equal status with GIGONDAS, a village that had achieved AC status many years earlier. The Vacqueyras AC is best known for its red wines, which generally exhibit dark color, spicy fruit, and enough TANNINS to age well. The main red-wine grapes are GRENACHE, SYRAH, CINSAUT, and MOURVÈDRE.

Vaillons *see* CHABLIS

Valais [va-LEH; va-LAY] Canton that contains one of Switzerland's best growing climates—dry and sunny—and is therefore one of the two main growing regions (the other being VAUD). The vineyards are located in the upper valley of the Rhône in the southwestern part of Switzerland not far from the Italian border. Valais produces mostly white wines, and CHASSELAS (locally known as *Fendant*) is the dominant grape. GAMAY and PINOT NOIR are the most popular red grapes in this area. They're often blended together in a wine called **Dôle**, which is similar to a light-bodied, red BURGUNDY. Dôle, which must contain 51 percent Pinot Noir, is regarded as one of Switzerland's best red wines. Lower-quality versions (those with less than 51 percent Pinot Noir) of this same blend are called **Goron**. Valais also grows Amigne, Arvine, Johannisberger (RIESLING), Humagne, and Malvoisie de Valais (PINOT GRIS) grapes.

Valcalepio DOC [vahl-kah-leh-PEE-oh] DOC located in the center of Italy's LOMBARDY region northeast of Milan and just east of Bergamo. Valcalepio makes a BIANCO wine from CHARDONNAY, Pinot Bianco (PINOT BLANC), and Pinot Grigio (PINOT GRIS); a ROSSO from MERLOT and CABERNET SAUVIGNON; and a PASSITO wine from Moscato (MUSCAT). The best wines come from the vineyards next to the FRANCIACORTA DOCG, along the Oglio River.

Valdadige DOC [vahl-DAH-dee-jay] This DOC, which covers vineyards scattered throughout northeastern Italy's TRENTINO-ALTO ADIGE region and into the VENETO region, is considered the lowest-quality DOC in the Adige Valley. Valdadige (*Etschtaler* in German) has four VARIETAL WINES—CHARDONNAY, Pinot Bianco (PINOT BLANC), Pinot Grigio (PINOT GRIS), and SCHIAVA—and three basic wines—BIANCO, ROSSO, and ROSATO. The Bianco, Rosso, and Rosato wines, which can be DRY or AMABILE, have many approved varieties from which they can be made.

Valdeorras DO [bahl-deh-AWR-rahs] A DO of about 3,800 vineyard acres located in the mountainous area east of the town of Orense in the Galica region in northwestern Spain. Valdeorras produces mostly red wines made primarily from Alicante (GRENACHE) and much of it is sold off in BULK. The MENCÍA grape is now being planted in larger numbers, and wines made from it are gaining a following and are more likely to show up with a Valdeorras DO label. White wines are made mainly from PALOMINO grapes, which produce rather ordinary TABLE WINES. The real rising star of Valdeorras, however, is the white wine made from the local grape Godello (VERDELHO). This high-quality grape grows well in this area and produces CRISP, FRESH, AROMATIC wines.

Valdepeñas DO [bahl-deh-PEH-nyahss] A large DO located south of Madrid in the southern part of Spain's CASTILLA-LA MANCHA region. The Valdepeñas DO, which is named after the town of the same name, is almost fully surrounded by the huge LA MANCHA DO. Traditionally, Valdepeñas ("valley of stones") is best known for a wine that's been made here for centuries—clarete, a light red wine made from both red (Cencibel or TEMPRANILLO) grapes and white (AIRÉN) grapes. Even though Airén grapes are planted in more than 80 percent of the vineyards, the red claretes make up the majority of Valdepeñas production. That's because the DO requirements state that the minimum amount of Cencibel to be used is 20 percent, which means that Airén could comprise up to 80 percent of the blend. This ratio produces wines that are light in both color and flavor. Nonetheless, red Valdepeñas wines are popular throughout Spain. The region's best wines have very high percentages of Cencibel, and more producers are making red wines solely from Cencibel in CRIANZA, RESERVA, and GRAN RESERVA styles using American OAK. Authorities are now requiring that any new vineyard planting consist only of red Cencibel grapevines. These moves are helping to improve Valdepeñas wine in both quality and image.

Valdepeñera Blanca *see* AIRÉN

Val di Cornia DOC [vahl dee KOHR-nyah] A coastal DOC zone located along the Cornia River south of Livorno in Italy's TUSCANY region. It's just south of its famous neighbor, the BOLGHERI DOC. This area's attracting a lot of attention, particularly around the subzone of Suvereto, where wines from grapes grown here can use **Val di Cornia Suvereto DOC** on the label. The quality of Val di Cornia's wines has improved dramatically since the DOC was approved in 1989. Initially, the DOC included ROSSO, ROSATO, and BIANCO wines, but recent DOC changes have added both white and red VARIETAL WINES. The area is gaining a reputation for its high-quality CABERNET SAUVIGNON, MERLOT, and SANGIOVESE wines. Red wines require a minimum of 18 months AGING, RISERVA red wines require 24 months, and red wines from the Suvereto subzone (considered the best) require 26 months of aging.

Valdiguie *see* GAMAY

Vale do São Francisco *see* BRAZIL

Vale dos Vinhedos *see* BRAZIL

Valencia DO [vah-LEHN-shee-uh; Sp. bahl-LEHN-thyah] DO area that is located just west of the coastal city of Valencia in eastern Spain's region called the Levante. There are over 40,000 vineyard acres spread over three subzones: the smallest, **Alto Turia**, which is situated northwest of the city of Valencia; **Clariano**, which is southwest of the city; and the largest area, **Valentino**, which includes vineyards from the former DO, Cheste, and is located directly west of the city of Valencia. The Valencia DO produces more white wines than reds or ROSÉS. Merseguera is the most widely planted white grape, but there are a variety of others including MALVASIA, Planta Fina, Moscatel (MUSCAT), and PEDRO XIMÉNEZ. Red and rosé wines are made mainly from Monastrell (MOURVÈDRE), blended with Garnacha (GRENACHE), and TEMPRANILLO.

Valgella *see* VALTELLINA DOC

Valle d'Aosta; Valle d'Aosta DOC [VAHL-lay DAWSS-tuh] With less than 2000 vineyard acres, Valle d'Aosta is Italy's smallest wine-producing region. It's located in the northwestern section of the country, with France on the west, Switzerland on the north, and PIEDMONT surrounding it on the south and east. Because of its location, the region is officially bilingual and part of the area (known as *Vallée d'Aoste* in French) is French-speaking. Valle d'Aosta is surrounded by tall Alpine peaks, and the vineyards are planted primarily on hilly slopes and terraces near the valley floor. There is currently only one DOC area, **Valle d'Aosta DOC**. The previous DOC areas of Donnaz and Enfer d'Arvier were incorporated into it and are now regarded as two of the seven subzones. The other five subzones are Arnad-Montjovet, Chambave,

Morgex et La Salle, Nus, and Torrette. The Valle d'Aosta DOC covers ROSSO, BIANCO, ROSATO, and a large group of VARIETAL wines. Twenty-two approved grape varieties can be grown throughout this DOC. The most popular white grapes are Blanc de Morgex, Moscato (MUSCAT), MÜLLER-THURGAU, and Pinot Grigio (PINOT GRIS). For red and rosé wines, the most prominent grapes are Fumin, GAMAY, NEBBIOLO, Petit Rouge, Pinot Nero (PINOT NOIR), and Vien de Nus.

Valle de Guimar DO *see* CANARY ISLANDS

Valle de la Orotava DO *see* CANARY ISLANDS

Vallée de la Marne *see* CHAMPAGNE

Valley of the Moon *see* SONOMA VALLEY AVA

Valmur [vahl-MEW*R*] One of the seven GRAND CRU vineyards in CHABLIS. It consists of just over 29 acres and is located between GRENOUILLES and LES CLOS.

Val Nure *see* COLLI PIACENTINI

Valpaços IPR *see* TRÁS-OS-MONTES

Valpantena [vahl-pahn-TEH-nah] A term referring to the Pantena Valley, which lies within the VALPOLICELLA DOC area near Verona in Italy's VENETO region. The name can be used on the label as Valpolicella-Valpantena.

Valpolicella DOC [vahl-paw-lee-CHEHL-lah] A very important red-wine DOC zone located in northeastern Italy's VENETO region. It's situated between BARDOLINO and SOAVE, just north of Verona. Valpolicella ranks just after the CHIANTI DOCG for Italy's total DOC red-wine production. The wine is made primarily from Corvina Veronese (CORVINA), CORVINONE, Rondinella, and Molinara grapes, although four other varieties can comprise up to 15 percent of the blend. Valpolicella's standard DOC wines are rather LIGHT and very fragrant and fruity. Those labeled SUPERIORE have a 1 percent higher minimum ALCOHOL content and are AGED for a minimum of 1 year; AMARONE must be aged for 2 years. The best wines are generally those labeled CLAS-SICO, indicating they're from the inner classico zone with its steeply terraced vineyards. **Valpolicella-Valpantena** on the label indicates that the wines come from a separate area called the Pantena Valley. Valpolicella wines made by the RIPASSO PROCESS are richer in flavor and more full-bodied (*see* BODY) than standard renditions. To make a ripasso wine, the juice is FERMENTED in the usual way and then placed in casks containing the LEES from a prior batch of RECIOTO DELLA VALPO-LICELLA or RECIOTO DELLA VALPOLICELLA AMARONE. This ripasso process, which lasts from 2 to 3 weeks, adds color, TANNINS, and complex flavors. Unfortunately, the term *ripasso* is not allowed on wine labels, so the consumer must know the producers who make this style of wine. Among the wines using this process are Boscaini's Le Canne, Masi's CAMPO FIORIN, and Santi's Castello.

Valréas *see* CÔTES DU RHÔNE

Valtellina DOC; Valtellina Superiore DOCG [vahl-teh-LEE-nah] Demarcated zone located in the LOMBARDY region in northern Italy, very close to the Swiss border. The special MACROCLIMATE of this Alpine area allows the grapes to ripen properly. Only red wines are covered by this DOC. Standard Valtellina wines are made from at least 80 percent Chiavennasca (the local name for NEBBIOLO), and the rest are made from a variety of red grapes; they require 1 year of AGING. Valtellina SUPERIORE wines, which were upgraded to DOCG status in 1998, must be made with at least 90 percent Chavennasca grapes and have 2 years of aging, one of which is in wood. Bottles labeled "RIS-ERVA" have had 3 years of aging. Valtellina Superiore can be made only from vineyards surrounding four of Valtellina's villages—**Grumello**, **Inferno**, **Valgella**, and **Sassella**, the latter being considered best. The word *Sforzato, Sfursat,* or *Sfurzat* on the label indicates the wine was made by the PASSITO process and has a minimum ALCOHOL content of 14½ percent.

Vancouver Island VA *see* BRITISH COLUMBIA

vanilla; vanillin *see* Glossary of Wine Tasting Terms, page 655

varietal *see* VARIETAL WINE

varietal character The unique traits of a given grape variety once it's made into wine is called its varietal character. These traits include AROMA, flavor, COLOR, and BODY. Many elements, like soil, climate, winemaking techniques, and storage can influence a wine, but the grape variety is the dominant component. With practice, one can learn these characteristics and begin to identify VARIETAL WINES. For example, the characteristics of PINOT NOIR and CABERNET SAUVIGNON are distinct enough that, once the differences are understood, they usually can be distinguished even in a BLIND TASTING. Other grape varieties have characteristics so similar that they may be difficult to identify for all except a practiced palate. With some grapes, the varietal characteristics are simply not very distinctive, making identification extremely difficult. *See also* CHARACTER.

varietal wine; varietal [vuh-RI-ih-tuhl] A wine that uses the name of the dominant grape from which it's made, such as CABERNET SAUVIGNON, CHARDONNAY, and RIESLING. This practice occurs primarily in areas where many different grape varieties are grown in close proximity, principally in growing regions of North and South America, Australia, New Zealand, and recently in parts of Europe. There are rules in most areas about what can be called a varietal wine. For example, in the United States, at least 75 percent of the wine must come from the grape variety named on the label, while it's 85 percent in Australia and Europe. Instead of using varietal names, Europeans have long labeled their better wines with the names of regions, districts, or villages, thereby giving the wine's origin utmost importance. In Europe, most quality wines are governed by each country's APPELLATION system, which defines what grapes can be grown in specific areas and encourages the production of quality wines.

variety; varieties The single type of grape within a species that has its own distinct recognizable characteristics. Some of the better-known grape varieties (also called *cultivars*) include CABERNET SAUVIGNON, CHARDONNAY, CHENIN BLANC, MERLOT, PINOT NOIR, RIESLING, SAUVIGNON BLANC, SYRAH, and ZINFANDEL. Almost all grape varieties used in winemaking are part of the VITIS VINIFERA species. In the United States, it's common practice to include the name of the grape variety on the label (*see* VARIETAL WINE), whereas in Europe the name of the producing region is the common identifier. Over 185 of the most popular grape varieties are defined in this book (for a detailed list *see* Grape Varieties, page 595).

Varois *see* COTEAUX VAROIS AC

Varosa IPR *see* TRÁS-OS-MONTES

Varresana Bianca *see* VERMENTINO

Vaucoupin *see* CHABLIS

Les Vaucrains *see* NUITS-SAINT-GEORGES

Vaud [VOH] One of Switzerland's two main wine-producing cantons—the other is VALAIS. Vaud's vineyards are located along the Rhône, starting north of Valais, and along the north shore of Lake Geneva. The three main growing areas are CHABLAIS, just south of Lake Geneva on the Rhône; LAVAUX, which is east of Lausanne on the lake's north shore; and LA CÔTE, which is on the lake's north shore west of Lausanne. Vaud is primarily a white-wine area, and CHASSELAS (locally known as *Dorin*) is the dominant grape. The most popular red grapes are GAMAY and PINOT NOIR. These two grapes are often blended together in a wine called **Salvagnin**, which is similar in style (like a light-bodied, red BURGUNDY) to the Valais canton's *Dôle*. Other varieties grown in this region include PINOT GRIS, PINOT BLANC, and Riesling-Sylvaner (MÜLLER-THURGAU). Vaud has implemented a rudimentary APPELLATION system, which simply defines the region, the grape varieties, and the required sugar levels (*see* APPELLATION D'ORIGINE CONTROLEE for an explanation of the more extensive French system).

Vaudésir [voh-day-ZEE*R*] One of the seven GRAND CRU vineyards in CHABLIS. It consists of just under 32 acres, which are situated between LES PREUSES and GRENOUILLES.

Vau de Vey *see* CHABLIS

VCGI *see* VINOS DE CALIDAD CON INDICACIÓN GEOGRÁFICA

VdM *see* VINHO DE MESA

VDN *see* VIN DOUX NATUREL

VDQS *see* VIN DÉLIMITÉ DE QUALITÉ SUPÉRIEURE

vecchio [VEHK-ee-oh] Italian for "old," the word *vecchio* is used in the wine world to mean "aged." It can appear on DOC wines that have met certain aging conditions.

vegetal *see* Glossary of Wine Tasting Terms, page 655

Velletri DOC [vay-LEH-tree] A DOC area located northeast of Lake Albano and northeast of Rome in Italy's LATIUM region. The area produces BIANCO and ROSSO wines. The Bianco, which is made from MALVASIA and TREBBIANO, may be DRY, AMABILE or DOLCE, and STILL or SPUMANTE. The Rosso is made primarily from SANGIOVESE, MONTEPULCIANO, and Cesanese and may be dry or amabile. Bottles labeled RISERVA are higher in ALCOHOL and have been AGED for 2 years.

velouté *see* Glossary of Wine Tasting Terms, page 655

Veltliner *see* GRÜNER VELTLINER

Veltlini *see* GRÜNER VELTLINER

velvety *see* Glossary of Wine Tasting Terms, page 655

vendange [vahn-dahn-ZH] French for "VINTAGE," referring to the grape harvest. The Spanish equivalent is *vendimia;* the Italian is *vendemmia.*

Vendange Tardive [vahn-dahn-ZH tahr-DEEV] French for "LATE HARVEST," referring to wines made from late-picked grapes with higher sugar levels and more pronounced flavors. Such wines, which are a specialty of the ALSACE region, are generally VINIFIED totally DRY and are rich and very flavorful. They're made from several varieties—RIESLING, GEWÜRZTRAMINER, PINOT GRIS, and MUSCAT.

vendemmia [vayn-DAYM-myah] Italian for "VINTAGE," referring to the time of the grape harvest. The Spanish equivalent is *vendimia;* the French is *vendange.*

vendimia [bayn-DEE-myah] Spanish for "VINTAGE," referring to the grape harvest. The French equivalent is *vendange;* the Italian is *vendemmia.*

Veneto [VEH-neh-toh] A large wine-producing region in northeastern Italy. Its capital, Venice, sits on the Adriatic Sea. Directly west of Venice is this area's other important city, Verona, which isn't far from Lake Garda on this region's western edge. Veneto has about 185,000 vineyard acres and is one of Italy's top three or four regions in total wine production. It's also the top producer of DOC-approved wines, with almost 19 percent of Italy's total DOC production, although many would question how well this truly reflects the production of "quality" wine. The best-known wines are from the three DOCs of BARDOLINO, SOAVE, and VALPOLICELLA, all of which are located around Verona. This region has three DOCGS—BARDOLINO SUPERIORE, RECIOTO DI SOAVE, and SOAVE SUPERIORE. Its twenty-two DOC areas include BIANCO DI CUSTOZA, BREGANZE, COLLI BERICI, COLLI EUGANEI, GAMBELLARA, and LISON-PRAGAGGIORE (shared with FRIULI-VENEZIA GIULIA). Popular red grapes in the Veneto include CABERNET FRANC, CABERNET SAUVIGNON, CORVINA, MERLOT, Molinara, and Rondinella. Among the favored white grapes are CHARDONNAY, GARGANEGA, Pinot Bianco (PINOT BLANC), Pinot Grigio (PINOT GRIS), PROSECCO, and TREBBIANO.

Vennentino *see* VERMENTINO

Ventoux *see* CÔTES DU VENTOUX

veraison [vay-ray-ZON] The point in the growing season when ripening grapes begin to soften and change color from green to either red or yellow, depending on the VARIETY. In the northern hemisphere, veraison typically occurs anywhere from late June to mid August, depending on the climate. *See also* VITICULTURE.

Vérargues *see* GRÉS DE MONTPELLIER

Verbesco *see* BARBERA

Verdejo; Verdejo Palido [vehr-DAY-yoh pah-LEE-doh] A white-wine grape grown in and indigenous to Spain's RUEDA region. It's also cultivated in the neighboring regions of Toro and RIBERA DEL DUERO. Verdejo produces full-bodied (*see* BODY), yet CRISP wine with a rich, nutty flavor. Rueda's top category of wine, Rueda SUPERIOR, must contain at least 60 percent Verdejo; the very best wine is 100 percent Verdejo. The Rueda region also produces a SHERRY-style wine from Verdejo grapes.

Verdelho [vehr-DEH-lyoh] 1. Once MADEIRA'S most widely planted white-wine grape, Verdelho is slowly being phased out (*see also* second definition). This same variety is found in the Azores and in Australia. On the Portuguese mainland, a different variety, also called Verdelho, is recommended in the DÃO region's white wines and in the production of white PORT. The official Portuguese name for this VARIETY is now *Gouveio*. The *Godello* grown in northwest Spain is believed to be the same variety as Gouveio. 2. A medium-DRY style of Madeira wine, slightly richer than SERCIAL but less opulent than BOAL or MALMSEY. Originally made primarily with Verdelho grapes, this style of Madeira has recently utilized more TINTA NEGRA MOLE (which is considered only a *good* grape), especially in the cheaper versions. In 1986, however, Portugal entered the Common Market, whose regulations required that by 1993 any Madeira wine naming a variety on its label will have to contain at least 85 percent of that grape. Wines labeled "Verdelho-style" can contain less than the required 85 percent, and most likely contain more Tinta Negra Mole.

Verdicchio [vehr-DEEK-kyoh] A white-wine grape grown mainly in Italy's MARCHES region where it's been cultivated since the fourteenth century. Verdicchio's name is derived from *verde* (meaning green), referring to the yellow-green skin of the grape, which gives the wine a subtle greenish hue. The wines are generally CRISP and DRY, with a light but elegant aroma and flavor. The best known of the Verdicchio wines come from the DOC of VERDICCHIO DEI CASTELLI DE JESI, which can include small amounts of TREBBIANO and MALVASIA. Part of the notability of these wines comes from the unusual green, amphora (two-handled urn)-shaped bottle in which it comes. The wines from the DOC of

VERDICCHIO DEI MATELICA are not as well known as those from Verdicchio dei Castelli di Jesi but are thought by many to be as good or better because they're more full-bodied (*see* BODY) and have better aging potential. The high ACID levels of the Verdicchio grape makes it a good candidate for SPARKLING WINES, and the SPUMANTE made from this variety receives good reviews. Verdicchio is also known as *Marchigiano* and *Verdone.*

Verdicchio dei Castelli di Jesi DOC [veh*r*-DEEK-kyoh day kahs-TEHL-lee dee YEH-zee] Area that encompasses the hilly sites west of the town of Jesi in Italy's MARCHES region. This is the best known of the DOCs making wine from the VERDICCHIO grape. The wines, which can also contain up to 15 percent MALVASIA and TREBBIANO grapes, are generally CRISP and DRY, with a light but elegant aroma and flavor. The CLASSICO zone covers all but a small section of the regular DOC area. SPUMANTE versions are made as well, some using the MÉTH-ODE CHAMPENOISE.

Verdicchio di Matelica DOC [veh*r*-DEEK-kyoh dee mah-TAY-lee-kah] Another DOC that produces wines based on the VERDICCHIO grape. It's located south of the better-known VERDICCHIO DEI CASTELLI DI JESI DOC in central Italy's MARCHES region. The wines of these two DOCs are similar, although some believe that the Matelica wines are more full-bodied (*see* BODY). In addition to Verdicchio, the wines can also contain up to 15 percent of MALVASIA and TREBBIANO grapes.

Verdone *see* VERDICCHIO

Verdot Rouge *see* PETIT VERDOT

Verduno Pelaverga DOC [veh*rr*-DOO-noh peh-lah-VEH*RR*-gah] DOC zone that encompasses areas around the village of Verduno and parts of the neighboring villages of La Morra and Roddi d'Alba in northern Italy's PIEDMONT region. The northern tip overlaps the famous BAROLO DOCG and some Barolo wines are produced around Verduno, although they aren't generally as well regarded as those made from vineyards to the south. The wines from the Verduno Pelaverga are DRY wines (STILL or SPARKLING) that must be made of at least 85 percent of the PELAVERGA grape variety. The wines are generally light and spicy with floral and red fruit aromas. They have moderate alcohol levels with a minimum of 11 percent and are best drunk young.

Verduzzo; Verduzzo Friulano [vehr-DOOT-soh froo-LAH-noh] A white-wine grape indigenous to Italy's FRIULI-VENEZIA GIULIA region. Verduzzo is best known for its AMABILE (semisweet) and DOLCE (sweet) wines, which exhibit floral and rich honey characteristics, balanced by good ACIDITY. The best of these sweet wines comes from the RAMANDOLO DOCG. Verduzzo is also used in the production of DRY white wines. The *Verduzzo Trevigiano* grown in Italy's VENETO region is thought to be a different variety.

Aux Vergelesses *see* SAVIGNY-LÈS-BEAUNE

Les Vergelesses *see* PERNAND-VERGELESSES

Les Vergennes *see* CORTON

Les Vergers *see* CHASSAGNE-MONTRACHET AC

Vergine *see* MARSALA DOC

verjuice; *Fr.* verjus [VER-joos; *Fr.* vehr-ZHOO] An acidic, slightly sour liquid made from unripe fruit, primarily grapes. The word derives from *vert jus,* French for "green juice," referring to the fact that the juice comes from high-acid, low-sugar semiripe grapes that were thinned from the vines. Verjuice is used in preparations like sauces and mustards to heighten flavor, much as lemon juice or vinegar would be employed, though it's a more gentle acidulant. Not widely used since medieval and Renaissance times, verjuice is now enjoying a comeback in many dishes.

Vermentino [ver-mehn-TEE-noh] A white-wine grape thought to be related to MALVASIA and to a variety grown in Italy's PIEDMONT known as *Favorita*. Vermentino is most often associated with the French island of CORSICA. However, it's also grown on the neighboring Italian island SARDINIA and on Italy's mainland in the LIGURIA region. On Corsica, Vermentino is usually blended with Ugni Blanc (TREBBIANO). Corsica's best wines, however, are made with 100 percent Vermentino grapes and are deep-colored, fruity, and full-bodied (*see* BODY). In Liguria, where Vermentino is DOC classified as **Riviera Ligure di Ponente**, the wines are LIGHTER and CRISPER than the Corsican versions. Sardinian renditions, which are classified as **Vermentino di Gallura DOCG** and **Vermentino di Sardegna DOC**, are similar to those from Liguria, but not as ACIDIC. Vermentino, known in France as *Rolle*, is also called *Varresana Bianca* and *Vennentino*.

Vermentino di Gallura DOCG *see* VERMENTINO

Vermentino di Sardegna DOC *see* VERMENTINO

vermouth [ver-MOOTH] White wine that has been FORTIFIED and flavored with various herbs and spices. The name *vermouth* comes from the German *wermut* ("wormwood"), which, before it was declared poisonous, was once the principal flavoring ingredient. There are several types of this wine, the most popular being **dry white vermouth**, commonly thought of as French, although it's made in other countries including the United States. It's served as an APÉRITIF and used in nonsweet cocktails like martinis. The reddish brown **sweet vermouth** (which is colored with caramel) is also served as an apéritif as well as used in slightly sweet cocktails such as the Manhattan. A third style called **Bianco** is white and slightly sweet, and not as popular as the other two.

Vernaccia di Oristano [ver-NAHT-chah dee aw-riss-TAH-noh] 1. A white-wine grape grown on the island of SARDINIA, primarily north of the city of Oristano. Vernaccia di Oristano grapes are processed much like those for sherry, producing good-quality, amber-colored wines reminiscent of DRY, aged Olorosos (*see* SHERRY). These wines are AGED in wood for a minimum of 2 years—3 years for SUPERIORE, and 4 years for RISERVA. Although not as distinctive, there are also LIQUOROSO (FORTIFIED) versions that are vinified both sweet and dry. Vernaccia di Oristano is not related to VERNACCIA DI SAN GIMIGNANO. 2. A DOC encompassing the city of Oristano and areas to the north of the city, which is located on the western side of Sardinia.

Vernaccia di San Gimignano; Vernaccia di San Gimignano DOCG [ver-NAHT-chah dee sahn jee-mee-NYAH-noh] 1. A white-wine grape grown in Italy's TUSCANY region, primarily southwest of Florence around the medieval hilltop town of San Gimignano. Vernaccia di San Gimignano dates back as far as the thirteenth century, and its origins are thought to be Greek. The wines produced from this variety vary tremendously. Traditionally made, they're golden in color, rich, and full-bodied (*see* BODY), with an OXIDIZED style and a slightly bitter edge to the flavor. More modern winemaking techniques produce paler-colored wines with crisper, lighter characteristics. 2. A DOCG area based around the town of San Gimignano that was the very first to receive DOC status when Italy began implementing its wine-classification system in 1966. It was upgraded to DOCG status in 1993, and at the same time approval was given for up to 10 percent CHARDONNAY grapes to be added. In addition to the reputation for the wines produced from its namesake grape, the town of San Gimignano is renowned for its medieval atmosphere. It's replete with tall, narrow towers that were built during a time when higher was considered better and safer.

vernache *see* FEDERWEISSER

Vernatsch *see* SCHIAVA

Les Verroilles *see* GEVREY CHAMBERTIN

Vertical Shoot Positioning *see* TRELLIS SYSTEM

vertical tasting *see* WINE TASTING

Vesuvio DOC [veh-SOO-vee-oh] DOC zone located east of Naples in Italy's CAMPANIA region. Actually, there are two DOCs in the area—the Vesuvio DOC and the **Lacryma Christi del Vesuvio DOC (LCV)**, which means "tears of Christ." Both make BIANCO, ROSSO, and ROSATO and use the same grapes. The difference is that the Lacryma Christi del Vesuvio DOC requires a minimum ALCOHOL level to be 1 to 1½ percent higher. The varieties used for the red and ROSÉ wines are Piedirosso, Sciascinoso, and AGLIANICO. The white wines are made from Verdeca, Coda di Volpe, Falanghina, and GRECO. There is also an LCV LIQUOROSO, a white FORTIFIED WINE made from the same white grapes. Lacryma is sometimes spelled *Lacrima* or *Lachryma*.

Vézelay AC [vay-zuh-lay] Appellation located southeast of CHABLIS in BURGUNDY. Vineyards in and around the villages of Asquins, Saint-Père, Tharoiseau, and Vézelay produce white wines made from CHARDONNAY grapes that may be labeled BOURGOGNE VÉZELAY. There are approximately 160 acres under vine in the appellation, most planted in the 1970s and later because of PHYLLOXERA. Even though that insect hit the vineyards here in the late 1800s, vineyards weren't replanted until much later. The wines from Vézelay are viewed as an inexpensive alternative to the wines from Chablis. They are CRISP and FLINTY like those from Chablis, but they mature earlier.

Victoria Victoria, Australia's second-smallest state, is located in the southeastern corner of the country, bounded on the south and east by the Indian Ocean, Bass Strait, and Tasman Sea. NEW SOUTH WALES is to the north, SOUTH AUSTRALIA to the south. Melbourne is Victoria's capital and most populous city, and Australia's second most populous city after Sydney. Victoria's wine industry started slowly in the 1840s, followed the gold boom of the 1850s, and continued to expand for several decades. In the 1890s Victoria produced over half of Australia's wines. Then PHYLLOXERA infested many of the growing regions and a depression hit; the wine industry faltered well into the twentieth century. Victoria's viticultural revival gathered strength in the 1970s and 1980s and today it's the third most important wine state after South

Australia and New South Wales. Under the Australian GEOGRAPHIC INDI-CATIONS system, Victoria officially has six major ZONES and nineteen REGIONS. In the Northwest corner of the state, farthest from Melbourne, is the **North West Victoria Zone**. Here you'll find the highly productive regions of MURRAY DARLING and SWAN HILL, which rely on irrigation from Murray River water and which produce large quantities of inexpensive but decent quality wines. Farther south is the **Western Victoria Zone** with three regions (east to west)—GRAMPIANS, PYRENEES, and HENTY. Moving east and slightly north there is the **Central Victoria Zone** with, east to west, the BENNDIGO, GOULBURN VALLEY, and CENTRAL VICTORIAN HIGH COUNTRY regions. Southward, circling Melbourne, is the **Port Phillip Zone**, which is divided into five regions—GEELONG, MACEDON RANGES, MORNINGTON PENINSULA, SUNBURY, and the most famous of all, YARRA VALLEY. Just east is GIPPSLAND, which is both a zone and region. The sixth zone is the **North East Victoria Zone**, which hosts the RUTHERGLEN, KING VALLEY, and ALPINE VALLEYS regions. Victoria grapes can make their way into wines designated as SOUTH EASTERN AUSTRALIA, a gigantic zone that covers three states and parts of two others.

Vidal 256 *see* VIDAL BLANC

Vidal Blanc [vee-dahl BLAHN (BLAHNGK)] A French-American HYBRID grape developed by crossing Ugni Blanc (TREBBIANO) and Seibel 4986 (another hybrid). Vidal Blanc (officially known as *Vidal 256*) is grown in the eastern United States and Canada. The grapes have high sugar and good ACID levels, with nice but rather neutral flavors. The wines are vinified in a variety of styles from DRY to sweet. ICE WINES with good flavor and richness have been made from frozen Vidal Blanc grapes in a style similar to German EISWEIN.

VIDE *see* VINTIVINICOLTORI ITALIANI D'ECCELLENZA

Vidigueira DOC *see* ALENTEJO

Vidure *see* CABERNET SAUVIGNON

vieilles vignes [vee-ay-VEE-nyuh] *see* OLD VINE

vigna [VEE-nyah] Italian for "vineyard."

vignaiolo [vee-NYAH-loh] Italian for "grape grower."

Vigne au Saint; La Vigne au Saint *see* CORTON

vigneron [vee-nyeh-ROHN] French for "vine grower."

vignoble [vee-NYOHBL] French for "vineyard."

Vignoles *see* RAVAT

vigorous *see* Glossary of Wine Tasting Terms, page 655

Vijariego Grape VARIETIES grown primarily on the CANARY ISLANDS. **Vijariego Blanco** is the primary white grape in the El Hierro DO. It's also grown in the Tacoronte-Acentejo DO, where it's one of the allowed white varieties that can be blended with the red wines produced in that DO, and in the Ycoden-Daute-Isora DO. It can produce fairly interesting dry white wines. Vijariego **Negro** is the red-wine variety. It's grown throughout the Canary Islands and produces fairly RUSTIC wines. The Canary Islands escaped the PHYLLOXERA epidemic that struck most of Europe so these varieties survived here.

Vila Nova de Gaia [vee-lah noh-vah deh GAH-yah] A quaint old town in northern Portugal that sits on the Douro River across from the city of OPORTO. PORT wines have been stored and matured in the LODGES (warehouses) in Vila Nova de Gaia for over 200 years.

Le Village *see* CORTON

Villány-Siklós [vihl-lan sheek-lohsh] Wine region located in southwest Hungary, just west of the Danube River. Vineyards dot the slopes of the Villány and Siklós hills. The eastern section surrounding Villány is best known for its red wines, particularly its PINOT NOIR and BORDEAUX BLENDS, but Kékfarnkos (BLAUFRÄNKISH) and PORTUGEISER are also grown. White varieties such as CHARDONNAY, HÁRSLEVELŰ, Italian Riesling (WELSCHRIESLING), and LEÁNYKA are grown mainly in the Siklós area.

Villard Blanc [vee-yahr BLAHN; BLAHNGK] A white French-American HYBRID once widely grown in the south of France, particularly in the LANGUEDOC-ROUSSILLON region. It was developed by French hybridizers Seyve and Villard, who also created SEYVAL BLANC. Villard Blanc, also known as *Seyve Villard 12.375,* is grown in the eastern United States as well. It's highly productive and produces medium-quality wine with a flavor so pronounced that it's usually blended with other grape varieties to produce a more neutral wine. Villard Blanc acreage has declined over the last few decades because French authorities are encouraging its replacement with higher-quality white grape varieties.

Villard Noir [vee-yahr NWAHR] Although once quite popular in France, this red French-American HYBRID is gradually being replaced by higher-quality red varieties at the encouragement of French authorities. Villard Noir, which is still planted in southwestern France, produces wines of medium to low quality. Much of the crop is now distilled (*see* DISTILLATION) into SPIRITS. Villard Noir, also known as *Seyve Villard 18.315,* can be found in the eastern United States as well.

vin [VAN] French for "wine."

viña [BEE-nyah] Spanish for "vineyard."

vin blanc [van BLAHN] French for "white wine."

vin bourru [van boo-REW] A French term for wine that is drawn from the vat or barrel just shortly after FERMENTATION is completed. Vin bourru wine has a fresh, slightly effervescent character and is a favorite in many European countries.

vin de carafe *see* CARAFE WINE

Vin de Consommation Courante [van duh kawn-saw-mah-SYAWN koo-RAHN] French for "Wine for Current Consumption," once the official name for France's VIN ORDINAIRE ("ordinary wine"). Vin de Consommation Courante has been replaced by the term VIN DE TABLE.

Vin de Corse AC *see* CORSICA

vin de cuvée [van duh koo-VAY] A term used in France's CHAMPAGNE region to describe the juice produced from the first PRESSING of the grapes. The presses in champagne hold 4,000 kilograms (about 8,800 pounds) of grapes, which, up until 1990, were given four separate pressings. The first pressing (*serre*) could produce up to 2,050 liters (541 gallons) of *vin de cuvée,* which is the best juice and goes into the premium champagnes. The second pressing could yield up to 410 liters (108 gallons) of juice called *première taille.* The third pressing could produce up to 205 liters (54 gallons) of juice called *deuxième taille.* Both the second and third pressings were of lesser quality than the *vin de cuvée* and were used in lower-quality wines or sold off. The fourth pressing, called *rebêche,* was made from moistened grapes and produced insipid juice used by the workers for homemade wine. As of 1990, the deuxième taille (juice from the third pressing) category was officially eliminated and the maximum amount of juice for the première taille (juice from the second pressing) was increased from 410 liters to 500 liters (132 gallons).

vin de garde [van duh GAHRD] A French term that means "wine for guarding" or "keeping," referring to a wine with the proper attributes for long AGING. A vin de garde will improve and develop character as it matures.

vin de goutte *see* FREE-RUN JUICE; FREE-RUN WINE

vin de l'année [va*n* duh lah-NAY] French term that means "this year's wine" and refers to wine from the latest VINTAGE. The expression is used in areas like BEAUJOLAIS, where many of the wines are drunk quite young.

Vin Délimité de Qualité Supérieure (VDQS) [va*n* deh-lee-mee-TAY duh kah-lee-TAY soo-pehr-YUR] French for "Delimited Wine of Superior Quality." This is the second-highest classification level for French wines, the top category being APPELLATION D'ORIGINE CONTRÔLÉE (AC). There are two categories below VDQS—VIN DE PAYS and VIN DE TABLE. VDQS wines are controlled by regulations similar to AOC wines. Many VDQS wines are of excellent quality, and the French have promoted over twenty VDQS areas to AOC status. This classification is shrinking in size as the VDQS are being promoted and few new ones are being created.

vin de liqueur [va*n* duh lee-KEW*R*] Similar to a VIN DOUX NATUREL in that FERMENTATION is stopped by the addition of BRANDY (a vin doux naturel must be stopped by a neutral alcohol). The brandy is usually added to the grape juice before fermentation has begun, but it can be added during the process. The resulting FORTIFIED WINE is sweet and high in ALCOHOL, generally ranging between 16 and 22 percent. FLOC DE GASCOGNE, PINEAU DES CHARENTES, and RATAFIA are all vins de liqueur.

vin de paille [va*n* duh PAH-yuh] French for "straw wine," referring to wines made from grapes that are dried by spreading them out on mats or trays or by hanging them in bunches. The name comes from the original practice of using straw mats during the drying process. The dried grapes are full of sweet, concentrated juice. Once FERMENTATION begins, the sugar content is usually high enough to take the wine to a reasonable alcohol level (*see* ALCOHOL BY VOLUME) and still retain enough RESIDUAL SUGAR to make these wines fairly sweet.

vin de pays [va*n* deu pay-YEE] French for "country wine." Officially, this is the third-highest wine-quality level in France's quality control system. The two higher categories are APPELLATION D'ORIGINE CONTRÔLÉE (AOC) and VIN DÉLIMITÉ DE QUALITÉ SUPÉRIEURE (VDQS); VIN DE TABLE is lower. The rules for vin de pays are similar to the two higher categories, but they are slightly more relaxed in that higher YIELDS and lower minimum ALCOHOL levels are allowed. There are three types of geographically defined categories within vin de pays. The largest are *vin de pays régionaux,* which encompass entire regions. Within a region, there may be several *vin de pays départementaux* (DÉPARTE-MENTS), and within those, there are numerous *vin de pays de zone* (a localized area or community), the smallest defined areas. Some of the better-known vin de pays regions are Vin de Pays du Jardin de la France and Vin de Pays D'Oc. Départements include Vin de Pays de l'Aude (AUDE) and Vin de Pays de l'Hérault (L'HÉRAULT). The term **Vin du pays**, which simply means "local wine," isn't the same as *vin de pays* and has no legal meaning.

vin de presse *see* FREE-RUN JUICE; FREE-RUN WINE

Vin de Qualité Produits dans des Régions Déterminées (VQPRD) [va*n* deu kah-lee-TAY proh-DWEE dah*n* day ray-ZHAW*N*S day-tehr-mee-NEES] A French expression that literally means "Quality Wine Produced in Determined Regions," and that is commonly short-ened to simply "quality wine." Though "VQPRD" may be found on the label of some top-quality wines from countries in the EUROPEAN UNION, each member country has their own program to encourage the produc-tion of quality wines. For example, in France the APPELLATION D'ORIGINE CONTRÔLÉE and VIN DÉLIMITÉ DE QUALITE SUPÉRIEUR are such programs, as are Italy's DENOMINAZIONE DI ORIGINE CONTROLLATA and DENOMINAZIONE DI ORIGINE CONTROLLATA E GARANTITA, Spain's DENOMINACIÓN DE ORIGEN, and Germany's QUALITÄTSWEIN and QUALITÄTSWEIN MIT PRÄDIKAT.

Vin de Savoie AC *see* SAVOIE

vin de table [va*n* deu TAH-bl] French for "TABLE WINE," also referred to as *vin ordinaire* ("ordinary wine"). This is France's lowest category of wine and includes all the wines that don't fit into the higher cate-gories of APPELLATION D'ORIGINE CONTRÔLÉE (AOC), VIN DÉLIMITÉ DE QUALITE SUPÉRIEURE (VDQS), and VIN DE PAYS. The labels on vin de table wines don't mention regional or local origin and bear only the country's name. They're often sold with a proprietary brand name with the sim-ple indication that they're either VIN ROUGE, VIN BLANC, or VIN ROSÉ. Vin de table replaces the term VIN DE CONSOMMATION COURANTE.

vin doux naturel (VDN) [va*n* doo nah-tew-REHL] French for "naturally sweet wine." This refers to a category of sweet, FORTIFIED WINES made from grapes that are high in natural sugar (capable of reaching 15 percent ALCOHOL) and whose FERMENTATION is stopped by the addition of a neutral alcohol (no more than 10 percent of the vol-ume). The resulting wines are usually 15 to 18 percent alcohol but can range as high as 21½ percent. VDNs vary in sweetness, with white wines generally being sweeter and less alcoholic than reds. Most VDN white wines are made from MUSCAT, usually Muscat à Petits Grains or Muscat of Alexandria. APPELLATION D'ORIGINE CONTRÔLÉES (ACS) noted for their VDN whites include MUSCAT DE BEAUMES-DE-VENISE, MUSCAT DE FRONTIGNAN, Muscat de Lunel, Muscat de Mireval, MUSCAT DE RIVESALTES, and Muscat de St-Jean-de-Minervois. The best known VDN red and ROSÉ wines, produced primarily from GRENACHE, are from the ACs of BANYULS, MAURY, RASTEAU, and RIVESALTES.

Vin du Bugey VDQS *see* BUGEY VDQS

vin du pays [va*n* doo pay-YEE] The French term for "local wine." *See also* VIN DE PAYS.

vineal [vihn-EE-uhl] A general term describing anything characteristic of grapes, grapevines, wine, or winemaking. *See also* VINOUS.

vinegary *see* Glossary of Wine Tasting Terms, page 655

vine variety *see* VARIETY

vineyard An area planted with grapevines.

vineyard designated A term indicating that a wine is made with grapes from the specific vineyard named on a wine's label. In the United States, a vineyard name on a label means that 95 percent of the grapes in the wine came from the named vineyard and that the named vineyard is located in the AVA indicated on the label.

vin fin [va*n* FA*N*] French for "wine of quality." This is not an official term, however, and, because it's so freely used for marketing purposes, it doesn't have much meaning.

vin gris [va*n* GREE] French for "gray wine," but referring to very pale ROSÉ wines. Vin gris wines are produced in various parts of France and are made from lightly pressed red grapes (CABERNET SAUVIGNON, PINOT NOIR, or GAMAY), which are separated from the juice before much color is transferred from the skins.

vinha [VEE-nyer] Portuguese for "vineyard."

Vinhão *see* SOUZÀO

vinho [VEE-nyoo] Portuguese for "wine."

vinho consumo [VEE-nyoo KAW*N*-soo-myoh] Portuguese for "wine to consume" or ordinary wine. Similar in meaning to the French VIN ORDINAIRE.

vinho de mesa (VdM) [VEE-nyoo der MAY-zer] The lowest quality-level designation for Portuguese wine, indicating a simple table wine. It's similar to the French category of VIN DE TABLE. VINHO REGIONAL (VR) is the next quality level up followed by the INDICAÇÃO DE PROVENIENCIA REGULAMENTADA (IPR). The highest Portuguese quality category is DENOMINAÇÃO DE ORIGEM CONTROLADA (DOC). Currently vinho de mesa wines are not allowed to have VINTAGE dates.

vinho generoso [VEE-nyoo zher-ner-ROA-zoo] Portuguese for "fortified wine."

vinho regional (VR) [VEE-nyoo rree-zhyoo-NAHL] A regional designation for Portuguese wine quality with a connotation similar to that of the French VIN DE PAYS. Vinho regional is the third level in the Portuguese quality hierarchy—below the DENOMINAÇÃO DE ORIGEM CONTROLADA (DOC) and the INDICAÇÃO DE PROVENIENCIA REGULAMENTADA (IPR) and above the VINHO DE MESA (VDM) category. Some producers are opting to use "vinho regional" labeling in order to take advantage of less stringent rules, such as those for the use of grape varieties not allowed by DOCs or IPRs and permission to use varietal names on wine labels. The current Portuguese vinho regional designates are ALENTEJO, Algrave, BEIRAS, ESTREMADURA, MADEIRA, Rios do Minho, RIBATEJO, TERRAS DO SADO, and Trás-os-Montes.

Vinho Verde DOC [VEE-nyoh VEHR-deh] Portugal's largest DOC, Vinho Verde is located in the Minho region in the northwestern part of the country. The term *vinho verde* means "green wine," referring not to this wine's color, but to its fresh, fruity youthfulness. These slightly effervescent wines can be red or white, each representing about half the production. The red wines, which are often harsh with a SOUR, ACIDIC character, are primarily consumed by the Portuguese and are not exported in large quantities. The white wines are also acidic, but the acidity helps make them FRESH and CRISP. Although the best white wines are DRY, some are made in a sweet style. Both red and white wines are meant to be drunk young. The main grapes used for the red wines are Azal Tinto, Borraçal, and Espadeiro; the white wines use ALVARINHO, LOUREIRO, and Trajadura grapes.

viniculture [VIHN-ih-kuhl-cher] Synonymous with ENOLOGY, viniculture is the study or science of winemaking. One who does so is called a viniculturist, enologist, or simply a winemaker. The term viniculture is not as popular as its counterpart enology. *See also* ACETALDE-HYDE; ACETIFICATION; ACETOBACTER; ACIDITY; ACIDS; ACIDULATION; AGING; ALCOHOL; AMELIORATION; ANTHOCYANINS; ANTIOXIDANT; ASSEMBLAGE; AUTO-CLAVE; AUTOLYSIS; BAKING; BARREL; BARREL FERMENTATION; BRIX; BENTONITE; BLENDING; BORDEAUX BLEND; BOTTLE FERMENTATION; BOTTLE SICKNESS; BUNG; CAMPDEN TABLETS; CAP; CAPSULE; CARBON DIOXIDE; CARBONIC MACERATION; CARBOY; CHAPTALIZATION; CHARMAT PROCESS; COOPERAGE; CORKS; CRUST; CRY-OEXTRACTION; CUSTOM CRUSHING; DEACIDIFICATION; DESTEMMING; DISGORGE-MENT; DOSAGE; ENOLOGY; ESTERS; ESTUFAGEM; FERMENTATION; FERMENTATION CONTAINERS; FERMENTATION LOCK; FIELD BLEND; FILTERING; FINING; FLAVONOIDS; FLOR; FORTIFICATION; FRUCTOSE; GLUCOSE; GLYCEROL; GRAPE CONCENTRATE; GRAPES; HYDROGEN SULFIDE; HYDROMETER; INOCULATE; ISINGLASS; LEAF REMOVAL; LEES; MACERATION; MALOLACTIC FERMENTATION; MÉTHODE CHAMP-ENOISE; MUST; MUST WEIGHT; MUTAGE; MUTÉ; MYCODERMA; OAKING; OXIDATION; PASSITO; PASTEURIZATION; PH; PHENOLIC COMPOUNDS; PLASTERING; POMACE; POTASSIUM METABISULFITE; POTENTIAL ALCOHOL; PRESS; PULP; PUMPING OVER; PUNCHING DOWN; RACKING; RESIDUAL SUGAR; RIDDLING; RIPASSO PROCESS; SEC-ONDARY FERMENTATION; SEDIMENT; SKIN CONTACT; SOLERA SYSTEM; SPECIFIC GRAVITY; STABILIZATION; STAINLESS STEEL TANKS; STARTER; SULFUR DIOXIDE; SUR LIE; TANNINS; TOPPING; TARTRATES; ULLAGE; VARIETY; VINTAGE; VITICULTURE; VOLATILE ACIDITY; WHOLE BERRY FERMENTATION; WINEGROWER; YEAST.

vinifera *see* VITIS VINIFERA

viniferous [vi-NIHF-uhr-us] Suitable for use in winemaking, as in a viniferous grape variety.

vinification [vihn-ih-fih-KAY-shuhn] The process of making wines. *See also* ENOLOGY; VINICULTURE.

vinify; vinified [VIHN-uh-fi] To produce wine from grapes or other fruit.

vin jaune [va*n* ZHOHN] French for "yellow wine," referring to a type of wine made in eastern France's JURA region. AGED for 6 years, vin jaune undergoes a process similar to a fino-style SHERRY whereby a film of FLOR (a yeast) covers the wine's surface. This layer prevents OXI-DATION while allowing evaporation, thereby creating the wine's subsequent concentration. The result is a sherrylike wine with a delicate, nutty richness that can age for decades. The best-known vin jaune, made from SAVAGNIN grapes, is from the CHÂTEAU-CHALON AC.

vin mousseux *see* MOUSSEUX

vin nature *see* NATURE

vin nouveau *see* NOUVEAU

vino [It. VEE-noh; Sp. BEE-noh] Italian and Spanish for "wine."

vino borracho *see* MALAGA DO

vino corriente [BEE-no koh-rree-AYN-tay] Spanish for "plain wine," referring to one that's young, inexpensive, and ordinary. Vino corriente is equivalent in meaning to France's VIN ORDINAIRE.

vino da pasto [VEE-noh dah PAH-stoh] Italian for TABLE WINE or "wine of the meal." This term has no official significance and is used to categorize wines served during the meal versus those taken as an APÉRITIF or DESSERT WINE. VINO DA TAVOLA, which also means "table wine," is an official category.

vino da taglio *see* TAGLIO

vino da tavola (VdT); pl. vini [VEE-noh dah TAH-voh-lah; pl. VEE-nee] Italian for "TABLE WINE," referring to Italy's lowest category of wine. The term is similar to France's VIN DE TABLE and Germany's TAFEL-WEIN. Generally, VdT wines are fairly ordinary; however, there are a number of surprises because many top producers don't conform to DOC regulations and make excellent wines that they register in this category. This occurs mainly when producers use unapproved grape varieties or when the proportions don't meet DOC regulations. Examples of such excellent wines are Tuscany's Solaia and Tignanello (both are a blend of CABERNET SAUVIGNON and SANGIOVESE).

vino de color *see* MALAGA DO

vino de la tierra [BEE-noh day lah TYEH*R*-*r*ah] Spanish for "country wine," a category that's equivalent to the French VIN DE PAYS. These are defined vineyard areas that have not yet achieved a DENOMINACIÓN DE ORIGEN (DO) standing.

vino de licór [BEE-noh day lee-KOHR] A sweet Spanish FORTIFIED WINE with an alcohol range of between 15 percent and 22 percent.

vino de mesa [BEE-noh day MAY-sah] Spanish for "TABLE WINE," which is Spain's lowest official category of wine. This term has a similar status to France's VIN DE TABLE, Italy's VINO DA TAVOLA, and Germany's TAFELWEIN. These wines do not qualify for the higher quality categories, VINO DE LA TIERRA or DENOMINACIÓN DE ORIGEN (DO). Occasionally a label may indicate **"vino de mesa de—"** followed by the name of a region or province. Nonconforming winemakers often use these categories for high-quality wines that don't meet DO or vino de la tierra requirements, much in the same manner as Italian winemakers do for their SUPER TUSCANS.

vino de pago [BEE-noh day PAH-goh] Term used in Spain for single-estate wines that are known for their consistently high quality. A few of the very top estates have been granted DO status and label their wines with Denominación de Origen de Pago.

vino de pasto [BEE-noh day PAHS-toh] An unofficial Spanish term for "wine of the meal" or "TABLE WINE." It's used to designate wines served during the meal versus those consumed as an APÉRITIF or DESSERT WINE. VINO DE MESA (which also means "table wine") is the official category.

vino espumoso natural método tradicional *see* CAVA DO

Vino-Lok *see* CLOSURES

vino maestro *see* MÁLAGA DO

vinometer [vih-NAHM-ih-ter] A simple calibrated instrument used to measure the alcoholic content of finished DRY wines. A vinometer isn't accurate for sweet wines.

Vino Nobile di Montepulciano DOCG [VEE-noh NAW-bee-lay dee mawn-teh-pool-CHAH-noh] DOCG that is located in the hilly area around the town of Montepulciano, southeast of Siena in the eastern portion of Italy's TUSCANY region. The designated area is actually situated inside the large CHIANTI subzone of Colli Senesi. Vino Nobile di Montepulciano is named after the town and the historic notion that the wine was available only for the tables of nobility. This was the very first DOCG in Italy. Unfortunately, its first VINTAGE in 1983 was met with disappointing reviews. That and the fact that over 250,000 cases of this wine are now produced yearly has somewhat diminished its noble aspect. Quality since that 1983 vintage has improved, however, and wines from the top producers are viewed as some of Italy's best. Vino Nobile di Montepulciano wines are made from a minimum of 70 percent Prugnolo (SANGIOVESE), 10 to 20 percent CANAIOLO, and up to 20 percent of other varieties (although no more than 10 percent of white grapes). One of the other red varieties most often used is the Mammolo, which scents the wine with the essence of violets. White grapes like TREBBIANO and MALVASIA are no longer required, which allows winemakers to produce wines that are more intense and longer-lived. The wines of this DOCG must be AGED for 2 years (there are several options for the amount of wood aging, but the minimum is 12 months), 3 years for RISERVA wines. In 1989, a new DOC—ROSSO DI MONTEPULCIANO—was formed. It's located in exactly the same area and uses the exact same grape varieties as those used for the Vino Nobile di Montepulciano DOCG. This change has allowed producers to reclassify some of the wines originally intended for Vino Nobile di Montepulciano to the Rosso di Montepulciano DOC. As a result, lesser wines can be used in the new DOC, which should raise the overall quality of wines coming from the Vino Nobile di Montepulciano DOCG.

vino novello [VEE-noh noh-VEHL-oh] Italian for "new wine," used in the same sense as the French NOUVEAU to refer to light, fruity red wines. By law, vino novello (also called simply *novello*) must be bottled within the year of the harvest, but in practice they're bottled within a few weeks.

vin ordinaire [va*n* or-dee-NEH*R*] French for "ordinary wine." *See also* VIN DE TABLE.

vino rosso *see* ROSSO

Vinos de Calidad con Indicación Geográfica (VCIG) [BEE-nohs day kah-lee-DAHD kon een-dee-kah-THIH-ohn gee-oh-GRAH-fee-kah] Spanish for "Quality Wines with a Geographical Indication." This is a wine classification level for Spanish wines that comes between the higher level DENOMINACIÓN DE ORIGEN (DO) and the lower level VINO DE LA TIERRA designated wines. These wines are essentially from regions that are working their way to becoming a DO. The classification is similar to the French VIN DÉLIMITÉ DE QUALITÉ SUPÉRIEURE (VDQS).

Vinos de Madrid DO Established in 1990, this DO comprises the vineyards surrounding Spain's capital city Madrid. Sometimes referred to as *Tierra de Madrid,* this area consists of three subzones—**Arganda**, **Navalcarnero**, and **San Martín de Valdeiglesias**. Arganda—in which there are almost 30,000 vineyard acres—is by far the most important in terms of wine quantity and quality. The majority of wine in this zone is white, traditionally made from Malvar, Albillo, and AIRÉN. Recently, in an attempt to improve quality, the varieties of Viura (MACABEO), Torrontés, and PARELLADA were approved. But Arganda is best known for its red wines, which are made from Tinto Fino (TEMPRANILLO) with a little Garnacha Tinta (GRENACHE). CABERNET

SAUVIGNON and MERLOT are now being grown as well. The better reds can be full-flavored and full-bodied.

vinosity *see* Glossary of Wine Tasting Terms, page 655

vino tipico [VEE-noh TEE-pee-koh] Initiated in 1989, this quality category for Italian wines ranks between the VINO DA TAVOLA and DENOMINAZIONE DI ORIGINE CONTROLLATA (DOC) categories. It's similar to France's VIN DE PAYS and Germany's LANDWEIN. Vino tipico wines are officially approved as being representative of their area.

vinous [VI-nuhs] A general term describing anything characteristic of wine. For example, a vinous color or vinous fragrance. *See also* VINEAL; Glossary of Wine Tasting Terms, page 655.

vin rosé [van roh-ZAY] French for "rosé wine."

vin rouge [van ROOZH] French for "red wine."

Vin Santo; Vino Santo [VEEN SAHN-toh; VEE-noh] Vin Santo ("holy wine") is produced primarily in TUSCANY but also in Italy's UMBRIA, TRENTINO-ALTO ADIGE, and VENETO regions. It's made by partially drying grapes either by hanging them up or by airing them on trays in well-ventilated rooms or barns for 3 to 6 months. The semidried grapes, which are full of concentrated sugars and flavors are PRESSED before being FERMENTED in small oak or chestnut barrels (called **caratelli**), which contain a small amount of **madre**—thick wine left from the prior year. The wine is typically kept in these barrels for 2 to 3 years, sometimes as long as 6 years. The barrels, which are not completely full, are exposed to varying temperatures (hot in the summer, cool in the winter), an OXIDATION treatment that's part of the AGING process. The resulting wine has a characteristic nutty-caramel flavor, a deep golden color, and an ALCOHOL content that ranges from 14 to 17 percent. Most Vin Santo is sweet and served as DESSERT WINE, although some versions are DRY, similar to SHERRY, and better suited for an APERITIF. The grapes used to make Vin Santo vary. For example, in Tuscany the grapes are primarily TREBBIANO, MALVASIA, and CANAIOLO. The POMINO DOC, however, makes a red Vin Santo from SANGIOVESE, CABERNET SAUVIGNON, CABERNET FRANC, and MERLOT, and a white version from PINOT BLANC and CHARDONNAY. In TRENTINO, the Noisiola grape is used, while in the VENETO region's GAMBELLARA DOC, GARGANEGA is the main grape.

Vin Santo di Gambellara *see* GAMBELLARA DOC

vins de garage *see* GARAGE WINES

Vino-Seal *see* CLOSURES

vins mousseux *see* MOUSSEUX

Vinsobres *see* CÔTES DU RHÔNE

vintage [VIHN-tihj] Term that describes both the year of the actual grape harvest and the wine made from those grapes. In the United States, the label may list the **vintage year** if 95 percent of the wine comes from grapes harvested that year. If a blend of grapes from 2 years or more is used, the wine is called *non-vintage* or *NV*. Some CHAMPAGNE and SPARKLING WINE producers are using the term *multi-vintage* to describe wines made from a blend of 2 or more years. The multi-vintage designation is to reflect the fact that the vintners are purposefully blending cuvees from different years to achieve a superior house style. Although it's often assumed that a **vintage wine** is one of superior quality, that's not necessarily true. Some vintages are simply considered better overall than others. That's because the quality of the harvest varies from one year to another. In addition, an individual wine may be better or worse than others of a particular vintage because of the originating vineyard's MESOCLIMATE or because of the winemaking process it underwent. An excellent year for a growing region translates to a generally superior quality, which means there are more choices for fine wines of that vintage. So consumers should view a vintage year only as a general guideline. In the end, each wine must be judged on its own merit.

vintage Champagne *see* CHAMPAGNE; MILLÉSIME

vintage port *see* PORT

vinted by [VIHN-ted] Occasionally seen on labels, this phrase has no legal or established significance. In general, it means "made by." *See also* BOTTLED BY; ESTATE BOTTLED; GROWN, PRODUCED, AND BOTTLED BY; MADE AND BOTTLED BY; PRODUCED AND BOTTLED BY.

Vintivinicoltori Italiani d'Eccellenza; VIDE [veen-tee-vee-nee-koh-loh-TOH-ree ih-tah-lee-AH-nee dayt-chayl-LEHN-tzuh] Italian for "Italian growers and makers of excellence," a voluntary group of wine producers that has established more stringent standards than those imposed by DOC or DOCG regulations. Vintivinicoltori Italiani d'Eccellenza (VIDE) member organizations market only ESTATE BOTTLED wines, which can be submitted for demanding chemical analysis and tasting panel review. Approval by the Vintivinicoltori Italiani d'Eccellenza entitles the wine bottle to bear the VIDE neck label, indicating its high quality. Wines from each new VINTAGE must be submitted for testing in order to earn the VIDE neck label so members can't rest on the reputation of the prior year's wine.

vintner [VIHNT-ner] One who makes or sells wine.

Vintners Quality Alliance (VQA) An independent Canadian regulatory organization implemented to improve the quality of Canadian wines. The VQA is currently established in two provinces, ONTARIO and BRITISH COLUMBIA, but there are efforts underway to add Quebec and Nova Scotia to the list. The VQA establishes standards at a provincial level and for approved designated VITICULTURAL AREAS (VA). Winery participation in the VQA system is voluntary, but it's required if the winery wants to label their wines with the VA designation or with the VQA symbol, which indicates wine has been certified. Use of terms like "Icewine" or "Estate Bottled" is also restricted because they have precise definitions under the VQA authority. The certification process is fairly strict—it requires extensive record keeping on the wine seeking approval, as well as a blind tasting by a panel of experts looking for defects. There are numerous other rules, such as the percentage of wine required from the growing area and BRIX levels for grapes. The Canadian VQA system's rules are much closer to the French APPELLATION D'ORIGINE CONTRÔLÉE (AOC or AC) and far more demanding than the AMERICAN VITICULTURAL AREA in the United States where wine quality is not addressed.

Vintner's Reserve *see* RESERVE

Vinum Optimu Rare Signatum *see* SHERRY

Vinum Optimu Signatum *see* SHERRY

Vinzelles *see* POUILLY-VINZELLES AC

Viognier; Vionnier [vee-oh-NYAY] An esteemed white-wine grape that was once very rare because of the limited acreage planted throughout the world. Its low yield and susceptibility to vineyard DISEASES made Viognier wines extremely difficult to find. This has all changed in the last decade as Viognier became very popular and growers around the world have been adding it to their vineyards. This grape gained its distinguished reputation from the northern RHÔNE wines of CHÂTEAU-GRILLET and CONDRIEU. Connoisseurs crave these intense, DRY white wines with vibrant floral qualities and an intriguing BOUQUET reminiscent of apricots, peaches, and pears. Within the CÔTE RÔTIE vineyards, a small amount of Viognier is interplanted with SYRAH, a red grape. The Viognier grapes are harvested and vinified with the Syrah to produce the highly valued CÔTE-RÔTIE red wines. It's extremely rare for France to sanction officially the use of a white grape in such high-quality red wines. California has gone from less than 100 acres in the early 1990s to over 2,000 acres with Calera Wine Company and Joseph Phelps Vineyards being early innovators with this variety. Similar interest in this variety has taken place in the LANGUEDOC-ROUSSILLON region of France and in parts of Australia, Italy, Spain, South Africa, and South America

Vionnier *see* VIOGNIER

Viré-Clessé AC [vee-reh klehs-SAY] APPELLATION established in 1998 from one of the MÂCON AC's better producing areas around the COMMUNES of Clessé, Laizé, Montbellet, and Viré in France's BURGUNDY region. Only white wines from CHARDONNAY are allowed here.

Virginia In the early 1600s, Virginia was one of the first states to plant grapes and make wines. Starting in 1773, Thomas Jefferson made repeated attempts (with little success) to grow VITIS VINIFERA vines on his estate, Monticello. By the end of the nineteenth century, Virginia was one of the more important wine-producing areas in the United States. Unfortunately, the temperance movement and PROHIBITION destroyed most of the existing industry. A resurgence began in the early 1970s when VINTNER Dr. Archie Smith III first planted HYBRIDS like SEYVAL BLANC and then later VITIS VINIFERA vines at his Meredyth Vineyards. After New York, Virginia is considered the most important producer of quality wines on the East Coast. In 2002, more than seventy licensed wineries were producing wines from over 2,000 vineyard acres. More than 70 percent of this acreage is planted with *Vitis vinifera* grapes like BARBERA, CABERNET FRANC, CABERNET SAUVIGNON, CHARDONNAY, GEWÜRZTRAMINER, MERLOT, PINOT GRIS, PINOT NOIR, RIESLING, SAUVIGNON BLANC, and VIOGNIER. Chardonnay is the most popular variety and seems to do best in this climate. Hybrids like CHAMBOURCIN, Seyval Blanc, and VIDAL BLANC are also popular. Virginian vineyards are scattered throughout the state, but the majority are between Charlottesville and the Maryland border, on the eastern slopes of the Blue Ridge Mountains. Virginia has six designated VITICULTURAL AREAS: MONTICELLO AVA, NORTH FORK OF ROANOKE AVA, NORTHERN NECK GEORGE WASHINGTON BIRTHPLACE AVA, ROCKY KNOB AVA, SHENANDOAH VALLEY AVA, and VIRGINIA'S EASTERN SHORE AVA.

Virginia's Eastern Shore AVA Approved in 1991, this AVA encompasses 436,480 acres on the Virginia section of the Delmarva

Peninsula. The Eastern Shore area is separated from Virginina's mainland by the Chesapeake Bay and is located in Accomack and Northampton Counties.

Virginia Seedling *see* NORTON

Visan *see* CÔTES DU RHÔNE

viscous; viscosity *see* Glossary of Wine Tasting Terms, page 655

vite [VEE-tay] Italian for "vine."

viticulteur [vee-tee-kuhl-TEW*R*] French for "vine grower."

viticultural area [VIHT-ih-kuhl-cher-uhl] A region where grapes are grown, the abbreviation for which is VA. *See also* AMERICAN VITICULTURAL AREA.

viticulture; viticultural [VIHT-ih-kuhl-cher] The cultivation of grapevines, or the study or science of grapes and their culture. *See also* AISLE; AMERICAN VITICULTURAL AREA; BERRY; BOTRYTIS CINEREA; BUD BREAK; BUDWOOD; BUNCH; CANE; CANOPY; CANOPY MANAGEMENT; CLIMAT; CLIMATE REGIONS OF CALIFORNIA; CLONAL SELECTION; CLONE; CLUSTER; CRUSH; CRUSHER; CUTTING; DISEASES, VINEYARD; FLOWERING; FRUIT SET; GRAFTING; GREEN PRUNING; HANG TIME; HECTARE; HECTOLITER; HYBRID; MACROCLIMATE; MESOCLIMATE; MICROCLIMATE; OVERCROPPING; PARENT VINE; PRUNING; ROOTSTOCK; SCION; SECOND CROP; SHATTER; SHELLING; SHOOT; SUMMER PRUNING; T-BUDDING; TRELLIS SYSTEM; VERAISON; VINTAGE; VITICULTURAL AREA; WINEGROWER; YIELD.

vitigno [VEE-tee-nyoh] Italian for "vine variety" or "grape variety."

vitis [VEE-tihs] The botanical genus to which grapevines belong. *See also* VITIS AESTIVALIS; VITIS LABRUSCA; VITIS RIPARIA; VITIS ROTUNDIFOLIA; VITIS VINIFERA.

Vitis aestivalis [VEE-tihs ehs-tuh-VEHL-uhs] A species of vine native to America and grown primarily in the area in and around Missouri, Arkansas, and Tennessee. The best-known variety is the red grape NORTON, sometimes called *Cynthiana*.

Vitis labrusca [VEE-tihs luh-BRUHS-kuh] One of the main North American vine species, *Vitis labrusca* is found primarily in Canada and the northeastern United States, although some grapes of this species are grown in South America. The CONCORD variety is the best known, followed by the CATAWBA and the Delaware. Grapes from this species have a pronounced musky, grapey, FOXY quality that's often criticized by VITIS VINIFERA aficionados.

Vitis riparia [VEE-tihs rih-PEHR-ee-uh] A native America vine species noted for its resistance to PHYLLOXERA and best known for breeding ROOTSTOCKS that can withstand this disease. There are some grape VARIETIES of this species used in winemaking, although the best known are HYBRIDS (such as BACO NOIR) that have been developed from breeding *Vitis riparia* with VITIS VINIFERA varieties.

Vitis rotundifolia [VEE-tihs roh-tuhn-dih-FOHL-ee-uh] Vine species that is native to the region around the Gulf of Mexico and is part of the MUSCADINE family. This species, whose name is attributed to the vines' round leaves, produces grapes with a strong, musky flavor. The best-known VARIETY—the bronze-colored SCUPPERNONG—is used to make sweet wines that are still popular in some areas of the South.

Vitis vinifera [VEE-tihs vihn-IHF-uh-ruh] The vine species that produces over 99 percent of the world's wines today. It is native to Europe as well as East and Central Asia, but it has been planted all over the world. There are estimated to be thousands of VARIETIES of this species, some of the best known being CABERNET SAUVIGNON, CHARDON-NAY, CHENIN BLANC, MERLOT, PINOT NOIR, RIESLING, SAUVIGNON BLANC, SYRAH, and ZINFANDEL.

Viura *see* MACABEO

Vivarais *see* CÔTES DU VIVARAIS VDQS

Vlassky Riesling; Vlassky Rizling *see* WELSCHRIESLING

VLM *see* RIDDLING

Vogelsang *see* JOHANNISBERG

volatile acid *see* ACIDS

volatile acidity Also called simply *VA*, volatile acidity is as much a part of wine as body temperature is in a human. A balanced amount of VA is necessary for aroma and flavor but, just as a fever indicates a problem in man, excess volatile acidity in wine signals trouble. VA can be caused by several acids, even though its primary source is acetic acid (*see* ACIDS) and is the result of bacteriological infection through OXIDATION during winemaking. In quantities of less than 0.05 percent, volatile acidity doesn't affect a wine's quality. At higher levels, how-ever, VA can give wine a sharp, vinegary tactile sensation, which is caused by acetic acid. In wines with excessive volatile acidity, the acetic acid is accompanied by ETHYL ACETATE, which contributes a sweet, vinegary smell. Extreme volatile acidity signifies a seriously flawed wine. Such a wine can be referred to as *volatile*. *See also* VOLATILE in the Glossary of Wine Tasting Terms, page 655.

Volnay AC; Volnay-Santenots AC [vawl-NAY sah*n*-tuh-NOH] The village of Volnay sits high up on the hill between MEURSAULT and POMMARD in the CÔTE DE BEAUNE area of France's BURGUNDY region. As one heads south, the **Volnay AC** is the last APPELLATION in the Côte de Beaune (until the SANTENAY AC) that focuses on red wines. These PINOT NOIR-based wines are generally of high quality, and the Volnay AC has an above-average reputation. Their reputation extends back to the 1300s, when they were a favorite of Phillipe de Valois, the Duke of Burgundy. In the 1400s, these wines were a favorite of Louis XI. Although Volnay has no GRAND CRU vineyards, it has more acreage assigned to PREMIER CRU vineyards than to those for the regular Volnay AC. The better premier cru vineyards include **Bousse d'Or**, **Les Caillerets**, **Les Champans**, **Clos des Chênes**, and **Clos des Ducs**. The wines range from a LIGHTER, elegant, silky style to those that are more full-bodied (*see* BODY) and TANNIC. The **Volnay-Santenots AC** is for six red-wine-producing vineyards that, although actually located in Meursault, are allowed to use Volnay-Santenots AC on their label.

voros Hungarian for "red."

VORS *see* SHERRY

VOS *see* SHERRY

Vosgros *see* CHABLIS

Vosne-Romanée AC [vohn raw-ma-NAY] The village of Vosne-Romanée is located in the CÔTE DE NUIT area of BURGUNDY. The top red wines from this village are considered to be the finest in BURGUNDY—possibly in all of France—with wines from the PAUILLAC AC in BORDEAUX the most often mentioned contenders. Vosne-Romanée contains six prestigious GRAND CRU vineyards, which produce some of the world's highest-priced wines: RICHEBOURG, LA ROMANÉE, ROMANÉE-CONTI, ROMANÉE-SAINT-VIVANT, LA TÂCHE, and, recently promoted from PREMIER CRU status, LA GRAND RUE. The grands crus ÉCHEZEAUX and GRANDS-ÉCHEZEAUX, which are located in the neighboring village of Flagey-Échezeaux, are also often associated with Vosne-Romanée. This is because the Flagey-Échezeaux village wines can be sold with the Vosne-Romanée appellation. In addition to the grands crus, there are seventeen Premier Cru vineyards that have a reputation for producing generally high-quality wine. Of these, **Les Beaux Monts**, **Clos des Réas**, **Les Gaudichots**, **Aux Malconsorts**, and **Les Suchots** are considered some of the best.

High-quality wines from Vosne-Romanée demonstrate richness and elegance, along with a spiciness that's difficult to find in other red Burgundies. Many critics believe that the quality of standard Vosne-Romanée AC wines is variable and inconsistent, which is disappointing because they're expensive. More often than not, these wines coast on the reputation of the grands crus and premiers crus of this village.

Vougeot AC [voo-ZHOH] The village of Vougeot, which is located in the CÔTE DE NUITS area of BURGUNDY, is most often associated with the 124-acre GRAND CRU vineyard, CLOS DE VOUGEOT. There are about 40 other acres in this APPELLATION, split between the village vineyards and several PREMIER CRU vineyards. The premier cru of **Les Petits Vougeots** and its subvineyard of **Clos de la Perrière** are thought to be the best. Most of the wine is red, made from PINOT NOIR, although there's a small amount of white made from CHARDONNAY. These white wines are produced from the premier cru vineyard Le Clos Blanc and labeled **Clos Blanc de Vougeot**.

Vouvray AC [voo-VREH; voo-VRAY] APPELLATION that is just east of Tours in the center of France's LOIRE Valley. CHENIN BLANC, which is noted for its high ACID levels, is the only variety grown in the vineyards that surround the village of Vouvray. The white wines vary greatly in style—they can be very sweet to very DRY, and STILL or SPARKLING. The best are generally well-made, medium-dry wines, with a touch of sweetness to help balance the sharp ACIDITY. Very sweet wines, especially those created from BOTRYTIS CINEREA-infected grapes, can also be wonderful because Chenin Blanc's acidity cuts what could be an overbearing sweetness and heightens the COMPLEX, HONEYED flavors. It also enables many of these wines to age quite well, with some lasting 40 to 50 years. The same high acidity that benefits sweet wines can make DRY wines harsh and sharp when young. The best of these will SOFTEN, and their flavors will evolve as they mature. CRISP, dry wines are usually the best choice for further processing into fully sparkling (MOUSSEUX) or slightly sparkling (PETILLANT) wines. Vouvray Moussex AC and Vouvray Petillant AC are both made via MÉTHODE CHAMPENOISE.

VQA see VINTNERS QUALITY ALLIANCE

VQPRD see VIN DE QUALITÉ PRODUITS DANS DES RÉGIONS DÉTERMINÉES

VR see VINHO REGIONAL

VSP see TRELLIS SYSTEM

Wachenheim [VAHKH-uhn-hime] One of the top wine-producing villages of Germany's PFALZ region. Wachenheim is located south of BAD DÜRKHEIM in the BEREICH Mittelhaardt/Deutsche Weinstrasse. The wines from Wachenheim, although slightly lighter than those from the neighboring villages of DEIDESHEIM and Forst, are still full-bodied (*see* BODY) and RIPE. They're often described as ELEGANT. The best individual vineyard sites (EINZELLAGEN) are **Goldbächel** and **Gerümpel**, followed by **Böhlig** and **Rechbächel**.

Wahluke Slope AVA [WAH-look] Eastern Washington APPELLATION established in January 2006, covering 81,000 acres north of the tri-city area of Richland, Pasco, and Kennewick. Wahluke is a Native American word meaning "watering place." The AVA lies within the huge COLUMBIA VALLEY AVA and is one of the warmest and driest areas. There are over 5,200 acres planted, mostly to red-grape varieties such as BARBERA, CABERNET FRANC, CABERNET SAUVIGNON, MALBEC, MERLOT, SANGIOVESE, SYRAH, and ZINFANDEL, although some CHARDONNAY and VIOGNIER are also grown. Two wineries, Fox Estate Winery and Ginkgo Forest Winery, and three custom crush facilities currently operate in the area.

Waiheke Island *see* AUCKLAND

Waikato [why-KAH-toh] New Zealand's smallest winegrowing region, which lies around the Waikato River, about 90 minutes south of the city of Auckland. This area typically includes the **Bay of Plenty**, which adjoins Waikato on its western boundary just over the Kaimai Range, and where a few wineries are scattered along the Bay. The vineyards here are still quite small, with a little over 300 acres planted between them. The most widely cultivated varieties are CABERNET SAUVIGNON, CHARDONNAY, and SAUVIGNON BLANC, but there is also CHENIN BLANC, GEWÜRZTRAMINER, MERLOT, PINOT NOIR, and RIESLING. This area is warm, humid, and wet, which creates numerous growing challenges. On the other hand, such conditions also create an environment conducive to BOTRYTIS CINEREA, the result of which is delicious DESSERT WINE made from Riesling and Chardonnay.

Wairarapa *see* WELLINGTON

Walker Bay WO *see* OVERBERG WO

Walla Walla Valley AVA A 340,000-acre VITICULTURAL AREA located in the southern part of the large COLUMBIA VALLEY AVA. Most of this region is in southeast Washington but a tiny portion dips into northeast Oregon. The area, which had only four wineries and sixty planted acres in the

W

mid-1980s, is growing rapidly. In 2001, approval was given to increase the region's official size, thus adding wineries and planted vineyards that were previously outside the approved AVA boundaries. There are now over 35 wineries and 1,200 planted acres. The Walla Walla region is highly regarded for its very diverse climate. Dominant varieties are CABERNET SAUVIGNON, CHARDONNAY, MERLOT, and SYRAH, plus a small amount of GEWÜRZTRAMINER. Leonetti Cellars and Woodward Canyon Winery are highly regarded pioneers in this region.

Walporzheim/Ahrtal, Bereich *see* AHR

Walschriesling *see* WELSCHRIESLING

ward *see* SOUTH AFRICA

Warren Hills AVA *see* NEW JERSEY

Washington Washington winemaking is thought to have begun in the 1870s, although the first VITIS VINIFERA vines weren't planted until the early 1900s. PROHIBITION and Washington state laws managed to put a damper on most activity from 1920 to the 1960s. However, Washington has blossomed since the mid-1960s and now has over 200 wineries and 30,000 acres of *Vitis vinifera* vineyards. It's the second largest producer (after California) of high-quality wine in the United States. Most of Washington's better vineyards are located in the eastern portion of the state, where the Cascade Mountains block the cool, damp weather prevalent in the western part. Washington's three primary growing regions are here—COLUMBIA VALLEY AVA, YAKIMA VALLEY AVA, and WALLA WALLA AVA (the latter two are encompassed by the huge Columbia Valley AVA). RED MOUNTAIN AVA is a small subregion of the Yakima Valley AVA approved in 2001. These APPELLATIONS are the warmest growing areas in the Pacific Northwest, ranging from Region I to Region III (*see* CLIMATE REGIONS OF CALIFORNIA). The eastern region has the dry climate that is ideal for grapes and requires some irrigation during the growing season. Because of the varying temperatures throughout the eastern part of Washington, different grape varieties do well in its various locations. This means that MERLOT, a warm-weather grape, and RIESLING, a cool-weather grape, can both flourish. CABERNET SAUVIGNON, CHENIN BLANC, SAUVIGNON BLANC, and SÉMILLON are also grown, as well as CONCORD and other VITIS LABRUSCA varieties. Another large area with limited acreage is the PUGET SOUND AVA, located around Puget Sound in western Washington. Although not a designated area, a region worth noting is in southwestern Washington (Clark County) just north of Portland, Oregon. Its climate is similar to Oregon's

Willamette Valley, which has great success with PINOT NOIR, Riesling, and CHARDONNAY.

watering back Low-tech method of lowering the alcohol level in wine. In California this is illegal in most cases, according to the California Administrative Code, which indicates "no water in excess of the minimum amount necessary to facilitate normal fermentation may be used in the production or cellar treatment of any grape wine." This phraseology essentially applies to a stuck fermentation (*see* FERMENTATION). Europeans also frown upon its use. But watering back is being practiced more frequently as grapes are picked with higher and higher sugar content to achieve optimum ripeness and flavors. The higher sugar content obviously translates to higher alcohol content, which is not always desirable. *See also* REVERSE OSMOSIS; SPINNING CONE.

watery *see* Glossary of Wine Tasting Terms, page 655

weeper Term describing a bottle of wine that is leaking slightly (*weeping*) around the cork. This can be caused by a faulty cork or by poor storage where a cork that wasn't kept moist shrank. Weepers aren't necessarily bad bottles of wine, although it's possible that spoilage and/or OXIDATION could have occurred. This occurrence of weeping is also called *seepage*.

Wehlen [VAY-luhn] A small wine-producing town located between BERNKASTEL and ZELTINGEN in Germany's MOSEL-SAAR-RUWER region. It's considered one of the region's top producers, primarily because of the wines from the famous vineyard site (EINZELLAGE) **Sonnenuhr** (which means "sundial," after the massive sundial on the property). Wehlen owes much of its reputation to the high-quality wines from the Prüm family, who've made wine in Wehlen since the eighteenth century.

weighty *see* Glossary of Wine Tasting Terms, page 655

Wein [VINE] German for "wine."

Weinbaugebiet [vine-BOW-geh-beet] The term for a basic wine region designated for DEUTSCHER TAFFELWEIN (German TABLE WINE) production. There are four *Weinbaugebiete*—BAYERN, NECKAR, OBERHEIN, and RHEIN MOSEL. They are further divided into eight Untergebiet (subdistricts) and nineteen Gebiet (districts identified for LANDWEIN production).

Weinberg [VINE-behrk] German for "vineyard." *See also* WEINGARTEN.

Weingarten [VINE-gahr-tuhn] Term for "vineyard" used in Germany's WÜRTTEMBERG region. *See also* WEINBERG.

Weingärtnergenossenschaft [VINE-gahrt-nuhr-geh-NAW-sehn-shahft] Term for "cooperative cellar" in Germany's WÜRTTEMBERG region. *See also* WINZERGENOSSENSCHAFT

Weingut [VINE-goot] German for "wine estate." The term *weingut* usually refers to a winemaking facility, its cellar, and the vineyards. It can be used on a label only if the wine and any SUSSRESERVE have been made exclusively from estate-grown grapes.

Weinkellerei [vine-KEHL-ler-ri] German for "wine cellar." Use of this term on a label usually means that the producer buys their grapes, MUST, or wine and may not have their own vineyards. Use of *Weingut-Weinkellerei* on a label indicates the producer owns his vineyards but also buys grapes from others.

Weinsiegel [VINE-zee-gerl] German wine seal for wines that have won quality awards. *Deutsches Weinsiegel* is for national awards. *Badisches Weinsiegel* is an example of a regional wine seal from Baden.

Weinsteins [VINE-schtines] German for "wine stones" (*see* TARTRATES).

Weinviertel DAC *see* DISTRICTUS AUSTRIA CONTROLLATUS

Weissburgunder *see* PINOT BLANC

Weisserburgunder *see* MELON DE BOURGOGNE; PINOT BLANC

Weisser Gutedel *see* CHASSELAS

Weisser Klevner *see* PINOT BLANC

Weisser Riesling *see* RIESLING

Weissherbst [VICE-hehrbst] German for "white autumn" or "white harvest." It originally referred to red grapes that had lost their color because of Edelfaüle (BOTRYTIS CINEREA). Today *Weissherbst* refers to ROSÉ wines produced from a single grape variety and of at least QUALITÄTSWEIN quality. The best-known wines of this type are made from Spätburgunder (PINOT NOIR) in Germany's BADEN and WÜRTTEMBERG regions.

Wellington The official name for the New Zealand winegrowing region that is also referred to as *Wairarapa* or *Martinborough*. It's located at the southern end of the North Island close to Wellington,

New Zealand's capital city. Martinborough, the primary town in the region, is a little over 50 miles west of Wellington. Vines were first planted here in the 1880s, but it wasn't until a century later that Wellington began to be noted on the world wine stage. The Tararua Mountains, which lie west of the vineyards between Wellington and Martinborough, block much of the wet weather that blows across most of the North Island's south end. This drier environment plus the cool winds blowing off Cook's Strait (which is between the North and South Islands) provides a climate many feel is similar to MARLBOROUGH, New Zealand's largest growing region. The Wellington region, with just over a thousand acres, was New Zealand's seventh largest growing area in 2002. PINOT NOIR has established the region's reputation and is its most planted variety. However, CHARDONNAY, GEWÜRZTRAMINER, PINOT GRIS, SAUVIGNON BLANC, and RIESLING can also be very successful. And, although not planted on a large scale, CABERNET SAUVIGNON and MERLOT are have produced distinguished wines.

well rounded *see* ROUND

Welschriesling [VELSH-reez-ling; VELSH-rees-ling; velsh-REEZ-ling] A white-wine grape that—in spite of its spelling—is not related to the true RIESLING of Germany; it is a distinctly separate variety. Welschriesling's origin is a mystery, but it is well suited for the climate of central Europe, where it's extensively cultivated. It's known as Welshriesling (or *Walschriesling*) in Austria, *Vlassky Riesling* or *Vlassky Rizling* in Czechoslovakia, *Olaszriesling* in Hungary, *Riesling Italico (or Italian Riesling)* in Italy, and *Grasevina* or *Laskiriesling* or *Laski Rizling* in Slovenia and other areas of the former Yugoslavia. Welschriesling is a high-yielding vine that, in most cases, produces fairly bland wines. At its best, this grape delivers LIGHT wines with pronounced flowery aromas, but it's quite different from the true Riesling. Some areas, like northeast Italy, blend Welschriesling with true Riesling and label the result "Riesling," which causes some confusion. In parts of Romania, Welschriesling is used in SPARKLING WINES, whereas Austria occasionally turns it into a delightful TROCKENBEERENAUSLESE.

West Connecticut Highlands AVA *see* CONNECTICUT

West Elks AVA *see* COLORADO

Western Australia Australia's largest state, with the Indian Ocean to the west and SOUTH AUSTRALIA and the Northern Territory to the east. Western Australia (popularly known as "W.A.") covers about a third of the country but only hosts about 10 percent of Australia's population.

Perth, its capital city and also the most populous, has about two thirds of the states' population. Although Western Australia comprises Australia's entire western portion, its vineyard areas occupy only a tiny section of the state's southwestern corner; most of the rest of the state is inhospitable to grape cultivation. The 27,000 planted acres represent about 7 percent of the nation's total, with wine production only 3.5 percent, the latter indicative of the smaller yields and high-quality wines this state produces. Western Australia's wine history started in the early 1830s and was centered almost exclusively in the Swan Valley (SWAN DISTRICT) for over 140 years. The Swan Valley is one of Australia's hottest growing areas. For over 30 years Western Australia vine growers have been seeking cooler growing areas, most of which lie south of Perth. According to the Australian GEOGRAPHIC INDICATIONS system, Western Australia has five major zones and eight regions. Around Perth is the **Greater Perth Zone** with the aforementioned Swan District region north of the city, the PERTH HILLS region to the east, and the PEEL region just south of Perth. South of this area is the **South West Australia Zone**, which includes the following regions: the famous MARGARET RIVER, BLACKWOOD VALLEY, GEOGRAPHE, GREAT SOUTHERN, and PEMBERTON. At this writing, Western Australia's other three zones (Central Western Australia Zone; West Australian South East Coastal Zone; and Eastern Plains, Inland and North of Western Australia Zone) don't have much viticultural activity.

Western Victoria Zone *see* VICTORIA

white port *see* PORT

White Riesling *see* RIESLING

white wine Any wine that's made from light-skinned grapes or from dark-skinned grapes whose juice doesn't contain any extracted color (which happens when the juice is immediately separated from the grape skins, seeds, and pulp). A white wine's hue may range from almost no color to very pale yellow to golden yellow to amber. As white wines age, they tend to darken.

White Zinfandel White Zinfandel is not a white wine but rather what's called a BLUSH WINE in the United States and a ROSÉ or BLANC DE NOIR in France. It's made from ZINFANDEL (a red-wine grape) and kept pale in color by quickly removing the skins from the juice after the grapes are pressed, which stops the transfer of color from the grape skin's dark pigments. The wine is then processed as for white wine. The resulting color generally varies from pale pink to apricot to salmon. Most White Zinfandels are slightly sweet, although some are quite DRY with just a whisper of RESIDUAL SUGAR. Introduced in the United States in the late 1970s, White Zinfandel wines found a niche in the early 1980s as the white-wine boom took off and producers searched for a channel for the red-grape surplus.

whole berry fermentation Fermentation method that could be considered a variation of the CARBONIC MACERATION technique but differs in that it's normally used with full-bodied (*see* BODY), TANNIC red wines. Whole berry fermentation consists of leaving some of the grape berries intact during the CRUSHING process. Some winemakers like to hold some of these whole berries back and add them at various points, thereby extending the FERMENTATION process. The chemical process involved with whole berry fermentation lends these sturdy red wines a lively, berryish character with fewer TANNINS and less ALCOHOL.

whole bunch fermentation *see* WHOLE CLUSTER FERMENTATION

whole cluster fermentation A traditional but controversial technique of FERMENTATION using intact clusters of grapes and stems. It's the reverse of DESTEMMING, which removes the stems and often includes CRUSHING, which breaks down the grapes. Proponents of whole cluster fermentation, also called *whole bunch fermentation*, say that it extends fermentation time because the grapes break down slower. Advocates indicate this especially helps PINOT NOIR, which ferments very quickly. By extending fermentation, higher EXTRACT is achieved. In addition, the stems provide added flavor, body, and weight. The result is a bigger, more complex wine with deeper color. Detractors indicate that the stems must be fully mature or they will contribute unwelcome GREEN, STEMMY, and VEGETAL characteristics to the wine. They don't think the risk is worth it and indicate there are other techniques to slow fermentation and develop complexity in their wines. In addition, the stems release TANNINS that are undesirable in some wines. Whole cluster fermentation is popular in BURGUNDY, where about half the winemakers use this technique.

Wild Horse Valley AVA A small California AVA established in 1988 and located about 5 miles east of the city of Napa. It lies along Wild Horse Valley at the point where the Solano County line juts into Napa before heading directly east. This region encompasses 3,300 acres in portions of both Napa and Solano counties. It has a cool climate that's affected by air drawn off San Pablo Bay. Although not currently well planted, some Chardonnay and Pinot Noir are grown here.

Willamette Valley AVA [wuh-LAM-iht] This Oregon VITICULTURAL AREA is in the state's northern portion, starting north of Portland and stretching to just south of Eugene. The Willamette Valley AVA nestles between the coastal range to the west and the Cascade Mountains to the east in Oregon's best-known grape-growing areas. It stretches for about 175 miles and is this state's main wine-producing region. Although not officially divided, this area is typically thought of as being split into the North Willamette Valley, which has the largest concentration of wineries, and the South Willamette Valley, which is slightly warmer. The dividing line is just south of Salem. The Willamette Valley is a cool growing region and the most popular grape varieties here are PINOT NOIR, PINOT GRIS, RIESLING, and CHARDONNAY. It is because of this area that Oregon now has a worldwide reputation for excellent Pinot Noir. Other grapes, planted in small amounts, include CABERNET SAUVIGNON, GEWÜRZTRAMINER, MÜLLER-THURGAU, SÉMILLON, and ZINFANDEL. The DUNDEE HILLS AVA, with its red soil and steep hills, is considered one of the best, as is the EOLA-AMITY HILLS AVA. CHEHALEM MOUNTAINS, MCMINNVILLE, RIBBON RIDGE, and YAMHILL-CARLTON DISTRICT have also been approved as AVAs. All are located in the northern part of the region.

Willow Creek AVA Established in 1983, this California VITICULTURAL AREA is east and slightly north of Eureka, where the Trinity River and the Trinity River South Fork converge. It encompasses 6,000 acres in Humboldt and Trinity Counties, but there are less than 10 acres planted.

Wiltingen [VIHL-ting-uhn] A famous wine-producing village located on the SAAR River in Germany's MOSEL-SAAR-RUWER region. Wiltingen is surrounded by numerous vineyards, including the 67-acre SCHARZHOFBERG vineyard, which produces the village's best wines. Scharzhofberg is classified as an ORTSTEIL, and its wines, therefore, don't use Wiltingen in the name but are simply labeled Scharzhofberg. Wiltingen gives its name to the GROSSLAGE covering the area Wiltingener Scharzberg, which can cause some confusion with the Scharzhofberg name. Other good vineyards include **Braune Kupp**, **Braunfels**, **Hölle**, **Kupp**, and **Rosenberg**. Area vineyards are planted with a high proportion of RIESLING.

Wiltinger Scharzberg *see* SAAR

wine The naturally fermented juice of grapes, unless otherwise specified. More broadly, the term can include alcoholic beverages created from other fruits and even vegetables and grains. Such potables are usually specified with the name of the fruit, as in "apricot wine." Wine has a rich history that has evolved along with that of man. Its historical roots reach back almost 12,000 years. As various cultures spread out into new parts of the world, so did the grapevine and the art of winemaking. Today there are vineyards throughout the world with good wine being produced in far-ranging locations from the United States to South Africa to Australia to South America to Europe. Wine is broadly classified in the following categories: 1. STILL (nonsparkling) WINES—including red, white, and ROSÉ—which can be DRY (nonsweet), semisweet, and sweet; 2. SPARKLING WINES, including French CHAMPAGNES as well as effervescent wines from other parts of the world; 3. FORTIFIED WINES (such as SHERRY, PORT, and some DESSERT WINES), which have been augmented with BRANDY or other spirit; and 4. Aromatic Wines, like VERMOUTH, which have been flavored with ingredients like herbs or spices. *See also* DEALCOHOLIZED WINES.

wine bottles *see* Wine Bottles, page 609

wine bucket *see* Temperatures for Serving Wine, page 641; Optimum Serving Temperatures by Wine Type, page 642

wine, buying *see* Tips on Buying Wine, page 607

wine cellar A term that can refer to both a storage area for wines and the wines stored there. Traditionally, wine cellars were underground because such a location keeps the wines at the proper temperature. Subterranean cellars certainly aren't a requirement today with air-cooling and the advent of temperature-controlled units that can be placed anywhere. No matter where wine is stored, the bottles should be lying on their sides so that the cork stays moist and airtight. A drying cork can shrink and expose the wine to oxygen (*see* OXIDATION), which can ruin a wine. Ideally, a wine cellar should be dry (but not overly, since a modicum of moisture helps keep the corks from drying out), well ventilated, vibration free, cool, and dark. The cellar's temperature should remain fairly constant—if it changes, it shouldn't do so drastically. The ideal temperature for storing wine is around 55°F, but a reasonably consistent temperature between 45 and 70°F is acceptable. However, the warmer the temperature, the faster a wine will change. UNIVERSITY OF CALIFORNIA, DAVIS researchers discovered that every 18°F increase in temperature can double the rate of a wine's chemical changes. In short, the characteristics of a wine stored at 72°F could possibly change twice as fast as one stored at 54°F. The term **active wine cellar** refers to one with a climate control system that maintains the temperature and humidty. A **passive wine cellar** does

W

not have a climate control system and relies on its natural environment to control humidity and reduce temperature swings. Many of these are built underground.

wine consumption *see* Main Wine Producing Countries—Production and Consumption, page 688

wine cooler An alcoholic beverage based on wine, fruit juice, sugar, and carbonated water. Wine coolers were first introduced in the United States during the early 1980s and became very popular over the next 5 to 6 years.

wine futures *see* FUTURES

wineglasses *see* Glassware, page 647

winegrower; winegrowing Narrowly defined, a winegrower is a person who cultivates grapes and makes wine from them. But this doesn't really convey the full meaning. The implication is that this person is not simply a grower interested in maximizing yield and profits. A winegrower is someone who understands that the quality of the grapes produced has a huge impact on the quality of the finished wine—wine is "made" in the vineyard. He or she is familiar with the latest viticultural practices and uses them. Winegrowing employs procedures to keep YIELDS down; CANOPY MANAGEMENT techniques to create the optimal grape-growing environment for maximum flavor, color, and ripeness of the grapes; limited use of chemicals; and meticulous harvesting practices to pick all fruit at optimal ripeness levels.

wine lake A reference to the low-quality wine produced in huge volumes from the warmer growing areas in the European Economic Community. Unlike quality wines, these potables don't fit into any of the supervised quality categories; therefore, the vineyards where these wines are grown are not governed by YIELD limitations. In addition, the grape VARIETIES are usually high producers of neutral character. Authorities in the various European countries are encouraging improvements through advanced VINIFICATION techniques and replanting with higher-quality grape varieties.

winemaker An expert at making wine, who's usually in charge of all the steps of wine production at a winery. Also called an *enologist* or *viniculturist*. *See also* ENOLOGY; VINICULTURE.

Wine of Origin *see* SOUTH AFRICA

wine press *see* PRESS

wine production *see* Principal Wine Producing Countries, page 686 and Main Wine Producing Countries—Production and Consumption, page 688

winery The American name for the place, including the building and required winemaking equipment, where wine is made.

wine-serving temperatures *see* Temperatures for Serving Wine, page 641; Optimum Serving Temperatures by Wine Type, page 642

wine steward *see* SOMMELIER

wine-storing temperatures *see* WINE CELLAR

wine taster 1. A person who evaluates wine by tasting. Generally, the term is applied to professionals or serious amateurs who have knowledge of and experience in the proper evaluation techniques. It can apply to writers, critics, buyers, and judges of wine tasting events. 2. Another name for a TASTEVIN. *See also* Tasting Wine, page 648; Glossary of Wine Tasting Terms, page 655.

wine tasting *see* Tasting Wine, page 648; Glossary of Wine Tasting Terms, page 655

wine tasting terms *see* Glossary of Wine Tasting Terms, page 655

wine thief A long glass or metal tube used for withdrawing samples of wine from barrels or CARBOYS.

Winkel [VINGK-uhl] A prominent wine-producing village located near the Rhine River in Germany's RHEINGAU region. It's situated in an area of premium vineyards, along with other villages like GEISENHEIM, Mittelheim, OESTRICH, and HATTENHEIM. Winkel's most famous vineyard is the 125-acre Schloss Vollrads, which is situated in the hills above the village. Schloss Vollrads is classified as an ORTSTEIL and, therefore, simply uses its name on wine labels. Other quality vineyard sites (EINZELLAGEN) are **Hasensprung** and **Jessuitengarten**.

Winkler Scale *see* CLIMATE REGIONS OF CALIFORNIA

Winzergenossenschaft [vine-zer-geh-NAW-sehn-shahft] The literal translation of this German term is "wine grower association," although it's more generally known as a "cooperative cellar." Wines sold by cooperative cellars can use the term ERZEUGERABFÜLLUNG—which has the same connotation as ESTATE BOTTLED—on labels. Although most of the better wines come from private estates, some of the *winzergenossenschaft* wines, particularly in Germany's PFALZ and BADEN regions, can be quite good. *Winzerverein* ("wine grower society") sometimes appears on labels and has the same meaning as *Winzergenossenschaft*. *See also* ZENTRALKELLEREI.

Winzerverein *see* WINZERGENOSSENSCHAFT

Wisselbrunnen *see* HATTENHEIM

withered *see* Glossary of Wine Tasting Terms, page 655

WO *see* SOUTH AFRICA

Wonnegau, Bereich *see* RHEINHESSEN

wood-aged port *see* PORT

wood aging *see* AGING

woody *see* Glossary of Wine Tasting Terms, page 655

Worcester WO A large demarcated wine district of SOUTH AFRICA that's part of the Breede River Valley Region. It's located about 70 miles northeast of Cape Town around the town of Worcester. This is a hot, dry area that requires irrigation from water supplied from the Breede River. With almost 44,000 planted acres, Worcester has just under 17 percent of the nation's vineyard acreage. This high-yielding area is able to produce as much as 25 percent of South Africa's total wine production, much of which ends up as FORTIFIED WINE or BRANDY. White varieties dominate here, with CHENIN BLANC (called *Steen* locally) taking up about 25 percent of all the vineyard area. Next comes Columbar (COLUMBARD), Hanepoot (MUSCAT), and CHARDONNAY. Red varieties, which take up less than one-third of the vineyards, are led by Shiraz (SYRAH), CABERNET SAUVIGNON, PINOTAGE, CINSAUT, and MERLOT.

Wrattonbully [RAT-tuhn-bul-lee] An Australian wine-producing region located about 200 miles southeast of Adelaide in SOUTH AUSTRALIA'S Limestone Coast Zone. It's situated near the town of Naracoorte, between the better-known regions of PADTHAWAY and COONAWARRA. It lies in the foothills of the Naracoorte Ranges and has soil—terra rossa over limestone—similar to the famous Coonawarra region, just to the south. Its climate is warmer than Coonawarra but cooler than Padthaway. Viticultural development started in the late 1960s and early 1970s, but dramatic growth didn't occur until the 1990s. There are about 3,300 acres planted in the Wrattonbully region. CABERNET SAUVIGNON and SHIRAZ are the primary VARIEITES followed by MERLOT, CHARDONNAY, SAUVIGNON BLANC, and PINOT NOIR. Before this region was officially named Wrattonbully, it was called by several different names including **Naracoorte Ranges** and **Koppamurra**.

Wülfen *see* RAUENTHAL

Württemberg [VU*R*T-uhm-beh*r*k] One of Germany's thirteen ANBAUGEBIETE (quality-wine regions), located along the Neckar River and its tributaries where they flow east of the Rhine River before turning west to join the Rhine. The majority of the region's 28,000 acres of vineyards are situated just north of the city of Stuttgart. The region is divided into three main BEREICHE—**Kocher-Jagst-Tauber**, **Remstal-Stuttgart**, and **Württembergisch Unterland**. There are many small vineyards in the region and almost 90 percent of the crop is processed by grower's cooperatives. Unlike most Anbaugebiete, red varieties make up over 50 percent of the planted acreage in Württemberg. RIESLING is the most widely planted grape, but there are several widely planted red varieties—Trollinger (SCHIAVA), Müllerrebe (MEUNIER), Limberger, PORTUGIESER, and Spätburgunder (PINOT NOIR). Red wines are generally slightly sweet and light in both color and TANNINS. Because many of the red grapes lack adequate color, they're made into WEISSHERBST (a ROSÉ) rather than red wine. This region's other specialty is SCHILLERWEIN, a pink wine made by combining red and white grapes prior to FERMENTATION.

Württembergisch Unterland, Bereich *see* WÜRTTEMBERG

Würzburg [VUH*R*TS-beh*r*k] University city that is the capital of Germany's FRANKEN region and the site of many of the old cellars of the region's finest wine-producing estates. Among the best cellars are the Staatlicher Hofkeller, which is the Bavarian State Domain; the Juliusspital, the local church charity; and Bürgerspital, a city-run charitable institution. The vineyards on the city's outskirts along the Main River are planted primarily with MÜLLER-THURGAU, RIESLING, and SYLVANER. **Stein** is the most famous vineyard (EINZELLAGE) in Würzburg (and Franken). Its 210 acres cover the best sections, which have an ideal southern exposure and look down on Würzburg. Wines from the Franken region are sometimes called Steinwein, in reference to this famous vineyard.

Würzburger Stein *see* FRANKEN; WÜRZBURG

Würzgarten *see* HALLGARTEN; ÜRZIG

Wyndruif *see* SÉMILLON

Xarel-lo [sah-REHL-loh] Grown extensively in Spain's CATALONIA region, this white-wine grape is one of the three main varieties used to make most Spanish SPARKLING WINES. It is considered a medium- to low-quality grape, used mainly to add BODY, and is customarily blended with the higher-quality MACABEO and PARELLADA grapes. Xarel-lo is also used to make a STILL WINE, which is usually a blend of these same grapes. It's the primary grape in the Alella DO, where it's known as *Pansa Blanca*.

Xérès [seh-REHS] The former name for JEREZ DE LA FRONTERA.

Xinómavro [ksee-NOH-mah-vroh] A red-grape variety grown in various parts of Greece, particularly the northern portion. Xinómavro is known for its high ACIDITY and deep red color; in fact its name indicates just that—*xino* means "sour" and *mavro* means "black." Xinómavro is the primary grape in the wines of Náousa and Gouménissa. The red wines, which are generally TOUGH and TANNIC with high acidity in their youth, require 5 or more years of AGING. Grapes grown in cooler regions and handled by capable winemakers can be rich and full-bodied with relatively high alcohol that's balanced by good acidity. This grape is also used in SPARKLING WINES.

X

Y **Yakima Valley AVA** [YAK-uh-maw] Although Yakima Valley, which is in the south central part of Washington State, was the first designated AVA in the northwest, it's now encompassed by the much larger COLUMBIA VALLEY AVA. The Yakima Valley AVA covers approximately 665,600 acres, starting just southwest of the city of Yakima and flowing southeast almost reaching Kennewick in the Tri-Cities area. It has some of the coolest weather in the Columbia Valley and grows a great number of CONCORD grapes, most of which are used for juice. In 2001, a small 4,000-acre section in the southeastern portion overlooking Benton City was approved as the **Red Mountain AVA**—named after this area's Red Mountain, the name of which comes from the red-hued native grasses on its slopes. Yakima Valley has over 10,000 planted acres, 700 of which are in the Red Mountain area. In 2006, the RATTLESNAKE HILLS AVA was established as a sub-appellation. In order of popularity, the vineyards are planted to CHARDONNAY, MERLOT, CABERNET SAUVIGNON, RIESLING, SYRAH, GEWÜRZTRAMINER, SAUVIGNON BLANC, CABERNET FRANC, PINOT GRIS, and CHENIN BLANC.

Yamhill-Carlton District AVA APPELLATION created in February 2005 within the larger WILLAMETTE VALLEY AVA. Its horseshoe-shaped hills contain 51,500 acres, of which about 1,200 are planted with grapes. Vineyards must be planted between 200 and 1,000-foot elevations. There are over 20 wineries located in the AVA, plus a number of wineries that source fruit from the area vineyards. PINOT NOIR is the star from this AVA but CHARDONNAY, DOLCETTO, MUSCAT, PINOT BLANC, PINOT GRIS, and PINOT MEUNIER are also grown. Notable vineyards include Belle Pent, McCrone, Reed & Reynolds, Shea, and WillaKenzie.

Yarra Valley An Australian growing region located in VICTORIA'S Port Phillip Zone. It's situated about 30 miles northeast of Melbourne around the towns of Yarra Glen and Lilydale. Its winemaking history dates back to the early 1890s when vines were planted at Yering Station. Today, after many starts and stops, the Yarra Valley is recognized as one of Australia's premier wine regions and has over 6,000 acres of vineyard. The terrain is undulating, with some of Australia's steepest slopes. The climate is warm to cool, depending on altitude and location. The principal grape varieties here are CHARDONNAY, PINOT NOIR, and CABERNET SAUVIGNON, followed by MERLOT, SAUVIGNON BLANC, Shiraz (SYRAH), RIESLING, and SÉMILLON. Yarra Valley is best known for Pinot Noir and Cabernet Sauvignon wines. There are over 45 producers in the area.

Ycoden-Daute-Isora DO *see* CANARY ISLANDS

yeast [YEEST] A living, microscopic, single-cell organism. Wild yeast spores are always floating in the air. Just when these wild spores first interacted with foods and liquids is uncertain, but we do know that Egyptians used yeast as a leavening agent over 5,000 years ago and that wine and other fermented beverages were made for millennia before that. It was in 1857 that France's famous microbiologist Louis Pasteur discovered that FERMENTATION was caused by yeasts. During fermentation, yeast converts food (in the form of sugar or starch) into ALCOHOL and CARBON DIOXIDE. In the production of wine, the conversion of yeast to alcohol is necessary for the final product, and carbon dioxide is what makes SPARKLING WINES effervescent. To multiply and grow, all yeast needs is the right environment—moisture, food, and a warm, nurturing temperature. Today, scientists have been able to isolate and identify the specific yeasts that are best for winemaking. Modern winemakers carefully choose the yeasts they use in combination with different varieties of grapes. Various yeasts have specific properties and are better suited for particular winemaking styles. For example, some yeasts produce less foam and are therefore well suited for BARREL FERMENTATION. Those styles of yeast that are resistant to cold temperatures are best for making white wines. Other yeasts ferment more rapidly, tolerate alcohol better, or impart flavors to the wine (some desirable, others not). Popular commercially available yeasts used today include Champagne, Epernay, Montrachet, Pasteur Champagne, and Steinberg. Rather than resorting to using cultivated yeasts, some winemakers prefer **native yeast fermentation**, which relies simply on natural wild yeast spores. *See also* BRETTANOMYCES.

yeasty *see* Glossary of Wine Tasting Terms, page 655

Yecla DO [YAY-klah] A small DO located in the Levante region in eastern Spain, northwest of the city of Alicante. Yecla mainly produces high-ALCOHOL (14 to 16 percent) red wines, primarily from Monastrell (MOURVÈDRE) grapes, along with some Garnacha (GRENACHE). The white varieties grown in this DO are AIRÉN, MACABEO, and Merseguera. Experimental plots of CABERNET SAUVIGNON, MERLOT, and TEMPRANILLO have also been planted. Current efforts suggest that a shift toward lower-alcohol (12 to 13 percent) wines may be underway.

yeso *see* PLASTERING

yield [YEELD] A term used in grape-growing and winemaking circles to express the productivity of a set amount of vineyard land. Yield is a way of comparing the relative productivity of different grape varieties in different locations. In the United States and Australia, grape yield is generally expressed in terms of tons per acre; in Europe and South America, it's expressed in HECTOLITERS per HECTARE. In comparing European yields to U.S. yields, 1 hectoliter of grapes per hectare would be equivalent to 0.0741 tons of grapes per acre; 1 ton per acre is equivalent to 13.5 hectoliters per hectare. A hectoliter produces approximately 133 bottles or 11.1 cases of wine (a standard bottle is 750 milliliters). A ton of grapes produces about 727 bottles or just over 60 cases of wine. Therefore, a vineyard in France that produces 50 hectoliters of grapes per hectare would be equivalent to one in the United States that produces 3.7 tons of grapes per acre. A U.S. vineyard producing 5 tons per acre is equivalent to a European vineyard producing 67.5 hectoliters per hectare. A 50-hectare vineyard producing 45 hectoliters of grapes per hectare would produce just under 25,000 cases of wine. Yield is important because the higher the yield, the more productive the vines and the more grapes the grower has to sell. However, it's generally agreed that lower yields produce higher-quality wines and that the higher the yield, the more diluted the resulting wine will be. With that in mind, one of the criteria for meeting French APPELLATION D'ORIGINE CONTRÔLÉE (AC) regulations is permissible yield. Each AC area has a maximum allowable yield, depending on the grape variety and quantity of land. Yields are kept down by PRUNING the vines so that there's an optimum ratio between fruit production and vegetative growth (important for the next year's production). As more is learned about VITICULTURE, higher yields are being achieved without loss of quality. However, it still holds true that higher yields from the same set of vines grown the same way will dilute the concentration in the grapes. Some vineyards in Germany's RHINE and MOSELLE district can yield 100 hectoliters per hectare without loss of quality. On the other hand, in Spain much of the vineyard land is very arid and can't be densely planted because the vines won't get enough moisture. This climate, plus rather antiquated viticultural practices, limits yields in most parts of Spain where the average is around 23 hectoliters of grapes per hectare. In California's coastal areas, where higher-quality wines are made, growers expect 3 to 6 tons per acre (equivalent to 40 to 80 hectoliters per hectare), depending on the location and grape variety.

York Mountain AVA Approved in 1987, this 9,360-acre California APPELLATION is located just west of the PASO ROBLES AVA in SAN LUIS OBISPO COUNTY. It sits east of the San Lucia Mountains and, at higher elevations, receives the ocean breezes that are typically blocked from the Paso Robles area. Therefore, York Mountain is considered a cool

Region I area (*see* CLIMATE REGIONS OF CALIFORNIA) and does well with PINOT NOIR grapes. It currently has only one winery, York Mountain Vineyard, whose history dates back to the 1880s when Andrew York established it as the Ascension Winery.

Yorkville Highlands AVA Approved in 1998, this California APPELLATION is in MENDOCINO COUNTY, running northwest from the Mendocino-Sonoma County line just above the ALEXANDER VALLEY AVA in SONOMA COUNTY until it meets the ANDERSON VALLEY AVA. It includes about 40,000 acres in areas on both sides of Highway 128, from just above Cloverdale toward Boonville. The MENDOCINO AVA was expanded to include the Yorkville Highlands AVA as part of the approved petition for the area. SAUVIGNON BLANC and red BORDEAUX varieties are being grown. The area is still relatively new with only a couple of wineries.

young; youthful *see* Glossary of Wine Tasting Terms, page 655

Yountville AVA A California VITICULTURAL AREA approved in 1999 and located north of the city of Napa around the town of Yountville. Its boundaries were primarily established by those of the other existing or proposed AVAS in the large NAPA VALLEY AVA—OAK KNOLL DISTRICT on the south, OAKVILLE on the north, STAGS LEAP DISTRICT on the east, and MOUNT VEEDER on the west. The town of Yountville takes its name from George C. Yount (its founding father), who had a large land grant in the Napa Valley and who was the first to plant grapes there. The Yountville AVA is warmer than the CARNEROS AVA, but cooler than areas to the west and north of it. The area encompasses about 8,260 acres with not quite half of that planted to vineyards. CHARDONNAY is the dominant variety, especially in vineyards to the south where it's coolest. MERLOT and CABERNET FRANC do well here, as does CABERNET SAUVIGNON in the AVA's northern portion.

Yvorne [ee-VAW*R*N] A wine named for a village in the CHABLAIS district in Switzerland's VAUD canton. Yvorne wines are produced from CHASSELAS grapes, locally called *Dorin*. They're known for their ripe fruit and FLINTY character and are considered some of the best of the district.

ZAP *see* ZINFANDEL ADVOCATES AND PRODUCERS

Zapponara Bianca *see* BOMBINO BIANCO

Zell [TSEHL] Although there are a number of German towns and villages named Zell, the best known in wine circles is the village on the Mosel River in Germany's MOSEL-SAAR-RUWER region. It's this village that's the genesis of Zeller Schwarze Katz, the wine with the familiar black cat (Schwarze Katz) on the label. In 1971, Zeller Schwarze Katz became the name of the GROSSLAGE covering vineyards around Zell, and only wines from this Grosslage can use the name. Most wines using the Zeller Schwarze Katz name are simple, light wines, although quality can vary immensely. Zell also lends its name to the BEREICH that covers this region, Bereich Zell/Mosel, which encompasses the land from Zell northeast to Koblenz. This area is also referred to as *Untermosel* or *Lower Mosel.*

Zeller Schwarze Katz *see* ZELL

Zell/Mosel, Beriech *see* ZELL

Zeltingen [TSEHL-tihn-guhn] A top wine-producing village in Germany's MOSEL-SARR-RUWER region. It's located in the same area as other esteemed villages of the Mosel—BERNKASTEL, GRAACH, and WEHLEN. The vineyards of Zeltingen-Rachtig (its full name) exist on both sides of the Mosel River. Top EINZELLAGEN include Deutschherrenberg, Himmerlreich, Schlossberg, and Sonnenuhr (which lies adjacent to the Sonnenuhr vineyard of Wehlen). Zeltingener RIESLING wines are known to be full-bodied (*see* BODY) yet ELEGANT.

Zentralkellerei [TSEHN-trahl-KEHL-lehr-ri] A German term meaning "central cellar," referring to a very large cooperative cellar that gets its wine or MUST from smaller cooperative cellars (*see* WINZERGENOSSEN-SCHAFT). A large *Zentralkellerei* may have as many as 4,000 to 5,000 members and produce their own brand names of wine.

Zibibbo *see* MUSCAT

Zinfandel [ZIHN-fuhn-dehl] Grape that is considered California's red-wine grape because it's not widely grown in other parts of the world. Zinfandel vines were brought to California in the 1850s. By the 1880s, this variety was rapidly gaining acceptance by California growers, and it is now that state's second most extensively planted red grape behind CABERNET SAUVIGNON. For years Zinfandel's origins were very mysterious. Initially, research confirmed a relationship between Zinfandel and Primitivo (a variety grown in Italy's PUGLIA region), causing speculation that Zinfandel might have originated in Italy. However, in late 2001, DNA FINGERPRINTING determined that Crljenak Kastelanski (a little-known grape from Croatia) and Zinfandel had identical DNA profiles. Further analysis proved that a more popular Croatian grape, PLAVAC MALI, was a descendant of Crljenak Kastelanski. The current thinking is that Crljenak is the parent of both Zinfandel and Primitivo. Outside of the Zinfandel grown in California (and Italy's Primitivo), there are only isolated plantings of this grape, mainly in South Africa and Australia. Zinfandel is vinified in many styles, which vary greatly in quality. One popular style is WHITE ZINFANDEL, a fruity-flavored BLUSH WINE that's usually slightly sweet and ranges in color from light to dark pink. The Zinfandel grape is also used as a base for SPARKLING WINES. When made into red wine, Zinfandel can produce wines ranging from light, NOUVEAU styles to hearty, robust reds with berrylike, spicy (sometimes PEPPERY) flavors, plenty of TANNINS and ALCOHOL, and enough DEPTH, COMPLEXITY, and LONGEVITY to be compared to CABERNET SAUVIGNONS. Another style is LATE-HARVEST Zinfandel, which exhibits higher alcohol levels and some RESIDUAL SUGAR. Occasionally, Zinfandel is FORTIFIED and marketed as a California PORT-style wine. Large Zinfandel plantings exist in California's CENTRAL VALLEY where the hot weather tends to produce lower-quality grapes, which often make their way into JUG WINE. The Italian DOC, PRIMITIVO DI MANDURIA, produces DRY red Primitivo grape-based wines that are similar to some California Zins. As Zinfandel's popularity increases, more and more enterprising Italian Primitivo growers are labeling their wines "Zinfandel" and exporting them to the United States.

Zinfandel Advocates and Producers (ZAP) A nonprofit, educational organization formed in 1991 to promote wines made from ZINFANDEL. It was established in the United States but now also includes international members. Today there are about 310 producer members and some 6,500 advocates that attend various organization-sponsored events. ZAP also supports a study at the UNIVERSITY OF CALIFORNIA, DAVIS to document Zinfandel's DNA, as well as a Heritage Vineyard at the University's research vineyards in Oakville in the Napa Valley. The Heritage Vineyard is a collection of Zinfandel vine cuttings from all over California.

Zitsa *see* GREECE

Zonda Valley *see* ARGENTINA

zone *see* GEOGRAPHIC INDICATIONS

zucchero [TSOOK-kay-roh] Italian for "sugar." *Zuccheraggio* is the Italian term for "CHAPTALIZATION" and *residuo* refers to RESIDUAL SUGAR.

Appendix

Listing of Contents

Grape Varieties

Following are the names of the grape varieties defined in *The New Wine Lover's Companion*. The primary listings with full definitions are in **boldface**. Other entries are typically the grape's regional or country names, which are cross-referenced to the main listing.

Ablan *see* PALOMINO

Acolon *see* DORNFELDER

Aghiorghitiko; Agiorgitiko

Aglianico

Agliano *see* ALEATICO

Airén

Albana

Albariño *see* ALVARINHO

Alcanol *see* MACABEO

Alcayata *see* MONASTRELL

Aleatico

Alicante *see* ALICANTE BOUSCHET; GRENACHE

Alicante Bouschet

Alicante Ganzin *see* RUBIRED

Aligoté

Allianico *see* ALEATICO

Altesse

Alvarinho

Americano *see* ISABELLA

Amorgiano *see* MANDELARIA

Aramon

Arinto

Arneis

Arnsburger

Assyyrtiko

Aurora; Aurore

Auxerrois *see* MALBEC

Auxerrois Blanc

Auxerrois Gris *see* PINOT GRIS

Bacchus

Baco Blanc

Baco Noir

Baga

Balbi *see* PROSECCO

Balzac *see* MOURVÈDRE

Barbera

Beaunois *see* CHARDONNAY

Beli Pinot *see* PINOT BLANC

Bellina *see* ISABELLA

Bergeron *see* ROUSSANNE

Bermejuela *see* MARMAJUELO

Biancame *see* ALBANA

Bigney *see* MERLOT

Black Hamburg *see* MUSCAT

Black Muscat *see* MUSCAT

Blanca-Roja *see* MALVASIA

Blanc de Troyes *see* ALIGOTE

Blanc Fumé

Blanquette *see* CLAIRETTE

Blauburgunder *see* PINOT NOIR

Blauer Klevner *see* PINOT NOIR

Blauer Limberger *see* BLAUFRÄNKISCH

Blauer Portugieser *see* PORTUGIESER

Blauer Spätburgunder *see* PINOT NOIR

Blaufränkisch

Boal

Bobal

Bombino Bianco

Bonarda

Bonarda di Chieri *see* BONARDA

Bonarda di Gattinara *see*
    BONARDA
Bonarda Piemontese *see*
    BONARDA
Bordo *see* CABERNET FRANC
Bouche *see* CABERNET FRANC;
    CABERNET SAUVIGNON
Bouchet *see* CABERNET FRANC;
    CABERNET SAUVIGNON
Bourguignon Noir *see* GAMAY
Brachet
Braquet *see* BRACHET
Brenton *see* CABERNET FRANC
Brown Muscat *see* MUSCAT
Brunello *see* SANGIOVESE
Bual *see* BOAL
Buisserate *see* JACQUÈRE
Burger *see* ELBLING
Burgundac Crni *see* PINOT NOIR
Burgunder

Cabernet Dorsa *see* DORNFELDER
Cabernet Dorio *see* DORNFELDER
Cabernet Franc
Cabernet Sauvignon
Caccione Nero *see* CANAIOLO
Cadarca *see* KADARKA
Calabrese *see* NERO D'AVOLA
Camobraque *see* FOLLE BLANCHE
Canaiolo
Cannonau *see* GRENACHE
Cape Riesling *see* CROUCHEN
Carignan; Carignane
Carignan Rosos *see* GRENACHE
Cariñena *see* CARIGNAN
Carmelin *see* PETIT VERDOT
Carmenet *see* CABERNET FRANC
Carnelian
Castelhão, Castelhão Frances
    see PERIQUITA
Catarratto
Catawba

Cayuga White
Cencibel *see* TEMPRANILLO
Centurian; Centurion
Chambourcin
Chancellor
Charbono
Chardonel
Chardonnay
Chasselas
Chaudenet Gris *see* ALIGOTÉ
De Chaunac
Chelois
Chenin Blanc
Chevrier *see* SÉMILLON
Chiavennasca *see* NEBBIOLO
Cienna
Cinsaut, Cinsault
Clairette
Clairette Ronde *see* TREBBIANO
Clairette Rosé *see* TREBBIANO
Clare Riesling *see* CROUCHEN
Clevner *see* PINOT BLANC; PINOT
    NOIR
Colombar *see* COLOMBARD
Colombard; Columbard
Colorino
Complexa
Concord
Cordisco *see* MONTEPULCIANO
Cortese
Corvina
Corvinone
Cot *see* MALBEC
Crabutet *see* MERLOT
Criolla *see* MISSION
Crljenak Kastelanski *see*
    ZINFANDEL
Croatina; Croattina
Crouchen
Cruian *see* CORVINA
Cugnette *see* JACQUÈRE
Cynthiana *see* NORTON

De Chaunac
Dolcetto
Dolsin; Dolsin Nero *see* DOLCETTO
Dorin *see* CHASSELAS
Dornfelder
Durif
Dutchess

Edeltraube *see* GEWÜRZTRAMINER
Ehrenfelser
Elbling
Elysium *see* MUSCAT
Emerald Riesling
Erbaluce
Espagne *see* CINSAUT
Esparte *see* MOURVÈDRE
Essencia *see* MUSCAT

Faber
Falanghina; Falangina
Favorita *see* VERMENTINO
Fendant *see* CHASSELAS
Feteasca *see* LEÁNYKA
Flora
Folgasão
Folle Blanche
Freisa
French Colombard *see*
    COLOMBARD
Fresa *see* FREISA
Fresia *see* FREISA
Friulara *see* RABOSO
Friulano *see* SAUVIGNONASSE
Friularo *see* RABOSO
Frontenac
Frontignan *see* MUSCAT
Frühburgunder *see* PINOT NOIR
Früher Roter Malvasier *see*
    MALVASIA
Fumé Blanc *see* SAUVIGNON
    BLANC
Furmint

Gaglioppo
Gamaret
Gamay
Gamay Beaujolais
Gamay Blanc *see* CHARDONNAY
Gamza *see* KADARKA
Gargana *see* GARGANEGA
Garganega
Garanoir *see* GAMARET
Garnaccia *see* GRENACHE
Garnacha *see* GRENACHE
Garnacha Blanca *see* GRENACHE
Garnacha Tinta *see* GRENACHE
Garnacha Tintorera *see* ALICANTE
    BOUSCHET
Garnacho Tinto *see* GRENACHE
Gelber Muskateller *see* MUSCAT
Gewürztraminer
Glera *see* PROSECCO
Godello *see* VERDELHO
Golden Chasselas *see* PALOMINO
Gold Hamburg *see* MUSCAT
Goldmuskateller *see* MUSCAT
Gordo Blanco *see* MUSCAT
Gouveio *see* VERDELHO
Graciano
Grasevina *see* WELSCHRIESLING
Grauburgunder *see* PINOT GRIS
Grauvernatsch *see* SCHIAVA
Grechetto; Greghetto
Greco
Greco Bianco di Perugia *see*
    GRECHETTO
Greco del Vesuvio *see* GRECO
Greco delle Torre *see* GRECO
Greco di Ancona *see* ALBANA
Greco Spoletino *see* GRECHETTO
Green Grape *see* SÉMILLON
Green Hungarian
Grenache
Grignolino
Grillo

Gringet *see* SAVAGNIN
Gris Meunier *see* MEUNIER
Grolleau *see* GROSLOT
Groppello
Groslot
Gros Plant *see* FOLLE BLANCHE
Grosse Roussette *see* MARSANNE
Grosse Syrah *see* MONDEUSE
Grossriesling *see* ELBLING
Grossvernatsch *see* SCHIAVA
Grüner *see* GRÜNER VELTLINER
Grüner Veltliner
Grünmuskateller *see* GRÜNER
   VELTLINER
Gutedel *see* CHASSELAS

Hanepoot *see* MUSCAT
Hárslevelü
Helfensteiner
Hermitage *see* CINSAUT
Hermitage Blanc *see* MARSANNE
Heroldrebe
Huxelrebe

Isabella
Italian Riesling *see*
   WELSCHRIESLING

Jacquère
Joannes Seyve 26205 *see*
   CHAMBOURCIN
João de Santarem *see* PERIQUITA
Johannisberger *see* RIESLING
Johannisberg Riesling *see* RIESLING
Juan Garcia

Kadarka
Kékfrankos *see* BLAUFRÄNKISCH
Kékmedoc *see* MENOIRE
Kéknyelü
Kerner
Kleinberger *see* ELBLING

Kleinvernatsch *see* SCHIAVA
Klingelberger *see* RIESLING
Kuhlmann 1882 *see* MARÉCHAL
   FOCH
Kuhlmann 1942 *see* LEON MILLOT

Lacrima Nera see GAGLIOPPO
Landot
Lagarino *see* LAGREIN
Lagrain *see* LAGREIN
Lagrein
Lairén *see* AIRÉN
Lambrusco
Lardot *see* MACABEO
Laskiriesling *see* WELSCHRIESLING
Leányka
Leon Millot
Lexia *see* MUSCAT
Listan *see* PALOMINO
Lizzana *see* GARGANEGA
Lyonnaise Blanche *see* MELON
   DE BOURGOGNE
Macabeo
Maccabeu *see* MACABEO
Mâconnais *see* ALTESSE
Mädchentraube *see* LEÁNYKA
Málaga *see* CINSAUT
Malbec
Malmsey *see* MALVASIA
Malvasia
Malvoisie *see* MALVASIA
Manchega *see* AIRÉN
Mandelaria; Mandelari
Marchigiano *see* VERDICCHIO
Maréchal Foch
Marmajuelo
Marsanne
Marselan
Marzemina Bianca *see* CHASSELAS
Mataro *see* MOURVÈDRE
Mavrodaphne
Mazuelo *see* CARIGNAN

Médoc Noir *see* MERLOT; MENOIRE
Melon d'Arbois *see* CHARDONNAY
Melon de Bourgogne
Mencía
Menoire
Merlau *see* MERLOT
Merlau Blanc *see* MERLOT BLANC
Merlot
Merlot Blanc
Meunier
Mission
Mittervernatsch *see* SCHIAVA
Molette Noire *see* MONDEUSE
Monastrell
Mondeuse
Monestel *see* CARIGNAN
Montepulciano
Montonec *see* PARELLADA
Morastel *see* MONASTRELL
Morellone *see* MONTEPULCIANO
Morillon *see* NEGRETTE
Morne Noir *see* MENOIRE
Morio-Muskat
Morrastal *see* MONASTRELL
Morrastel *see* GRACIANO
Mortágua *see* TOURIGA NACIONAL
Moscatel *see* MUSCAT
Moscatel de Málaga *see* MUSCAT
Moscatel Gordo *see* MUSCAT
Moscatello *see* ALEATICO
Moscatel Rose *see* MUSCAT
Moscato Bianco *see* MUSCAT
Moscato di Amburgo *see*
    MUSCAT
Moscato Giallo *see* MUSCAT
Moscato Rosa *see* MUSCAT
Mourvèdre
Müllerrebe *see* MEUNIER
Müller-Thurgau
Muscadelle
Muscadet *see* MELON DE
    BOURGOGNE

Muscadet Doux *see* MUSCADELLE
Muscadine
Muscat
Muscat Blanc *see* MUSCAT
Muscat Blanc à Petits Grains
    see MUSCAT
Muscat Canelli *see* MUSCAT
Muscat d'Alsace *see* MUSCAT
Muscatel de Grano Menudo *see*
    MUSCAT
Muscateller *see* ALEATICO
Muscat Frontignan *see* MUSCAT
Muscat Hamburg *see* MUSCAT
Muscat of Alexandria *see*
    MUSCAT
Muscat Ottenel *see* MUSCAT
Muskateller *see* MUSCAT
Muskotaly *see* MUSCAT
Musquette *see* MUSCADELLE

Nagyburgundi *see* PINOT NOIR
Napa Gamay *see* GAMAY
Nebbiolo
Negra Mole
Negramoll *see* NEGRA MOLE
Negrette
Negron *see* RABOSO
Nerello
Neretto *see* CROATINA
Nero d'Avola
Niagara
Nielluccio *see* SANGIOVESE
Norton

Oeillade *see* CINSAUT
Ojo de Liebre *see* TEMPRANILLO
Olaszriesling *see* WELSCHRIESLING
Oporto *see* PORTUGIESER
Optima
Orange Muscat
Oremasco *see* DOLCETTO

Ortega
Ottaianello *see* CINSAUT

Paarl Riesling *see* CROUCHEN
Païen *see* GEWÜRZTRAMINER
Pais *see* MISSION
Palomino
Parellada
Pedernão *see* ARINTO
Pedro Jiménez *see* PEDRO
XIMÉNEZ
Pedro Ximen *see* PEDRO
XIMÉNEZ
Pedro Ximénez
Pelaverga
Periquita
Perlan *see* CHASSELAS
Petite-Cabernet *see* CABERNET
SAUVIGNON
Petite Sirah; Petite Syrah
Petit Gamai *see* GAMAY
Petit Gris *see* PINOT GRIS
Petit Noir *see* NEGRETTE
Petit Verdau *see* PETIT VERDOT
Petit Verdot
Picardan Noir *see* CINSAUT
Picolit
Picotener *see* NEBBIOLO
Picpoule *see* FOLLE BLANCHE
Pigato
Pignolo
Pignul *see* PIGNOLO
Pineau *see* PINOT NOIR
Pineau d'Anjou *see* CHENIN
BLANC
Pineau de la Loire *see* CHENIN
BLANC
Pinotage
Pinot Beurot *see* PINOT GRIS
Pinot Bianco *see* PINOT BLANC
Pinot Blanc
Pinot Buot *see* PINOT GRIS

Pinot Chardonnay *see*
CHARDONNAY
Pinot de l'Ermitage *see* DURIF
Pinot de Romans *see* DURIF
Pinot Grigio *see* PINOT GRIS
Pinot Gris
Pinot Meunier *see* MEUNIER
Pinot Nero *see* PINOT NOIR
Pinot Noir
Piqupoul de Pays *see* BACO
BLANC
Pisse-vin *see* ARAMON
Plante Riche *see* ARAMON
Plant Gris *see* ALIGOTÉ
Plant Meunier *see* MEUNIER
Plavac Mali
Portugais Bleu *see* PORTUGIESER
Portugieser
Pressac *see* MALBEC
Primaticcio *see* MONTEPULCIANO
Primitivo *see* ZINFANDEL
Prosecco
Prugnolo *see* SANGIOVESE
Prunella *see* CINSAUT
Pugent *see* NEBBIOLO

Raboso
Raisinotte *see* MUSCADELLE
Ravat
Rebula *see* RIBOLLA
Refosco
Refosco del Peduncolo Rosso
see MONDEUSE
Refosco Nostrano *see* MONDEUSE
Requena *see* BOBAL
Rheinelbe *see* ELBLING
Rhine Riesling *see* RIESLING
Ribolla
Riesling
Riesling Italico *see*
WELSCHRIESLING
Riesling Renano *see* RIESLING

Riesling-Sylvaner *see* MÜLLER-
  THURGAU
Rivaner *see* MÜLLER-THURGAU
Riviera Ligure di Ponente *see*
  VERMENTINO
Rizlingszilvani *see* MÜLLER-
  THURGAU
Rkatsiteli
Robola *see* RIBOLLA
Rolle *see* VERMENTINO
Romondolo Classico *see*
  VERDUZZO
Rosenmuskateller *see* MUSCAT
Rotor Traminer *see*
  GEWÜRZTRAMINER
Rougeon
Roussanne
Rousselet *see* GEWÜRZTRAMINER
Roussette
Roussillon *see* GRENACHE
Roussillonen *see* CARIGNAN
Royalty
Rubienne
Rubin
Rubired
Ruby Cabernet
Rufete
Rülander *see* PINOT GRIS
Rusa *see* GEWÜRZTRAMINER

Saint-Émilion *see* TREBBIANO
Sangiovese
San Gioveto *see* SANGIOVESE
Sangioveto *see* SANGIOVESE
Sangrantino
Sanvicetro *see* SANGIOVESE
Sauvignon *see* SAUVIGNONASSE;
  TOCAI FRIULANO
Sauvignonasse
Sauvignon Blanc
Sauvignon Gris *see* SAUVIGNON
  BLANC

Sauvignon Jaune *see* SAUVIGNON
  BLANC
Sauvignon Musqué *see*
  SAUVIGNON BLANC
Sauvignon Rose *see* SAUVIGNON
  BLANC
Sauvignon Rouge *see* CABERNET
  SAUVIGNON; SAUVIGNON BLANC
Sauvignon Vert *see*
  SAUVIGNONASSE
Savagnin
Savagnin Noir *see* PINOT NOIR
Savagnin Rosé *see*
  GEWÜRZTRAMINER
Savoyance *see* MONDEUSE
Scheurebe
Schiava
Schioppettino
Schwarzriesling *see* MEUNIER
Scuppernong
Seibel 5279 *see* AURORA
Siebel 5898 *see* ROUGEON
Seibel 7053 *see* CHANCELLOR
Seibel 9549 *see* DE CHAUNAC
Seibel 10878 *see* CHELOIS
Sémillon
Sercial
Serprina *see* PROSECCO
Seyre-Villard 5276 *see* SEYVAL
  BLANC
Seyval Blanc
Silvaner *see* SYLVANER
Skadarska *see* KADARKA
South African Riesling *see*
  CROUCHEN
Souzão, Sousão
Spanna *see* NEBBIOLO
Spätburgunder *see* PINOT NOIR
Steen *see* CHENIN BLANC
Stein *see* CHENIN BLANC
Sultana
Sumarello *see* UVA DI TROIA

Sylvaner
Symphony
Syrah
Szekszárd
Szükerbarat *see* PINOT GRIS

Talia *see* TREBBIANO
Tannat
Tempranilla *see* TEMPRANILLO
Tempranillo
Terrano *see* REFOSCO
Thalia *see* TREBBIANO
Thompson Seedless *see* SULTANA
Tindilloro *see* CANAIOLO
Tinta *see* GRENACHE
Tinta Caiada
Tinta Lameira *see* TINTA CAIADA
Tinta Madeira
Tinta Negra Mole *see* NEGRA
    MOLE
Tinta Roriz *see* TEMPRANILLO
Tinto *see* GRENACHE
Tinto Cão
Tinto del Pais *see* TEMPRANILLO
Tinto de Toro *see* TEMPRANILLO
Tinto Fino *see* TEMPRANILLO
Tocai Friulano; Tocai
Tocai Italico *see* TOCAI FRIULANO
Tokai *see* TOCAI FRIULANO
Tokay *see* MUSCADELLE
Tokay d'Alsace *see* PINOT GRIS
Tondo *see* PROSECCO
Touriga Francesa
Touriga Nacional
Traminac *see* GEWÜRZTRAMINER
Traminer *see* GEWÜRZTRAMINER
Traminer Aromatico *see*
    GEWÜRZTRAMINER
Traminer Aromatique *see*
    GEWÜRZTRAMINER
Traminer Musqué *see*
    GEWÜRZTRAMINER

Traminer Parfumé *see*
    GEWÜRZTRAMINER
Tramini *see* GEWÜRZTRAMINER
Trebbiano
Trebbiano Abruzzo *see* BOMBINO
    BIANCO
Trebbiano d'Abruzzo *see*
    BOMBINO BIANCO
Trebbiano Romagnolo *see*
    TREBBIANO
Trebbiano Toscano *see*
    TREBBIANO
Trollinger *see* SCHIAVA
Trouchet Noir *see* CABERNET
    FRANC
Tschaggel *see* SCHIAVA
Tschaggelevernatsch *see*
    SCHIAVA
Tyrian

Ugni Blanc *see* TREBBIANO
Ugni Noir *see* ARAMON
Ull de Llebre *see* TEMPRANILLO
Uva Abruzzi *see*
    MONTEPULCIANO
Uva Canina *see* CANAIOLO
Uva della Marina *see* UVA DI
    TROIA
Uva di Troia
Uva Merla *see* CANAIOLO
Uva Vermiglia *see* CROATINA

Valcarcelia *see* MONASTRELL
Valdepeñera Blanca *see* AIRÉN
Varresana Bianca *see*
    VERMENTINO
Veltliner *see* GRÜNER VELTLINER
Veltlini *see* GRÜNER VELTLINER
Vennentino *see* VERMENTINO
Verdejo; Verdejo Palido
Verdelho
Verdicchio

Verdone *see* VERDICCHIO
Verdot Rouge *see* PETIT VERDOT
Verduzzo; Verduzzo Friulano
Vermentino
Vernaccia di Oristano
Vernaccia di San Gimignano
Vernatsch *see* SCHIAVA
Vidal 256 *see* VIDAL BLANC
Vidal Blanc
Vidure *see* CABERNET SAUVIGNON
Vignoles *see* RAVAT
Villard Blanc
Villard Noir
Vinhão *see* SOUZÃO
Viognier
Vionnier *see* VIOGNIER
Viura *see* MACABEO
Vlassky Riesling; Vlassky
 Rizling *see* WELSCHRIESLING

Walschriesling *see*
 WELSCHRIESLING
Weissburgunder *see* PINOT BLANC
Weisserburgunder *see* MELON DE
 BOURGOGNE; PINOT BLANC
Weisser Gutedel *see* CHASSELAS
Weisser Klevner *see* PINOT BLANC
Weisser Riesling *see* RIESLING
Welschriesling
White Riesling *see* RIESLING
Wyndruif *see* SÉMILLON

Xarel-lo
Xinómavro

Zapponara Bianca *see* BOMBINO
 BIANCO
Zibibbo *see* MUSCAT
Zinfandel

Wine Styles

In most instances, when pairing wine with food, you should drink a better wine and forgo its compatibility with the food rather than settle for a mediocre wine just to achieve a food-wine match. But it's also worth the extra effort to try to balance the style of the wine with that of the food. A hearty dish like osso buco, for example, is better paired with a rich, intense wine like a CABERNET SAUVIGNON, ZINFANDEL, or red RHÔNE. On the other hand, a lighter dish like a simple pasta primavera (fresh vegetables and olive oil) is better complemented with a white wine or even a lighter red wine such as PINOT NOIR, BEAUJOLAIS, LAMBRUSCO, or VALPOLICELLA. The goal in pairing wine with food is compatibility—neither should overpower the other.

The following information provides a general guide to the style of various wines in terms of the BODY they typically exhibit. Keep in mind that individual winemaking styles and a given VINTAGE may influence the weight of these wines.

Note: White and red wines are noted separately and grouped into one of three sections—light-, medium-, and full-bodied. In each section, the wines are ordered (top to bottom) from the lightest to the heaviest.

White Wines

Light-Bodied (from Lightest to Heaviest)

- Italian, such as those from FRASCATI, GALESTRO, ORVIETO, SOAVE, TREBBIANO D'ABRUZZO, and VERDICCHIO DEI CATELLIDI DI JESI

- German, nonsweet (TROCKEN or HALBTROCKEN) from grape varieties such as MÜLLER-THURGAU, SYLVANER, or SCHEUREBE

- PINOT GRIS (also called *Pinot Grigio*)

- German, nonsweet (TROCKEN or HALBTROCKEN) from RIESLING grapes

- MELON DE BOURGOGNE—like French MUSCADET, America's Melon de Bourgogne, and some U.S. PINOT BLANCS (some of which are actually made from Melon de Bourgogne grapes)

- CHAMPAGNE and other better SPARKLING WINES—Blanc de Blanc (lighter, less-yeasty styles)

- Riesling from the United States and ALSACE

- Pinot Blanc (unoaked) from Alsace and the United States

Medium-Bodied (from Lightest to Heaviest)

- CHENIN BLANC—French from SAVENNIÈRES and VOUVRAY, from the United States
- Champagne and other better sparkling wines—all but the less-yeasty-style Blanc de Blanc
- U.S. Pinot Blanc (oaky styles)
- Southern Rhône wines like CÔTE DU RHÔNE
- U.S. SAUVIGNON BLANC wines (unoaked)
- Bordeaux
- U.S. and Alsatian GEWÜRZTRAMINERS
- POUILLY-FUMÉ, SANCERRE, and U.S. Sauvignon Blanc (oaky styles)
- Italian—like those from GAVI
- CHARDONNAY—unoaked U.S. or French (like those from CHABLIS)
- BURGUNDY—those from POUILLY-FUISSÉ, SAINT VÉRAN, and other MÂCONNAIS wines (MÂCON, MÂCON-VILLAGES)

Full-Bodied (from Lightest to Heaviest)

- Chardonnay—United States, BARREL-FERMENTED and AGED in oak
- Burgundy—those from premier Burgundian villages like CHASSAGNE-MONTRACHET, PULIGNY-MONTRACHET, MEURSAULT
- Northern Rhône wines, especially those from HERMITAGE but also SAINT JOSEPH and CROZES-HERMITAGE

Red Wines

Light-Bodied (from Lightest to Heaviest)

- BARDOLINO
- Lambrusco
- NOUVEAU-style—French, United States, and others
- Beaujolais (except for CHÉNAS, JULIÉNAS, MORGON, MOUIN-À-VENT, and RÉGNIÉ)
- Most German red wines—like SPÄTBURGUNDER or PORTUGIESER

- Valpolicella (except AMARONE-style)
- DOLCETTO—United States and Italian
- Beaujolais from CHÉNAS, JULIÉNAS, MORGON, MOUIN-À-VENT, and RÉGNIÉ
- Burgundy—most CÔTE DE BEAUNE

Medium-Bodied (from Lightest to Heaviest)

- Valpolicella (Amarone-style only)
- RIOJA
- BARBERA—U.S. and Italian
- CHIANTI CLASSICO
- U.S. PINOT NOIR
- Burgundy—most CÔTE DE NUITS
- Bordeaux—most vintages

Full-Bodied (from Lightest to Heaviest)

- Burgundy—from the better vintages of top GRAND CRU and PREMIER CRU vineyards
- U.S. Merlot
- U.S. SYRAH and Australian Shiraz
- U.S. Zinfandel
- Bordeaux (the best vintages)
- U.S. Cabernet Sauvignon
- AGLIANICO wines from southern Italy, particularly TAURASI and AGLIANICO DEL VULTURE
- Rhône (especially Hermitage, CÔTE ROTIE, and CORNAS)
- BRUNELLO DI MONTALCINO
- BARBARESCO
- BAROLO

Tips on Buying Wine

Buying wine can be an interesting and endlessly adventurous journey of discovery. However, unlike other consumables, which generally have a predictable level of consistency year after year, wine VINTAGES can be noticeably different in varying degrees from subtle to conspicuous. Such annual differences could have any of myriad reasons including diverse weather conditions, changes in winemaker or winemaking style, or grapes from a different supplier. Newcomers needn't be intimidated, however, and the following tips should help facilitate wine-buying forays.

Plan ahead: Read about wines—unplanned or spur-of-the-moment purchases are often disappointing, not to mention costly. Put your name on several wine shop mailing lists or internet sites that offer newsletters and updates on current releases, award-winning wines, and what's new in the wine world in general. Compare several different stores/sites for the best prices.

Where to shop: Whereas specialty wine shops were once the only place to find a large selection of wines, today wine is available everywhere from discount chain stores to supermarkets. But remember that light, heat, and erratic temperature fluctuations are wine's enemies so note the store's environment. It should be fairly cool, and the wine should be stored well away from heat outlets or the glare of bright, intense light, such as a sun-drenched window. You want a retailer with rapid turnover, which isn't always the case in supermarkets or drug stores. Ideally, the wine should be stored horizontally so the cork doesn't dry out, but this may not be an issue in a store whose inventory moves briskly.

The store's staff: Shopping for wine will be a lot easier if you choose a merchant with a well-informed staff. They should be able to advise you on everything (especially what's new and interesting), suggest a special vintage, and recommend a wine to go with a particular dish. You'll generally get more personalized and informed service at a wine shop than you will at a store where wine isn't the focus. And you'll get to know the salespeople better if you limit most of your shopping to two to three merchants. Many retailers will keep an eye out for wines they know their customers are looking for and let them know when it comes in.

Learn a store's system: Familiarizing yourself with the way a merchant organizes the wines will give you a head start the next time you need to make a last-minute purchase. For American wines, most stores arrange their wines by grape variety (CABERNET SAUVIGNON,

CHARDONNAY, ZINFANDEL, etc.); foreign wines are typically shelved by country of origin (France, Italy, Spain, etc.). There are also often sections for discounted wines, odd lots, special promotions, and the like.

Know what you want: A little advance thought will make life easier, particularly for beginning wine shoppers. Is the wine for a party or a meal? If the wine's to accompany food, what will be served? What are your personal preferences? How much do you want to spend? A little forethought will help the store's staff direct you to exactly what you want.

Try before you buy: Trust your personal taste—it should always be the final word. You're potentially setting yourself up for trouble (not to mention wasted money) if you buy a case of wine simply because a co-worker, friend, or wine writer likes it. *You* might think it's dreck. Many wine stores have tasting bars that let you sample selected wines. If that isn't possible, buy a single bottle and try it at home before buying several bottles or a case.

Making that purchase: Inspect the wine you buy to make sure that the bottle's FILL LEVEL isn't lower than other bottles—it should be up to the neck. Also check to be sure the wine doesn't show any sign of leakage. Both are a warning that air (one of wine's worst enemies) is getting into the bottle. Buying wine in case lots generally saves you money because many wine stores offer discounts of 10 percent or more on case purchases. But only buy in case lots if you *know* you like the wine.

See also Demystifying the Wine Label, page 612; Grape Varieties, page 595; Opening and Serving Wine at Home, page 636; Optimum Serving Temperatures by Wine Type, page 642; Wine Bottles, page 609; WINE CELLAR; Wine Styles, page 604.

Wine Bottles

Common Wine Bottle Shapes

Wine bottles come in myriad sizes, shapes, and colors, all of which have some traditional usage, though there are no hard and fast rules. The thickness of a bottle's glass may also vary. For example, many California wineries are using Bordeaux-shaped bottles that not only are slightly taller than the standard but also have much thicker glass and deeper punts. A large format bottle refers to anything larger than the standard 750 ml size.

 **Bordeaux bottle:** Straight-sided with high, steep shoulders. The Bordeaux bottle is excellent for wines that throw SEDI-MENT, as the shoulders serve to dam it back. Dark green glass is the standard for red wines, and this bottle is classically used for BORDEAUX, CABERNET SAUVIGNON, MERLOT, ZINFANDEL, and Italy's higher-quality CHIANTI. A pale green glass version is used for Bordeaux white wines and around the world for wines made from SAUVIGNON BLANC and SÉMILLON. A clear glass version is used for DESSERT WINES. Some of these bottles are now show-ing up in taller versions that are slightly wider at the shoulders than at the bottom and have deeper PUNTS.

Burgundy bottle: Pale green colored glass (occasionally clear) with gently sloping shoulders. This bottle is used throughout BURGUNDY and the RHÔNE, as well as throughout most of the world for wines made from grape varieties asso-ciated with those regions, such as CHARDONNAY, PINOT NOIR, and SYRAH (although Australian Syrah generally comes in Bordeaux-style bottles). Many Italian and Spanish wines also come in sloped-shouldered bottles. **Rhône bottles** are simi-lar in style to Burgundy bottles, but they are not so fat; some have a coat of arms embossed into the bottle's neck.

Alsace/Mosel/Rhine bottle: Tall and slender with gently sloping shoulders. It's used in the RHINE region (where it's brown colored) and in ALSACE and the MOSEL (where it is typically green). This shape is used elsewhere for wines made with grape varieties associated with Germany, like RIESLING and GEWÜRZTRAMINER. European ROSÉ wines generally use this same bottle, only it's made of clear glass.

Champagne (sparkling wine) bottle: This bottle design has a long neck, gently sloping shoulders, very thick glass, and a deep punt, all devised to retain carbonation pressure (which is three times that of an average car tire) from bursting the bottle. The glass in such bottles may be either green or clear.

Fortified wine bottles: Stocky, sturdy bottles made of dark green (sometimes black) glass are the norm for FORTIFIED WINES such as MADEIRA, PORT, and SHERRY. Such bottle designs have steep shoulders (very steep for vintage ports) for catching sediment.

Common Wine Bottle Sizes

Half-Split: 187 ml (typically for SPARKLING WINE)

Half-Bottle; Split; Tenth: 375 ml (half a standard bottle).

Standard Bottle: 750 ml; customary size for most wines around the world.

Magnum: 1.5 liters (equivalent of two standard bottles).

Double Magnum: 3.0 liters (equivalent of four standard bottles).

Jeroboam: There are two sizes—the SPARKLING WINE version used in CHAMPAGNE and BURGUNDY is 3.0 liters (equivalent of four standard bottles). The STILL WINE version, common in BORDEAUX, is 4.5 liters (equivalent of six standard bottles).

Imperial: 6.0 liters (equivalent of eight standard bottles). Imperials are typically shaped like Bordeaux bottles and are used for STILL WINE.

Methuselah: 6.0 liters (equivalent of eight standard bottles). Methuselahs are traditionally shaped like Burgundy bottles and are used for SPARKLING WINE.

Salmanazar: 9.0 liters (equivalent of twelve standard bottles—one case).

Balthazar: 12.0 liters (equivalent of sixteen standard bottles); typically used for SPARKLING WINE.

Nebuchadnezzar: 15.0 liters (equivalent of twenty standard bottles); typically used for SPARKLING WINE.

Demystifying the Wine Label

The information on a wine label can provide the consumer with pertinent details about the wine in the bottle. Unfortunately, some foreign wine labels can be extremely confusing. In the United States, however, certain label information is required, even for imported wines (on which the data must be in English). The following information should bolster your wine label knowledge and help decipher even the most complicated label.

Label Information for Wines Sold in the United States

1. Brand Name
2. Name of the Producer
3. Name and Address of the Bottler
4. Name of the Importer
5. Name of the Shipper
6. Alcohol Content
7. Volume of the Bottle's Contents
8. Country of Origin
9. Sulfite Advisory
10. Government Warning
11. Quality of the Wine
12. Vintage of the Wine
13. Type of Wine
14. Appellation or Growing Region
15. Varietal designations
16. Descriptive Information

Wine Label Details

1. Brand Name The brand name is a name used by the producer to identify the wine. Almost any brand name is acceptable except for those that mislead the consumer.

- In many cases the brand name is the actual name of the winery, producer, or bottler.

- A brand name might be a made-up name used to identify a particular quality level of wines from a large winery or a second label of a small or medium-sized producer. Liberty School from

Caymus Vineyards and Hawk Crest from Stag's Leap Wine Cellars are examples of second labels.

- It may also be a name created specifically by a winery for a retailer or restaurant. For example, Bronco Wine Company produces Charles Shaw wines for California's Trader Joe's chain of markets.

- Proprietary brand names are sometimes used for high-quality wine that doesn't meet the criteria to be labeled as a varietal wine. For example, *Insignia* (by Joseph Phelps Vineyards) is so named because it's a blend of Cabernet Sauvignon, Cabernet Franc, and Merlot. Because it doesn't contain 75 percent of one grape variety, it cannot (in the United States) be named after any grape variety.

2. Name of the Producer The producer's name is often the most important information on the label. That's because some producers have a reputation for producing high-quality wines year after year, whereas others have sporadic or less than stellar records. For example, a single GRAND CRU vineyard in BURGUNDY can have numerous producers, with some making consistently higher-quality wine than others. The producer's name can be the name of a winery (in countries like the United States and Australia), of a CHÂTEAU (in some parts of France, like BORDEAUX), of a DOMAINE in other French areas like Burgundy, and of wine estates in Italy, Spain, and Germany. The exact name of the producer is important because in areas like France and Germany, there are a number of producers with the same surname. Therefore, knowledge of both Christian name and surname is necessary to differentiate producers. For instance, the name of the Prüm family is attached to numerous wine estates in Germany's MOSEL-SAAR-RUWER region, the best known of which is Joh. Jos. Prüm.

3. Name and Address of the Bottler The bottler is often the same as the producer, but occasionally a company other than the producer actually bottles the wine. In such a case the label would read something like: "Bottled for ABC Winery by XYZ Company." A label that says "Estate Bottled" means the wine was bottled by the producer.

4. Name of the Importer When wines are brought into the United States, an importer handles the arrangements for shipping and storing the wines until they reach the next level in the U.S. distribution system.

5. Name of the Shipper If a company other than the importer handles the shipping, that organization's name is also listed on the label.

6. Alcohol Content The United States requires that ALCOHOL BY VOLUME information be included on wine labels. For TABLE WINE, the U.S. requirement is a minimum alcohol level of 7 percent, a maximum of 14 percent. The label variance can be up to 1.5 percent. For example, a wine label stating "Alcohol 12.5% By Volume" can legally range anywhere from 11 to 14 percent. However, wines cannot exceed the upper or lower limit. The alcohol-by-volume range for SHERRIES is 17 to 20 percent and for PORTS 18 to 20 percent; both have a label variance of 1 percent.

7. Volume of the Bottle's Contents The volume figure, such as 750 ml (milliliters) or 1.5 l (liters), is sometimes molded into the bottle glass rather than printed on the label. Therefore, if the label doesn't designate the bottle size, look along the base of the bottle for the indication. For details on the various bottle sizes allowed in the United States, *see* Wine Bottles, page 609.

8. Country of Origin This tells you the country where the wine was produced. However, depending on that country's laws, it may not necessarily be where all the grapes were grown.

9. Sulfite Advisory The words "Contains Sulfites" indicate that SULFUR DIOXIDE (SO_2)—a colorless, water-soluble, nonflammable gas—was used somewhere in the grape-growing or winemaking process and that the resulting wine contains 10 ppm or more of sulfites, which can cause severe allergic reactions in certain individuals.

10. Government Warning A caveat required on all alcoholic beverages containing 0.5% or more alcohol by volume. It warns that drinking alcoholic beverages can 1. cause birth defects, 2. impair ability to drive a car or operate machinery, and 3. cause health problems.

11. Quality of the Wine A wine's quality is often implied by the rating it receives in the producing country's appellation system. For example, at the lowest level of Italy's quality ranking are the VINO DA TAVOLA wines, followed by VINO TIPICO, DENOMINAZIONE DI ORIGINE CONTROLLATA (DOC), and the highest level, DENOMINAZIONE DI ORIGINE CONTROLLATA E GARANTITA (DOCG). Although choosing an Italian DOCG wine doesn't always mean it will be better than those of lesser rankings, it usually indicates a wine of high quality. See individual country entries for their hierarchy of quality rankings.

12. Vintage of the Wine The year indicated on a wine label is the VINTAGE, or the year the grapes were harvested. In the United States, a wine label may only list the vintage if 95 percent of the wine comes from grapes harvested that year. If a blend of grapes from two or more years is used, the wine is either labeled "non-vintage" (NV) or there's no date mentioned.

13. Type of Wine This information is typically very general, usually in the form of basic terms like "red table wine," "dry red wine," "white wine," "still white wine," or "sparkling wine." Such terms simply place the wine in a generic category. Don't assume, however, that because a wine is described as, say, a "red table wine" that it's simple or mediocre. In the United States, for example, unless a wine contains at least 75 percent of a particular grape variety, it cannot use the grape's name on the label. As an example, for its premium red wine *Cain Five* (a blend of the five Bordeaux grape varieties—CABERNET SAUVIGNON, CABERNET FRANC, MERLOT, MALBEC, and PETIT VERDOT), Cain Cellars simply calls it "red table wine." The name of a grape variety may be used as the type of wine if that variety is on the approved variety list of the TAX AND TRADE BUREAU.

14. Appellation or Growing Region As mentioned previously under "Name of the Wine," the actual growing area or APPELLATION becomes the name of many European wines. In other areas like the United States and Australia, where the wine is more often named for the grape variety, some producers also list the growing region (particularly if it's prestigious) on the label. The NAPA VALLEY in the United States and the HUNTER VALLEY in Australia are examples of such well-known growing regions. In the United States, where such growing regions are called AMERICAN VITICULTURAL AREAS (AVA), at least 85 percent of the grapes must come from a single AVA for the region's name to be used on the label. If a grape variety is listed on the label, the appellation must also be listed.

15. Varietal Designations A wine that uses the name of a single VARIETY on the label (such as CABERNET SAUVIGNON, CHARDONNAY, MERLOT, SAUVIGNON BLANC, or ZINFANDEL) must contain at least 75 percent of that variety. The one exception is if a VITIS LABRUSCA variety such as CONCORD or CATAWBA is used, in which case the wine must contain at least

51 percent of that variety. If a label lists two or more varieties, all the grapes used must be of those varieties, which must be listed in dominant order. A label that includes a varietal designation must also list the appellation or growing region.

16. Descriptive Information   Occasionally, wine labels include descriptive words or phrases designed to give the consumer added information. For example, a label might indicate the wine was barrel-fermented, a process thought to imbue a wine with rich, creamy flavors, delicate oak characteristics, and better aging capabilities. Many terms, however, are simply marketing jargon with no legal or standard usage.

See the labels on the following pages for examples of information that typically appears on wine labels.

Sample Wine Labels

Wine labels contain a wealth of interesting and informative facts. Although each label is distinctive, most feature the same basic information, such as

1. Brand name
2. Name of the producer
3. Name and address of the bottler
4. Name of the importer
5. Name of the shipper
6. Alcohol content
7. Volume of the bottle's contents
8. Country of origin
9. Sulfite advisory
10. Government warning
11. Quality of the wine
12. Vintage of the wine
13. Type of wine
14. Appellation or growing region
15. Varietal designation
16. Descriptive information

Obviously, not all of this information will necessarily be found on every wine label, but much of it will. On the following pages you'll see a variety of wine labels from U.S. and foreign producers with callouts that highlight important information.

Brand name

Apellation or growing region

Varietal designation

Vintage of the wine

GRGICH HILLS

Napa Valley
CHARDONNAY
1979
PRODUCED AND BOTTLED BY
GRGICH HILLS CELLAR, RUTHERFORD, CA
ALCOHOL 13.4% BY VOLUME

Name of the producer

Alcohol content

Apellation or growing region

Brand name

Name of the producer

Volume of the bottle's contents

Vintage of the wine

Country of origin

Type of wine

Sulfite advisory

Name of the importer

Alcohol content

Brand name

Vintage of the wine

Apellation or growing region

Name of the producer

Volume of the bottle's contents

Alcohol content

Country of origin

Type of wine

Name of the shipper

Name of the importer

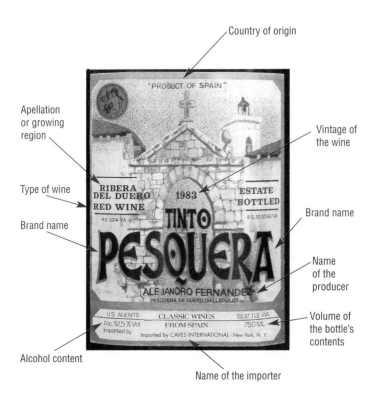

Country of origin

Apellation or growing region

Vintage of the wine

Type of wine

Brand name

Brand name

Name of the producer

Volume of the bottle's contents

Alcohol content

Name of the importer

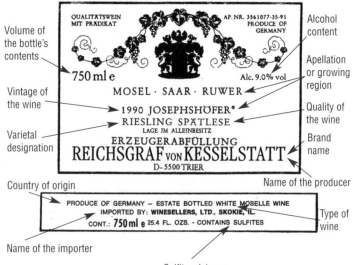

Volume of the bottle's contents

Vintage of the wine

Varietal designation

Alcohol content

Apellation or growing region

Quality of the wine

Brand name

Country of origin

Name of the producer

Name of the importer

Type of wine

Sulfite advisory

QUALITÄTSWEIN MIT PRÄDIKAT

AP. NR. 3561077-35-91 PRODUCE OF GERMANY

750 ml e

Alc. 9.0% vol

MOSEL · SAAR · RUWER

1990 JOSEPHSHÖFER*
RIESLING SPÄTLESE
LAGE IM ALLEINBESITZ

ERZEUGERABFÜLLUNG
REICHSGRAF VON KESSELSTATT
D-5500 TRIER

PRODUCE OF GERMANY – ESTATE BOTTLED WHITE MOSELLE WINE
IMPORTED BY: WINESELLERS, LTD., SKOKIE, IL.
CONT.: 750 ml e 25.4 FL. OZS. - CONTAINS SULFITES

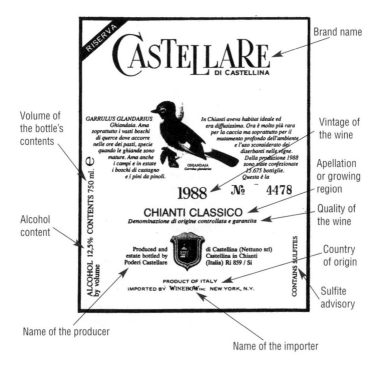

Brand name

Volume of the bottle's contents

Vintage of the wine

Apellation or growing region

Alcohol content

Quality of the wine

Country of origin

Sulfite advisory

Name of the producer

Name of the importer

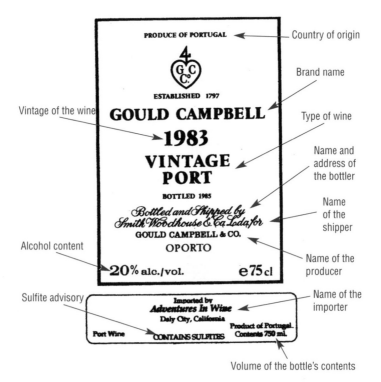

Country of origin

Brand name

Vintage of the wine

Type of wine

Name and address of the bottler

Name of the shipper

Alcohol content

Name of the producer

Sulfite advisory

Name of the importer

Volume of the bottle's contents

PRODUCE OF PORTUGAL

ESTABLISHED 1797

GOULD CAMPBELL

1983

VINTAGE PORT

BOTTLED 1985

Bottled and Shipped by Smith Woodhouse & Ca Lda for

GOULD CAMPBELL & CO,

OPORTO

20% alc./vol.   e 75 cl

Imported by
Adventures In Wine
Daly City, California

Product of Portugal
Contents 750 ml.

Port Wine   CONTAINS SULFITES

Pronunciation Guide for Wine Producers and Proprietary Brands

Following is a pronunciation guide for some producers and proprietary brands for wines commonly found in restaurants and wine stores in the United States.

Acacia Winery [uh-KAY-shuh]
Amézola de la Mora [ah-meh-ZOH-lah deh lah MOR-uh]
L'Angélus, Château [sha-TOH lahn-zhay-LEUS]
d'Angludet, Château [sha-toh dahn-gloo-DAY]
Antinori [ahn-tih-NOH-ree]
d'Arche, Château [sha-TOH DAHRSH]
L'Arrosée, Château [sha-TOH lah-roh-SAY]
Au Bon Climat [oh bohn klee-MAHT]
Ausone, Château [sha-TOH oh-sohn]

Balestard-la-Tonnelle, Château [sha-TOH bah-les-STAR lah toh-NELL]
Barbacarlo [bahr-bah-KAHR-loh]
Barbadillo, Antonio [bahr-bah-DEE-lyoh]
Bassermann-Jordan, Weingut Dr. von [VINE-goot]
Batailley, Château [sha-TOH bah-TIE-yay]
Beaucastel, Château [sha-TOH boh-kahs-tehl]
Beaulieu Vineyards (BV) [BOOL-yuh]
Beauregard, Château [sha-TOH boh-ruh-GAHR]
Beauséjour, Château [sha-TOH boh-say-ZHOOR]
Beau-Séjour-Bécot, Château [sha-TOH boh-say-ZHOOR-bay-koh]
Belair, Château [sha-TOH bel-EHR]
Belgrave, Château [sha-TOH bel-GRAHV]
Bellevue Mondotte, Château [sha-TOH bel-vew mawn-DAWT]
Berliquet, Château [sha-TOH behr-lee-KAY]
Beychevelle, Château [sha-TOH beh-shuh-VEHL]
Bischöflichen Weingüter [BIHSH-uhf-lihkh-uhn VINE-goot-uhr]
Bollinger [BAWL-in-jer; BOHL-in-jer]
Le Bon Pasteur, Château [sha-TOH luh bawn pahs-tuhr]
Bouchaine; Bouchaine Vineyards; Chateau Bouchaine [boo-SHAYN; sha-TOH boo-SHAYN]

Bouscaut, Château [sha-TOH boo-SKOH]
Boyd-Cantenac, Château [sha-TOH boyd kah*n*-tuh-NACK]
Branaire-Ducru, Château [sha-TOH brah-NEHR doo-KROO]
Brane-Cantenac, Château [sha-TOH brah*n* kahn-teh-NAHK]
Broustet, Château [sha-TOH broo-STEH]
Buehler Vineyards [BYOO-ler]
Buena Vista Winery [BWAY-nuh VIHS-tah]
Burgess Cellars [BER-jihss]

Cadet-Piola, Château [sha-TOH kah-DAY PYOH-luh]
Le Caillou, Château [sha-TOH luh kah-YOO]
Cain Cellars [KAYN]
Calera Wine Company [ka-LEHR-uh]
Calon-Ségur, Château [sha-TOH kah-law*n*-say-GYOO*R*]
De Camensac, Château [sha-TOH kah-mahn-SAHK]
Campo Fiorin [KAHM-poh FYOH-rihn]
Campo Viejo [KAHM-poh VYAY-hoh]
Canon, Château [sha-TOH kah-NAW*N*]
Canon-la-Gaffelière, Château [sha-TOH kah-NAW*N* lah gahf-LYEH*R*]
Cantemerle, Château [sha-TOH kahn-teh-MEH*R*L]
Cantenac-Brown, Château [sha-TOH kahn-teh-NAK BROWN]
Caramino [kah-rah-MEE-noh]
Carbonnieux, Château [sha-TOH kar-baw-NYEUH]
Carmenet Vineyard [kar-meh-NAY]
Les Carmes Haut-Brion, Château [sha-TOH lay KAHRM oh-bree-OH*N*]
Carneros Creek Winery [kahr-NEH-rohs]
Carrudes de Lafite, Château [sha-TOH hrew-ahd duh laf-FEET]
Caymus Vineyards [KAY-muhss]
Certan-de-May, Château [sha-TOH seh*r*-TAH*N* duh MEH]
Certan-Giraud, Château [sha-TOH seh*r*-TAH*N* zhee-ROH]
Chalone Vineyard [shah-LOHN]
Chapoutier [shah-poo-TYAY]
Chappellet Vineyard [shap-pehl-LAY]
Chasse-Spleen, Château [sha-TOH shahs SPLEEN]
Chateau Montelena [sha-TOH mawn-teh-LEE-nuh]
Chateau Ste. Michelle [sha-TOH saynt mih-SHELL]
Chateau St. Jean [sha-TOH saynt JEEN]
Chateau Woltner [sha-TOH WALT-ner]
Cheval Blanc, Château [sha-TOH shuh-vahl BLA*N*]
Citran, Château [sha-TOH see-TRAH*N*]

La Clémence, Château [sha-TOH kley- maw*n*s]
Clerc-Milon-Rothschild, Château [sha-TOH kleh*r* mee-LAW*N* rawt-SHEELD (rawth-CHILD)]
Climens, Château [sha-TOH klee-MAHS]
Clinet, Château [sha-TOH klee-NAY]
Clos de Sarpe [kloh duh sahrp]
Clos des Jacobins [kloh day zha-koh-BA*N*]
Clos du Bois [kloh duh BWAH]
Clos du Val [kloh deu VAHL]
Clos Fourtet [kloh foor-TEH]
Clos l'Eglise [kloh lay-GLEEZ]
Clos Pegase [kloh pay-GAHS]
Codorníu [koh-dor-NOO]
B. R. Cohn [KOHN]
Coltassala [kohl-tahs-SAH-lah]
Compañía Vinícola del Norte de España (CVNE) [kohm-pah-NYEE-ah vihn-ee-KOH-luh dehl NOR-tay day ehs-PAHN-yah] (CVNE is pronounced KOO-nay and spelled *Cune* on labels)
La Conseilante, Château [sha-TOH lah kaw*n*-seh-YAH*N*T]
Cos d'Estournel, Château [sha-TOH kaws dehss-toor-NEHL]
Cos Labory, Château [sha-TOH kaws lah-baw-REE]
Coutet, Château [sha-TOH koo-TEE]
Couvent-des-Jacobins, Château [sha-TOH koo-vah*n* day zhah-koh-BA*N*]
Croizet-Bages, Château [sha-TOH k*r*wah-zeh BAHZH]
Cronin Vineyards [KROH-nihn]
Croque-Michotte, Château [sha-TOH krawk mee-SHAWT]
Curé-Bon-la-Madeleine, Château [sha-TOH kyoo-ray bawn lah mad-uh-LEHN]
Cuvaison Winery [KOO-vay-sawn (Fr. koo-veh-ZOH*N*)]

Dauzac, Château [sha-TOH doh-ZAHK]
Dehlinger Winery [DAY-leen-ger]
Delas Frères [duh-lah frehr]
De Loach Vineyards [deh LOHSH]
Doisy-Daëne, Château [sha-TOH dwah-zee DAYN]
Doisy-Védrines, Château [sha-TOH dwah-zee vay-DREEN]
Domaine Carneros [doh-MAYN (Fr. daw-MEHN) kahr-NEH-rohs]
Domaine Chandon [doh-MAYN (Fr. daw-MEHN) shahn-DAWN]
Domaine de Chevalier [doh-MAYN duh shuh-vah-LYAY]
Domaine des Remizières [doh-MAYN dayz hruh-MEE-zyehr]
Domaine Drouhin [doh-MAYN (Fr. daw-MEHN) DROO-ah*n*]

Domecq, Pedro [PAY-droh doh-MAYK]
La Dominique, Château [sha-TOH lah daw-mee-NEEK]
Dominus Estate [DAHM-ih-nuhs]
Ducru-Beaucaillou, Château [sha-TOH doo-KROO boh-kah-YOO]
Duhart-Milon-Rothschild, Château [sha-TOH doo-AHR mee-LAW*N* rawt-SHEELD (rawth-CHILD)]
Durfort-Vivens, Château [sha-TOH dyoo*r*-faw*r* vee-VAH*N*S (vee-VAH*N*)]

L'Eglise-Clinet, Château [sha-TOH leh-GLEEZ klee-NAY]
Etude [ay-TEWD]
L'Evangile, Château [sha-TOH lay-vahn-ZHEEL]

Faustino Martínez [faws-TEE-noh mahr-TEE-nehz]
Ferrari-Carano Vineyards [fuh-RAHR-ree kuh-RAH-noh]
Ferreira [feh-RRAY-rah]
Ferrière, Château [sha-TOH feh-*R*YEH*R*]
Fetzer Vineyards [FEHT-zer]
Feytit Clinet, Château [sha-TOH feh-TEE klee-NAY]
de Fieuzal, Château [sha-TOH deh fyuh-ZAHL]
Figeac, Château [sha-TOH fee-ZHAHK]
Fiorano [fee-oh-RAH-noh]
Flaccianello [flahk-kee-ah-NEHL-loh]
La Fleur-Pétrus, Château [sha-TOH lah fluh*r* pay-T*R*EWSS]
Folie à Deux Winery [FOH-lee ah doo]
Fonseca Guimaraens [fawn-SAY-kuh GIH-mah-rah*ns*]
Franciscan Vineyards [fran-SIHS-kuhn]
Freixenet [fresh-ehn-EHT]

La Gaffelière, Château [sha-TOH gah-fuh-LYEH*R*]
E & J Gallo Winery [GA-loh]
Le Gay, Château [sha-TOH luh GAY]
Gazin, Château [sha-TOH gah-ZA*N*]
Geyser Peak [GI-ser]
Giscours, Château [sha-TOH zhees-KOO*R*]
Gloria, Château [sha-TOH glaw-*R*YAH]
Grand Corbin, Château [sha-TOH grah*n* kohr-bah]
Grand Corbin-Despagne, Château [sha-TOH grah*n* kohr-bah dehs-PAH-nyuh]
Grand-Mayne, Château [sha-TOH grah*n* MEHN]
Grand-Puy-Ducasse, Château [sha-TOH grah*n* pwee doo-KAHSS]

Grand-Puy-Lacoste, Château [sha-TOH grah*n* pwee lah-KAWST]
Grange Hermitage [GRAH*N*ZH ehr-mee-TAHZH]
Grgich Hills Cellar [GER-gihch]
Grifi [GREE-fee]
Gruaud-Larose, Château [sha-TOH gr*o*o-oh lah-*R*OHZ]
Guenoc Winery [GWEN-ahk]
Guigal [gee-gahl]
Guiraud, Château [sha-TOH gee-*R*OH]

Hanzell Vineyards [han-ZELL]
Haut-Bages-Libéral, Château [sha-TOH oh BAHZH lee-bay-*R*AHL]
Haut-Bailly, Château [sha-TOH oh bah-YEE]
Haut-Batailley, Château [sha-TOH oh bah-tah-YEH]
Haut-Brion, Château [sha-TOH oh-bree-OH*N*]
Haut-Maurbuzet, Château [sha-TOH oh mar-boo-ZEH]
Hogue Cellars [HOHG]
Husch Vineyards [HUHSH]

d'Issan, Château [sha-TOH dee-SAH*N*]

Kesselstatt, Weingut Reichsgraf von [KEHSS-uhl-shtaht]
Kirwan, Château [sha-TOH kee*r*-WAH*N*]
Krug [KROOG]
Charles Krug Winery [KROOG]
Kunde Estate Winery [KUHN-dee]

Lafaurie-Peyraguey, Château [sha-TOH lah-foh-*R*EE peh-rah-GEH]
Lafite-Rothschild, Château [sha-TOH laf-FEET rawt-SHEELD
    (rawth-CHILD)]
Lafleur, Château [sha-TOH lah-FLEW*R*]
Lafon-Rochet, Château [sha-TOH lah-FAW*N* raw-SHAY]
Lagrange, Château [sha-TOH la-G*R*AHNZH]
La Lagune, Château [sha-TOH lah lah-GEWN]
Lamothe, Château [sha-TOH lah-MOTT]
Lanessan, Château [sha-TOH lah-neh-SAH*N*]
Langoa-Barton, Château [sha-TOH lah*n*-GWAH bahr-TAW*N*]
Larcis Ducasse, Château [sha-TOH lah*r*-see doo-KAHSS]
Larmande, Château [sha-TOH lah*r*-MAH*N*D]
Lascombes, Château [sha-TOH lahs-KAW*M*B]
Latour, Château [sha-TOH lah-TOO*R*]
Latour à Pomerol, Château [sha-TOH lah-TOO*R* ah paw-muh-
    *R*AWL]

Laurent-Perrier [law-RAH*N* pehr-RYAY]
Leonetti Cellar [lee-oh-NEH-tee]
Léoville-Barton, Château [sha-TOH lay-aw-VEEL bah*r*-TAW*N*]
Léoville-Las-Cases, Château [sha-TOH lay-aw-VEEL lahss KAHZ]
Léoville-Poyferré, Château [sha-TOH lay-aw-VEEL pwah-fuh-*R*AY]
López de Heredia [LOH-pehz day ay-ray-DYAH]
La Louvière, Château [sha-TOH lah loo-VYEH*R*]
Lynch-Bages, Château [sha-TOH la*n*sh BAZH (lihnsh-BAHZH)]
Lynch-Moussas, Château [sha-TOH la*n*sh moo-SAH (lihnsh moo-SAH)]
Lytton Springs Winery [LIHT-uhn]

Magdelaine, Château [sha-TOH mahg-duh-LEHN]
Malartic-Lagravière, Château [sha-TOH mah-lah*r*-TEEK lah-g*r*a-VYEH*R*]
Malescot-St. Exupéry, Château [sha-TOH mah-less-KOH sa*n* teg-zew-pay-REE]
de Malle, Château [sha-TOH duh MAHL]
Margaux, Château [sha-TOH mah*r*-GOH]
Marqués de Cáceres [mahr-KAYSS deh kah-THAY-rehs]
Marqués de Murrieta [mahr-KAYSS deh myoor-ree-EHT-uh]
Marqués de Riscal [mahr-KAYSS deh rees-KAHL]
Marquis d'Alesme-Becker, Château [sha-TOH mah*r*-KEE dah-lehm beh-KEH*R*]
Marquis de Terme, Château [sha-TOH mah*r*-KEE duh TEH*R*M]
Louis M. Martini Winery [LOO-ee mahr-TEE-nee]
Matanzas Creek Winery [muh-TAN-zuhs]
Maucaillou, Château [sha-TOH mow-kah-YOO]
Mayacamas Vineyards [mi-yuh-KAH-muhs]
Mazzocco Vineyards [muh-ZAH-koh]
Meyney, Château [sha-TOH may-NAY]
La Mission-Haut-Brion, Château [sha-TOH lah mee-SYAW*N* oh-bree-OH*N*]
Moët et Chandon [moh-EHT ay Shahn-DAWN]
Monbousquet, Château [sha-TOH mawn-boos-KEH]
Monbrison, Château [sha-TOH mawn-bree-SAW*N*]
Mondavi, Robert; Robert Mondavi Winery [mawn-DAH-vee]
La Mondotte, Château [sha-TOH lah maw*n* -DAWT]
Monticello Cellars [mawn-tih-CHEHL-oh]
Montrose, Château [sha-TOH maw*n*-*R*OHZ]
Mouton-Cadet [moo-TAW*N* kah-DAY]

Mouton d'Armailhacq, Château [sha-TOH moo-TAW*N* dah*r*-mah-YAK]
Mouton-Rothschild, Château [sha-TOH moo-TAW*N* rawt-SHEELD (RAWTH-child)]
Musar, Château [sha-TOH moo-SAHR]
Myrat, Château [sha-TOH mee-*R*AH]

Nairac, Château [sha-TOH neh-*R*AK]
Nalle Winery [NAHL]
Nenin, Château [sha-TOH neh-NA*N*]
Niebaum-Coppola Estate [NEE-bowm KOH-puh-luh]

Olivier, Château [sha-TOH aw-lee-VYAY]
Opus One [OH-puhs]

Palazzo Altesi [pah-LAHT-tsoh ahl-TAY-see]
Palmer, Château [sha-TOH pahl-MEH*R* (PAHL-muhr)]
Pape-Clément, Château [sha-TOH pahp klay-MAH*N*]
Paul Jaboulet Aîné [pol ZHAH-boo-leh eh-nay]
Pavie, Château [sha-TOH pah-VEE]
Pavie-Decesse, Château [sha-TOH pah-vee day-SEHS]
Pavie-Macquin, Château [sha-TOH pah-vee mah-KEE*N*]
Robert Pecota Winery [peh-KOH-tuh]
Pedesclaux, Château [sha-TOH pay-dehs-KLOH]
Perrier, Joseph [peh-RYAY]
Perrier-Jouët [peh-RYAY zhoo-AY]
Petit-Village, Château [sha-TOH puh-TEE vee-LAHZH]
Pétrus, Château [sha-TOH pay-T*R*EWSS]
Pichon-Longueville Baron, Château [sha-TOH pee-SHAW*N* law*n*g-VEEL beh*r*-ON]
Pichon-Longueville-Comtesse de Lalande, Château [sha-TOH pee-SHAW*N* law*n*g-VEEL koh*m*-TEHSS duh lah-LAH*N*D]
Le Pin, Château [sha-TOH luh paw*n*]
Piper Heidsieck [PIPE-er HIDE-sehk]
La Pointe, Château [sha-TOH lah PWAH*N*T]
Pol Roger [pawl roh-ZHAY]
Pontet-Canet, Château [sha-TOH paw*n*-teh kah-NEH]
Potensac, Château [sha-TOH poh-tahn-SAK]
Pouget, Château [sha-TOH poo-ZHEH]
Poujeaux, Château [sha-TOH poo-ZHOH]
Prieuré-Lichine, Château [sha-TOH p*r*ee-uh-RAY lee-SHEEN]
Prüm [P*R*OOM]

Quinta do Noval [KEEN-tah doh NOH-vahl]
Quivira Vineyards [kee-VEER-uh]

Rabaud-Promis, Château [sha-TOH ra-BOH praw-mee]
A. Rafanelli Winery [ra-fuh-NEHL-lee]
Rausan-Ségla, Château [sha-TOH roh-ZAHN say-GLAH]
Rauzan-Gassies, Château [sha-TOH roh-ZAHN gah-SEE (gah-SEES)]
Raymond-Lafon, Château [sha-TOH ray-MAWN lah-FAWN]
Rayne-Vigneau, Château [sha-TOH rayn vee-NYOH]
Regaleali [reh-gah-leh-AH-lee]
Rieussec, Château [sha-TOH ree-uh-SEHK]
J. Rochioli Vineyards [roh-kee-OH-lee]
Roederer, Louis [loo-EE ROH-duh-rer]
Roederer Estate [ROH-duh-rer]
Romer du Hayot, Château [sha-TOH raw-MEHR doo hay-OH]
Rosenblum Cellars [ROH-suhn-bloom]

St. Clement Vineyards [saynt KLIH-muhnt]
Saint-Pierre, Château [sha-TOH san PYEHR]
Saintsbury Cellars [SAYNTS-behry]
Schloss Groenesteyn [SHLAWSS GRUH-nuh-shtine]
Schloss Johannisberg [SHLAWSS yoh-HAHN-ihss-berk]
Schloss Reinhartshausen [SHLAWSS RINE-harts-how-zuhn]
Schloss Schönborn [SHLAWSS SHOEN-born]
Schloss Vollrads [SHLAWSS FAWL-rahts]
Schramsberg Vineyards [SHRAMS-berg]
Sebastiani Vineyards [seh-bas-tee-YAH-nee]
Sequoia Grove [sih-KWOY-uh]
Sigalas Rabaud, Château [sha-TOH see-gah-LAH rah-BOH]
Silverado Vineyards [sihl-vuh-RAH-doh]
Simi Winery [SEE-mee]
Simmern, Langwerth von [LAHNG-vayrt fuhn ZIHM-uhrn]
Robert Sinskey Vineyards [SIHN-skee]
Smith-Haut-Lafitte, Château [sha-TOH smeet oh lah-FEET]
Sociando-Mallet, Château [sha-TOH soh-syahn-DOH mah-LAY]
Il Sodaccio [eel soh-DAH-tchoh]
I Sodi di San Niccolo [ee SOH-dee dee sahn nee-KOH-loh]
Solaia [soh-LEH-yuh]
Sonoma-Cutrer [soh-NOH-muh koo-TREHR]
Soutard, Château [sha-TOH soo-TAHR]
Spottswoode Vineyard [SPOTS-wood]
Steltzner Vineyards [STEHLT-sner]

Suau, Château [sha-TOH soo-OH]
Suduiraut, Château [sha-TOH soo-dwee-ROH]

Taittinger [taht-teen-ZHEH*R*]
Talbot, Château [sha-TOH tahl-BOH]
Tavernelle [tah-vehr-NEHL]
du Tertre, Château [sha-TOH doo teh*r*-T*R*UH]
Le Tertre-Roteboeuf, Château [sha-TOH luh teh*r*-T*R*UH roht-BU*R*F]
Thanisch, Wwe, Dr. H. [TAH-nihsh]
Tignanello [tee-nyah-NELL-oh]
Torbato di Alghero [tohr-BAH-toh dee ahl-GEH-roh]
Torcolato [tohr-koh-LAH-toh]
Torres [TAWR-rehs]
La Tour-Carnet, Château [sha-TOH lah too*r* kah*r*-nay]
La Tour Blanche, Château [sha-TOH lah too*r* BLAH*N*SH]
La Tour Figeac, Château [sha-TOH lah too*r* fee-ZHAHK]
Tour du Haut-Moulin, Château [sha-TOH too*r* doo oh moo-LAH*N*]
La Tour-Martillac, Château [sha-TOH lah too*r* mah*r*-tee-YAHK]
Trefethen Vineyards [treh-FEH-thihn]
Troplong-Mondot, Château [sha-TOH troh-LAW*N* maw*n*-DOH]
Trotanoy, Château [sha-TOH t*r*aw-tah-NWAH]
Trottevieille, Château [sha-TOH t*r*awt-VYEH-yuh]
Tudal Winery [too-DAHL]

Vega Sicilia [BAY-gah see-SEE-lyah]
Venegazzu [veh-neh-GAHD-dzoo]
Veuve Clicquot-Ponsardin [vu*r*v klee-KOH paw*n*-sah*r*-DA*N*]
Vichon Winery [vee-SHAWN]
Vieux-Château-Certan [vyew shah-TOH seh*r*-TAH*N*]
Villa Mt. Eden [VIHL-luh mownt EE-dn]
Vintage Tunina [too-NEE-nah]
Vita Nova [VEE-tuh NOH-vuh]

Warre [WEHR]
Wente Bros. [WIHN-tee]

d'Yquem, Château [sha-TOH dee-KEHM]

Ordering Wine in a Restaurant

Ordering wine in a restaurant isn't really much different from buying it in a wine store; the main distinction is that you have an audience— your dining companion(s). There is a certain procedure, however, that the following tips should help you quickly master.

Be prepared. If you're a novice and have the time, do a little reading to get some idea of what you might want to order.

The wine list. Today, most restaurants have a wine list, no matter how abbreviated. Some establishments might simply offer a red and white HOUSE WINE, while others have a daily "blackboard" with a small selection of wines. Most wine lists are presented as a printed menu, with the wines arranged by color (red, white, rosé) and region or country (American, French, Italian, etc.). A good wine list will indicate the wine's name, vintage, and region or winemaker, such as: "1989 Heitz Cabernet Sauvignon, Napa Valley, Martha's Vineyard." Some even add a descriptive comment about the wine, such as: "Dark, rich, and intensely flavorful, with hints of mint and cherries and a long-lasting finish." Additionally, many wine lists number their wines, which facilitates the server in locating them in the cellar. Numbers are also a help if you don't know how to pronounce a wine—you can simply say, "I'd like a bottle of number 13." If you order the house wine (which should be available by glass or carafe), ask what it is. The server should be able to tell you the variety (Chardonnay, Merlot, etc.), brand name, and VINTAGE. Lastly, expect the standard markup for wines in restaurants to be two to three times retail.

Need some help? You've perused the wine list and made a selection. Or, maybe you've reviewed the list, know that you want a Pinot Noir, but are unfamiliar with those on the list. This is where the SOMMELIER or wine steward can help. A *good* one will assist you in choosing a wine in your price range, while at the same time making you feel comfortable, never uninformed. In some restaurants, the server will perform the sommelier's duties.

Presentation. When the wine's presented to you, examine the label to make sure it's the wine you ordered. Be sure to check the vintage—sometimes a restaurant will deplete its supply of one vintage and simply bring out the succeeding year. This may not make a difference, but if you love a wine's 1997 vintage and are shown a 1998 instead, know there will most certainly be some difference. In such an instance, you may decide to order a different wine.

Cork sniffers beware. After opening the wine, the sommelier or server typically presents the cork to the person who ordered the wine. Please don't sniff it. Doing so is likely to tag you as dilettantish or pompous and, unless the cork itself is bad (and smells like moldy, damp cardboard), tells you little. But you can check the cork to be sure the wine end is wet—a signal that the wine was stored properly. On the other hand, if a cork is crumbly, it's certainly a sign of deterioration—order another bottle.

Smelling and tasting. The sommelier's next step is to pour a small amount of wine for the person who ordered it. Smell and taste are the best criteria of whether or not a wine is sound so you want to gently swirl the wine in the glass to release the aroma, give it a sniff, and then take a sip. If the wine doesn't emit any rank or off-putting odors (such as vinegar) or flavors, it is most probably fine. Remember that the flavor and aroma of wine will expand and develop as it aerates. It's not appropriate to return a wine simply because you don't like it as much as you thought you would. Lastly, the tasting process should not be a long, involved procedure—the server has other tables to attend. Once you've tasted and approved of a wine, simply say "thank you," a signal to pour the wine for the others in your party.

Corkage. Many restaurants will open and serve a bottle of wine brought by the diner. A quick call to the restaurant will confirm if this is possible and, if so, the amount of the corkage fee—a charge for opening and serving the wine. Some restaurants charge a lower fee if the wine brought is not on their wine list, such as might be the case with an older or particularly distinctive wine.

See also Demystifying the Wine Label, page 612.

Opening and Serving Wine at Home

A bottle of wine begs to be shared;
I have never met a miserly wine lover.
–Clifton Fadiman, American author

Serving wine at home does not need to be difficult or overly formal. The first thing to consider is a wine's serving temperature, which depends on the style of the wine as well as your personal preference. Serving wine overly cold can mute its aroma and flavor, while serving it inordinately warm can make the wine seem dull and harshly ALCO-HOLIC. For more details on temperature, *see* Temperatures for Serving Wine, page 641; Optimum Serving Temperatures by Wine Type, page 642. *See also* Tasting Wine, page 648; GLASSWARE.

Still Wine

Detaching the capsule: The first step in opening most wine is to remove the CAPSULE, a casing (most often made of metal or plastic) that covers the bottle's lip and cork. Using a sharp knife or special foil-cutting tool (available at wine or gourmet shops), cut through the capsule about ¼ inch below the bottle's lip. Remove the capsule at the point it's cut. Wipe the rim of the bottle and the top of the cork with a damp towel to remove any residue.

Removing the cork: Most better wines are sealed with a CORK (although some producers are exploring alternative CLOSURES), so you'll need a corkscrew or corkpuller (*see* Wine Openers, page 639). Position the tip of the corkscrew on the cork, just slightly off center. Slowly spiral the worm (screw) into the cork as far as it will go. Once the worm is firmly seated, gently ease the cork out of the bottle. Wipe the lip of the bottle again to remove any cork residue. If part of the cork breaks off during opening, carefully reinsert the corkscrew at an angle, gently easing out the cork. Or, use the thin prongs of a corkpuller to capture and remove the remnant. If you mistakenly push the cork end into the wine, try extracting it with a special cork retrieval tool, available at wine and gourmet shops. If the cork can't be recovered, decant the wine through a fine sieve.

Decanting wine: Red wines over 8 years old often have a natural SEDIMENT, which, though harmless, leaves an unpleasant grittiness on the palate. Holding the wine bottle up to or over a strong light will usually reveal this sediment—decanting is a simple way to remove it. Decanting is also done to allow wine to AERATE (breathe) before it's served, a process many believe enhances a wine's flavor. When decanting an older wine, try not to disturb the sediment. A wine basket (also called *cradle* or *Burgundy basket*) can be used to move the bottle in a horizontal position from where it was stored to where it will be decanted. This position keeps the sediment from disseminating throughout the wine. Or you can stand the bottle upright for an hour so that the sediment can settle to the bottom. To decant the wine, slowly pour it into a DECANTER, placing a strong light (a candle is theatrical, a flashlight more practical) behind or below the neck of the bottle so that you can see the wine. The light lets you see the first signs of sediment, at which point you stop pouring.

Glassware: The wineglass you use should have a rim that curves in slightly (some champagne FLUTES are an exception), which captures the aroma and BOUQUET and makes it possible to swirl the wine properly in order to release its fragrance. A wineglass should always be made of clear glass so that the wine's true color and clarity are plainly visible. *See* Glassware, page 647, for more information.

Pouring the wine: Fill the glass only about a third to half full, again to leave room for swirling. Just as you finish pouring each glass and are returning the bottle to the upright position, give the bottle a slight twist, which forestalls dripping. All that's left to serving wine is to savor and enjoy it!

Sparkling Wine

SPARKLING WINE should be served quite cold, between 39 and 50°F, depending on the wine's quality. Cold mutes flavor so a less expensive wine should be served colder than a superior sparkler. Conversely, VINTAGE champagnes—with their complexity and delicate balance of flavors—are much better served at between 45 and 50°F.

It's best not to chill sparkling wines for much more than 2 hours before serving. Longer chilling can dull both flavor and bouquet. To speed-chill a wine, submerge the bottle in an ice bucket filled with equal amounts of ice and cold water. This procedure chills the wine much faster than ice alone.

The first step in opening champagne is to remove the CAPSULE (foil), which sometimes has a "zipper" or perforation to expedite the process. Untwist and remove the wire cage that encloses the cork. Keep the cork covered with your hand—you don't want it to pop out prematurely (a rare occurrence) and smack someone in the eye.

Holding the bottle at a 45° angle (pointed away from anyone), and with the fingers of one hand over the cork, gently rotate the bottle (not the cork) with your other hand. As you feel the cork begin to loosen and lift, use your thumb to gently ease it from the bottle. If properly handled, the cork should release from the bottle with a muted "poof," not a loud "POP." Although properly opened champagne should never gush from the bottle, it's a good idea to have a glass standing by, just in case.

Sparkling wines should always be served in flutes (*see* Glassware, page 647). These tall, slender glasses have a relatively small surface from which bubbles can escape. Their shape also showcases more of the wine's bouquet. The old-fashioned shallow, "saucer" champagne glass allows both effervescence and bouquet to escape twice as fast as the flute.

Wine Openers

There are many types of wine opener, the most common and traditional style being the corkscrew. Typically, a corkscrew has a pointed metal worm (spiral or screw) with a transverse handle at one end. The most important part of the corkscrew is the worm itself, which should be rounded, thin, and tapered, with a needle-sharp point. The spiral-shaped worm is not itself centered but wrapped around an imaginary perpendicular line—it's a helix. Fine wines generally have long corks so you want to choose an opener with a worm about 2½ inches long, which will help ensure that the bottom of an older (possibly fragile) cork doesn't break off. Choose a corkscrew that will give you some leverage to pull out the cork. More importantly, choose one that's easy for you to use. *See also* Opening and Serving Wine at Home, page 636.

There are many varieties of corkscrews, some of which are quite elaborate. Following are the most common styles:

Waiter's corkscrew Also called a *waiter's friend*, this small, classic corkscrew contains a worm, a knife, and a lever that doubles as a bottle opener. All of these handy tools fold up like a pocket knife. To use this style of corkscrew, insert the worm slightly off center and screw it all the way into the cork. Prop the lever against the bottle rim and pull straight upwards, easing out the cork.

Winged corkscrew This style has a center worm, with a winglike lever on each side. To operate, simply place the mouth of the corkscrew over the bottle's lip and turn the center handle until the worm is fully inserted into the cork. As the handle's turned, the "wings" ratchet upwards. Pushing on the upraised wings removes the cork.

Ah-so Also called a *butler's friend*, this is a corkpuller, rather than a corkscrew. It's comprised of two parallel flat metal prongs connected by a handle. The prongs are pushed down between the inside of the bottle neck and the sides of the cork; then the device is pulled and turned at the same time until the cork comes out.

Screwpull Invented by space and oil industry engineer Herbert Allen, the Screwpull corkscrew is nearly infallible, which is why it's so frequently copied. Screwpulls, which have extremely long, Teflon-coated worms, come in two basic styles. The **Screwpull table model** is comprised of a worm surrounded by a plastic frame, which fits over the bottle's neck. Continuous turning of the handle inserts the worm into the cork, then lifts the cork out. The **Screwpull lever model** is a more automated style. It's comprised of a lever, gripper handles and a rack-and-pinion mechanism. You simply place the opener over the bottle, tighten the gripping handles with one hand, and use the other hand to work the lever, which inserts the worm and pulls out the cork. It's effortless.

Temperatures for Serving Wine

The serving temperature for wine varies depending on the style of wine and one's personal preference. Serving wine too cold masks its aroma and flavor and highlights any bitterness. Serving it too warm can make wine seem harshly ALCOHOLIC, the flavors FLAT and DULL.

A wine storage area's temperature dictates how a wine should be handled before serving. If the storage isn't cool enough, some wine will require chilling; others may need to be removed from the cellar early so they can gradually warm to the proper temperature. "Room temperature" can and probably will be warmer than the maximum temperature (62 to 67°F) suggested for some red wines. Keep in mind that wine will warm up a little through the natural effects of air, swirling the wine in the glass, and the heat of one's hands (though a wine glass should always be held by the stem).

White wines are served cold, but how cold is a matter of individual taste. Generally, SPARKLING WINES and young, sweet white wines are served at from 40 to 50°F. On the other hand, rich, full-bodied whites like California and Australian CHARDONNAYS and French white BURGUNDIES are better served at around 50 to 55°F. Other white wines should be served somewhere in the 43 to 53°F range, depending on the complexity of their flavor. More intricately flavored wines should be served on the warmer side of this range in order to reveal their full scope of aromas and flavors. Because cold masks flavor, flawed or less expensive wines (except those with a bitter characteristic) should be served slightly cooler so weaknesses aren't so glaringly obvious.

Lighter red wines like BEAUJOLAIS or VALPOLICELLA are best served at 50 to 60°F, whereas **bolder reds** like BORDEAUX, RHÔNE, BAROLO, CHIANTI, and California CABERNET SAUVIGNON and ZINFANDEL are best at about 62 to 67°F. **Other reds**, such as California PINOT NOIR and red Burgundies, are best served in the 55 to 65°F range, depending on how rich and full-bodied they are.

Chilling or cooling wine can be accomplished by 1 to 2 hours of refrigeration, depending on the desired final temperature. **Quick-chill** wine by submerging the bottle in an ice (or wine) bucket filled with half cold water and half ice for about 20 minutes. If the bucket isn't tall enough for the ice and water to cover the bottle's neck, invert the bottle (only if sediment isn't a problem) for the last 5 minutes. Wines that are too cold can be quickly warmed by placing the bottle in a bucket of warm (70°F) water for about 5 minutes.

Optimum Serving Temperatures by Wine Type

Champagne and Other Sparkling Wines

Type of Wine	Serving Temperature (°F)
Inexpensive versions	40 to 44
Better non-vintage	42 to 47
The best vintages	45 to 50

Sweet and Semisweet White Wines

Type of Wine	Serving Temperature (°F)
Dessert wines (younger)	45 to 50
German semisweet wines—QbA (Qualitätswein Bestimmter Anbaugebiet), Spätlese, and Auslese	45 to 50
German sweet wines (older)—Auslese, Beerenauslese, Eisewein, and Trockenbeerenauslese	50 to 55
Sauternes (older)	50 to 55
Vouvray	43 to 48

White Wines (Dry and Off-Dry)

Type of Wine	Serving Temperature (°F)
Bordeaux—like those from Graves	45 to 50
Burgundy—medium quality	45 to 50
Burgundy—premium quality	50 to 55
Chardonnay—medium quality	45 to 50
Chardonnay—premium quality	50 to 55
Chenin Blanc U.S.	43 to 48
German, high-quality, nonsweet (Trocken or Halbtrocken)	48 to 53
Gewürztraminer—U.S. and Alsatian	45 to 50
Italian—like those from Frascati, Galestro, Orvieto, Soave, Trebbiano d'abruzzo, Verdicchio dei Catellidi di Jesi	42 to 47
Italian—like those from Gavi	45 to 50
Melon de Bourgogne	43 to 48
Muscadet	43 to 48
Pinot Blanc from Alsace and the United States	45 to 50
Pinot Gris (also called *Pinot Grigio*)	45 to 50
Pouilly-Fumé	43 to 48
Rhône (northern)	48 to 53
Rhône (southern)	45 to 50
Sancerre	43 to 48
Sauvignon Blanc	43 to 48
Savenniers	43 to 48

Rosé and Blush Wines

Type of Wine	Serving Temperature (°F)
Almost all Rosé and Blush Wines	40 to 45
High-quality dry rosé	43 to 48

Red Wines

Type of Wine	Serving Temperature (°F)
Aglianico wines from southern Italy, particularly Taurasi and Aglianico Del Vulture	62 to 67
Barbaresco	60 to 65
Barbera—U.S. and Italian	57 to 62
Bardolino	48 to 53
Barolo	62 to 67
Beaujolais (except for Chénas, Juliénas, Morgon, Moulin-à-Vent, and Régnié)	50 to 55
Beaujolais from Chénas, Juliénas, Morgon, Moulin-à-vent, and Régnié	53 to 58
Bordeaux (most vintages)	58 to 63
Bordeaux (the best vintages)	62 to 67
Brunello di Montalcino	62 to 67
Burgundy—from the better vintages of top grand cru and premier cru vineyards	58 to 63
Burgundy—most Côte de Beaune	55 to 60
Burgundy—most Côte de Nuits	58 to 63
Cabernet Sauvignon—U.S.	62 to 67
Chianti Classico	57 to 62
Chianti Classico Reserva	60 to 65
Côtes du Rhône (and other southern Rhônes)	53 to 58
Dolcetto—U.S. and Italian	53 to 58
German red wines—like Spätburgunder or Portugieser	52 to 57
Lambrusco	48 to 53
Merlot—U.S.	59 to 64
Nouveau-style—French, U.S., and others	48 to 53
Pinot Noir—U.S.	58 to 63
Rhône (northern)	62 to 67
Rioja	57 to 62
Rioja Reserva	60 to 65
Shiraz, Australian	59 to 64
Syrah—U.S.	59 to 64
Valpolicella (Amarone-style only)	55 to 60
Valpolicella (except Amarone-style)	52 to 57
Zinfandel (light)	57 to 62
Zinfandel (heavy)	62 to 67

Fortified Wines

Type of Wine	Serving Temperature (°F)
Madeira	55 to 60
Muscat de Beaumes de Venise	42 to 47
Port, Ruby	57 to 62
Port, Tawny (older)	55 to 60
Port, Tawny (younger)	50 to 55
Port, Vintage	62 to 67
Port, white	45 to 50
Sherry, amontillados	60 to 65
Sherry, most finos, except amontillados	45 to 50
Sherry, olorosos	60 to 65

How to Store Leftover Wine

Careful handling of an unfinished bottle of wine is necessary because prolonged contact with air will ruin a wine's flavor. One way to save leftover wine is to transfer it to a smaller bottle, thereby minimizing airspace. Save splits (*see* Wine Bottles, page 609) just for this purpose, or use other clean small bottles. Always seal the bottle tightly to keep more air from getting in.

Another option is to "gas" leftover wine. There are several canned pressurized gases on the market today (Private Preserve is the most commonly available) that are a combination of nitrogen (N_2) and carbon dioxide (CO_2). This heavier-than-air combination is squirted directly into a partially full bottle of wine, thereby blanketing the wine's surface and protecting it from flavor-destroying oxygen. Such products are available in cans (which feel empty because gas is weightless) in most wine stores and many gourmet specialty shops.

There's another gadget on the market called a vacuum wine saver (VacuVin), which is designed to remove excess air from a partially full wine bottle. To use it, you simply insert a specially designed reusable rubber stopper in the bottle neck, position a pump over the stopper, and pump up and down until you can feel some resistance (some pumps have an audible "click" when the proper vacuum's been reached), an indication that the air has been sucked from the bottle, meaning that the bottle is vacuum sealed.

For SPARKLING WINES, a champagne stopper can be found at gourmet shops and wine stores for only about five dollars. This special spring-loaded stopper comes in a couple of styles. One has two metal wings that fold down and over the neck of a sparkling wine bottle; the other simply fits over the bottle neck and a fold-down lever locks in the bubbles.

Store leftover wine—red, white, and sparkling—in the refrigerator and, if possible, drink it within a day or two. If the room temperature is cool (65°F), red wine does not need to be refrigerated.

Glassware

The right glassware (also called *stemware*) can greatly enhance the flavor and bouquet of wine. There are distinct sizes and shapes of glasses designed for STILL WINES (red and white) and SPARKLING WINES. Many glass manufacturers (such as the Austrian firm, Riedel) produce different glasses for every major wine type. However, it's difficult (and expensive) for most of us to have all these glasses on hand.

There are four basic styles of glassware:

Bordeaux/   Burgundy/   White Wine   Sparkling Wine
Cabernet   Pinot Noir

A good all-purpose glass can be used for both red and white wines. Choose one that's clear—the depth and richness of a wine's color shouldn't be distorted by colored or cut glass. The bowl's shape should be ample to allow room for swirling and for the wine's flavor to evolve; the rim should be thin. The bowl should narrow slightly at the rim, which focuses the aromas toward your nose. The glass stem should be long enough so that your hand doesn't touch the bowl and warm the wine.

The perfect size glass for an average 4-ounce serving of either red or white wine is 10 to 12 ounces. That leaves you plenty of room for swirling. A slightly smaller glass is fine (just serve slightly less wine), and larger bowls are quite good as long as their shape and balance are appropriate.

SPARKLING WINES should be served in a FLUTE—a stemmed glass with a tall, slender cone- or tulip-shaped bowl. These narrow glasses provide less surface from which the bubbles can escape and retain effervescence much better than all-purpose glasses and markedly better than the shallow, wide-brimmed "champagne" glasses that were once so popular. Like all-purpose wineglasses, flutes should be thin and long stemmed. A flute should hold 6 ounces or more.

See also Tasting Wine, page 648.

Tasting Wine

*Wine is alive, and when you offer it to your fellow man you are
offering him life. More than that, you are calling out more life
in him, you are engaging in what might be called a creative
flattery, for you are asking him to summon up his powers of
discrimination, to exercise his taste, or perhaps merely to evince
curiosity of a desire to learn. I know no other liquid that,
placed in the mouth, forces one to think.*
—Clifton Fadiman, American author

There's drinking wine and tasting wine, the latter being a more serious (but still enjoyable) endeavor.

Ground Rules for Wine Tastings

The primary objective of a wine tasting is to analyze the wine to determine its quality. The most simple, straightforward approach is to
assess whether a wine *tastes* good. However, dedicated wine tasters
(who vary broadly in their degree of seriousness) have more exacting
criteria.

To begin with, it should be noted that evaluating wine is a very
personal process. Besides individual likes and dislikes, everyone has
varying levels of tolerance for qualities like sweetness, bitterness, tannins, and acid. Such personal variables can result in passionate dis-
agreements at a wine tasting, where some participants think a wine is
outstanding and others consider it mediocre. There are really no
wrong answers when it comes to your particular preferences. It all
comes down to whether you like the particular wine you're tasting.

There are many guidelines on how to taste wine formally: using
the proper equipment (such as white tablecloths and appropriate
glasses), having the wines at the right temperature, and decanting the
wine, if necessary. Tastings can include flights of from six to eight
wines. The average amount of each wine to pour is about 1 ounce.
Use at least 8-ounce wineglasses to allow plenty of room for swirling.

Caveat: Don't brush your teeth or eat anything sweet, tart, or acidic
within an hour of a wine tasting.

There are numerous descriptors used for wine tasting (*see* Glossary
of Wine Tasting Terms, page 655). Knowing these terms is certainly
not a requirement for enjoying wine, but knowing a little terminology
will help you better understand wine newsletters, magazine and
newspaper articles on wine, wine reviews, and restaurant wine lists.
See also Glassware, page 647; Opening and Serving Wine at Home,

page 636; Optimum Serving Temperatures by Wine Type, page 642; Wine Openers, page 639.

Types of Wine Tastings

When planning a wine tasting, the first thing to consider is the type, of which there are several.

Blind tastings: The tasters don't know the identity of the wines, which is often done so that knowledge of the wine's origin doesn't influence opinions. In some blind tastings, participants know what type of wines are being tasted, but not which producer they're from. For example, the wines might all be 1985 California cabernet sauvignons, or the same vintage of California and Bordeaux wines. In other blind tastings, participants might know they're sampling six chardonnays from six named wineries, but not which glass each wine is in. Part of the fun and educational value of a blind tasting is learning how to determine the regional traits of wines and, eventually, those of the individual wineries and châteaux.

Double blind tastings: Different varietal wines are tasted together, adding the challenge of trying to ascertain the varietal character of each wine, in addition to the country of origin and producer.

Horizontal tastings: Where all the wines are from the same vintage but from different wineries, wine estates, or châteaux.

Vertical tastings: Wines are from different (often contiguous) years but from the same winery, wine estate, or château. For example, a vertical tasting could include the 1981, 1982, 1983, 1984, 1985, and 1986 vintages of Silver Oak Napa Valley cabernet sauvignon. The idea of a vertical tasting is to try to identify traits that exist in the same wine year after year.

The Wine Tasting Process

The tasting process itself involves three basic components—the wine's appearance, smell, and, of course, taste, each of which possesses distinct and important nuances.

A Wine's Appearance

A wine's appearance tells an experienced wine taster several things including how it's aging (whether it may be past its prime) and possible quality. Start by slightly tilting the glass away from you at about a 45° angle, preferably over a white background so the wine's color, clarity, and brilliance are obvious. When comparing several similar wines, the color intensity can also be examined by placing glasses (with the same fill level) on a white background and viewing them from the top.

Next, with the glass in an upright position, begin gently swirling the wine. This technique can be learned initially by leaving the wineglass on the table, holding it by the stem and rotating it in small circles. The object is to get the wine to move up the sides of the glass at least halfway. Once you can swirl on the table without sloshing, lift the glass off the table and use the same technique (the noise of moving the glass around on the table can be distracting or annoying to other tasters). Swirling is done to help release a wine's aroma. It also wets the inside of the glass, leaving a coating that separates into viscous-looking rivulets called legs. Rivulets that take a long time to slide down the glass are a clue that the wine is probably rich and full-bodied (*see* body).

What to look for in a wine's appearance:

Clarity is an important factor in a wine's appearance. Wines should be brilliant without any cloudiness or haziness, factors that generally signal a flaw in the wine. A clear wine will occasionally have some sediment in the shoulder or the bottom of the bottle, which is acceptable, especially in older wines. Decanting a wine prior to serving will remove the sediment.

Color depth (or intensity) is an indicator of quality that, in most instances, accurately predicts (particularly with red wine) how full-bodied a wine will be. Grape varieties and their intrinsic degree of color most certainly influence the depth of color, which can confuse the issue when comparing wines made from different varieties. When comparing like wines, however, the rule of thumb is that the deeper-colored wines are generally made from higher-quality grapes and will therefore have fuller flavor and body. A pale color intensity, especially in red wine, can have several meanings—from overplanted vineyards to underripe grapes—any of which diminish a wine's character and flavor.

Color hue is an extremely important gauge of how well a wine has aged. As wine matures, the small amount of oxygen in the bottle affects its color, which therefore becomes an indicator of whether the wine is aging at an appropriate rate. If the wine's color seems older than it should, it could indicate a problem, such as mishandling during production or bottling or possibly a bad cork. Likewise, an older wine that still exhibits the bright color of one much younger most certainly has aged well and will probably also have a youthful aroma and taste. Following is a brief description of the color changes wines undergo during aging.

White wine color transitions during aging

- *Pale greenish-yellow* is common in very young wines that are still exhibiting small amounts of chlorophyll (found in grapes); this generalization is especially true of wines from cooler growing climates.

- *Straw color* is representative of many recently released dry white wines.

- *Yellow-gold* is found in younger sweet dessert wines and in dry wine with 3 to 4 years of aging.

- *Gold* is indicative of dry wines with substantial (6 years or more) bottle-aging and of full-bodied dessert wines with additional age. Dessert wines of considerable age and good condition will exhibit an even deeper golden color.

- *Brown tinging* indicates excessive aging and the flavor and smell of such a wine will most probably be somewhat oxidized. The only exceptions are some sherries that are still quite good.

Red wine color transitions during aging

- *Purple* is indicative of a very young wine.

- *Crimson* or ruby is common in dry tables wines with brief aging, as well as very young vintage ports.

- *Red* is indicative of table wines with several years of bottle age, such as a 2- to 5-year-old Cabernet Sauvignon or red Bordeaux or a 1- to 3-year-old Pinot Noir or red Burgundy. This is the optimum stage for most red wines unless they're made for long aging.

- *Brick-red* (the red color begins to fade and assume a hint of brown) is an indicator of maturity in a wine. Examples are Bordeaux wines that are generally 6 years or older and Burgundies over 3 years old.

- *Reddish-brown* (even lighter than brick-red, with more brownish hues) suggests a very mature bottle of wine, such as a Bordeaux over 10 years old or a Burgundy over 7 years. This stage is about as far as a dry table wine can go and still be good; those capable of long aging can remain in this stage for years.

- *Tawny* is only desirable with old tawny ports; tawny-colored dry table wines are generally not worth drinking.

- *Amber-brown* is an indication in most cases of deterioration and oxidization, which produces a stale, sherrylike character.

A Wine's Smell

Because smell and taste have a symbiotic relationship, just smelling a wine can reveal much of its character. If there's something inherently wrong or wonderful, the nose will usually detect it. Swirling a wine releases its aroma and bouquet, which can be perceived by putting your nose just inside the glass and inhaling gently. If you don't get much odor from a wine, cover the top of the glass with one palm and swirl again, quickly removing your palm just before you smell again. The caliber of an aroma or bouquet can be gauged by its intensity, quality, and character.

Intensity of a wine's aroma or bouquet can vary greatly and is generally reflective of the taste that will follow. A light aroma usually heralds a light taste; wines with a more intense or aromatic nose, assuming other factors are favorable, are considered desirable.

Quality can be stated in generalities such as pleasant versus unpleasant smell, complex versus simple, and harmonious versus unbalanced. The best wines are pleasant, complex, and harmonious, with no off odors.

Character pertains more specifically to the various odors that are detectable in a wine. The nose of a complex wine might exhibit many smells including black cherries, chocolate, violets, leather, and cinnamon. On the other hand, a simple wine might reveal only a couple of scents, such as raspberry and vanilla. Experienced tasters usually have better-developed sensory memories than beginners and are therefore more adept at identifying the intricacies of a wine's aroma. Training your "aroma memory" can be helpful when trying to determine a wine's characteristics, and you can do so by spending time in a garden smelling (and tasting) various fruits, vegetables, and flowers. Or, gather a variety of items representative of other smells that can be found in wine, such as leather, rubber, or tobacco. Some wine specialty shops have kits that will help you identify various smells found in wine. *See also* the Glossary of Wine Tasting Terms, page 655.

A Wine's Taste

Now it's time for the final evaluation step—tasting the wine. By this time, a number of clues about the wine will already have been revealed. Begin by taking a small sip of wine—some serious tasters suck in a little air just as they do so, a technique that aerates the wine (accentuating the flavor) but that, unless done discreetly, creates a loud slurping noise. Other tasters "chew" or slosh the wine around in their mouth. Both techniques are intended to expose the wine's full flavors while bringing the olfactory senses into play. As you swallow the wine, notice the impression that lingers in your mouth and throat.

The wine's flavors are often forecasted by the smell, although different or additional flavor characteristics may be detected while tasting. Certain important properties affect the final evaluation of the wine that only tasting can determine. These include discernible levels of sweetness or dryness, acidity, bitterness, tactile sensations generated by the wine's body, tannins (in red wine), alcohol level, finish, and, finally, the overall balance of these combined properties. Now, let's talk about these tasting properties in detail.

Sweetness or dryness levels are generally more important in white wines because most reds are vinified DRY (no residual sugar). The style of wine usually dictates the level of sweetness. For example, most CHARDONNAY and SAUVIGNON BLANC wines are dry, whereas CHENIN BLANC, GEWÜRZTRAMINER, and RIESLING wines often have a touch of sweetness, and dessert wines like SAUTERNES or LATE HARVEST WINES are usually very sweet. Sometimes sweetness, which is most recognizable at the tip of the tongue, is required to balance the high acidity of a particular grape, such as the highly acidic Chenin Blanc used in France's VOUVRAY wines. Occasionally, a completely dry but very fruity wine has a seemingly sweet quality to it, which is the result of the ETHYL ALCOHOL produced during fermentation.

Acidity, which is detected by tartness, accomplishes several things. It contributes to a wine's aging capabilities by working as a preservative, protecting both color and flavor; it enlivens the flavor—wines with low acid are usually flat; and it gives a wine that would ordinarily be cloyingly sweet enough balance to be desirable. Excess acid, however, can give a wine a sharp, harsh edge and throw it off kilter.

Bitterness, which is most evident on the back of the tongue, is not a desirable character in most wines. In young reds, however, a small amount is not generally considered a fault.

Body, which is perceived in the mouth as texture or weight, is produced by a combination of elements including ALCOHOL, GLYCEROL,

ACID, and EXTRACT. A rich, complex wine that feels luxuriously heavy in the mouth is considered full-bodied, whereas one that seems watery or flimsy is light-bodied or thin. A medium-bodied wine falls somewhere between the two. Not all wines seek to be full-bodied, however, particularly those like CHAMPAGNE, which strive for finesse. Rich DESSERT WINES like Sauternes are generally full-bodied partly because their RESIDUAL SUGAR adds weight and texture.

Tannins are detectable by a dry, sometimes puckery, sensation in the mouth and back of the throat. They're noticeable in many red wines but not whites. That's because, during red winemaking, the juice is left in contact with the grape skins, seeds, and stems, all of which contribute astringent substances known as TANNINS. The length of contact partially determines the amount of tannins in a wine, but additional tannins are extracted from oak barrels (especially new ones) during extended aging. Although tannins are noticeable in young red wines, they are generally most prominent in high-quality red wines meant for aging and give such wines structure as well as an antioxidant (preservative) capability. The harsh, rough qualities of tannins diminish over time, producing a wine that has backbone without being overtly tannic. Ideally, this process occurs while the wine still has other positive attributes like good flavor, fruit, and acidity. Occasionally, wines have excess tannins that never come into balance before the rest of the components fade.

Alcohol plays a role in giving a wine more body, but it shouldn't be singularly noticeable in a balanced wine. Excess alcohol that isn't balanced by other components can produce a warm, sometimes even hot, burning sensation in the mouth and throat. Such a wine is referred to as HOT or ALCOHOLIC.

Finish is the lingering impression of flavor and tactile sensation that remains in the mouth after the wine is swallowed. The palate impression should be favorable, and the longer the finish, the higher the quality of the wine. This length of time, sometimes referred to as *persistence*, is often described in terms such as "it had a long finish," "the finish was lacking," or "the finish was short."

Balance is the relationship of all the individual factors of a wine's flavor. A wine where none of the components overpowers the others is considered well balanced. For example, a wine with a very light fruit flavor could easily be overpowered by alcohol or tannins, whereas a fruity, full-flavored wine with the same levels of alcohol and tannins would be well balanced. A sweet wine with moderate acid might not be balanced, but a dry wine with that same acid level might be excellent.

Glossary of Wine Tasting Terms

There's a special wine tasting vocabulary, and knowing the language will help you better understand wine-related newsletters, magazine and newspaper articles, wine reviews, and even wine lists. Terms analogous to the word (such as butterscotch, candylike, coffee, cranberry, licorice, mushroom, and raspberry) won't be found in this glossary unless they relate to a specific wine characteristic or type. *See also* WINE TASTER; Tasting Wine, page 648.

How to use this glossary: Throughout the main A-to-Z section of *Wine Lover's Companion*, SMALL CAPS are used to indicate cross-references to other terms in the body (*see* How to Use This Book, page xiii). But there are exceptions to every rule. So, in this Glossary of Wine Tasting Terms, terms in SMALL CAPS still point you to the main A-to-Z portion of the book, but underlined SMALL CAPS tell you to look within this glossary. One more thing: In cases where a wine tasting term has a tangential or expanded definition in the A-to-Z portion, "*see* main listing" will be parenthetically noted.

acescence; acescent [uh-SEHS-uhns; uh-SEHS-uhnt] Wines with acescence have a sharp, sweet-and-sour tang, sometimes accompanied by a vinegary smell. Such *acescent* characteristics signal the presence of ACETIC ACID and ETHYL ACETATE.

acetic [uh-SEE-tihk] At a level of 0.07 percent and above, ACETIC ACID gives wine a sweet, slightly vinegary odor. Above 0.1 percent and the vinegar components become exceedingly sharp—the wine is flawed. Such wine may be variously described as "acetic" or "vinegary" or may be said to have ACESCENCE.

acetone [ASS-ih-tohn] A wine with a sharp but slightly sweet and somewhat fruity smell (akin to that of nail polish), typically caused by ETHYL ACETATE.

acidity; acidic; acid Terms describing levels of ACIDITY (*see* main listing, page 2) in a wine. When acidity is too high, a wine tastes tart and feels slightly harsh and acerbic on the palate; too low and wine tastes dull and flat—FLABBY. High-acidity wines are often described as "acidic" or "acid."

acrid Excessive SULFUR DIOXIDE added during winemaking can cause wine to have a pungent smell or harsh bitter taste described as "acrid."

adolescent phase *see* DUMB

aftertaste The flavor that lingers in the mouth (sometimes detectable in the back of the throat and nasal passages) after a wine is tasted. A long aftertaste is the hallmark of a complex wine. *See also* FINISH; LENGTH.

aggressive Slightly harsh on the palate, usually resulting from high TANNINS or ACIDITY or both.

alcoholic; alcohol, high An undesirable trait revealed by a sharp, burning (almost biting) palate sensation caused by an elevated ALCOHOL level out of proportion to a wine's other components. *See also* HOT.

angular Wine that leaves a tart flavor impression on the palate, typically because it's young and DRY or too acidic. The opposite is SOFT or SUPPLE.

appley; apples This term describes a wine's smell in several ways. **Green apples** are typically a signal that immature grapes were used for the wine, **ripe apples** are indicative of some CHARDONNAYS, and an **old apple** fragrance is often found in sweet TOKAY wines.

aroma In wine parlance, the established definition of aroma is the simple, fruity smell of the grape variety. Today's broader definition combines a wine's varietal fragrance plus any changes that develop during FERMENTATION and AGING. The traditional difference is that a young wine will show its varietal aroma in a more pronounced way, whereas in a mature wine—where some of the grape's intrinsic fragrance has been replaced by other characteristics—the smell transmutes into a BOUQUET. *See also* NOSE.

aromatic A wine with a rich, spicy, or herbaceous aroma and flavor, generally derived from grape varieties such as SAUVIGNON BLANC and MUSCAT.

astringent; astringency A harsh, dry, mouth-puckering effect created by excess TANNINS. High ACIDITY can produce a similar reaction. Astringent wines may mellow as they mature.

attack Wine tasting parlance for the first impression of a wine on the palate.

attenuated [uh-TEN-yoo-ay-td] A wine that's heading over the hill, demonstrated by a loss of FRUIT and BODY.

austere; austerity Wine with excessive TANNINS or ACIDITY accompanied by a lack of richness, FRUIT, and BODY. Austerity is most often found in young, immature wines that may mellow during AGING.

awkward A wine whose components are out of balance is considered clumsy or awkward. *See also* DUMB.

backbone Wine with a strong, balanced structure of ALCOHOL, ACIDITY, and TANNINS.

backward Not as developed as expected for its VINTAGE, style, and type.

baked A warm-earth smell sometimes found in VINTAGES produced during a hot growing season when extreme sun exposure can cause moisture-deprived grapes to dehydrate. In MADEIRA wines, a process called *estufagem* "bakes" the wines, which produces their characteristic tangy, burnt-caramel flavor.

balance; balanced When all the components—fruit, ACIDITY, ALCOHOL, TANNINS, and the like—are in perfect harmony (depending on the wine's origin and style), with no element overpowering another.

barnyard *see* BRETTANOMYCES

berrylike; berries An intense, ripe, sweet-fruit characteristic found particularly in young ZINFANDEL, CABERNET SAUVIGNON, and MERLOT wines. Such a trait most often suggests blackberries, black cherries, mulberries, raspberries, or strawberries.

big A rich, full-bodied (*see* BODY) wine that's concentrated and intensely flavored. Such wines are typically high in ALCOHOL but well balanced. The term *massive* describes exceptionally big (and magnificent) wines.

bite Assertive acid in a wine can give the FINISH a "bite." In rich, full-bodied wine, this can be positive, but overt acid in a lesser wine is a fault.

bitter; bitterness Bitterness in wine can be due to TANNINS, chemical salts, oxidized polyphenols, bacteria, and even some grapes (such as GEWÜRZTRAMINER), which have an intrinsically bitter note. Slight bitterness can contribute BALANCE to a sweet wine. Overt bitterness that dominates a wine's flavor or AFTERTASTE is considered a fault.

blackcurrant; black currant A marked black currant (*cassis* in French) smell found in some wines, such as CABERNET SAUVIGNON and red BORDEAUX. This essence can range from subtle to rich. *See also* REDCURRANT.

blunt A strongly flavored wine that delivers little else in the way of AROMA and FINISH.

body The impression of texture or weight in the mouth, comprising an amalgam of elements including ALCOHOL, EXTRACT, GLYCEROL, and ACID. A wine with a rich, complex, well-ROUNDED, lingering flavor is considered **full-bodied**; one that's watery or lacking in body is called **light-bodied** or THIN; a **medium-bodied** wine ranks in between. Not all wines strive for a full-bodied characteristic, namely those whose hallmark may be FINESSE, such as CHAMPAGNE.

Dessert wines, like rich SAUTERNES, are considered full-bodied partly because the RESIDUAL SUGAR adds weight and texture.

botrytised [boh-TRY-tihsd] A sweet, uniquely aromatic, honeyed characteristic in both flavor and smell, caused by grapes that have been infected with BOTRYTIS CINEREA.

bottle stink A stale, somewhat stinky odor that sometimes exists when a cork is first withdrawn from the bottle. Bottle stink usually dissipates fairly quickly.

bouquet The complex fragrance that develops in a wine through fermentation and aging, specifically bottle aging. *See also* AROMA; NOSE.

brambly *see* BRIARY

brawny Young red wines that are full-bodied (*see* BODY) but high in TANNINS and ALCOHOL and still somewhat raw. AGING helps SOFTEN such wines and produces a degree of finesse.

breed The best and most refined wines, prized for their CHARACTER, COMPLEXITY, and high quality. A wine of *breed* will have a superior heritage and be made from the best varieties. The French term for breed is *race*.

brettanomyces; brett [breht-tan-uh-MI-sees; BREHT] Brettanomyces is a spoilage YEAST that produces a horsey, barnyard aroma that some people love (saying it adds richness to the wine), others detest, and many don't even detect. It's typically caused by less-than-sanitary barrels or winemaking procedures. Other odor descriptors for wine degraded by brett include mouse droppings, a sweaty saddle, or burnt beans. A wine overly imbued with brett tends to get worse as it AGES.

briary [BRI-uh-ree] An AGGRESSIVE wine—usually with high TANNINS and ALCOHOL—that produces a palate impression of spiciness akin to black pepper. Also sometimes called *brambly* or *bramble*.

brick red The color of some red wines, a signal of maturity. The brick-red hue is detectable most obviously at the MENISCUS, or rim of the wine in a glass.

bright; brightness Describing wines (generally young ones) with fresh, fruity, lively flavors.

brilliant A wine of superior clarity, sparkling clear. This is typically the result of intense filtering.

browning An older red wine will be a deep ruby color with a tinge of brown on the edges (MENISCUS). Although it may be quite enjoyable, a wine that shows browning will usually not improve with additional AGING. Considerable browning indicates the wine has FADED. Browning in a young wine is a flaw.

brut *see* BRUT main listing, page 76.

burning *see* HOT

burnt A singed or smoky essence, often relating to overcharred barrels.

burnt matches *see* SULFUR

buttery The smell and, sometimes, flavor of melted butter in a wine, most often used with mature CHARDONNAY. *Buttery* is also used to describe the golden color of some wines.

butyric [byoo-TIHR-ihk] A characteristic derived from butyric acid (*see* ACIDS) and found in some spoiled wines, evidenced by the odor of rancid butter.

caramel Wine, such as MADEIRA, with a rich, burnt-sugar aroma and flavor.

cardbord A CORKED wine often takes on the smell of musty wet cardbord.

cassis [ka-SEES] *see* BLACKCURRANT

cat pee A classic aroma description for SAUVIGNON BLANC (more often found in those from the LOIRE, rather than from southern hemisphere wines), which could be compared to a whiff of ammonia.

cedar Also called *cigar box,* a smell characteristic of cedarwood, most often found in the BOUQUET of fine red wines, such as those from BORDEAUX and some California CABERNET SAUVIGNONS. It can also be detected in some OAK-aged white wines.

character A term applied to a wine with distinctive, obvious features, either pertaining to its style or its variety. Although character has nothing to do with a wine's quality, one without it is considered dull. *See also* VARIETAL CHARACTER.

cherry An aroma and flavor characteristic reminiscent of fresh cherries that is often found in ZINFANDELS and PINOT NOIRS. On the other hand, black cherries are more evocative of CABERNET SAUVIGNONS.

chewy Wines (generally red) that are so RICH, DENSE, INTENSE, and full-bodied (*see* BODY) that they produce a mouth-filling impression that make them seem almost *chewy.* Such wines can also be referred to as FLESHY or MEATY.

chocolaty; chocolate A rich chocolate aroma and flavor sometimes found in CABERNET SAUVIGNONS, ZINFANDELS, and other red wines.

cigar box *see* CEDAR

citrusy; citrus Describes wine with citrusy characteristics (generally grapefruit, lemon, or lime) in both flavor and smell. Such wines aren't necessarily high in ACID.

clarity Wines that are brilliantly clear, without any cloudiness or haziness are said to have *clarity.* A clear wine will occasionally have some sediment in the shoulder or the bottom of the bottle, which is perfectly fine, especially in older wines.

classic A broad wine term used to suggest that a wine is consistent with the established characteristics of that particular wine's type and style. Even though the term is sometimes used on wine labels (for example, "Classic Cabernet"), it has no official definition except in GERMANY where it has a specific meaning.

clean A wine that tastes and smells fresh, with no off nuances.

closed; closed-in Used for wine that doesn't show its full potential, most likely because of its youth. AGING will usually open up such a wine as it develops CHARACTER and intensity. *See also* DUMB.

cloudy; cloudiness Describes a wine that's visually murky. Cloudiness is considered a defect in young wines and is most often due to faulty winemaking. An older wine with SEDIMENT, though not absolutely clear, should not be confused with a cloudy wine.

cloying Wine that lacks the balance of ACIDITY to keep it from becoming unappetizingly sweet.

clumsy *see* AWKWARD

coarse A description for mediocre or poor-quality wine that may have BODY, but little else, often the result of inferior grape varieties or growing methods. In SPARKLING WINES, coarseness generally refers to effervescence with large, rough bubbles.

color A wine's color is an indicator of its condition, quality, age, and even style. In general, the less intense a wine's color, the more delicate the flavor and body. The color of any good wine should be clear. As wines age, their colors change—white wines become darker, often with traces of amber; red wines begin to fade and often assume a tawny, brick-red cast. A change of color in a young wine signals premature aging. See also Tasting Wine, page 648.

complex; complexity Complexity is a hallmark of quality in a wine. A complex wine is one with multiple layers and nuances of bouquet and flavor. Its myriad elements are perfectly balanced, completely harmonious, and eminently interesting. Such a wine is the diametric opposite of one that is simple and one-dimensional.

concentrated A wine with intensely rich, full fruity flavors.

confectionary Term used to describe wine that has sweet flavors and/or aromas that are sometimes cloying, much to the wine's detriment. This trait is not related to RESIDUAL SUGAR, but rather to intense fruitness and/or the sweet vanilla essence sometimes imparted by oak AGING.

cooked Wine with a heavy, sweet, sometimes caramelly smell and flavor is said to have a "cooked" characteristic. This trait can have several causes including an unusually high temperature during vinification or the addition of some form of sugar.

corked; corky A wine that's been affected by a faulty cork has an distinctly musty odor and flavor reminiscent of moldy, wet cardboard or newspapers. *See also* CORKED WINE.

creamy An adjective sometimes used to describe the creamlike impression left on the palate from a SPARKLING WINE's rich, smooth froth.

crisp Wine that has a fresh, lively ACIDITY that, although noticeable, doesn't overpower the other components. Crispness is a desirable trait in white wines.

deep Many aspects of a wine (its COLOR, flavor, or BOUQUET) can be deep, which, in the wine world, is a word that signifies intensity. *See also* DEPTH.

delicate; delicacy A quality wine that is light to medium-bodied, well-BALANCED, and REFINED. Delicate may also apply to a fine wine that's poised to decline.

depth A wine with flavor depth is full-bodied (*see* BODY) and INTENSE and has multiple dimensions of flavor and BOUQUET. In this context, depth is similar in meaning to COMPLEXITY. *Depth of color* refers to the color intensity, a quality indicator that, in most instances, accurately predicts (particularly with red wine) how full-bodied a wine will be. The intrinsic degree of color in various grape varieties most certainly influences the depth of a wine's color. The rule of thumb when comparing like wines is that the deeper-colored wines are generally made from higher-quality grapes and will therefore have fuller flavor and body. A pale color intensity, especially in a red wine, can have several meanings—from overplanted vineyards to underripe grapes—any of which diminish a wine's character and flavor. *See also* DEEP.

developed Referring to a wine's state of maturity and drinkability. A *well-developed* wine is perfectly matured and ready to drink, while one that's *underdeveloped* needs AGING before being consumed. An *overdeveloped* wine is just that—over the hill and on the decline.

dirty Wine with a distinctly disgusting, rank odor, typically caused by poor winemaking.

dirty sox Term sometimes used to describe wines imbued with a good dose of BRETTANOMYCES.

distinguished A wine of exceptional CHARACTER, REFINEMENT, and quality.

dried out Wine whose fruit has faded, which lets the ACID, TANNINS, and ALCOHOL dominate.

dry A term that describes wine that isn't sweet at all; its French counterpart is SEC. In a fully dry wine, all the sugar has been converted to ALCOHOL during FERMENTATION. A medium-dry wine has a small amount of RESIDUAL SUGAR, but not enough to prevent the wine from being enjoyed with a meal. A wine with the barest hint of sweetness is referred to as OFF DRY. *See also* EXTRA DRY, page 199.

dull Just as it sounds, a dull wine is lackluster and devoid of zest and interest.

dumb; dumb phase Though *dumb* is sometimes used as a synonym for CLOSED, it really has a more complex meaning. The dumb phase of a wine (generally red) is that period of transition from its youth to maturity. Shortly after bottling, a wine may be luscious, with rich, ripe aromas and flavors. However, after a certain period of time (usually several months), such a wine may begin to close down—the fruit begins to decrease before the complexities of maturity have fully developed. The combination of declining fruit and preemergent complexity cancel each other out, creating a wine that simply doesn't taste very good. VINTNERS have no idea what causes this phenomenon but do agree that the time frame for this dumb phase, which can last for several years, is completely unpredictable. The dumb phase of a wine is also referred to as the *flat spot* or the *awkward, transformational,* or *adolescent phase.*

dusty A palate impression of solid flavor particles. By the nose, a dusty smell is reminiscent of an earthen-floored cellar.

earthy; earthiness An aroma or flavor evocative of damp, rich soil. Earthy is typically used in a positive sense, unless the characteristic is emphatic, at which point it can become DIRTY.

eggs *see* SULFUR

elegant; elegance Wines with FINESSE, lightness, and flair—they're gracefully BALANCED and of exceedingly high quality.

empty *see* HOLLOW

esters [EHS-tuhrs] A wine that smells of ESTERS (*see* main listing, page 197) has a sweet and slightly fruity aroma.

ethyl acetate A slightly sweet, fruity, vinegary smell that can be quite complementary in rich wines. Overt amounts, however, can smell like nail polish and are considered a flaw. *See also* ETHYL ACETATE (main listing, page 198).

eucalyptus [yoo-kuh-LIHP-tuhs] A spicy, aromatic, mintlike aroma found in certain red wines, such as Heitz Martha's Vineyard CABERNET SAUVIGNON. Some vineyards that produce such wines are surrounded by eucalyptus trees, which some contend contribute their essence to the grapes.

extract [EHKS-trakt] A wine described as having good "extract" is typically full-bodied (*see* BODY), and has dense, CONCENTRATED flavors and intense (for the type), opaque colors. A wine that's "overextracted" is usually quite TANNIC. *See also* EXTRACT (main listing, page 199).

extra dry *see* EXTRA DRY (main listing, page 199).

exuberant [ehk-ZOO-buhr-uhnt] Wines that are LIVELY, with lavish fruit.

faded; fading Such a wine has typically lost color, its COMPLEXITY and CHARACTER diminished, typically through the ravages of age.

fat A positive descriptor sometimes used for wine that, although CONCENTRATED, RICH, and high in GLYCEROL, has low to average ACIDITY. The impression on the palate is full and *fat*. A wine with *almost* the same qualities, but not in the same concentration, might be referred to as **plump.** A fat wine with exceedingly low acidity is referred to as FLABBY. A fat sweet wine can be overwhelmingly unctuous. *See also* LEAN.

feeble A wine that lacks distinction in all respects—flavor, AROMA, BODY, CHARACTER, and so on.

finesse Describes wine with distinction, grace, and perfect harmony among its components.

finish The final flavor and TEXTURE impression that remains on the palate after a wine is swallowed. The finish is part of a wine's overall balance. A distinctive, lingering (or LONG) finish is the ideal. A wine with a weak or nonexistent finish is considered lacking.

firm A positive term (the opposite of FLABBY) describing the palate impression of a wine that's fairly high in TANNIN and ACIDITY but still well-BALANCED.

flabby Wine that's heavy on the palate, caused by a serious deficiency in ACIDITY, STRUCTURE and, subsequently, in flavor. *See also* FAT.

flat 1. For STILL WINE, *flat* describes a dull flavor and CHARACTER due to a lack of ACIDITY. 2. A SPARKLING WINE sans bubbles is *flat*.

flat spot *see* DUMB

fleshy Describes a full-bodied (*see* BODY), smooth wine with high ALCOHOL, EXTRACT and, usually, GLYCEROL. *Fleshy* is comparable to CHEWY, the opposite of LEAN.

fliers Tiny visible but tasteless particles that occasionally appear in wine. Usually caused by a cold environment, fliers generally disappear when the wine is warmed.

flinty An aroma and flavor reminiscent of flint striking steel, also referred to as *gunflint*. This characteristic, which the French call *pierre-à-fusil*, comes from grapes grown in certain soils and is considered a positive trait. It's found in extremely dry white wines such as certain French CHABLIS and SAUVIGNON BLANCS.

floral; flowery An aroma reminiscent of flowers, such as violets, citrus blossoms, or roses. This impression can also be sensed on the palate. Floral characteristics are more likely to be found in white wines like JOHANNISBERG RIESLING and GEWÜRZTRAMINER than in reds, although those made from NEBBIOLO grapes are known to be suggestive of violets.

forward A term for wine that has matured earlier than expected for its age and style. The opposite of BACKWARD.

foxy A pronounced musky, earthy quality found in wines made with grapes from the North American vine species VITIS LABRUSCA.

fresh; freshness A well-balanced wine that's LIVELY, CLEAN, and FRUITY.

frizzante [freet-TSAHN-teh] An Italian term for wines with light effervescence. *Pétillant* is the French equivalent: *spritzig,* the German.

fruity; fruitiness; fruit Used for wines that have the characteristic flavor and smell of fresh fruit—a quality primarily displayed in young wines. But fruitiness doesn't necessarily reflect grapes—it can be characteristic of apples, blackberries, cherries, raspberries, you name it. For example, the taste and aroma of GEWÜRZTRAMINER is reminiscent of litchis. Fruity wines typically have a FRESH quality and distinctive CHARACTER.

full-bodied *see* BODY

gamey; game Some very old wines have a BOUQUET that resembles the flesh of game birds or animals, sometimes with a nuance of decay. Though this descriptor is considered positive, wines it applies to can be an acquired taste.

garrigue [GAH-*r*eeg] This French word translates to "scrubland" and refers to hills and plateaus around the Mediterranean that are dry, windswept, and grow scattered, uncultivated pockets of vegetation such as juniper, lavender, sage, scrubby oak, rockrose, and thyme. The term is used in the wine world to describe wines, usually from southern France, that portray aromas and flavors of this vegetation, meaning the wine displays traits of lavender, sage, thyme, etc., sort of a herbs de Provence with an earthy quality. A number of wines from this area use *garrigue* on their label.

gassy A negative term for wines with unexpected carbonation produced by bottle FERMENTATION.

geranium Red wines smelling of geraniums (more accurately, a split geranium leaf) suffer from SORBIC ACID degeneration. On the other hand, a geranium smell in GEWURZTRAMINER is not considered a fault but is simply one of the grape's many spicy-floral nuances.

glycerol; glycerine [GLYS-uh-rawl; GLYS-uh-rihn] Describes a wine that feels smooth and silky on the palate. *See also* GLYCEROL (main listing, page 231).

gooseberry A term used to describe the spicy-tart flavor of some SAUVIGNON BLANCS, specifically those from cool regions.

goût [GOO] French for "taste," *goût* is used (in the wine world) with other words to identify a particular characteristic. For example, *goût de terroir* refers to the sensory aspects of smell and taste that come from the TERROIR—the geographic factors that influence the grapes from which the wine was made. *Goût de bouchon* (*bouchon* being French for "stopper") refers to a wine that's CORKED.

grapey A term for wines with the simple flavors and aromas of fresh grapes, rather than the complex panoply of flavors found in fine wines. A *grapey* characteristic is exemplified in wines made from certain varieties such as the MUSCAT and CONCORD.

grassy; grassiness Also sometimes referred to as GREEN, this is the characteristic smell of freshly cut grass or hay (found in some SAUVIGNON BLANCS). A balanced amount is pleasant; too much is detrimental.

gravelly A term that describes wine with a clean, earthy smell. This gravelly characteristic is most often associated with the wines of GRAVES. *See also* EARTHY.

green Term used in several ways—to describe a very young wine that's not ready to drink, or a wine made from underripe grapes, or sometimes to indicate a GRASSY quality. It generally suggests a wine with high ACIDITY and reduced fruity richness.

grip Wine with a firm (as opposed to FLABBY) TEXTURE, typically the result of robust TANNINS and ACIDITY.

gunflint *see* FLINTY

hard A young wine that's excessively TANNIC (with reds), or ACIDIC (typically with whites), or both. Such wines often MELLOW and soften (*see* SOFT) with AGING.

harmonious A wine that's perfectly BALANCED and ready to drink.

harsh A wine that's HARD in the extreme, usually as a result of high astringency, which gives it a rough, tactile sensation on the palate.

hazy Describes a relatively clear wine that has a moderate amount of suspended particulates, common in some UNFILTERED or UNFINED wines. *See also* CLOUDINESS.

heady A wine that's high in ALCOHOL.

hearty Generally applied to LIVELY, ROBUST, high-ALCOHOL red wines.

heavy Wine that's out of BALANCE as a result of high ALCOHOL and proportionately low ACIDITY for the fruit.

herbaceous; herbal [her-BAY-shuhss] A term for wines that smell of fresh herbs (basil, oregano, rosemary), which can vary, depending on the wine. Sometimes an herbal quality can be sensed on the palate. An herbal characteristic can be a VARIETAL trait in some CABERNET SAUVIGNONS, as well as MERLOTS and SAUVIGNON BLANCS. It's considered desirable unless it becomes overpowering or turns VEGETAL.

high toned Term used to describe wines that display significant aromas that can be delightful but, in some cases, too excessive. These wines often have higher levels of VOLATILE ACIDITY and if there's too much they can become unpleasant.

hollow Used for a wine that lacks DEPTH and BODY—it may taste fine going in, but the flavor rapidly disappears. Also called *empty* and *shallow*.

honeyed Sweet, often BOTRYTISED, wines (such as SAUTERNES and TROCKENBEERENAUSLESEN) that have a honeylike fragrance and flavor.

hot Used for wines with excessive ALCOHOL that, unless balanced with strong FRUIT, creates a burning, prickly sensation in the mouth and throat. A "hot" sensation may be acceptable in FORTIFIED wines such as PORT and SHERRY, but is not desirable in most wines.

inky 1. Used for red wine with an offensive metallic, often THIN flavor. Such a trait is often caused by TANNINS coming in contact with iron (such as a nail). 2. Visually, *inky* is also used to indicate the deep, seemingly impenetrable color of some red wines.

insipid Wines that lack CHARACTER, flavor, BODY, and most other positive attributes.

jammy; jamlike An intensely ripe, FRUITY, CONCENTRATED flavor and aroma.

leafy The smell of leaves, the type of which can vary depending on the wine. Unless this characteristic is overpowering or turns VEGETAL, it's not considered objectionable.

lean The opposite of FLESHY, describing a wine that's somewhat sparse in FRUIT and, sometimes, moderately ASTRINGENT. Such characteristics, however, don't necessarily translate into an unenjoyable wine. *See also* FAT.

leathery Wines (usually BIG, TANNIC reds) that have the rich smell of new leather, typically the result of the wine's exposure to wooden barrels.

legs After a glass of wine is swirled, it often leaves a coating on the inside of the glass that separates into viscous-looking rivulets called *legs* or *tears*. These streams slowly slide down the glass, returning to the wine's surface. Legs generally indicate a RICH, full-bodied (*see* BODY) wine with relatively high alcohol (12 percent or more). Very wide legs are sometimes called *sheets.*

length Also known as *persistence*, the length of a wine is measured (in seconds) by the amount of time its BOUQUET and flavor linger after swallowing. The longer it lingers, the finer the wine.

light A term with several connotations. It can refer to a wine that's light-bodied (*see* BODY), one that's young, fruity, and drinkable, or one that's relatively low in ALCOHOL. *See also* LIGHT WINE.

limpid; limpidity A wine that's crystalline, luminous, and bright. *See also* BRILLIANT.

lively Most often used for white wine, "lively" refers to fresh, youthful, fruity characteristics, usually the result of good ACIDITY.

long A reference to the length of time a wine's presence remains in the mouth after swallowing. A long (or *lingering*) FINISH is an indicator of a fine wine. *See also* SHORT.

luscious *see* LUSH

lush Used for wines that are RICH, SOFT, VELVETY, sweet, and FRUITY—in other words, exceedingly drinkable. Synonymous with *luscious.*

lychee An exotically spicy-sweet flavor evocative of the lychee fruit (also called lychee nut) and distinctively characteristic of the GEWÜRZTRAMINER grape.

maderized [MAD-uh-rized] A term for mature wine that assumes a MADEIRA-like character, undesirable in most TABLE WINE. Maderization, which occurs primarily in white and ROSÉ wine, is typically caused by OXIDATION, often combined with overly warm storage. Its aroma characteristics can range from caramelized and nutty to the slightly stale nuance of overripe apples; the wine's color takes on a brownish tinge. Though *maderized* is often used synonymously with OXIDIZED, the latter doesn't infer warm storage. In France, the term is *maderisé;* in England, it's SHERRIFIED.

masculine *see* MUSCULAR

massive *see* BIG

mature; maturity A complimentary term for wine that's perfectly DEVELOPED, AGED, and ready to drink—it's not too young, and it's not headed over the hill.

meaty Wine (primarily red) that's so RICH and full-bodied (*see* BODY) that it seems almost *chewable*. A synonym for CHEWY.

mellow A MATURE, well-AGED wine that's pleasantly SOFT but not FLABBY.

meniscus [mih-NIHS-kuhs] The rim of a wine in a glass. The COLOR intensity of the meniscus is an indicator of several of the wine's characteristics including concentration, MATURITY, and RICHNESS. Also simply called *rim color.*

mercaptans [mer-KAP-tuhns] A wine that smells of MERCAPTANS (*see* main listing) has a pungent, sour odor with any number of offensive characteristics including that of garlic, sweat, skunk, rotten eggs, or rubber. Sometimes this odor can be diminished by AERATION.

metallic An unpleasant tinny characteristic, generally the result of a wine's contact with metal.

minerally; mineral Lick a stone and you'll get an impression of this classic characteristic found in true SAUVIGNON BLANCS from France's Loire Valley, or DRY German RIESLINGS, or the trademark flavor of the red wines of Château HAUT-BRION.

minty; mint An appealing mintlike characteristic found in some California CABERNETS and ZINFANDELS. As long as it isn't predominant, a minty smell (similar to that of EUCALYPTUS) is considered desirable.

moldy A moldy smell or flavor is generally a signal that a wine was either made from moldy grapes or stored in deteriorating or improperly cleaned barrels. *See also* CORKED.

monolithic A massive, solid wine with very concentrated flavors, lots of power. Same vein as ROBUST and BIG but even more so. It may or may not have good balance and/or complexity to go along with its bigness.

mousy; mousey [MOW-see] An ACETIC, though flat smell and flavor caused by bacterial contamination.

mouthfeel A self-explanatory term describing the tactile palate impressions of a wine, such as rough or velvety.

mouth-filling Used for wines that are so BIG, RICH, and intensely flavored that they produce textural tactile impressions on the palate. Such wines typically have a high ALCOHOL and GLYCEROL content.

muscular Big, bold, full-bodied (*see* BODY) red wine. Synonymous with *masculine.*

musky An earthy-spicy aroma characteristic.

musty An undesirable damp, moldy smell and flavor, usually caused by wine being stored in unclean barrels. Sometimes mustiness can be attributed to a faulty cork, in which case it may disappear on AERATION.

naked Term used to describe wines that are unoaked—they haven't been matured in oak barrels or been treated with other oak alternatives (oak chips, flavorings or staves).

nail polish *see* ACETONE

nerveux [nehr-VEUH] French term that literally means "nervous," "energetic," or "vigorous." In wine tasting circles, it describes wines that are full-bodied (*see* BODY), lively, and well-BALANCED, with excellent AGING qualities.

nervy Wines that have enough acidity that it's perceptible, but not so much that it's out of balance with the other components of a wine. It applies to dry, white wines with enough fruit and alcohol to have good structure.

neutral Wine that lacks distinction and, though perfectly acceptable, is simple and ordinary.

noble A term used to describe a superior wine of remarkable CHARACTER and great BREED. *Noble* may also be used to describe eminent vineyards or grape varieties (such as CABERNET SAUVIGNON, PINOT NOIR, and SÉMILLON) known for producing superlative wines.

nose *n.* A wine's "nose" is the general term for its detectable odor. Depending on its state of maturity, the nose may reflect a young wine's simple varietal AROMA or the more complex BOUQUET of a mature wine. **nose** *v.* To smell a wine in order to detect its nuances, you nose it.

nutty Some wines, such as SHERRY or tawny PORT, have a crisp, nutty (typically hazelnut or walnut) characteristic. Full-bodied (*see* BODY) CHARDONNAYS sometimes also have a very subtle nutty trait. An overt nutty trait in TABLE WINE is considered a flaw.

oaky; oakiness A toasty, vanillin flavor and fragrance in wines that have been aged in new or lightly toasted (*see* TOAST) oak barrels. An oaky characteristic is wonderful in the proper balance. However, exaggerated oakiness can be TANNIC (sometimes almost VEGETAL) and overwhelm a wine's other components—it's considered undesirable. *See also* OAK.

off Wine that's obviously spoiled or seriously flawed. Some wine tasters also use *off* to describe a wine that's not true to CHARACTER.

off dry Used for wine that has the barest hint of sweetness—from 0.6 to 1.4 percent RESIDUAL SUGAR.

oily This term can refer to either texture or flavor, although it's more commonly applied to the former. A wine with an oily "texture" produces a smooth, slightly slippery impression in the mouth, which is usually the result of relatively high GLYCEROL, often combined with low ACIDITY. This tactile characteristic is often found in FAT wines. The term oily is also used sometimes to describe the BOUQUET of a wine like a mature RIESLING, although the term PETROL is more appropriate in this instance.

open A term describing wine that's accessible or ready to drink.

opening A wine's "opening" (which can apply to smell, flavor, or both) is the first impression it gives. Such opening characteristics can change from the first taste to one a few minutes later. For instance, the smell of SULFUR on the opening may be entirely indistinguishable on subsequent passes.

overripe Used to describe wine made from grapes that have remained on the vine too long before being picked, which makes them high in sugar and low in ACID. In some wines, such as ZINFANDELS, slightly overripe grapes can be desirable; a CHARDONNAY made with such grapes, however, can be HEAVY and out of BALANCE. *See also* PRUNEY.

oxidized Describing deterioration through OXIDATION (exposure to air), either during production or aging. The chemical changes caused by oxidation produce a brownish color and stale, flat sherrylike smell and flavor, all of which can render a TABLE WINE undrinkable. Though *oxidized* is often used synonymously with MADERIZED, the latter infers that, in addition to air exposure, the wine has also endured storage in an overly warm environment.

pelure d'oignon [peh-LEWR dohn-YAWN] French for "onion skin" which, in wine parlance, refers to the brownish-orange tint that some older red wines develop as they age. The term is also sometimes used with light red or ROSÉ wines.

penetrating A wine with an intense, almost tactile aroma, generally the result of high ALCOHOL and overt ESTERS.

peppery A trait found in wines (such as some RHÔNE wines and vintage PORTS) with spicy, black-pepper characteristics, sometimes accompanied by high ALCOHOL.

perfumed; perfumy Primarily used to describe white wine with an intensely fragrant aroma, often representative of the grapes from which it was made.

perlant [PEHR-law*n*] A French term for a wine with an extremely slight sparkle—so trivial that it feels more like a tickle.

persistence *see* LENGTH

pétillant; pétillance [pay-tee-YAW*N*] A French term meaning "slightly sparkling," referring to wines with extremely light effervescence. *Pétillance* is the noun form. The Italian equivalent is *frizzante*; the German is *spritzig.*

petrol; petroleum; petrolly A generally positive term used to describe the faint smell of petroleum found in some wines, such as mature RIESLINGS.

pierre-à-fusil [pee-AIR ah FOO-zee] French for "FLINTY."

piqué [pee-KAY] A French term for a wine that has gone sour and is turning vinegary. The English synonym is PRICKED.

plump *see* FAT

powerful Wines (typically red) that are BOLD, high-ALCOHOL, and full-flavored. Synonymous with *strong*.

pricked Wine that has an off-putting sharpness caused by VOLATILE ACIDITY. In an extreme state, such wines have almost turned to vinegar.

prickly; prickle A subtle sparkle from residual carbon dioxide gas.

pruney A negative term sometimes used to describe wines made from extremely overripe grapes, which contribute an undesirable pungent characteristic.

puckery Used for wines that are so TANNIC that they make the mouth and teeth feel extremely dry. The term ASTRINGENT is more aptly used for the same sensation.

race [*R*AHSS] The French term for "BREED."

racy A wine (typically white) with agreeably high acidity balanced by lively fruit flavors.

raisiny Positive description of a rich, concentrated, almost caramelly flavor in some LATE HARVEST and FORTIFIED WINES. Such a trait is considered a fault in DRY wines because it's typically the result of being made with dried-out grapes grown in an excessively hot climate.

raw A term for wine that's young, undeveloped, and harsh, typically caused by unresolved TANNINS and ACIDITY. With time, such wines usually become BALANCED and quite drinkable.

redcurrant; red currant A sweetly tart, tangy flavor similar to the fresh fruit in some PINOT NOIRS.

reduced; reductive *see* REDUCED; REDUCTION; REDUCTIVE, main listing, page 420

refined A refined wine (or one of refinement) is high in quality, as well as being in perfect CHARACTER and BALANCE for its origin and style.

resinous; resiny A characteristic found in wines, predominantly Greek, that have been treated with pine-tree resin, which lends a distinctive turpentine-like flavor and smell. *See also* RETSINA.

rich; richness Used for wine with an opulently full and balanced complement of intense flavor, FRUIT, ALCOHOL, and EXTRACT.

rim color *see* MENISCUS

ripe Wine made from perfectly ripened grapes, which contribute RICH, ROUND, naturally sweet, FRUITY characteristics. *See also* UNRIPE.

robe Term used to discuss elements of a wine's color, including the depth and hue.

robust Similar in meaning to BIG, describing wine (more likely red than white) that's full-bodied (*see* BODY), ROUND, and full of FRUIT—in short, a big mouthful.

rotten eggs *see* SULFUR

rough; roughness Used for COARSE, generally ordinary wines that are overly TANNIC and/or ACIDIC. However, some wines that exhibit roughness eventually mature and become full-bodied (*see* BODY) and well-BALANCED.

round; rounded A well-BALANCED, MELLOW, full-bodied (*see* BODY) wine is sometimes referred to as *round;* its flavor is *rounded.* The term is similar to FAT.

rubbery A negative term describing the odor of rubber, which is caused by the presence of MERCAPTANS.

rustic Wines that lack sophistication or elegance. These wines might also be described as BRAWNY, EARTHY, HEARTY, and/or ROUGH. Rustic's not necessarily a negative term but rather one used to differentiate a wine that doesn't fit the typical model of refinement and polish found in many of today's wines.

sappy This term is used to describe wine in two ways. 1. Lots of upfront fruit flavors, succulent, and juicy as is found in some high quality young wines. 2. A term similar to STEMMY and/or GREEN but not as extreme—either underripe grapes are the cause or the juice remained in contact with stems for a prolonged period during winemaking.

sauvage *see* SAUVAGE (main listing, page 466)

sec *see* DRY; *see also* SEC (main listing, page 472).

shallow *see* HOLLOW

sharp A wine that has a biting sensation due to excess ACIDITY or ACETIC ACID. Some sharp wines will mellow with age.

sheets *see* LEGS

sherrified [SHEHR-rih-fide] Used for TABLE WINE with a heavy, stale smell and flavor and a color with a brownish tinge. Such wines are said to have a SHERRYlike character, which is typically caused by OXIDATION (exposure to air). Unless it was specifically produced to achieve this character, a sherrified wine is faulty.

short A wine that has an abrupt FINISH—not an admirable quality. *See also* LONG.

silky Wine that is incredibly smooth, LUSH, and finely TEXTURED. VELVETY is a similar term.

simple Wine that, though not COMPLEX, is forthright and quite good.

sinewy Wine that lacks fruit but other aspects—ALCOHOL, ACIDITY, and TANNINS—are BALANCED.

skunky A term for the analogous smell, which is caused by MERCAPTANS. *See also* SULFUR.

smoky A subtle smoky character that can be attributed to the soil in which the grapes were grown (as with some reds from GRAVES) or to the barrels in which the wine was aged.

smooth A general term used to describe a variety of things including a wine's TEXTURE, FINISH, and the tactile impression of FLAVOR and BODY.

soapy Wine with a dull, disagreeable flavor, generally caused by a lack of ACIDITY.

soft; softening A wine described as "soft" is well BALANCED, fruity, mellow, and pleasant—generally the result of lower ACIDITY and/or TANNINS (or the perfect fusion of the two). It's the opposite of HARD. The mellowing process that a young (TANNIC and/or ACIDIC) wine undergoes during AGING is called softening.

solid Wine that's full-bodied (*see* BODY) and loaded with ACIDITY, ALCOHOL, FRUIT, and TANNINS. The term sometimes refers to youthful wines that will develop well with AGING.

sound A wine that's without faults in clarity, color, aroma, or flavor is sound.

sour A term for a spoiled wine that's making its turn toward vinegar. A wine with high acidity is more aptly referred to as ACIDIC or TART than sour.

spicy An umbrella term for the lively, fragrant aroma and flavor of some wines. This word may cover any of many spices including allspice, cinnamon, cloves, mace, nutmeg, and pepper. A spicy characteristic is usually related to the grape (GEWÜRZTRAMINER is known for its spiciness) but can also come from the wine's contact with new oak barrels.

spritzig [SHPRIH-tsihg] A German term describing slightly SPARKLING WINES that produce a gentle prickling sensation on the tongue. *Spritzig* corresponds to the French *pétillant* and the Italian *frizzante*.

spritzy A word describing a tiny degree of pinpoint effervescence; undesirable in a STILL WINE.

stale Used for wine that's lost its vitality and freshness, the result of which is a dull flavor and BOUQUET.

stalky *see* STEMMY

steely Wine tasting term that describes pure-flavored white wines that are LEAN but well BALANCED and quite high in ACIDITY.

stemmy Also called *stalky,* this term describes wines that have an astringently harsh, "green" leaflike flavor, usually due to the juice's prolonged contact with grape stems during winemaking.

stickie Australian term for DESSERT WINE that's often FORTIFIED.

strong *see* POWERFUL

structure A wine's architecture—its plan—which includes all the main building blocks of ACID, ALCOHOL, FRUIT, GLYCEROL, and TANNINS. It's not enough, however, to say that a wine simply has "structure" (which all do). The term should be clarified with adjectives such as *inadequate* or *strong;* one can also refer to a wine as *well structured.*

sturdy Descriptor for a wine that is generally substantial, powerful, and assertive.

sulfur; sulphur There are two distinct sulfurous characteristics that affect a wine's smell. One, which occurs when there are excessive amounts of SULFUR DIOXIDE, has the smell of a burnt matchstick just after it's lit. This pungent odor is often accompanied by a prickling sensation in the back of the throat and upper part of the nose. A sulphur dioxide characteristic will generally dissipate through aeration, either by DECANTING the wine or swirling it in the glass. The other form of sulfur that can negatively influence wine is HYDROGEN SULFIDE (H_2S), which creates the distinctively foul odor of rotten eggs, sometimes rubber. H_2S that stays too long in wine combines with other constituents to form MERCAPTANS (which smell skunky) and, eventually, DISULFIDES, which reek of sewage.

supple Well-STRUCTURED wines that are HARMONIOUS, SOFT, and VELVETY—in short, extremely pleasing.

surmaturité; sur maturité [soor mah-teu-ree-TAY] Term used to describe a stage in a grape's development when it becomes overripe, starts to shrivel, sugar levels climb, and acid levels fall. Some winemakers like to pick just as grapes begin this stage, believing that grapes have reached their maximum maturity and their fullest flavors. Wines made from grapes picked at this stage are sometimes described as *surmaturité.* Wines made from grapes picked a bit later might be described as FLABBY and/or PRUNEY.

sweet A term used for both flavor and BOUQUET. Though it generally applies to the sense of taste, certain components—such as oakiness, which contributes a sweet vanilla essence, or intense fruitiness—can give wine a seemingly sweet smell. *See also* SWEETNESS.

syrupy Describing RICH, almost thick sweet wines such as a TROCKENBEERENAUSLESE.

tannic Wine in which TANNINS are excessive. Tannins are detectable by a dry, occasionally puckery, sensation in the mouth and back of the throat, sometimes accompanied by a bitter AFTERTASTE.

tar A positive term sometimes used to describe the smell of hot tar; occasionally found in some CABERNETS and ZINFANDELS.

tart A harsh, sharp impression on the palate, an indicator for wines that are high in ACIDITY.

tears *see* LEGS

terroir *see* GOUT; TERROIR, main listing, page 232.

texture Used for wines that are DENSE, INTENSE, and full-bodied (*see* BODY)—so much so that they seem to produce a weighty, mouth-filling palate impression that feels almost thick.

thick Wines that are extremely RICH, almost HEAVY, combined with a lack of ACIDITY.

thin Used for wine lacking BODY, with the perception of being watery.

tight; tightly knit Describing a young, undeveloped wine that seems HARD on the palate. Such a wine will generally MELLOW with AGING.

tired Wine that's DULL, past its prime, and generally uninteresting.

toasty The appealing smell of bread when darkly toasted, which is particularly desirable in some CHARDONNAYS and SPARKLING WINES. Stronger toasty flavors, found in some red wines, reflect spicy, roasted coffee flavors and aromas. This characteristic is the result of the wine being stored in toasted barrels (*see* TOAST).

tobacco Used to describe the BOUQUET of some complex, mature wines (such as many reds from GRAVES), which is uniquely similar to that of freshly lit pipe tobacco. Such a characteristic is considered desirable.

toe curler Term attributed to Sharon Tyler Herbst for wines so delicious you just can't get enough of them.

tough A full-bodied (see BODY), excessively tannic wine. Such wine will often mellow with proper aging.

transformational phase *see* DUMB

truffles The subtle fragrance of fresh white truffles, most often detected in NEBBIOLO wines of Italy's PIEDMONT region (which is also known for its truffles).

typicity [tih-PIH-sih-tee] From the French *typicité* ("typical of its kind"). Description of a wine that possesses the expected qualities and characteristics relating to the grape variety from which it was made, the region from which it came, and/or the traits of a particular VINTAGE. A wine "lacking typicity" may be quite wonderful, yet not correspond characteristically.

unctuous [UHNK-choo-uhs] This term is similar to oily and refers to wines that are rich and full-bodied with a smooth, slippery mouthfeel. Unctuous is often associated with sweet dessert wines like sauternes.

unripe; underripe Terms used for wine made from grapes that have been picked before they're fully ripe. Such grapes generally have high acidity, green flavors, and a lack of CHARACTER which, of course, translates to the wine.

vanilla; vanillin A sensory term for the sweet, distinctively vanilla-like smell that's associated with some wines that have been AGED in American OAK.

vegetal [VEHJ-ih-tl] A taste and smell characteristic of fresh or cooked vegetables, particularly bell peppers and asparagus. Some grape varieties—such as CABERNET SAUVIGNON—have a natural degree of vegetal character. However, a dominant vegetal quality is considered a fault. *See also* HERBACEOUS.

velouté [veh-loo-TAY] *see* VELVETY.

velvety A term for opulently HARMONIOUS wines that have a LUSH, smooth TEXTURE. In French the term is *velouté*.

vigorous Wines that are full-bodied (*see* BODY), lively, and youthful.

vinegary The sharp smell and/or flavor of vinegar in wine is a sign of bacteriological breakdown or excessive acetic acid (*see* ACIDS)—and the wine's demise.

vinosity [vi-NAHS-ih-tee] The collective characteristics of a wine, such as aroma and taste.

vinous [VI-nuhs] When used as a wine tasting term, this term describes a generically winey flavor and/or aroma—a pleasant but not terribly interesting wine. *See also* VINOUS (main listing, page 563).

viscous; viscosity [VIHS-kuhs; vih-SKAH-sih-tee] A viscous wine is generally RICH, CONCENTRATED, and high in GLYCEROL and EXTRACT. Viscosity leaves a strong impression of TEXTURE on the palate and is discernible visually by distinct LEGS or SHEETS on the sides of the glass.

volatile A wine with excessive VOLATILE ACIDITY, which produces a sharp, vinegary edge and signifies a seriously flawed wine.

watery Synonymous with THIN—a wine lacking BODY.

weighty Describes a powerful, full-bodied (*see* BODY) wine.

withered An over-the-hill wine that's lost its FRUITY characteristics, both in flavor and smell.

woody A wine that's been kept too long in barrels can assume an exaggerated <u>OAKY</u> flavor and aroma that can overwhelm the wine's other components.

yeasty Used for the yeasty, fresh-bread <u>BOUQUET</u> found in certain wines that have been aged *sur lie*—"on the LEES" (the fermentation-created sediment that consists mainly of dead yeast cells and small grape particles). Some wines—such as CHARDONNAY or SAUVIGNON BLANC—are aged this way to add complexity. SPARKLING WINES made via MÉTHODE CHAMPENOISE can also assume a yeasty characteristic because they undergo a second fermentation in the bottle. In most wines, however, a yeasty smell is considered a flaw.

young; youthful A descriptor for fresh, light, generally fruity wine.

Official Wine Classifications of Bordeaux

The famous Classification of 1855 was created as part of the World Exhibition in Paris that same year. It was intended as a means to determine which BORDEAUX wines would be exhibited—they had to be France's best. Although unofficial rankings had long been in practice, for some reason the Classification of 1855 took hold as a hallmark of excellence. Only the red wines of the MÉDOC and white wines of SAUTERNES were rated. At the time, the wines from other Bordeaux growing areas—like GRAVES, POMEROL, and SAINT-ÉMILION—were not deemed prestigious enough for consideration (the only exception being Château Haut-Brion of Graves).

To arrive at the rankings, a group of wine brokers used a system based on the price each wine traditionally brought in the marketplace—the most expensive wines had the highest rankings. Among the myriad Bordeaux châteaux, only sixty-one were chosen for their red wines—sixty from the Médoc and one from Graves received a CRU CLASSÉ (classed growths) ranking. This red-wine category was further divided into five subcategories: four châteaux were classified as PREMIERS CRUS (first growths); fifteen as DEUXIÈMES CRUS (second growths); fourteen as TROISIÈMES CRUS (third growths); ten as QUARTIÈMES CRUS (fourth growths); and eighteen as CINQUIÈMES CRUS (fifth growths). These rankings have held firm, with the exception of the 1973 upgrade of Château Mouton-Rothschild from a second to a first growth.

For white wines from Sauternes and Barsac, there are only two cru classé categories—first growth and second growth. Of the twenty-four classified châteaux, eleven were designated as first growth and twelve as second growth. Since then, some of the second-growth châteaux have split, making the current total fifteen. Château d'Yquem was elevated to a class all by itself—known variously as *Premier Grand Cru*, *Grand Premier Cru*, and *Premier Cru Supérieur*—and is allowed to put "Premier Grand Cru Classé" on its label, although it doesn't.

Because cru classé rankings are tied to a château and not to a specific vineyard, wine from a particular site can actually change classifications if the vineyard should change hands from one château to another. Therefore, wines from a vineyard that was previously classified as fifth-growth can rise to first-growth status if a first-growth château purchases the land from which the wine is made.

Many argue that the 1855 Classification is now more academic than representative, while others believe that, on the whole, the Classification is still very valid. What's true is that much has changed since then, including winemaking techniques, superior wine coming from new châteaux not included in the Classification, and expanded production as adjacent vineyards are purchased.

That being said, it's the marketplace that, in the end, determines quality, much as pricing was the initial criteria for the 1855 rankings. Today many SUPER SECONDS (Bordeaux's most lauded second growths) are considered better than some first-growth wines and are priced accordingly. And it's not uncommon to find some fourth- and fifth-growth wines selling for more than those higher ranked. For a breakdown of how many first- through fifth-growths are in each appellation, *see* the chart below.

SUMMARY OF THE 1855 CLASSIFICATION						
Growth	1st Growth	2nd Growth	3rd Growth	4th Growth	5th Growth	*Appellation Total*
Appellation						
Margaux	1	5	10	3	2	21
Pauillac	3	2	0	1	12	18
Saint-Julien	0	5	2	4	0	11
Saint-Estèphe	0	2	1	1	1	5
Haut-Médoc	0	0	1	1	3	5
Graves	1	0	0	0	0	1
Growth Total	5	14	14	10	18	
Total Châteaux						61

The 1855 Classification of Bordeaux

The Médoc

Premiers Crus (First Growths)	Appellation
Château Lafite-Rothschild	Pauillac
Château Latour	Pauillac
Château Margaux	Margaux
Château Haut-Brion	Pessac-Léognan (Graves)
Château Mouton-Rothschild (upgraded in 1973)	Pauillac

Deuxièmes Crus (Second Growths)	Appellation
Château Rausan-Ségla	Margaux
Château Rauzan-Gassies	Margaux
Château Léoville-Las Cases	Saint-Julien
Château Léoville-Poyferré	Saint-Julien
Château Léoville-Barton	Saint-Julien
Château Durfort-Vivens	Margaux
Château Lascombes	Lascombes
Château Gruaud-Larose	Saint-Julien
Château Brane-Cantenac	Margaux
Château Pichon-Longueville Baron	Pauillac
Château Pichon-Longueville Lalande	Pauillac
Château Ducru-Beaucaillou	Saint-Julien
Château Cos d'Estournel	Saint-Estèphe
Château Montrose	Saint-Estèphe

Troisièmes Crus (Third Growths)	Appellation
Château Giscours	Margaux
Château Kirwan	Margaux
Château d'Issan	Margaux
Château Lagrange	Saint-Julien
Château Langoa-Barton	Saint-Julien
Château Malescot-St. Exupéry	Margaux
Château Cantenac-Brown	Margaux

Château Palmer	Margaux
Château La Lagune	Haut-Médoc
Château Desmirail	Margaux
Château Calon-Ségur	Saint-Estèphe
Château Ferrière	Margaux
Château Marquis d'Alesme-Becker	Margaux
Château Boyd-Cantenac	Margaux

Quatrièmes Crus (Fourth Growths)	Appellation
Château St.-Pierre	Saint-Julien
Château Branaire-Ducru	Saint-Julien
Château Talbot	Saint-Julien
Château Duhart-Milon-Rothschild	Pauillac
Château Pouget	Margaux
Château La Tour-Carnet	Haut-Médoc
Château Lafon-Rochet	Saint-Estèphe
Château Beychevelle	Saint-Julien
Château Prieuré-Lichene	Margaux
Château Marquis-de-Terme	Margaux

Cinquièmes Crus (Fifth Growths)	Appellation
Château Pontet-Canet	Pauillac
Château Batailley	Pauillac
Château Grand-Puy-Lacoste	Pauillac
Château Grand-Puy-Ducasse	Pauillac
Château Haut-Batailley	Pauillac
Château Lynch-Bages	Pauillac
Château Lynch-Moussas	Pauillac
Château Dauzac	Margaux
Château d'Armailhac (previously Mouton-Baron-Philippe)	Pauillac
Château du Tertre	Margaux
Château Haut-Bages-Libéral	Pauillac
Château Pédesclaux	Pauillac
Château Belgrave	Haut-Médoc
Château de Camensac	Haut-Médoc
Château Cos Labory	Saint-Estèphe
Château Clerc-Milon-Rothschild	Pauillac
Château Croizet-Bages	Pauillac
Château Cantermerle	Haut-Médoc

The 1855 Classification of Bordeaux

Sauternes/Barsac

The original 1855 Classification for Sauternes/Barsac included only twelve Deuxièmes Crus. That number has now increased to fifteen because some châteaux have been divided.

Premier Grand Cru (First Great Growth)	Appellation
Château d'Yquem	Sauternes

Premiers Crus (First Growths)	Appellation
Château La Tour Blanche	Sauternes
Château Lafaurie-Peyraguey	Sauternes
Château Haut-Peyraguey	Sauternes
Château de Rayne-Vigneau	Sauternes
Château Suduiraut	Sauternes
Château Coutet	Barsac
Château Climens	Barsac
Château Guiraud	Sauternes
Château Rieussec	Sauternes
Château Rabaud-Promis	Sauternes
Château Sigalas-Rabaud	Sauternes

Deuxièmes Crus (Second Growths)	Appellation
Château d'Arche	Sauternes
Château Doisy-Védrines	Barsac
Château Caillou	Barsac
Château Filhot	Sauternes
Château Doisy-Daëne	Barsac
Château Nairac	Barsac
Château Lamothe	Sauternes
Château Lamothe-Guignard	Sauternes
Château Suau	Barsac
Château de Malle	Sauternes
Château de Myrat	Barsac
Château Broustet	Barsac
Château Romer-du-Hayot	Sauternes
Château Doisy-Dubroca	Barsac

Graves (Pessac-Léognan) Classification of 1959

The châteaux of Graves were originally classified for red wines in 1953 (with the exception of Château Haut-Brion, which was included in the 1855 Classification). The Graves Classification was updated in 1959, when white wines were added and selected châteaux were given CRU CLASSÉ status (with no hierarchical ranking within this category). Thirteen châteaux were deemed crus classés for their red wines; six of those thirteen plus two additional estates also received this honor for their white wines. The following listing indicates the name of the château and whether its cru classé status is for red wine, white wine, or both.

Château Bouscaut (red and white wines)
Château Carbonnieux (red and white wines)
Château Domaine de Chevalier (red and white wines)
Château Couhins-Lurton (white wine)
Château de Fieuzal (red wine)
Château Haut-Bailly (red wine)
Château Haut-Brion (red and white wines)
Château La Mission-Haut-Brion (red wine)
Château La Tour-Haut-Brion (red wine)
Château La Tour-Martillac (red and white wines)
Château Laville-Haut-Brion (white wine)
Château Malartic-Lagravière (red and white wines)
Château Olivier (red and white wines)
Château Pape-Clément (red wine)
Château Smith-Haut-Lafitte (red wine)

Saint-Émilion Classification of 1955 (revised 1996)

The wines of Saint-Émilion were classified for the first time in 1955, a century after wines of the Médoc were classified. Unlike the Médoc, Saint-Émilion's classification system can be revised every 10 years, at which time châteaux could be elevated or downgraded. The most recent review, completed in 1996, lists thirteen châteaux as PREMIERS GRANDS CRUS CLASSÉS (the highest level). Two of the thirteen, Château Ausone and Château Cheval Blanc, were elevated into Category A— they're both generally considered comparable in quality to the Médoc FIRST GROWTHS. The next level—GRANDS CRUS CLASSÉS—is comprised of fifty-five estates. The number of châteaux in the third level—GRANDS CRUS—varies from 150 to 200 because châteaux must qualify annually by submitting their wines for tastings.

Premiers Grands Crus Classés (First Great Classed Growths)

Category A

Château Ausone

Château Cheval Blanc

Category B

Château L'Angélus
Château Beau-Séjour-Bécot
Château Beauséjour-Duffau-Lagarrosse
Château Belair
Château Canon
Château Figeac

Château La Gaffelière
Château Magdelaine
Château Pavie
Château Trottevieille
Clos Fourtet

Grand Crus Classés
(Great Classed Growths)

Château l'Arrosée
Château Balestard-La-Tonnelle
Château Bellevue
Château Bergat
Château Berliquet
Château Cadet-Bon
Château Cadet-Piola
Château Canon-La-Gaffelière
Château Cap de Mourlin
Château Chauvin
Château Clos des Jacobins
Clos de l'Oratoire
Clos Saint-Martin
Château la Clotte
Château la Clusière
Château Corbin
Château Corbin-Michotte
Château la Couspaude
Château Curé-Bon
Château Dassault
Couvent des Jacobins
Château la Dominique
Château Faurie-de-Souchard
Château Fonplégade
Château Fonroque
Château Franc-Mayne
Château les Grandes Murailles
Château Grand Mayne
Château Grand Pontet

Château Guadet Saint-Julien
Château Haut-Corbin
Château Haut-Sarpe
Château Lamarzelle
Château Laniote
Château Larcis-Ducasse
Château Larmande
Château Laroque
Château Laroze
Château Matras
Château Moulin du Cadet
Château Pavie-Decesse
Château Pavie-Macquin
Château Petit Faurie de Soutard
Château le Prieuré
Château Ripeau
Château Saint-Georges-Côte-
    Pavie
Château la Serre
Château Soutard
Château Tertre-Daugay
Château La Tour-Figeac
Château la Tour du Pin Figeac
    (Giraud-Bélivier)
Château la Tour du Pin Figeac
    (Moueix)
Château Troplong-Mondot
Château Villemaurine
Château Yon-Figeac

Principal Wine Producing Countries

(in thousands of gallons)

Country	2005		2004		2003		2002	
Italy	1,427,127	1	1,404,936	2	1,184,794	2	1,178,348	2
France	1,376,510	2	1,516,023	1	1,224,738	1	1,330,226	1
Spain	955,222	3	1,135,657	3	1,105,408	3	884,422	3
USA	604,655	4	531,240	4	515,151	4	536,285	4
Argentina	402,135	5	408,528	5	349,378	5	335,377	5
Australia	377,804	6	387,790	6	286,239	7	321,454	6
China	317,016	7	309,091	7	306,449	6	295,882	7
Germany	241,804	8	265,422	8	216,390	9	261,142	8
South Africa	222,070	9	245,133	9	233,879	8	189,919	9
Chile	208,332	10	166,460	11	176,525	11	148,548	11
Portugal	191,953	11	197,633	10	193,908	10	176,393	10
Russia	133,015	12	135,260	13	119,674	13	107,257	13
Greece	106,385	13	112,224	15	100,362	15	81,500	16
Hungary	94,233	14	114,654	14	102,502	14	88,051	14
Brazil	84,511	15	103,691	16	69,215	17	84,855	15
Romania	68,740	16	162,893	12	146,752	12	144,269	12
Moldavia	60,761	17	79,941	17	84,934	16	59,467	19
Ukraine	60,761	18	51,251	20	62,875	19	64,196	18
Austria	59,810	19	72,253	18	66,732	18	68,660	17
Bulgaria	45,122	20	51,489	21	61,131	20	52,360	21
Croatia	44,646	21	41,238	22	46,707	22	55,346	20
Yugoslavia	34,370	22	61,712	19	60,339	21	51,515	22

Adapted from data provided by the Organisation Internationale de la Vigne et du Vin (O.I.V.)

2001		2000		2000–1996		1995–1991		1990–1986	
1,381,476	2	1,363,697	2	1,436,769	2	1,605,369	1	1,736,059	1
1,410,431	1	1,520,118	1	1,486,567	1	1,397,142	2	1,707,686	2
805,749	3	1,101,419	3	902,492	3	698,439	3	885,505	3
507,226	4	567,987	4	538,557	4	465,459	4	479,936	5
418,329	5	331,202	5	355,481	5	411,804	5	526,088	4
283,492	7	213,035	8	194,965	9	127,071	11	113,201	12
285,314	6	277,389	6	253,111	7	135,789	10	72,227	16
234,882	8	260,270	7	263,889	6	274,509	6	264,497	7
170,951	10	183,579	9	207,038	8	217,367	7	204,528	9
144,031	12	176,314	11	133,834	12	87,866	17	109,238	14
205,770	9	177,265	10	180,382	10	192,217	8	223,364	8
90,614	15	80,575	17	66,362	18	88,447	16		
91,855	14	93,995	15	101,234	14	96,901	14	112,118	13
145,669	11	113,571	13	109,001	13	100,996	13	289,911	6
78,409	16	96,109	14	77,141	15	81,764	18	78,409	15
134,468	13	144,137	12	163,078	11	146,065	9	188,440	10
32,336	22	66,045	18	56,825	20	105,883	12		
47,024	21	34,079	22	37,355	22	45,994	22		
66,864	17	61,765	19	62,109	19	65,649	20	72,200	17
59,705	18	87,311	16	74,261	16	91,459	15	117,137	11
51,542	20	49,956	21	55,372	21	51,621	21		
55,663	19	52,123	20	70,959	17	69,083	19		

Main Wine Producing Countries— Production and Consumption

(in thousands of gallons)

Country		2005	2004	2003
Italy	Wine Production	1,427,127	1,404,936	1,184,794
	Wine Consumption	713,709	747,629	775,183
	Difference	713,418	657,306	409,611
	Percentage Difference	50%	47%	35%
France	Wine Production	1,376,510	1,516,023	1,224,738
	Wine Consumption	885,796	877,553	900,352
	Difference	490,714	638,497	324,387
	Percentage Difference	36%	42%	26%
Spain	Wine Production	955,222	1,135,657	1,105,408
	Wine Consumption	361,557	367,157	364,516
	Difference	593,665	768,500	740,893
	Percentage Difference	62%	68%	67%
United States	Wine Production	604,655	531,240	515,151
	Wine Consumption	663,356	642,169	628,775
	Difference	(58,701)	(110,929)	(113,624)
	Percentage Difference	−10%	−21%	−22%
Argentina	Wine Production	402,135	408,528	349,378
	Wine Consumption	289,858	293,583	325,945
	Difference	112,277	114,945	23,433
	Percentage Difference	28%	28%	7%

Adapted from data provided by the Organisation Internationale de la Vigne et du Vin (O.I.V.)

2002	2001	2000–1996	1995–1991	1990–1986
1,178,348	1,381,476	1,436,769	1,605,369	1,736,059
732,016	796,503	844,055	927,853	967,454
446,332	584,974	592,688	677,516	768,605
38%	42%	41%	42%	44%
1,330,226	1,410,431	1,486,567	1,397,142	1,707,686
919,875	896,072	932,687	985,656	1,102,027
410,351	514,358	553,880	411,513	605,659
31%	36%	37%	29%	35%
884,422	805,749	902,492	698,439	885,505
368,795	376,139	381,132	407,868	459,726
515,627	429,610	521,333	290,545	425,779
58%	53%	58%	42%	48%
536,285	507,226	538,557	465,459	479,936
595,409	561,383	549,864	495,575	549,257
(59,123)	(54,157)	(11,307)	(30,117)	(69,321)
–11%	–11%	–2%	–6%	–14%
335,377	418,329	355,481	411,804	526,088
316,699	317,967	340,766	415,291	470,346
18,678	100,362	14,715	(3,487)	55,742
6%	24%	4%	–1%	11%

Main Wine Producing Countries— Production and Consumption (cont'd)

(in thousands of gallons)

Country		2005	2004	2003
Australia	Wine Production	377,804	387,790	286,239
	Wine Consumption	119,489	115,209	110,850
	Difference	258,315	272,581	175,389
	Percentage Difference	68%	70%	61%
China	Wine Production	317,016	309,091	306,449
	Wine Consumption	356,643	350,990	306,079
	Difference	(39,627)	(41,899)	370
	Percentage Difference	−13%	−14%	0%
South America	Wine Production	222,070	245,133	233,879
	Wine Consumption	91,142	92,701	92,120
	Difference	130,928	152,432	141,759
	Percentage Difference	59%	62%	61%
Chile	Wine Production	208,332	166,460	176,525
	Wine Consumption	69,849	67,287	67,419
	Difference	138,483	99,173	109,106
	Percentage Difference	66%	60%	62%

Adapted from data provided by the Organisation Internationale de la Vigne et du Vin (O.I.V.)

2002	2001	2000–1996	1995–1991	1990–1986
304,045	273,347	194,965	127,071	113,201
105,857	105,038	95,263	84,749	87,100
198,188	168,309	99,702	42,322	26,101
65%	62%	51%	33%	23%
295,882	285,314	253,111	135,789	72,227
303,014	292,025	260,429	134,679	72,359
(7,133)	(6,710)	(7,318)	1,110	(132)
–2%	–2%	–3%	1%	0%
189,919	170,951	207,038	217,367	204,528
102,608	104,932	104,642	96,452	88,738
87,311	66,019	102,396	120,915	115,790
46%	39%	49%	56%	57%
148,548	149,473	133,834	87,866	109,238
60,682	59,441	63,667	62,082	92,437
87,866	90,033	96,584	25,784	16,802
59%	60%	52%	29%	15%

Bibliography

Adams, Leon D. *Leon D. Adams' Commonsense Book of Wine (3rd ed.).* Boston: San Francisco Book Company/Houghton Mifflin, 1975.

_____. *The Wines of America.* New York: McGraw-Hill, 1985.

Amerine, M. A., and V. L. Singleton. *Wine (2nd ed.).* Berkeley: University of California Press, 1977.

Anderson, Burton. *The Simon & Schuster Guide to the Wines of Italy.* New York: Simon & Schuster, 1992.

_____. *The Wine Atlas of Italy.* New York: Simon & Schuster, 1990.

Anderson, Stanley F., and Raymond Hull. *The Art of Making Wine.* New York: Hawthorn Books, 1970.

Arkell, Julie. *New World Wines.* London: Ward Lock, 1999.

Ashley, Maureen. *The Encyclopedia of Italian Wines.* New York: Fireside/Simon & Schuster, 1991.

Barr, Andrew. *Pinot Noir.* London: Viking/Penguin, 1992.

Bastianich, Joseph, and David Lynch. *Vino Italiano: The Regional Wines of Italy.* New York: Clarkson Potter, 2002.

Benson, Jeffrey, and Alastair Mackenzie. *Sauternes (2nd ed.).* London: Philip Wilson Publishers Ltd., 1990.

Bespaloff, Alexis. *Alexis Bespaloff's Complete Guide to Wine.* New York: Signet/Penguin, 1994.

_____. *The New Frank Schoonmaker Encyclopedia of Wine.* New York: William Morrow and Company, 1988.

Bradford, Sarah. *The Story of Port.* London: Christie's Wine Publications, 1983.

Broadbent, Michael. *The New Great Vintage Wine Book.* New York: Alfred A. Knopf, 1991.

_____. *The Simon & Schuster Pocket Guide to Wine Tasting.* New York: Fireside/Simon & Schuster, 1988.

Cass, Bruce, editor, and Jancis Robinson, consulting editor. *The Oxford Companion to the Wines of North America.* Oxford: Oxford University Press, 2000.

Cernilli, Daniele, and Marco Sabellico. *The New Italy.* London: Mitchell Beazley, 2000.

Clark, Corbet. *American Wines of the Northwest.* New York: William Morrow, 1989.

Clarke, Oz. *New Classic Wines.* New York: Simon & Schuster, 1991.

_____. *Oz Clarke's New Encyclopedia of French Wines*. New York: Simon & Schuster, 1990.

_____. *Oz Clarke's New Encyclopedia of Wine*. New York: Harcourt Brace & Company, 1999.

Clarke, Oz, and Margaret Rand. *Oz Clarke's Encyclopedia of Grapes*. New York: Harcourt, Inc., 2001.

Coates, Clive. *The Wines of France*. South San Francisco: The Wine Appreciation Guild, 1999.

Conaway, James. *Napa*. Boston: Houghton Mifflin Company, 1990.

Cooke, George M., and James T. Lapsley. *Making Table Wine at Home*. Oakland, CA: University of California, 1988.

Cooper, Michael. *Wines of New Zealand*. London: Mitchell Beazley, 1997.

Cooper, Rosalind. *The Wine Book*. Tucson: HPBooks, 1981.

Cox, Jeff. *From Vines to Wines: The Complete Guide to Growing Grapes and Making Your Own Wine*. Pownal, VT: Storey Books, 1999.

Dallas, Phillip. *Italian Wines (3rd ed.)*. London: Faber and Faber, 1989.

Dominé, André. *Wine*. Königswinter: Könemann, 2004.

Dovaz, Michel, and Steven Spurrier. *Académie du Vin Wine Course—The Complete Course in Wine Appreciation, Tasting, and Study of the Paris Académie du Vin (2nd ed.)*. London: Mitchell Beazley, 1990.

Duijker, Hubrecht. *The Wine Atlas of Spain and Traveller's Guide to the Vineyards*. New York: Simon & Schuster, 1992.

Eyres, Harry. *Cabernet Sauvignon*. London: Viking/Penguin, 1991.

Faith, Nicholas. *The Story of Champagne*. New York: Facts On File, 1989.

Forrestal, Peter, consultant editor. *The Global Encyclopedia of Wine*. Willoughby, NSW, Australia: Global Book Publishing, 2001.

Friedrich, Jacqueline. *A Wine and Food Guide to the Loire*. New York: Henry Holt and Company, 1996.

Galhano, A. A. Moreira da Fonseca, J. R.-P. Rosas, and E. Serpa Pimentel. *Port Wine: Notes on Its History, Production and Technology (4th ed.)*. Oporto: Instituto do Vinho Porto, 1991.

George, Rosemary. *The Simon & Schuster Pocket Wine Label Decoder*. New York: Fireside/Simon & Schuster, 1989.

_____. *The Wine Dictionary*. Essex, England: Longman, 1989.

Gleave, David. *The Wines of Italy.* London: Salamander, 1989.

Gregutt, Paul, and Jeff Prather. *Northwest Wines: A Pocket Guide to the Wines of Washington, Oregon, and Idaho.* Seattle: Sasquatch Books, 1994.

Halliday, James. *Wine Atlas of Australia and New Zealand.* Sydney: HarperCollins Publishers (Australia), 1998.

_____. *Wine Atlas of California.* New York: Viking/Penguin, 1993.

Hazan, Victor. *Italian Wine.* New York: Alfred A. Knopf, 1982.

Herbst, Sharon Tyler, and Ron Herbst. *The Deluxe Food Lover's Companion.* Hauppauge, NY: Barron's Educational Series, Inc., 2009.

_____. *The New Food Lover's Companion, Fourth Edition.* Hauppauge, NY: Barron's Educational Series, Inc., 2007.

Hernandez, Alejandro, and Gonzales Contreras. *Wine and Vineyards of Chile.* Santiago: Ediciones Copygraph Publishers, 1993.

Howkins, Ben. *Rich, Rare & Red: A Guide to Port.* London: Christopher Helm, 1987.

Iland, Patrick, and Peter Gago. *Australian Wine From the Vine to the Glass.* Adelaide: Patrick Iland Wine Promotions Publishers, 1997.

Jackisch, Philip. *Modern Winemaking.* Ithaca, NY: Cornell University Press, 1985.

Jamieson, Ian. *German Wines.* London: Faber and Faber, 1991.

_____. *The Simon & Schuster Guide to the Wines of Germany.* New York: Fireside/Simon & Schuster, 1992.

Jeffs, Julian. *Sherry.* London: Faber and Faber, 1982.

_____. *The Wines of Spain.* London: Faber and Faber, 1999.

Johnson, Hugh. *Hugh Johnson's Modern Encyclopedia of Wine (4th ed.).* New York: Simon & Schuster, 1998.

_____. *The Atlas of German Wines and Traveller's Guide to the Vineyards.* New York: Simon & Schuster, 1986.

Johnson, Hugh, and James Halliday. *The Vintner's Art—How Great Wines Are Made.* New York: Simon & Schuster, 1992.

Johnson, Hugh, and Jancis Robinson. *The World Atlas of Wine (5th ed.).* London: Mitchell Beazley, 2001.

Joseph, Robert. *French Wines: The Essential Guide to the Wines and Wine-growing Regions of France.* New York: DK Publishing, Inc., 1999.

_____. *The Ultimate Encyclopedia of Wine*. London: Prion, 1996.

_____. *The Wines of the Americas*. Los Angeles: HPBooks, 1990.

Kaufman, William I. *The Pocket Encyclopedia of Pacific Northwest Wines and Wineries*. San Francisco: The Wine Appreciation Guild, 1992.

Kolpan, Steven, Brian H. Smith, and Michael A. Weiss. *Exploring Wine—The Culinary Institute of America's Complete Guide to Wines of the World*. New York: Van Nostrand Reinhold, 1996.

Kramer, Matt. *Making Sense of Burgundy*. New York: Quill/William Morrow, 1990.

_____. *Making Sense of California Wine*. New York: William Morrow and Company, 1992.

Lambert-Gocs, Miles. *The Wines of Greece*. Boston: Faber and Faber, 1990.

Librarie Larousse. *Larousse Wines and Vineyards of France*. New York: Arcade Publishing/Little, Brown and Company, 1991.

Lichine, Alexis. *Alexis Lichine's New Encyclopedia of Wines & Spirits (5th ed.)*. New York: Alfred A. Knopf, 1987.

Livingstone-Learmouth, John, and Melvyn Master. *The Wines of the Rhône*. London: Faber and Faber, 1983.

Loftus, Simon. *Puligny-Montrachet: Journal of a Village in Burgundy*. New York: Alfred A. Knopf, 1993.

MacDonogh, Giles. *The Wine and Food of Austria.* London: Mitchell Beazley, 1992.

MacQuitty, Jane. *The Simon & Schuster Pocket Guide to Australian & New Zealand Wines*. New York: Fireside/Simon & Schuster, 1990.

May, Oliver. *The Wines of Australia (new ed.)*. London: Faber and Faber, 1991.

Mayson, Richard. *Portugal's Wines and Wine Makers*. San Francisco: The Wine Appreciation Guild/Ebury Press, 1992.

McGovern, Patrick E., Stuart J. Fleming, and Solomon H. Katz, editors. *The Origins and Ancient History of Wine.* Philadelphia: Gordon and Breach Publishers, 1995.

McWhirter, Kathryn, and Charles Metcalfe. *Encyclopedia of Spanish and Portuguese Wines*. New York: Fireside/Simon & Schuster, 1991.

Metcalfe, Charles, and Kathryn McWhirter. *The Wines of Spain & Portugal*. Los Angeles: HPBooks, 1988.

Norman, Remington. *Rhône Renaissance.* San Francisco: Wine
Appreciation Guild, 1996.
_____. *The Great Domaines of Burgundy.* New York: Henry Holt
and Company, 1992.

Parker, Robert M. *Bordeaux: A Comprehensive Guide to the Wines
Produced from 1961–1997.* New York: Simon & Schuster, 1998.
_____. *Burgundy: A Comprehensive Guide to the Producers,
Appellations, and Wines.* New York: Simon & Schuster, 1990.
_____. *Wines of the Rhône Valley; Revised and Expanded Edition.*
New York: Simon & Schuster, 1997.
Peppercorn, David. *Bordeaux (2nd ed.).* London: Faber and Faber,
1991.
Peynaud, Émile. *The Taste of Wine: The Art and Science of Wine
Appreciation.* San Francisco: The Wine Appreciation Guild, 1987.
Philpott, Don. *The Vineyards of France.* Chester, CT: The Globe
Pequot Press, 1987.
Pigott, Stuart. *Riesling.* London: Viking/Penguin, 1991.
Platter, John. *John Platter's South African Wine Guide.* Edited by
Erica Platter. Stellenbosch, South Africa: J. & E. Platter, 1992, and
2nd ed., 1997.
**Prial, Frank J. II, with Rosemary George and Michael Edwards,
editors.** *The Companion to Wine.* New York: Prentice Hall
General Reference, 1992.

Radford, John. *The New Spain.* London: Mitchell Beazley, 1998.
Ray, Cyril. *The New Book of Italian Wines.* London: Sidgwick &
Jackson, 1982.
Read, Jan. *The Simon & Schuster Guide to the Wines of Spain.* New
York: Simon & Schuster, 1992.
_____. *The Wines of Portugal.* London: Faber and Faber, 1987.
Ribéreau-Gayon, Pascal (ed.). *The Wines and Vineyards of France.*
New York: Viking/Penguin, 1990.
Robinson, Jancis. *Vines, Grapes and Wines.* New York: Alfred A.
Knopf, 1986.

Spurrier, Steven. *French Country Wines.* London: Collins Willow,
1984.
Stevenson, Tom. *Champagne.* London: Sotheby's, 1986.
_____. *Sotheby's World Wine Encyclopedia (4th ed.).* London:
Sotheby's/Dorling Kindersley, 2007.
_____. *The Wines of Alsace.* London: Faber and Faber, 1993.

Style, Sue. *A Taste of Alsace.* New York: William Morrow, 1990.

Suckling, James. *Vintage Port: The Wine Spectator's Ultimate Guide for Consumers, Collectors, and Investors.* San Francisco: Wine Spectator Press, 1990.

Sullivan, Charles L. *A Companion to California Wine: An Encyclopedia of Wine and Winemaking From the Mission Period to the Present.* Berkeley: University of California Press, 1998.

_____. *Like Modern Edens: Winegrowing in Santa Clara Valley and Santa Cruz Mountains 1798–1981.* Cupertino, CA: California History Center, 1982.

Sutcliffe, Serena. *The Wine Handbook.* New York: Fireside/Simon & Schuster, 1987.

_____. *The Wines of Burgundy.* New York: Fireside/Simon & Schuster, 1992.

Thompson, Bob. *The Simon & Schuster Pocket Guide to California Wines.* New York: Fireside/Simon & Schuster, 1990.

_____. *The Wine Atlas of California and the Pacific Northwest.* New York: Simon & Schuster, 1993.

Voss, Roger. *The Simon & Schuster Pocket Guide to Fortified and Dessert Wines.* New York: Fireside/Simon & Schuster, 1989.

_____. *Wines of the Loire.* London: Faber and Faber, 1995.

Wagner, Philip M. *Grapes into Wine: A Guide to Winemaking.* New York: Alfred A. Knopf, 1987.

Wasserman, Sheldon and Pauline. *Italy's Noble Red Wines.* New York: MacMillan Publishing Company, 1991.

Young, Alan. *Wine Routes of Argentina.* San Francisco: International Wine Academy, 1998.

Zraly, Kevin. *Windows On The World Complete Wine Course.* New York: Sterling Publishing Company, 2002.

About the Authors

Ron Herbst, long a passionate and dedicated wine connoisseur and foodie, is a food and wine journalist and consultant. He started his career in the restaurant business and graduated with a BSBA with a major in Hotel and Restaurant Management. His best-selling first and second editions of the popular *Wine Lover's Companion*, co-authored with Sharon Tyler Herbst, received rave reviews and it's the wine dictionary on the "Epicurious" and Food Network Internet sites. Ron collaborated with Sharon on *The Deluxe Food Lover's Companion*, as well as the fourth edition of *The New Food Lover's Companion*, and contributed to many of her other books on food and drink. He and Sharon have been called "the dynamic duo of food and drink."

Sharon Tyler Herbst, dubbed the foremost writer of user-friendly food and drink reference works, was an award-winning author of seventeen books. *The Food Lover's Companion* (broadly hailed as "A must for every cook's library") earned her reputation as a culinary powerhouse. Many internet sites (including Condé Nast's "Epicurious," "TV Food Network," and Amazon.com) feature *Food Lover's Companion* as their online dictionary.